An Introduction to Programming with

C++

Second Edition

Diane Zak

COURSE TECHNOLOGY

★

THOMSON LEARNING ™

Australia • Canada • Mexico • Singapore • Spain • United Kingdom • United States

An Introduction to Programming with C++, Second Edition,
is published by Course Technology.

Managing Editor:
Jennifer Normandin

Acquisitions Editor:
Christine Guivernau

Senior Product Manager:
Jennifer Muroff

Developmental Editor:
Amanda Brodkin

Production Editor:
Kristen Guevara

Associate Product Manager:
Tricia Coia

Editorial Assistant:
Janet Aras

Associate Product Marketing Manager:
Meagan Walsh

Manufacturing Coordinator:
Denise Widjeskog

Cover Designer:
MaryAnn Southard

Disclaimer

Course Technology reserves the right to revise this publication and make changes from time to time in its content without notice.

The Web addresses in this book are subject to change from time to time as necessary without notice.

ISBN 0-619-03359-2

Contents

tutorial 4
VARIABLES, CONSTANTS, ARITHMETIC OPERATORS, AND ASSIGNMENT STATEMENTS *111*

tutorial 5
BUILT-IN FUNCTIONS *157*

tutorial 6
PROGRAM-DEFINED VALUE-RETURNING FUNCTIONS *185*

tutorial 7
PROGRAM-DEFINED VOID FUNCTIONS *225*

tutorial 8

THE SELECTION STRUCTURE 265

tutorial 9

MORE ON THE SELECTION STRUCTURE 299

tutorial 10

THE REPETITION STRUCTURE 339

tutorial 11

MANIPULATING CHARACTERS AND STRINGS 379

tutorial 12

CLASSES AND OBJECTS *419*

tutorial 13

SEQUENTIAL ACCESS FILES *447*

t u t o r i a l   1 4

ARRAYS *491*

a p p e n d i c e s

Preface

An Introduction to Programming with C++ is designed for a beginning programming course. This book uses the C++ programming language to teach programming concepts. Although the book assumes that the student is using the Microsoft Visual C++ 6.0 Introductory Edition compiler, the student will be able to create the programs in the book using most C++ compilers, often with little or no modification.

Organization and Coverage

An Introduction to Programming with C++ contains 14 tutorials that present hands-on instruction. In these tutorials, students with no previous programming experience learn how to plan and create well-structured programs. By the end of the book, students will have learned how to write programs using the sequence, selection, and repetition structures, as well as how to create and manipulate functions, classes, objects, sequential access files, and arrays.

Approach

An Introduction to Programming with C++ is distinguished from other textbooks because of its unique approach, which motivates students by demonstrating why they need to learn the concepts and skills. This book teaches programming concepts using a task-driven, rather than a command-driven, approach. By working through the tutorials—which are each motivated by a realistic case—students learn how to create programs that solve problems they are likely to encounter in the workplace. This is much more effective than memorizing a list of commands out of context.

Features

An Introduction to Programming with C++ is an exceptional textbook because it also includes the following features:

- **"Read This Before You Begin" Section** This section is consistent with Course Technology's unequaled commitment to helping instructors introduce technology into the classroom. Technical considerations and assumptions about hardware, software, and default settings are listed in one place to help instructors save time and eliminate unnecessary aggravation.

- **Lessons** Each tutorial is divided into two lessons—Concept and Application. The Concept Lesson introduces various programming concepts, including programming syntax and code examples. All of the examples are shown in C++, and many examples are provided for the Java and Visual Basic programming languages as well, emphasizing the application of the programming concepts to multiple programming languages. The Application Lesson begins with a case, or business-related problem that the student could reasonably expect to encounter in business. In the remainder of the Application Lesson, the student creates the program that solves the case problem. Concepts are combined in later Application Lessons so that the student has the opportunity to use multiple programming features to efficiently solve programming tasks.

- **Step-by-Step Methodology** The unique Course Technology methodology keeps students on track. They click or press keys always within the context of solving a specific problem or the Application Lesson case. The text constantly guides students, letting them know where they are in the process of solving the problem. The numerous illustrations include labels that direct students' attention to what they should look at on the screen.

- **Help?** paragraphs anticipate problems students might encounter and help them resolve these problems on their own. This feature facilitates independent learning and frees the instructor to focus on substantive conceptual issues, rather than on common procedural errors.

- **Tips** provide additional information about a procedure—for example, an alternative method of performing the procedure.

- **Mini-Quizzes** are strategically placed to test the student's knowledge at various points in each tutorial. Answers to the quiz questions are provided in the tutorials, allowing the student to determine if he or she has mastered the material covered thus far before continuing with the lesson.

- **Summaries** follow each Concept Lesson and recap the programming concepts and commands covered in the lesson.

- **Questions and Exercises** Each Concept Lesson concludes with meaningful Questions that test students' understanding of what they learned in the lesson. The Questions are followed by Exercises, which provide students with additional practice of the skills and concepts they learned in the lesson. Each Application Lesson also includes Exercises, many of which provide practice in applying cumulative programming knowledge or allow the student to explore alternative solutions to programming tasks. The answers to the even-numbered exercises (except Discovery and Debugging exercises) can be found at www.course.com in the "Downloads" section.

- **Discovery Exercises** are designated by a "Discovery" icon in the margin, and encourage students to challenge and independently develop their own programming skills.

- **Debugging Exercises** One of the most important programming skills a student can learn is the ability to correct problems, called "bugs," in an existing program. Debugging Exercises, which are designated by a Debugging icon, provide an opportunity for students to detect and correct errors in an existing program.

Microsoft Visual C++ 6.0 Introductory Edition

Microsoft Visual C++ 6.0 Introductory Edition is an optional item available with this text. The Introductory Edition of the Visual C++ development system (formerly called the Standard Edition) targets developers learning the C++ language. It is designed for entry-level programmers who want to take advantage of the powerful C++ language and the Microsoft Foundation Classes (MFC). The Visual C++ 6.0 Introductory Edition includes step-by-step tutorials, wizards, and MFC object-oriented libraries that make it easy to create powerful Windows-based applications. Version 6.0 includes a variety of professional tools to help the programmer learn C, C++, and many other professional technologies such as MFC, OLE, ODBC, DAO, ActiveX, and COM.

There are some differences between the Introductory Edition, which is an optional item available with this book, and the Enterprise and Professional

Editions, which are offered by Microsoft. The Professional Edition targets professional software developers who need features such as code optimization and statically linked libraries. These features are not found in the Introductory Edition. The Enterprise Edition is provided to corporate developers. It provides a complete toolset for developing C++ applications and components that access remote databases, including SQL databases, and takes advantage of the latest Internet and ActiveX technologies.

Teaching Tools

- **Instructor's Manual** The Instructor's Manual has been quality assurance tested. It is available in printed form and through the Course Technology Faculty Online Companion on the World Wide Web. (Call your customer service representative for the URL and your password.) The Instructor's Manual contains the following items:

  - Cases that can be assigned as semester projects.
  - Answers to all of the Questions and solutions to all of the Exercises. Suggested solutions are also included for Discovery Exercises.
  - Tutorial Notes, which contain background information from the author about the Tutorial Case and the instructional progression of the tutorial.
  - Technical Notes, which include troubleshooting tips as well as information on how to customize the students' screens to closely emulate the screen shots in the book.

- **Course Test Manager Version 1.21 Engine and Test Bank** Course Test Manager (CTM) is a cutting-edge Windows-based testing software program, developed exclusively for Course Technology, that helps instructors design and administer examinations and practice tests. This full-featured program allows students to generate practice tests randomly that provide immediate on-screen feedback and detailed study guides for questions incorrectly answered. Instructors can also use Course Test Manager to create printed and online tests. You can create, preview, and administer a test on any or all tutorials of this textbook entirely over a local area network. Course Test Manager can grade the tests students take automatically at the computer and can generate statistical information on individual as well as group performances. A CTM test bank has been written to accompany your text and is included on the CD-ROM. The test bank includes multiple-choice, true/false, short answer, and essay questions.

- **Solutions Files** Solutions Files contain every file or answer students are asked to create or modify in the tutorials, Questions, and Exercises.

- **Data Files** Data Files, containing all of the data that students will use for the tutorials and Exercises, are provided through Course Technology's Web site and are available as part of the Instructor's Resource Kit . A ReadMe file includes technical tips for lab management. See the inside covers of this book and the "Read This Before You Begin" section before the Overview for more information on Data Files.

- **MyCourse.com** MyCourse.com is an online syllabus builder and course-enhancement tool. Hosted by Course Technology, MyCourse.com adds value to courses by providing additional content that reinforces what students are learning. Most importantly, MyCourse.com is flexible, allowing instructors to choose how to organize the material—by date, by class session, or by using the default organization, which organizes content by chapter. MyCourse.com allows instructors to add their own materials, including hyperlinks, school logos, assignments, announcements, and other course content. Instructors using more than one textbook can build a course that includes all of their Course Technology texts in one easy-to-use site. Instructors can start building their own courses today at *www.mycourse.com/instructor*.

Acknowledgments

I would like to thank all of the people who helped to make this book a reality, especially Amanda Brodkin (Development Editor) and Jennifer Muroff (Product Manager). Amanda, thank you for your great suggestions and for always making my deadlines for me. You truly are a fantastic Development Editor, and I am so happy to have had the opportunity to work with you. I will miss talking and laughing with you almost daily. Jennifer, thank you for your understanding, patience, and encouraging words. And thank you for working behind the scenes to help me complete this project.

I also want to thank Kristen Guevara (Production Editor), John Bosco (Quality Assurance Project Leader), Nicole Ashton (Quality Assurance Manuscript Reviewer), and Alex White (Quality Assurance Manuscript Reviewer). Kristen, you did a great job on this project. How you managed to keep track of all of the different phases of this project is beyond me. Nicole, thank you for your invaluable suggestions, and for finding my errors.

I am grateful to the many reviewers who provided invaluable comments on the manuscript, in particular: Joseph DeLibero, Arizona State University; James McGuffee, Austin Community College; Stan Pushkarsky, Austin Community College; and Terrance Walsh, McDowell Technical Community College.

Finally, I dedicate this book in loving memory of Mary Clare Karnick. We all loved you more.

Diane Zak

Read This Before You Begin

To the User

Using Your Own Computer

If you are going to work through this book using your own computer, you will need:

- **Computer System** Microsoft Visual C++ 6.0 Professional Edition, Learning Edition, Introductory Edition, or Enterprise Edition for Windows 95 or Microsoft Windows NT 4.0 or later must be installed on your computer. This book assumes a complete installation of Microsoft Visual C++.
- Microsoft Visual C++ 6.0 Introductory Edition is an optional item with your book. The following system requirements apply.
  - Personal computer with a 486 or higher processor
  - Microsoft Windows 95 or later or Windows NT 4.0 or later
  - 32 MB of RAM
  - VGA or higher-resolution monitor (Super VGA recommended)
  - Microsoft Mouse or compatible pointing device
  - 225 MB hard disk space for installation
  - A CD-ROM drive with 32-bit protected mode CD-ROM drivers
  - Modem or other connection to the World Wide Web (recommended)

Data Files

Ask your instructor or lab manager for details on how to get Data Files. You will not be able to complete the tutorials or exercises in this book using your own computer until you have Data Files. The Data Files may also be obtained electronically through the Internet. See the inside front or back cover of this book for more details. The Data Files will be stored in a folder named "Cpp" which you must copy to your computer's hard drive.

Important note: The `getline` function in Microsoft Visual C++ Version 6.0 contains an error that will cause some of the programs in this book to run incorrectly. You can work around this error by completing the following steps:

1. Copy the Data Files to your computer's hard disk.
2. Use Windows to open the Include folder, which typically is located in the Program Files/Microsoft Visual Studio/VC98 folder on your computer's hard disk.
3. Right-click String in the list of filenames. (Be sure to right-click the String filename, and not the String.h filename.)
4. Click Rename on the shortcut menu. Type String.old and press the Enter key.
5. Open the Cpp folder on your computer's hard disk.
6. Copy the String file from the Cpp folder to the Include folder.

Visit Our World Wide Web Site

The appendices that accompany this book can be found on the World Wide Web. Additional materials designed especially for you are also available on the World Wide Web. Go to *www.course.com*.

To the Instructor

To complete the tutorials in this book, your students must use a set of Data Files. These files are included in the Instructor's Resource Kit. They may also be obtained electronically through the Internet. Go to *http://www.course.com/* to download the Data Files that accompany this book.

Course Technology Data Files

You are granted a license to copy the data files to any computer or computer network used by students who have purchased this book.

An Overview of a Microcomputer System

objectives

After completing this overview, you will be able to:

- Describe the components of a microcomputer system
- Explain the relationship between hardware and software
- Explain the history of programming languages

An Introduction to a Microcomputer System

In 1975, the first **microcomputers**, also called **personal computers**, appeared in the marketplace. Since then, the microcomputer has become so popular that it is difficult to imagine what a person ever did without one. Imagine typing a letter on a typewriter, or keeping track of your investments manually, or drawing the blueprints for a house without the aid of a computer!

Since the introduction of the microcomputer, situations and tasks that once were considered impossible are now commonplace. For example, **telecommuting**, where an employee works from home and uses a microcomputer to communicate with his or her office, is now an option available to many business professionals. Microcomputers also allow you to access information from around the world, via the Internet and the World Wide Web, from the comfort of your home, office, or school.

Figure 1 shows a typical microcomputer system found in most businesses and homes.

software

3.5" floppy disk drive

screen or monitor

system unit

CD-ROM

3.5" storage media

keyboard

hard disk drive

CD-ROM drive

mouse

printer

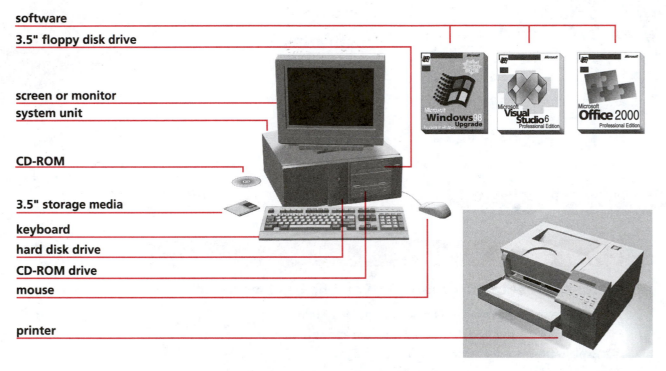

Figure 1: A typical microcomputer system

Notice that a **microcomputer system** is composed of both hardware and software. **Hardware** refers to the physical components of the microcomputer system. **Software** refers to the programs (step-by-step instructions) that tell the hardware how to perform a task. In the next section, you will learn about the hardware and software found in a microcomputer system and how they interact.

An Overview of Hardware and Software

As Figure 1 shows, the hardware in a microcomputer system consists of a **system unit,** which is the case or box that contains the main circuit boards and storage devices, and other devices called peripheral devices.

Peripherals

A **peripheral device** is a device that is attached to the system unit. Peripheral devices extend the capabilities of the computer system, and they provide the user a means by which he or she can communicate with the computer. The three categories of peripheral devices are input devices, output devices, and auxiliary storage devices.

An **input device** allows you to communicate with the computer by entering data into it. Examples of commonly used input devices are a keyboard, mouse, and scanner. As you are working through the lessons and exercises in this book, you will use an input device—the keyboard—to enter your C++ program instructions into the computer.

An **output device** allows the computer to communicate with you by displaying or printing information. Examples of commonly used output devices are a monitor and printer. You will use a monitor to display the C++ instructions you enter into the computer, and you will use a printer to print the instructions. You also will use a monitor and printer to display and print the results of your C++ programs.

Auxiliary storage devices, the third category of peripheral devices, allow you to permanently store information. Floppy disk drives and hard disk drives are the two most common auxiliary storage devices. These storage devices use an auxiliary storage media—either a floppy disk or a hard disk—to store the information. You will use an auxiliary storage device to save your C++ program instructions. By doing so, you will be able to use the program again without having to retype it.

Internal Memory

Now look inside the system unit to see what it contains. See Figure 2.

▶ Auxiliary (which means "additional" or "secondary") storage devices and auxiliary storage media are so named because they provide storage capability in addition to that available in the internal memory of the computer.

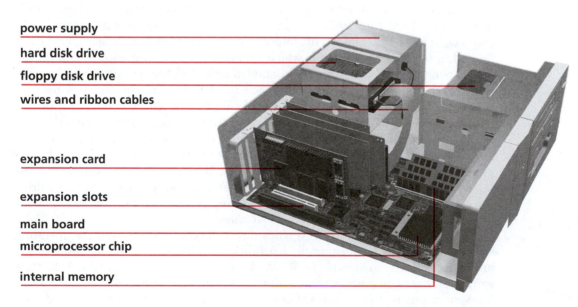

power supply

hard disk drive

floppy disk drive

wires and ribbon cables

expansion card

expansion slots

main board

microprocessor chip

internal memory

Figure 2: The inside of the system unit

The system unit houses an area called **internal memory**, which is simply an ordered sequence of memory cells contained on chips—integrated circuits residing on silicon. Internal memory is like a large post office, where each memory cell, like each post office box, has a unique address, and each can contain mail. Figure 3 illustrates this comparison.

each post office box
has a unique address

each memory cell has
a unique address

Figure 3: Comparison of post office boxes to internal memory

Unlike a post office box, which can contain many pieces of mail at the same time, a memory cell can store only one piece of mail at any time. The mail found in a memory cell is typically either a program instruction or an item of data. **Data** refers to the information processed by a program. The data may be input by the user, such as the number of hours an employee worked, or it may be the result of a calculation made by the computer, such as an employee's gross pay.

Some of the chips in internal memory are **Random-Access Memory (RAM)** chips; others are **Read-Only Memory (ROM)** chips. There are two major differences between a RAM chip and a ROM chip. First, while the computer is on, the user can both write information to and read information from the memory cells located on a RAM chip. In contrast, a user can only read information from a ROM chip's cells; he or she cannot write information to the memory cells on a ROM chip. Second, a RAM chip is volatile, which means that any information stored on the chip is temporary. The information contained on a RAM chip is lost when the computer is turned off or loses power unexpectedly. A ROM chip, on the other hand, is nonvolatile; instructions remain on a ROM chip even when the computer is off.

The memory cells located on ROM chips contain instructions written there by the manufacturer. When you turn a computer on, these instructions perform an automatic self-test of the computer. The self-test makes sure that the different components of the computer are working properly. If all is well, the instructions contained on the ROM chips search either the computer's hard drive or a floppy drive for a set of instructions known as the operating system, which is discussed in the Types of Software section later in this Overview.

The instructions on the ROM chips direct the computer to read the operating system instructions from either the hard disk or a floppy disk. As the instructions are read, they are written to the RAM chips in internal memory, where they are stored until the computer is turned off (or loses power). In addition to the operating system instructions, the RAM chips also store program instructions and data entered from the keyboard or read from a file previously saved on a disk.

The Central Processing Unit

Besides internal memory, the system unit also houses the **Central Processing Unit** (**CPU**), which is the brain of the computer. The CPU resides on a microprocessor chip, which is a single integrated circuit, and it contains two principal components—the control unit and the Arithmetic/Logic Unit (ALU). It also contains special high-speed storage locations called **registers**.

The **control unit** in the CPU directs the flow of information from one part of the computer to another. The control unit is responsible for making sure that the computer correctly processes the program instructions and data stored in internal memory.

The second component of the CPU, the **Arithmetic/Logic Unit** (**ALU**), performs the arithmetic calculations and comparison operations for the computer. If the control unit instructs the computer to add two numbers, it is the ALU that performs the addition. The ALU also would be responsible for comparing the number of hours an employee worked with the number 40 to determine whether the employee should receive overtime pay.

The ALU uses the registers in the CPU to hold the data that is being processed. It uses a special register, called an **accumulator**, to temporarily store the result of an arithmetic or comparison operation. Figure 4 illustrates how the CPU processes an instruction to add the numbers 4 and 5.

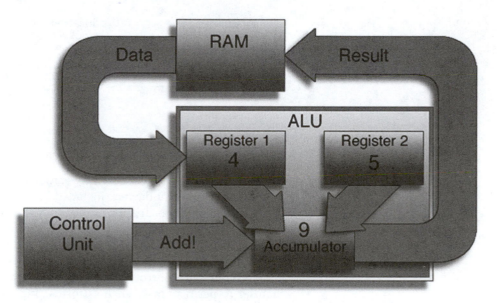

Figure 4: Diagram of how the CPU processes an instruction to add two numbers

First, the control unit sends the data to be processed—in this case, the numbers 4 and 5—from RAM to the ALU, where it is held in registers. The control unit then sends a signal to the ALU, directing it to add both numbers. After performing the necessary operation, the ALU stores the result—in this case, the number 9—in the accumulator. The control unit then sends the contents of the accumulator to RAM so it can be output, saved on a disk, or used for further processing.

Types of Software

The hardware component of a computer system isn't much use without software. Recall that the term *software* refers to the instructions that tell the computer how to perform a task. Software typically is divided into two general categories: system software and application software. Each of these categories contains various types of software, as shown in Figure 5.

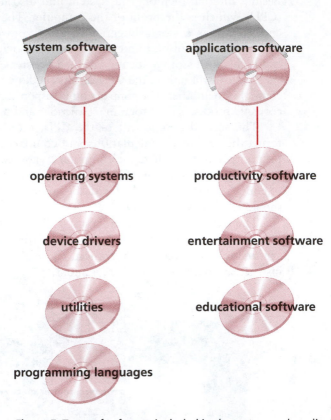

Figure 5: Types of software included in the system and application software categories

The purpose of **system software** is to manage the computer and its peripheral devices. As Figure 5 indicates, included in the system software category are operating systems, device drivers, utilities, and programming languages. **Operating systems** are programs that coordinate the activities within the computer and allow you and the computer to communicate with each other. Windows, Mac OS, UNIX, Linux, and DOS are popular operating systems. **Device drivers** are programs that help the computer control a peripheral device, and **utilities** are programs that allow the user to perform tasks such as formatting a disk, copying data from one disk to another, and protecting the computer from viruses. **Programming languages** are programs that allow a user to control how the computer processes data to produce the information that he or she wants. You will learn more about programming languages in the next section.

Unlike system software, **application software** allows a user to computerize a task that he or she might otherwise perform manually, such as writing a letter, preparing a budget, or playing a game. Included in the application software category are productivity software (such as word processors, spreadsheets, databases, and graphics programs), entertainment software (such as computer games), and educational software (such as math tutors and encyclopedias).

In the next section, you will learn more about the programming language component of system software.

mini-quiz

Mini-Quiz 1

1. The two components of a microcomputer system are _____ and _____ .

2. The three categories of peripheral devices are _____ , _____ , and _____ .

3. The information processed by a program is called _____ .

4. When you enter a program into the computer, the program is stored on _____ chips in internal memory.

5. The CPU contains the _____ , _____ , and special high-speed storage locations called _____ .

6. Word processors belong to a category of software called _____ software.

7. Programming languages belong to a category of software called _____ software.

8. The data to be processed is stored in _____ in the ALU.

A Brief History of Programming Languages

Although computers appear to be amazingly intelligent machines, they cannot yet think on their own. Computers still rely on human beings to give them directions. These directions are called **programs**, and the people who write the programs are called **programmers**.

Just as human beings communicate with each other through the use of languages such as English, Spanish, Hindi, or Chinese, programmers use a variety of special languages, called **programming languages**, to communicate with the computer. Some popular programming languages are C++, Java, Visual Basic, C, COBOL (Common Business Oriented Language), and BASIC (Beginners All-purpose Symbolic Instruction Code). In the next sections, you will follow the progression of programming languages from machine languages to assembly languages, then to high-level procedure-oriented languages, and finally to high-level object-oriented languages.

Machine Languages

A computer represents each character in its **character set**—the letters, numerals, and special symbols that can be entered into the computer—by a series of microscopic electronic switches. Like the light switches in your house, each electronic switch can be either on or off. Computers use the binary number system to represent the two switch states. Unlike the decimal number system, with which you are familiar, the **binary number system** uses only the digits 0 and 1, rather than the digits 0 through 9. A 0 in the binary number system indicates that the switch is off; a 1 indicates that it is on. Each character in the computer's character set is represented by a series of these off and on switches—in other words, by a series of 0s and 1s.

Each switch—each 0 or 1—is called a **bit**, which is short for *binary digit*. Most computers use eight switches—in other words, eight bits or binary digits—to represent each number, letter, or symbol. Which of the eight switches are on and which are off is determined both by the character being represented and by the coding scheme used by the computer. Microcomputers typically use a coding scheme called **ASCII** (pronounced *ASK-ee*), which stands for American Standard Code for

Information Interchange. The letter X, for example, is represented in the ASCII coding scheme by the eight bits 01011000. The collection of eight bits used to represent a character is called a **byte**. Appendix A in this book shows the ASCII codes for the letters, numerals, and special symbols included in a computer's character set.

Because computers can understand only these on and off switches, the first programmers had to write the program instructions using nothing but combinations of 0s and 1s. Instructions written in 0s and 1s are called **machine language** or **machine code**. The machine languages (each type of machine has its own language) represent the only way to communicate directly with the computer. Figure 6 shows a segment of a program written in a machine language.

```
0100
001101 100000 001101 110001
00101 10001 10000
01110
111001
111001 001 11000 001
11000
0011100
100010 00110
```

Figure 6: A segment of a program written in a machine language

As you can imagine, programming in machine language is very tedious and error-prone and requires highly trained programmers.

Assembly Languages

Slightly more advanced programming languages are called **assembly languages**. Figure 7 shows a segment of a program written in an assembly language.

```
main proc pay
      mov ax, dseg
      mov ax, 0b00h
      add ax, dx
      mov a1, b1
      mul b1, ax
      mov b1, 04h
```

Figure 7: A segment of a program written in an assembly language

The assembly languages simplify the programmer's job by allowing the programmer to use mnemonics in place of the 0s and 1s in the program. **Mnemonics** are memory aids—in this case, alphabetic abbreviations for instructions. For example, most assembly languages use the mnemonic ADD to represent an add operation and the mnemonic MUL to represent a multiply operation. The mnemonic MOV is used to move data from one area of memory to another. Programs written in an assembly language require an **assembler**, which also is a program, to convert the assembly instructions into machine code—the 0s and 1s the computer can understand.

Although it is much easier to write programs in assembly language than in machine language, programming in assembly language still is tedious and requires highly trained programmers.

The next major development in programming languages was the introduction of the high-level languages. The first high-level languages were procedure-oriented.

High-Level Procedure-Oriented Languages

High-level languages allow the programmer to use instructions that more closely resemble the English language. In **high-level procedure-oriented languages**, the emphasis of a program is on *how* to accomplish a task. The programmer must instruct the computer every step of the way, from the start of the task to its completion. The programmer determines and controls the order in which the computer processes the instructions. You may have either heard or read about the COBOL, BASIC, or C procedure-oriented languages.

Figure 8 shows a segment of a program written in BASIC. Notice how closely most of the instructions resemble the English language. Even if you do not know the BASIC language, it is easy to see that the program shown in Figure 8 tells the computer, step by step, *how* to compute and display an employee's net pay.

```
input "Enter name";names$
input "Enter hours worked";hours
input "Enter pay rate";rate
grossPay = hours * rate
federalTax = .2 * grossPay
socSecTax = .07 * grossPay
stateTax = .06 * grossPay
netPay = grossPay – federalTax – socSecTax – stateTax
print names$, netPay
end
```

Figure 8: A program written in BASIC—a high-level procedure-oriented language

tip

Almost everyone, at one time or another, has used top-down design to create a solution to a problem. You probably used top-down design when you planned your last vacation. Your overall goal was to "take a vacation." To accomplish that goal, you divided the solution into small tasks, such as "choose vacation spot," "make hotel reservations," "make airline reservations," and "call kennel."

In all procedure-oriented programs, the order of the instructions is extremely important. For example, in the program shown in Figure 8, you could not put the instruction to display the net pay before the instruction to calculate the net pay, and then expect the computer to display the correct results. When writing programs in a procedure-oriented language, the programmer must determine not only the proper instructions to give the computer, but the correct sequence of those instructions as well. A programmer typically will use a design methodology called **top-down design** to assist him or her in planning a procedure-oriented program.

When using top-down design to create a procedure-oriented program, the programmer begins with a statement that describes the overall purpose or goal of the program—in other words, it describes what the program is supposed to do. The purpose of the program shown in Figure 8, for example, is to determine the amount an employee should be paid. The program's purpose states *what* needs to be done, but it does not tell *how* to get it done. The programmer tells *how* to accomplish the program's purpose by dividing the solution into small, manageable tasks. The payroll program shown in Figure 8, for example, is broken up into small tasks that input the employee name, hours worked, and pay rate; calculate the gross pay, taxes, and net pay; and display the employee name and net pay. These tasks describe how to reach the program's goal—in this case, determining how much to pay the employee. You will learn more about top-down design in Tutorial 2.

High-level procedure-oriented languages require a compiler to convert the English-like instructions into the 0s and 1s the computer can understand. Like assemblers, compilers are separate programs. A **compiler** translates the entire program into machine code before running the program.

High-level procedure-oriented languages are a vast improvement over the low-level machine and assembly languages. Some of the high-level procedure-oriented languages—for example, the BASIC language—do not require a great amount of technical expertise to write simple programs.

High-Level Object-Oriented Languages

Recently, more advanced high-level languages, referred to as object-oriented languages, have become popular. Java, Smalltalk, C++, and Visual Basic are examples of popular object-oriented languages. Unlike procedure-oriented languages, which view a problem solution simply as a set of ordered tasks, **object-oriented languages** view a problem solution as a set of interacting objects. A programmer typically uses a design methodology called **object-oriented design** (**OOD**) to assist him or her in planning an object-oriented program. As with top-down design, the programmer begins with a statement that describes the purpose of the program. However, rather than breaking up the program into one or more tasks, the programmer divides the program into one or more objects, resulting in programs whose code is very different from those created using the procedure-oriented approach.

The objects in an object-oriented program can take on many different forms. For example, the menus, option buttons, and command buttons included in many Windows programs are objects. An object also can represent something encountered in real life. For example, a payroll program may include objects that represent a time card, an employee, and a date. The partial program shown in Figure 9 shows how you can use the C++ language to create a Date object named payDay.

tip

Some high-level languages—for example, some versions of the BASIC language—use a program called an interpreter, instead of a compiler, to convert the English-like instructions into machine code. Unlike a compiler, an interpreter translates the high-level instructions into machine code, line by line, as the program is running.

```
class Date                                        //defines what a Date object looks like
{
public:
        void changeDate(int month, int day, int year);   //changes the month, day, and year
        void displayDate( );                      //displays the month, day, and year
private:
        int month;                                //a Date object contains a month,
        int day;                                  //a day, and a year
        int year;
};

Date payDay;                                      //creates a Date object named payDay
```

Figure 9: A partial program written in C++—a high-level object-oriented language

All but the last instruction shown in Figure 9 simply describe what a Date object looks like. You describe an object by specifying its characteristics and behaviors. In this case, a Date object is composed of a month, day, and year. The Date object's month, day, and year can be both changed and displayed. The last instruction shown in Figure 9—Date payDay;—uses the object's description to create the object named payDay.

The object-oriented languages offer two advantages over the procedure-oriented languages. First, object-oriented languages allow a programmer to use familiar objects to solve problems. The ability to use objects that model things found in the real world makes problem solving much easier. Assume, for example, that your task is to create a program that handles the checking account transactions for a bank. Thinking in terms of the objects used by the bank—checking accounts, withdrawal slips, deposit slips, and so on—will make this task easier to accomplish. Second, because each object is viewed as an independent unit, an object can be used in more than one application, with either little or no modification; this saves programming time and money. For example, you can use the Date object shown in Figure 9 in any program that requires a date. In a personnel program, for instance, you could use a Date object to represent a hire date. In an airline reservation program, on the other hand, a Date object might represent a departure date.

Many object-oriented languages, such as C++ and Visual Basic, are direct descendants of existing procedure-oriented languages. The C++ language, for example, is a superset of the procedure-oriented C language; the procedure-oriented predecessor of Visual Basic is the QBasic language. Because both C++ and Visual Basic are based on procedure-oriented languages, you can use either C++ or Visual Basic to create not only object-oriented programs, but procedure-oriented programs as well.

Like procedure-oriented languages, object-oriented languages need a compiler to translate the high-level instructions into machine code.

tip

▶ Languages that can be used to create both procedure-oriented and object-oriented programs are often referred to as hybrid languages.

mini-quiz

Mini-Quiz 2

1. The collection of letters, numerals, and symbols that you can enter into a computer is called the computer's _____ .

2. Instructions written in 0s and 1s are called _____ language.

3. _____ languages allow a programmer to use mnemonics in place of the 0s and 1s in a program.

4. In _____ languages, the emphasis of a program is on *how* to accomplish a task.

5. In _____ languages, the programmer breaks up a problem into interacting objects.

6. When designing programs, procedure-oriented languages use a design methodology called _____ , whereas object-oriented languages use a design methodology called _____ .

As you can see, programming languages have come a long way since the first machine languages. What hasn't changed about programming languages, however, are the three basic control structures used by programmers: sequence, selection, and repetition. These structures are referred to as **control structures** because they control the flow of the program; in other words, they control the order in which the program instructions are processed. You will learn about these three structures in Tutorial 1.

You now have completed the Overview. You can either take a break or complete the end-of-lesson questions and exercises.

SUMMARY

A microcomputer system contains both hardware and software. Hardware refers to the physical components of the system, and consists of the system unit, input devices, output devices, and peripheral devices. The system unit houses internal memory, which is composed of both RAM and ROM chips, and the Central Processing Unit (CPU), which is the brain of the computer.

The CPU contains two principal components—the control unit and the Arithmetic/Logic Unit (ALU)—and special high-speed storage locations called registers. The control unit is responsible for making sure that the computer correctly processes the program instructions and data stored in internal memory. The ALU performs the arithmetic calculations and comparison operations for the computer. The data to be processed is stored in registers in the CPU. The result of arithmetic or comparison operations is stored in a special register, called the accumulator.

Software refers to the step-by-step instructions, called programs, that tell the hardware how to perform a task. Software typically is divided into two categories: system software and application software. System software includes operating systems, device drivers, utilities, and programming languages. Application software includes productivity software, entertainment software, and educational software.

A computer represents each character in its character set—the letters, numerals, and special symbols that can be entered into the computer—by a series of microscopic electronic switches that can be either on or off. Computers use the binary number system to represent the two switch states. The binary number system uses the digit 0 to indicate that a switch is off; it uses a 1 to indicate that the switch is on.

Each switch—each 0 or 1—is called a bit, which is short for *binary digit*. Most computers use eight bits, referred to as a byte, to represent each number, letter, or symbol. Which of the eight bits are on and which are off is determined both by the character being represented and by the coding scheme used by the computer. Microcomputers typically use a coding scheme called ASCII (pronounced ASK-ee), which stands for American Standard Code for Information Interchange.

Programs are the step-by-step instructions that tell a computer how to perform a task. Programmers, the people who write computer programs, use various programming languages to communicate with the computer. The first programming languages were machine languages, also called machine code. The assembly languages came next, followed by the high-level procedure-oriented languages, and then the high-level object-oriented languages.

ANSWERS TO MINI-QUIZZES

Mini-Quiz 1

1. hardware, software
2. input devices, output devices, auxiliary storage devices
3. data
4. RAM
5. ALU, control unit, registers
6. application (or productivity)
7. system
8. registers

Mini-Quiz 2

1. character set

2. machine

3. Assembly

4. high-level procedure-oriented

5. high-level object-oriented

6. top-down design, object-oriented design

Q U E S T I O N S

1. Which of the following is not a peripheral device?
a. auxiliary storage device
b. input device
c. output device
d. system unit

2. A computer's system unit contains _____ .
a. the ALU
b. the control unit
c. internal memory
d. all of the above

3. A storage cell in the internal memory of a computer can store _____ at a time.
a. one instruction
b. one piece of data
c. two or more pieces of data
d. either a or b

4. While the computer is on, you can both write information to and read information from a storage cell located on _____ .
a. a RAM chip
b. a ROM chip
c. either a RAM chip or a ROM chip

5. Which of the following is responsible for making sure that the program instructions stored in internal memory are processed correctly?
a. ALU
b. control unit
c. internal memory unit
d. RAM chip

6. Which of the following performs the arithmetic calculations and logic operations for the computer?
a. ALU
b. control unit
c. internal memory unit
d. ROM chip

7. Where is the result of an arithmetic or comparison operation stored?
a. accumulator
b. adder
c. compiler
d. control unit

8. The set of step-by-step directions given to a computer is called _____.
   a. computerese
   b. a command
   c. a collection
   d. a program

9. Using the binary number system, which of the following indicates that a switch is off?
   a. 0
   b. 1
   c. 2
   d. 3

10. Which of the following is a program that translates high-level instructions into machine code?
    a. assembler
    b. compiler
    c. source program
    d. translator

EXERCISES

1. Briefly explain the history of programming languages as outlined in the Overview.

2. Make a list of your computer system's input devices, output devices, and auxiliary storage devices. Which operating system is your computer using?

3. Appendix A in this book lists the ASCII codes for the letters, numerals, and special symbols included in a computer's character set. What are the ASCII codes for the ampersand (&), the letter S, and the letter s?

4. Explain the difference between top-down design and object-oriented design.

5. List and explain two advantages of using object-oriented languages.

   Exercises 6 and 7 are Discovery Exercises. Discovery Exercises, which may include topics that are not covered in this lesson, allow you to "discover" the solutions to problems on your own.

 6. Research the C++ programming language. Where did it originate? Who developed it? What is the meaning of the two plus signs in the C++ name? (You can use either the Internet or the library to do your research.)

 7. Research both the decimal number system and the binary number system. Explain how both systems work. For example, why do the digits 10100 represent a different number in each system? What number do those digits represent in each system? How can you convert a binary number to its decimal equivalent? How can you convert a decimal number to its binary equivalent?

An Introduction to Control Structures

Concept Lesson

Defining Control Structures

All computer programs, no matter how simple or how complex, are written using one or more of three basic structures: sequence, selection, and repetition. These structures are called **control structures** or **logic structures**, because they control the flow of a program's logic. You will use the sequence structure in every program you write. In most programs, you also will use both the selection and repetition structures.

This tutorial will give you an introduction to the three control structures used in computer programs. It also will introduce you to a computerized mechanical man named Rob, who will help illustrate the control structures. More detailed information about each structure, as well as how to implement these structures using the C++ language, is provided in subsequent tutorials. Begin by learning about the sequence structure.

The Sequence Structure

You already are familiar with the sequence structure—you use it each time you follow a set of directions, in order, from beginning to end. A cookie recipe, for example, provides a good example of the sequence structure. To get to the finished product—edible cookies—you need to follow each recipe instruction in order, beginning with the first instruction and ending with the last. Likewise, the **sequence structure** in a computer program directs the computer to process the program instructions, one after another, in the order listed in the program. You will find the sequence structure in every program.

You can observe how the sequence structure works by programming a mechanical man named Rob. Like a computer, Rob has a limited instruction set—in other words, Rob can understand only a specific number of instructions, also called commands. Rob's instruction set includes the following three commands: `walk`, `turn`, and `sit`. When told to `walk`, Rob takes one complete step forward; in other words, Rob moves his right foot forward one step, then moves his left foot to meet his right foot. When told to `turn`, Rob turns 180 degrees, which is half of a full turn of 360 degrees. When told to `sit`, Rob simply sits down.

For this first example, assume that Rob is facing a chair that is two steps away from him. Your task is to write the instructions, using only the commands that Rob understands, that will direct Rob to sit in the chair. Figure 1-1 shows Rob, the chair, and the instructions that will get Rob seated in the chair.

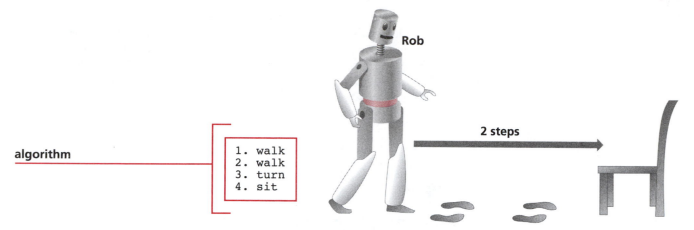

algorithm

```
1. walk
2. walk
3. turn
4. sit
```

2 steps

Figure1-1: An example of the sequence structure

The four instructions shown in Figure 1-1 are called an algorithm. An **algorithm** is simply the set of step-by-step instructions that accomplish a task. Figure 1-1's algorithm, for example, contains the instructions that are necessary to get Rob seated in the chair. Notice that it is important that Rob follow the instructions in the list in order—in other words, in sequence. Rob first must walk two times, then turn, and then sit; he cannot turn first, then walk two times, and then sit.

Learn about the repetition structure next.

mini-quiz

Mini-Quiz 1

1. The three basic control structures are _____ , _____ , and _____ .

2. All programs contain the _____ structure.

3. When using the _____ structure, instructions are followed in the order that they appear in the program.

4. The step-by-step instructions that accomplish a task are called a(n) _____ .

The Repetition Structure

As with the sequence structure, you already are familiar with the repetition structure. For example, shampoo bottles typically include the repetition structure in the directions for washing your hair. Those directions usually tell you to repeat the "apply shampoo to hair," "lather," and "rinse" steps until your hair is clean. When used in a program, the **repetition structure**, also referred to as a **loop**, directs the computer to repeat one or more instructions until some condition is met, at which time the computer should stop repeating the instructions.

You can observe how the repetition structure works by programming Rob, the mechanical man. In this example, Rob is facing a chair that is 50 steps away from him. Your task is to write the algorithm that will sit Rob in the chair. If the sequence structure was the only control structure available to you, you would need to write the `walk` instruction 50 times, followed by `turn`, then `sit`. Although that algorithm would work, it is quite cumbersome to write. Imagine if Rob were 500 steps away from the chair! The best way to write the algorithm to get Rob seated in a chair that is 50 steps away from him is to use the repetition structure. To do so, however, you will need to add another instruction to Rob's instruction set: in addition to `walk`, `turn`, and `sit`, Rob now can understand the command `repeat x times:`, where `x` is the number of times you want him to repeat something. The illustration of Rob and the chair, along with the correct algorithm, is shown in Figure 1-2. Notice that the algorithm contains both the sequence and repetition structures.

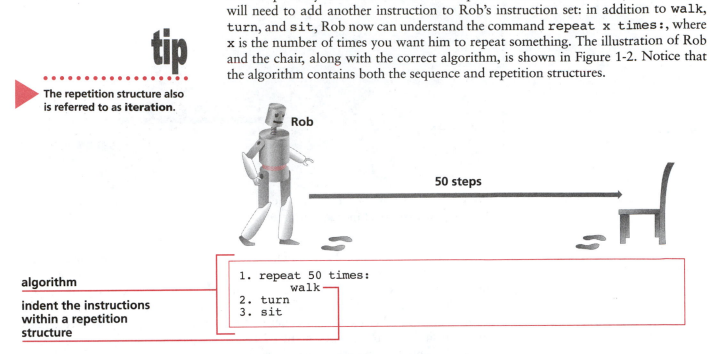

tip

▶ The repetition structure also is referred to as **iteration**.

algorithm

indent the instructions within a repetition structure

Figure 1-2: An example of the repetition structure

Rather than writing the `walk` instruction 50 times, this algorithm uses the `repeat 50 times:` instruction to direct Rob to walk 50 times before he turns and then sits. Notice that the instruction to be repeated—in this case, `walk`—is indented below the `repeat 50 times:` instruction. Indenting in this manner indicates the instructions that are part of the repetition structure and, therefore, are to be repeated. Because the `turn` and `sit` instructions are not part of the repetition structure—in other words, they are to be followed only once, not 50 times—they are not indented. The algorithm shown in Figure 1-2 is both easier to write and much clearer than one containing 50 `walk` instructions.

Recall that the repetition structure repeats one or more instructions until some condition is met, at which time the repetition structure ends. In the example shown in Figure 1-2, the repetition structure ends after Rob walks 50 times. Rob is then free to continue to the next instruction in the algorithm—in this case, `turn`, followed by `sit`. But what if you don't know precisely how many steps there are between Rob and the chair? In that case, you need simply to change the repetition structure's condition.

In the next example, assume that Rob is facing a chair and you don't know how far away from the chair he is. As before, your task is to write the algorithm that will get Rob seated in the chair. In order to accomplish this task, you will need to add another instruction to Rob's instruction set: Rob now can understand the instruction `repeat until you are directly in front of the chair:`. The new algorithm is shown in Figure 1-3.

tip

▶ Although the repetition structure shown in Figure 1-2 includes only one instruction, a repetition structure can include many instructions.

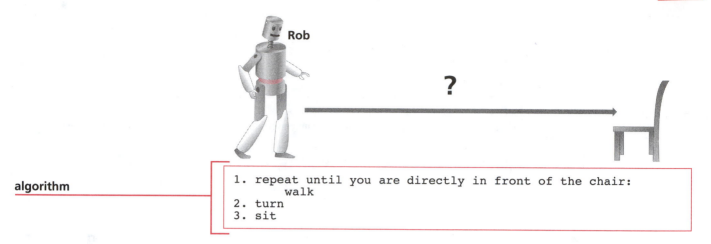

Rob

algorithm

```
1. repeat until you are directly in front of the chair:
       walk
2. turn
3. sit
```

Figure 1-3: Another example of the repetition structure

The repetition structure shown in Figure 1-3's algorithm ends when Rob is standing directly in front of the chair. If Rob is 10 steps away from the chair, the repetition structure directs him to walk 10 times before he turns and then sits. If Rob is 500 steps away from the chair, the repetition structure directs him to walk 500 times before he turns and then sits. If Rob is directly in front of the chair, the repetition structure is bypassed, and Rob simply turns and then sits.

The last of the three control structures is the selection structure.

The Selection Structure

Like the sequence and repetition structures, you already are familiar with the **selection structure**, also called the **decision structure**. The selection structure makes a decision, and then takes an appropriate action based on that decision. You use the selection structure every time you drive your car and approach an intersection. Your decision, as well as the appropriate action, is based on whether the intersection has a stop sign. If the intersection has a stop sign, then you stop your car; otherwise, you proceed with caution through the intersection. When used in a computer program, the selection structure alerts the computer that a decision needs to be made. The selection structure also provides the appropriate action to take based on the result of that decision.

As before, Rob can demonstrate the selection structure, although you will need to add to his instruction set to do so. In this example, assume that Rob is holding either a red or yellow balloon, and that he is facing two boxes. One of the boxes is colored yellow and the other is colored red. The two boxes are located 20 steps away from Rob. Your task is to have Rob drop the balloon into the appropriate box—the yellow balloon belongs in the yellow box, and the red balloon belongs in the red box. After Rob drops the balloon, you then should return him to his original position. To write an algorithm to accomplish the current task, you will need to add four more instructions to Rob's instruction set. The new instructions will allow Rob to make a decision about the color of the balloon he is holding, and then take the appropriate action based on that decision. Rob's new instruction set is shown in Figure 1-4.

four new
instructions

```
walk
turn
sit
repeat x times:
repeat until you are directly in front of the chair:
if the balloon is red, do this:
otherwise, do this: (This instruction can be used only in combination with an if instruction)
drop the balloon in the red box
drop the balloon in the yellow box
```

Figure 1-4: Rob's new instruction set

Figure 1-5 shows an illustration of this example, along with the correct algorithm.

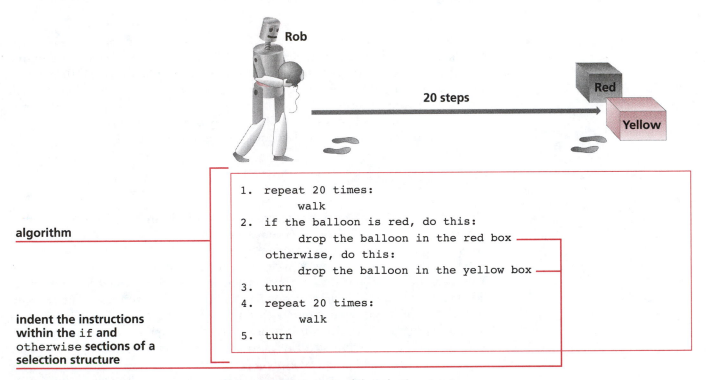

algorithm

```
1.  repeat 20 times:
        walk
2.  if the balloon is red, do this:
        drop the balloon in the red box
    otherwise, do this:
        drop the balloon in the yellow box
3.  turn
4.  repeat 20 times:
        walk
5.  turn
```

indent the instructions
within the if and
otherwise sections of a
selection structure

Figure 1-5: An example of the selection structure

Notice that the instruction to be followed when the balloon is red—in this case, drop the balloon in the red box—and the instruction to be followed when the balloon is not red—in this case, drop the balloon in the yellow box—are indented. As you do with the instructions contained in a repetition structure, you also indent the instructions contained within the if and otherwise sections of a selection structure. Indenting in this manner makes it clear which instructions are to be followed when the balloon is red and which should be followed when the balloon is not red. Also indented in Figure 1-5 is the walk instruction contained in both repetition structures.

Notice that the algorithm shown in Figure 1-5 contains all three control structures: sequence, selection, and repetition. The repetition structure, which directs Rob to walk 20 times, is processed first. After Rob walks the 20 steps, the repetition structure ends and Rob proceeds, sequentially, to the next instruction listed in the algorithm; that instruction involves a decision. If the balloon Rob is holding is red, then Rob should drop it into the red box; otherwise, he should drop it into the yellow box. Once the decision is made and the proper action is taken, the selection structure ends and Rob proceeds to the next instruction listed in the algorithm—turn. After turning 180 degrees, the second repetition structure, which directs Rob to walk 20 times, and the last instruction, which turns Rob 180 degrees, return Rob to his original position.

mini-quiz

Mini-Quiz 2

1. You use the _____ structure to repeat one or more instructions in a program.

2. The _____ structure ends when its condition has been met.

3. The _____ structure, also called the decision structure, instructs the computer to make a decision, and then take some action based on the result of the decision.

You now have completed Tutorial 1's Concept lesson. You can either take a break or complete the end-of-lesson questions and exercises before moving on to the Application lesson.

SUMMARY

An algorithm is the set of step-by-step instructions that solve a problem. The algorithms for all computer programs contain one or more of the following three control structures: sequence, selection, and repetition. The control structures, also called logic structures, are so named because they control the flow of a program's logic.

The sequence structure directs the computer to process the instructions, one after another, in the order listed in the program. The repetition structure directs the computer to repeat one or more instructions until some condition is met. The selection structure, also called the decision structure, directs the computer to make a decision, and then selects an appropriate action to take based on that decision. The sequence structure is used in all programs. Most programs also contain both the selection and repetition structures.

ANSWERS TO MINI-QUIZZES

Mini-Quiz 1

1. sequence, selection, repetition

2. sequence

3. sequence

4. algorithm

Mini-Quiz 2

1. repetition

2. repetition

3. selection

QUESTIONS

1. Which of the following is not a programming control structure?
   a. repetition
   b. selection
   c. sequence
   d. sorting

2. Which of the following control structures is used in every program?
   a. repetition
   b. selection
   c. sequence
   d. switching

3. The set of instructions for how to add two numbers is an example of the _____ structure.
   a. control
   b. repetition
   c. selection
   d. sequence

4. The step-by-step instructions that solve a problem are called _____.
   a. an algorithm
   b. a list
   c. a plan
   d. a sequential structure

5. The recipe instruction "Beat until smooth" is an example of the _____ structure.
   a. control
   b. repetition
   c. selection
   d. sequence

6. The instruction "If it's raining outside, then take an umbrella to work" is an example of the _____ structure.
   a. control
   b. repetition
   c. selection
   d. sequence

7. Which control structure would an algorithm use to determine whether a credit card holder is over his or her credit limit?
   a. repetition
   b. selection
   c. both repetition and selection

8. Which control structure would an algorithm use to calculate a 5% commission for each of a company's salespeople?
   a. repetition
   b. selection
   c. both repetition and selection

9. Assume a company pays a 3% annual bonus to employees who have been with the company over 5 years; other employees receive a 1% bonus. Which control structure would an algorithm use to calculate each employee's bonus?
   a. repetition
   b. selection
   c. both repetition and selection

E X E R C I S E S

You will use Rob, the mechanical man, to complete Exercises 1 and 2. Rob's instruction set is shown in Figure 1-6.

walk   (**Rob moves his right foot forward one step, then moves his left foot to meet his right foot**) sit turn   (**180-degree turn**) jump   (**allows Rob to jump over anything in his path**) throw the box out of the way if the box is red, do this: otherwise, do this: (**this instruction can be used only in combination with an** `if` **instruction**) repeat x times:

Figure 1-6

1. Rob is five steps away from a box, and the box is 10 steps away from a chair, as illustrated in Figure 1-7. Create an algorithm, using only the instructions shown in Figure 1-6, that will sit Rob in the chair. Assume that Rob must jump over the box before he can continue toward the chair.

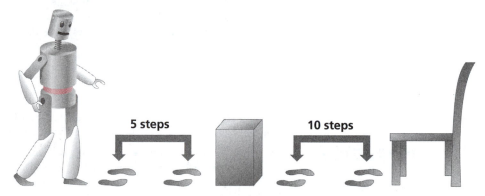

5 steps   10 steps

Figure 1-7

2. Rob is five steps away from a box, and the box is 10 steps away from a chair, as illustrated in Figure 1-7. Create an algorithm, using only the instructions shown in Figure 1-6, that will sit Rob in the chair. Assume that Rob will need to jump over the box if the box is red; otherwise he will need to throw the box out of the way.

3. Assume a company pays an annual bonus to its employees. The bonus is based on the number of years the employee has been with the company. Employees working at the company for less than 5 years receive a 1% bonus; all others receive a 2% bonus. Write two versions of an algorithm that will print each employee's bonus. Use only the instructions shown in Figure 1-8 to do so. Be sure to indent the instructions appropriately.

calculate the bonus by multiplying the salary by 1%
calculate the bonus by multiplying the salary by 2%
if the years employed are greater than or equal to 5, do this:
if the years employed are less than 5, do this:
otherwise, do this:
print the bonus
read the salary and years employed
repeat for each employee:

Figure 1-8

4. Assume a store gives a 10 percent discount to customers who are at least 65 years old. Write two versions of an algorithm that will print the amount of money a customer owes. Use only the instructions shown in Figure 1-9 to do so. Be sure to indent the instructions appropriately.

assign 10% as the discount rate
assign 0 as the discount rate
calculate the amount due by multiplying the item price by (1 minus the discount rate)
if the customer's age is greater than or equal to 65, do this:
if the customer's age is less than 65, do this:
otherwise, do this:
print the amount due
read the customer's age and item price

Figure 1-9

Exercise 5 is a Discovery Exercise. Discovery Exercises, which may include topics that are not covered in this lesson, allow you to "discover" the solutions to problems on your own.

discovery

5. Create an algorithm that tells someone how to evaluate the following expression (the / operator means division and the * operator means multiplication). (*Hint*: As you may remember from your math courses, division and multiplication are performed before addition and subtraction.)

    12 / 2 + 3 * 2 – 3

A computer program is good only if it works. Errors in either an algorithm or programming code can cause a program to run incorrectly. Therefore, a programmer needs to know how to locate and fix these errors. Exercise 6 is a Debugging Exercise. Debugging Exercises allow you to practice recognizing and solving errors in a program.

debugging

6. The algorithm shown in Figure 1-10 should evaluate the expression x + y / z * 3, but it is not working correctly. Correct the algorithm.

1. add x to y
2. divide the result of step 1 by z
3. multiply the result from step 2 by 3

Figure 1-10

Application Lesson

Using the Control Structures

case ▶ Rob, the mechanical man, is standing in front of a flower bed that contains six flowers. Your task in this lesson is to create an algorithm that will direct Rob to pick the flowers as he walks to the other side of the flower bed. Rob should pick all red flowers with his right hand. Flowers that are not red should be picked with his left hand.

Programming Rob the Mechanical Man

Before you can complete this lesson, the Rob the Mechanical Man files must be installed on your computer's hard disk; the installation process is described in the following eight steps.

> **Important note:** If you are working on a computer in your school's computer lab, the files may already be installed on the computer. If they are installed, you can skip the following eight steps. If you are unsure whether the files are installed, ask your instructor or technical support person before completing the eight steps.

To install the Rob the Mechanical Man files on your computer's hard disk:

1 Click the **Start** button on the taskbar, and then click **Run** to open the Run dialog box.

2 Click the **Browse** button to open the Browse dialog box. Open the **Rob Installation Files** folder, which is located in the Cpp folder on your computer's hard drive.

3 Click **Setup** (Setup.exe) in the list of filenames, and then click the **Open** button to return to the Run dialog box.

4 Click the **OK** button in the Run dialog box. A message box appears and indicates that seven files are being copied to your computer's hard disk. After the files are copied, the Rob the Mechanical Man Setup dialog box opens.

5 Read the message in the dialog box. If necessary, close any open files, then click the **OK** button in the dialog box. A message concerning installation appears in the dialog box, as shown in Figure 1-11.

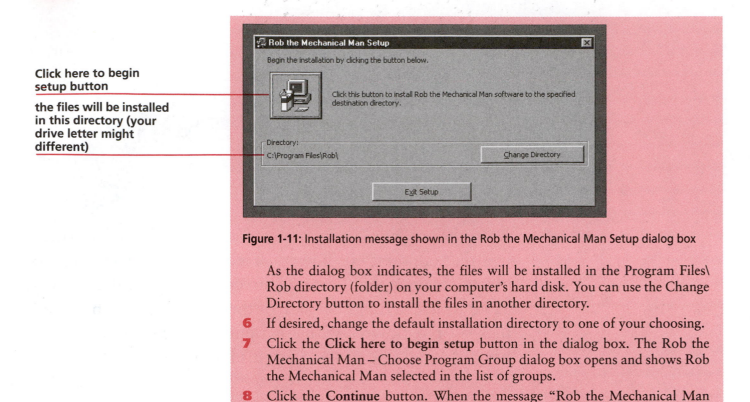

Click here to begin setup button

the files will be installed in this directory (your drive letter might different)

Figure 1-11: Installation message shown in the Rob the Mechanical Man Setup dialog box

As the dialog box indicates, the files will be installed in the Program Files\ Rob directory (folder) on your computer's hard disk. You can use the Change Directory button to install the files in another directory.

6 If desired, change the default installation directory to one of your choosing.

7 Click the **Click here to begin setup** button in the dialog box. The Rob the Mechanical Man – Choose Program Group dialog box opens and shows Rob the Mechanical Man selected in the list of groups.

8 Click the **Continue** button. When the message "Rob the Mechanical Man Setup was completed successfully" appears, click the **OK** button.

Figure 1-12 shows an illustration of Rob and the flower bed.

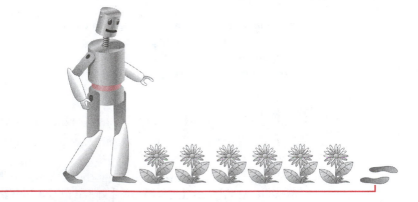

Rob should end up on the other side of the flower bed

Figure 1-12: Rob and the flower bed

Your computer's hard disk contains an application that you can use to create the algorithm that directs Rob to pick the flowers as he walks to the other side of the flower bed.

To run the application that you will use to create Rob's algorithm:

1 Click the **Start** button on the taskbar, and then point to **Programs** on the Start menu.

2 Point to **Rob the Mechanical Man** on the Programs menu, and then click **Application Lesson**. The Rob the Mechanical Man application shown in Figure 1-13 appears on your screen.

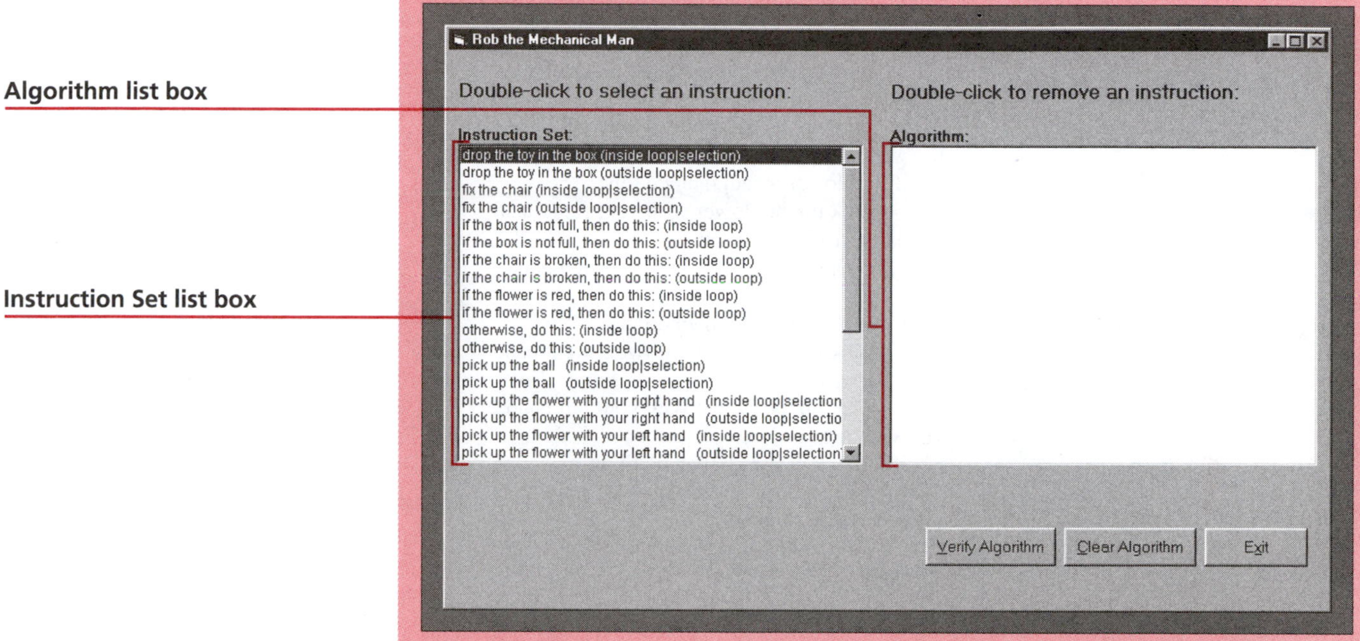

Algorithm list box

Instruction Set list box

Figure 1-13: Rob the Mechanical Man application

The application shown in Figure 1-13 contains two list boxes, identified by the labels Instruction Set and Algorithm. The Instruction Set list box displays the set of instructions that Rob can understand. Double-clicking an instruction in the Instruction Set list box copies the instruction to the Algorithm list box, which currently is empty. If you make a mistake and want to remove an instruction from the Algorithm list box, you do so simply by double-clicking the instruction in the Algorithm list box. When you are finished adding the appropriate instructions to the Algorithm list box, you can click the Verify Algorithm button to verify that the algorithm is correct. Clicking the Clear Algorithm button removes all of the instructions from the Algorithm list box, and clicking the Exit button ends the application.

As Figure 1-12 indicates, Rob is standing in front of a flower bed that contains six flowers. If the first flower is red, Rob should pick the flower with his right hand; otherwise, he should pick it with his left hand. He then should walk one step forward to position himself in front of the second flower. If the second flower is red, Rob should pick it with his right hand; otherwise, he should use his left hand. He then should walk one step forward to position himself in front of the third flower. Rob will need to follow the same procedure for each flower in the flower bed. After picking the last flower, Rob will need to walk two steps forward, rather than one step, to end up on the other side of the flower bed. Figure 1-14 shows the initial algorithm for Rob.

```
1. if the flower is red, then do this:
       pick up the flower with your right hand
   otherwise, do this:
       pick up the flower with your left hand
2. walk
3. if the flower is red, then do this:
       pick up the flower with your right hand
   otherwise, do this:
       pick up the flower with your left hand
4. walk
5. if the flower is red, then do this:
       pick up the flower with your right hand
   otherwise, do this:
       pick up the flower with your left hand
6. walk
7. if the flower is red, then do this:
       pick up the flower with your right hand
   otherwise, do this:
       pick up the flower with your left hand
8. walk
9. if the flower is red, then do this:
       pick up the flower with your right hand
   otherwise, do this:
       pick up the flower with your left hand
10. walk
11. if the flower is red, then do this:
       pick up the flower with your right hand
   otherwise, do this:
       pick up the flower with your left hand
12. walk
13. walk
```

Figure 1-14: Initial algorithm for Rob

Although the algorithm shown in Figure 1-14 will work correctly, notice that it is quite long. Imagine if Rob had 50 flowers to pick—you would need to repeat the selection structure and the `walk` instruction 50 times! Figure 1-15 shows a more efficient and convenient way of writing this algorithm.

```
1. repeat 6 times:
       if the flower is red, then do this:
           pick up the flower with your right hand
       otherwise, do this:
           pick up the flower with your left hand
       walk
2. walk
```

Figure 1-15: Final algorithm for Rob

tip
• • • • • • • • • • • • • • •
You can remove an instruction from the Algorithm list box by double-clicking the instruction in the list box.

Rather than listing the instructions to determine the color, pick the flower, and then walk for each of the six flowers, the algorithm shown in Figure 1-15 uses the repetition structure to direct Rob to repeat those instructions six times.

Now use the application on your screen to enter the algorithm shown in Figure 1-15 and verify that it works correctly.

To enter the algorithm shown in Figure 1-15, and then verify that it works correctly:

1 Scroll down the Instruction Set list box until you see the `repeat 6 times:` instruction. Double-click **repeat 6 times:** in the Instruction Set list box. The instruction appears in the Algorithm list box, as shown in Figure 1-16.

the instruction is copied here

double-click this instruction

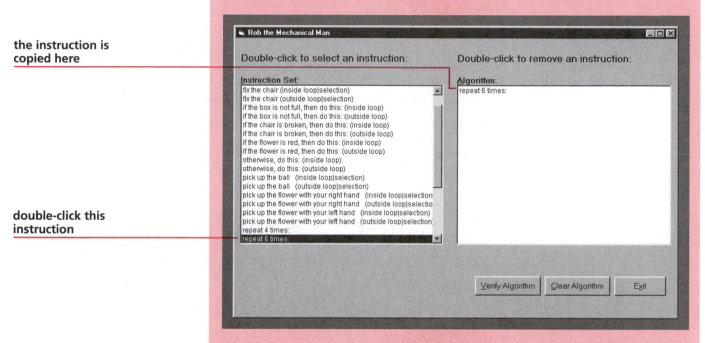

Figure 1-16: First instruction shown in the Algorithm list box

HELP? If you inadvertently selected the wrong instruction, double-click the incorrect instruction in the Algorithm list box to remove the instruction, then repeat Step 1.

According to the algorithm shown in Figure 1-15, Rob needs to use a selection structure to determine if the color of the current flower is red. The Instruction Set list box contains two instructions that can be used to determine this: `if the flower is red, then do this: (inside loop)` and `if the flower is red, then do this: (outside loop)`. The instruction you use will depend on whether you want the instruction to be part of a repetition structure (loop). If the instruction should be included in a repetition structure, you would choose `if the flower is red, then do this: (inside loop)`; otherwise, you would choose `if the flower is red, then do this: (outside loop)`. In this case, you want the instruction that determines the flower's color to be inside the loop.

2 Double-click **if the flower is red, then do this: (inside loop)** to copy this instruction to the Algorithm list box. Notice that the instruction appears indented below the `repeat 6 times:` instruction. The indentation indicates that the `if the flower is red, then do this: (inside loop)` instruction is included in the repetition structure.

tip

As you learned in the Concept lesson, the repetition structure also is referred to as a loop.

▶ Technically, the `pick up the flower with your right hand (inside loop|selection)` instruction also is inside the `repeat 6 times:` **loop.** This is because the selection structure in which the instruction is contained is inside the loop.

If the flower is red, then Rob needs to pick it with his right hand. The instruction to pick the flower should be included in the selection structure. You can do so using the `pick up the flower with your right hand (inside loop|selection)` instruction. (The `loop|selection` in an instruction means that you can use the instruction within either a loop or a selection structure.)

3 Double-click **pick up the flower with your right hand (inside loop | selection)** to copy this instruction to the Algorithm list box. Because this instruction is part of the selection structure, it appears indented below the `if the flower is red, then do this: (inside loop)` instruction.

If the flower is not red, then Rob needs to pick it with his left hand.

4 Double-click **otherwise, do this: (inside loop)**, then double-click **pick up the flower with your left hand (inside loop|selection)**.

After picking a flower, Rob needs to walk one step forward. This instruction should be part of the `repeat 6 times:` repetition structure, because it needs to be done after picking each of the six flowers.

5 Scroll down the Instruction Set list box, if necessary, until you locate the `walk (inside loop|selection)` instruction, then double-click **walk (inside loop|selection)**.

The last instruction in the algorithm shown in Figure 1-15 is to have Rob walk one step forward; this will position him at the end of the flower bed. Because this instruction should be followed only once, after Rob has picked the six flowers, you will need to place the instruction outside the `repeat 6 times:` repetition structure.

6 Double-click **walk (outside loop|selection)**. Figure 1-17 shows the completed algorithm in the Algorithm list box.

completed algorithm

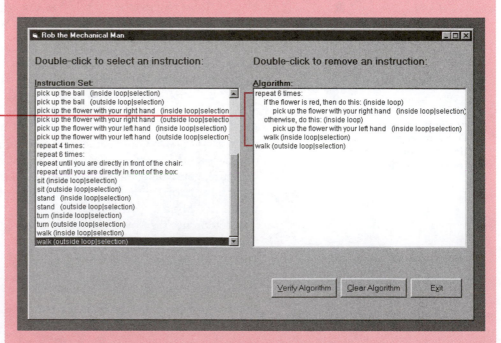

Figure 1-17: The completed algorithm shown in the Algorithm list box

You can verify that the algorithm is correct by clicking the Verify Algorithm button.

7   Click the **Verify Algorithm** button. A dialog box containing the message "Great job!" opens. Click the **OK** button to close the dialog box.

8   Click the **Exit** button to close the application.

You now have completed Tutorial 1's Application lesson. You can either take a break or complete the end-of-lesson exercises.

> **Important note:** Rob, the mechanical man, is used only in this tutorial. When you have completed this lesson's Exercises, you can remove the Rob the Mechanical Man files from your computer's hard disk. However, if you are working on a computer in your school's computer lab, check with your instructor or technical support person before removing the files.

To uninstall the Rob the Mechanical Man program:

1   Click the **Start** button, point to **Settings**, then click **Control Panel**.

2   Double-click **Add/Remove Programs** to open the Add/Remove Programs Properties dialog box.

3   Scroll down the list box, if necessary, then click **Rob the Mechanical Man** in the list. Click the **Add/Remove** (**Change/Remove** in Windows 2000) button. When you are asked if you are sure you want to remove Rob the Mechanical Man and all of its components, click the **Yes** button.

4   When the "Program installation removed" message appears, click the **OK** button.

5   Click the **OK** (**Close** in Windows 2000) button to close the Add/Remove Programs Properties dialog box, then close the Control Panel window.

E X E R C I S E S

1.   In this exercise, you will create an algorithm that directs Rob, the mechanical man, to perform a set of tasks.

    a. Click the Start button, and then point to Programs on the Start menu. Point to Rob the Mechanical Man on the Programs menu, and then click Application Exercises.

    b. Rob is facing a box that is located zero or more steps away from him. Rob is carrying a toy in his right hand. Create an algorithm, using only the instructions shown in the Instruction Set list box, that will direct Rob to drop the toy in the box.

    c. When you have completed the algorithm, click the Exercise 1 button to verify that the algorithm is correct.

    d. When the algorithm is working correctly, click the Exit button to end the application.

2.   In this exercise, you will create an algorithm that directs Rob, the mechanical man, to perform a set of tasks.

    a. Click the Start button, and then point to Programs on the Start menu. Point to Rob the Mechanical Man on the Programs menu, and then click Application Exercises.

    b. Rob is seated in a chair and is four steps away from a table. A ball is resting on the top of the table, as illustrated in Figure 1-18. Create an algorithm, using only the instructions shown in the Instruction Set list box, that will direct Rob to pick up the ball, and then return him to his original position.

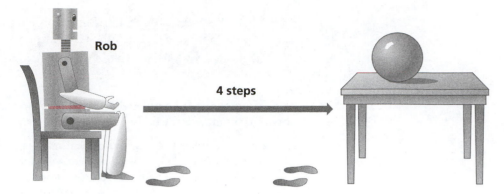

Figure 1-18

    c. When you have completed the algorithm, click the Exercise 2 button to verify that the algorithm is correct.

    d. When the algorithm is working correctly, click the Exit button to end the application.

3. In this exercise, you will create an algorithm that directs Rob, the mechanical man, to perform a set of tasks.

    a. Click the Start button, and then point to Programs on the Start menu. Point to Rob the Mechanical Man on the Programs menu, and then click Application Exercises.

    b. Rob is facing a chair that is located zero or more steps away from him. Create an algorithm, using only the instructions shown in the Instruction Set list box, that will sit Rob in the chair, but only if the chair is not broken. If the chair is broken, the algorithm should instruct Rob to fix the chair.

    c. When you have completed the algorithm, click the Exercise 3 button to verify that the algorithm is correct.

    d. When the algorithm is working correctly, click the Exit button to end the application.

4. In this exercise, you will create an algorithm that directs Rob, the mechanical man, to perform a set of tasks.

    a. Click the Start button, and then point to Programs on the Start menu. Point to Rob the Mechanical Man on the Programs menu, and then click Application Exercises.

    b. Rob, who is seated in a chair, is facing a box that is zero or more steps away from him. Rob is holding a toy in his left hand. Create an algorithm, using only the instructions shown in the Instruction Set list box, that will direct Rob to drop the toy in the box—but only if the box is not full. The algorithm also should return Rob to his original position.

    c. When you have completed the algorithm, click the Exercise 4 button to verify that the algorithm is correct.

    d. When the algorithm is working correctly, click the Exit button to end the application.

5. Using only the instructions shown in Figure 1-19, create an algorithm that shows the steps an instructor takes when grading a test that contains 25 questions.

> if the student's answer is not the same as the correct answer, do this:
> repeat 25 times:
> read the student's answer and the correct answer
> mark the student's answer incorrect

Figure 1-19

6. You have just purchased a new personal computer system. Before putting the system components together, you read the instruction booklet that came with the system. The booklet contains a list of the components that you should have received. The booklet advises you to verify that you received all of the components by matching those that you received with those on the list. If a component was received, you should cross its name off the list; otherwise, you should draw a circle around the component's name in the list. Using only the instructions shown in Figure 1-20, create an algorithm that shows the steps you should take to verify that the package contains the correct components.

cross the component name off the list
read the component name from the list
circle the component's name on the list
search the package for the component
if the component was received, do this:
otherwise, do this: (**this instruction can be used only in combination with an if instruction**)
repeat for each component name on the list:

Figure 1-20

Exercises 7 and 8 are Discovery Exercises. Discovery Exercises, which may include topics that are not covered in this lesson, allow you to "discover" the solutions to problems on your own.

7. Complete the algorithm shown in Figure 1-21. The algorithm should show a payroll clerk how to calculate and print the gross pay for five workers. If an employee works more than 40 hours, he or she should receive time and one-half for the hours worked over 40.

1. _____
   read the employee's name, hours worked, and pay rate
   _____
         calculate the gross pay by multiplying the hours worked by the pay rate
   otherwise, do this:
         calculate the overtime hours by subtracting 40 from the number of hours worked
         calculate the overtime pay by multiplying the overtime hours by the pay rate
         divided by 2
         calculate the gross pay by _____
   print the employee's name and gross pay

Figure 1-21

8. Create an algorithm that tells someone how to evaluate the following expression (the / operator means division and the * operator means multiplication):

   12 / 2 + 3 * (4 – 2) + 1

A computer program is good only if it works. Errors in either an algorithm or programming code can cause a program to run incorrectly. Therefore, a programmer needs to know how to locate and fix these errors. Exercises 9 and 10 are Debugging Exercises. Debugging Exercises allow you to practice recognizing and solving errors in a program.

debugging

9. The algorithm shown in Figure 1-22 is not working correctly; it does not get Rob seated in the chair. Correct the algorithm.

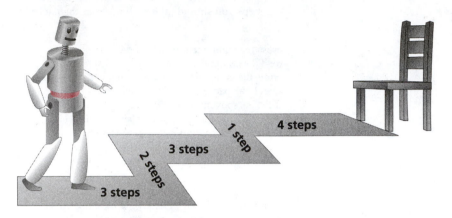

```
 1.  repeat 3 times:
          walk
 2.  turn left 90 degrees
 3.  repeat 2 times:
          walk
 4.  turn right 90 degrees
 5.  repeat 2 times:
          walk
 6.  turn right 90 degrees
 7.  walk
 8.  turn right 90 degrees
 9.  repeat 4 times:
          walk
10.  turn around 180 degrees
11.  sit
```

Figure 1-22

debugging   **10.** The algorithm shown in Figure 1-23 does not get Rob through the maze. Correct the algorithm.

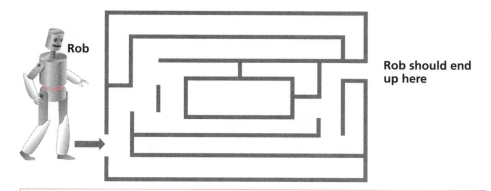

```
 1.  walk into maze
 2.  turn left 90 degrees
 3.  repeat until you are directly in front of a wall:
        walk
 4.  turn right 90 degrees
 5.  repeat until you are directly in front of a wall:
        walk
 6.  turn right 90 degrees
 7.  repeat until you are directly in front of a wall:
        walk
 8.  turn right 90 degrees
 9.  repeat until you are directly in front of a wall:
        walk
10.  turn right 90 degrees
11.  repeat until you are directly in front of a wall:
        walk
12.  turn left 90 degrees
13.  repeat until you are directly in front of a wall:
        turn right 90 degrees
14.  repeat until you are out of the maze:
        walk
```

Figure 1-23

Beginning the Problem-Solving Process

objectives

After completing this tutorial, you will be able to:

- Explain the problem-solving process used to create a computer program
- Analyze a problem
- Complete an IPO chart
- Plan an algorithm using pseudocode and flowcharts
- Desk-check an algorithm

Concept Lesson

Problem Solving

In this tutorial, you will learn the process that programmers follow to solve problems using a computer. Although you may not realize it, you use a similar process to solve hundreds of small problems every day, such as how to get to school and what to do when you are hungry. Because most of these problems occur so often, however, you typically solve them almost automatically, without giving much thought to the process your brain goes through to arrive at the solutions. Unfortunately, problems that are either complex or unfamiliar usually cannot be solved so easily; most require extensive analysis and planning. Understanding the thought process involved in solving simple and familiar problems will make solving complex or unfamiliar ones easier.

First, you will explore the thought process that you follow when solving common, daily problems. Then, you will learn how to use a similar process to create a computer solution to a problem—in other words, to create a computer program. The computer solutions you will create in this tutorial will contain the sequence control structure only, where each instruction will be processed in order, from beginning to end.

In Tutorials 8 and 9, you will learn how to include the selection structure in a program. Then, in Tutorial 10, you will learn how to include the repetition structure.

Solving Everyday Problems

The first step in solving a familiar problem is to analyze the problem. You then plan, review, implement, evaluate, and modify (if necessary) the solution. Consider, for example, how you solve the everyday problem of being hungry. First, your mind analyzes the problem to identify its important components. One very important component of any problem is the goal of solving the problem; in this case, the goal is to stop the hunger pangs. Other important components of a problem are the things that you can use to accomplish the goal. For example, you can use the lettuce, tomato, cucumber, and salad dressing that are in your refrigerator to relieve your hunger pangs.

After analyzing the problem, your mind plans an algorithm. Recall from Tutorial 1 that an algorithm is simply the step-by-step instructions that describe how to accomplish a task. In other words, an algorithm is a solution to a problem. The hunger problem's algorithm, for example, describes how to use the lettuce, tomato, cucumber, and salad dressing to stop your hunger pangs. Figure 2-1 shows a summary of the analysis and planning steps for the hunger problem.

result of analysis step

Items used to accomplish the goal	Algorithm	Goal
lettuce tomato cucumber salad dressing	1. rinse the lettuce, tomato, and cucumber 2. cut up the lettuce, tomato, and cucumber 3. place the lettuce, tomato, and cucumber in a salad bowl 4. pour the salad dressing on the salad 5. eat the salad	stop the hunger pangs

result of planning step

Figure 2-1: Summary of the analysis and planning steps for the hunger problem

After planning the algorithm, you review it (in your mind) to verify that it will work as intended. When you are satisfied that the algorithm is correct, you implement the algorithm by following each of its instructions in the order indicated. In this case, for example, you rinse the lettuce, tomato, and cucumber, and then cut them up, place them in a salad bowl, pour salad dressing on the salad, and then eat the salad.

Finally, after implementing the algorithm, you evaluate it and, if necessary, you modify it. In this case, if your hunger pangs are gone after eating the salad, then your algorithm is correct because it accomplishes its goal. If, on the other hand, you still are hungry, then you know that you need to modify the algorithm for the next time. An example of a modified algorithm for the hunger problem is shown in Figure 2-2.

Items used to accomplish the goal	Algorithm	Goal
lettuce tomato cucumber salad dressing apple	1. rinse the lettuce, tomato, and cucumber 2. cut up the lettuce, tomato, and cucumber 3. place the lettuce, tomato, and cucumber in a salad bowl 4. pour the salad dressing on the salad 5. eat the salad 6. rinse the apple 7. eat the apple	stop the hunger pangs

modifications made to original algorithm

Figure 2-2: Modified algorithm for the hunger problem

In the next section, you will learn that a similar thought process is used to create computer solutions to problems.

Creating Computer Solutions to Problems

In the previous section, you learned how you create a solution to a problem that occurs every day. A similar problem-solving process is used to create a computer program. A computer program is also a solution, but one that is implemented with a computer. The problem-solving process that computer programmers use when creating a computer program is shown in Figure 2-3.

1. Analyze the problem.

2. Plan the algorithm.

3. Desk-check the algorithm.

4. Code the algorithm into a program.

5. Desk-check the program.

6. Evaluate and modify (if necessary) the program.

Figure 2-3: The problem-solving process for creating a computer program

Just like you do, a computer programmer also first analyzes the problem. He or she then plans the algorithm—the steps that tell the computer how to solve the problem. Programmers use tools such as IPO (Input, Processing, Output) charts, pseudocode, and flowcharts to help them analyze problems and develop algorithms. You will learn about these tools in this lesson.

After the analysis and planning steps, the programmer then desk-checks the algorithm. **Desk-checking**, also called **hand-tracing**, means that you use pencil and paper, along with sample data, to walk through each of the steps in the algorithm manually, just as if you were the computer. Programmers desk-check the algorithm to verify that it will work as intended. If any errors are found in the algorithm, the errors are corrected before the programmer continues to the next step in the problem-solving process. Eliminating errors at this pencil and paper stage will make it much easier to produce a correct program in the later steps of the problem-solving process.

When the programmer is satisfied that the algorithm is correct, he or she then translates the algorithm into a language that the computer can understand. Programmers refer to this step as **coding** the algorithm. You will begin learning how to code an algorithm in Tutorial 3. A coded algorithm is called a **program**. In this book, you will use the C++ programming language to code your algorithms.

After creating the program—the coded version of the algorithm—the programmer desk-checks the program to make sure that he or she translated each of the algorithm's steps correctly. If any errors are found in the program, the errors are corrected before the programmer continues to the final step in the problem-solving process.

The final step in the problem-solving process is to evaluate and modify (if necessary) the program. A programmer evaluates a program by running it, along with sample data, on the computer. If the program does not work as intended, then the programmer makes the necessary modifications until the program works correctly.

In this tutorial, you will learn how to use the first three problem-solving steps to create a computer program; you will explore the last three steps in Tutorial 3. Begin with the first step in the problem-solving process, which is to analyze the problem.

The term *desk-checking* refers to the fact that the programmer is seated at his or her desk, rather than in front of the computer, when reviewing the algorithm. The term *hand-tracing* refers to the fact that the programmer uses a pencil and paper to follow each of the steps in the algorithm by hand.

The importance of the first three steps in the problem-solving process cannot be stressed enough. If a programmer does not take the time to analyze the problem, then plan and desk-check the algorithm, the computer program he or she creates typically will contain errors that are difficult to find and expensive to correct.

Analyzing the Problem

You cannot solve a problem unless you understand it, and you cannot understand a problem unless you analyze it—in other words, unless you identify its important components. The purpose of analyzing a problem is to determine the goal of solving the problem, and the items that are needed to achieve that goal. Programmers refer to the goal as the **output**, and the items needed to achieve the goal as the **input**. When analyzing a problem, you always search first for the output, and then for the input. Many times you will need to consult with the program's user—the person for whom you are creating the program—to determine the output and the input. This is especially true if the problem specification provided by the user is unclear or incomplete. Analyze the problem specification shown in Figure 2-4.

> Sarah Martin has been working for Quality Builders for four years. Last year, Sarah received a 4% raise, which brought her current weekly pay to $250. Sarah is scheduled to receive a 3% raise next week. She wants you to write a program that will display, on the computer screen, the amount of her new weekly pay.

Figure 2-4: Problem specification

When analyzing a problem, you always determine the output first. A helpful way to identify the output is to search the problem specification for an answer to the following question: *What does the user want to see either printed on paper, displayed on the screen, or stored in a file?* The answer to this question typically will be stated as nouns and adjectives in the problem specification. The problem specification shown in Figure 2-4, for instance, indicates that Sarah (the program's user) wants to see her new weekly pay displayed on the screen; the output, therefore, is the new weekly pay. Notice that the words *new* and *weekly* are adjectives, and that the word *pay* is a noun.

IPO Charts

Programmers use an **IPO** (**Input, Processing, Output**) chart to organize and summarize the results of a problem analysis. Figure 2-5 shows a partially completed IPO chart for Sarah's problem. Notice that you list the output items in the Output column of the IPO chart.

Input	Processing	Output
	Processing items: Algorithm:	new weekly pay

Figure 2-5: Partially completed IPO chart showing the output

tip

You can draw an IPO chart by hand, or you can use the table feature in a word processor (such as Microsoft Word) to draw one.

After determining the output, you then determine the input. A helpful way to identify the input is to search the problem specification for an answer to the following question: *What information will the computer need to know in order to either print, display, or store the output items?* As with the output, the input is typically stated as nouns and adjectives in the problem specification. When determining the input, it helps to think about the information that you would need to use to solve the problem manually, because the computer will need to know the same information. For example, to determine Sarah's new weekly pay, both you and the computer will need to know Sarah's current weekly pay, as well as her raise rate; both of these items, therefore, are the input. Here again, notice that *current*, *weekly*, and *raise* are adjectives, and *pay* and *rate* are nouns. Figure 2-6 shows the partially completed IPO chart listing the problem's input and output. Notice that you list the input items in the Input column of the IPO chart.

result of analysis step

Input	Processing	Output
current weekly pay raise rate	Processing items: Algorithm:	new weekly pay

Figure 2-6: Partially completed IPO chart showing the input and output items

You now have completed the analysis step for the current problem. Keep in mind that analyzing real-world problems will not always be as easy as analyzing the ones found in a textbook. You will find that the analysis step is the most difficult of the problem-solving steps. This is primarily because most problem specifications contain either too much information or too little information.

A problem specification that contains too much information—more than is necessary to solve the problem—can be confusing to analyze. If you are not sure if an item of information is important, ask yourself this question: *If I didn't know this information, could I still solve the problem?* If your answer is "Yes," then the information is superfluous and you simply can ignore it. The current problem specification, for example, tells you that Sarah works for Quality Builders. Now ask yourself the following question: *If I didn't know that Sarah worked for Quality Builders, could I still solve the problem?* The answer is "Yes," so you can ignore this information.

When reading a problem specification, it helps to use a pencil to lightly cross out the information that you feel is unimportant to the solution, thereby reducing the amount of information you need to consider in your analysis. If you later find that the information is important, you can always erase the pencil line. In the current problem, for example, you can cross out the unimportant information as shown in Figure 2-7.

~~Sarah Martin has been working for Quality Builders for four years. Last year, Sarah received a 4% raise, which brought her~~ current weekly pay to $250. Sarah is scheduled to receive a 3% raise next week. ~~She wants you to~~ write a program that will display, on the computer screen, the amount of her new weekly pay.

Figure 2-7: Problem specification with unimportant information crossed out

Worse than having too much information in a problem specification is not having enough information to solve a problem. Consider, for example, the problem specification shown in Figure 2-8.

Jack Osaki, one of the shipping clerks at Quality Builders, earns $7 per hour. Last week, Jack worked 40 hours. He wants you to write a program that will display his weekly net pay.

Figure 2-8: Problem specification that does not contain enough information

It is clear from reading the problem specification that the output is the weekly net pay. The input appears to be both the hourly pay and the number of hours worked during the week. However, is that the only information the computer needs to know to display Jack's net pay? Although you can display a person's gross pay if you know only the hours worked and the hourly pay, a net pay calculation typically involves deducting federal and state taxes, as well as insurance, from the gross pay. What taxes and insurance, if any, will you need to deduct from Jack's gross pay to calculate his net pay? There is no way to know, because the problem specification does not contain enough information. Before you can solve this problem, you will need to ask Jack to be more specific about how his net pay is to be calculated.

As a programmer, it is important to distinguish between information that truly is missing in the problem specification, and information that simply is not stated, explicitly, in the problem specification—that is, information that is implied. For example, consider the problem specification shown in Figure 2-9.

Sharon Begay, who works for Quality Builders, needs a program that will display the area of any rectangle. The dimensions of the rectangle will be given in feet.

Figure 2-9: Problem specification in which the input is not explicitly stated

As you may remember from your math courses, you calculate the area of a rectangle by multiplying its length by its width. Therefore, the length and width of the rectangle are the input items for this problem. Notice, however, that the words *length* and *width* do not appear in the problem specification. Although neither item is stated explicitly in the problem specification, the items are not considered missing information, because the formula for calculating the area of a rectangle is common knowledge—or, at least, the formula can be found in any math book. With practice, you also will be able to "fill in the gaps" in a problem specification.

If you are having trouble analyzing a problem, try reading the problem specification several times, as it is easy to miss information during the first reading. If the problem still is not clear to you, do not be shy about asking the user for more information. Remember, the greater your understanding of a problem, the easier it will be for you to write a correct and efficient solution to the problem.

mini-quiz

Mini-Quiz 1

For each problem specification that follows, identify the output and the input. Also identify what information, if any, is missing from the problem specification.

1. Paul Eisenstein lives in a state that charges a 3% state income tax on his yearly taxable wages. He wants you to write a program that will display the state income tax he would need to pay at the end of the year.

2. Deepa Charna belongs to a CD (compact disc) club. The club requires Deepa to purchase 10 CDs each year, at a reduced cost of $8 per CD. Deepa wants to know how much she saves each year by buying the CDs through the club rather than through a store.

3. Penny Long saves $1.25 per day. Penny would like to know the total amount she saved during the month of January.

4. If Jerry Rides saves $1.45 per day, how much will he save in one year?

After analyzing a problem, you then plan its algorithm—its solution.

Planning the Algorithm

The second step in the problem-solving process is to plan the algorithm—the step-by-step instructions that the computer needs to follow to transform the problem's input into its output. You record the algorithm in the Processing column of the IPO chart.

Most algorithms begin with an instruction that enters the input items into the computer. The input items are the items listed in the Input column of the IPO chart. To determine Sarah Martin's new weekly pay, for example, you will record the instruction "enter the current weekly pay and raise rate" as the first step in the algorithm. You will record this instruction in the Processing column of the IPO chart, below the word "Algorithm."

After the instruction to enter the input items, you usually record instructions to process those items, typically by performing some calculations on them, to achieve the problem's required results. The required results are listed in the Output column of the IPO chart. In Sarah's problem specification, consider how you can use the input items (current weekly pay and raise rate) to achieve the output item (new weekly pay).

Before you can display the new weekly pay, you must compute it. To compute the new weekly pay, you first calculate the weekly raise by multiplying the current weekly pay by the raise rate; you then add the weekly raise to the current weekly pay. You will record the instructions "calculate the weekly raise by multiplying the current weekly pay by the raise rate" and "calculate the new weekly pay by adding the weekly raise to the current weekly pay," as Steps 2 and 3 in the IPO chart. Notice that both calculation instructions state both *what* is to be calculated and *how* to calculate it.

Unlike the current weekly pay, raise rate, and new weekly pay, the weekly raise amount calculated within the algorithm is neither an input item nor an output item; rather, it is a special item, commonly referred to as a processing item. A **processing item** represents an intermediate value that the algorithm uses when processing the input into the output. In this case, the algorithm uses the two input items (current weekly pay and raise rate) to calculate the intermediate value—weekly raise—which the algorithm then uses to compute the new weekly pay. Not all algorithms require a processing item. If one or more processing items are required, they are listed in the Processing column of the IPO chart, below the words "Processing items." You will enter "weekly raise" as a processing item used in the current algorithm.

Most algorithms end with an instruction either to print, display, or store the output items, which are listed in the Output column of the IPO chart. (*Display*, *print*, and *store* refer to the screen, the printer, and a file on a disk, respectively.) In this case, you need simply to display Sarah's new weekly pay, so you will record the instruction "display the new weekly pay" as the last step in the IPO chart. The completed IPO chart is shown in Figure 2-10. Notice that the algorithm begins by entering some data (the input items), then processing that data (the two calculations), and ends by displaying some data (the output item). Most algorithms will follow this same format.

Input	Processing	Output
current weekly pay raise rate	Processing items: weekly raise Algorithm: 1. enter the current weekly pay and raise rate 2. calculate the weekly raise by multiplying the current weekly pay by the raise rate 3. calculate the new weekly pay by adding the weekly raise to the current weekly pay 4. display the new weekly pay	new weekly pay

Figure 2-10: Completed IPO chart

Notice that the algorithm shown in Figure 2-10 is composed of short English statements. The statements represent the steps the computer needs to follow to display the new weekly pay. In programming terms, the list of steps shown in Figure 2-10 is called pseudocode. **Pseudocode** is a tool programmers use to help them plan an algorithm. Pseudocode is not standardized—every programmer has his or her own version—but you will find some similarities among the various versions.

Although the word *pseudocode* might be unfamiliar to you, you already have written pseudocode without even realizing it. Think about the last time you gave directions to someone. You wrote down each direction on paper, in your own words. These directions were a form of pseudocode. As you will learn in Tutorial 3, a programmer uses the pseudocode as a guide when coding the algorithm.

In addition to using pseudocode, programmers also use flowcharts to help them plan the algorithm for a problem. Unlike pseudocode, which consists of short English statements, a **flowchart** uses standardized symbols to show the steps the computer needs to take to accomplish the program's goal. Figure 2-11 shows the current problem's algorithm in flowchart form.

Input	Processing	Output
current weekly pay raise rate	Processing items: weekly raise Algorithm: (**start**) ↓ / **enter the current weekly pay and the raise rate** / ↓ [**weekly raise = current weekly pay multiplied by raise rate**] ↓ [**new weekly pay = weekly raise plus current weekly pay**] ↓ / **display the new weekly pay** / ↓ (**stop**)	new weekly pay

Figure 2-11: IPO chart shown with a flowchart in the Processing column

tip
....

▶ You can draw the flowchart symbols by hand, or you can use the drawing feature in a word processor; you also can use a flowcharting program, such as SmartDraw.

tip
....

▶ Many programmers prefer flowcharts over pseudocode, since a picture is sometimes worth a thousand words.

Notice that the flowchart shown in Figure 2-11 contains three different symbols: an oval, a rectangle, and a parallelogram. The symbols are connected with lines, called **flowlines**. The oval symbol is called the **start/stop symbol**. The start oval indicates the beginning of the flowchart, and the stop oval indicates the end of the flowchart. Between the start and the stop ovals are two rectangles, called **process symbols**. You use the process symbol to represent tasks such as calculations.

The parallelogram is called the **input/output symbol** and is used to represent input tasks, such as getting information from the user, and output tasks, such as displaying or printing information. The first parallelogram shown in Figure 2-11 represents an input task. The last parallelogram represents an output task.

When planning the algorithm, you do not need to create both a flowchart and pseudocode; you need to use only one of these planning tools. The tool you use is really a matter of personal preference. For simple algorithms, pseudocode works just fine. When an algorithm becomes more complex, however, the program's logic may be easier to see in a flowchart. In this book, you usually will use pseudocode in planning algorithms.

Keep in mind that a problem can have more than one solution. For example, you could have solved Sarah's problem without using a processing item, as shown in Figure 2-12.

Input	Processing	Output
current weekly pay raise rate	Processing items: none Algorithm: 1. enter the current weekly pay and raise rate 2. calculate the new weekly pay by multiplying the current weekly pay by the raise rate, and then adding the result to the current weekly pay 3. display the new weekly pay	new weekly pay

Figure 2-12: Another way of solving Sarah's problem

Rather than calculating the weekly raise separately, the algorithm shown in Figure 2-12 includes the calculation in the one that computes the new weekly pay.

In the next section, you will learn some hints for writing algorithms.

Hints for Writing Algorithms

It is important to remember that you don't need to "reinvent the wheel" each time you create a solution to a problem. Before you write an algorithm, consider whether the problem you are solving is similar to one you have already solved. If it is, you then can use that problem's algorithm to solve the current problem, often with very little modification. For example, consider the problem specification shown in Figure 2-13.

Quality Builders is increasing each of its prices by 3%. The owner of the company wants you to write a program that will display the amount of the increase and the new price.

Figure 2-13: Problem specification similar to one you worked with in this lesson

Although it may not be obvious at first glance, the problem specification shown in Figure 2-13 is almost identical to the one shown earlier in Figure 2-4—only the terminology is different. As you may remember, the problem specification shown in Figure 2-4 required you to calculate and display both the increase in Sarah's pay and her new pay. That is no different than calculating and displaying both an increase in an item's price and a new price, which Figure 2-13's problem specification requires you to do. The IPO chart for Figure 2-13's problem is shown in Figure 2-14. If you compare this IPO chart to the one shown in Figure 2-12, you will notice the similarity between both solutions.

Input	Processing	Output
current price increase rate	Processing items: none Algorithm: 1. enter the current price and increase rate 2. calculate the increase amount by multiplying the current price by the increase rate 3. calculate the new price by adding the increase amount to the current price 4. display the increase amount and new price	increase amount new price

Figure 2-14: IPO chart for the problem specification shown in Figure 2-13

Even if the problem you are trying to solve is not identical to one that you already solved, you may be able to use a portion of a previous solution to solve the current problem. Consider, for example, the problem specification shown in Figure 2-15.

> At the end of every year, Quality Builders gives each of its employees a bonus. This year the bonus rate is 6% of the employee's current yearly salary. Mary Vasko wants you to write a program that will display her bonus.

Figure 2-15: Problem specification that contains a portion that is similar to one you worked with in this lesson

Although the problem specified in Figure 2-15 is not identical to any that you solved in this lesson, you can use a part of a previous algorithm to solve it; more specifically, you can use the raise calculation part of Figure 2-10's algorithm.

Calculating a bonus, which you need to do now, is no different than calculating a raise; both calculations require you to take an amount and multiply it by a percentage rate. Recall that you calculated Sarah's raise by multiplying her current weekly pay by her raise rate. Similarly, in Figure 2-15's problem, you will calculate Mary's bonus by multiplying her yearly salary by her bonus rate. The IPO chart for the current problem is shown in Figure 2-16.

Input	Processing	Output
current yearly salary bonus rate	Processing items: none Algorithm: 1. enter the current yearly salary and bonus rate 2. calculate the bonus by multiplying the current yearly salary by the bonus rate 3. display the bonus	bonus

Figure 2-16: IPO chart for the problem specification shown in Figure 2-15

If you have not solved a similar problem, and you cannot find a portion of an existing algorithm that you can use, try solving the problem manually, writing down on paper every step you take to do so. If you were to solve Figure 2-15's problem manually, for example, you would need first to read Mary's yearly salary and her bonus rate into your mind. You then would need to calculate her bonus by multiplying the bonus rate by the yearly salary. Finally, you would write the bonus amount down on a piece of paper. You can use the steps that you wrote down as a guide when creating your algorithm.

Figure 2-17 summarizes what you learned in this section about planning algorithms.

1. Before writing an algorithm, consider whether you have already solved a similar problem. If you have, you can use the same solution, often with little modification, to solve the current problem.

2. If you have not solved a similar problem, consider whether you can use a portion of an existing algorithm to solve the current problem.

3. If you have not solved a similar problem, and if you cannot use a portion of an existing algorithm, solve the problem manually, noting each step you take to do so.

Figure 2-17: Hints for planning algorithms

mini-quiz

After analyzing a problem and planning its algorithm, you then desk-check the algorithm, using either the flowchart or the pseudocode, along with sample data.

Desk-Checking the Algorithm

A programmer reviews an algorithm by desk-checking, or hand-tracing, it—in other words, by completing each step in the algorithm manually. You desk-check an algorithm to verify that it is not missing any steps, and that the existing steps are correct and in the proper order. Before you begin the desk-check, you first choose a set of sample data for the input values, which you then use to manually compute the expected output values. For example, you will use input values of $250 and .03 (3%) as Sarah Martin's current weekly pay and raise rate, respectively. Sarah's new weekly pay should be $257.50, which is her current weekly pay of $250 plus her weekly raise of $7.50 (250 multiplied by .03); the 257.50 is the expected output value. You now use the sample input values (250 and .03) to desk-check the algorithm. If the algorithm produces the expected output value of 257.50, then the algorithm appears to be correct.

You can use a desk-check table to help you desk-check an algorithm. The table should contain one column for each input item shown in the IPO chart, as well as one column for each output item and one column for each processing item. Figure 2-18 shows a partially completed desk-check table for Sarah Martin's problem.

tip

········· ▶ You can draw a desk-check table by hand, or you can use the table feature in a word processor (such as Microsoft Word) to draw one.

current weekly pay	raise rate	weekly raise	new weekly pay

Figure 2-18: Desk-check table showing columns for the input, processing, and output items from the IPO chart

You can desk-check an algorithm using either its pseudocode or its flowchart. The pseudocode for Sarah Martin's problem is shown in Figure 2-10, and the flowchart is shown in Figure 2-11. In both figures, the first step is to enter the input values—in this case, the current weekly pay of 250 and the raise rate of .03. You record the results of this step by writing 250 and .03 in the current weekly pay and raise rate columns, respectively, in the desk-check table, as shown in Figure 2-19.

current weekly pay	raise rate	weekly raise	new weekly pay
250	.03		

Figure 2-19: Desk-check table showing input values entered in the appropriate columns

The second step in the algorithm is to calculate the weekly raise by multiplying the current weekly pay by the raise rate. The desk-check table shows that the current weekly pay is 250 and the raise rate is .03. Notice that you use the table to determine what the current weekly pay and raise rate values are; this helps to verify the accuracy of the algorithm. If, for example, the table did not show any amount in the raise rate column, you would know that your algorithm missed a step—in this case, it would have missed entering the raise rate.

Multiplying the current weekly pay of 250 by the raise rate of .03 results in a 7.50 raise. You record the number 7.50 in the weekly raise column, as shown in Figure 2-20.

current weekly pay	raise rate	weekly raise	new weekly pay
250	.03	7.50	

Figure 2-20: Weekly raise entry included in the desk-check table

The next step in the algorithm is to calculate the new weekly pay by adding the weekly raise to the current weekly pay. According to the desk-check table, the weekly raise is 7.50 and the current weekly pay is 250. Added together, those amounts result in a new weekly pay of 257.50. You write the 257.50 in the new weekly pay column, as shown in Figure 2-21.

current weekly pay	raise rate	weekly raise	new weekly pay
250	.03	7.50	257.50

Figure 2-21: New weekly pay entry included in the desk-check table

After calculating the new weekly pay, the last instruction in the algorithm is to display the new weekly pay on the screen. In this case, 257.50 will be displayed, because that is what appears in the table's new weekly pay column. Notice that this amount agrees with the manual calculation you performed prior to desk-checking the algorithm, so the algorithm appears to be correct. The only way to know for sure, however, is to test the algorithm a few more times with different input values.

For example, you will test the algorithm with a current weekly pay of $100 and a raise rate of .10 (10%). The new weekly pay should be $110, which is the current weekly pay of $100 plus the weekly raise of $10 (100 multiplied by .10).

Recall that the first instruction in the algorithm is to enter the current weekly pay and the raise rate. Therefore, you would write 100 in the current weekly pay column and .10 in the raise rate column, as shown in Figure 2-22.

cross out the previous values

current weekly pay	raise rate	weekly raise	new weekly pay
~~250~~	~~.03~~	7.50	257.50
100	.10		

Figure 2-22: Desk-check table for the second set of input values

Notice that you cross out the previous values of these two items in the table before recording the new values; this is because each column should contain only one value at any time.

The next step in the algorithm is to calculate the weekly raise. Multiplying the current weekly pay, which is listed in the table as 100, by the raise rate, which is listed as .10, results in a weekly raise of 10. So you then would cross out the 7.50 that appears in the weekly raise column in the table and write 10 immediately below it.

The next step is to calculate the new weekly pay. Adding the raise, which is listed in the table as 10, to the current weekly pay, which is listed in the table as 100, results in a new weekly pay of 110. Therefore, you would cross out the 257.50 that appears in the new weekly pay column in the table and write 110 immediately below it. The completed desk-check table is shown in Figure 2-23.

current weekly pay	raise rate	weekly raise	new weekly pay
~~250~~	~~.03~~	~~7.50~~	~~257.50~~
100	.10	10	110

Figure 2-23: Desk-check table showing the results of the second desk-check

The last step in the algorithm is to display the new weekly pay. In this case, the algorithm will display 110, because that is what appears in the table's new weekly pay column. The amount in the table agrees with the manual calculation you performed earlier, so the algorithm still appears to be correct. To be sure, however, you should desk-check it a few more times.

In addition to desk-checking the algorithm using valid data, you also should desk-check it using invalid data, because users sometimes make mistakes when entering data. **Valid data** is data that the programmer is expecting the user to enter. For example, in the algorithm that you just finished desk-checking, the programmer expects the user to provide positive numbers for the input values (current weekly pay and raise rate). **Invalid data** is data that the programmer is not expecting the user to enter. In this case, the programmer is not expecting the user to enter a negative value as the current weekly pay. A negative weekly pay is obviously an input error, because an employee cannot earn a negative amount for the week. Beginning in Tutorial 8, you will learn how to create algorithms that correctly handle input errors. For now, however, you can assume that the user of the program will always enter valid data.

As a way of summarizing what you learned in this lesson, you will use the first three steps in the problem-solving process to solve another problem.

The Gas Mileage Problem

Figure 2-24 shows the problem specification for the gas mileage problem, which you will solve next.

> When Jacob Steinberg began his trip from California to Vermont, he filled his car's tank with gas and reset its trip meter to zero. After traveling 324 miles, Jacob stopped at a gas station to refuel; the gas tank required 17 gallons. Create a program that Jacob can use to display his car's gas mileage—the number of miles his car can be driven per gallon of gas—at anytime during the trip.

Figure 2-24: Problem specification for the gas mileage problem

First, analyze the problem, looking for nouns and adjectives that represent both the output and the input. The output should answer the question *What does the user want to see either printed on paper, displayed on the screen, or stored in a file?* The input should answer the question *What information will the computer need to know in order to either print, display, or store the output items?* In the gas mileage problem, the output is the miles per gallon, and the input is the number of miles driven and the number of gallons used.

Next, plan the algorithm. Recall that most algorithms begin with an instruction that enters the input items into the computer, followed by instructions that process the input items and then print, display, or store the output items. Figure 2-25 shows the completed IPO chart for the gas mileage problem.

Input	Processing	Output
number of miles driven number of gallons used	Processing items: none Algorithm: 1. enter the number of miles driven and the number of gallons used 2. calculate the miles per gallon by dividing the number of miles driven by the number of gallons used 3. display the miles per gallon	miles per gallon

Figure 2-25: Completed IPO chart for the gas mileage problem

After planning the algorithm, you then desk-check it, which is the third step in the problem-solving process. You will desk-check the algorithm twice, first using 324 and 17 as the miles driven and number of gallons, respectively, and then using 200 and 12. Figure 2-26 shows the completed desk-check table for the gas mileage problem.

number of miles driven	number of gallons used	miles per gallon
~~324~~	~~17~~	~~19.06~~
200	12	16.67

Figure 2-26: Completed desk-check table for the gas mileage problem

mini-quiz

Mini-Quiz 3

1. Desk-check the following algorithm. Use a yearly taxable wage of $20,000 and a 3% state income tax rate, and then use a yearly taxable wage of $10,000 and a 2% state income tax rate.

Input	Processing	Output
yearly taxable wages state income tax rate	Processing items: none Algorithm: 1. enter the yearly taxable wages and the state income tax rate 2. calculate the annual state income tax by multiplying the yearly taxable wages by the state income tax rate 3. display the annual state income tax	annual state income tax

2. Desk-check the following algorithm. Use 5 and 7 as the first set of input values, then use 6 and 8 as the second set of input values.

Input	Processing	Output
first number second number	Processing items: sum Algorithm: 1. enter the first number and the second number 2. calculate the sum by adding together the first number and the second number 3. calculate the average by dividing the sum by 2 4. display the average	average

You now have completed the first three of the six steps required to create a computer program: analyze the problem, plan the algorithm, and desk-check the algorithm. You will complete the last three steps—code the algorithm into a program, desk-check the program, and evaluate and modify (if necessary) the program—in Tutorial 3. You can either take a break or complete the end-of-lesson questions and exercises before moving on to the Application lesson.

SUMMARY

If you are like most people, you probably do not pay much attention to the problem-solving process that you use when solving everyday problems. This process typically involves analyzing the problem, and then planning, reviewing, implementing, evaluating, and modifying (if necessary) the solution. You can use a similar problem-solving process to create a computer program, which also is a solution to a problem.

Programmers use tools such as IPO (Input, Processing, Output) charts, pseudocode, and flowcharts to help them analyze problems and develop algorithms. During the analysis step, the programmer first determines the output, which is the goal or purpose of solving the problem. The programmer then determines the input, which is the information he or she needs to reach the goal. During the planning step, programmers write the steps that will transform the input into the output. Most algorithms begin by entering some data (the input items), then processing that data (usually by doing some calculations), and then displaying some data (the output items).

After the analysis and planning steps, a programmer then desk-checks the algorithm to see if it will work as intended. Desk-checking means that the programmer follows each of the steps in the algorithm by hand, just as if he or she were the computer. When the programmer is satisfied that the algorithm is correct, he or she then codes the algorithm. Coding refers to translating the algorithm into a language that the computer can understand. A coded algorithm is called a program. After coding the algorithm, the programmer then desk-checks the program to be sure that he or she correctly translated each of the steps in the algorithm. The programmer then evaluates and modifies (if necessary) the program by executing it, along with sample data, using the computer. If the program does not work as intended, then the programmer makes the necessary modifications until the program works correctly.

Before writing an algorithm, you should consider whether you have already solved a similar problem. If you have, you can use that solution, often with little modification, to solve the current problem. If you have not solved an identical problem, consider whether a portion of an existing algorithm is similar enough to use in the current problem. If no existing algorithms help, try solving the problem manually, being sure to write down every step you take to do so, because the computer will need to follow the same steps.

ANSWERS TO MINI-QUIZZES

Mini-Quiz 1

1. Output: annual state income tax
   Input: yearly taxable wages, state income tax rate
   Missing information: none

2. Output: annual savings
   Input: number of CDs purchased each year, CD cost when purchased through the club, CD cost when purchased through the store
   Missing information: CD cost when purchased through the store

3.   Output: total amount saved in January
      Input: amount saved per day, number of days in January
      Missing information: none (Although the number of days in January is not specified in the problem specification, that information can be found in any calendar.)

4.   Output: yearly savings
      Input: amount saved per day, number of days in the year
      Missing information: number of days in the year (Because some years are leap years, you would need to know the number of days in the year.)

Mini-Quiz 2

1.   parallelogram

2.   rectangle

3.

Input	Processing	Output
yearly taxable wages state income tax rate	Processing items: none Algorithm: 1. enter the yearly taxable wages and the state income tax rate 2. calculate the annual state income tax by multiplying the yearly taxable wages by the state income tax rate 3. display the annual state income tax	annual state income tax

Input	Processing	Output

number of CDs purchased each year club's CD price store's CD price	Processing items:
	  amount spent through the club
	  amount spent at the store
	
	Algorithm:
	1. enter the number of CDs purchased each year, the club's CD price, and the store's CD price
	2. calculate the amount spent through the club by multiplying the number of CDs purchased each year by the club's CD price
	3. calculate the amount spent at the store by multiplying the number of CDs purchased each year by the store's CD price
	4. calculate the annual savings by subtracting the amount spent through the club from the amount spent at the store
	5. display the annual savings
		annual savings

Mini-Quiz 3

1.

yearly taxable wages	state income tax rate	annual state income tax
~~20000~~	~~.03~~	~~600~~
10000	.02	200

2.

first number	second number	sum	average
~~5~~	~~7~~	~~12~~	~~6~~
6	8	14	7

QUESTIONS

1. The first step in the problem-solving process is to _____.
   a. plan the algorithm
   b. analyze the problem
   c. desk-check the algorithm
   d. code the algorithm

2. Programmers refer to the goal of solving a problem as the _____.
   a. input
   b. output
   c. processing
   d. purpose

3. Programmers refer to the items needed to reach a problem's goal as the _____
   a. input
   b. output
   c. processing
   d. purpose

4. A problem's _____ will answer the question "What does the user want to see either printed on paper, displayed on the screen, or stored in a file?"
   a. input
   b. output
   c. processing
   d. purpose

5. Programmers use _____ to organize and summarize the results of their problem analysis.
   a. input charts
   b. IPO charts
   c. output charts
   d. processing charts

6. A problem's _____ will answer the question "What information will the computer need to know in order to either print, display, or store the output items?"
    a. input
    b. output
    c. processing
    d. purpose

7. Most algorithms begin by _____.
    a. displaying the input items
    b. entering the input items into the computer
    c. entering the output items into the computer
    d. processing the input items by doing some calculations on them

8. You record the algorithm in the _____ column of the IPO chart.
    a. Input
    b. Output
    c. Processing
    d. Purpose

9. The calculation instructions in an algorithm should state _____.
    a. only *what* is to be calculated
    b. only *how* to calculate something
    c. both *what* is to be calculated and *how* to calculate it
    d. both *what* is to be calculated and *why* is it calculated

10. Most algorithms follow the format of _____.
    a. entering the input items, then displaying, printing, or storing the input items, and then processing the output items
    b. entering the input items, then processing the output items, and then displaying, printing, or storing the output items
    c. entering the input items, then processing the input items, and then displaying, printing, or storing the output items
    d. entering the output items, then processing the output items, and then displaying, printing, or storing the output items

11. The short statements that represent the steps the computer needs to follow to solve a problem are called _____.
    a. flow diagrams
    b. IPO charts
    c. pseudocharts
    d. pseudocode

12. _____ use standardized symbols to represent an algorithm.
    a. Flowcharts
    b. Flow diagrams
    c. IPO charts
    d. Pseudocharts

13. The _____ symbol is used in a flowchart to represent a calculation task.
    a. input
    b. output
    c. process
    d. start

14. The _____ symbol is used in a flowchart to represent a step that gets information from the user.
    a. input/output
    b. process
    c. selection/repetition
    d. start/stop

15. The process symbol in a flowchart is the _____.
   a. ◇
   b. ⬭
   c. ▱
   d. ▭

16. The input/output symbol in a flowchart is the _____.
   a. ◇
   b. ⬭
   c. ▱
   d. ▭

17. The start/stop symbol, which marks both the beginning and ending of a flowchart, is a(n) _____.
   a. ◇
   b. ⬭
   c. ▱
   d. ▭

18. After planning an algorithm, you should _____ to verify that it will work correctly.
   a. analyze the algorithm
   b. code the algorithm
   c. desk-check the algorithm
   d. evaluate and modify (if necessary) the program

19. When desk-checking an algorithm, you should set up a table that contains _____.
   a. one column for each input item
   b. one column for each output item
   c. one column for each processing item
   d. all of the above

EXERCISES

1. Hai Chang needs a program that will calculate and display the square of a number. Complete an IPO chart for this problem. Use pseudocode in the Processing column. Also complete a desk-check table for your algorithm. Use 4 as the number for the first desk-check, then use the number 6.

2. Mingo Sales needs a program that the company can use to enter the sales made in each of two states. The program should display the commission, which is 5% of the total sales. (In other words, if you have sales totaling $3000, your commission is $150.) The commission rate may change in the future, so you should treat it as an input item. Complete an IPO chart for this problem. Use pseudocode in the Processing column. Also complete a desk-check table for your algorithm. For the first desk-check, use 1000 and 2000 as the two state sales, and use .05 (the decimal equivalent of 5%) as the commission rate. Then use 3000 and 2500 as the two state sales, and use .06 as the commission rate.

3. Joan Brimley is the accountant at Paper Products. The salespeople at Paper Products are paid a commission, which is a percentage of the sales they make. The current commission rate is 10%, but that rate may change in the future. (In other words, if you have sales totaling $2000, your commission is $200.) Joan wants you to create a program that will display the commission after she enters the salesperson's sales and commission rate. Complete an IPO chart for this problem. Use a flowchart in the Processing column. Also complete a desk-check table for your algorithm. Use 2000 and .1 (the decimal equivalent of 10%) as the salesperson's sales amount and commission rate, respectively. Then use 5000 and .06.

4. RM Sales divides its sales territory into three regions: 1, 2, and 3. Robert Gonzales, the sales manager, wants a program in which he can enter the current year's sales for each region and the projected increase (expressed as a percentage) in sales for each region. He then wants the program to display the following year's projected sales for each region. (For example, if Robert enters 10,000 as the current sales for region 1, and then enters a 10% projected increase, the program should display 11,000 as next year's projected sales.) Complete an IPO chart for this problem. Use pseudocode in the Processing column. Also complete a desk-check table for your algorithm.

    Use the following information for the first desk-check:

Region	Sales	Increase rate
1	10000	.1 (the decimal equivalent of 10%)
2	3000	.09 (the decimal equivalent of 9%)
3	6000	.1 (the decimal equivalent of 10%)

    Use the following information for the second desk-check:

Region	Sales	Increase rate
1	5000	.02 (the decimal equivalent of 2%)
2	2000	.03 (the decimal equivalent of 3%)
3	1000	.02 (the decimal equivalent of 2%)

Exercise 5 is a Discovery Exercise. Discovery Exercises, which may include topics that are not covered in this lesson, allow you to "discover" the solutions to problems on your own.

5. Modify the algorithm that you created in Exercise 1 so that it calculates and displays the square of positive numbers only. If the number entered by the user is either zero or less than zero, the algorithm should display an error message. Desk-check the algorithm using the numbers 10 and –3.

A computer program is good only if it works. Errors in either an algorithm or programming code can cause the program to run incorrectly. Therefore, a programmer needs to know how to locate and fix these errors. Exercises 6 and 7 are Debugging Exercises. Debugging Exercises allow you to practice recognizing and solving errors in a program.

6. Etola Systems wants a program that will display the ending inventory amount, given the beginning inventory amount, the amount sold, and the amount returned. The algorithm shown in Figure 2-27 is supposed to solve this problem, but it is not working correctly. First calculate the expected results using a beginning inventory of 50, an amount sold of 10, and an amount returned of 2. Then use these values to desk-check the algorithm. Rewrite the algorithm correctly, then desk-check it again.

Input	Processing	Output
beginning inventory amount sold amount returned	Processing items: none Algorithm: 1. enter the beginning inventory, amount sold, and amount returned 2. calculate the ending inventory by adding the amount sold to the beginning inventory, then subtracting the amount returned from the result 3. display the ending inventory	ending inventory

Figure 2-27

debugging   7. The algorithm shown in Figure 2-28 should calculate an employee's gross pay. Correct any errors in the algorithm. (You do not have to worry about overtime pay.)

Input	Processing	Output
hours worked rate of pay	Processing items: none Algorithm: 1. enter the hours worked and pay rate 2. calculate the gross pay by multiplying the hours by the rate of pay 3. display the gross pay	gross pay

Figure 2-28

Application Lesson

Using the First Steps in the Problem-Solving Process

case ▶ Last year, Mark Williams opened a new wallpaper store named The Paper Tree. Business is booming at the store, and Mark and his salesclerks are always busy. Recently, however, Mark has received several complaints from customers about the store's slow service, and he has decided to ask his salesclerks for suggestions on how the service can be improved. The overwhelming response from the salesclerks is that they need a more convenient way to calculate the number of single rolls of wallpaper required to cover a room. Currently, the salesclerks perform this calculation manually, using pencil and paper. Doing this for so many customers, however, takes a great deal of time, and service has begun to suffer. Mark has asked for your assistance in this matter. He would like you to create a program that the salesclerks can use to quickly calculate and display the required number of rolls.

The Problem Specification

Before you begin the problem-solving process, you meet with Mark to develop an appropriate problem specification—one that contains all of the information needed to solve the problem. You also ask Mark to show you how the clerks currently calculate the required number of rolls. As you learned in the Concept lesson, the computer will need to make the same calculations as you do. Figure 2-29 shows the final problem specification and a sample calculation.

Problem specification:

Create a program that calculates and displays the number of single rolls of wall-paper needed to cover a room. The salesclerk will provide the length, width, and ceiling height of the room, in feet. He or she also will provide the number of square feet a single roll will cover.

Sample calculation:
> Room size: 10 feet by 12 feet, with a ceiling height of 8 feet
> Single roll coverage: 30 square feet

1. Calculate the perimeter of the room by adding together its length and width, and then multiplying the sum by 2:   (10 feet + 12 feet) * 2 = 44 feet

2. Calculate the wall area by multiplying the room's perimeter by its height:
   44 feet * 8 feet = 352 square feet

3. Calculate the required number of single rolls by dividing the wall area by the number of square feet a single roll provides: 352 square feet / 30 square feet = 11.73 (rounded to two decimal places), or approximately 12 single rolls

---

Figure 2-29: Problem specification and sample calculation

Armed with this information, you now can begin the problem-solving process.

Analyze the Problem

As you learned in the Concept lesson, the first step in the problem-solving process is to analyze the problem. You do so to determine the goal of solving the problem (output), and the items that are needed to achieve the goal (input). Recall that you always search the problem specification first for the output, and then for the input. The input and output typically are stated as nouns and adjectives in the problem specification.

Asking yourself the question *What does the user want to see either printed on paper, displayed on the screen, or stored in a file?* will help you determine the output. In this case, the user wants to see the number of single rolls of wallpaper needed to cover a room, so you will record "number of single rolls" in the Output column of this problem's IPO chart.

The question *What information will the computer need to know in order to either print, display, or store the output items?* will help you determine the input. In this case, the input is the length, width, and ceiling height of the room, as well as the coverage provided by a single roll of wallpaper. Figure 2-30 shows the IPO chart with the Input and Output columns completed.

Input	Processing	Output
room length room width ceiling height single roll coverage	Processing items: Algorithm:	number of single rolls

Figure 2-30: IPO chart showing input and output items

The next step in the problem-solving process is to plan the algorithm.

Planning the Algorithm

After determing a problem's input and output, you then plan its algorithm, which is the step-by-step instructions that will transform the input into the output. Recall that most algorithms begin by entering the input items into the computer. You will record "enter the room length, room width, ceiling height, and single roll coverage" as the first step in the current problem's algorithm. Notice that the instruction refers to the input items using the same names listed in the Input column of the IPO chart.

After the instruction to enter the input items, you usually record instructions to process those items, typically by performing some calculations on them. According to the sample calculation shown in Figure 2-29, first you need to calculate the room's perimeter. You do so by adding together the room's length and width, and then multiplying that sum by two. You will notice that the room perimeter does not appear in either the Input or Output column in the IPO chart. This is because the room perimeter is neither an input item nor an output item; rather, it is a processing item. As you learned in the Concept lesson, a processing item represents an intermediate value that the algorithm uses when processing the input into the output. For this problem, you will enter "room perimeter" in the Processing items section of the IPO chart and "calculate the room perimeter by adding together the room length and room width, and then multiplying the sum by 2" in the Algorithm section, as shown in Figure 2-31.

Input	Processing	Output
room length room width ceiling height single roll coverage	Processing items: room perimeter Algorithm: 1. enter the room length, room width, ceiling height, and single roll coverage 2. calculate the room perimeter by adding together the room length and room width, and then multiplying the sum by 2	number of single rolls

Figure 2-31: IPO chart showing the partially completed algorithm

Next, you need to calculate the wall area by multiplying the room's perimeter by the height of its ceiling. This calculation will give you the total number of square feet to be covered. Like the perimeter, the wall area is a processing item. Therefore, you will enter "wall area" in the Processing items section of the IPO chart, and "calculate the wall area by multiplying the room perimeter by the ceiling height" in the Algorithm section.

The last calculation you need to make is to divide the wall area by the coverage provided by a single roll. This calculation will give you the required number of single rolls. You will enter "calculate the number of single rolls by dividing the wall area by the single roll coverage" in the Algorithm section of the IPO chart.

Recall that most algorithms end with an instruction either to print, display, or store the output items. In this case, you need simply to display the number of single rolls. You will record "display the number of single rolls" in the Algorithm section of the IPO chart. The completed IPO chart is shown in Figure 2-32.

Input	Processing	Output
room length room width ceiling height single roll coverage	Processing items: room perimeter wall area Algorithm: 1. enter the room length, room width, ceiling height, and single roll coverage 2. calculate the room perimeter by adding together the room length and room width, and then multiplying the sum by 2 3. calculate the wall area by multiplying the room perimeter by the ceiling height 4. calculate the number of single rolls by dividing the wall area by the single roll coverage 5. display the number of single rolls	number of single rolls

Figure 2-32: Completed IPO chart for the wallpaper store problem

After completing the IPO chart, you then move on to the third step in the problem-solving process, which is to desk-check the algorithm that appears in the chart.

Desk-Checking the Algorithm

You desk-check an algorithm to verify that it is not missing any steps, and that the existing steps are correct and in the proper order. Recall that, before you begin the desk-check, you first choose a set of sample data for the input values, which you then use to manually compute the expected output values. In this case, you will use the input values shown earlier in Figure 2-29. In that figure, the values 10 feet, 12 feet, 8 feet, and 30 square feet are specified as the room length, room width, ceiling height, and single roll coverage, respectively. The sample calculation provided in Figure 2-29 shows that the required number of single rolls, using those input values, is 11.73 (rounded to two decimal places), or approximately 12 single rolls. Now see if the algorithm shown in Figure 2-32 results in the same amount.

First, create a desk-check table that contains a column for each input, processing, and output item, as shown in Figure 2-33.

room length	room width	ceiling height	single roll coverage	room perimeter	wall area	number of single rolls

Figure 2-33: Desk-check table for the wallpaper store problem

Now you can begin desk-checking the algorithm. The first instruction in the algorithm is to enter the room length, room width, ceiling height, and single roll coverage. Figure 2-34 shows these values entered in the desk-check table.

room length	room width	ceiling height	single roll coverage	room perimeter	wall area	number of single rolls
10	12	8	30			

Figure 2-34: Input values entered in the desk-check table

The next instruction is to calculate the room perimeter by adding together the room length and room width, and then multiplying the sum by 2. The room length column in the desk-check table contains the number 10, and the room width column contains the number 12. When you add together the numbers 10 and 12, you get 22. And when you multiply the 22 by 2, you get 44, which you enter in the room perimeter column in the table, as shown in Figure 2-35.

room length	room width	ceiling height	single roll coverage	room perimeter	wall area	number of single rolls
10	12	8	30	44		

Figure 2-35: Room perimeter value entered in the desk-check table

The third instruction in the algorithm is to calculate the wall area by multiplying the room perimeter by the ceiling height. The room perimeter column in the table contains the number 44, and the ceiling height column contains the number 8. When you multiply 44 by 8, you get 352, which you enter in the wall area column in the table, as shown in Figure 2-36.

room length	room width	ceiling height	single roll coverage	room perimeter	wall area	number of single rolls
10	12	8	30	44	352	

Figure 2-36: Wall area value entered in the desk-check table

The fourth instruction in the algorithm is to calculate the number of single rolls by dividing the wall area by the single roll coverage. The wall area column in the table contains the number 352, and the single roll coverage column contains the number 30. When you divide 352 by 30, you get 11.73 (rounded to two decimal places), which you enter in the number of single rolls column in the table. The completed desk-check table is shown in Figure 2-37.

room length	room width	ceiling height	single roll coverage	room perimeter	wall area	number of single rolls
10	12	8	30	44	352	11.73

Figure 2-37: Desk-check table showing the results of the first desk-check

The last instruction in the algorithm is to display the number of single rolls. According to the desk-check table, the number of single rolls is 11.73, which agrees with the manual calculation shown earlier in Figure 2-29. Although the algorithm appears to be correct, recall that you should test it several times using different data to be sure. Figure 2-38 shows the desk-check table using input values of 12 feet, 14 feet, 10 feet, and 37 square feet as the room length, room width, ceiling height, and single roll coverage, respectively.

room length	room width	ceiling height	single roll coverage	room perimeter	wall area	number of single rolls
~~10~~ 12	~~12~~ 14	~~8~~ 10	~~30~~ 37	~~44~~ 52	~~352~~ 520	~~11.73~~ 14.05

Figure 2-38: Desk-check table showing the results of the second desk-check

Almost every problem—no matter how simple it is—can be solved in more than one way. For example, rather than using the algorithm shown in Figure 2-32 to solve the wallpaper problem, you also could have used the algorithm shown in Figure 2-39.

Input	Processing	Output
room length room width ceiling height single roll coverage	Processing items: room perimeter Algorithm: 1. enter the room length, room width, ceiling height, and single roll coverage 2. calculate the room perimeter by adding together the room length and room width, and then multiplying the sum by 2 3. calculate the number of single rolls by multiplying the room perimeter by the ceiling height, and then dividing the result by the single roll coverage 4. display the number of single rolls	number of single rolls

Figure 2-39: Another correct algorithm for the wallpaper store problem

You now have completed Tutorial 2's Application lesson. You can either take a break or complete the end-of-lesson exercises.

E X E R C I S E S

1. Rewrite the IPO chart shown in Figure 2-32 using a flowchart, rather than pseudocode, in the Algorithm section.

2. John Lee wants a program in which he can enter the following three pieces of information: his savings account balance at the beginning of the month, the amount of money he deposited during the month, and the amount of money he withdrew during the month. He wants the program to display his balance at the end of the month. Complete an IPO chart for this problem, using pseudocode in the Processing column. Also complete a desk-check table for your algorithm.

   Use the following information for the first desk-check:

savings account balance at the beginning of the month:	2000
money deposited during the month:	775
money withdrawn during the month:	1200

   Use the following information for the second desk-check:

savings account balance at the beginning of the month:	500
money deposited during the month:	100
money withdrawn during the month:	610

3. Lana Jones wants a program that will display the average of any three numbers she enters. Complete an IPO chart for this problem, using pseudocode in the Processing column. Also complete a desk-check table for your algorithm. Use the following three numbers for the first desk-check: 25, 76, 33. Use the following three numbers for the second desk-check: 10, 15, 20.

4. Jackets Unlimited is having a sale on all of its merchandise. The store manager asks you to create a program that requires the clerk simply to enter the original price of a jacket and the discount rate. The program should then display both the sales discount and the new sales price. Complete an IPO chart for this problem, using pseudocode in the Processing column. Also complete a desk-check table for your algorithm. For the first desk-check, use 100 as the jacket price and .25 (the decimal equivalent of 25%) as the discount rate. For the second desk-check, use 50 as the jacket price and .1 as the discount rate.

5. Typing Salon currently charges $.10 per typed envelope and $.25 per typed page, although those prices may change in the future. The company accountant wants a program that will help her prepare the customer bills. She will enter the number of typed envelopes and the number of typed pages, as well as the current charges per typed envelope and per typed page. The program should display the total amount due from the customer. Complete an IPO chart for this problem, using pseudocode in the Processing column. Also complete a desk-check table for your algorithm.

   Use the following information for the first desk-check:

number of typed envelopes:	100
number of typed pages:	100
charge per typed envelope:	.10
charge per typed page:	.25

   Use the following information for the second desk-check:

number of typed envelopes:	10
number of typed pages:	15
charge per typed envelope:	.20
charge per typed page:	.30

6. Management USA, a small training center, plans to run two full-day seminars on December 1. (Because each seminar lasts the entire day, a person can register for only one of the two seminars at a time.) The current seminar price is $200, but that price could change in the future. Registration for the seminars will be taken by telephone. When a company calls to register its employees, the Management USA telephone representative will ask for the following two items of information: the number of employees registering for the first seminar and the number registering for the second seminar. Claire Jenkowski, the owner of Management USA, wants a program that will display the total number of employees the company is registering and the total cost. Complete an IPO chart for this problem, using pseudocode in the Processing column. Also complete a desk-check table for your algorithm.

Use the following information for the first desk-check:

number registering for the first seminar:	10
number registering for the second seminar:	10
seminar price:	200

Use the following information for the second desk-check:

number registering for the first seminar:	30
number registering for the second seminar:	10
seminar price:	100

7. Suman Gadhari, the payroll clerk at Sun Projects, wants a program that will compute an employee's net pay. Suman will enter the hours worked, the hourly rate of pay, the federal withholding tax (FWT) rate, the Social Security (FICA) tax rate, and the state income tax rate. For this program, you do not have to worry about overtime, as this company does not allow anyone to work more than 40 hours per week. Suman wants the program to display the employee's gross pay, FWT, FICA, state income tax, and net pay. Complete an IPO chart for this problem, using pseudocode in the Processing column. Also complete a desk-check table for your algorithm.

Use the following information for the first desk-check:

hours worked:	20
hourly pay rate:	6
FWT rate:	.2
FICA rate:	.08
state income tax rate:	.02

Use the following information for the second desk-check:

hours worked:	30
hourly pay rate:	10
FWT rate:	.2
FICA rate:	.08
state income tax rate:	.04

8. Perry Brown needs a program that will allow him to enter the length of four sides of a polygon. The program should display the perimeter of the polygon. Complete an IPO chart for this problem, using pseudocode in the Processing column. Also complete a desk-check table. Desk-check the algorithm twice, using your own sample data.

9. Builders Inc. needs a program that will allow its sales clerks to enter both the diameter of a circle and the price of railing material per foot. The program should display the circumference of the circle and the total price of the railing material. (Use 3.14 as the value of pi.) Complete an IPO chart for this problem, using a flowchart in the Processing column. Also complete a desk-check table for your algorithm. Desk-check the algorithm twice, using your own sample data.

10. Tile Limited wants a program that will allow its sales clerks to enter the length and width, in feet, of a rectangle, and the price of a square foot of tile. The program should display the area of the rectangle and the total price of the tile. Complete an IPO chart for this problem, using pseudocode in the Processing column. Also complete a desk-check table for your algorithm. Desk-check the algorithm twice, using your own sample data.

11. Willow Pools wants a program that will allow its salespeople to enter the dimensions of a rectangle in feet. The program should display the volume of the rectangle. Complete an IPO chart for this problem, using pseudocode in the Processing column. Also complete a desk-check table for your algorithm. Desk-check the algorithm twice, using your own sample data.

12. IMY Industries needs a program that its personnel clerks can use to display the new hourly pay, given both the current hourly pay for each of three job codes (1, 2, and 3) and the raise rate (entered as a decimal). Complete an IPO chart for this problem, using pseudocode in the Processing column. Also complete a desk-check table for your algorithm.

    Use the following information for the first desk-check:

    current hourly pay for job code 1:   7.55
    current hourly pay for job code 2:   10.00
    current hourly pay for job code 3:   10.30
    raise rate: .02

    Use the following information for the second desk-check:

    current hourly pay for job code 1:   8.00
    current hourly pay for job code 2:   6.50
    current hourly pay for job code 3:   7.25
    raise rate: .02

13. Sue Chen attends Jefferson University in Kentucky. Students attending Jefferson University are considered full-time students if they are registered for at least 15 semester hours. Students registered for less than 15 hours are considered part-time students. Sue would like you to create a program that will display the total cost per semester. Tuition is $100 per semester hour. The cost of room and board is $3000. (Assume that all students live on campus and will have room and board charges.) Complete an IPO chart for this problem, using a flowchart in the Processing column. Also complete a desk-check table for your algorithm. Desk-check the algorithm twice. Use 20 semester hours for the first desk-check, and use 14 hours for the second desk-check.

Exercise 14 is a Discovery Exercise. Discovery Exercises, which may include topics that are not covered in this lesson, allow you to "discover" the solutions to problems on your own.

14. George Markos, the payroll clerk at Microstep Company, wants a program that will compute an employee's gross pay. George will enter the hours worked and the hourly rate of pay. Employees working over 40 hours receive time and one-half on the hours over 40. George wants the program to display the employee's gross pay. Complete an IPO chart for this problem, using pseudocode in the Processing column. Also complete a desk-check table for your algorithm. For the first desk-check, use 20 as the hours worked and 6 as the hourly pay rate. For the second desk-check, use 43 as the hours worked and 10 as the hourly pay rate.

A computer program is good only if it works. Errors in either an algorithm or programming code can cause the program to run incorrectly. Therefore, a programmer needs to know how to locate and fix these errors. Exercises 15 and 16 are Debugging Exercises. Debugging Exercises allow you to practice recognizing and solving errors in a program.

debugging

15. Jean Marie wants a program that will display the cube of a number. The algorithm shown in Figure 2-40 is supposed to solve this problem, but it is not working correctly. Rewrite the algorithm correctly, then desk-check it using the number 4.

Input	Processing	Output
number	Processing items: none Algorithm: 1. calculate the cube of the number by multiplying the number by itself three times	cube of the number

Figure 2-40

debugging

16. GeeBees Clothiers is having a sale. The manager of the store wants a program that will allow the clerk to enter the original price of an item and the discount rate. The program then will display the discount, as well as the sale price. The algorithm shown in Figure 2-41 is supposed to solve this problem, but it is not working correctly. Rewrite the algorithm correctly, then desk-check it using an original price of $100 and a discount rate of 25 percent.

Input	Processing	Output
original price discount rate	Processing items: none Algorithm: 1. enter the original price and the discount rate 2. calculate the sale price by subtracting the discount from the original price 3. display the discount and the sale price	discount sale price

Figure 2-41

Completing the Problem-Solving Process and Getting Started with C++

After completing this tutorial, you will be able to:

- Code an algorithm into a program
- Desk-check a program
- Evaluate and modify a program
- Understand the components of a C++ program
- Differentiate between source code, object code, and executable code
- Open a C++ source file
- Save, compile, build, and execute a C++ program

Concept Lesson

More on the Problem-Solving Process

In Tutorial 2, you learned how to analyze a problem, as well as how to plan and desk-check an algorithm designed to solve the problem. Recall that analyzing, planning, and desk-checking are the first three steps in the problem-solving process used to create a computer program. The entire process is shown in Figure 3-1.

1. Analyze the problem.

2. Plan the algorithm.

3. Desk-check the algorithm.

4. Code the algorithm into a program.

5. Desk-check the program.

6. Evaluate and modify (if necessary) the program.

Figure 3-1: The problem-solving process for creating a computer program

Only after the programmer is satisfied that an algorithm is correct does he or she then move on to Step 4 in the problem-solving process. As Figure 3-1 indicates, Step 4 is to code the algorithm—in other words, to translate the algorithm into a language that the computer can understand. As you may remember from Tutorial 2, a coded algorithm is called a **program**. In this book, you will use the C++ programming language to translate your algorithms into programs.

After completing the coding step, the programmer then desk-checks the program to make sure that the algorithm was translated correctly—this is Step 5 in the problem-solving process. Programmers typically desk-check the program using the same sample data used to desk-check the algorithm. If the program does not produce the same results as the algorithm, the programmer corrects the errors in the program before continuing to the final step in the problem-solving process.

The final step in the problem-solving process is to evaluate and modify (if necessary) the program. A programmer evaluates a program by running (executing) it on the computer. While the program is running, the programmer enters the same sample data he or she used when desk-checking the program. If the executed program does not work as intended, the programmer makes the necessary modifications until it does.

Now take a closer look at Steps 4 through 6 in the problem-solving process.

Coding the Algorithm into a Program

In Tutorial 2's Application lesson, you analyzed the problem specification shown in Figure 3-2 for The Paper Tree wallpaper store. You then created and desk-checked an appropriate algorithm.

<u>Problem specification:</u>

Create a program that calculates and displays the number of single rolls of wallpaper needed to cover a room. The salesclerk will provide the length, width, and ceiling height of the room, in feet. He or she also will provide the number of square feet a single roll will cover.

<u>Sample calculation:</u>

      Room size: 10 feet by 12 feet, with a ceiling height of 8 feet

      Single roll coverage: 30 square feet

1. Calculate the perimeter of the room by adding together its length and width, and then multiplying the sum by 2: (10 feet + 12 feet) * 2 = 44 feet
2. Calculate the wall area by multiplying the room's perimeter by its height: 44 feet * 8 feet = 352 square feet
3. Calculate the required number of single rolls by dividing the wall area by the number of square feet a single roll provides: 352 square feet / 30 square feet = 11.73 (rounded to two decimal places), or approximately 12 single rolls.

Figure 3-2: Problem specification for The Paper Tree wallpaper store

Figure 3-3 shows the IPO chart that you created for this problem.

Input	Processing	Output

room length
room width
ceiling height
single roll coverage
	Processing items:
	   room perimeter
	   wall area
	
	Algorithm:
	1. enter the room length, room width, ceiling height, and single roll coverage
	2. calculate the room perimeter by adding together the room length and room width, and then multiplying the sum by 2
	3. calculate the wall area by multiplying the room perimeter by the ceiling height
	4. calculate the number of single rolls by dividing the wall area by the single roll coverage
	5. display the number of single rolls
		number of single rolls

Figure 3-3: IPO chart for The Paper Tree wallpaper store problem

Recall that the IPO chart shows the problem's input, processing, and output items, as well as the algorithm needed to solve the problem. The algorithm shown in Figure 3-3, for example, shows the steps the computer will need to follow to calculate and display the number of single rolls of paper required to wallpaper a room. The calculation is based on the values of the room length, room width, ceiling height, and single roll coverage entered by the user. Notice that the algorithm also calculates two intermediate values: room perimeter and wall area. As you learned in Tutorial 2, an intermediate value, referred to as a processing item, is one that the algorithm uses when processing the input into the output.

Assigning Names, Data Types, and Initial Values to the IPO Items

Programmers use the information in the IPO chart to code the algorithm. First, the programmer assigns a descriptive name to each unique input, processing, and output item listed in the IPO chart. In most programming languages, these names can contain only letters, numbers, and the underscore; they cannot contain punctuation characters or spaces. Most C++ programmers use lowercase letters for the names. If a name contains more than one word, however, most C++ programmers capitalize the first letter in the second word. In this case, you will assign the names `length`, `width`, `height`, and `rollCoverage` to the four input items; `perimeter` and `area` to the two processing items; and `rolls` to the output item.

The programmer also assigns a data type to each input, processing, and output item. The data type specifies the type of data (for example, decimal or integer) each item represents. In this case, because the input, processing, and output items could contain decimal numbers, the proper data type to assign is `float`. You will learn more about data types in Tutorial 4.

In addition to assigning both a name and data type to each input, processing, and output item, the programmer also assigns an initial value. This is referred to as **initializing** the item. As you will learn in Tutorial 4, items declared using the `float` data type typically are initialized to zero using the value `0.0`, as shown in Figure 3-4.

The keyword `float` is short for floating-point, which refers to a number with a decimal place.

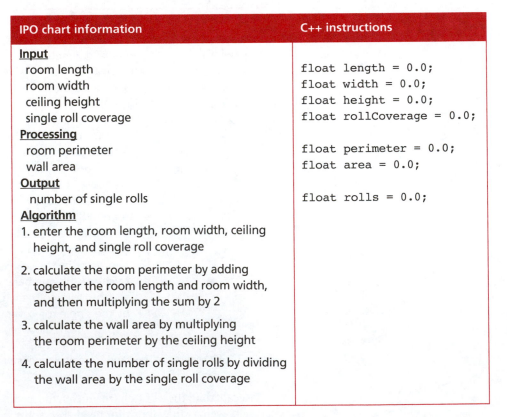

IPO chart information	C++ instructions
<u>Input</u>	
room length	`float length = 0.0;`
room width	`float width = 0.0;`
ceiling height	`float height = 0.0;`
single roll coverage	`float rollCoverage = 0.0;`
<u>Processing</u>	
room perimeter	`float perimeter = 0.0;`
wall area	`float area = 0.0;`
<u>Output</u>	
number of single rolls	`float rolls = 0.0;`
<u>Algorithm</u>	
1. enter the room length, room width, ceiling height, and single roll coverage	
2. calculate the room perimeter by adding together the room length and room width, and then multiplying the sum by 2	
3. calculate the wall area by multiplying the room perimeter by the ceiling height	
4. calculate the number of single rolls by dividing the wall area by the single roll coverage	

Figure 3-4: C++ instructions corresponding to the wallpaper store problem's input, processing, and output items

The seven instructions

```
float length = 0.0;
float width = 0.0;
float height = 0.0;
float rollCoverage = 0.0;
float perimeter = 0.0;
float area = 0.0;
float rolls = 0.0;
```

direct the computer to declare, or create, seven **variables**, which are simply computer memory locations that the program will use while it is running. The word `float`, which must be typed using lowercase letters, is a keyword in C++. A **keyword** is a word that has a special meaning in a programming language. In C++, the keyword `float` indicates that the variable (memory location) can store a number with a decimal place.

Notice that each of the variable declaration instructions ends with a semicolon (;). The instruction to declare a variable is considered a **statement**, which is simply a C++ instruction that causes the computer to perform some action after it is executed, or processed, by the computer. All C++ statements must end with a semicolon.

Translating the Algorithm Steps into C++ Code

After assigning a name, data type, and initial value to each input, processing, and output item, the programmer then translates each step in the algorithm into one or more C++ instructions, as shown in Figure 3-5.

Not all lines of code in a C++ program are statements. As you will learn in this tutorial's Application lesson, program comments, which are lines of code used to internally document a program, are not statements, because they do not cause the computer to perform any action.

Like most programming languages, the C++ language follows a specific format, referred to as its syntax. The **syntax** of a language, whether it is C++ or English, is simply the set of rules that you must follow to use the language. The syntax of the C++ language, like the syntax of the English language, will take some time and effort to learn.

IPO chart information	C++ instructions
Input	
room length	`float length = 0.0;`
room width	`float width = 0.0;`
ceiling height	`float height = 0.0;`
single roll coverage	`float rollCoverage = 0.0;`
Processing	
room perimeter	`float perimeter = 0.0;`
wall area	`float area = 0.0;`
Output	
number of single rolls	`float rolls = 0.0;`
Algorithm	

1. enter the room length, room width, ceiling height, and single roll coverage	`cout << "Enter room length: ";`
	`cin >> length;`
	`cout << "Enter room width: ";`
	`cin >> width;`
	`cout << "Enter ceiling height: ";`
	`cin >> height;`
	`cout << "Enter single roll coverage: ";`
	`cin >> rollCoverage;`

Figure 3-5: C++ instructions corresponding to the wallpaper store problem's algorithm

IPO chart information	C++ instructions
2. calculate the room perimeter by adding together the room length and room width, and then multiplying the sum by 2	`perimeter = (length + width) * 2;`
3. calculate the wall area by multiplying the room perimeter by the ceiling height	`area = perimeter * height;`
4. calculate the number of single rolls by dividing the wall area by the single roll coverage	`rolls = area / rollCoverage;`
5. display the number of single rolls	`cout << "Single rolls: " << rolls << endl;`

Figure 3-5: C++ instructions corresponding to the wallpaper store problem's algorithm (continued)

Do not be concerned if the C++ instructions shown in Figure 3-5 look confusing to you. Each instruction is described in this lesson with a minimal amount of explanation. You will learn more detail about each instruction in the following tutorials. For now, you need simply to pay attention to how each instruction corresponds to a step in the algorithm.

Step 1 in the algorithm is to enter the input items—room length, room width, ceiling height, and single roll coverage. You will have the user enter the input items at the keyboard. To do so, you first will use a C++ instruction that prompts the user for the information you want him or her to enter. You then will use a C++ instruction that allows him or her to enter the information.

In C++, you use **streams**, which are just sequences of characters, to perform standard input and output operations. The standard output stream is called `cout` (pronounced *see out*), which refers to the computer screen. The standard input stream, on the other hand, is called `cin` (pronounced *see in*), which refers to the keyboard. To make the concept of streams easier to understand, it may help to think of the `cout` stream as simply a sequence of characters sent "out" to the user through the computer screen, and think of the `cin` stream as a sequence of characters sent "in" to the computer through the keyboard.

The C++ statement `cout << "Enter room length: ";` prompts the user to enter the room's length by displaying an appropriate message on the computer screen. (You can tell that this line is a statement because it ends with a semicolon.) The `<<` that follows `cout` in the statement is called the **insertion operator**. It may help to think of the insertion operator as meaning "sends to." In this case, the insertion operator (`<<`) sends the "Enter room length: " message to the computer screen (`cout`). Keep in mind that this statement only displays the message on the screen. The statement does not allow the user to actually enter the room length; you will need to use the standard input stream `cin` to do so.

tip

Be certain to use the operator that is appropriate for the stream. You use the insertion operator (<<) with the `cout` stream and the extraction operator (>>) with the `cin` stream. The insertion operator *inserts* data into the `cout` stream (the computer screen), while the extraction operator *extracts* data from the `cin` stream (the keyboard).

The C++ statement `cin >> length;` uses the `cin` stream to allow the user to enter the length. The `>>` that follows `cin` is called the **extraction operator**. It may help to think of the `>>` operator as meaning "gets from." In this case, the statement `cin >> length;` gets the room length from the keyboard (`cin`), then stores that amount in the `length` variable (memory location).

After the user enters the length of the room, the statement `cout << "Enter room width: ";` prompts the user to enter the width. The statement `cin >> width;` then allows the user to enter the width, which the statement stores in the `width` variable.

The next four statements—`cout << "Enter ceiling height: ";`, `cin >> height;`, `cout << "Enter single roll coverage: ";`, and `cin >> rollCoverage;`—prompt the user to enter the height and roll coverage, and then store the user's responses in the `height` and `rollCoverage` variables, respectively.

Step 2 in the algorithm is to calculate the perimeter of the room by adding together the room's length and width, and then multiplying that sum by 2. The C++ statement `perimeter = (length + width) * 2;` accomplishes this task by adding the value stored in the `length` variable to the value stored in the `width` variable, and then multiplying that sum by 2. (Notice that a computer uses an asterisk to represent multiplication.) The statement stores the result of the calculation in the `perimeter` variable. Recall that the `perimeter` variable is one of the two processing items.

The third step in the algorithm is to calculate the wall area by multiplying the perimeter of the room by the height of the ceiling. This task is handled by the C++ statement `area = perimeter * height;`, which multiplies the contents of the `perimeter` variable by the contents of the `height` variable, and then stores the result in the `area` variable. Recall that the `area` variable is the second processing item.

Step 4 in the algorithm is to calculate the number of single rolls of wallpaper by dividing the wall area by the single roll coverage, which is the area that a single roll can cover. The C++ statement `rolls = area / rollCoverage;` accomplishes this by dividing the value stored in the `area` variable by the value stored in the `rollCoverage` variable. (Notice that a computer uses a forward slash [/] to represent division.) The quotient will be stored in the `rolls` variable.

The last step in the algorithm is to display the required number of single rolls of wallpaper, which was calculated in the previous step. You can do so using the C++ statement `cout << "Single rolls: " << rolls << endl;`. This statement will display the message "Single rolls: " along with the contents of the `rolls` variable. (Notice that you can use more than one insertion operator in a statement.) The `endl` (pronounced *end of line*) text that appears at the end of the statement is one of the C++ stream manipulators. A **stream manipulator** allows the program to manipulate, or manage, the input and output stream characters in some way. When outputting information to the computer screen, for example, you can use the `endl` stream manipulator to advance the cursor to the next line on the screen.

After the programmer finishes coding the algorithm into a program, he or she then moves on to the fifth step in the problem-solving process, which is to desk-check the program.

mini-quiz

Mini-Quiz 1

1. The programmer assigns a _____, _____, and _____ to each unique input, processing, and output item listed in the IPO chart.

2. A _____ is a location in the computer's memory that the program uses while it is running.

3. Write a C++ statement that declares a variable named `grossPay`. Use `float` as the data type, and use `0.0` as the initial value.

4. Write a C++ statement that stores the value entered at the keyboard in a variable named `grossPay`.

Desk-Checking the Program

The fifth step in the problem-solving process is to desk-check the program to make sure that each step in the algorithm was translated correctly. You should desk-check the program using the same sample data that you used to desk-check the algorithm. The results obtained when desk-checking the program should be identical to the results obtained when desk-checking the algorithm. For your convenience in comparing the results of both desk-checks later in this lesson, Figure 3-6 shows the desk-check table that you completed for the wallpaper store algorithm in Tutorial 2's Application lesson.

room length	room width	ceiling height	single roll coverage	room perimeter	wall area	number of single rolls
~~10~~ 12	~~12~~ 14	~~8~~ 10	~~30~~ 37	~~44~~ 52	~~352~~ 520	~~11.73~~ 14.05

Figure 3-6: Completed desk-check table for the wallpaper store algorithm

As Figure 3-6 indicates, you desk-checked the algorithm twice, using two sets of data. The first set of data used 10 as the room length, 12 as the room width, 8 as the ceiling height, and 30 as the single roll coverage. The second set of data used 12 as the room length, 14 as the room width, 10 as the ceiling height, and 37 as the single roll coverage. You will use both sets of data to desk-check the program.

When desk-checking the program, you first place the names of the input, processing, and output variables in a new desk-check table, along with each variable's initial value, as shown in Figure 3-7.

variable names

initial values

length	width	height	rollCoverage	perimeter	area	rolls
0.0	0.0	0.0	0.0	0.0	0.0	0.0

Figure 3-7: Variable names and initial values shown in the program's desk-check table

Next, you complete each of the C++ instructions in order, recording any changes made to the variables in the desk-check table. For example, the statement `cout << "Enter room length: ";` prompts the user to enter the length of the room. The statement does not make any changes to the program's variables, so no entry is necessary in the desk-check table as a result of the statement. However, recall that the next statement, `cin >> length;`, allows the user to enter the length, and it stores the user's response in the `length` variable. If the user enters the number 10 as the room length, for example, the statement stores the number 10 in the `length` variable. You record the result of the `cin >> length;` statement in the desk-check table by crossing out the 0.0 that appears as the initial value in the `length` column, and entering the number 10 there instead.

The statement `cout << "Enter room width: ";` prompts the user to enter the width of the room, and the statement `cin >> width;` stores the user's response in the `width` variable. Assuming the user enters the number 12, you cross out the 0.0 that appears in the desk-check table's `width` column, and record the number 12 there instead.

The statement `cout << "Enter ceiling height: ";` prompts the user to enter the ceiling height, and the statement `cin >> height;` stores the user's response in the `height` variable. Assuming the user enters the number 8, you cross out the 0.0 that appears in the desk-check table's `height` column, and record the number 8 there instead.

The statement `cout << "Enter single roll coverage: ";` prompts the user to enter the area covered by a single roll of wallpaper, and the statement `cin >> rollCoverage;` stores the user's response in the `rollCoverage` variable. Assuming the user enters the number 30, you cross out the 0.0 that appears in the desk-check table's `rollCoverage` column, and record the number 30 there instead, as shown in Figure 3-8.

> **tip**
> ● ● ● ● ● ● ● ● ● ● ● ● ● ● ●
> As you learned in Tutorial 2, each column in a desk-check table should contain only one value at a time.

length	width	height	rollCoverage	perimeter	area	rolls
~~0.0~~ 10	~~0.0~~ 12	~~0.0~~ 8	~~0.0~~ 30	0.0	0.0	0.0

Figure 3-8: Current status of the desk-check table

The next statement, `perimeter = (length + width) * 2;`, first adds the contents of the `length` variable (10 according to the desk-check table) to the contents of the `width` variable (12 according to the desk-check table), giving 22. It then multiplies that sum by 2, giving 44. The statement stores the number 44 in the `perimeter` variable. Notice that the calculation that appears on the right side of the equal sign in the statement is performed first, and then the result is stored in the variable whose name appears on the left side of the equal sign. As a result of this statement, you cross out the number 0.0 that appears in the desk-check table's `perimeter` column, and record the numer 44 there instead, as shown in Figure 3-9.

length	width	height	rollCoverage	perimeter	area	rolls
~~0.0~~ 10	~~0.0~~ 12	~~0.0~~ 8	~~0.0~~ 30	~~0.0~~ 44	0.0	0.0

Figure 3-9: Desk-check table showing the result of the perimeter calculation

The next statement, `area = perimeter * height;`, first multiplies the contents of the `perimeter` variable (44) by the contents of the `height` variable (8), and then stores the result (352) in the `area` variable. In the desk-check table, you cross out the 0.0 that appears in the `area` column, and record the number 352 there instead, as shown in Figure 3-10.

As you will learn in Tutorial 4, the equal sign in the statements that calculate the perimeter, area, and number of rolls is called the assignment operator, because it assigns a value to a variable.

length	width	height	rollCoverage	perimeter	area	rolls
~~0.0~~ 10	~~0.0~~ 12	~~0.0~~ 8	~~0.0~~ 30	~~0.0~~ 44	~~0.0~~ 352	0.0

Figure 3-10: Desk-check table showing the result of the area calculation

The next statement, `rolls = area / rollCoverage;`, first divides the contents of the `area` variable (352) by the contents of the `rollCoverage` variable (30), and then stores the result (11.73) in the `rolls` variable. In the desk-check table, you cross out the 0.0 that appears in the `rolls` column, and record the number 11.73 there instead, as shown in Figure 3-11.

length	width	height	rollCoverage	perimeter	area	rolls
~~0.0~~ 10	~~0.0~~ 12	~~0.0~~ 8	~~0.0~~ 30	~~0.0~~ 44	~~0.0~~ 352	~~0.0~~ 11.73

Figure 3-11: Desk-check table showing the result of the rolls calculation

The last statement, `cout << "Single rolls: " << rolls << endl;`, displays the message "Single rolls: ", along with the contents of the `rolls` variable (11.73), on the screen. The `endl` stream manipulator then advances the cursor to the next line on the screen.

If you compare the second row of values shown in Figure 3-11 with the first row of values shown earlier in Figure 3-6, you will notice that the results obtained when desk-checking the program are identical to the results obtained when desk-checking the algorithm. Recall, however, that you should perform several desk-checks, using different data, to make sure that the program is correct. Now desk-check the program using 12 as the room length, 14 as the room width, 10 as the ceiling height, and 37 as the single roll coverage; this is the same data used in the second desk-check shown in Figure 3-6. Each time you desk-check a program, keep in mind that you must complete all of the program's instructions, beginning with the first instruction. In this case, the first instruction initializes the `length` variable. The completed desk-check table is shown in Figure 3-12.

length	width	height	rollCoverage	perimeter	area	rolls
~~0.0~~ ~~10~~ ~~0.0~~ 12	~~0.0~~ ~~12~~ ~~0.0~~ 14	~~0.0~~ ~~8~~ ~~0.0~~ 10	~~0.0~~ ~~30~~ ~~0.0~~ 37	~~0.0~~ ~~44~~ ~~0.0~~ 52	~~0.0~~ ~~352~~ ~~0.0~~ 520	~~0.0~~ ~~11.73~~ ~~0.0~~ 14.05

Figure 3-12: Desk-check table showing the results of the second desk-check

Here again, if you compare the fourth row of values shown in Figure 3-12 with the second row of values shown earlier in Figure 3-6, you will notice that the program produced the same results as did the algorithm.

After desk-checking the program, the programmer then evaluates and modifies (if necessary) the program.

Evaluating and Modifying the Program

The final step in the problem-solving process is to evaluate and modify (if necessary) the program. Programmers often refer to this as the "testing and debugging" step. **Testing** refers to running (executing) the program, along with sample data, on the computer. The results obtained when the program is run on the computer should agree with those shown in the program's desk-check table. If the results of running the program differ from those of the desk-check, then the program contains errors that must be corrected.

Debugging refers to the process of locating and removing any errors, called **bugs**, in a program. Program errors can be either syntax errors or logic errors. You create a **syntax error** when you enter an instruction that violates the programming language's syntax—the set of rules that you must follow when using the language. Typing `ednl` rather than `endl` is an example of a syntax error. Most syntax errors occur as a result of mistyping a keyword or variable name, or forgetting to enter a semicolon at the end of a statement. Most syntax errors are easy to both locate and correct.

Logic errors, on the other hand, are much more difficult to find, because they can occur for a variety of reasons. The instruction `perimeter = length + width * 2;`, which is supposed to calculate the perimeter, is an example of a logic error. Although the instruction is syntactically correct, it is logically incorrect, because it tells the computer first to multiply the contents of the `width` variable by 2, then add that product to the contents of the `length` variable, and then assign the sum to the `perimeter` variable. This error occurs because, arithmetically, multiplication is performed before addition in an expression. The instruction to calculate the perimeter, written correctly, should be `perimeter = (length + width) * 2;`. Adding the parentheses to this instruction tells the computer first to add the contents of the `length` variable to the contents of the `width` variable, then multiply that sum by 2, and then assign the product to the `perimeter` variable. Other logic errors occur typically as a result of neglecting to enter a program instruction or entering the program instructions in the wrong order.

If a program contains an error, the programmer must locate and then correct the error. The programmer's job is not finished until the program runs without errors and produces the expected results.

tip

> You will learn about the precedence order for the arithmetic operators in Tutorial 4.

mini-quiz

Mini-Quiz 2

1. How many values can a variable contain at any time?
2. Errors in a program are also called _____.
3. Program errors can be either _____ errors or _____ errors.

You now have completed the six-step process for creating a computer program. Recall that those steps are to analyze the problem, then plan, desk-check, and code the algorithm, and then desk-check, evaluate, and modify (if necessary) the program. You can either take a break or complete the end-of-lesson questions and exercises before moving on to the Application lesson.

S U M M A R Y

After analyzing a problem, and then planning and desk-checking an appropriate algorithm, the programmer continues to the fourth step in the problem-solving process, which is to code the algorithm into a program, using the information in the IPO chart. First the programmer assigns a name, data type, and initial value to each unique input, processing, and output item listed in the IPO chart. He or she then translates each step in the algorithm into one or more C++ instructions.

In C++, you use streams, which are just sequences of characters, to perform standard input and output operations. The standard output stream is called cout (pronounced *see out*), which refers to the computer screen. The standard input stream is called cin (pronounced *see in*), which refers to the keyboard.

The << operator is called the insertion operator, and it is used to send information to the output stream. The >> operator is called the extraction operator, and it is used to get information from the input stream.

After coding the algorithm, the programmer then desk-checks the program to make sure that the algorithm was translated correctly. You should desk-check the program using the same sample data that you used to desk-check the algorithm. The results obtained when desk-checking the program should be identical to the results obtained when desk-checking the algorithm.

The final step in the problem-solving process is to evaluate and modify (if necessary) the program. A programmer evaluates, or tests, a program by running (executing) it, along with sample data, on the computer. If the executed program does not work as intended, the programmer makes the necessary modifications until it does.

Some programs have errors, called bugs. Program errors can be either syntax errors or logic errors. A syntax error occurs when you violate one of the rules of the programming language, referred to as the language's syntax. A logic error can occur for a variety of reasons—such as mistyping a keyword or variable name, forgetting to enter a semicolon at the end of a statement, neglecting to enter an instruction, or entering the program instructions in the wrong order. Debugging refers to the process of locating and removing the errors in a program.

A N S W E R S   T O   M I N I · Q U I Z Z E S

Mini-Quiz 1

1.   descriptive name, data type, initial value
2.   variable
3.   `float grossPay = 0.0;`
4.   `cin >> grossPay;`

Mini-Quiz 2

1.   one
2.   bugs
3.   syntax, logic

QUESTIONS

1. Which of the following is the fourth step in the problem-solving process?
   a. Evaluate and modify (if necessary) the program.
   b. Code the algorithm into a program.
   c. Plan the algorithm.
   d. Desk-check the program.

2. The rules of a programming language are called its _____.
   a. guidelines
   b. procedures
   c. regulations
   d. syntax

3. Which of the following statements declares a variable that can contain a decimal number?
   a. `dec payRate = 0.0;`
   b. `float payRate = 0.0`
   c. `float hourlyPay = 0.0;`
   d. none of the above

4. A C++ statement must end with a _____.
   a. : (colon)
   b. , (comma)
   c. ; (semicolon)
   d. none of the above

5. In C++, you use _____ to perform standard input and output operations.
   a. characters
   b. sequences
   c. streams
   d. none of the above

6. The standard output stream, which refers to the computer screen, is called
   _____.
   a. `cin`
   b. `cout`
   c. `stdin`
   d. `stdout`

7. The standard input stream, which refers to the keyboard, is called _____
   a. `cin`
   b. `cout`
   c. `stdin`
   d. `stdout`

8. Which of the following statements displays the word "Hello" on the computer screen?
   a. `cin << "Hello";`
   b. `cin >> "Hello";`
   c. `cout << "Hello";`
   d. `cout >> "Hello";`

9. Which of the following is the extraction operator?
   a. `>>`
   b. `<<`
   c. `//`
   d. `/*`

10. Which of the following statements allows the user to enter data at the keyboard?
    a. `cin << currentPay;`
    b. `cin >> currentPay;`
    c. `cout << currentPay;`
    d. `cout >> currentPay;`

11. Which of the following is the insertion operator?
    a. `>>`
    b. `<<`
    c. `//`
    d. `/*`

12. Which of the following stream manipulators advances the cursor to the next line on the computer screen?
    a. `advln`
    b. `edlin`
    c. `endl`
    d. `lineadv`

13. The final step in the problem-solving process is to _____.
    a. evaluate and modify (if necessary) the program
    b. code the algorithm into a program
    c. plan the algorithm
    d. desk-check the program

14. The process of locating and removing the errors in a program is called _____.
    a. analyzing
    b. correcting
    c. debugging
    d. tracking

15. Misspelling an instruction is an example of _____.
    a. an entry error
    b. a function error
    c. a logic error
    d. a syntax error

16. Typing the instruction `grossPay = hoursWorked - hourlyPay;` is an example of _____.
    a. an entry error
    b. a function error
    c. a logic error
    d. a syntax error

EXERCISES

1. Three C++ instructions are missing from the code shown in Figure 3-13. First study the algorithm, then complete the C++ code by entering the three missing instructions.

IPO chart information	C++ instructions

Input
   first number
   second number
 	
 Processing
	`float num1 = 0.0;`
	 `float num2 = 0.0;`

Figure 3-13

IPO chart information	C++ instructions
Output sum	`float sum = 0.0;`

Algorithm
1. enter the first number
   and the second number
	`cout << "Enter first number: ";`
	`cin >> num1;`
	_____
	_____

2. calculate the sum by
   adding the first number
   to the second number
	_____

3. display the sum	`cout << "The sum is " << sum << endl;`

Figure 3-13 (continued)

2. Desk-check the program you completed in Exercise 1 two times, using the numbers 3 and 5 first, and then using the numbers 50.5 and 31.3. Use the desk-check table shown in Figure 3-14.

num1	num2	sum

Figure 3-14

3. Study the algorithm shown in Figure 3-15, then complete the C++ code shown in the figure.

IPO chart information	C++ instructions
Input current weekly pay raise rate	`float currentPay = 0.0;` `float rate = 0.0;`
Processing weekly raise	_____
Output new weekly pay	_____

Algorithm
1. enter the current weekly
   pay and raise rate
	`cout << "Enter current weekly pay: ";`
	`cin >> currentPay;`
	`cout << "Enter raise rate: ";`
	_____

2. calculate the weekly raise
   by multiplying the current
   weekly pay by the raise rate
	`raise = _____`

Figure 3-15

IPO chart information	C++ instructions
3. calculate the new weekly pay by adding the weekly raise to the current weekly pay	newPay = _____
4. display the new weekly pay	_____

Figure 3-15 (continued)

4. Create a desk-check table for the program you completed in Exercise 3. Desk-check the program twice. For the first desk-check, use 250 as the current weekly pay and .03 as the raise rate. For the second desk-check, use 100 as the current weekly pay and .10 as the raise rate. When you are finished desk-checking, compare your desk-check table with the one shown in Tutorial 2's Figure 2-23; the results (other than the initialization rows) should be the same.

Exercise 5 is a Discovery Exercise. Discovery Exercises, which may include topics that are not covered in this lesson, allow you to "discover" the solutions to problems on your own.

5. In this exercise, you will learn about the int data type.
   a. Study the algorithm shown in Figure 3-16, then write the appropriate C++ code. The numbers the user will enter into the computer will be integers, which means they will not contain a decimal portion. Use the int data type to declare the appropriate variables, and initialize each to the number 0. (*int* stands for *integer*.)

IPO chart information	C++ instructions
Input	
first number	_____
second number	_____
third number	_____
Processing	
Output	
sum	_____
Algorithm	
1. enter the first number, second number, and third number	_____
	_____
	_____
	_____
	_____
	_____
2. calculate the sum by adding together the first number, second number, and third number	_____
3. display the sum	_____

Figure 3-16

   b. Create an appropriate desk-check table for the program. Desk-check the program twice. For the first desk-check, use the numbers 25, 76, and 33. For the second desk-check, use the numbers 10, 15, and 20.

A computer program is good only if it works. Errors in either an algorithm or programming code can cause the program to run incorrectly. Therefore, a programmer needs to know how to locate and fix these errors. Exercise 6 is a Debugging Exercise. Debugging Exercises allow you to practice recognizing and solving errors in a program.

debugging

6. In this exercise, you will debug C++ code.
    a. Study the algorithm and C++ code shown in Figure 3-17. Desk-check the C++ code using an original price of 100 and a discount rate of 25%.
    b. Make the necessary changes to the C++ code, then desk-check the code again, using the same sample data.

IPO chart information	C++ instructions

Input
  original price
  discount rate
	`float original = 0.0;`
	`float rate = 0.0;`

Processing discount	`float discount = 0.0;`
Output sale price	`float sale = 0.0;`

Algorithm
1. enter the original price
  and the discount rate
	`cout << "Original price: ";`
	`cin >> original;`
	`cout << "Discount rate: ";`
	`cin >> rate`

2. calculate the discount by
  multiplying the original
  price by the discount rate
	`discount = original * discRate;`

3. calculate the sale price
  by subtracting the discount
  from the original price
	`sale = discount - original;`

4. display the sale price	`cout << "Sales price: " << sale <<` `endl;`

Figure 3-17

Application Lesson

Creating a C++ Program

case ▶ In this lesson, you will use the C++ programming language to complete the program for Mark Williams and The Paper Tree wallpaper store. Recall that the program allows the store's salesclerks to calculate and display the number of single rolls of paper required to wallpaper a room.

The C++ Programming Language

C++ evolved from the procedure-oriented C programming language, which was developed in 1972 at Bell Laboratories by Dennis Ritchie. In 1985, Bjarne Stroustrup, also of Bell Laboratories, added, among other things, object-oriented features to the C language. This enhanced version of the C language was named C++.

C++ is a superset of C, which means that, with few exceptions, everything available in C also is available in C++. This means that you can use C++ as a procedural, as well as an object-oriented, language. Before using the object-oriented features of C++, you will learn how to use C++ to create procedure-oriented programs. The techniques you learn from procedural programming will help you create object-oriented programs later.

To create and execute a C++ program, you need to have access to a text editor, often simply called an editor, and a C++ compiler. You use the editor to enter the C++ instructions, called **source code**, into the computer. You then save the source code in a file on a disk, using the filename extension .cpp. (The *cpp* stands for *C plus plus*.) The file containing the source code is called the **source file**.

As you learned in the Overview, the computer cannot understand instructions written in a high-level language. Rather, a compiler is necessary to translate the high-level instructions into machine code—the 0s and 1s that the computer *can* understand. Machine code is usually called **object code**. When you compile a C++ program, the compiler generates the appropriate object code, saving it automatically in a file whose filename extension is .obj. (The *obj* stands for *object*.) The file containing the object code is called the **object file**.

After the compiler creates the object file, it then invokes another program called a linker. The **linker** combines the object file with other machine code necessary for the C++ program to run correctly—such as machine code that allows your program to communicate with input and output devices. The linker produces an **executable file**, which is a file that contains all of the machine code necessary to run your C++ program as many times as desired without the need for translating the program again. The executable file has an extension of .exe on its filename. (The *exe* stands for *executable*.)

Figure 3-18 illustrates the process the C++ compiler follows when translating source code into executable code.

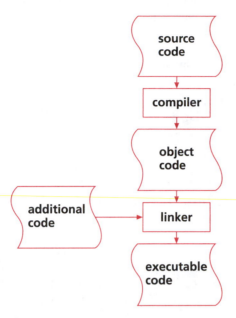

Figure 3-18: Process by which source code is translated into executable code

Many C++ systems, such as Microsoft Visual C++ and Borland C++ Builder, contain both the editor and compiler in one integrated environment, referred to as an IDE (Integrated Development Environment). Other C++ systems, called command-line compilers, contain only the compiler and require you to use a general-purpose editor (such as Notepad and WordPad) to enter the program instructions into the computer. Keep in mind that the different C++ systems, such as Visual C++ and C++ Builder, are not different languages. Rather, they are different implementations of the C++ language. Although this book assumes that you are using Microsoft Visual C++ 6.0 to create your programs, you will be able to use the C++ instructions that you learn in this book in most C++ systems.

mini-quiz

Mini-Quiz 3

1. The .cpp file that contains your C++ instructions is called the _____ file.

2. The compiler saves the machine code version of your C++ instructions in the _____ file.

3. The linker produces an _____ file, which is a file that contains all of the machine code necessary to run your C++ program.

Starting to Program in C++

Before you can create a C++ program, you need to start C++. The instructions for starting C++ depend on the C++ system you are using. The following instructions show you how to start Microsoft Visual C++ 6.0 Introductory Edition. If you are using a different C++ system, you might need to ask your instructor or your technical support person for the appropriate instructions to start that system. Before you begin the following steps, you should have copied the C++ data files for this book to your computer's hard disk, as specified in the Read This Before You Begin page found at the beginning of this book.

To start the Microsoft Visual C++ 6.0 program:

1 If necessary, start Windows. Click the **Start** button on the taskbar to display the Start menu, then point to **Programs**. The Programs menu appears to the right of the Start menu. Point to **Microsoft Visual C++ 6.0** on the Programs menu. The Visual C++ menu appears to the right of the Programs menu. Click **Microsoft Visual C++ 6.0** on the Visual C++ menu. The Microsoft Visual C++ 6.0 Introductory Edition copyright screen appears momentarily, and then the Microsoft Visual C++ window appears.

HELP? The copyright screen might not appear, or it will be different if you are not using Microsoft Visual C++ Introductory Edition.

2 If a Tip of the Day dialog box appears, click the **Show tips at startup** check box to deselect it, and then click the **Close** button to close the dialog box.

3 If necessary, click the **Maximize** button 🔲 on the Microsoft Visual C++ title bar to maximize the Microsoft Visual C++ window.

4 Right-click the **menu bar** to display the shortcut menu shown in Figure 3-19. You can use the shortcut menu to specify which windows you want opened. In this case, only the Standard toolbar window should be selected on the menu.

right-click the menu bar

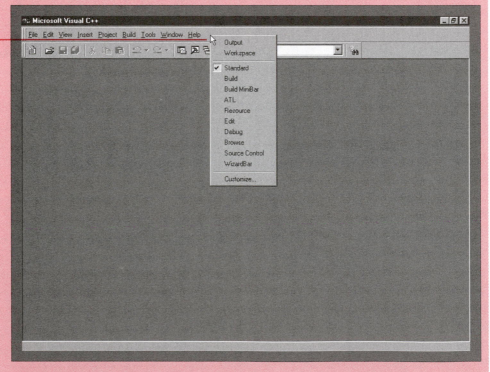

Figure 3-19: Shortcut menu

HELP? If Standard is not selected, click it to select it. If another item on the menu is selected, click it to deselect it. You may need to open the shortcut menu more than once.

5 If necessary, click the **menu bar** to close the shortcut menu. Figure 3-20 shows the Microsoft Visual C++ 6.0 window.

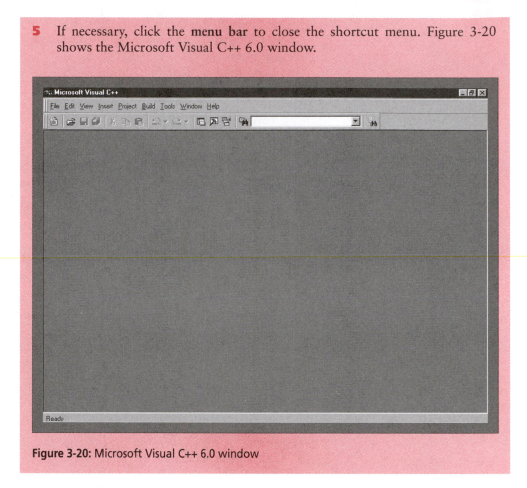

Figure 3-20: Microsoft Visual C++ 6.0 window

Important note: From this point of the book onward, you will be instructed simply to "start Visual C++."

Figure 3-21 shows the information from the IPO chart that you created for The Paper Tree wallpaper store in Tutorial 2's Application lesson. The figure also shows the corresponding C++ instructions, which you learned about in this tutorial's Concept lesson.

IPO chart information	C++ instructions
Input	
room length	`float length = 0.0;`
room width	`float width = 0.0;`
ceiling height	`float height = 0.0;`
single roll coverage	`float rollCoverage = 0.0;`
Processing	
room perimeter	`float perimeter = 0.0;`
wall area	`float area = 0.0;`
Output	
number of single rolls	`float rolls = 0.0;`

Figure 3-21: IPO chart information and the corresponding C++ instructions

IPO chart information	C++ instructions
Algorithm	

1. enter the room length, room width, ceiling height, and single roll coverage	```cout << "Enter room length: ";```
	```cin >> length;```
	```cout << "Enter room width: ";```
	```cin >> width;```
	```cout << "Enter ceiling height: ";```
	```cin >> height;```
	```cout << "Enter single roll coverage: ";```
	```cin >> rollCoverage;```

2. calculate the room perimeter by adding together the room length and room width, and then multiplying the sum by 2	```perimeter = (length + width) * 2;```
3. calculate the wall area by multiplying the room perimeter by the ceiling height	```area = perimeter * height;```
4. calculate the number of single rolls by dividing the wall area by the single roll coverage	```rolls = area / rollCoverage;```
5. display the number of single rolls	```cout << "Single rolls: " << rolls << endl;```

Figure 3-21: IPO chart information and the corresponding C++ instructions (continued)

Your hard disk contains a partially completed C++ program containing most of the instructions shown in Figure 3-21. Open that program now.

To open the partially completed C++ program:

1 Click **File** on the menu bar, and then click **Open**. The Open dialog box appears. Open the Cpp\Tut03\T3App folder on your computer's hard disk, then click **T3App.cpp** in the list of filenames. (The *T3App* in the filename stands for *Tutorial 3, Application lesson*; the *.cpp* stands for *C plus plus*.)

2 Click the **Open** button to open the file. If necessary, click the **Maximize** button ▣ on the T3App.cpp window's title bar to maximize the window. The program appears in the T3App.cpp window, as shown in Figure 3-22.

comment

directives

function data type

variables

function header

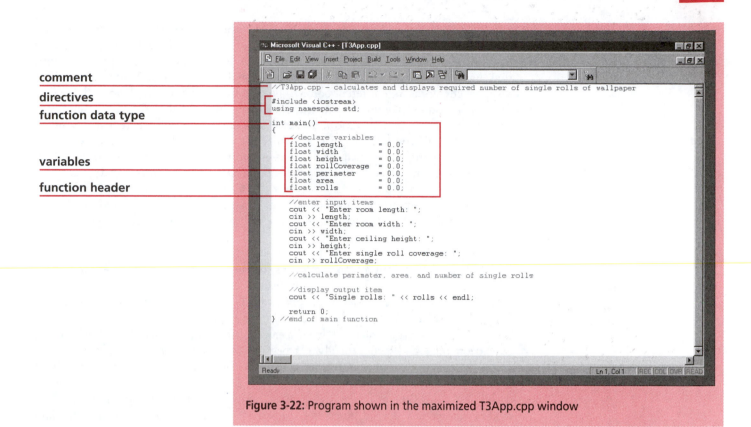

```
Microsoft Visual C++ - [T3App.cpp]
File  Edit  View  Insert  Project  Build  Tools  Window  Help

//T3App.cpp - calculates and displays required number of single rolls of wallpaper

#include <iostream>
using namespace std;

int main()
{
    //declare variables
    float length        = 0.0;
    float width         = 0.0;
    float height        = 0.0;
    float rollCoverage  = 0.0;
    float perimeter     = 0.0;
    float area          = 0.0;
    float rolls         = 0.0;

    //enter input items
    cout << "Enter room length: ";
    cin >> length;
    cout << "Enter room width: ";
    cin >> width;
    cout << "Enter ceiling height: ";
    cin >> height;
    cout << "Enter single roll coverage: ";
    cin >> rollCoverage;

    //calculate perimeter, area, and number of single rolls

    //display output item
    cout << "Single rolls: " << rolls << endl;

    return 0;
} //end of main function

Ready                                          Ln 1, Col 1   REC COL OVR READ
```

Figure 3-22: Program shown in the maximized T3App.cpp window

Do not be concerned if the program shown in Figure 3-22 looks confusing to you. Each program instruction is described in this lesson with a minimal amount of explanation. You will learn more detail about each instruction in the following tutorials.

The first line in the program is `//T3App.cpp - calculates and displays required number of single rolls of wallpaper`. The `//` (two forward slashes) in a C++ program tell you that what follows on that line is a **comment**, which is simply a message to the person reading the program. In this case, the comment reminds you of the program's name and purpose. Comments, which are referred to as **internal documentation**, make the program instructions more readable and easier to understand by anyone viewing the program. The C++ compiler ignores the comments when it translates the source code into object code.

If you are using a color monitor, you will notice that comments appear in a different color than the rest of the code. The Visual C++ editor displays comments in a different color to help you quickly identify them in the code.

The second line of code in the program, `#include <iostream>`, is called a directive. C++ programs typically include at least one directive, and most include many directives. The **#include directive** is a special instruction for the C++ compiler that tells the compiler to include the contents of another file, in this case the iostream file, in the current program. Files that are included in programs are called **include files** or **header files**. The `#include` directive provides a convenient way to merge the source code from one file with the source code in another file, without having to retype the code. Notice that the name of the file—in this case, iostream—is in angle brackets (< >). The angle brackets indicate that the file is located in C++'s include folder, which comes with the C++ compiler and includes C++'s standard header (include) files.

In C++, the iostream file contains the instructions (source code) needed to handle input and output operations, such as entering data from the keyboard and displaying information on the computer screen. If your program will perform either of those tasks, you will need to use the `#include <iostream>` directive to include the iostream file in the program.

tip

The term *header file* refers to the fact that the file is included at the beginning (head) of a program.

If you are using a color monitor, you will notice that `#include` appears in a different color than the comments or the rest of the code. Like `float`, which you learned about in the Concept lesson, `#include` is a C++ keyword, which is a word that has a special meaning in a programming language. The Visual C++ editor displays keywords in a different color to help you quickly identify them in the code.

When you enter your C++ instructions, keep in mind that the C++ compiler is case sensitive. Typing `#Include`, rather than `#include`, will create a syntax error, because the C++ compiler will not recognize the word `Include`. In other words, in the C++ programming language, `include` is not the same as `Include` or `INCLUDE`.

The third line of code in the program, `using namespace std;`, also is a directive, called a *using directive*. It tells the C++ compiler that the definition of standard C++ keywords—such as `cout`, `cin`, and `endl`—can be found in a namespace (a special area in the computer's internal memory) named std, which is short for "standard."

The fourth line of code in the program is `int main()`. The word `main`, which must be typed in lowercase letters, is the name of a function. A **function** is simply a block of code that performs a task. You can recognize a function in a C++ program by the parentheses immediately following the name. Some functions require you to enter information between the parentheses; others, like `main`, do not. Every C++ program must have a `main` function, because this is where the execution of a C++ program always begins. Most C++ programs contain many more functions in addition to the `main` function. You will learn more about functions in Tutorials 5, 6, and 7.

Some functions return a value after completing their assigned task, while others, referred to as **void functions**, do not. If a function returns a value, the data type of the value it returns will appear to the left of the function name; otherwise, the keyword `void` will appear to the left of the name. Notice that `int`, which stands for *integer* and is typed in lowercase letters, precedes `main` in the code shown in Figure 3-22. The `int` indicates that the `main` function returns a value of the integer data type—in other words, the function returns a number that does not contain a decimal place. The entire line of code, `int main()`, is referred to as a **function header**, because it marks the beginning of the function.

After the function header, you enter the code that directs the function on how to perform its assigned task. In C++, you enclose a function's code within a set of braces ({ }). The braces mark the beginning and the end of the code block that comprises the function. In the current program, the opening brace ({) is located immediately below the function header, and the closing brace (}) is located at the end of the program. Everything between the opening and closing braces is included, in this case, in the `main` function, and is referred to as the **function body**.

Immediately below the opening brace is the comment `//declare variables`, which describes the purpose of the next seven instructions. Those instructions declare, or reserve, seven variables, which are simply memory locations that the program uses while it is running. As you learned in the Concept lesson, the instruction to declare a variable is considered a statement in C++, and therefore ends with a semicolon.

Notice that each variable declaration begins with the keyword `float`, which tells the C++ compiler that the variable (memory location) can store a number with a decimal place. The keyword `float` must be typed in lowercase letters.

In C++, it is common to use lowercase letters when naming variables. If the variable name contains two words, however, you use an uppercase letter for the first letter in the second word, as shown in the variable name `rollCoverage`.

The line below the variable declaration statements, `//enter input items`, is a comment that informs the reader that the purpose of the next set of instructions is to enter the input items into the computer. Recall that entering the input items is the first step in the algorithm shown in Figure 3-21.

tip

In most programming languages, variable names cannot contain spaces.

Four of the eight statements below the //enter input items comment use the cout stream and the insertion operator (<<) to display messages that prompt the user to enter the room length, room width, ceiling height, and single roll coverage. The other four statements use the cin stream and the extraction operator (>>) to allow the user to enter values in response to each prompt.

The next line of program code is the comment //calculate perimeter, area, and number of single rolls. Notice that the instructions that perform these calculations are missing from the program. You will enter the missing instructions in the next set of steps.

To enter the missing instructions:

1 Click the **blank line immediately below the //calculate perimeter, area, and number of single rolls** comment. The insertion point appears in the blank line. If necessary, press the **Tab** key so that the insertion point is aligned with the comment.

According to Figure 3-21, you calculate the perimeter using the C++ statement perimeter = (length + width) * 2;.

2 Type **perimeter = (length + width) * 2;** (be sure to type the semicolon) and press the **Enter** key.

The C++ statements needed to calculate the area and single roll coverage are area = perimeter * height; and rolls = area / rollCoverage;, respectively.

3 Type the additional two instructions shown in Figure 3-23, which shows the completed T3App program.

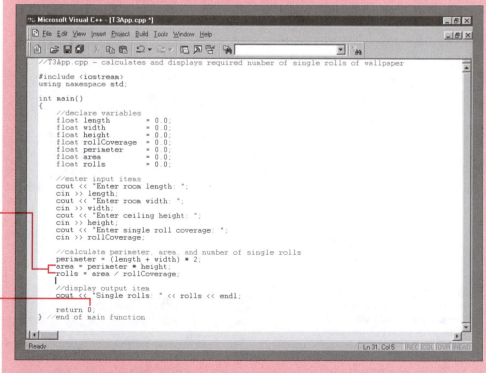

enter these two lines of code

indicates that the program ended normally

Figure 3-23: Completed T3App program

The next line of code is the comment //display output item, which describes the purpose of the statement located immediately below it. That statement, cout << "Single rolls: " << rolls << endl;, corresponds to the last step in the algorithm, and it displays the "Single rolls: " message along with the number of single rolls. As you learned in the Concept lesson, the endl that appears at the end of the statement is one of the C++ stream manipulators, and it advances the cursor to the next line on the computer screen.

The next line of code is the statement return 0;. As mentioned earlier, the main function returns an integer value—in this case, it returns the number 0 to the operating system to indicate that the program ended normally.

The last line in the program is the closing brace (}) that marks the end of the main function. You can include a comment—in this case, //end of main function—on the same line with any C++ instruction; however, you must be sure to enter the comment *after* the instruction, and not before it. Only text appearing after the // on a line is interpreted as a comment.

mini-quiz

Mini-Quiz 4

1. Write a C++ instruction that you could use to enter the message "My first program" as a comment in a program.

2. Write a C++ statement that declares a float variable named hoursWorked. Initialize the variable to 0.0.

3. Write a C++ statement that gets the number of hours worked from the user at the keyboard, and then stores the response in the hoursWorked variable.

4. Write a C++ statement that displays the message "Number of hours worked " on the screen, followed by the contents of the hoursWorked variable. The statement should then advance the cursor to the next line on the screen.

Next, learn how to use the Visual C++ 6.0 compiler to execute a C++ program.

Executing a C++ Program

Before you can execute a C++ program, you need to save it and then compile it. Recall that compiling refers to the process of translating the source code into object code. The method of telling C++ to save, compile, and execute a program varies with the different C++ systems. In the following steps, you will learn how to use the compiler included in the Microsoft Visual C++ 6.0 Introductory Edition to save, compile, and execute a program. If you are using a different C++ system, you might need to ask your instructor or your technical support person for the appropriate instructions for that system.

tip

You always should save a program before compiling the program. That way, if a fatal error occurs in the program, you will not lose the instructions you entered; you can simply reopen the file.

To save, compile, and then execute a C++ program using the Introductory Edition:

1 Click the **Save** button 🖫 on the Standard toolbar to save the file using its current name, T3App.cpp.

2 Click **Build** on the menu bar, then click **Compile T3App.cpp**. The Microsoft Visual C++ dialog box appears, as shown in Figure 3-24.

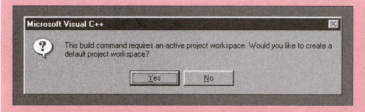

Figure 3-24: Microsoft Visual C++ dialog box

For the Visual C++ compiler to compile a program, the program must be in a project workspace. (You will learn about projects and workspaces in Tutorial 4.) Because you did not create a project workspace before opening the current program, Visual C++ asks if you would like to create a default workspace. You click the Yes button to do so.

3 Click the **Yes** button to create a default project workspace for the current program.

The compiler translates the C++ instructions (the source code) into the 0s and 1s (the object code) that the computer can understand. The Output window appears as the compiler is working. When the compiler is finished, the Output window will look like the one shown in Figure 3-25.

indicates that compiling step produced no errors or warnings

name of object file

Output window

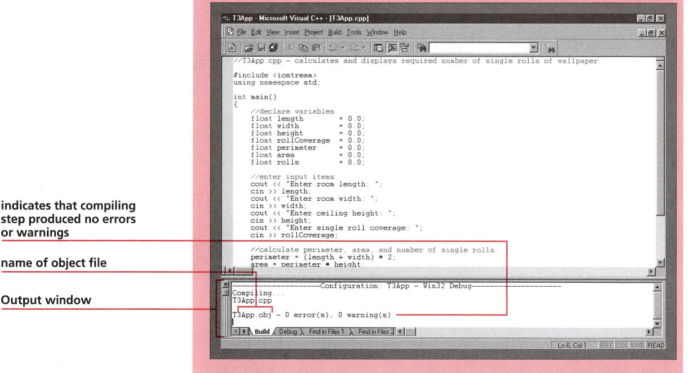

Figure 3-25: Output window at the end of the compile phase

The Output window indicates that the compiler translated the source code contained in the T3App.cpp file into object code, and stored that object code in the T3App.obj file. According to the Output window, the compiler found no errors or warnings during the compiling phase.

As you learned earlier in this lesson, after the compiler translates the source code into object code, it then needs to invoke the linker program, whose task is to link your program's object code to other machine code necessary for your program to run. You invoke the linker program using the Build *<filename.exe>* command on the Build menu.

4   Click **Build** on the menu bar, then click **Build T3App.exe**. When the build process is finished, the Output window appears as shown in Figure 3-26.

the title bar will look different in Windows 2000

indicates that linking step produced no errors or warnings

name of executable file

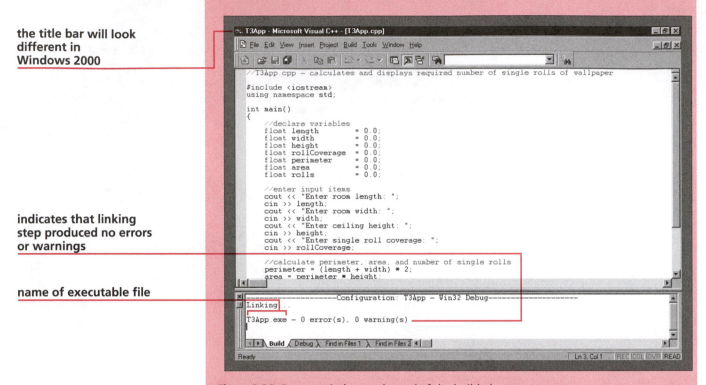

Figure 3-26: Output window at the end of the build phase

The Output window indicates that the linker performed its task and stored the results in an executable file named T3App.exe. According to the Output window, no errors or warnings occurred during the linking phase. Your program is now ready to execute.

5   Click **Build** on the menu bar, then click **Execute T3App.exe**. If you are using the Intoductory Edition of Visual C++ 6.0, the Microsoft (R) Visual C++ (R) dialog box appears on the screen and reminds you that you are not permitted to redistribute executable files created with the Introductory Edition. If necessary, click the **OK** button to close the dialog box. The "Enter room length: " prompt appears in a DOS window, as shown in Figure 3-27.

tip

In this book, you use Microsoft Visual C++ 6.0 to create console applications, which are explained in Tutorial 4. The ouput from console applications appears in a DOS window.

DOS window

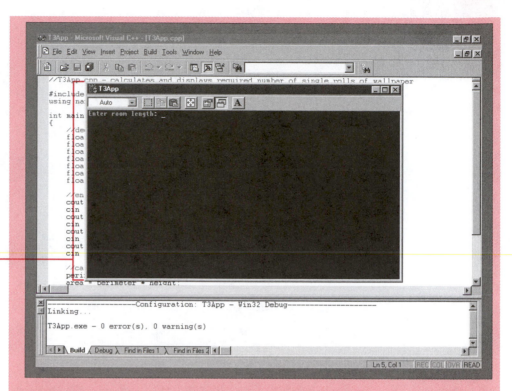

Figure 3-27: Prompt appears in a DOS window

You will test the program using 10 as the room length, 12 as the room width, 8 as the ceiling height, and 30 as the roll coverage. According to the desk-check table shown in the Concept lesson's Figure 3-11, the required number of single rolls should be 11.73.

6 Type **10** as the room length, and then press the **Enter** key. When the prompt to enter the room width appears, type **12** and then press the **Enter** key. When the prompt to enter the ceiling height appears, type 8 and then press the **Enter** key. When the prompt to enter the single roll coverage appears, type **30** and then press the **Enter** key. The required number of single rolls, 11.7333 (notice that the computer carried the answer out to four decimal places), appears on the screen, along with the "Press any key to continue" message. The Microsoft Visual C++ 6.0 editor automatically displays the "Press any key to continue" message on the screen when your program ends. See Figure 3-28.

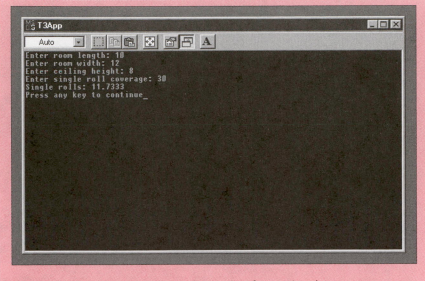

Figure 3-28: DOS window showing the results of executing the program

HELP? If your result was different, you probably made an error when entering the missing instructions. You will learn how to correct errors in C++ code in the next section.

7 Press the **Enter** key to close the DOS window.

Next, you will introduce a syntax error into the current program. You then will learn how to locate and correct the error; in other words, you will learn how to debug and modify the program.

Locating and Correcting an Error in a Program

It is extremely easy to make a typing error when entering a C++ program, thereby producing a syntax error in the program. Observe what happens when a C++ program contains a syntax error.

To introduce a syntax error, then locate and correct the error:

1 Click the Output window's **Hide docked window** button ⊠ to hide the window.

HELP? If you are having trouble locating the Hide docked window button, refer to Figure 3-29.

2 Position the pointer Ⅰ at the end of the `cin >> rollCoverage;` statement in the program, and then click at that location. The insertion point appears after the ; (semicolon) on that line.

3 Press the **Backspace** key to delete the ; (semicolon) that appears at the end of the statement. The statement now should say `cin >> rollCoverage` rather than `cin >> rollCoverage;`.

4 Click the **Save** button 💾 on the Standard toolbar to save the file using its current name.

To run a Visual C++ program, recall that you need to compile it, then build it, and then execute it. In the previous section, you ran the program by selecting three commands on the Build menu: Compile, Build, and Execute. Rather than using this three-step process, you can execute a Microsoft Visual C++ 6.0 program in two steps: by first selecting the Build command, and then selecting the Execute command. The Compile command is not necessary to select, because, in Microsoft Visual C++ 6.0, the Build command compiles the program, if necessary, before it builds the executable file.

5 Click **Build** on the menu bar, then click **Build T3App.exe.**

6 Scroll up the Output window as shown in Figure 3-29. (The drive letter and path in the instruction might be different from the one shown in the figure.)

Hide docked window button

your drive letter and path might be different

scroll to the right to see the entire message

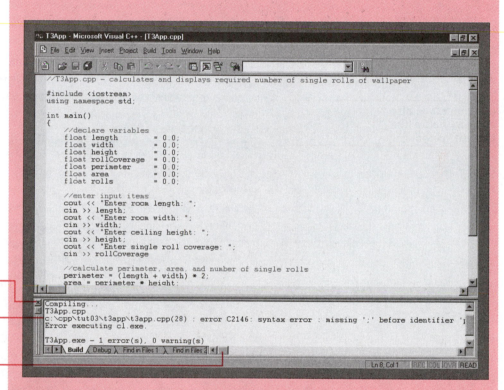

Figure 3-29: Output window showing an error

The Output window tells you that the compiler encountered a syntax error in the program. (You may need to scroll the Output window horizontally to see the full message.)

7 Double-click the **error message in the Output window** to select it, as shown in Figure 3-30.

tip

The number 28 that appears in parentheses in the error message is the number of the line where the error was encountered in the program. In this case, the `perimeter=(length + width) *2` statement is the 28th line in the T3App.cpp program.

location where error was encountered

double-click the error message

error message also appears below the Output window

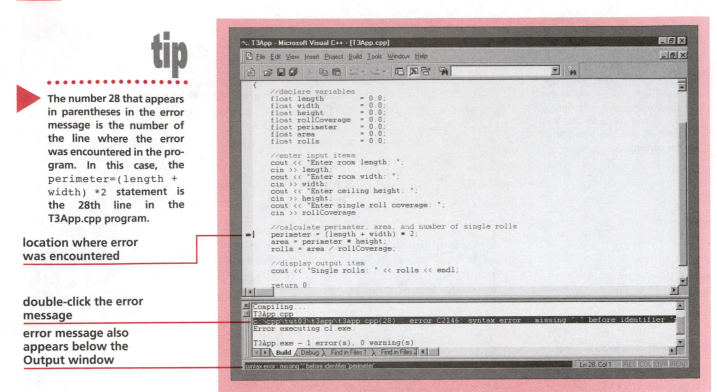

Figure 3-30: Screen showing the description and location of the syntax error

Notice that the error message "syntax error : missing ';' before identifier 'perimeter' " appears below the Output window. Visual C++ also displays an arrow at the location where the error was encountered in the program. In this case, the arrow is pointing to the statement `perimeter = (length + width) * 2;`. Although that is the statement where the compiler discovered the error, that is not the statement that actually caused the error. Rather, the error was caused by the previous statement, `cin >> rollCoverage`. Notice that the semicolon is missing from that statement.

8 Hide the Output window. Position the cursor at the end of the `cin >> rollCoverage` instruction in the program, and then type **;** (a semicolon).

Now save, build, and execute the program to verify that it is working correctly.

9 Save the program. Click **Build** on the menu bar, then click **Build T3App.exe**. The Output window indicates that no errors and no warnings were encountered during the compiling and linking phases. Click **Build** on the menu bar, then click **Execute T3App.exe**. C++ executes the T3App.exe file. If you are using the Introductory Edition, click the **OK** button to remove the Microsoft (R) Visual C++ (R) dialog box.

Important note: In the future, you will be instructed simply to "save, build, and execute the program."

You will test the program using 12 as the room length, 14 as the room width, 10 as the ceiling height, and 37 as the single roll coverage. According to the desk-check table shown in the Concept lesson's Figure 3-12, the required number of single rolls should be 14.05.

10 Type **12** as the room length, and then press the **Enter** key. When the prompt to enter the room width appears, type **14** and then press the **Enter** key. When the prompt to enter the ceiling height appears, type **10** and then press the **Enter** key. When the prompt to enter the single roll coverage appears, type **37** and then press the **Enter** key. The required number of single rolls, 14.0541 (notice that the computer carried out the answer to four decimal places), appears on the screen, along with the "Press any key to continue" message, as shown in Figure 3-31.

Figure 3-31: DOS window showing results of executing the program

11 Press the **Enter** key to continue.

Although the program is not designed currently to handle invalid data correctly, you will test it with invalid data simply to see the results. You will do so using a negative number as the room length. Because you did not make any changes to the program since the last time it was saved and built, you simply can execute the program; you do not need to save and build it again.

To test the program using invalid data:

1 Hide the Output window. Click **Build** on the menu bar, then click **Execute T3App.exe**. If you are using the Introductory Edition, click the **OK** button to close the Microsoft (R) Visual C++ (R) dialog box. Type **-10** (be sure to type the hyphen before the number 10) as the room length, and then press the **Enter** key.

Because the room length should not be a negative number, the program should respond at this point by prompting the user to enter a positive number, rather than by prompting the user to enter the room width; you will learn how to design a program that does so in a later tutorial.

2 Type **10** as the room width and then press the **Enter** key. Type **10** as the ceiling height and then press the **Enter** key. Type **30** as the single roll coverage and then press the **Enter** key. The number 0 appears as the number of single rolls. When the "Press any key to continue" message appears, press the **Enter** key to close the DOS window.

When you are sure that a program works correctly, you should keep your IPO chart and a printout of the program in a safe place, so you can refer to them if you need to change the program in the future. The IPO chart and printout are referred to as **external documentation**. You will learn how to print the program, as well as how to close the program, in the next section.

Printing and Closing a Program

The File menu on the Microsoft Visual C++ menu bar contains a Print command, which you can use to print the program. The File menu also contains the Close Workspace command, which allows you to close the current program without exiting C++. You use the Close Workspace command when you are finished with one program and you want to begin another program. Print the current program, then close the current program's workspace.

tip

The Close button ☒ on the .cpp program window's title bar closes the .cpp program window only; it does not close the workspace.

To print the program, and then close the program's workspace and exit Microsoft Visual C++:

1 If your computer is connected to a printer, click **File** on the menu bar, and then click **Print**. When the Print dialog box appears, click the **OK** button. The program prints on your printer.

2 Click **File** on the menu bar, and then click **Close Workspace**. The message "Do you want to close all document windows?" appears in the Microsoft Visual C++ dialog box. Click the **Yes** button. Visual C++ closes the current program's workspace. You now can open either a new or an existing program. (You will learn how to open a new program in Tutorial 4.)

3 Click **File** on the menu bar, and then click **Exit** to exit Microsoft Visual C++ 6.0.

You now have completed Tutorial 3's Application lesson. You can either take a break or complete the end-of-lesson exercises.

ANSWERS TO MINI-QUIZZES

Mini-Quiz 3

1. source

2. object (or .obj)

3. executable (or .exe)

Mini-Quiz 4

1. //My first program

2. float hoursWorked = 0.0;

3. cin >> hoursWorked;

4. cout << "Number of hours worked " << hoursWorked << endl;

EXERCISES

1. In this exercise, you will complete an existing program that calculates and displays the sum of two numbers. The IPO chart information, C++ code, and desk-check table for this problem are shown in Figures 3-13 and 3-14 in the Exercises section of the Concept lesson.

   a. Open the T3AppE01.cpp file contained in the Cpp\Tut03\T3AppE01 folder on your computer's hard disk. This program calculates and displays the sum of two numbers. Review the IPO chart and code shown in Figure 3-13. Notice that three instructions are missing from the program: the instruction that prompts the user to enter the second number, the instruction that allows the user to enter the number, and the instruction that calculates the sum. Enter the missing statements in the appropriate areas of the program.

   b. Save and then build the program. If necessary, correct any syntax errors, and then save and build the program again. Execute the program. Test the program twice, using the numbers 3 and 5 first, and then using the numbers 50.5 and 31.3. Compare your results to the desk-check table shown in Figure 3-14.

   c. When the program is working correctly, hide the Output window, then use the File menu to close the workspace.

2. In this exercise, you will complete an existing program that calculates and displays the new weekly pay based on the current weekly pay and raise rate entered by the user. The IPO chart information and C++ code for this problem are shown in Figure 3-15. You completed the desk-check in Exercise 4 in the Concept lesson.

   a. Open the T3AppE02.cpp file contained in the Cpp\Tut03\T3AppE02 folder on your computer's hard disk. This program calculates and displays the new weekly pay based on the current weekly pay and raise rate entered by the user. Review the IPO chart and code shown in Figure 3-15. Notice that six statements are missing from the program. Enter the missing statements in the appropriate areas of the program.

   b. Save and then build the program. If necessary, correct any syntax errors, and then save and build the program again. Execute the program. Test the program twice. For the first test, use 250 as the current weekly pay and .03 as the raise rate. For the second test, use 100 as the current weekly pay and .10 as the raise rate. Compare your results to the desk-check table that you created in Exercise 4 in the Concept lesson.

   c. When the program is working correctly, hide the Output window, then use the File menu to close the workspace.

3. In this exercise, you will complete an existing program that calculates and displays a commission amount based on the sales and commission rate entered by the user.

   a. Open the T3AppE03.cpp file contained in the Cpp\Tut03\T3AppE03 folder on your computer's hard disk. This program calculates and displays a commission amount.

   b. Study the existing code. Notice that the statements to calculate and display the commission are missing from the program. Enter the missing statements in the appropriate areas of the program. The statement that displays the commission amount should display the message "Your commission is $" followed by the commission amount; it also should move the cursor to the next line on the screen.

   c. Create an appropriate desk-check table, then desk-check the program twice. For the first desk-check, use 2000 as the sales and .10 as the commission rate. For the second desk-check, use 5000 as the sales and .06 as the commission rate.

   d. Save and then build the program. If necessary, correct any syntax errors, and then save and build the program again. Execute the program. Test the program twice, using the same data used in Step c. Compare your results to the desk-check table that you created in Step c.

   e. When the program is working correctly, hide the Output window, then use the File menu to close the workspace.

4. In this exercise, you will complete an existing program that calculates and displays an ending balance based on the beginning balance, deposit, and withdrawal amounts entered by the user.

    a. Open the T3AppE04.cpp file contained in the Cpp\Tut03\T3AppE04 folder on your computer's hard disk. This program calculates and displays the ending balance amount.

    b. Study the existing code. Notice that the statements to prompt the user to enter the beginning balance, deposit, and withdrawal amounts are missing from the program. The statements that allow the user to enter that data also are missing from the program. Enter the missing statements in the appropriate areas of the program.

    c. Create an appropriate desk-check table, then desk-check the program twice. For the first desk-check, use 2000 as the beginning balance amount, 775 as the deposit amount, and 1200 as the withdrawal amount. For the second desk-check, use 500 as the beginning balance amount, 100 as the deposit amount, and 610 as the withdrawal amount.

    d. Save and then build the program. If necessary, correct any syntax errors, and then save and build the program again. Execute the program. Test the program twice, using the same data used in Step c. Compare your results to the desk-check table that you created in Step c.

    e. When the program is working correctly, hide the Output window, then use the File menu to close the workspace.

Exercises 5 and 6 are Discovery Exercises. Discovery Exercises, which may include topics that are not covered in this lesson, allow you to "discover" the solutions to problems on your own.

5. In this exercise, you will complete an existing program that calculates and displays the average of three numbers.

    a. Open the T3AppE05.cpp file contained in the Cpp\Tut03\T3AppE05 folder on your computer's hard disk. This program calculates and displays the average of three numbers.

    b. Complete the program by entering the missing statements.

    c. Create an appropriate desk-check table, then desk-check the program twice. For the first desk-check, use the numbers 25, 76, and 33. For the second desk-check, use the numbers 10, 15, and 20.

    d. Save and then build the program. If necessary, correct any syntax errors, and then save and build the program again. Execute the program. Test the program twice, using the same data used in Step c. Compare your results to the desk-check table that you created in Step c.

    e. When the program is working correctly, hide the Output window, then use the File menu to close the workspace.

6. In this exercise, you will practice working with the `cout` stream.

    a. Open the T3AppE06.cpp file contained in the Cpp\Tut03\T3AppE06 folder on your computer's hard disk. The program shows three different ways to display the message "C++ is a programming language" on the screen.

    b. Build and execute the program. What differences, if any, do you see in the manner in which each of the three ways displays the message? What do these differences tell you about how the `cout` stream and the insertion operator handle the display of data on the screen?

    c. Hide the Output window, then use the File menu to close the workspace.

A computer program is good only if it works. Errors in either an algorithm or programming code can cause the program to run incorrectly. Therefore, a programmer needs to know how to locate and fix these errors. Exercise 7 is a Debugging Exercise. Debugging Exercises allow you to practice recognizing and solving errors in a program.

debugging

7. In this exercise, you will debug C++ code.

   a. Open the T3AppE07.cpp file contained in the Cpp\Tut03\T3AppE07 folder on your computer's hard disk. This program should calculate and display the sales discount and the new sales price.

   b. Create an appropriate desk-check table, then desk-check the program using 100 as the original price and .25 as the discount rate.

   c. Correct any errors in the program, then desk-check the program twice. For the first desk-check, use 100 as the original price and .25 as the discount rate. For the second desk-check, use 50 as the original price and .1 as the discount rate.

   d. Save and then build the program. If necessary, correct any syntax errors, and then save and build the program again. Execute the program. Test the program twice, using the data supplied in Step c. Compare your results to the desk-check table that you created in Step c.

   e. When the program is working correctly, hide the Output window, then use the File menu to close the workspace.

Variables, Constants, Arithmetic Operators, and Assignment Statements

objectives

After completing this tutorial, you will be able to:

- Distinguish between a variable, a named constant, and a literal constant
- Select an appropriate name, data type, and initial value for a memory location
- Explain how data is stored in memory
- Reserve and initialize a memory location
- Type cast data
- Use an assignment statement to assign data to a variable
- Include arithmetic operators in an expression
- Get string input using the `getline` function
- Create a console application

Concept Lesson

Program Components

In Tutorial 3's Application lesson, you completed a C++ program for The Paper Tree wallpaper store. The program is shown in Figure 4-1.

numeric literal constants

variables

arithmetic operators

numeric literal constant

string literal constant

```
Microsoft Visual C++ - [T3App1.cpp]
File  Edit  View  Insert  Project  Build  Tools  Window  Help

                                              double

//T3App1.cpp - calculates and displays required number of single rolls of wallpaper

#include <iostream>
using namespace std;

int main()
{
    //declare variables
    float length        = 0.0;
    float width         = 0.0;
    float height        = 0.0;
    float rollCoverage  = 0.0;
    float perimeter     = 0.0;
    float area          = 0.0;
    float rolls         = 0.0;

    //enter input items
    cout << "Enter room length: ";
    cin >> length;
    cout << "Enter room width: ";
    cin >> width;
    cout << "Enter ceiling height: ";
    cin >> height;
    cout << "Enter single roll coverage: ";
    cin >> rollCoverage;

    //calculate perimeter, area, and number of single rolls
    perimeter = (length + width) * 2;
    area = perimeter * height;
    rolls = area / rollCoverage;

    //display output item
    cout << "Single rolls: " << rolls << endl;

    return 0;
} //end of main function

Ready                                                    Ln 1, Col 1   REC COL OVR READ
```

Figure 4-1: C++ program for The Paper Tree wallpaper store

....

> You will learn about two other types of operators—logical and comparison—in Tutorial 8.

Most programs, like the one shown in Figure 4-1, include the following components: variables, constants, and operators. You began learning about variables in Tutorial 3. You will learn more about variables and you also will learn about two types of constants—named and literal—in this tutorial. In addition, you will learn about arithmetic operators, which are used to perform calculations that typically appear in assignment statements. An **assignment statement** is a statement that assigns a value to an existing variable. Begin by learning about variables and named constants.

Variables and Named Constants

Variables and named constants are locations (within the computer's internal memory) where a program can temporarily store data. The data may be entered by the user at the keyboard, or it may be read in from a file, or it may be the result of a calculation made by the computer. The program shown in Figure 4-1, for example, stores the user's input—room length, room width, ceiling height, and single roll coverage—in memory locations named `length`, `width`, `height`, and `rollCoverage`. The program also stores the results of the perimeter, area, and number of single rolls calculations in memory locations named `perimeter`, `area`, and `rolls`.

It may be helpful to picture a memory location as a small box inside the computer. You can enter and store data in the box, but you cannot actually see the box. Two types of memory locations (boxes) are available for your program to use: variable memory locations and named constant memory locations. The difference between the two types is that the contents of a variable memory location can change (vary) as the program is running, whereas the contents of a named constant memory location cannot.

You will need to reserve a memory location for each unique input, processing, and output item listed in a problem's IPO chart. But how do you determine which type of memory location to reserve—variable or named constant? If an item's value will change each time a program is executed, you will need to store the value in a variable memory location, referred to simply as a **variable**, because that is the only type of memory location whose contents can change while a program is running. In the program shown in Figure 4-1, for example, the values of the input, processing, and output items are stored in variables, because those values will be different for each customer. (The IPO chart for Figure 4-1's program is shown in Tutorial 3's Figure 3-3.)

You use a named constant memory location, referred to simply as a **named constant,** for any item whose value will remain the same each time the program is executed. For example, if every roll of wallpaper at The Paper Tree wallpaper store covered the same area—30 square feet—you would store the value of the single roll coverage (30) in a named constant rather than in a variable, because the value will be the same for each customer.

The problem specification and IPO chart shown in Figure 4-2 provide another example of using variables and named constants.

Problem specification:		
Mr. Johnson needs a program that he can use to calculate and display the area of a circle, based on the circle radius he enters. Use 3.141593 as the value for pi.		
Input	**Processing**	**Output**
radius pi (3.141593)	Processing items: radius squared Algorithm: 1. enter the radius 2. calculate the radius squared by multiplying the radius by itself 3. calculate the area by multiplying pi by the radius squared 4. display the area	area

Figure 4-2: Problem specification and IPO chart for the circle area problem

You will learn more about the C++ rules for naming memory locations in this tutorial's Application lesson.

A list of C++ keywords is shown in Figure 4-18.

Although you will use only the C++ language in this book, at times you will be given information pertaining to the Java and Visual Basic languages. This is done to show you that the programming concepts you are learning in this book can be applied, with slight modification, to any programming language.

The practice of capitalizing only the first letter in the second and subsequent words in a memory location's name is sometimes referred to as "hump notation." Because the uppercase letters in the name are taller than the lowercase letters, the uppercase letters appear as "humps" in the name.

The IPO chart indicates that the program, which calculates and displays the area of a circle, will require four memory locations: two for the input items (radius and pi), one for the processing item (radius squared), and one for the output item (area). The values of the radius, radius squared, and area items should be stored in variables, because those values will change each time the program is executed. The value of the pi item, however, will remain constant at 3.141593, and should be stored in a named constant.

The method of creating variables and named constants—in other words, the method of reserving memory locations in a program—differs in each programming language. However, most programming languages require the programmer to assign both a name and data type to each variable and named constant the program will use. The programmer also must assign a beginning value to each named constant. Although assigning a beginning value to a variable is optional in most programming languages, it is considered a good programming practice to do so and is highly recommended.

Before learning how to reserve variables and named constants in a program, you will learn how to select an appropriate name, data type, and initial value for the memory location.

Selecting a Name for a Memory Location

You should assign a descriptive name to each variable and named constant the program will use. The name, also called the **identifier**, should help you remember the purpose of the memory location—in other words, the meaning of the value stored therein. For example, the names length and width are much more meaningful than are the names x and y, because length and width remind you that the amounts stored in the memory locations represent a length and width measurement, respectively.

In addition to being descriptive, the name that a programmer assigns to a memory location must follow several specific rules, which vary with the different programming languages. However, in most programming languages, a memory location's name must begin with a letter and it can include only letters, numbers, and the underscore. Typically, no punctuation characters or spaces are allowed in a memory location's name. The name also cannot be the same as a keyword because, as you learned in Tutorial 3, a keyword has a special meaning in a programming language. For instance, return is a keyword in three of the most popular programming languages: C++, Java, and Visual Basic. Therefore, you cannot use return to name a memory location in a program written in those languages.

Each programming language has its own set of conventions that programmers follow when using the language. For example, many C++ and Java programmers use uppercase letters when naming named constants, and lowercase letters when naming variables; this allows them to distinguish between the named constants and variables in a program. If a variable's name contains two or more words, however, most C++ and Java programmers capitalize the first letter in the second and subsequent words, as shown in the names rollCoverage and rateOfPay. In comparison, many Visual Basic programmers use both uppercase and lowercase letters in the names of all memory locations. They distinguish between named constants and variables by beginning named constant names with the three lowercase letters *con* (short for *constant*), and beginning variable names with a three-character ID, entered in lowercase letters, that represents the variable's data type—*str* for String, *sng* for Single, and so on. In this book, you will follow the naming convention used by many C++ programmers.

Figure 4-3 lists possible names that you could use in a C++, Java, and Visual Basic program to identify the circle area problem's input, processing, and output items, which are shown in Figure 4-2's IPO chart.

Language	Memory location type	Name
C++ and Java	variable	`radius`
	variable	`radiusSquared`
	variable	`area`
	named constant	`PI`
Visual Basic	variable	`sngRadius`
	variable	`sngRadiusSquared`
	variable	`sngArea`
	named constant	`conPi`

Figure 4-3: Names of memory locations for the circle area problem

In addition to selecting an appropriate name for each variable and named constant the program will use, you also must determine the appropriate data type for each.

Selecting a Data Type for a Memory Location

Each variable and named constant must be assigned a **data type,** which controls the type of data the memory location can store. Figure 4-4 shows some of the data types available in the C++, Java, and Visual Basic programming languages.

Type of data the memory location can store	Data types available in each language		
	C++	**Java**	**Visual Basic**

Integer (a whole number)	`short`
	`int`
	`long`
		`short`
		`int`
		`long`
			`Integer`
			`Long`

Floating-point number (a number with a decimal place)	`float`
	`double`
	`long double`
		`float`
		`double`
			`Single`
			`Double`

One character enclosed in single quotation marks	`char`	`char`	
Zero or more characters enclosed in double quotation marks	`string`	`String`	`String`
Boolean value (True or False)	`bool`	`boolean`	`Boolean`

Figure 4-4: Some of the data types available in C++, Java, and Visual Basic

As Figure 4-4 indicates, each of the three programming languages contains one or more data types for storing **integers** (whole numbers), **floating-point numbers** (numbers with a decimal place), **characters** (letters, symbols, and numbers that will not be used in calculations), and **Boolean** values (True and False). The appropriate data type to use for a memory location depends on the values the memory location will need to store. Figure 4-5 on the next page shows the values that each of the C++ data types can store and the amount of memory required to store the values.

tip

Some programmers pronounce `char` as "care" because it is short for *character*, while others pronounce `char` as in the first syllable of the word *charcoal*.

tip

The names of data types in C++ and Java must be typed in lowercase letters; the only exception is the String data type in Java. The names of data types in Visual Basic always begin with an uppercase letter, and the remaining letters are lowercase.

tip

C++ uses the keywords `true` and `false` to represent the Boolean values True and False. These values are called Boolean values in honor of the English mathematician George Boole (1815-1864), who invented Boolean algebra.

Data type	Stores	Memory required	Values
`char`	one character	1 byte	one character
`short`	integer	2 bytes	-32,768 to 32,767
`int`	integer	4 bytes	-2,147,483,648 to 2,147,483,647
`long`	integer	4 bytes	-2,147,483,648 to 2,147,483,647
`float`	floating-point number	4 bytes	±3.4e-38 to ±3.4e38
`double`	floating-point number	8 bytes	±1.7e-308 to ±1.7e308
`long double`	floating-point number	10 bytes	±3.4e-4932 to ±1.1e4932
`string`	zero or more characters	1 byte per character	zero or more characters
`bool`	Boolean value	1 byte	`true`, `false`

Figure 4-5: Values and memory required for C++ data types

In this lesson's Discovery Exercise 13, you will run a program that will tell you the number of bytes your system uses for the data types shown in Figure 4-5.

As Figure 4-5 shows, memory locations assigned either the `short`, `int`, or `long` data type can store only integers. The differences among these three data types are in the range of integers each type can store and the amount of memory each type needs to store the integer. The range of values and the amount of memory are machine-dependent, so your system might have different values. For example, on some systems, the `int` data type has the same range and memory requirement as the `short` data type, rather than the long data type, as shown in Figure 4-5.

You can reduce the amount of internal memory that a program consumes, thereby improving the program's efficiency, by using memory locations with smaller memory requirements wherever possible. For example, although an `int` memory location can store numbers in the `short` range of -32,768 to 32,767, the `int` data type takes twice as much memory as the `short` data type to do so. Therefore, you can conserve internal memory by storing a person's age in a `short` variable rather than in an `int` variable.

Keep in mind, however, that memory usage is not the only important factor in determining a program's efficiency; the speed at which a program executes also is important. Although a `short` memory location uses less internal memory than does an `int` memory location, a calculation containing `int` memory locations takes less time to process than the equivalent calculation containing `short` memory locations. This is because the computer must convert `short` memory locations to the `int` data type while the calculation is being performed.

> **Important note:** In this book, you will use the int data type to store integers, and the `float` data type to store numbers with a decimal place.

Figure 4-6 shows the data types selected for the circle area problem's memory locations. These data types—`float` in C++ and Java, and `Single` in Visual Basic—allow each memory location to store a floating-point number.

Language	Memory location	Name	Data type
C++ and Java	variable	radius	float
	variable	radiusSquared	float
	variable	area	float
	named constant	PI	float
Visual Basic	variable	sngRadius	Single
	variable	sngRadiusSquared	Single
	variable	sngArea	Single
	named constant	conPi	Single

Figure 4-6: Data types assigned to memory locations for the circle area problem

Knowing how data is stored in the computer's internal memory will help you understand the importance of a memory location's data type.

How Data is Stored in Internal Memory

Numeric data—data assigned to memory locations that can store only numbers—is represented in internal memory using the binary (or *base 2*) number system. Recall from the Overview that the binary number system uses only the two digits 0 and 1. Although the binary number system may not be as familiar to you as the decimal (or *base 10*) number system, which uses the ten digits 0 through 9, it is just as easy to understand. Figure 4-7 compares both number systems.

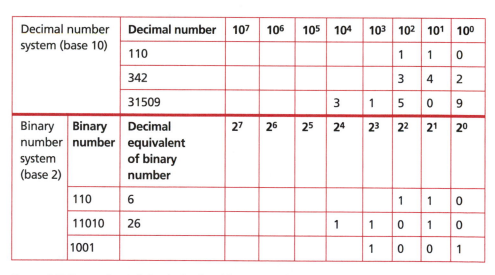

Decimal number system (base 10)		Decimal number	10^7	10^6	10^5	10^4	10^3	10^2	10^1	10^0
		110						1	1	0
		342						3	4	2
		31509				3	1	5	0	9
Binary number system (base 2)	Binary number	Decimal equivalent of binary number	2^7	2^6	2^5	2^4	2^3	2^2	2^1	2^0
	110	6						1	1	0
	11010	26				1	1	0	1	0
	1001						1	0	0	1

Figure 4-7: Comparison of the decimal and binary number systems

As Figure 4-7 illustrates, the position of each digit in the decimal number system is associated with the system's base number, 10, raised to a power. Starting with the right-most position, for example, the positions represent the number 10 raised to a power of 0, 1, 2, 3, and so on. The decimal number 110, therefore, means zero 1s (10^0), one 10 (10^1), and one 100 (10^2), and the decimal number 342 means two 1s (10^0), four 10s (10^1), and three 100s (10^2). The decimal number 31509 means nine 1s (10^0), zero 10s (10^1), five 100s (10^2), one 1000 (10^3), and three 10000s (10^4).

The position of each digit in the binary number system also is associated with the system's base number—in this case, 2—raised to a power. Starting with the right-most position, the positions represent 2 raised to a power of 0, 1, 2, 3, and so on. The binary number 110, therefore, means zero 1s (2^0), one 2 (2^1), and one 4 (2^2). The decimal equivalent of the binary number 110 is 6, which is calculated by adding together 0 + 2 + 4 (zero 1s + one 2 + one 4). The binary number 11010 means zero 1s (2^0), one 2 (2^1), zero 4s (2^2), one 8 (2^3), and one 16 (2^4). The decimal equivalent of the binary number 11010 is 26, which is calculated by adding together 0 + 2 + 0 + 8 + 16. On your own, calculate the decimal equivalent of the last binary number (1001) shown in Figure 4-7. If your answer is the decimal number 9 (one 1 + zero 2s + zero 4s + one 8), you are correct.

Unlike numeric data, character data—data assigned to memory locations that can store characters—is represented in internal memory using ASCII codes. ASCII (pronounced *ASK-ee*) stands for American Standard Code for Information Interchange. The ASCII coding scheme assigns a specific code to each character (letter, number, and symbol) on the keyboard. The ASCII codes for the letters, numbers, colon, and semicolon, along with the binary representation of these codes, are shown in Figure 4-8.

▶ The full ASCII chart is shown in Appendix A.

Character	ASCII	Binary	Character	ASCII	Binary	Character	ASCII	Binary
0	48	00110000	K	75	01001011	g	103	01100111
1	49	00110001	L	76	01001100	h	104	01101000
2	50	00110010	M	77	01001101	i	105	01101001
3	51	00110011	N	78	01001110	j	106	01101010
4	52	00110100	O	79	01001111	k	107	01101011
5	53	00110101	P	80	01010000	l	108	01101100
6	54	00110110	Q	81	01010001	m	109	01101101
7	55	00110111	R	82	01010010	n	110	01101110
8	56	00111000	S	83	01010011	o	111	01101111
9	57	00111001	T	84	01010100	p	112	01110000
:	58	00111010	U	85	01010101	q	113	01110001
;	59	00111011	V	86	01010110	r	114	01110010
A	65	01000001	W	87	01010111	s	115	01110011
B	66	01000010	X	88	01011000	t	116	01110100
C	67	01000011	Y	89	01011001	u	117	01110101
D	68	01000100	Z	90	01011010	v	118	01110110
E	69	01000101	a	97	01100001	w	119	01110111
F	70	01000110	b	98	01100010	x	120	01111000
G	71	01000111	c	99	01100011	y	121	01111001
H	72	01001000	d	100	01100100	z	122	01111010
I	73	01001001	e	101	01100101			
J	74	01001010	f	102	01100110			

Figure 4-8: Partial ASCII chart

As Figure 4-8 shows, the uppercase letter A is assigned the ASCII code 65, which is stored in internal memory using the eight bits ("binary digits") 01000001 (one 64 and one 1). Notice that the lowercase version of each letter on your keyboard is assigned a different ASCII code than the letter's uppercase version. The lowercase letter a, for example, is assigned the ASCII code 97, which is stored in internal memory using the eight bits 01100001. This fact indicates that the computer does not consider both cases of a letter to be equivalent—in other words, the uppercase letter A is not the same as the lowercase letter a. This concept will become important when you compare characters and strings in later tutorials.

At this point, you may be wondering why the numeric characters on your keyboard are assigned an ASCII code. Aren't they supposed to be stored using the binary number system, as you learned earlier? The answer is this: the computer uses the binary number system to store the *number* 9, but it uses the ASCII coding scheme to store the *character* 9. But how does the computer know whether the 9 is a number or a character? The answer to this question is simple: by the memory location's data type. For example, when you press the 9 key on your keyboard in response to the C++ statement `cin >> age;`, the computer uses the data type of the `age` memory location to determine whether to store the 9 as a number (using the binary number system) or as a character (using the ASCII coding scheme). If the memory location's data type is `int`, the 9 is stored as the binary number 1001 (one 1 + one 8). If the memory location's data type is `char`, on the other hand, the 9 is stored as a character using the ASCII code 57, which is represented in internal memory as 00111001 (one 1 + one 8 + one 16 + one 32).

The memory location's data type also determines how the computer interprets the data already stored in a memory location. For example, if a program instruction needs to access the value stored in a memory location—perhaps to display the value on the screen—the computer uses the memory location's data type to determine the value's data type. For instance, assume that a memory location named `inputItem` contains the eight bits 01000001. If the memory location's data type is `char`, the C++ statement `cout << inputItem;` displays the uppercase letter A on the screen. This is because the computer interprets the 01000001 as the ASCII code 65, which is equivalent to the uppercase letter A. However, if the memory location's data type is `int`, the C++ statement `cout << inputItem;` displays the number 65 on the screen, because the 01000001 is interpreted as the binary code for the decimal number 65.

As you can see, the data type of the memory location is important, because it determines how the data is stored when first entered into the memory location. It also determines how the data is interpreted when the memory location is used in an instruction later in the program.

In addition to assigning an appropriate name and data type to each variable and named constant, recall that you also should assign an initial value to each.

Selecting an Initial Value for a Memory Location

Assigning an initial, or beginning, value to a memory location is referred to as **initializing**. You typically initialize a memory location by assigning a literal constant to it. Unlike variables and named constants, literal constants are not memory locations. Rather, a **literal constant** is an item of data that can appear in a program instruction, and that can be stored in a memory location. Literal constants can have a data type that is either numeric, character, or string.

A **numeric literal constant** is simply a number. The numbers 0.0, 2, and 0 shown earlier in Figure 4-1's wallpaper program are examples of numeric literal constants. Numeric literal constants can consist only of numbers, the plus sign (+), the minus sign (−), the decimal point (.), and the letter e in uppercase or lowercase (for exponential notation). Numeric literal constants cannot contain a space, a comma, or a special character, such as the dollar sign ($) or the percent sign (%).

tip

Some programming languages—for example, Visual Basic—also recognize date literal constants, which are dates that typically are enclosed in number signs (#), like this: #12/25/2003#.

tip

Exponential notation, often referred to as e *notation*, provides a convenient way of writing very large and very small numbers by expressing the number as a multiple of some power of 10. For example, the large number 3,200,000,000 written using e notation is 3.2e9. The positive number after the e indicates the number of places to the right to move the decimal point. In this case, e9 says to move the decimal point nine places to the right, which is the same as multiplying the number by 10 to the ninth power. Numbers written using e notation also can have a negative number after the e; the negative number indicates the number of places to the left to move the decimal point. For example, 3.2e−9 says to move the decimal point nine places to the left (.0000000032), which is the same as dividing the number by 10 to the ninth power.

Character literal constants cannot be used in all programming languages. For example, unlike C++ and Java, Visual Basic does not recognize a character literal constant. In Visual Basic, you enclose one character in double quotation marks, and it is considered a string literal constant.

You can learn more about initializing `bool` variables by completing Discovery Exercise 15 at the end of the Application lesson.

You can learn more about implicit type conversion by completing Discovery Exercise 12 at the end of this lesson.

A **character literal constant** is one character enclosed in single quotation marks. The letter 'X' is a character literal constant, and so are the dollar sign '$' and a space ' ' (two single quotation marks with a space between). A **string literal constant**, on the other hand, is zero or more characters enclosed in double quotation marks, such as the word "Hello", the message "Enter room length: " (which appears in Figure 4-1's program), and the empty string "" (two double quotation marks with no space between). Figure 4-9 shows examples of numeric, character, and string literal constants.

Numeric literal constants	Character literal constants	String literal constants
2	'X'	"Hello"
3.14	'$'	"Enter room length: "
3.2e6	'b'	"450"
-2300	'2'	"345AB"
0	' ' (a space enclosed in single quotation marks)	"" (two double quotation marks with no space between)
Important note: Notice that character literal constants are enclosed in single quotation marks and string literal constants are enclosed in double quotation marks. Numeric literal constants, however, are not enclosed in any quotation marks.		

Figure 4-9: Examples of numeric, character, and string literal constants

When using a literal constant to initialize a memory location in a program, the data type of the literal constant should match the data type of the memory location to which it is assigned. In other words, you should use only integers to initialize memory locations having the `short`, `int`, or `long` data type in a C++ program, and only floating-point numbers to initialize memory locations having the `float`, `double`, or `long double` data type. Character literal constants should be used to initialize `char` memory locations, and string literal constants to initialize `string` memory locations. Memory locations having the `bool` data type typically are initialized using either the C++ keyword `true` or the C++ keyword `false`, which stand for the Boolean values True and False, respectively.

When a program instructs the computer to initialize a memory location, the computer first compares the data type of the value assigned to the memory location with the data type of the memory location itself to verify that the value is appropriate for the memory location. If the value's data type does not match the memory location's data type, most programming languages use a process called **implicit type conversion** to convert the value to fit the memory location. For example, if you use a floating-point number—such as 3.7—to initialize a memory location that can store only integers, the compiler will convert the floating-point number to an integer before storing the value in the memory location; it does so by truncating (dropping off) the decimal portion of the number. In this case, the compiler will convert the floating-point number 3.7 to the integer 3. As a result, the number 3, rather than the number 3.7, will be assigned to the memory location. It is not always possible to convert a value to match the memory location's data type. For example, using a string literal constant to initialize a memory location that can store only integers will produce an error during the compiling phase, because the compiler cannot convert a string literal constant to an integer.

When you distinguish between a literal constant, a named constant, and a variable, it is helpful to remember that a literal constant is simply an item of data. Variables and named constants, on the other hand, are memory locations where literal constants are stored. Unlike the value of a literal constant and the contents of a variable, the contents of a named constant cannot change while the program is running.

If a memory location is a named constant, the problem description and/or IPO chart will provide the appropriate initial value to use. For example, the problem description and IPO chart shown earlier in Figure 4-2 indicate that the PI named constant should be initialized to 3.141593. The initial value for a variable, on the other hand, typically is not stated in a problem description or IPO chart, because the value is supplied by the user while the program is running. As a result, `short`, `int`, and `long` variables in a C++ program generally are initialized to the integer 0. Variables of the `float`, `double`, and `long double` data types typically are initialized to the floating-point number 0.0. `char` variables usually are initialized to a space (' '), and `string` variables to the empty string (""). As mentioned earlier, the C++ keywords `true` and `false` are used to initialize `bool` variables.

Be aware that the C++ compiler might display the warning message *'initializing'* : *truncation from 'const double' to 'float'* when you initialize a `float` memory location to a number other than 0.0. This warning message appears because Visual C++ treats all numeric literal constants containing a decimal place as a `double` data type. When you assign a `double` number (which requires eight bytes of memory) to a `float` memory location (which can store only four bytes), Visual C++ warns you that it may need to truncate part of the number in order to store it in the memory location. Some programmers simply ignore the warning message, while others use a process called *type casting* to prevent Visual C++ from displaying the warning message.

Type Casting

Whether Visual C++ displays the warning message *'initializing'* : *truncation from 'const double' to 'float'* depends on the value used to initialize the `float` memory location. For example, the number 3.5 will not trigger the warning message; however, the number 3.7 will.

Type casting, also known as **explicit type conversion**, is the explicit conversion of data from one data type to another. You type cast, or explicitly convert, an item of data by enclosing the data in parentheses, and then preceding it with the C++ keyword that represents the desired data type. For example, to type cast the `double` number 3.7 to the `float` data type, you would use `float(3.7)`. The `float` in the type cast tells the C++ compiler to treat the number within parentheses as a `float` data type rather than as a `double` data type.

> **Important note:** In this book, you will always use a type cast when initializing a `float` memory location to a value other than 0.0.

Figure 4-10 shows the initial values appropriate for the circle area problem's memory locations. In each case, the data type of the initial value matches the data type of the memory location.

Language	Memory location	Name	Data type	Initial value
C++ and Java	variable	radius	float	0.0
	variable	radiusSquared	float	0.0
	variable	area	float	0.0
	named constant	PI	float	float(3.141593)
Visual Basic	variable	sngRadius	Single	0.0
	variable	sngRadiusSquared	Single	0.0
	variable	sngArea	Single	0.0
	named constant	conPi	Single	3.141593

Figure 4-10: Initial values assigned to memory locations for the circle area problem

Mini-Quiz 1

1. Which of the following is an invalid name for a variable?

    a. `class2003`

    b. `gallons`

    c. `88TaxAmt`

    d. `tuition`

2. The letter 'w' is a _____.

    a. character literal constant

    b. named constant

    c. numeric literal constant

    d. string literal constant

3. "Jacob Motors" is a _____.

    a. character literal constant

    b. named constant

    c. numeric literal constant

    d. string literal constant

4. In the binary number system, the decimal number 23 is represented as _____.

    a. 10111

    b. 10011

    c. 11000

    d. 10001

5. The lowercase letter b is stored in internal memory using the eight bits _____.

    a. 01100010

    b. 01100011

    c. 01100000

    d. 01010001

Now that you know how to select an appropriate name, data type, and initial value for a memory location, you will learn how to use that information to reserve a memory location in a program. Begin by learning how to reserve a named constant.

Reserving a Named Constant

The instruction you use to reserve, or declare, a named constant differs in each programming language. However, the instruction typically will allow you to specify the named constant's name, data type, and initial value. Figure 4-11 shows the syntax and examples of instructions used to reserve named constants in C++, Java, and Visual Basic.

Language	Syntax	Examples

C++	**const** *datatype constantname* **=** *value***;**	`const int AGE = 65;`
		`const float MAXPAY = float(15.75);`
		`const char YES = 'Y';`
		`const string TITLE = "IMG"`

Java	**final** *datatype constantname* **=** *value***;**	`final int AGE = 65;`
		`final float MAXPAY = float(15.75);`
		`final char YES = 'Y';`
		`final String TITLE = "IMG";`

Visual Basic	**Const** *constantname* **As** *datatype* **=** *value*	`Const conAge As Integer = 65`
		`Const conMaxPay As Single = 15.75`
		`Const conYes As String = "Y"`
		`Const conTitle As String = "IMG"`

Figure 4-11: Syntax and examples of instructions that reserve named constants

In the syntax for each language, *datatype* is the type of data the named constant will store, *constantname* is the name of the named constant, and *value* is a literal constant that represents the value you want stored in the named constant. Words and symbols in bold—for example, `const`, `final`, `Const`, `As`, the = sign, and the ; (semicolon)—in an instruction's syntax are required parts of the syntax. Notice that the C++ and Java programming languages require the instruction to end with a semicolon. This is because the instruction to reserve a named constant is considered a statement in C++ and Java, and both languages require statements to end with a semicolon.

The C++ statement that you use in a program to reserve a named constant whose name is `PI` and whose value is 3.141593 is `const float PI = float(3.141593);`. This statement tells the computer to set aside a small box in internal memory, and to name the box `PI`. The `PI` box (memory location) will have a data type of `float` and an initial value of 3.141593. The keyword `const` at the beginning of the statement indicates that the `PI` memory location is a named constant, which means that its value cannot be changed later in the program. If the program contains a statement that attempts to change the value stored in the `PI` named constant, the C++ compiler will display an error message.

After you reserve, or declare, a named constant, you then can use its name, instead of its value, in another statement. For example, you can use the C++ statement `cout << PI;` to display the contents of the `PI` named constant on the screen; this instruction will display the value 3.141593. You also can use the `PI` named constant in a C++ statement that calculates the area of a circle, like this: `area = radiusSquared * PI;`. C++ will use the value stored in the `PI` named constant (3.141593) to calculate the area.

Next, learn how to reserve a variable.

tip

Named constants make a program more self-documenting and, therefore, easier to modify because they allow you to use meaningful words in place of values that may be less clear.

Reserving a Variable

The instruction you use to reserve, or declare, a variable differs in each programming language. However, the instruction usually will allow you to specify the variable's name and data type. Some languages—for example, C++ and Java—also allow you to specify an initial value for the variable. Other languages—such as Visual Basic—perform the initialization task for you automatically when you declare the variable. Figure 4-12 shows the syntax and examples of instructions used to reserve and initialize variables in C++, Java, and Visual Basic.

Language	Syntax	Examples	Initial value

C++	*datatype variablename = initialvalue;*	`int age = 0;`
		`float rate = 0.0;`
		`char grade = ' ';`
		`string coName = "";`
			0
			0.0
			one space
			empty string

Java	*datatype variablename = initialvalue;*	`int age = 0;`
		`float rate = 0.0;`
		`char grade = ' ';`
		`String coName = "";`
			0
			0.0
			one space
			empty string

Visual Basic	**Dim** *variablename* **As** *datatype*
	(Visual Basic initializes variables
	automatically)
		`Dim intAge As Integer`
		`Dim sngRate As Single`
		`Dim strGrade As String`
		`Dim strCoName As String`
			0
			0.0
			empty string
			empty string

Figure 4-12: Syntax and examples of instructions that reserve and initialize variables

tip

▶ If you do not supply an initial value for a variable in a C++ or Java program, the variable will contain a meaningless value, referred to by programmers as "garbage". The garbage is the remains of what was last stored at the memory location that the variable now occupies.

In the syntax for each language, *datatype* designates the type of data the variable will store, *variablename* is the name of the variable, and *initialvalue* is usually a literal constant that represents the beginning (initial) value for the variable. Words and symbols in bold—for example, `Dim`, `As`, the = sign, and the ; (semicolon)—in an instruction's syntax are required parts of the syntax. Notice that C++ and Java require the instruction to end with a semicolon. This is because the instruction to reserve a variable is considered a statement in C++ and Java, and both languages require statements to end with a semicolon.

Figure 4-13 shows the C++ statements that you would use in a program to reserve the `radius`, `radiusSquared`, and `area` variables.

```
float radius = 0.0;
float radiusSquared = 0.0;
float area = 0.0;
```

Figure 4-13: C++ statements reserving the `radius`, `radiusSquared`, and `area` variables

tip

▶ Recall that C++ programmers typically initialize `int`, `float`, `char`, and `string` variables to 0 (zero), 0.0, ' ' (a space), and "" (the empty string), respectively.

The C++ statements shown in Figure 4-13 tell the computer to set aside three memory locations that can store floating-point numbers. The memory locations will be named `radius`, `radiusSquared`, and `area`, and each will be initialized to the numeric literal constant 0.0.

mini-quiz

Mini-Quiz 2

1. Write a C++ instruction that reserves a named constant named `CITY`. Use the string literal constant "Chicago" to initialize the memory location.

2. Write a C++ instruction that reserves a variable named `numberOfPeople`. Assign the data type `int` to the variable, and initialize it appropriately.

3. Write a C++ instruction that reserves a variable named `studentName`. Assign the data type `string` to the variable, and initialize it appropriately.

4. Write a C++ instruction that reserves a variable named `interestRate`. The variable will need to store a number with a decimal place. Select the appropriate data type and initial value for the variable.

In the next section, you will learn how to write an assignment statement, which you can use to change the contents of a variable while a program is running.

Using an Assignment Statement to Store Data in a Variable

If you want to change the contents of a variable while a program is running, you can use an assignment statement to do so. Figure 4-14 shows the syntax and examples of assignment statements written in the C++, Java, and Visual Basic languages. Notice that C++ and Java require a semicolon at the end of an assignment statement.

You cannot use an assignment statement to assign a value to a named constant, because the contents of a named constant cannot be changed while a program is running.

It is easy to confuse an assignment statement (`hoursWkd = 50;`) with a variable declaration statement (`int hoursWkd = 50;`) in C++. You use a variable declaration statement, which must begin with a data type, to create and initialize a new variable. You use an assignment statement to change the value stored in an existing variable. An assignment statement does not reserve a variable in memory.

Language	Syntax	Examples

C++ and Java	*variablename = expression;*	`hoursWkd = 50;`
		`overtime = hoursWkd - 40;`
		`age = age + 1;`
		`sales = float(6300.75);`
		`bonus = sales * RATE;`
		`name = "Jackie";`
		`middleInitial = 'P';`
		Note: `hoursWkd`, `overtime`, and `age` are `int` variables, and `sales` and `bonus` are `float` variables. `RATE` is a `float` named constant, `name` is a `string` (`String` in Java) variable, and `middleInitial` is a `char` variable.

Visual Basic	*variablename = expression*	`intHoursWkd = 50`
		`intOvertime = intHoursWkd - 40`
		`intAge = intAge + 1`
		`sngSales = 6300.75`
		`sngBonus = sngSales * conRate`
		`strName = "Jackie"`
		`strMiddleInitial = "P"`
		Note: `intHoursWkd`, `intOvertime`, and `intAge` are `Integer` variables, and `sngBonus` and `sngSales` are `Single` variables. `conRATE` is a `Single` named constant, and `strName` and `strMiddleInitial` are `String` variables. (Recall that Visual Basic does not have a `char` data type and it does not recognize character literal constants.)

Figure 4-14: Syntax and examples of assignment statements

When an assignment statement is encountered in a program, the computer assigns the value of the *expression* appearing on the right side of the assignment operator (=) to the variable whose *variablename* appears on the left side of the assignment operator (=). The data type of the *expression*—which can include literal constants, named constants, variables, arithmetic operators (you will learn more about these in the next section), and functions—must match the data type of the variable to which it is assigned. For example, you should assign only *expressions* that represent integers to memory locations declared using the `int` data type in C++, and only *expressions* that represent strings to memory locations declared using the `string` data type. As you learned earlier, if the data type of the *expression*'s value does not match the data type of the memory location to which the value is assigned, most programming languages use a process called implicit type conversion to convert the value to fit the memory location. Also recall that it is not always possible for the computer to convert a value to match the memory location's data type.

The first C++ assignment statement shown in Figure 4-14, `hoursWkd = 50;`, stores the integer 50 (a numeric literal constant) in an `int` variable named `hoursWkd`. The second assignment statement `overtime = hoursWkd - 40;`—whose *expression* contains a variable (`hoursWkd`), an arithmetic operator (-), and a numeric literal constant (40)—first subtracts the integer 40 from the contents of the `int` variable named `hoursWkd`, and then assigns the result to the `int` variable named `overtime`. Assuming the `hoursWkd` variable contains the number 50, the second assignment statement will assign the number 10 to the `overtime` variable.

The third C++ assignment statement shown in Figure 4-14, `age = age + 1;`, uses an arithmetic operator (+) to add the integer 1 to the value stored in the `int` variable named `age`; it then assigns the sum to the `age` variable. If the `age` variable contained the value 16 before this statement was processed by the computer, it would contain the value 17 after it was processed.

The fourth C++ assignment statement, `sales = float(6300.75);`, uses a type cast to assign the number 6300.75 to the `float` variable named `sales`. The type cast tells the C++ compiler to treat the number 6300.75 as a `float` rather than as a `double`.

The fifth C++ assignment statement, `bonus = sales * RATE;`, contains two `float` variables (`bonus` and `sales`), a `float` named constant (`RATE`), and an arithmetic operator (*). This assignment statement will multiply the contents of the `sales` variable by the contents of the `RATE` named constant, and then assign the result to the `bonus` variable.

The sixth C++ assignment statement shown in Figure 4-14, `name = "Jackie";`, simply stores the string literal constant "Jackie" in a `string` variable named `name`. The last C++ assignment statement, `middleInitial = 'P';`, stores the character literal constant 'P' in a `char` variable named `middleInitial`.

It is important to remember that a variable can store only one value at a time. When you assign another value to the variable, the new value replaces the existing value. For example, assume that a C++ program contains the following statements and comments:

tip

Recall that C++ treats all numbers with a decimal place as a `double` data type.

```
int number = 0;            //declare and initialize variable
cout << "Enter a number: "; //get user input
cin >> number;
number = number * 2;       //double the number
```

When you run the program containing these statements and comments, the four lines of code are processed as follows:

- The statement `int number = 0;` creates the `number` variable in the computer's internal memory and initializes the variable to the integer 0. Here again, you may want to picture the `number` variable as a small box inside the computer. This statement tells C++ to place a 0 (zero) inside the box.
- The statement `cout << "Enter a number: ";` displays the "Enter a number: " prompt on the screen.
- The statement `cin >> number;` waits for the user to enter a number. After the user does so, the computer replaces the 0 currently stored in the `number` variable with the user's response. If the user entered the number 4, for example, the `number` variable (box) now would contain the number 4, rather than the number 0.
- The assignment statement `number = number * 2;` first multiplies the contents of the `number` variable (4) by 2, giving 8. It then removes the number 4 from the `number` variable and stores the number 8 there instead. Notice that C++ evaluates the *expression* appearing on the right side of the assignment operator before assigning the result to the variable whose name appears on the left side; all programming languages process assignment statements in the same manner.

Several of the examples shown in this lesson contain arithmetic operators, which are used to perform calculations in a program. The next section provides a more thorough discussion of arithmetic operators.

Arithmetic Operators

Most programs require the computer to perform one or more calculations. You instruct the computer to perform a calculation by writing an arithmetic expression that contains one or more arithmetic operators. Figure 4-15 lists the arithmetic operators, along with their precedence numbers. The precedence numbers indicate the order in which a programming language performs the arithmetic operations in an expression. Operations with a precedence number of 1 are performed before operations with a precedence number of 2, which are performed before operations with a precedence number of 3, and so on. However, you can use parentheses to override the order of precedence, because operations within parentheses always are performed before operations outside parentheses.

Operator	Operation	Precedence number
()	override normal precedence rules	1
-	negation	2
*, /, %	multiplication, division, and modulus arithmetic (**Note:** The modulus arithmetic operator in Visual Basic is Mod, rather than %, and it is performed after multiplication and division, but before addition and subtraction in a Visual Basic program.)	3
+, -	addition and subtraction	4

Figure 4-15: Arithmetic operators and their order of precedence

Notice that some operators shown in Figure 4-15 have the same precedence number. For example, both the addition and subtraction operator have a precedence number of 4. If an expression contains more than one operator having the same priority, those operators are evaluated from left to right. In the expression 3 + 12 / 3 - 1, for instance, the division (/) is performed first, then the addition (+), and then the subtraction (-). In other words, the computer first divides 12 by 3, then adds the result of the division (4) to 3, and then subtracts 1 from the result of the addition (7). The expression evaluates to 6.

You can use parentheses to change the order in which the operators in an expression are evaluated. For example, the expression 3 + 12 / (3 - 1) evaluates to 9, not 6. This is because the parentheses tell the computer to subtract 1 from 3 first, then divide the result of the subtraction (2) into 12, and then add the result of the division (6) to 3.

One of the arithmetic operators listed in Figure 4-15, the modulus arithmetic operator (%), might be less familiar to you. The modulus arithmetic operator is used to divide two integers, and results in the remainder of the division. For example, 211 % 4 (read 211 mod 4) equals 3, which is the remainder of 211 divided by 4. One use for the modulus operator is to determine if a year is a leap year—one that has 366 days rather than 365 days. As you may know, if a year is a leap year, then its year number is evenly divisible by the number 4—in other words, if you divide the year number by 4 and the remainder is 0 (zero), then the year is a leap year. You can determine if the year 2004 is a leap year by using the expression 2004 % 4. This expression evaluates to 0 (the remainder of 2004 divided by 4), so the year 2004 is a leap year. Similarly, you can determine if the year 2005 is a leap year by using the expression 2005 % 4. This expression evaluates to 1 (the remainder of 2005 divided by 4), so the year 2005 is not a leap year.

tip

▶ Years ending in 00 are not leap years unless they also are evenly divisible by 400.

mini-quiz

Mini-Quiz 3

1. Write a C++ assignment statement that assigns the value 23.25 to a `float` variable named `price`.

2. Write a C++ assignment statement that assigns the letter T to a `char` variable named `insured`.

3. Write a C++ assignment statement that multiplies the number 10.75 by the contents of a `float` variable named `hours`, and then assigns the result to a `float` variable named `grossPay`.

4. The assignment statement `answer = 8 / 4 * 3 - 5 % 2` assigns the value _____ to the `answer` variable. (The `answer` variable is an `int` variable.)

5. What value will be assigned to the `answer` variable in question 4 if the variable is a `float` variable?

You now have completed Tutorial 4's Concept lesson. You can either take a break or complete the end-of-lesson questions and exercises before moving on to the Application lesson.

S U M M A R Y

Most programs include variables, constants (named and literal), and arithmetic operators (which are used to perform calculations). Variables and named constants are simply memory locations (inside the computer) where you can temporarily store data. The contents of a variable can change as the program is running, but the contents of a named constant cannot. You must assign a name, data type, and initial value to each named constant you declare. You also must assign a name and data type to each variable you declare. Although assigning an initial value to a variable is optional in most programming languages, it is considered a good programming practice to do so to ensure that the variable does not contain garbage.

In C++, you declare and initialize a named constant using the syntax **const** *datatype constantname = value;*. You declare and initialize a variable in C++ using the syntax *datatype variablename = initialvalue;*. You typically use a literal constant, which simply is an item of data, to initialize named constants and variables. C++ has three types of literal constants: numeric, character, and string. A numeric literal constant is a number. A character literal constant is one letter, number, or symbol enclosed in single quotation marks (' '). A string literal constant is zero or more characters enclosed in double quotation marks ("").

You can use an assignment statement, which must conform to the C++ syntax *variablename = expression;*, to store data in a variable. The data type of the *expression* must match the data type of the variable. When C++ encounters an assignment statement in a program, it assigns the value of the *expression* appearing on the right side of the assignment operator (=) to the variable whose *variablename* appears on the left side of the assignment operator. A variable can store only one item of data at any one time. When you assign another item to the variable, the new data replaces the existing data.

When assigning a value to a memory location, it is important that the value fit the memory location's data type. If you assign a value that does not match the data type of the memory location, most programming languages use a process called implicit type conversion to convert the value to fit the memory location. However, it is not always possible for the computer to make the conversion. You can use a type cast to explicitly convert data from one data type to another.

Most programs require the computer to perform one or more calculations. You instruct the computer to perform a calculation by writing an arithmetic expression that contains one or more arithmetic operators. Each arithmetic operator is associated with a precedence number, which controls the order in which the operation is performed in an expression. You can use parentheses to override the normal order of precedence, because operations within parentheses always are performed before operations outside parentheses.

A N S W E R S   T O   M I N I - Q U I Z Z E S

Mini-Quiz 1

1. c. 88TaxAmt

2. a. character literal constant

3. d. string literal constant

4. a. 10111

5. a. 01100010

Mini-Quiz 2

1. `const string CITY = "Chicago";`

2. `int numberOfPeople = 0;`

3. `string studentName = "";`

4. `float interestRate = 0.0;`

Mini-Quiz 3

1. `price = float(23.25);`

2. `insured = 'T';`

3. `grossPay = 10.75 * hours;`

4. *5*

5. 5.0 (*Note:* Data stored in `float`, `double`, and `long double` variables always contains at least one decimal place.)

QUESTIONS

1. A variable is _____.
   a. an item of data
   b. a literal constant
   c. a memory location whose value can change while the program is running
   d. a memory location whose value cannot change while the program is running

2. To create a named constant, you must assign _____ to it.
   a. a data type
   b. a name
   c. an initial value
   d. all of the above

3. Which of the following declares and initializes a C++ variable that can store whole numbers only?
   a. `int numItems = 0;`
   b. `int numItems = '0';`
   c. `int numItems = "0";`
   d. `numItems = 0;`

4. Which of the following is a valid name for a variable?
   a. `amt-Sold`
   b. `amt   Sold`
   c. `amt_Sold`
   d. `98SoldAmt`

5. Which of the following is not a valid name for a C++ variable?
   a. `float`
   b. `payRate`
   c. `total`
   d. `winnings`

6. The number 4.5e3 is a _____ literal constant.
   a. character
   b. named
   c. numeric
   d. string

7. Which of the following will store the letter H in a `char` variable named `initial`?
   a. `initial = 'H'`
   b. `initial = 'H';`
   c. `initial = "H"`
   d. `initial = "H";`

8. You typically initialize `int` variables in a C++ program to _____.
   a. the number 0 enclosed in double quotes
   b. the number 0 enclosed in single quotes
   c. the number 0
   d. the number 0.0

9. You typically initialize `char` variables in a C++ program to _____.
   a. a space enclosed in double quotation marks
   b. a space enclosed in single quotation marks
   c. the number 0
   d. the number 0.0

10. Which of the following C++ statements declares and initializes a `float` variable named `rate`?
   a. `float rate = 0.0`
   b. `float rate = '0.0';`
   c. `float rate = 0.0;`
   d. `rate = 0.0;`

11. Which of the following are valid characters for a numeric literal constant?
   a. a decimal point
   b. the letter e
   c. a minus sign
   d. all of the above

12. Which of the following are valid characters for a numeric literal constant?
   a. a comma
   b. a dollar sign ($)
   c. a percent sign (%)
   d. none of the above

13. Which of the following C++ statements creates a named constant called RATE whose value is 16.5?
   a. `const RATE = float(16.5);`
   b. `const float RATE = float(16.5);`
   c. `float RATE = float(16.5);`
   d. `RATE const = float(16.5);`

14. Assume that the following instructions are part of a valid C++ program. What is the value contained in the `number` variable after the instructions are processed?

   ```
   int number = 0;
   number = 10;
   number = number + 5;
   ```
   a. 0
   b. 5
   c. 10
   d. 15

15. What value will be assigned to the `answer` variable as a result of the `answer = 3 + 2 * 9 % (10 − 6);` statement? (The `answer` variable is an `int` variable.)
   a. 1
   b. 6
   c. 11
   d. none of the above

16. What value will be assigned to the `answer` variable as a result of the `answer = 3 + 2 * 9 % (10 − 6);` statement? (The `answer` variable is a `float` variable.)
   a. 1
   b. 6
   c. 11
   d. none of the above

EXERCISES

1. Assume a C++ program needs to store an item's price. The price will range from $15.50 to $20. Write the statement to declare and initialize the necessary variable. Name the variable `price`. Then write an assignment statement that assigns the value $16.23 to the variable.

2. Assume a C++ program needs to store an item's height and width. Both dimensions can contain decimal places. Write the statements to declare and initialize the necessary variables. Name the variables `height` and `width`. Then write an assignment statement that assigns the value 4.5 to the `height` variable. Also write an assignment statement that assigns the value 6.9 to the `width` variable.

3. Assume a C++ program needs to store the population of a city. Write the statement to declare and initialize the necessary variable. Name the variable `population`. Then write an assignment statement that assigns the value 60000 to the `population` variable.

4. Assume a C++ program needs to store a letter of the alphabet. Write the statement to declare and initalize the necessary variable. Name the variable `letter`. Then write an assignment statement that assigns the letter A to the `letter` variable.

5. Write a C++ statement to declare and initialize a named constant called `TAXRATE` whose value is .15.

6. Write a C++ statement to declare and initialize a named constant called `MAXPAY` whose value is 20.

7. Write a C++ statement to declare and initialize a `char` named constant called `INSURED` whose value is the letter Y.

8. Write a C++ statement to declare and initialize a named constant called `PROMPT` whose value is the string "Press any key to continue".

9. Assume a program needs to store the number of units in stock at the beginning of the current month, the number of units purchased during the current month, the number of units sold during the current month, and the number of units in stock at the end of the current month. (The number of units is always an integer.) Write the appropriate C++ statements to declare and initialize the necessary memory locations. Name the memory locations `beginStock`, `purchased`, `sold`, and `endStock`. Then write an assignment statement that calculates the number of units in stock at the end of the current month.

10. Assume a program needs to calculate a bonus. The bonus is always 5 % of the sales. Write the appropriate C++ statements to declare and initialize the necessary memory locations. Be sure to assign descriptive names to each memory location. Then write an assignment statement that calculates the bonus. (Use the `float` data type for all memory locations.)

11. Assume a program needs to calculate an employee's gross pay. The input items will be the employee's name, hours worked, and pay rate. Write the appropriate C++ statements to declare and initialize the necessary memory locations. (The hours worked and pay rate will always be integers.) Then write an assignment statement that calculates the gross pay. (You do not need to worry about overtime pay, because no employees work more than 40 hours.)

Exercises 12 and 13 are Discovery Exercises. Discovery Exercises, which may include topics that are not covered in this lesson, allow you to "discover" the solutions to problems on your own.

12. In this exercise, you will learn how C++ uses implicit type conversion to convert a value assigned within a declaration statement.

a. Open the T4ConE12.cpp file contained in the Cpp\Tut04\T4ConE12 folder on your computer's hard disk. This program initializes an **int** variable named **number** to the integer 9. It then displays the value stored in the **number** variable on the screen.

b. Build and then execute the program. If you are using the Introductory Edition of Microsoft Visual C++ 6.0, click the OK button to remove the dialog box that appears on the screen. The number 9 appears in the DOS window. Press the Enter key to close the DOS window.

c. Change the 9 in the variable declaration statement to 9.6, then save, build, and execute the program. If you are using the Introductory Edition of Microsoft Visual C++ 6.0, click the OK button to remove the dialog box that appears on the screen. The number 9 appears in the DOS window; this indicates that the C++ compiler converted the floating-point number 9.6 to an integer before storing it in the **number** variable. Press the Enter key to close the DOS window.

d. Change the 9.6 in the variable declaration statement to '9', then save, build, and execute the program. If you are using the Introductory Edition of Microsoft Visual C++ 6.0, click the OK button to remove the dialog box that appears on the screen. What value appears in the DOS window? What does this value represent? Press the Enter key to close the DOS window.

e. Change the '9' in the variable declaration statement to "9", then save and build the program. What happens when you assign a value whose data type cannot be converted to fit the memory location?

f. Change the "9" in the variable declaration statement to 9, then save and build the program.

g. Hide the Output window, then use the File menu to close the workspace.

13. In this program, you will discover the number of bytes of memory your system uses for the C++ data types shown in this lesson's Figure 4-5. Although the memory requirements are machine-dependent, in C++, the size of a **char** variable is always less than or equal to the size of a **short** variable. A **short** variable is always less than or equal to the size of an **int** variable, which is always less than or equal to the size of a **long** variable. In addition, the size of a **float** variable is always less than or equal to the size of a **double** variable, which is always less than or equal to the size of a **long double** variable.

a. Open the T4ConE13.cpp file contained in the Cpp\Tut04\T4ConE13 folder on your computer's hard disk. Build and execute the program. The amount of memory your system requires for each C++ data type shown in this lesson's Figure 4-5 appears in a DOS window. Press the Enter key to close the DOS window.

b. Hide the Output window, then use the File menu to close the workspace.

A computer program is good only if it works. Errors in either an algorithm or programming code can cause the program to run incorrectly. Therefore, a programmer needs to know how to locate and fix these errors. Exercise 14 is a Debugging Exercise. Debugging Exercises allow you to practice recognizing and solving errors in a program.

debugging

14. In this exercise, you will debug an existing C++ program.

a. Open the T4ConE14.cpp file contained in the Cpp\Tut04\T4ConE14 folder on your computer's hard disk. The program displays the total price of CDs purchased at a store. Study the program's code, then build and execute the program.

b. Correct any errors in the program, then save, build, and execute the program. When the program is working correctly, calculate the total price for the purchase of three CDs at a price of $10.99 per CD. (The answer should be 32.97.)

c. Hide the Output window, then use the File menu to close the workspace.

Application Lesson

Using Variables, Constants, Arithmetic Operators, and Assignment Statements in a C++ Program

case ▶ Jack Faye, the cashier at Jackson College, wants a program that the clerks can use to display each student's name and the total amount the student owes for the semester, including tuition and room and board. The tuition at Jackson College is $100 per semester hour, and room and board is $1800 per semester.

The Jackson College Algorithm

Figure 4-16 shows the IPO chart for the Jackson College problem.

Input	Processing	Output
name hours enrolled semester hour fee ($100) room and board fee ($1800)	Processing items: none Algorithm: 1. enter the name and hours enrolled 2. calculate the total amount owed by multiplying the hours enrolled by the semester hour fee, and then adding the room and board fee to the result 3. display the name and total amount owed	name total amount owed

Figure 4-16: IPO chart for the Jackson College problem

As Figure 4-16 indicates, the output is the student's name and the total amount the student owes for the semester. To display the output, the program needs to know the student's name, the number of hours the student is enrolled for the semester, the semester hour fee, and the room and board fee. Only the name and number of hours enrolled will vary with each student; the semester hour fee and the room and board fee will remain constant at $100 and $1800, respectively.

According to the algorithm, the program first will have the user enter the student's name and the number of hours the student is enrolled. The program then will calculate the total amount owed by multiplying the hours enrolled by the semester hour fee, and then adding the room and board fee to the result. Finally, the program will display both the student's name and total amount owed on the screen.

As you learned in Tutorial 2, you should desk-check the algorithm several times before you begin coding it. In this case, you will use the following two sets of data to desk-check the algorithm shown in Figure 4-16:

Data for first desk-check		Data for second desk-check	
Student's name:	Rachel Woods	Student's name:	Paul Pitowski
Hours enrolled:	15	Hours enrolled:	20
Semester hour fee:	$100	Semester hour fee:	$100
Room and board fee:	$1800	Room and board fee:	$1800

Figure 4-17 shows the completed desk-check table.

name	hours enrolled	semester hour fee	room and board fee	total amount owed
~~Rachel Woods~~	~~15~~	~~100~~	~~1800~~	~~3300~~
Paul Pitowski	20	100	1800	3800

Figure 4-17: Completed desk-check table for the Jackson College algorithm

After desk-checking the algorithm to verify its accuracy, you are ready to translate it into a language the computer can understand. The first step in the coding process is to determine how many memory locations the program requires.

Determining the Memory Locations

As you learned in the Concept lesson, you need to reserve a memory location—either a variable or a named constant—for each unique input, processing, and output item listed in the problem's IPO chart. In this case, you will use three variables to store the values of the name, hours enrolled, and total amount owed items, because the values of those items will be different for each student, and therefore the values will be different each time the program is executed. You will use two named constants to store the values of the semester hour fee and the room and board fee, because the values of those items ($100 and $1800, respectively) will be the same for each student, and therefore the values will remain the same each time the program is executed.

Recall that the programmer must assign a name to each variable and named constant. The name should be descriptive and it must follow the rules of the programming language. The C++ naming rules, along with examples of valid and invalid names in C++, are listed in Figure 4-18. Figure 4-18 also lists the keywords—often referred to as **reserved words**—in C++. You cannot use a keyword—for example, the word `float`—as the name of a variable or named constant in a C++ program, as indicated in the fourth rule shown in the figure.

Rules for names (identifiers) in a C++ program
1. The name must begin with a letter.
2. The name must contain only letters, numbers, and the underscore. No punctuation characters or spaces are allowed in the name.
3. The C++ compiler you are using determines the maximum number of characters in a name. In Microsoft Visual C++ 6.0, a name cannot be longer than 247 characters.
4. The name cannot be a keyword, such as double, because a keyword has a special meaning in C++. The C++ keywords, also called reserved words, are listed below.
5. Names in C++ are case sensitive.

Valid names	Invalid names	
deposit	98deposit	(the name must begin with a letter)
end_Balance	end Balance	(the name cannot contain a space)
withdrawal	withdrawal.amt	(the name cannot contain punctuation)
privateLocation	private	(the name cannot be a keyword)

C++ Keywords

asm	else	operator	throw
auto	enum	private	true
bool	explicit	protected	try
break	extern	public	typedef
case	false	register	typeid
catch	float	reinterpret_cast	typename
char	for	return	union
class	friend	short	unsigned
const	goto	signed	using
const_cast	if	sizeof	virtual
continue	inline	static	void
default	int	static_cast	volatile
delete	long	struct	wchar_t
do	mutable	switch	while
double	namespace	template	
dynamic_cast	new	this	

Figure 4-18: Naming rules, examples of valid and invalid names, and C++ keywords

tip

Variable names in C++ can begin with an underscore, but this naming convention usually is reserved for special variables used by the compiler. To avoid confusion, always begin your variable names with a letter.

Pay particular attention to the last rule shown in Figure 4-18: "Names in C++ are case sensitive." This rule means that, in a C++ program, the names hourlyFee, HourlyFee, and hourlyfee do not refer to the same location in memory. It is important to use the exact capitalization of a name throughout the entire C++ program; otherwise, the program will not work correctly. Figure 4-19 lists the names of the variables and named constants that you will use in the Jackson College program.

Memory location	Name
variable	name
variable	hours
variable	total
named constant	SEMHOURFEE
named constant	ROOMBOARD

Figure 4-19: Variables and named constants for the Jackson College program

In addition to selecting an appropriate name, you also must determine the appropriate data type for the variables and named constants. Figure 4-20 shows the data types you will use for the variables and named constants in the Jackson College program.

Memory location	Name	Data type
variable	name	string
variable	hours	int
variable	total	int
named constant	SEMHOURFEE	int
named constant	ROOMBOARD	int

Figure 4-20: Data types for the memory locations in the Jackson College program

As Figure 4-20 indicates, you will use the **string** data type for the **name** variable, because that memory location will need to store characters. You will use the **int** data type for the **hours** and **total** variables and for the **SEMHOURFEE** and **ROOMBOARD** named constants, because those memory locations will need to store only integers.

In addition to assigning a name and data type to each memory location, recall that you also must initialize each named constant. It is a good programming practice to initialize a program's variables, also. When you supply an initial value for a variable or named constant, that value, which should be the same data type as the memory location, overwrites (replaces) any garbage value stored at that memory location.

Figure 4-21 shows the initial values for the variables and named constants used in the Jackson College program.

Memory location	Name	Data type	Initial value
variable	name	string	"" (empty string)
variable	hours	int	0
variable	total	int	0
named constant	SEMHOURFEE	int	100
named constant	ROOMBOARD	int	1800

Figure 4-21: Initial values for the memory locations in the Jackson College program

tip

The initial values you select for a memory location will depend on the program you are writing. In most C++ programs, however, `short`, `int`, and `long` variables are initialized to 0, and `float`, `double`, and `long double` variables are initialized to 0.0. Similarly, `char` variables are initialized to a space enclosed in single quotation marks (' '), and `string` variables to the empty string (""). Finally, `bool` variables are usually initialized using either the C++ keyword `true` or the C++ keyword `false`.

As you learned in this tutorial's Concept lesson, you use the syntax **const** *datatype constantname = value;* to reserve a named constant in a C++ program, and you use the syntax *datatype variablename = initialvalue;* to reserve a variable. Figure 4-22 shows the C++ statements that you will use to reserve the variables and named constants in the Jackson College program.

IPO chart information	C++ instructions

Input
    name
    hours enrolled
    semester hour fee ($100)
    room and board fee ($1800)
Processing
    none
Output
    name
    total amount owed
	`string name = "";`
	`int hours = 0;`
	`const int SEMHOURFEE = 100;`
	`const int ROOMBOARD = 1800;`
	
	`int total = 0;`

Figure 4-22: C++ statements to reserve variables and named constants in the Jackson College program

Now you can begin translating the algorithm into C++ statements.

Coding the Jackson College Algorithm

The first step in the algorithm is to enter the name and hours enrolled. You can use the `cout` stream and the `<<` operator to prompt the user to enter the appropriate information. You can use the `cin` stream and the `>>` operator to get the hours enrolled from the user. Before you can write the instruction to enter the name, however, you need to learn about the `getline` function in C++.

The `getline` Function

As you observed in the previous programs in this book, you can use the `cin` stream and the `>>` operator to get a number from the user at the keyboard, and then store the number in a numeric variable. The `cin` stream and the `>>` operator also can be used to allow the user to enter one character, which then is stored in a `char` variable. Additionally, you can use the `cin` stream and the `>>` operator to get a string of characters from the user at the keyboard, as long as none of the characters is a space; this is because the `>>` operator stops reading characters from the keyboard when it encounters a space in the input. To get a string of characters that contains a space, you use the C++ `getline` function rather than the `cin` stream and the `>>` operator. Figure 4-23 shows the syntax and examples of the `getline` function.

Syntax	Examples

getline(cin, *variablename*);	`getline(cin, name);`
	`getline(cin, company);`
	`getline(cin, petName);`

Figure 4-23: Syntax and examples of the `getline` function

As you learned in Tutorial 3, you can recognize a function, which is simply a block of code that performs a specific task, by the parentheses immediately following the function's name. Some functions, such as the `getline` function, require you to enter information, called **arguments**, between the parentheses. The `getline` function requires two arguments: **cin** (which refers to the keyboard) and *variable-name* (which specifies the name of the variable in which to store the data entered at the keyboard). In the examples shown in Figure 4-23, the data entered by the user at the keyboard will be stored in the `name`, `company`, and `petName` variables. Notice that the `getline` function must end with a semicolon.

Figure 4-24 shows the C++ code corresponding to the first step in the Jackson College algorithm.

IPO chart information	C++ instructions
Input	
name	`string name = "";`
hours enrolled	`int hours = 0;`
semester hour fee ($100)	`const int SEMHOURFEE = 100;`
room and board fee ($1800)	`const int ROOMBOARD = 1800;`
Processing	
none	
Output	
name	
total amount owed	`int total = 0;`
Algorithm	
1. enter the name and hours enrolled	`cout << "Enter student name: ";`
	`getline(cin, name);`
	`cout << "Enter hours enrolled: ";`
	`cin >> hours;`

Figure 4-24: C++ instructions corresponding to the first step in the algorithm

The second step in the algorithm is to calculate the total amount due by multiplying the hours enrolled by the semester hour fee, and then adding the room and board fee to the result. You will need to use the `hours` variable, the `SEMHOURFEE` and `ROOMBOARD` named constants, and two arithmetic operators (* and +) in the calculation. You will assign the result of the calculation to the `total` variable, using the assignment statement `total = hours * SEMHOURFEE + ROOMBOARD;`.

The last step in the algorithm is to display the student's name and total amount owed on the screen; you can use the `cout` stream and the `<<` operator to do so. Figure 4-25 shows the C++ instructions for the Jackson College program.

IPO chart information	C++ instructions

Input
  name
  hours enrolled
  semester hour fee ($100)
  room and board fee ($1800)
	`string name = "";`
	`int hours = 0;`
	`const int SEMHOURFEE = 100;`
	`const int ROOMBOARD = 1800;`

Processing none	

Output
  name
  total amount owed
	
	`int total = 0;`

Algorithm
1. enter the name and
   hours enrolled
	`cout << "Enter student name: ";`
	`getline(cin, name);`
	`cout << "Enter hours enrolled: ";`
	`cin >> hours;`

2. calculate the total
   amount owed by
   multiplying the hours
   enrolled by the semester
   hour fee, and then
   adding the room and
   board fee to the result
	`total = hours * SEMHOURFEE + ROOMBOARD;`

3. display the name and total amount owed	`cout << "Student name: " << name << endl;` `cout << "Total due: " << total << endl;`

Figure 4-25: C++ instructions for the Jackson College program

As you learned in Tutorial 3, after coding the algorithm, you then need to desk-check the program, using the same data you used to desk-check the algorithm. Figure 4-26 shows the data and the completed desk-check table for the program.

Data for first desk-check		Data for second desk-check	
Student's name:	Rachel Woods	Student's name:	Paul Pitowski
Hours enrolled:	15	Hours enrolled:	20
Semester hour fee:	$100	Semester hour fee:	$100
Room and board fee:	$1800	Room and board fee:	$1800

Desk-check table

name	hours	SEMHOURFEE	ROOMBOARD	total
~~————~~	0	~~100~~	~~1800~~	~~0~~
~~Rachel Woods~~	~~15~~			~~3300~~
~~————~~	~~0~~	100	1800	~~0~~
Paul Pitowski	20			3800

Figure 4-26: Data and completed desk-check table for the Jackson College program

The results obtained when desk-checking the program agree with the results obtained when desk-checking the algorithm, so it appears that the algorithm was coded correctly. (The algorithm's desk-check table is shown in Figure 4-17.) You now are ready to enter the C++ instructions into the computer.

mini-quiz

Mini-Quiz 4

1. Write a C++ statement that gets a string of characters from the keyboard, and stores the characters in a variable named `streetAddress`.

2. Write a C++ statement that subtracts the number 40 from an `int` variable named `hours`, and stores the result in an `int` variable named `overtimeHours`.

3. Write a C++ statement that gets a number from the keyboard, and stores the number in a `float` variable named `taxRate`.

Up to this point, you have been opening existing C++ programs. In the next section, you will learn how to use Microsoft Visual C++ 6.0 to create a C++ version of the Jackson College program.

Creating a Console Application in C++

Although you can create many different types of applications in Visual C++, in this book you will create only console applications. A **console application** is a program that runs in a DOS window.

To create a console application in Visual C++:

1 Start Visual C++.

HELP? If you do not remember how to start Visual C++, you can refer to Tutorial 3's Application lesson for the appropriate instructions.

2 Click **File** on the menu bar, and then click **New**. The New dialog box opens. Click the **Projects** tab, if necessary, then click **Win32 Console Application** in the list of project types. If necessary, click the **Create new workspace** option button to select it. See Figure 4-27.

HELP? If the Location text box does not display the location of the Tut04 folder on your computer's hard disk (the location typically will be C:\CPP\TUT04\), click the ellipsis button that appears to the right of the Location text box to open the Choose Directory dialog box. Use the Choose Directory dialog box to open the Tut04 folder on your computer's hard disk, then click the OK button.

this should display the location of the Tut04 folder on your computer's hard disk

your list might be different

be sure this option is selected

select this project type

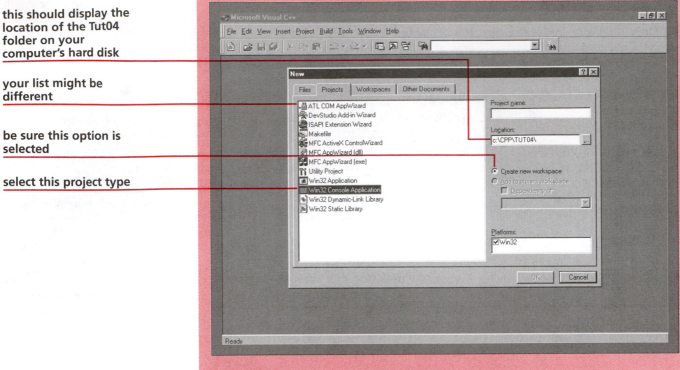

Figure 4-27: Projects tab in the New dialog box

3   Click the **Project name** text box, then type **T4App** in the text box, as shown in Figure 4-28. (The *T4App* stands for *Tutorial 4, Application lesson*.)

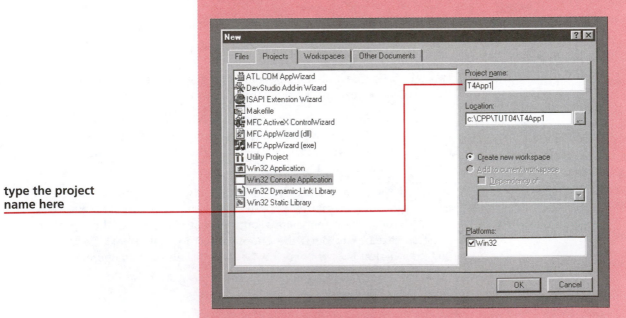

type the project name here

Figure 4-28: Project name entered in the New dialog box

4   Click the **OK** button to close the New dialog box. The Win32 Console Application - Step 1 of 1 window appears, If necessary, click the **An empty project** option button to select it, as shown in Figure 4-29.

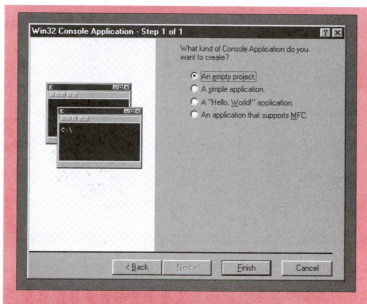

Figure 4-29: Win32 Console Application - Step 1 of 1 window

5 Click the **Finish** button. The New Project Information window appears, as shown in Figure 4-30.

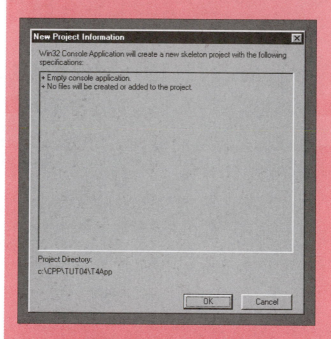

Figure 4-30: New Project Information window

6 Click the **OK** button to close the New Project Information window. The T4App - Microsoft Visual C++ window appears, as shown in Figure 4-31.

Close button

Project Workspace window

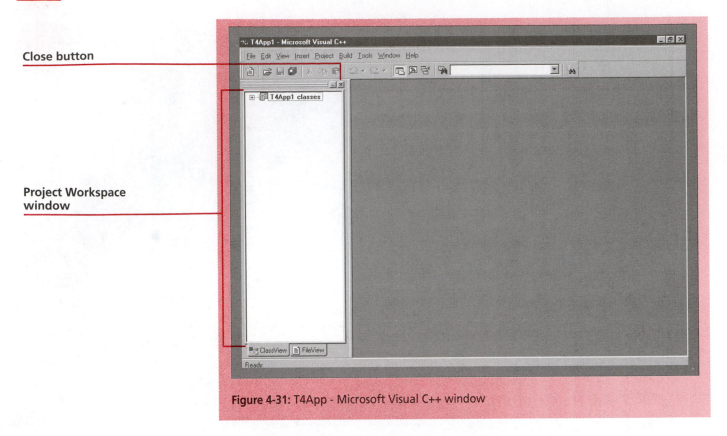

Figure 4-31: T4App - Microsoft Visual C++ window

When you use the New dialog box to create a console application, Visual C++ creates both a workspace and a project. A **workspace** is a container for one or more projects, and a **project** is a container for one or more files that contain source code, usually referred to as source files. (The current project does not yet contain any source files.) Although the idea of workspaces, projects, and source files may sound confusing, the concept of placing things in containers is nothing new to you. Think of a workspace as being similar to a drawer in a filing cabinet. A project then is similar to a file folder that you store in the drawer, and a file that contains source code is similar to a document that you store in the file folder. You can place many file folders in a filing cabinet drawer, just as you can place many projects in a workspace. You also can store many documents in a file folder, similar to the way you can store many source files in a C++ project. Figure 4-32 illustrates this analogy.

source file

project

workspace

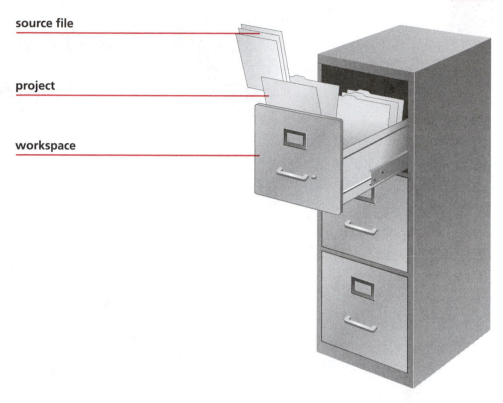

Figure 4-32: Illustration of a workspace, project, and source file

After you create the workspace and the project, you then add a source file to the project. You can add either a new source file or an existing source file. You will add a new source file to the project.

To add a new source file to the project:
1   Click **Project** on the menu bar, point to **Add To Project**, and then click **New** to open the New dialog box.
2   If necessary, click the **Files** tab, then click **C++ Source File** in the list of file types.

   If a project contains only one source file, most programmers give the file the same name as the project.
3   Click the **File name** text box, then type **T4App** in the File name text box, as shown in Figure 4-33.

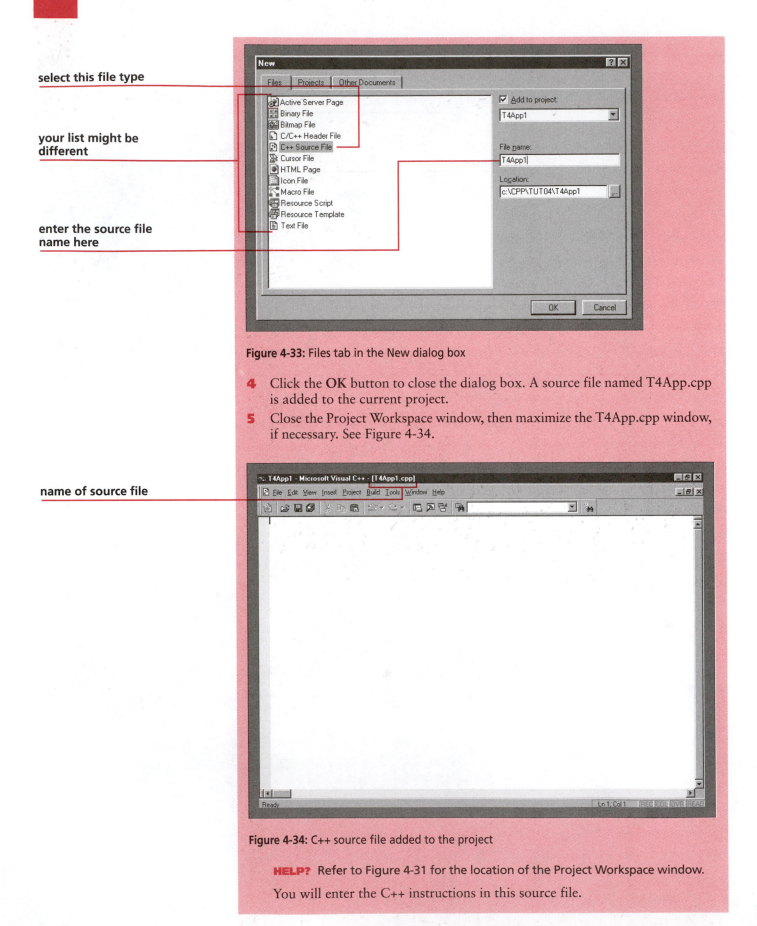

select this file type

your list might be different

enter the source file name here

Figure 4-33: Files tab in the New dialog box

4 Click the **OK** button to close the dialog box. A source file named T4App.cpp is added to the current project.

5 Close the Project Workspace window, then maximize the T4App.cpp window, if necessary. See Figure 4-34.

name of source file

Figure 4-34: C++ source file added to the project

HELP? Refer to Figure 4-31 for the location of the Project Workspace window.

You will enter the C++ instructions in this source file.

Figure 4-35 shows the basic structure of a C++ program. Items in square brackets ([ ]) in the structure are optional. Items in **bold**, on the other hand, are required. Items in *italics* represent places where the programmer must supply information relative to the program.

```
[comments that identify the program]

#include directives
using namespace std;

int main( )
{
        [named constant declarations]
        [variable declarations]

        [input statements]
        [calculation statements]
        [output statements]

        return 0;
} //end of main function
```

Figure 4-35: Basic structure of a C++ program

You will follow this basic structure when entering the Jackson College program instructions. According to the structure, you first enter comments that identify the program.

tip

Recall that the angle brackets (< >) in the `#include` directive tell the compiler that the header file is located in the C++ include folder.

To begin entering the Jackson College program instructions:

1   Type **//T4App.cpp - displays student's name and total due** and press the **Enter** key twice.

Next, enter the `#include` directives needed by the program. As you learned in Tutorial 3, a directive is a special instruction for the C++ compiler. A `#include` directive tells C++ to include the contents of another file, typically a header file that contains source code, in the current program. Most C++ programs include at least one header file, and many include several. You will need to include two header files in the T4App program: iostream and string. As you learned in Tutorial 3, the iostream header file contains the instructions needed for input and output operations in a C++ program. The string header file contains the instructions needed to reserve and access string memory locations. The name of both header files must be enclosed in angle brackets (< >).

2   Type **#include <iostream>** and press the **Enter** key, then type **#include <string>** and press the **Enter** key.

Now you will enter the `using namespace std;` statement. As you learned in Tutorial 3, this statement tells the compiler that the definition of standard C++ keywords—such as `cout`, `cin`, and `endl`—can be found in a namespace (a special area in the computer's internal memory) named std. (std is short for *standard*.)

3   Type **using namespace std;** and press the **Enter** key twice.

Recall that every C++ program must have a `main` function, because this is where the execution of a C++ program always begins. According to Figure 4-35, the function header for the `main` function is entered below the `using namespace std;` statement.

4   Type **int main()** and press the **Enter** key. (Do not type a space between the parentheses.)

Recall that the `main` function's instructions must be enclosed in a set of braces. The last instruction in the `main` function should be `return 0;`. It is a good practice to type the opening and closing braces and the `return 0;` statement right away, so that you don't forget to do it.

5   Type **{** (the opening brace) and press the **Enter** key twice. Notice that the Visual C++ editor indents the next line in the window.

6   Type **return 0;** and press the **Enter** key, then type **}** (the closing brace). Notice that the Visual C++ editor enters the closing brace at the window's left margin to align it with the opening brace.

7   Press the **Tab** key, then type **//end of main function** and press the **Enter** key.

8   Position the cursor in the blank line below the opening brace. Press the **Tab** key if necessary to position the insertion point as shown in Figure 4-36.

position the insertion
point here

Figure 4-36: Current status of the T4App program

Mini-Quiz 5

1.   You must include the _____ header file to use a `string` variable in a C++ program.

2.   You must include the _____ header file to use the `cout` keyword in a C++ program.

3.   The execution of every C++ program begins with the _____.

Next, you will enter the `main` function's instructions. According to the structure shown in Figure 4-35, you should declare the named constants first, then declare the variables.

The named constants are listed first so they are easier to locate if you need to change their values in the future.

To continue coding the T4App program:

1 Type the declaration statements shown in Figure 4-37, then position the insertion point as shown in the figure. Although C++ does not require you to align the assignment operators (=) in a list of declaration statements, doing so helps to make the program easier to read.

enter these five line of code

position the insertion point here

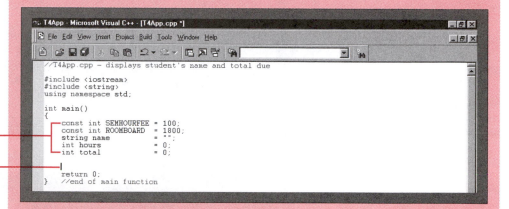

Figure 4-37: Instructions to declare and initialize the named constants and variables

Now enter the instructions that get the name and hours enrolled from the user.

2 Type the comment and additional statements shown in Figure 4-38, then position the insertion point as shown in the figure. (Don't be concerned about the box that might appear when you type the open parenthesis in the `getline` function.)

When you type the open parenthesis after the name of a C++ function, the Visual C++ editor might display a box containing information about the function's arguments, also called parameters. To turn this feature off, click Tools, then click Options. Click the Editor tab, then click the Auto parameter info check box to deselect it.

enter these five line of code

position the insertion point here

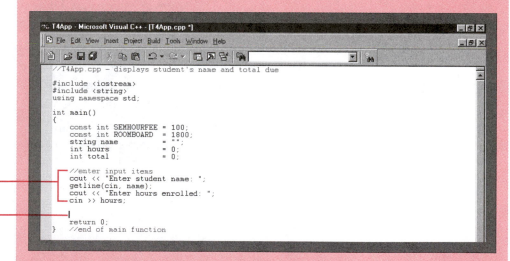

Figure 4-38: Instructions to enter the name and hours enrolled

Next, enter the instructions to calculate the tuition and the total amount owed, and the instructions to output the data.

3 Type the comments and additional statements shown in Figure 4-39, which shows the completed T4App program.

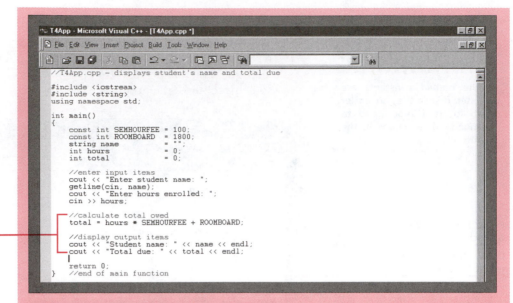

Figure 4-39: Completed T4App program

enter these five line of code

Now use the sample data shown earlier in Figure 4-26 to verify that the program code works correctly.

4   Save, build, and execute the program.

HELP? If you do not remember how to save, build, and execute a C++ program, you can refer to Tutorial 3's Application lesson for the appropriate instructions.

5   If you are using the Introductory Edition of Microsoft Visual C++ 6.0, press the **Enter** key to remove the message box that appears on the screen.

> **Important note:** In future steps, you will not be instructed specifically to press the Enter key to remove the message box.

6   When you are prompted for the student's name, type **Rachel Woods** and press the **Enter** key. The "Enter hours enrolled: " prompt appears.

HELP? If the hours enrolled prompt does not appear, press the Enter key again. If you needed to press the Enter key twice, refer to the Read This Before You Begin section found at the beginning of this book.

7   When you are prompted for the hours enrolled, type **15** and press the **Enter** key. The program calculates the total amount owed. It then displays the student's name and the total amount owed in a DOS window, as shown in Figure 4-40.

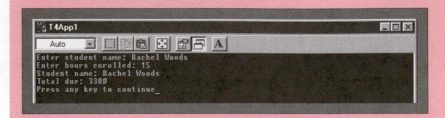

Figure 4-40: DOS window showing results of first test

> The DOS window shows that the total amount owed is 3300, which agrees with the results shown earlier in Figure 4-26's desk-check table; the program appears to be working correctly. You should, however, test it several more times with different data.
>
> **8** Press the **Enter** key to close the DOS window.
>
> **9** Execute the program again. Type **Paul Pitowski** as the student's name and press the **Enter** key. Type **20** as the hours enrolled and press the **Enter** key. The DOS window shows that the total amount owed is 3800, which agrees with the results shown in Figure 4-26's desk-check table. Press the **Enter** key to close the DOS window.
>
> **10** Close the Output window, click **File** on the menu bar, and then click **Close Workspace**. When prompted to close all document windows, click the **Yes** button.
>
> **11** Exit Visual C++.

You now have completed Tutorial 4's Application lesson. You can either take a break or complete the end-of-lesson exercises.

ANSWERS TO MINI-QUIZZES

Mini-Quiz 4

1. `getline(cin, streetAddress);`

2. `overtimeHours = hours - 40;`

3. `cin >> taxRate;`

Mini-Quiz 5

1. `string`

2. `iostream`

3. `main function`

EXERCISES

1. Write a C++ statement that uses the `getline` function to get a string of characters from the keyboard. Store the characters in a `string` variable named `company`.

2. Write a C++ statement that uses the `getline` function to get a string of characters from the keyboard. Store the characters in a `string` variable named `bookTitle`.

3. Write a C++ statement that multiplies a variable named `taxRate` by a variable named `grossPay`, and assigns the result to a variable named `tax`.

4. Write a C++ statement that multiplies a variable named `numItems` by a variable named `price`, and assigns the result to a variable named `totalPrice`.

5. Acme Appliances needs a program to calculate a bonus, which is always 5 percent of the sales.
   a. Complete an IPO chart for this problem.
   b. Desk-check the algorithm. Use 330.50 as the sales.

c. Use the IPO chart to code the program.

d. Desk-check the program using the data specified in Step b.

e. Create a console application. Name the project workspace T4AppE05, and save it in the Cpp\Tut04 folder on your computer's hard disk. Add a new C++ source file to the project. Name the source file T4AppE05.

f. Enter the appropriate C++ instructions into the source file.

g. Save, build, and execute the program. Test the program using the data specified in Step b.

h. When the program is working correctly, hide the Output window, then use the File menu to close the workspace.

6. Write a program to calculate the square of a number. The number will always be an integer.

a. Complete an IPO chart for this problem.

b. Desk-check the algorithm. Use 10 as the number.

c. Use the IPO chart to code the program.

d. Desk-check the program using the data specified in Step b.

e. Create a console application. Name the project workspace T4AppE06, and save it in the Cpp\Tut04 folder on your computer's hard disk. Add a new C++ source file to the project. Name the source file T4AppE06.

f. Enter the appropriate C++ instructions into the source file.

g. Save, build, and execute the program. Test the program using the data specified in Step b.

h. When the program is working correctly, hide the Output window, then use the File menu to close the workspace.

7. Builders Inc. needs a program that will allow the company's salesclerks to enter both the diameter of a circle (in feet) and the price of railing material per foot. (The diameter and the price may contain decimal places.) The program should display both the circumference of the circle and the total price of the railing material. Use 3.141593 as the value of pi.

a. Complete an IPO chart for this problem.

b. Desk-check the algorithm. Use 36.5 feet as the diameter, and $2.35 as the price per foot of railing material.

c. Use the IPO chart to code the program.

d. Desk-check the program using the data specified in Step b.

e. Create a console application. Name the project workspace T4AppE07, and save it in the Cpp\Tut04 folder on your computer's hard disk. Add a new C++ source file to the project. Name the source file T4AppE07.

f. Enter the appropriate C++ instructions into the source file.

g. Save, build, and execute the program. Test the program using the data specified in Step b.

h. When the program is working correctly, hide the Output window, then use the File menu to close the workspace.

8. A-1 Appliances needs a program that will allow the store clerks to enter the number of dishwashers in stock at the beginning of the current month, the number of dishwashers purchased by A-1 during the current month, and the number of dishwashers sold to customers during the current month. The program should calculate and display the number of dishwashers in stock at the end of the current month.

a. Complete an IPO chart for this problem.

b. Desk-check the algorithm, using 5000 as the number of dishwashers at the beginning of the month, 1000 as the number of dishwashers purchased during the month, and 3500 as the number of dishwashers sold during the month.

c. Use the IPO chart to code the program.

d. Desk-check the program using the data specified in Step b.

e. Create a console application. Name the project workspace T4AppE08, and save it in the Cpp\Tut04 folder on your computer's hard disk. Add a new C++ source file to the project. Name the source file T4AppE08.

f. Enter the appropriate C++ instructions into the source file.

g. Save, build, and execute the program. Test the program using the data specified in Step b.

h. When the program is working correctly, hide the Output window, then use the File menu to close the workspace.

9. Tile Limited wants a program that will allow the company's salesclerks to enter the length and width, in feet, of a rectangle, and the price of a square foot of tile. (The length, width, and price may contain decimal places.) The program should display the area of the rectangle and the total price of the tile.

a. Complete an IPO chart for this problem.

b. Desk-check the algorithm. Use 12.5 feet as the length, 14.5 feet as the width, and $3.10 as the price per square foot of tile.

c. Use the IPO chart to code the program.

d. Desk-check the program using the data specified in Step b.

e. Create a console application. Name the project workspace T4AppE09, and save it in the Cpp\Tut04 folder on your computer's hard disk. Add a new C++ source file to the project. Name the source file T4AppE09.

f. Enter the appropriate C++ instructions into the source file.

g. Save, build, and execute the program. Test the program using the data specified in Step b.

h. When the program is working correctly, hide the Output window, then use the File menu to close the workspace.

10. Jerome Symanski wants a program that he can use to display the number of cubic feet of water contained in a rectangular pool. (*Hint*: Find the volume of the rectangle.)

a. Complete an IPO chart for this problem.

b. Desk-check the algorithm, using 100 feet as the length, 30.5 feet as the width, and 4 feet as the depth.

c. Use the IPO chart to code the program. (Use `float` variables for the length, width, depth, and volume.)

d. Desk-check the program using the data specified in Step b.

e. Create a console application. Name the project workspace T4AppE10, and save it in the Cpp\Tut04 folder on your computer's hard disk. Add a new C++ source file to the project. Name the source file T4AppE10.

f. Enter the appropriate C++ instructions into the source file.

g. Save, build, and execute the program. Test the program using the data specified in Step b.

h. When the program is working correctly, hide the Output window, then use the File menu to close the workspace.

11. Temp Employers wants a program that will allow the company's clerks to enter an employee's name and the number of hours the employee worked during the month. (The number of hours worked will always be an integer.) The program will display the name, number of weeks (assume a 40-hour week), days (assume an eight-hour day), and hours worked. For example, if the employee enters the number 70, the program will display the employee's name, then 1 week, 3 days, and 6 hours.

a. Complete an IPO chart for this problem.

b. Desk-check the algorithm three times, using the following data:

Mary Claire, 88 hours worked

Jackie Smith, 111 hours worked

Sue Jones, 12 hours worked

c. Use the IPO chart to code the program.

d. Desk-check the program using the data specified in Step b.

e. Create a console application. Name the project workspace T4AppE11, and save it in the Cpp\Tut04 folder on your computer's hard disk. Add a new C++ source file to the project. Name the source file T4AppE11.

f. Enter the appropriate C++ instructions into the source file.

g. Save, build, and execute the program. Test the program using the data specified in Step b.

h. When the program is working correctly, hide the Output window, then use the File menu to close the workspace.

12. Colfax Industries needs a program that allows its shipping clerk to enter an item's name, the quantity of the item in inventory, and how many units of the item can be packed in a box for shipping. The program should display the item's name, the number of full boxes that can be packed from the quantity on hand, and the quantity of items left over.

    a. Complete an IPO chart for this problem.

    b. Desk-check the algorithm three times, using the following data:

       Cleanser, 45 in inventory, six can be packed in a box

       Hair Spray, 100 in inventory, three can be packed in a box

       Comb, 78 in inventory, five can be packed in a box

    c. Use the IPO chart to code the program.

    d. Desk-check the program using the data specified in Step b.

    e. Create a console application. Name the project workspace T4AppE12, and save it in the Cpp\Tut04 folder on your computer's hard disk. Add a new C++ source file to the project. Name the source file T4AppE12.

    f. Enter the appropriate C++ instructions into the source file.

    g. Save, build, and execute the program. Test the program using the data specified in Step b.

    h. When the program is working correctly, hide the Output window, then use the File menu to close the workspace.

13. Your friend Joe saves pennies in a jar, which he empties every month when he goes to the bank. You decide to create a program that allows him to enter the number of pennies, and then calculates and displays the number of dollars, quarters, dimes, nickels, and pennies he will receive when he trades in the pennies at the bank.

    a. Complete an IPO chart for this problem.

    b. Desk-check the algorithm two times, using the following data: 2311 pennies and 7333 pennies.

    c. Use the IPO chart to code the program.

    d. Desk-check the program using the data specified in Step b.

    e. Create a console application. Name the project workspace T4AppE13, and save it in the Cpp\Tut04 folder on your computer's hard disk. Add a new C++ source file to the project. Name the source file T4AppE13.

    f. Enter the appropriate C++ instructions into the source file.

    g. Save, build, and execute the program. Test the program using the data specified in Step b.

    h. When the program is working correctly, hide the Output window, then use the File menu to close the workspace.

14. A third-grade teacher at Hinsbrook Elementary School would like you to create a program that will help her students learn how to make change. The program should allow the student to enter the amount of money the customer owes and the amount of money the customer paid. The program should calculate and display the amount of change, as well as how many dollars, quarters, dimes, nickels, and pennies to return to the customer. For now, you do not have to worry about the situation where the price is greater than what the customer pays. You can always assume that the customer paid either the exact amount or more than the exact amount.

    a. Complete an IPO chart for this problem.

   b. Desk-check the algorithm three times, using the following data:
      75.34 as the amount due and 80.00 as the amount paid
      39.67 as the amount due and 50.00 as the amount paid
      45.55 as the amount due and 45.55 as the amount paid
   c. Use the IPO chart to code the program.
   d. Desk-check the program using the data specified in Step b.
   e. Create a console application. Name the project workspace T4AppE14, and save it in the Cpp\Tut04 folder on your computer's hard disk. Add a new C++ source file to the project. Name the source file T4AppE14.
   f. Enter the appropriate C++ instructions into the source file.
   g. Save, build, and execute the program. Test the program using the data specified in Step b.
   h. When the program is working correctly, hide the Output window, then use the File menu to close the workspace.

Exercise 15 is a Discovery Exercise. Discovery Exercises, which may include topics that are not covered in this lesson, allow you to "discover" the solutions to problems on your own.

discovery

15. As you learned in the Concept lesson, you can initialize a `bool` variable in C++ using either the keyword `false` or the keyword `true`. You also can use an integer—either 0 or 1—to initialize a `bool` variable. Initializing a `bool` variable to the number 0 is the same as initializing it to the keyword `false`. Initializing a `bool` variable to the number 1 is the same as initializing it to the keyword `true`. Although you can use an integer to initialize a `bool` variable, the keywords make your program more self-documenting.
   a. Open the T4AppE15.cpp file contained in the Cpp\Tut04\T4AppE15 folder on your computer's hard disk. The program initializes a `bool` variable named `insured` and then displays its value. Build and execute the program. What does the program display in the DOS window? Press the Enter key to close the DOS window.
   b. Change the `bool insured = false;` statement to `bool insured = true;`. Save, build, and then execute the program. What does the program display in the DOS window? Press the Enter key to close the DOS window.
   c. Change the `bool insured = true;` statement to `bool insured = 0;`. Save, build, and then execute the program. What does the program display in the DOS window? Press the Enter key to close the DOS window.
   d. Change the `bool insured = 0;` statement to `bool insured = 1;`. Save, build, and then execute the program. What does the program display in the DOS window? Press the Enter key to close the DOS window.
   e. Hide the Output window, then use the File menu to close the workspace.

A computer program is good only if it works. Errors in either an algorithm or programming code can cause the program to run incorrectly. Therefore, a programmer needs to know how to locate and fix these errors. Exercises 16 and 17 are Debugging Exercises. Debugging Exercises allow you to practice recognizing and solving errors in a program.

debugging

16. In this exercise, you will debug C++ code.
   a. Open the T4AppE16.cpp file contained in the Cpp\Tut04\T4AppE16 folder on your computer's hard disk. The program first initializes the `temp` variable. It then adds 1.5 to the `temp` variable before displaying its value.
   b. Build the program. Correct any errors. Save, build, and then execute the program. When the program is working correctly, hide the Output window, then use the File menu to close the workspace.

debugging

17. In this exercise, you will debug C++ code.
   a. Open the T4AppE17.cpp file contained in the Cpp\Tut04\T4AppE17 folder on your computer's hard disk. The program should calculate the average of the three sales amounts entered by the user.
   b. Build and then execute the program. Use the following sales amounts to test the program: 110.55, 203.45, and 100.68. Correct the program so that it produces the proper output. Save, build, and then execute the program. When the program is working correctly, hide the Output window, then use the File menu to close the workspace.

Built-In Functions

After completing this tutorial, you will be able to:

■ Use built-in mathematical functions
■ Generate random numbers
■ Format the numeric output in a C++ program
■ Send program output to a file in a C++ program

Concept Lesson

Functions

In Tutorial 3, you learned that a function is a block of code that performs a task. You can recognize a function in a program by the parentheses immediately following the function's name. The Jackson College program created in Tutorial 4's Application lesson and shown in Figure 5-1 contains two functions: `main` and `getline`.

```cpp
//T4App.cpp - displays student's name and total due

#include <iostream>
#include <string>
using namespace std;

int main()
{
     const int SEMHOURFEE = 100;
     const int ROOMBOARD  = 1800;
     string name          = "";
     int hours            = 0;
     int total            = 0;

     //enter input items
     cout << "Enter student name: ";
     getline(cin, name);
     cout << "Enter hours enrolled: ";
     cin >> hours;

     //calculate total owed
     total = hours * SEMHOURFEE + ROOMBOARD;

     //display output items
     cout << "Student name: " << name << endl;
     cout << "Total due: " << total << endl;

     return 0;
}    //end of main function
```

functions

actual arguments

Figure 5-1: Jackson College program from Tutorial 4's Application lesson

Some functions, such as `getline`, require you to enter information between the parentheses. The information can be one or more variables, named constants, literal constants, or keywords. Each item of information within a function's parentheses is called an **actual argument**. Each actual argument represents information that the function needs in order to perform its task. As indicated in Figure 5-1, the `getline` function—which you use to get string input from the keyboard—requires two actual arguments: the source of the input and the name of a variable in which to store the input. Not all functions require actual arguments; the `main` function, for example, does not require any actual arguments.

Programmers can include two different types of functions in a program: program-defined functions and built-in functions. A **program-defined function**, which you will learn more about in Tutorials 6 and 7, is a function whose task is determined by the programmer and whose code is defined, or specified, within the program in which the function is used. The `main` function in a C++ program is an example of a program-defined function, because the task it performs is determined by the code the programmer enters between the function's opening and closing braces in a program. The code entered in Figure 5-1's `main` function, for instance, tells the function how to perform the task of displaying the student's name and total due, given the student's name, hours enrolled, semester hour fee, and room and board fee.

Different from a program-defined function, a **built-in function** is a function whose task is predefined, and whose **function definition**—the code that guides the function in completing its task—is prewritten and appears outside of the program in which the function is used. The C++ `getline` function is an example of a built-in function. The function definitions for built-in functions are contained in files, called **libraries**, that come with the language compiler and reside on your computer's hard disk. The Visual C++ compiler comes with many library files—each containing the function definitions for a specific collection of functions. The cmath library file, for example, contains the function definitions for the built-in mathematical functions, which you will learn about in the next section. The string library file, on the other hand, contains the function definitions for built-in functions that operate on strings. The function definition for the built-in `getline` function, for example, is contained in the string library file.

In order for a program to use a built-in function, the appropriate library file must be included in the program. To use the `getline` function, for example, a program must contain the `#include <string>` directive. This directive allows the program to access the string library's source code, which contains the function definition for the `getline` function.

You tell a built-in function to perform its task by calling, or invoking, it in a program. You call (invoke) a built-in function by including its name and actual arguments (if any) in a statement. Although the idea of calling something and providing it with information may sound confusing at first, the concept is really nothing new to you. When you register for classes at school, you typically call the registrar and provide him or her with your Social Security number, name, and list of classes you want to take. As you do with a function, you call the registrar to perform a task for you. The registrar's task is to register you for the next semester; the `getline` function's task is to get string input from the keyboard and store it in a variable. Before either can perform its designated task, you must provide each with some very specific information. The registrar uses the information you provide—your Social Security number, name, and so on—to register you for the next semester's classes. The `getline` function uses the information you provide—the actual arguments—to get string input from the keyboard and store it in a variable.

When the computer processes a statement containing a built-in function, the computer first locates the function's code in the appropriate library. The computer then passes to the code any actual arguments listed in the statement. In the case of the `get-line` function shown in Figure 5-1, the computer passes two actual arguments to the function's code: `cin` and `name`. Both actual arguments are necessary for the `getline` function to perform appropriately, because they tell the function the source of the input (in this case, the keyboard) and where to store the input in memory (in this case, in the `name` variable). The computer then processes the function's code, which contains the instructions necessary to accomplish the function's task. Recall that you do not need to code a built-in function, because the code is prewritten and exists in a library file.

tip

You also can purchase library files from third-party vendors, or create your own library files.

tip

Recall from Tutorial 3 that the `#include` directive merges the source code from one file with the source code in another file.

tip

Built-in functions speed up program writing by allowing programmers to use existing code to perform common tasks.

The program statement processed by the computer after a built-in function completes its task depends on whether the built-in function is a value-returning function or a void function. A **value-returning function** is a function that returns a value to the statement that called the function; the computer continues processing with that statement. All of the built-in functions you will learn about in this lesson, except for the `srand` function, are value-returning functions. A **void function**, on the other hand, is a function that does not return a value. After processing a void function's code, the computer continues processing with the statement immediately following the statement that called the function. The `srand` function covered in this lesson is an example of a built-in void function.

In this lesson, you will learn how to use some of the numeric functions built into programming languages. More specifically, first you will learn about the built-in mathematical functions, which perform numerical calculations and then return the result, and then you will learn about the functions used to generate random numbers in a program. (The built-in functions that operate on characters and strings are covered in Tutorial 11.)

Using Built-In Mathematical Functions

Certain mathematical tasks—such as raising a number to a power or finding the square root of a number—are common in programs. Rather than have each programmer start from scratch and create functions to perform these tasks, most programming languages include a set of mathematical functions that any programmer can use in his or her programs. Figure 5-2 lists some of the mathematical functions built into most programming languages, along with the purpose of each function.

Function	Purpose
Power	raise a number to a power
Square Root	calculate the square root of a number
Cosine	calculate the cosine of an angle expressed in radians
Sine	calculate the sine of an angle expressed in radians
Tangent	calculate the tangent of an angle expressed in radians

Figure 5-2: Mathematical functions

In the following sections, you will be given a brief explanation and several examples of using these functions in a C++ statement.

The Power and Square Root Functions

The power and square root functions belong to a group commonly referred to as the exponential functions. Both functions are value-returning functions, because both return a value after performing their assigned task. The **power function**, for example, raises a number to a power, and then returns the result. The **square root function**, on the other hand, returns the square root of a number. Figure 5-3 shows the syntax of the power and square root functions in C++, Java, and Visual Basic. It also describes the value returned by each function.

tip

Appendix B contains a complete list of the mathematical functions available in C++.

Function	Value returned	C++ and Java syntax	Visual Basic syntax
Power	*x* raised to power *y*	**pow(*x*, *y*)**	*x* ^ *y*
Square root	square root of *x*	**sqrt(*x*)**	**Sqr(*x*)**

Note: In Visual Basic, you use the exponentiation operator (^) to raise a number (*x*) to a power (*y*).

Figure 5-3: Syntax of the power and square root functions in C++, Java, and Visual Basic

Figure 5-4 shows examples of using the pow and sqrt functions in a C++ statement.

C++ statements	Results
`cube = pow(4, 3);`	the number 64 assigned to the cube variable
`cout << pow(100, .5);`	the number 10 displayed on the screen
`cout << 10 * pow(2, 4);`	the number 160 displayed on the screen
`sqRoot = sqrt(16);`	the number 4 assigned to the sqRoot variable
`cout << pow(sqrt(4), 5);`	the number 32 displayed on the screen

Figure 5-4: Examples of the pow and sqrt functions in C++

tip

As you learned in Tutorial 4, when an assignment statement is encountered in a program, the computer assigns the value of the *expression* appearing on the right side of the assignment operator to the variable whose *variablename* appears on the left side of the assignment operator.

The `cube = pow(4, 3);` statement shown in Figure 5-4 first raises the number 4 to the third power—in other words, it multiplies the number 4 by itself three times (4 * 4 * 4). The statement assigns the result (64) to the cube variable.

The second statement shown in Figure 5-4, `cout << pow(100, .5);`, raises a number—in this case, 100—to to the .5 power, which is the same as finding the square root of the number. The statement will display the number 10 on the screen.

The third statement shown in Figure 5-4, `cout << 10 * pow(2, 4);`, raises the number 2 to the fourth power; it then multiplies the result (16) by 10, giving 160. The number 160 then is displayed on the screen.

The fourth statement, `sqRoot = sqrt(16);`, calculates the square root of the number 16, and then assigns the result (4) to the sqRoot variable.

The last statement shown in Figure 5-4, `cout << pow(sqrt(4), 5);`, first calculates the square root of 4, which is 2. It then raises the number 2 to the fifth power, and displays the result (32) on the screen.

The C++ pow and sqrt functions are defined in the cmath library file, so you will need to include the `#include <cmath>` directive in any program that uses these functions.

The Cosine, Sine, and Tangent Functions

The **cosine**, **sine**, and **tangent functions**, referred to as the trigonometric functions, can be used to calculate the cosine, sine, and tangent of *x*, where *x* is an angle expressed in radians. Because angles typically are expressed in degrees, you usually will need to convert the degrees to radians before using these functions. You convert degrees to radians using the equation radians = degrees * pi / 180, where the value of pi is 3.141593. For example, using this equation, 30 degrees is approximately .5 radians (30 * 3.141593 / 180), and 90 degrees is approximately 1.6 radians (90 * 3.141593 / 180).

Figure 5-5 shows the syntax of the cosine, sine, and tangent functions in C++, Java, and Visual Basic. Like the exponential functions, the trigonometric functions are value-returning functions because they return a value after completing their assigned task; these values are described in Figure 5-5.

Function	Value returned	C++ and Java syntax	Visual Basic syntax
Cosine	cosine of *x*	**cos(***x***)**	**Cos(***x***)**
Sine	sine of *x*	**sin(***x***)**	**Sin(***x***)**
Tangent	tangent of *x*	**tan(***x***)**	**Tan(***x***)**

Figure 5-5: Syntax of the cosine, sine, and tangent functions in C++, Java, and Visual Basic

Figure 5-6 shows examples of using the cos, sin, and tan functions in a C++ statement.

C++ statements	Results
`angleCos = cos(60 * 3.141593 / 180);`	the number .5 assigned to the `angleCos` variable
`cout << sin(1.57);`	the number 1 displayed on the screen
`cout << tan(31 * 3.141593 / 180);`	the number .6 displayed on the screen

Figure 5-6: Examples of the cos, sin, and tan functions in C++

tip

As you may remember from your math courses, one radian is equal to 180 / pi degrees, and one degree is equal to pi / 180 radians.

The `angleCos = cos(60 * 3.141593 / 180);` statement shown in Figure 5-6 first converts 60 degrees into radians by multiplying 60 by pi and then dividing the result by 180. This calculation results in approximately 1.05 radians. The statement then calculates the cosine of an angle that is 1.05 radians and assigns the result (.5) to the `angleCos` variable.

The second statement shown in Figure 5-6, `cout << sin(1.57);`, calculates the sine of an angle that is 1.57 radians, and displays the result (1) on the screen. The third example shown in the figure, `cout << tan(31 * 3.141593 / 180);`, converts 31 degrees into radians, and then finds the tangent of the angle. The statement displays the result (.6) on the screen.

Like the exponential functions, the trigonometric functions are defined in the cmath library file in C++. Every C++ program that uses a trigonometric function must include the `#include <cmath>` directive.

In addition to the mathematical functions, most programming languages also provide functions that you can use to generate random numbers.

Mini-Quiz 1

1. Write the C++ statement that raises the number 3 to the fifth power, and then stores the result in an int variable named answer.

2. Write the C++ statement that displays the square root of 25 on the screen.

3. Write the C++ statement that cubes the square root of 16, and then displays the result on the screen.

4. Write the C++ statement that squares the value stored in the number variable, and then displays the result on the screen.

5. Write the C++ statement that displays the cosine of a 15 degree angle.

6. Write the C++ statement that displays the tangent of an angle that is 1.3 radians.

Generating Random Numbers

Many programs require the use of random numbers. Lotto programs, backgammon programs, and programs used to practice elementary math skills are just a few examples of programs that utilize random numbers. Most programming languages have a built-in function for generating random numbers; the function is referred to as the **random number generator**. In C++, the random number generator is the rand function. In Java it is the random function, and in Visual Basic it is the Rnd function. The random number generator is a value-returning function in C++, Java, and Visual Basic. The range of numbers returned by the random number generator is language-dependent. In C++, the rand function returns a positive integer that is greater than or equal to zero, but less than or equal to RAND_MAX, a constant defined in the C++ cstdlib library file. Although the value of RAND_MAX varies with different systems, its value is always at least 32767. Unlike the random number generator in C++, the random number generator in Java and Visual Basic returns a positive number that is greater than or equal to zero, but less than 1.

In some programming languages—for example, C++ and Visual Basic—you must initialize (assign a beginning value to) the random number generator in each program in which it is used; this typically is done at the beginning of the program. If you do not initialize the random number generator, the same series of numbers will be generated each time the program is executed. This repetition occurs because the random number generators in C++ and Visual Basic do not generate true random numbers; rather, they generate pseudorandom numbers based on a mathematical formula included in the random number generator's code. In C++, you use the built-in srand function to initialize the random number generator; in Visual Basic, you use the Randomize statement. The C++ srand function is a void function, because it does not return a value.

Figure 5-7 shows the functions and statement you use to initialize the random number generator and generate random numbers in C++, Java, and Visual Basic.

tip

▶ If you want to view the value of RAND_MAX on your computer system, complete Discovery Exercise 11 at the end of this lesson.

tip

▶ You do not need to initialize the random number generator in Java.

Purpose	C++ syntax	Java syntax	Visual Basic syntax
Initialize random number generator	**srand(*seed*)**	No initialization is necessary	**Randomize**
Generate random number	**rand()**	**random()**	**Rnd**

Figure 5-7: Syntax of the random number functions and statement in C++, Java, and Visual Basic

As Figure 5-7 shows, the syntax of the C++ `srand` function is **srand**(*seed*), where *seed* is a number that represents the starting point for the `rand` function—the random number generator in C++. The `srand` and `rand` functions are defined in the C++ cstdlib library file. To use these functions, a program must contain the `#include <cstdlib>` directive.

When generating random numbers in a C++ program, most programmers use the built-in `time` function as the *seed* value in the `srand` function. The `time` function, which is defined in the ctime library file, is a value-returning function that returns the number of seconds that have elapsed since midnight of January 1, 1970, according to your computer system's clock. This ensures that the random number generator always is initialized with a unique number. The syntax for using the `time` function as the *seed* for the `srand` function is **srand**(**time**(NULL));. NULL, a constant defined in both the cstdlib and ctime library files, has a value of 0 (zero), and it tells the `time` function to simply return its value, but not store the value anywhere in memory.

Recall that the C++ `rand` function returns a positive integer that is greater than or equal to zero, but less than or equal to RAND_MAX. In most programs that use random numbers, you will need to generate numbers within a more specific range—for example, numbers from 1 through 10 only, or numbers from 10 through 100. You can use the formula *lowerbound* + **rand**() **%** (*upperbound - lowerbound* **+ 1**) to specify the range of numbers you want the program to generate. In the formula, *lowerbound* is the lowest number in the range, and *upperbound* is the highest number in the range. Figure 5-8 shows the syntax of this formula and two C++ statements that use the formula to generate random integers.

Formula: *lowerbound* + **rand()** **%** (*upperbound – lowerbound* **+ 1**)	
Examples	**Result**
`cout << 1 + rand() % (10 — 1 + 1);`	displays a random integer from 1 through 10 on the screen
`num = 10 + rand() % (100 — 10 + 1);`	assigns a random integer from 10 through 100 to the `num` variable
Note: The examples assume that the random number generator was initialized using `srand(time(NULL))`.	

Figure 5-8: Syntax and two examples of the random number formula in C++

Recall from Tutorial 4 that % is the modulus arithmetic operator, which is used to divide two integers and results in the remainder of the division.

You can use the first statement shown in Figure 5-8, `cout << 1 + rand() % (10 — 1 + 1);`, to display a random integer from 1 through 10 on the screen. Before displaying the random integer, the computer first evaluates the expression within parentheses; in this case, the `10 — 1 + 1` expression evaluates to 10. The computer then finds the remainder after dividing the random number (generated by the `rand` function) by 10. If the `rand` function generated the number 7, for instance, the remainder after performing the division would be 7. Finally, the computer adds the number 1 to the remainder (7), and displays the result (8) on the screen. Figure 5-9 shows the results of the `cout << 1 + rand() % (10 — 1 + 1);` statement using sample values produced by the `rand` function.

rand function value	Statement containing rand function value	Result
7	`cout << 1 + 7 % (10 — 1 + 1);` Evaluation of random number formula: Step 1: 1 + 7 % 10 Step 2: 1 + 7 Step 3: 8	displays the number 8 on the screen
323	`cout << 1 + 323 % (10 — 1 + 1);` Evaluation of random number formula: Step 1: 1 + 323 % 10 Step 2: 1 + 3 Step 3: 4	displays the number 4 on the screen
30000	`cout << 1 + 30000 % (10 — 1 + 1);` Evaluation of random number formula: Step 1: 1 + 30,000 % 10 Step 2: 1 + 0 Step 3: 1	displays the number 1 on the screen

Figure 5-9: Results of the `cout << 1 + rand() % (10 — 1 + 1);` statement using sample rand function values (continued)

You can use the second statement shown in Figure 5-8, `num = 10 + rand() % (100 — 10 + 1);`, to assign a random integer from 10 through 100 to the num variable. Before assigning the random integer, the computer first evaluates the expression within parentheses; in this case, the `100 — 10 + 1` expression evaluates to 91. The computer then finds the remainder after dividing the random number (generated by the `rand` function) by 91. If the `rand` function generated the number 352, for instance, the remainder after performing the division would be 79. Finally, the computer adds the number 10 to the remainder (79), and assigns the result (89) to the num variable. Figure 5-10 shows the results of the `num = 10 + rand() % (100 — 10 + 1);` statement using sample values produced by the rand function.

rand function value	Statement containing rand function value	Result
352	num = 10 + 352 % (100 − 10 + 1); Step 1: 10 + 352 % 91 Step 2: 10 + 79 Step 3: 89	assigns the number 89 to the num variable
4	num = 10 + 4 % (100 − 10 + 1); Step 1: 10 + 4 % 91 Step 2: 10 + 4 Step 3: 14	assigns the number 14 to the num variable
2500	num = 10 + 2500 % (100 − 10 + 1); Step 1: 10 + 2500 % 91 Step 2: 10 + 43 Step 3: 53	assigns the number 53 to the num variable

Figure 5-10: Results of the num = 10 + rand() % (100 − 10 + 1); statement using sample rand function values

mini-quiz

Mini-Quiz 2

1. Write the statement that programmers use to initialize the random number generator in C++.

2. Write the C++ formula that will generate integers in the range 1 through 25.

3. Write the C++ formula that will generate integers in the range 100 through 500.

4. If the rand function returns the number 12, what will the statement cout << 3 + rand() % (15 − 3 + 1); display on the screen?

You now have completed Tutorial 5's Concept lesson. You can either take a break or complete the end-of-lesson questions and exercises before moving on to the Application lesson.

SUMMARY

A function is a block of code that performs a task. Some functions require you to enter information, called actual arguments, between the parentheses following the function's name; others, like main, do not.

Programmers can include two different types of functions in a program: program-defined functions and built-in functions. A program-defined function is a function whose task is determined by the programmer and defined within the program in which the function is used. A built-in function, on the other hand, is a function whose task is predefined, and whose code is contained in a library file that comes with the language compiler and resides on your computer's hard disk. To use a built-in function in a program, you must call, or invoke, it by including its name and actual arguments (if any) in a statement. You also must include the appropriate library file in the program.

Built-in functions can be value-returning functions or void functions. A value-returning function returns a value after completing its assigned task. A void function, on the other hand, does not return a value.

Most programming languages include a set of built-in functions for performing common mathematical tasks. The power function, for example, raises a number to a power, and then returns the result. The square root function, on the other hand, returns the square root of a number. The cosine, sine, and tangent functions, referred to as the trigonometric functions, can be used to calculate the cosine, sine, and tangent of *x*, where *x* is an angle expressed in radians. In C++, the power (**pow**), square root (**sqrt**), cosine (**cos**), sine (**sin**), and tangent (**tan**) functions are defined in the cmath library file.

The built-in function used to generate random numbers is referred to as the random number generator. The **rand** function, which is defined in the cstdlib library file, is the random number generator in C++.

In some programming languages, you must initialize the random number generator in each program in which it is used; otherwise, the same series of numbers will be generated each time the program is executed. In C++, you use the statement **srand(time(NULL));** to initialize the random number generator. Like the **rand** function, the **srand** function is defined in the cstdlib library. The **time** function, on the other hand, is defined in the ctime library. The **NULL** constant is defined in both the cstdlib and ctime libraries.

You can use the formula *lowerbound* **+ rand**() **%** (*upperbound* - *lowerbound* **+ 1**) to specify the range of integers you want to generate in a program. In the formula, *lowerbound* is the lowest number in the range, and *upperbound* is the highest number in the range.

ANSWERS TO MINI-QUIZZES

Mini-Quiz 1

1. `answer = pow(3, 5);`
2. `cout << sqrt(25);`
3. `cout << pow(sqrt(16), 3);`
4. `cout << pow(number, 2);`
5. `cout << cos(15 * 3.141593 / 180);`
6. `cout << tan(1.3);`

Mini-Quiz 2

1. `srand(time(NULL));`
2. `1 + rand() % (25 − 1 + 1)`
3. `100 + rand() % (500 − 100 + 1)`
4. `15`

QUESTIONS

1. The items that appear between the parentheses following a function's name are called _____.

   a. actual arguments
   b. formal arguments
   c. passed arguments
   d. sent arguments

2. To use one of the mathematical functions built into C++, you must include the _____ directive in your program.
   a. #include <calculation>
   b. #include <compute>
   c. #include <cmath>
   d. #include <mathematical>

3. Which of the following C++ functions is equivalent to the mathematical expression 5^3?
   a. cube(5)
   b. pow(3, 5)
   c. pow(5, 3)
   d. sqrt(5, 3)

4. Which of the following C++ functions returns the square root of 100?
   a. pow(100, 2)
   b. sqroot(100)
   c. sqrt(100, 2)
   d. sqrt(100)

5. Which of the following C++ statements displays the sine of a 55 degree angle?
   a. cout << sin(55 * 3.141593 / 180);
   b. cout << sin(55 / 3.141593 * 180);
   c. cout << sine(55 * 3.141593 / 180);
   d. cout << sin(55);

6. The random number generator in C++ is the _____ function.
   a. rand
   b. random
   c. rnd
   d. srand

7. Which of the following C++ statements displays a random number in the range 3 through 9?
   a. 1 + rand() % (9 − 3 + 1)
   b. 3 + rand() % (9 − 3 + 1)
   c. 3 + rand() % (9 + 3 − 1)
   d. 9 + rand() % (9 + 1 − 3)

8. In C++, you use the _____ statement to initialize the random number generator.
   a. init(time(NULL));
   b. rand(time(NULL));
   c. srand(time(NULL));
   d. srand(time(null));

EXERCISES

1. Write the C++ statement that adds the square of the number stored in the num1 variable to the square of the number stored in the num2 variable, and assigns the result to the total variable.

2. Write the C++ statement that displays the square root of the number contained in the number variable.

3. Write the C++ statement that displays the square root of the sum of $num1^2$ and $num2^2$.

4. Write the C++ statement that assigns to the `answer` variable the result of the following formula: $x^2 * y^3$.

5. Write the C++ statement that assigns to the `rate` variable the result of the following formula: $(future / present)^{1\text{-}term} - 1$.

6. Write the C++ statement that displays the tangent of a 25 degree angle.

7. Write the C++ statement that displays the cosine of an angle that is .9 radians.

8. Write the C++ statement that displays a random number in the range 50 through 100.

Exercises 9 through 11 are Discovery Exercises. Discovery Exercises, which may include topics that are not covered in this lesson, allow you to "discover" the solutions to problems on your own.

9. Included in the cmath library in C++ is the definition of the absolute value function, which calculates and returns the absolute value of a number. The function's syntax is **abs**(*number*). Write the C++ statement that displays the absolute value of the number stored in the `difference` variable.

10. Included in the cmath library in C++ are the definitions of the logarithm and logarithm10 functions. The logarithm function, whose syntax is **log**(*number*), calculates the natural logarithm of a number. The logarithm10 function, whose syntax is **log10**(*number*), calculates the base 10 logarithm of a number. Write the C++ statement that displays the natural logarithm and the base 10 logarithm of the number 100.

11. In this exercise, you will learn more about the RAND_MAX constant.
    a. Open the T5ConE11.cpp file contained in the Cpp\Tut05\T5ConE11 folder on your computer's hard disk.
    b. The program should display the value of the RAND_MAX constant, which is defined in the cstdlib library. Complete the program appropriately.
    c. Save, build, and execute the program. What is the value of RAND_MAX on your system?
    d. Hide the Output window, then use the File menu to close the workspace.

A computer program is good only if it works. Errors in either an algorithm or programming code can cause the program to run incorrectly. Therefore, a programmer needs to know how to locate and fix these errors. Exercises 12 and 13 are Debugging Exercises. Debugging Exercises allow you to practice recognizing and solving errors in a program.

12. In this exercise, you will debug an existing C++ program.
    a. Open the T5ConE12.cpp file contained in the Cpp\Tut05\T5ConE12 folder on your computer's hard disk. The program should display a random number in the range 200 through 500, but it is not working correctly. Study the program's code, then build and execute the program.
    b. Correct any errors in the program, then save, build, and execute the program. When the program is working correctly, hide the Output window, then use the File menu to close the workspace.

13. In this exercise, you will debug an existing C++ program.
    a. Open the T5ConE13.cpp file contained in the Cpp\Tut05\T5ConE13 folder on your computer's hard disk. The program should display three random numbers in the range 1 through 10. Study the program's code, then build and execute the program. Note the three numbers displayed on the screen.
    b. Execute the program again. Why does the program display the same three random numbers? Correct this error in the program, then save, build, and execute the program again. When the program is working correctly, hide the Output window, then use the File menu to close the workspace.

Application Lesson

Using Built-In Functions in a C++ Program

case ▶ David Liu is in the market for a new car; however, he is not sure how much money he can spend on it. David will need to finance all but $2000 of the car price. He would like to pay off the car loan in four years, but the most he can afford to pay each month is $360. Currently, interest rates are in the range of 6% to 8%. He has asked you to create a program that he can use to compute the largest amount he can borrow using these constraints.

Analyzing, Planning, and Desk-Checking the Present Value Algorithm

You need to calculate the present value of a loan, referred to as the **principal**, for David. The formula to calculate the principal based on a series of periodic payments is *payment* * $(1 - (rate + 1)^{-term})$ / *rate*, where *payment* is the periodic payment (usually expressed in whole dollars), *rate* is the periodic interest rate, and *term* is the number of periodic payments. Figure 5-11 shows two examples of using the present value formula to calculate the loan principal.

Present value formula: *payment* * $(1 - (rate + 1)^{-term})$ / *rate*

Note: When you apply for a loan, the lender typically will quote you an annual interest rate, and the term will be expressed in years.

Example 1 – calculate the present value of a series of annual payments of $2000 for 4 years at 5% interest

Annual payment: 2000
Annual rate: .05
Term (years):   4
Formula: $2000 * (1 - (.05 + 1)^{-4}) / .05$
Present value (principal) rounded to the nearest whole dollar: $7092

Figure 5-11: Present value formula and examples

> **Example 2** – calculate the present value of a series of monthly payments of $250 for 5 years at 6% interest
>
> Monthly payment: 250
> Monthly rate: .005 (annual rate of .06 divided by 12)
> Term (months): 60 (5 years multiplied by 12)
> Formula: $250 * (1 - (.005 + 1)^{-60}) / .005$
> Present value (principal) rounded to the nearest whole dollar: $12,931

Figure 5-11: Present value formula and examples (continued)

Example 1 uses the present value formula to calculate the present value of a series of annual payments of $2000 for four years at 5 percent interest; the present value (principal) rounded to the nearest whole dollar is $7092. In other words, if you borrow $7092 for four years at 5 percent interest, you would need to make four annual payments of $2000 to pay off the loan.

Example 2 uses the present value formula to calculate the present value of a series of monthly payments of $250 for five years at 6 percent interest; in this case, the present value (principal) rounded to the nearest whole dollar is $12,931. The $12,931 represents the most you can borrow assuming a $250 monthly payment on a five-year loan at 6% interest. Notice that, before you can calculate the present value of a series of monthly payments, you need to convert the annual interest rate to a monthly interest rate by dividing the annual rate by 12. You also need to convert the term, which is expressed in years, to months by multiplying the number of years by 12.

You will use the present value formula to calculate the largest amount David Liu can borrow. Recall that David wants to pay off the loan in four years (48 months), and he doesn't want his monthly payment to exceed $360. Figure 5-12 shows the IPO chart for the David Liu problem.

Input	Processing	Output
payment (360 per month) term (48 months) rate (annual)	Processing items: none Algorithm: 1. enter the rate 2. convert the rate to a monthly rate by dividing the rate by 12 3. calculate the principal using the present value formula: payment $*(1 - (rate + 1)^{-term}) / rate$ 4. display the principal	principal

Figure 5-12: IPO chart for the David Liu problem

As Figure 5-12 indicates, the output is the principal, which is the present value of the loan. To display the output, the program needs to know the periodic payment, term, and rate. In this case, only the rate and principal will vary each time the program is executed. The periodic payment and term will remain constant at $360 per month and 48 months, respectively.

According to the algorithm, the program first will have the user enter the annual interest rate. The program then will convert the annual rate to a monthly rate by dividing the annual rate by 12. After making this conversion, the program will use the present value formula to calculate the principal, displaying the result on the screen.

Recall that you should desk-check the algorithm several times before you begin coding it. In this case, you will use the following two sets of data to desk-check the algorithm shown in Figure 5-12:

Data for first desk-check		Data for second desk-check	
Payment:	360	Payment:	360
Rate:	.06	Rate:	.08
Term:	48 months	Term:	48 months

Figure 5-13 shows the completed desk-check table, with the principal amounts rounded to the nearest whole dollar.

payment	term	rate	principal
~~360~~	~~48~~	~~.06~~	~~15329~~
360	48	.08	14746

Figure 5-13: Completed desk-check table for the algorithm

After desk-checking the algorithm to verify its accuracy, you are ready to translate it into a language the computer can understand.

Coding the Present Value Algorithm

The first step in the coding process is to determine how many memory locations the program requires. You need to reserve (declare) a memory location—either a variable or a named constant—for each unique input, processing, and output item listed in the problem's IPO chart. In this case, you will store the values of the rate and principal items in variables, because the values of those items probably will be different each time the program is executed. However, you will store the payment and term values in named constants, because those values ($360 and 48, respectively) will not change. You will use the `float` data type for the two variables, as these memory locations will need to store numbers containing a decimal place. You will use the `int` data type for the two named constants, which will need to store integers only. Figure 5-14 shows the C++ statements that you will use to reserve the variables and named constants in the David Liu program.

IPO chart information	C++ instructions
Input	
payment	`const int PAYMENT = 360;`
term	`const int TERM = 48;`
rate	`float rate = 0.0;`
Processing	
none	
Output	
principal	`float principal = 0.0;`

Figure 5-14: C++ statements to reserve variables and named constants

Now you can begin translating the algorithm into C++ statements. The first two steps in the algorithm are to enter the annual rate, and then convert the annual rate to a monthly rate. You can use the statement `cout << "Enter the annual interest rate: ";` to prompt the user to enter the rate, and you can use the statement `cin >> rate;` to get the rate from the user. You can use the assignment statement `rate = rate / 12;` to convert the annual rate to a monthly rate, as shown in Figure 5-15.

IPO chart information	C++ instructions

Input
  payment
  term
  rate
	`const int PAYMENT = 360;`
	`const int TERM = 48;`
	`float rate = 0.0;`

Processing none	
Output principal	`float principal = 0.0;`
Algorithm 1. enter the rate	`cout << "Enter the annual interest rate: ";` `cin >> rate;`
2. convert the rate to a monthly rate by dividing the rate by 12	`rate = rate / 12;`

Figure 5-15: C++ statements corresponding to the first two steps in the algorithm

The third step in the algorithm is to calculate the principal and assign the result to the `principal` variable. Recall that you will need to use the present value formula—$payment * (1 - (rate + 1)^{-term}) / rate$—to calculate the principal. Before you can use this formula in a C++ statement, you will need to replace the $(rate + 1)^{-term}$ portion, which raises $(rate + 1)$ to the $-term$ power, with the C++ **pow** function. As you learned in the Concept lesson, the syntax of the pow function is **pow**(x, y), where x is the number you want raised to the yth power. In this case, x will be `rate + 1`, and y will be `-TERM`. Figure 5-16 shows how you convert the present value formula into an arithmetic expression that can be used in a C++ statement.

Present value formula:	$payment * (1 - (rate + 1)^{-term}) / rate$
C++ expression:	`PAYMENT * (1 - pow(rate + 1, -TERM)) / rate`

Figure 5-16: Present value formula converted to a C++ expression

In the current program, you will use the assignment statement `principal = PAYMENT * (1 - pow(rate + 1, -TERM))/rate;` to assign the present value to the `principal` variable.

The last step in the algorithm is to display the principal on the screen. You can use the statement `cout << "You can borrow up to $" << principal << endl;` to do so. Figure 5-17 shows the C++ instructions for the David Liu program.

IPO chart information	C++ instructions

Input
  payment
  term
  rate
	`const int PAYMENT = 360;`
	`const int TERM = 48;`
	`float rate = 0.0;`

Processing none	
Output principal	`float principal = 0.0;`
Algorithm 1. enter the rate	`cout << "Enter the annual interest rate: ";` `cin >> rate;`

2. convert the rate to a
   monthly rate by
   dividing the rate by 12
	`rate = rate / 12;`

3. calculate the principal
   using the formula:
   payment * (1 −
   (rate + 1)$^{-term}$) / rate
	`principal = PAYMENT * (1 — pow(rate + 1,`
	`—TERM)) / rate;`

4. display the principal	`cout << "You can borrow up to $" <<` `principal << endl;`

Figure 5-17: C++ instructions for the David Liu program

After coding the algorithm, you then need to desk-check the program, using the same data you used to desk-check the algorithm. Figure 5-18 shows the data and the completed desk-check table for the program. The principal amounts in the figure are rounded to the nearest whole dollar.

Data for first desk-check Payment: 360 Rate: .06 Term: 48		Data for second desk-check Payment: 360 Rate: .08 Term: 48	
Desk-check table			
PAYMENT	TERM	rate	principal
~~360~~ 360	~~48~~ 48	~~0.0~~ ~~0.6~~ ~~0.0~~ .08	~~0.0~~ ~~15329~~ ~~0.0~~ 14746

Figure 5-18: Data and completed desk-check table for the program

The results obtained when desk-checking the program agree with the results obtained when desk-checking the algorithm. You now are ready to enter the C++ instructions into the computer.

Completing the David Liu Program

Your computer's hard disk contains a partially completed C++ program containing most of the instructions shown in Figure 5-17. Open that program now.

To open the partially completed C++ program:

1 Start Visual C++. Open the **T5App.cpp** file contained in the Cpp\Tut05\T5App folder on your computer's hard disk.

2 If necessary, click the **Maximize** button ▢ on the T5App.cpp window's title bar to maximize the window. The partially completed program appears in the T5App.cpp window, as shown in Figure 5-19.

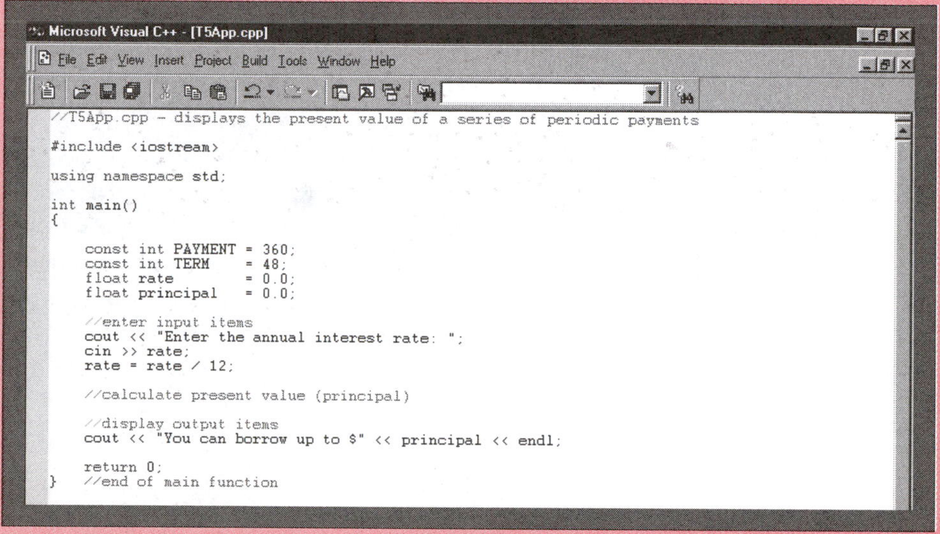

```
//T5App.cpp - displays the present value of a series of periodic payments

#include <iostream>

using namespace std;

int main()
{
    const int PAYMENT = 360;
    const int TERM    = 48;
    float rate        = 0.0;
    float principal   = 0.0;

    //enter input items
    cout << "Enter the annual interest rate: ";
    cin >> rate;
    rate = rate / 12;

    //calculate present value (principal)

    //display output items
    cout << "You can borrow up to $" << principal << endl;

    return 0;
}   //end of main function
```

Figure 5-19: Partially completed program shown in the maximized T5App.cpp window

Recall that the pow function, which is used in the C++ statement that calculates the principal, is defined in the cmath library file, so you will need to include the `#include <cmath>` directive in the program. Currently, the `#include <cmath>` directive and the statement to calculate the principal are missing from the program. You will enter the missing instructions in the next set of steps, and then you will test the program to verify that it is working correctly.

To complete the David Liu program, then test the program:

1 Position the insertion point in the blank line below the `#include <iostream>` directive. Type **#include <cmath>** and press the **Enter** key.

2 Position the insertion point in the blank line below the `//calculate present value (principal)` comment. Press the **Tab** key, if necessary, then type **principal = PAYMENT * (1 − pow(rate + 1, -TERM)) / rate;** (be sure to type the minus sign before the TERM constant) and press the **Enter** key.

3 Save, build, and execute the program.

4 When you are prompted for the annual interest rate, type **.06** and press the **Enter** key. The program calculates and displays the principal, as shown in Figure 5-20.

Figure 5-20: DOS window showing results of first test

The DOS window shows that the principal is $15328.9, rather than 15329 as shown in the desk-check tables. However, recall that the desk-check tables display the principal amounts rounded to the nearest integer; 15328.9 rounded to the nearest integer is 15329, so the program's output agrees with the amount shown in the desk-check tables. You will learn how to display numeric output rounded to the nearest integer in the next section.

Recall that you should test a program several times with different data. In this case, you will test it once more using an interest rate of 8 percent.

5 Press the **Enter** key to close the DOS window.

6 Execute the program again. Type **.08** as the annual interest rate and press the **Enter** key. The DOS window shows that the principal is $14746.3, which agrees with the results shown earlier in the desk-check tables. (The number 14746.3 rounded to the nearest integer is 14746—the amount shown in the desk-check tables.)

7 Press the **Enter** key to close the DOS window.

8 Hide the Output window.

Numbers representing monetary amounts typically are displayed with either no decimal places or two decimal places. You can accomplish this in a C++ program using the `fixed` stream manipulator and the `precision` function, which you will learn about in the next section.

Formatting Numeric Output

C++ displays numbers that contain a decimal point in either fixed-point or e (exponential) notation; the notation used is determined by the size of the number. Smaller numbers—those containing six or fewer digits to the left of the decimal point—usually are displayed in fixed-point notation. For example, the number 1234.56 would be displayed in fixed-point notation as 1234.56. Larger numbers—those containing more than six digits to the left of the decimal point—typically are displayed in e notation. The number 1225000.00, for example, would be displayed in e notation as 1.225e+006. Unless you are a scientist, engineer, or mathematician, you are used to viewing numbers in fixed-point notation rather than in e notation.

You can use the C++ `fixed` stream manipulator to display a program's numeric output in fixed-point notation only. To do so, you use the manipulator in a C++ statement, as follows: `cout << fixed;`. This statement tells the computer to use fixed-point notation when displaying numbers on the screen.

tip

As you learned in Tutorial 3, a stream manipulator allows the program to manipulate, or manage, the input and output stream characters in some way. You already are familiar with one of the C++ stream manipulators, endl, which advances the cursor to the next line on the computer screen.

In addition to using the fixed stream manipulator to format a C++ program's numeric output, you also must use the built-in precision function. The precision function uses the syntax **precision**(*numberOfDecimalPlaces*) to specify the number of decimal places to display in each number. The statement cout.precision(2);, for example, tells the computer to display two digits to the right of the decimal point for any number displayed on the screen. The statement cout.precision(0);, on the other hand, tells the computer to display numbers as integers. The precision function is defined in the iostream library; to use this function, a program must include the #include <iostream> directive.

The fixed stream manipulator and precision function must appear before the first cout statement that displays a number. Both settings remain in effect until the program encounters another statement that changes the setting. You will use the fixed stream manipulator and precision function in the current program to display the principal as a whole number in fixed-point notation.

To display the principal as a whole number in fixed-point notation:

1 Type the two additional statements shown in Figure 5-21.

enter these two
lines of code

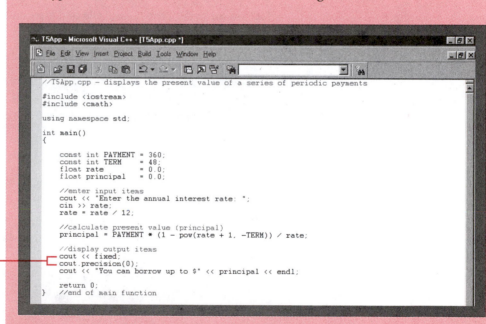

```
//T5App.cpp - displays the present value of a series of periodic payments

#include <iostream>
#include <cmath>

using namespace std;

int main()
{
    const int PAYMENT = 360;
    const int TERM    = 48;
    float rate        = 0.0;
    float principal   = 0.0;

    //enter input items
    cout << "Enter the annual interest rate: ";
    cin >> rate;
    rate = rate / 12;

    //calculate present value (principal)
    principal = PAYMENT * (1 - pow(rate + 1, -TERM)) / rate;

    //display output items
    cout << fixed;
    cout.precision(0);
    cout << "You can borrow up to $" << principal << endl;

    return 0;
}   //end of main function
```

Figure 5-21: Formatting statements shown in the program

2 Save, build, and execute the program.

3 When you are prompted for the annual interest rate, type **.06** and press the **Enter** key. The DOS window shows that the principal is $15329.

4 Press the **Enter** key to close the DOS window.

5 Execute the program again. Type **.08** as the annual interest rate and press the **Enter** key. The DOS window shows that the principal is $14746.

6 Press the **Enter** key to close the DOS window.

7 Hide the Output window.

tip

The cout.precision(0); function rounds up to the nearest integer if the number after the decimal point is 5 or more; otherwise, it simply truncates the decimal portion of the number. This explains why 15328.9 is rounded up to 15329, and 14746.3 is truncated to 14746.

Many times, you will need to print a program's output in addition to (or instead of) displaying it on the screen. You can print the output by first sending it to a file on a disk, and then using the C++ editor to open the file and print its contents.

Sending Program Output to a File

In addition to sending a program's output to the screen, you also can send the output to a file on a disk—a process referred to as "writing to the file." The file to which the output is written is called an **output file**. In this lesson, you will learn only the basics of creating an output file and writing data to it. You will learn much more about files in Tutorial 13.

Figure 5-22 shows the steps you must follow to create an output file and write data to it.

---

1. Enter the `#include <fstream>` directive in the program.

2. Create an object that represents the output file in the program.

3. Open (or create) the output file and associate it with the output file object created in Step 2.

4. Write the program's output to the output file.

5. Close the output file.

Figure 5-22: Steps for creating an output file and writing data to it

To begin entering the code to send the current program's output to a file:

1 Position the insertion point in the blank line below the `#include <cmath>` directive.

Step 1 in Figure 5-22 is to enter the `#include <fstream>` directive in the program. This directive gives the program access to the code contained in the fstream library file.

2 Type **#include <fstream>** and press the **Enter** key.

The fstream library file contains code that allows you to accomplish Step 2 in Figure 5-22, which is to create an object that represents the output file in the program. As you may remember from the Overview, programs written in an object-oriented language can contain objects that represent something encountered in real life—such as a timecard, a date, or, in this case, a file on a disk. You create the output file object using the syntax **ofstream** *objectName*;, where *objectName* is the name you want assigned to the object. In the current program, you will assign the name `outFile` to the output file object.

3 Position the insertion point in the blank line below the `float principal = 0.0;` statement. Press the **Tab** key, if necessary, then type **ofstream outFile;** and press the **Enter** key.

► You will learn more about objects in Tutorial 13.

► The *of* in `ofstream` stands for *output file*.

If the *filename* argument in the open function does not include a path, the computer will open the output file in the same folder as the program file. In the David Liu program, for example, the open function will open and store the T5App.dat output file in the Cpp\Tut05\T5App folder on your computer's hard disk, assuming that is the location of the T5App.cpp program file. You can change the output file's location by including a path in the *filename* argument. For example, to open the Loan.dat file contained in the Data folder on the A drive, you use "a:\Data\Loan.dat" as the *filename* in the open function.

The open function is one of the built-in functions defined in the fstream library file.

The .dat extension on a filename stands for *data*.

Step 3 in Figure 5-22 is to open an output file and associate it with the object created in Step 2. You do so using the open function in the following syntax: *objectName*.**open**(*filename* [, *mode*]);. In the syntax, *objectName* is the name of the output file object, and *filename*, which must be enclosed in quotation marks, is the name of the output file you want to open (or create) on the computer's hard disk. The *mode* argument, which is optional in the open function's syntax, tells the computer how the file is to be opened. You can open an output file for either output or append. When you open a file for output, the computer creates a new, empty file to which data can be written. If the file already exists, its contents are erased before any data is written to the file. You can open a file for output by using `ios::out` as the *mode* in the open function, or by simply omitting the *mode* argument. In other words, the two statements `outfile.open("T5App.dat", ios::out);` and `outfile.open("T5App.dat");` are equivalent and will produce the same result.

Many times, rather than writing a program's output to a new file, you just want to add the output to the end of an existing file. In those cases, you will need to open the output file for append rather than for output. You can do so using `ios::app` as the *mode* argument in the open function. The statement `outFile.open("T5App.dat", ios::app);`, for example, tells the computer to open the T5App.dat file for append. Any data the program sends to the T5App.dat file will be added to the end of the file. If a file opened for append does not exist, the computer creates the file before writing any data to it.

In the current program, you will open an output file named T5App.dat for output.

To complete the T5App.cpp program:

1 In the blank line below the `ofstream outFile;` statement, type **outFile.open("T5App.dat");** and press the **Enter** key.

Step 4 in Figure 5-22 is to write the program's output—in this case, the principal—to the output file. Before doing so, you will use the `fixed` stream manipulator and `precision` function to format the principal as a whole number in fixed-point notation.

2 Position the insertion point in the blank line below the `cout << "You can borrow up to $" << principal << endl;` statement. Press the **Tab** key, if necessary, then type **outFile << fixed;** and press the **Enter** key. This statement tells the computer that numbers written to the output file should be written in fixed-point notation.

3 Type **outFile.precision(0);** and press the **Enter** key. This statement tells the computer that numbers written to the output file should be written as integers.

4 Type **outFile << "You can borrow up to $" << principal << endl;** and press the **Enter** key.

Notice that the three statements you just entered are identical to the ones found immediately above them, except `cout` was replaced with `outFile`. The `cout` in the statements tells the computer to format and send the output to the screen, and the `outFile` tells the computer to format and send the output to the file associated with the file object.

▶ Recall that the open function opens the output file and associates it with the file object named *objectName*.

▶ The close function is one of the built-in functions defined in the fstream library file.

The last step shown in Figure 5-22 is to close the output file, which you can do using the close function. The syntax of the close function is *objectName*.**close**();, where *objectName* is the name of the file object. Notice that unlike the open function, the close function does not require a *filename* within the parentheses. This is because the computer automatically closes the file associated with the file object specified in *objectName*. In the current program, you will use the statement outFile.close(); to close the T5App.dat file, which is the file associated with the outFile file object.

5 Type the additional line of code shown in Figure 5-23, which shows the completed T5App.cpp program.

enter this line of code

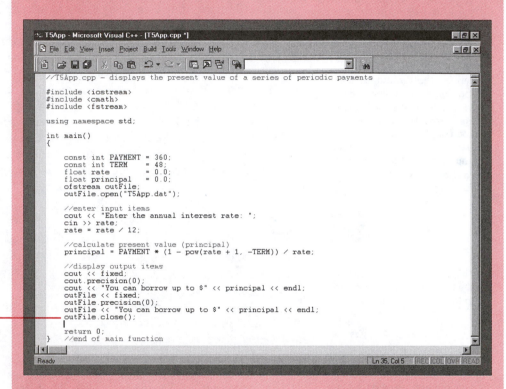

```
//T5App.cpp - displays the present value of a series of periodic payments

#include <iostream>
#include <cmath>
#include <fstream>

using namespace std;

int main()
{
    const int PAYMENT = 360;
    const int TERM    = 48;
    float rate        = 0.0;
    float principal   = 0.0;
    ofstream outFile;
    outFile.open("T5App.dat");

    //enter input items
    cout << "Enter the annual interest rate: ";
    cin >> rate;
    rate = rate / 12;

    //calculate present value (principal)
    principal = PAYMENT * (1 - pow(rate + 1, -TERM)) / rate;

    //display output items
    cout << fixed;
    cout.precision(0);
    cout << "You can borrow up to $" << principal << endl;
    outFile << fixed;
    outFile.precision(0);
    outFile << "You can borrow up to $" << principal << endl;
    outFile.close();

    return 0;
}   //end of main function
```

Figure 5-23: Completed T5App.cpp program

6 Verify the accuracy of your code by comparing the code on your screen to the code shown in Figure 5-23.

7 Save, build, and execute the program. Type **.08** as the annual interest rate and then press the **Enter** key. The program displays the principal ($14746) in a DOS window. It also creates and opens the T5App.dat output file on your computer's hard disk and then writes the principal amount to the file.

8 Press the **Enter** key to close the DOS window.

9 Hide the Output window.

Next, you will verify that the principal amount was written to the T5App.dat output file by opening the file in the C++ editor. You also will print the contents of the file.

To open the T5App.dat file and print its contents:

1 Click **File** on the menu bar, then click **Open**. The Open dialog box appears. Click the **Files of type list arrow**, then click **All Files (*.*)**, which appears at the bottom of the list. Click **T5App.dat** in the list of filenames, then click the **Open** button. The T5App.dat file appears in the T5App window, as shown in Figure 5-24.

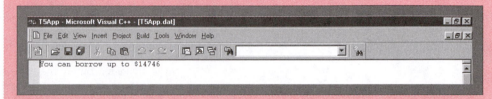

Figure 5-24: T5App window showing the contents of the T5App.dat output file

2 If your computer is connected to a printer, click **File** on the menu bar, then click **Print**, and then click the **OK** button.

3 Use the File menu to close the workspace. When prompted to close all document windows, click the **Yes** button.

4 Exit Visual C++.

You now have completed Tutorial 5's Application lesson. You can either take a break or complete the end-of-lesson exercises.

EXERCISES

1. In this exercise, you will modify the program you created in this lesson so that it also allows the user to enter the monthly payment and term (in years).
   a. Open the T5AppE01.cpp file contained in the Cpp\Tut05\T5AppE01 folder on your computer's hard disk.
   b. Modify the program appropriately, then save, build, and execute the program. Use the program to calculate the largest amount of money that can be borrowed (principal) assuming a monthly payment of $360, a four-year loan, and a 6% annual interest rate. The principal should be $15329.
   c. Execute the program again. What is the largest amount of money that can be borrowed (principal) assuming a monthly payment of $400, a three-year loan, and a 10% annual interest rate?
   d. When the program is working correctly, close the Output window, then use the File menu to close the workspace.

2. Assume you plan to deposit $2000 into your savings account at the end of each year for the next 20 years. Your bank is paying 10% interest, compounded annually and paid on the last day of each year. You want to create a program that will compute the value of your account in 20 years. You will need to use the future value formula in the program. The future value formula is $(payment * ((1 + rate)^{term} - 1)) / rate$, where *payment* is the periodic payment, *rate* is the periodic interest rate, and *term* is the number of periodic payments.
   a. Create a console application. Name the project workspace T5AppE02, and save it in the Cpp\Tut05 folder on your computer's hard disk. Add a new C++ source file to the project. Name the source file T5AppE02.

b. Enter the appropriate C++ instructions into the source file. Allow the user to enter the periodic payment, interest rate, and term (in years). Display the program output on the screen, and also save it to a file named T5AppE02.dat. The future value should be displayed as an integer in fixed-point notation.

c. Save, build, and execute the program. Use the program to calculate the future value of $2000 deposited at the end of each year for 20 years at a 10% interest rate. The future value should be $114,500.

d. Execute the program again. What is the future value of $5000 deposited at the end of each year for 10 years at a 6% interest rate?

e. When the program is working correctly, hide the Output window, then use the File menu to close the workspace.

3. Assume you are considering taking out a $60,000 mortgage for 25 years at an 8% interest rate. You want to create a program that will compute your monthly payment on this loan. You can use the following formula to make the appropriate calculation: *principal* * (*rate* / (1 − (*rate* + 1)^{-term})), where *principal* is the loan amount, *rate* is the monthly interest rate, and *term* is the number of monthly payments.

a. Create a console application. Name the project workspace T5AppE03, and save it in the Cpp\Tut05 folder on your computer's hard disk. Add a new C++ source file to the project. Name the source file T5AppE03.

b. Enter the appropriate C++ instructions into the source file. Allow the user to enter the principal, annual interest rate, and term (in years). Display the program output on the screen. Save the program input—the principal, term (in years), and the annual interest rate—and the program output in a file named T5AppE03.dat. The future value should be displayed and saved in fixed-point notation with two decimal places.

c. Save, build, and execute the program. Use the program to calculate the monthly payment for a $60,000 mortgage for 25 years at an 8% interest rate. The monthly payment should be $463.09.

d. Execute the program again. What is the monthly payment for a $120,000 mortgage for 30 years at a 9% interest rate?

e. When the program is working correctly, hide the Output window, then use the File menu to close the workspace.

4. In this exercise, you will create a program that calculates the sine, cosine, and tangent of an angle.

a. Create a console application. Name the project workspace T5AppE04, and save it in the Cpp\Tut05 folder on your computer's hard disk. Add a new C++ source file to the project. Name the source file T5AppE04.

b. Enter the appropriate C++ instructions into the source file. Create a named constant for the value of pi (3.141593). Allow the user to enter the angle in degrees, then calculate and display the angle's sine, cosine, and tangent. Display the output in fixed-point notation with two decimal places.

c. Save, build, and execute the program. Use the program to calculate the sine, cosine, and tangent of a 45 degree angle.

d. When the program is working correctly, hide the Output window, then use the File menu to close the workspace.

5. Assume you want to create a lottery program that generates six random numbers in the range 1 through 54.

a. Create a console application. Name the project workspace T5AppE05, and save it in the Cpp\Tut05 folder on your computer's hard disk. Add a new C++ source file to the project. Name the source file T5AppE05.

b. Enter the appropriate C++ instructions into the source file. Display the six random numbers on the screen and also save them to a file named T5AppE05.dat. Open the file so that it will append the program's output to the end of an existing file.

c. Save, build, and execute the program, which should display and save six random numbers. Execute the program again, which should display and save another six random numbers.

d. When the program is working correctly, hide the Output window, then use the File menu to close the workspace.

6. In this exercise, you will modify the program you created in this lesson so that it also calculates, displays, and saves (to the output file) the total amount paid and the total interest paid, assuming a monthly payment of $360 for four years.

    a. Open the T5AppE06.cpp file contained in the Cpp\Tut05\T5AppE06 folder on your computer's hard disk.

    b. Modify the program appropriately, then save, build, and execute the program. Enter .06 as the interest rate. What is the total amount David Liu paid for the car? How much of this amount was interest?

    c. When the program is working correctly, close the Output window, then use the File menu to close the workspace.

Exercises 7 and 8 are Discovery Exercises. Discovery Exercises, which may include topics that are not covered in this lesson, allow you to "discover" the solutions to problems on your own.

7. You have just won 1 million dollars in the lottery. You can choose either a single lump sum payment of $450,000, or 20 annual payments of $50,000. If you choose the annual payments of $50,000, you can invest the money at a rate of 10%, compounded annually. In this exercise, you will create a program that will allow you to determine which option is worth more in present dollars—the lump sum payment or the annuity.

    a. Create a console application. Name the project workspace T5AppE07, and save it in the Cpp\Tut05 folder on your computer's hard disk. Add a new C++ source file to the project. Name the source file T5AppE07.

    b. Enter the appropriate C++ instructions into the source file. (*Hint*: Use the present value formula that you learned in this tutorial's Application lesson to calculate the present value of the annuity.)

    c. Save, build, and execute the program. How much is the annuity worth in present dollars? Which option is better—the single lump sum or the annuity?

    d. When the program is working correctly, hide the Output window, then use the File menu to close the workspace.

8. In this exercise, you will determine the number of years it takes to double an investment. The formula to do so is $\log(2) / \log(1 + rate)$, where *rate* is the annual rate of interest.

    a. Create a console application. Name the project workspace T5AppE08, and save it in the Cpp\Tut05 folder on your computer's hard disk. Add a new C++ source file to the project. Name the source file T5AppE08.

    b. Enter the appropriate C++ instructions into the source file. Allow the user to enter the interest rate as a decimal number. Display the number of years in fixed-point notation with one decimal place. (*Hint*: You will need to use the C++ **log** function, whose syntax is **log**(*number*), in the formula.)

    c. Save, build, and execute the program. Enter .08 as the rate. The number of years should be 9.0.

    d. Execute the program again. How many years will it take to double an investment using a 6% interest rate?

    e. When the program is working correctly, hide the Output window, then use the File menu to close the workspace.

A computer program is good only if it works. Errors in either an algorithm or programming code can cause the program to run incorrectly. Therefore, a programmer needs to know how to locate and fix these errors. Exercise 9 is a Debugging Exercise. Debugging Exercises allow you to practice recognizing and solving errors in a program.

 debugging

9. In this exercise, you will debug an existing C++ program.

    a. Open the T5AppE09.cpp file contained in the Cpp\Tut05\T5AppE09 folder on your computer's hard disk. The program should calculate and display the square and square root of the number entered by the user, but it is not working correctly. Study the program's code, then build and execute the program.

    b. Correct any errors in the program, then save, build, and execute the program again. When the program is working correctly, hide the Output window, then use the File menu to close the workspace.

Program-Defined Value-Returning Functions

After completing this tutorial, you will be able to:

- Create and invoke a function that returns a value
- Pass information, by value, to a function
- Understand a variable's scope and lifetime
- Write a function prototype

Concept Lesson

More About Functions

As you learned in Tutorial 5, programmers can include two different types of functions in a program: built-in functions and program-defined functions. Recall that a **built-in function** is a function whose task is predefined, and whose **function definition**—the code that guides the function in completing its task—is prewritten and appears outside the program in which the function is used. The function definitions for built-in functions are contained in library files that come with the language compiler and reside on your computer's hard disk. The C++ pow function, whose function definition is contained in the cmath library, is an example of a built-in function.

A **program-defined function**, on the other hand, is a function whose task is determined by the programmer and defined within the program in which the function is used. Every C++ program contains at least one program-defined function, main, and most contain many more. Programmers use program-defined functions for two reasons. First, program-defined functions allow the programmer to avoid duplicating code in different parts of a program. If a program needs to perform the same task several times, it is more efficient to enter the appropriate code once, in a program-defined function, and then simply call the function to perform its task when needed. Second, program-defined functions allow large and complex programs, which typically are written by a team of programmers, to be broken into small and manageable tasks; each member of the team can be assigned one of the tasks to code as a function. When each programmer has completed his or her function, all of the functions then are gathered together into one program. Typically, the main function in the program is responsible for calling each of the other functions when needed. You call a program-defined function in exactly the same way as you call a built-in function—by including its name and actual arguments (if any) in a statement.

All built-in and program-defined functions are categorized as either value-returning functions or void functions. Value-returning functions return a value to the statement that called the function, whereas void functions do not return a value. You will learn how to create value-returning functions in this tutorial, and how to create void functions in Tutorial 7.

Creating Value-Returning Functions

A **value-returning function** is a function that returns a value after completing its assigned task. The numerical functions you learned about in Tutorial 5's Concept lesson are examples of value-returning functions built into most programming languages. The main function in a C++ program also is an example of a value-returning function, but one that is defined within the program itself. All value-returning functions return precisely one value to the statement that called the function. The only exception to this rule is the main function, which returns its one value to the operating system.

tip

The ability to create functions within a program allows more than one programmer to work on a program at the same time, decreasing the time it takes to write the program.

tip

Any program-defined function, not just main, can call another program-defined function.

tip

Recall that the items of information appearing within parentheses when you call a function are called actual arguments.

tip

You do not have to call the main function in a C++ program, as this is handled by the operating system when you execute the program. When the main function completes its task, the statement return 0; returns the number 0 to the operating system to indicate that the program ended successfully.

Figure 6-1 shows the syntax used to create (or define) a value-returning function in C++, Java, and Visual Basic. The figure also shows an example of a program-defined value-returning function whose task is to cube a number and then return the result.

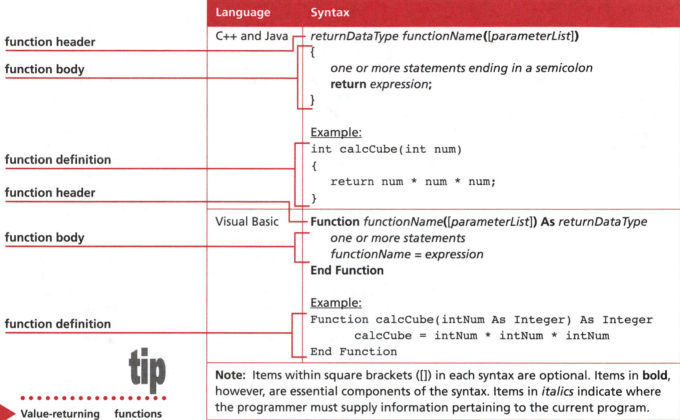

Language	Syntax

C++ and Java	*returnDataType functionName*(**[***parameterList***]**)
	 {
	     one or more statements ending in a semicolon
	     return *expression;*
	 }
	
	 <u>Example:</u>
	 `int calcCube(int num)`
	 `{`
	     `return num * num * num;`
	 `}`

Visual Basic	**Function** *functionName*(**[***parameterList***]**) **As** *returnDataType*
	     one or more statements
	     functionName = expression
	 End Function
	
	 <u>Example:</u>
	 `Function calcCube(intNum As Integer) As Integer`
	     `calcCube = intNum * intNum * intNum`
	 `End Function`

function header

function body

function definition

function header

function body

function definition

Note: Items within square brackets ([]) in each syntax are optional. Items in **bold**, however, are essential components of the syntax. Items in *italics* indicate where the programmer must supply information pertaining to the current program.

Figure 6-1: Syntax and an example of a program-defined value-returning function in C++, Java, and Visual Basic

As Figure 6-1 indicates, a program-defined function is composed of a function header and a function body.

Function Headers

The **function header,** which is the first line in a function definition, is so named because it appears at the top (head) of the function. The function header specifies the type of data the function will return (if any), as well as the function's name and an optional *parameterList*. The *parameterList* lists the data type and name of memory locations used by the function to store information passed to it.

In C++ and Java, the function header for a value-returning function begins with *returnDataType*, where *returnDataType* indicates the data type of the value returned by the function. If the function returns an integer, as does the `calcCube` function shown in Figure 6-1, *returnDataType* will be `int`; however, it will be `char` if the function returns a character. Unlike function headers in C++ and Java, function headers in Visual Basic begin with the keyword `Function`, and end with the *returnDataType*.

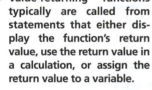

▶ Value-returning functions typically are called from statements that either display the function's return value, use the return value in a calculation, or assign the return value to a variable.

▶ Notice that a function header in C++ does not end with a semicolon. This is because a function header is not considered a statement.

▶ As you will learn in Tutorial 7, you use the C++ keyword `void` as the *returnDataType* for program-defined functions that do not return a value.

You can use any of the C++ data types listed in Tutorial 4's Figure 4-4 as the *returnDataType* for a program-defined value-returning function.

The rules for naming variables in C++, which also should be followed for naming C++ functions, are shown in Tutorial 4's Figure 4-18.

The function header also specifies the name of the function. The rules for naming program-defined functions are the same as for naming variables. To make your programs more self-documenting and easier to understand, you should use meaningful names that describe the task the function is to perform. In the examples shown in Figure 6-1, the name `calcCube` indicates that the function calculates the cube of a number.

In Tutorial 5, you learned how to pass (send) information—called actual arguments—to a built-in function; you also can pass actual arguments to a program-defined function. The actual arguments can be one or more variables, named constants, literal constants, or keywords. When the actual argument is a variable, the variable can be passed either *by value* or *by reference*. When a variable is passed **by value**, only the value stored in the variable is passed to the function. When a variable is passed **by reference**, on the other hand, the address of the variable in the computer's internal memory is passed. Unless you specify otherwise, C++ automatically passes variables *by value*. For now, you do not need to concern yourself with passing *by refererence*, because all variables passed to functions in this tutorial will be passed *by value*. You will learn how to pass variables *by reference* in Tutorial 7.

Recall that you pass information to a function when you want the function to process the information in some way. In the case of the `calcCube` function shown in Figure 6-1, you pass the number you want the function to cube. To cube the number 3, for example, you use the expression `calcCube(3)` in a C++ statement; this expression calls the `calcCube` function, passing it the literal constant 3. Similarly, to cube the number stored in the `number` variable, you use the expression `calcCube(number)` in a C++ statement. The `calcCube(number)` expression calls the `calcCube` function, passing it the value stored in the `number` variable.

When you pass a literal constant, a keyword, a named constant, or a variable's value to a function, the function stores the value it receives in a memory location. The name and data type of the memory locations that a function uses to store the values passed to it are listed in the function's *parameterList*, which appears within parentheses in the function header. The `calcCube` function's *parameterList* in Figure 6-1, for example, indicates that the function will use an `int` (`Integer` in Visual Basic) variable named `num` (`intNum` in Visual Basic) to store the value passed to it.

Each memory location listed in the *parameterList* is referred to as a **formal parameter**. The number of formal parameters included in the *parameterList* must agree with the number of actual arguments passed to the function. If you pass one actual argument, then the function will need only one formal parameter to store the value of that argument. Similarly, a function that is passed three actual arguments when called will require three formal parameters in its *parameterList*; each formal parameter must be assigned a data type and name. If a *parameterList* contains more than one formal parameter, you use a comma to separate one parameter from another.

In addition to having the same number of formal parameters as actual arguments, the data type and position of each formal parameter in the *parameterList* must agree with the data type and position of its corresponding actual argument in the *argumentList*. For instance, if the actual argument is an integer, then the formal parameter in which the integer will be stored should have a data type of `int` (`Integer` in Visual Basic). Likewise, if two actual arguments are passed to a function—the first one being a character and the second one being a number having a decimal place—the first formal parameter should have a data type of `char` (`String` in Visual Basic), and the second formal parameter should have a data type of `float` (`Single` in Visual Basic).

Not every function requires information to be passed to it, so not every function will have formal parameters listed in its function header. Functions that do not require a *parameterList* will have an empty set of parentheses after the function's name.

Rather than using an empty set of parentheses to indicate that a function does not receive any information, some C++ programmers enter the keyword `void` within the parentheses.

In addition to a function header, a function definition also includes a function body.

Function Body

The **function body** contains the instructions the function must follow to perform its assigned task. In C++ and Java, the function body begins with the opening brace ({) and ends with the closing brace (}). In Visual Basic, the function body begins with the line below the function header, and it ends with the keywords `End Function`. Although only one statement appears in each function body shown in Figure 6-1, a function body typically contains many statements.

In most cases, the last statement in the function body of a value-returning function in C++ and Java is **return** *expression*;, where *expression* represents the value the function returns to the statement that called it. The `return` statement alerts the computer that the function has completed its task, and it ends the function. In Visual Basic, you use the statement *functionName* = *expression* to return the function's value to the calling statement. A Visual Basic function ends when the computer processes the function's `End Function` statement. The data type of the *expression* in each syntax shown in Figure 6-1 must agree with the *returnDataType* specified in the function header.

mini-quiz

Mini-Quiz 1

1. Assume a program uses the statement `discount = calcDisc(300.45);` to call the `calcDisc` function. The function returns a number having a decimal place. Which of the following is a valid function header for the `calcDisc` function?

   a. `calcDisc(float sales)`

   b. `float calcDisc(sales);`

   c. `float calcDisc(float sales)`

   d. `float calcDisc(float sales);`

2. Write a function header for a C++ function named `calcTotal`. The function will be passed two integers when it is called; use the variable names `sale1` and `sale2` as the formal parameters. The function will return an integer.

3. Assume a program uses the C++ statement `cout << gross(hours, rate);` to call the `gross` function. (`hours` is an `int` variable, and `rate` is a `float` variable.) The function header used in the program is `float gross(float hoursWkd, payRate)`, which is incorrect. Correct the function header.

4. Write the C++ statement that instructs the `gross` function to return the contents of the `grossPay` variable.

In the next section, you will learn how the computer processes a program-defined function when the function is called by a statement within the program.

Processing a Program-Defined Function

As mentioned earlier, you call a program-defined function in exactly the same way as you call a built-in function—by including its name and actual arguments (if any) in a statement. When the computer processes a statement containing a program-defined function, the computer first locates the function's code in the program; in a C++ program, this code typically is located after the `main` function. If the function call contains an *argumentList*, the computer passes the values of the actual arguments (assuming variables included in the *argumentList* are passed *by value*) to the called function. Recall that the function receives these values and stores them in the memory locations listed in the function's *parameterList*. After doing so, the computer processes the function's code and, in the case of a value-returning function, the computer returns the appropriate value to the statement that called the function. This is the same process the computer uses when processing a statement containing a built-in value-returning function. The only difference is that the computer locates a program-defined function's code in the current program rather than in a library file.

Figure 6-2 shows examples of calling and defining program-defined value-returning functions in C++. The function calls, which appear in the main function in both examples, are shaded in the figure.

typically located below the main **function in a C++ program**

Function call	Function definition

`//Example 1`
`int main()`
`{`
`    int number = 0;`
`    cout << "Enter an integer: ";`
`    cin >> number;`
`    cout << calcCube(number);`
`    return 0;`
`}`
	`//*****program-defined functions*****`
	`int calcCube(int num)`
	`{`
	`        return num * num * num;`
	`}`

`//Example 2`
`int main()`
`{`
`    int salesAmt   = 0;`
`    float bonusAmt = 0.0;`
`    salesAmt = getSales( );`
 	
`    bonusAmt = bonus(salesAmt, .05);`
`    cout << bonusAmt;`
`    return 0;`
`}`
	`//*****program-defined functions*****`
	`int getSales( )`
	`{`
	`    int sales = 0;`
	`    cout << "Enter sales: ";`
	`    cin >> sales;`
	`    return sales;`
	`}`
	
	`float bonus(int dollars, float rate)`
	`{`
	`    float bonusAmt = 0.0;`
	`    bonusAmt = dollars * rate;`
	`    return bonusAmt;`
	`}`

one actual argument, one formal parameter

no actual arguments, no formal parameters

two actual arguments, two formal parameters

Figure 6-2: Examples of calling and defining program-defined value-returning functions in C++

Recall that most C++ programmers enter the function definitions below the `main` function in a C++ program. Many programmers also use a comment (such as `//*****program-defined functions*****`) to separate the `main` function's code from the code for the function definitions.

Notice that the quantity and data type of the actual arguments match the quantity and data type of the corresponding formal parameters. Also notice that the names of the formal parameters do not need to be identical to the names of the actual arguments to which they correspond. In the first example, for instance, the function call contains one actual argument named `number`, and the corresponding function header contains one formal parameter named `num`; both the actual argument and the formal parameter are of data type `int`.

In the second example, the call to the `getSales` function contains no actual arguments, and the corresponding function header contains no formal parameters. In that same example, the call to the `bonus` function contains two actual arguments: an `int` variable and a number with a decimal place. The `bonus` function header correctly contains two formal parameters to receive the information passed to the function: an `int` variable named `dollars` and a `float` variable named `rate`.

Desk-checking the two programs shown in Figure 6-2 will help you understand how the computer processes a program-defined function when it appears in a statement. Begin with the first program shown in the figure.

Desk-Checking Example 1

The first statement in Example 1's `main` function reserves and initializes an `int` variable named `number`. The next two statements prompt the user to enter an integer, and then store the user's response in the `number` variable. Assume that the user enters the number 4. Figure 6-3 shows the contents of memory after the first three statements in the `main` function are processed.

main function's variable

number
~~0~~
4

Figure 6-3: Contents of memory after the first three statements in the `main` function are processed

The fourth statement, `cout << calcCube(number);`, calls the `calcCube` function, passing it one actual argument: an `int` variable named `number`. Recall that unless specified otherwise, variables in C++ are passed *by value*, which means that only the contents of the variables are passed to the function. In this case, the computer passes the number 4 to the `calcCube` function.

At this point, the computer temporarily leaves the `main` function to process the code contained in the `calcCube` function, beginning with the function header. In this case, the *parameterList* in the `calcCube` function header tells the computer to reserve one memory location—an `int` variable named `num`. After reserving the `num` variable, the computer stores the value passed to the function—in this case, the number 4—in the variable, as shown in Figure 6-4.

calcCube **function's
variable**

main **function's
variable**

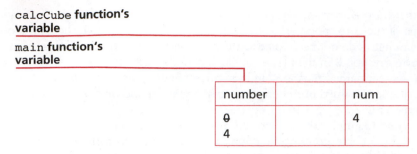

Figure 6-4: Contents of memory after the calcCube function header is processed

Next, the computer processes the return num * num * num; statement contained in the calcCube function body. This statement cubes the value stored in the num variable (4), and returns the result (64) to the statement that called the function—the cout << calcCube(number); statement in the main function. After processing the calcCube function's return statement, the computer removes the num variable from memory, and then the calcCube function ends. Figure 6-5 shows the contents of memory after the calcCube function has completed its task and returned its value. Notice that only the main function's number variable is still in the computer's memory.

main **function's
variable**

Figure 6-5: Contents of memory after the calcCube function completes its task and returns its value

The cout << calcCube(number); statement in the main function displays the value returned to it (64) on the screen. The computer then processes the main function's return 0; statement, which returns the number 0 to the operating system to indicate that the program ended normally. After processing this statement, the computer removes the number variable from memory, and then the program ends.

At this point, you may be wondering why the program needs to pass the contents of the number variable to the calcCube function. Why can't the function just use the number variable in its return statement, like this: return number * number * number;? You also may be wondering why the computer removes the num variable from memory after it processes the calcCube function's return statement, but waits until after it processes the main function's return statement before it removes the number variable. Why are the variables removed from memory at different times? To answer these questions, you need to learn about the scope and lifetime of a variable.

tip

▶ As you will learn in future tutorials, any variable that is declared in a statement block in a C++ program is considered a local variable. A statement block is simply a group of instructions enclosed in braces; a function, for example, is a statement block. C++ also allows you to create statement blocks that are not functions. Variables declared within these statement blocks can be used only by the statement block, and they are removed from memory when the statement block ends, which is when the computer encounters the statement block's closing brace. Later in this book you will learn more about statement blocks that are not functions.

tip

▶ You can experiment with the concepts of scope and lifetime by completing Discovery Exercise 8 at the end of this lesson.

The Scope and Lifetime of a Variable

A variable's **scope**, which can be either local or global, indicates which portions of a program can use the variable. A variable's **lifetime**, on the other hand, indicates how long the variable remains in the computer's memory. The scope and lifetime typically are determined by where you declare the variable in the program. Variables declared within a function, and those that appear in a function's *parameterList*, have a local scope and are referred to as **local variables**. Local variables can be used only by the function in which they are declared or in whose *parameterList* they appear. Local variables remain in memory until the function ends. In the case of a value-returning function, the function ends after the computer processes the `return` statement.

Global variables, on the other hand, typically are declared outside of any function in the program, and they remain in memory until the program ends. Unlike a local variable, a global variable can be used by any statement in the program. Declaring a variable as global rather than local allows unintentional errors to occur when a function that should not have access to the variable inadvertently changes the variable's contents. Because of this, you should avoid using global variables in your programs. If more than one function needs access to the same variable, it is better to create a local variable in one of the functions and then pass that variable only to the other functions that need it.

In the Example 1 program shown earlier in Figure 6-2, the `number` variable is local to the `main` function, because `main` is the function in which the `number` variable is declared. Therefore, only the `main` function can use the `number` variable; the `calcCube` function is not even aware of the variable's existence in memory. If you want the `calcCube` function to cube the value stored in the `number` variable, you must pass the variable's value to the function.

The num variable, which appears in the `calcCube` function's *parameterList* in Example 1, is local to the `calcCube` function. Therefore, only the `calcCube` function can use the num variable.

As mentioned earlier, local variables remain in memory until the function in which they are created ends. This explains why the num variable is removed from memory after the computer processes the `calcCube` function's `return` statement, and why the computer waits until after it processes the `main` function's `return` statement before it removes the `number` variable from memory.

Now that you understand the concepts of scope and lifetime, desk-check the second example shown earlier in Figure 6-2.

Desk-Checking Example 2

Figure 6-6 shows the program that you will desk-check in this section. This program appeared earlier as Example 2 in Figure 6-2.

typically located below the main function in a C++ program

Function call	Function definition
```//Example 2 int main() { int salesAmt = 0; float bonusAmt = 0.0; salesAmt = getSales( ); bonusAmt = bonus(salesAmt, .05); cout << bonusAmt; return 0; } ```	```//*****program-defined functions***** int getSales( ) { int sales = 0; cout << "Enter sales: "; cin >> sales; return sales; } } float bonus(int dollars, float rate) { float bonusAmt = 0.0; bonusAmt = dollars * rate; return bonusAmt; } ```

no actual arguments, no formal parameters

two actual arguments, two formal parameters

Figure 6-6: Code from Example 2

The first two statements in the **main** function declare and initialize two local variables: an **int** variable named **salesAmt** and a **float** variable named **bonusAmt**. Both variables can be used only by the **main** function, and both will remain in memory until the **main** function's **return** statement is processed. Figure 6-7 shows the contents of memory after the first two statements in the **main** function are processed.

main function's variables

salesAmt	bonusAmt
0	0.0

Figure 6-7: Contents of memory after the first two statements in the **main** function are processed

When the computer encounters the third statement, **salesAmt = getSales();**, it temporarily leaves the **main** function to process the instructions in the **getSales** function, beginning with the function header. The **getSales** function header does not contain any formal parameters, which indicates that the function will not receive any information when it is called.

The first statement in the getSales function body declares and initializes a local int variable named sales. The sales variable can be used only by the getSales function, and it will remain in memory until the getSales function's return statement is processed.

The next two statements in the getSales function body prompt the user to enter a sales amount, and then store the user's response in the sales variable. Figure 6-8 shows the contents of memory at this point, assuming the user entered the number 1575 as the sales amount.

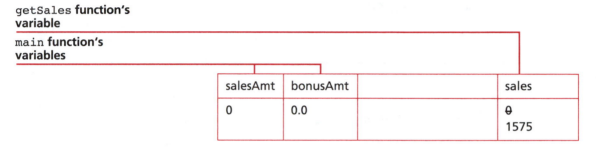

Figure 6-8: Contents of memory after the user enters the sales amount

Next, the computer processes the return sales; statement contained in the getSales function body. The statement returns the contents of the sales variable (1575) to the statement that called the function—the salesAmt = getSales(); statement in the main function—which assigns the return value (1575) to the salesAmt variable, as shown in Figure 6-9.

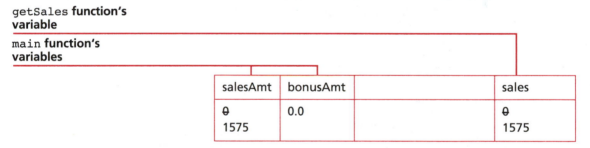

Figure 6-9: Contents of memory after the return sales; statement is processed

After processing the getSales function's return statement, the computer removes the sales variable from memory, and then the getSales function ends. Figure 6-10 shows the contents of memory after the getSales function has completed its task and returned its value. Notice that only the main function's variables are still in memory.

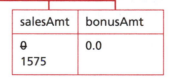

Figure 6-10: Contents of memory after the getSales function completes its task and returns its value

The next statement to be processed is the `main` function's `bonusAmt = bonus(salesAmt, .05);` statement. Here again, the computer temporarily leaves the `main` function; in this case, it does so to process the code in the `bonus` function. The *parameterList* in the `bonus` function header tells the computer to reserve two local variables—an `int` variable named `dollars` and a `float` variable named `rate`. After reserving both variables, the computer stores the first value passed to the function (the contents of the `salesAmt` variable) in the first formal parameter (the `dollars` variable). It then stores the second value passed to the function (the number .05) in the second formal parameter (the `rate` variable), as shown in Figure 6-11.

bonus function's variables

main function's variables

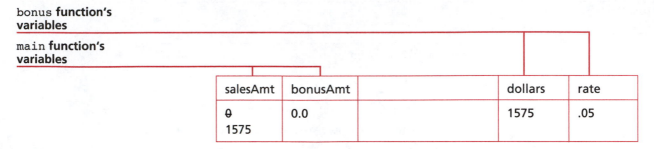

salesAmt	bonusAmt			dollars	rate
~~0~~ 1575	0.0			1575	.05

Figure 6-11: Contents of memory after the bonus function header is processed

The first statement in the `bonus` function body reserves an additional local variable. The variable, named `bonusAmt`, has a data type of `float`. The second statement in the function body multiplies the contents of the `dollars` variable (1575) by the contents of the `rate` variable (.05), and assigns the result (78.75) to the `bonusAmt` variable, as shown in Figure 6-12.

bonus function's variables

main function's variables

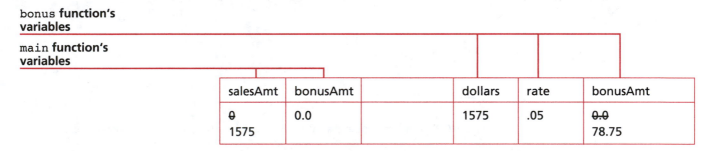

salesAmt	bonusAmt		dollars	rate	bonusAmt
~~0~~ 1575	0.0		1575	.05	~~0.0~~ 78.75

Figure 6-12: Contents of memory after the bonus is calculated

tip

For clarity, it is recommended that you use unique variable names throughout the program.

Notice that the computer's memory contains two locations having the same name, `bonusAmt`. When the variable's name appears in a statement, the computer knows which of the two locations to use by the position of the statement in the program. If the program statement appears in the `main` function, the computer uses the `bonusAmt` variable located in the `main` function's section in memory. However, if the program statement appears in the `bonus` function, the computer uses the `bonusAmt` variable located in the `bonus` function's section of memory.

Next, the computer processes the `return bonusAmt;` statement, which returns the contents of the `bonus` function's `bonusAmt` variable (78.75) to the statement that called the function—the `bonusAmt = bonus(salesAmt, .05);` statement in the `main` function. The `bonusAmt = bonus(salesAmt, .05);` statement assigns the value returned to it to the `bonusAmt` variable. At this point, the computer removes the `bonus` function's local variables (`dollars`, `rate`, and `bonusAmt`) from memory. Figure 6-13 shows the contents of memory after the `bonus` function completes its task and returns its value. Notice that only the variables local to the `main` function are still in memory.

`main` function's variable

salesAmt	bonusAmt
~~0~~	~~0.0~~
1575	78.75

Figure 6-13: Contents of memory after the `bonus` function completes its task and returns its value

After processing the `bonusAmt = bonus(salesAmt, .05);` statement, the computer processes the `cout << bonusAmt;` statement, which displays the contents of the `main` function's `bonusAmt` variable (78.75) on the screen. The `return 0;` statement then returns the number 0 to the operating system, indicating that the program ended normally. After processing the `return 0;` statement, the computer removes the `main` function's local variables (`salesAmt` and `bonusAmt`) from memory, and then the program ends.

mini-quiz

Mini-Quiz 2

1. The data type and name of each formal parameter must match the data type and name of its corresponding actual argument.

    a. True

    b. False

2. Unless specified otherwise, variables are passed _____, which means that only the contents of the variables are passed.

3. A variable's _____ indicates which portions of a program can use the variable.

4. Assume two functions declare a variable having the same name. How does the computer know which variable to use?

You now have completed Tutorial 6's Concept lesson. You can either take a break or complete the end-of-lesson questions and exercises before moving on to the Application lesson.

S U M M A R Y

A built-in function is a function whose task is predefined and whose code resides in a library file on your computer's hard disk. A program-defined function, on the other hand, is a function whose task is defined within the program itself. Programmers use program-defined functions for two reasons: program-defined functions allow the programmer to avoid duplicating code in different parts of a program, and they allow large and complex programs to be broken into small and manageable tasks. You call a program-defined function in exactly the same way as you call a built-in function—by including its name and actual arguments (if any) in a statement.

All functions are classified as either value-returning functions or void functions. A value-returning function is a function that returns a value after completing its assigned task; a void function does not return a value.

A program-defined function is composed of a function header and a function body. The function header is the first line in the function definition. It specifies the type of data the function returns, as well as the name of the function and an optional *parameterList* enclosed in parentheses. The *parameterList* contains the data type and name of each formal parameter the function will use to store the data passed to it. The number and sequence of formal parameters included in the *parameterList* must agree with the number and sequence of actual arguments passed to the function. Additionally, the data type of each formal parameter must agree with the data type of its corresponding actual argument. The name of each formal parameter typically is different than the name of the actual argument to which it corresponds. Functions that do not require a *parameterList* will have an empty set of parentheses after the function's name. Unless specified otherwise, variables in C++ are passed to the function *by value*, which means that only the contents of the variables are passed.

The function body in a function definition contains the instructions the function must follow to perform its assigned task. The last statement in the function body of a value-returning function typically is one that instructs the function to return its value.

A variable's scope, which can be either local or global, indicates which portions of a program can use the variable. A variable's lifetime, on the other hand, indicates how long the variable remains in the computer's memory. Local variables can be used only by the function in which they are created, and they remain in memory until the function ends. (As you will learn in future tutorials, variables declared in a statement block in a C++ program are local to the statement block, and they remain in memory until the statement block ends.) Global variables, which you should avoid using, can be used anywhere in the program, and they remain in memory until the program ends.

If more than one memory location within a program has the same name, and the name appears in a statement, the computer will use the position of the statement within the program to determine which memory location to use. For clarity, you should use unique variable names within a program.

A N S W E R S   T O   M I N I - Q U I Z Z E S

Mini-Quiz 1

1. c. `float calcDisc(float sales)`
2. `int calcTotal(int sale1, int sale2)`
3. `float gross(int hoursWkd, float payRate)`
4. `return grossPay;`

Mini-Quiz 2

1. b. False
2. by value
3. scope
4. By the position of the statement that refers to the variable in the program.

QUESTIONS

1. A function whose function header is `int main()` is an example of a
   _____ function.
   a. built-in
   b. program-defined value-returning
   c. program-defined void
   d. void

2. Value-returning functions can return _____.
   a. one value only
   b. one or more values
   c. the number 0 only
   d. none of the above

3. The function header specifies _____.
   a. the data type of the function's return value
   b. the name of the function
   c. the function's formal parameters
   d. all of the above

4. Which of the following is false?
   a. The number of actual arguments should agree with the number of formal parameters.
   b. The data type of each actual argument should match the data type of its corresponding formal parameter.
   c. The name of each actual argument should be identical to the name of its corresponding formal parameter.
   d. When you pass information to a function by value, the function stores the value of each item it receives in a separate memory location.

5. Each memory location listed in the *parameterList* in the function header is referred to as _____.
   a. an actual argument
   b. an actual parameter
   c. a formal argument
   d. a formal parameter

6. In a C++ function, the function body ends with the _____.
   a. {
   b. }
   c. ;
   d. `return` statement

7. Assume a program uses the statement `tax = calcTax(sales);` to call the `calcTax` function. (`sales` is a `float` variable.) The function returns a number having a decimal place. Which of the following is a valid function header for the `calcTax` function?
   a. `calcTax(float sales);`
   b. `float calcTax(salesAmount)`
   c. `float calcTax(float salesAmount)`
   d. `float calcTax(float sales);`

8. Which of the following is a valid function header for a C++ function that receives an integer first and a number with a decimal place second, and then returns a number with a decimal place?
    a. `fee(int base, float rate);`
    b. `int fee(int base, float rate)`
    c. `float fee(float base, int rate)`
    d. `float fee(int base, float rate)`

9. Which of the following instructs a function to return the contents of the `stateTax` variable to the `main` function?
    a. `restore stateTax;`
    b. `return stateTax`
    c. `return to main stateTax;`
    d. none of the above

10. If the statement `cout << net(gross, taxes);` passes the contents of the `gross` and `taxes` variables to the `net` function, the variables are said to be passed _____.
    a. by address
    b. by content
    c. by reference
    d. by value

11. Assume a program contains a program-defined function named `gross`. When the computer encounters the `gross` function's `return` statement, _____.
    a. it removes the function's local variables (if any) from memory, then continues program execution with the statement immediately following the one that called the function
    b. it removes the function's local variables (if any) from memory, then continues program execution with the statement that called the function
    c. it removes the function's global variables (if any) from memory, then continues program execution with the statement immediately following the one that called the function
    d. it removes the function's global variables (if any) from memory, then continues program execution with the statement that called the function

12. A variable's _____ indicates which portions of a program can use the variable.
    a. lifetime
    b. range
    c. scope
    d. span

13. Assume a variable named `beginBalance` appears in a function's *parameterList*. Which of the following statements is true?
    a. The `beginBalance` variable will remain in memory until the computer encounters the function's `return` statement.
    b. The `beginBalance` variable is called a functional variable.
    c. The `beginBalance` variable can be used anywhere in the program.
    d. both a and b

14. Assume a program contains three functions named `main`, `calcGross`, and `displayGross`. Both the `main` and `calcGross` functions declare a variable named `pay`. The `pay` variable name also appears in the `displayGross` function header. When the computer processes the `pay = hours * rate;` statement in the `calcGross` function, it will multiply the contents of the `hours` variable by the contents of the `rate` variable, and then _____.
    a. store the result in the `calcGross` function's `pay` variable
    b. store the result in the `displayGross` function's `pay` variable
    c. store the result in the `main` function's `pay` variable
    d. display an error message because you can't have three memory locations with the same name

E X E R C I S E S

1. Write the C++ code for a function that receives an integer passed to it. The function, named `halveNumber`, should divide the integer by 2, and then return the result (which may contain a decimal place).

2. Write the C++ code for a function that prompts the user to enter a character, and then stores the user's response in a `char` variable. The function should return the character entered by the user. (The function will not have any actual arguments passed to it.) Name the function `getChar`.

3. Write the C++ code for a function that receives four integers. The function should calculate the average of the four integers, and then return the result (which may contain a decimal place). Name the function `calcAverage`.

4. Write the C++ code for a function that receives two numbers that both have a decimal place. The function should divide the first number by the second number, and then return the result. Name the function `quotient`.

5. Write the C++ code for a function that prompts the user to enter a name, and then stores the user's response in a `string` variable. The function should return the name entered by the user. (The function will not have any actual arguments passed to it.) Name the function `getName`.

6. Write the C++ code for a function that generates a random integer within the range *lowerbound* to *upperbound*. As you learned in Tutorial 5, you can use the formula *lowerbound* **+ rand**() **%** (*upperbound - lowerbound* **+ 1**) to specify the range of integers you want to generate. The function will need to receive two integers. The first integer represents the *lowerbound*, and the second integer represents the *upperbound*. The function should return the random number.

7. Desk-check the program shown in Figure 6-14. Show the desk-check table after the first four instructions in the `main` function are processed, after the `calcEnd` function's `return` statement is processed (but before local variables are removed from memory), and after the `calcEnd` function's local variables are removed from memory.

main function	**Function definition**
```cpp int main() { int begVal = 1000; int purchase = 500; int sale = 200; int endVal = 0; endVal = calcEnd(begVal, purchase, sale); cout << endVal << endl; return 0; } ```	```cpp //*****program-defined functions***** int calcEnd(int b, int p, int sale) { int endValue = 0; endValue = b + p - sale; return endValue; } ```

Figure 6-14

Exercise 8 is a Discovery Exercise. Discovery Exercises, which may include topics that are not covered in this lesson, allow you to "discover" the solutions to problems on your own.

8. In this exercise, you will experiment with the concepts of scope and lifetime.

   a. Open the T6ConE08.cpp file contained in the Cpp\Tut06\T6ConE08 folder on your computer's hard disk.

   b. Build the program. The C++ compiler displays an error message indicating that the `calcDoubleNumber` function does not recognize the `number` variable. This error occurs because the `number` variable is local to the `main` function. To fix this error, you can either pass the `number` variable's value to the `calcDoubleNumber` function, or create a global variable named `number`. Passing the variable's value is the preferred way for the `main` function to communicate with the `calcDoubleNumber` function. However, to give you an opportunity to see how global variables work in a program, you will fix the program's error by creating a global variable named `number`.

   c. Change the `int number = 0;` statement in the `main` function to a comment by preceding the statement with `//`.

Recall that global variables are declared outside of any functions in the program. In the blank line below the `//declare global variable` comment, type `int number = 0;` and press the Enter key. Because the `number` variable is now a global variable, both the `main` and `calcDoubleNumber` functions have access to it. You can verify this by executing the program.

   d. Save, build, and execute the program. When prompted for a number, type 5 and press the Enter key. The DOS window shows that doubling the number 5 results in the number 10.

   e. Hide the Output window, then use the File menu to close the workspace.

A computer program is good only if it works. Errors in either an algorithm or programming code can cause the program to run incorrectly. Therefore, a programmer needs to know how to locate and fix these errors. Exercise 9 is a Debugging Exercise. Debugging Exercises allow you to practice recognizing and solving errors in a program.

debugging

9. Assume a C++ function named `calcCommission` is passed three items of information when it is called by the `main` function: a `string` variable followed by two `float` variables. (The variables are passed *by value*.) The `calcCommission` function returns a number with a decimal place. Rewrite the following function header correctly.

   ```
   calcCommission(name, float sales, float rate);
   ```

Application Lesson

Using Program-Defined Value-Returning Functions in a C++ Program

case ▶ After weeks of car shopping, David Liu still hasn't decided what car to purchase. Recently, David has noticed that many car dealers, in an effort to boost sales, are offering buyers a choice of either a large cash rebate or an extremely low financing rate, much lower than the rate David would pay by financing the car through his local credit union. David is not sure whether to take the lower financing rate from the dealer, or take the rebate and then finance the car through the credit union. He has asked you to create a program that he can use to calculate and display the monthly payments using both options.

Analyzing, Planning, and Desk-Checking the Periodic Payment Algorithm

You need to calculate a periodic payment on a loan for David. The formula to calculate the payment is *principal* * *rate* / (1 − (*rate* + 1)$^{-term}$), where *principal* is the amount of the loan, *rate* is the periodic interest rate, and *term* is the number of periodic payments. Figure 6-15 shows two examples of using the periodic payment formula to calculate the periodic payment on a loan.

Periodic payment formula: *principal* * *rate* / (1 − (*rate* + 1)$^{-term}$)

Note: When you apply for a loan, the lender typically quotes you an annual interest rate, and the term is expressed in years.

Example 1 – calculate the annual payment for a loan of $9000 for 3 years at 5% interest

Principal:	9000
Annual rate:	.05
Term (years):	3
Formula:	9000 * .05 / (1 − (.05 + 1)$^{-3}$)
Annual payment:	$3304.88 (rounded to two decimal places)

Figure 6-15: Periodic payment formula and examples

<u>**Example 2**</u> – calculate the monthly payment for a loan of $12,000 for 5 years at 6% interest

Principal:	12,000
Monthly rate:	.005 (annual rate of .06 divided by 12)
Term (months):	60 (5 years multiplied by 12)
Formula:	12,000 * .005 / (1 − (.005 + 1)$^{-60}$)
Monthly payment:	$231.99 (rounded to two decimal places)

Figure 6-15: Periodic payment formula and examples (continued)

Example 1 uses the periodic payment formula to calculate the annual payment for a $9000 loan for three years at 5% interest; the annual payment is $3304.88 (rounded to two decimal places). In other words, if you borrow $9000 for three years at 5% interest, you would need to make three annual payments of $3304.88 to pay off the loan.

Example 2 uses the periodic payment formula to calculate the monthly payment for a $12,000 loan for five years at 6% interest. To pay off this loan, you would need to make 60 payments of $231.99. Notice that, before you can calculate the monthly payment, you need to convert the annual interest rate to a monthly interest rate by dividing the annual rate by 12. You also need to convert the term, which is expressed in years, to months by multiplying the number of years by 12.

You will use the periodic payment formula to calculate David Liu's monthly car payment if he accepts the dealer's rebate and finances the car through his credit union. You also will use the formula to calculate David's monthly payment if he chooses the car dealer's lower financing rate instead of the rebate. Figure 6-16 shows the IPO chart for the David Liu problem.

Input	Processing	Output

car price
rebate
credit union rate (annual)
dealer rate (annual)
term (years)
	Processing items:
	    monthly credit union rate
	    monthly dealer rate
	    number of months
	
	Algorithm:
	1. enter the car price,
	   rebate, credit union rate,
	   dealer rate, and term
	2. calculate the monthly
	   credit union rate by
	   dividing the credit union
	   rate by 12
		credit union payment
		dealer payment

Figure 6-16: IPO chart for the David Liu problem

Input	Processing	Output
	3. calculate the monthly dealer rate by dividing the dealer rate by 12 4. calculate the number of months by multiplying the term by 12 5. calculate the credit union payment using the periodic payment formula: (car price - rebate) * monthly credit union rate / (1 - (monthly credit union rate + 1)$^{-\text{number of months}}$) 6. calculate the dealer payment using the periodic payment formula: car price * monthly dealer rate / (1 - (monthly dealer rate + 1)$^{-\text{number of months}}$) 7. display the credit union payment and the dealer payment	

Figure 6-16: IPO chart for the David Liu problem (continued)

As Figure 6-16 indicates, the output is the monthly payment to the credit union and the monthly payment to the car dealer. To display the output, the program needs to know the car price, rebate, credit union rate, dealer rate, and term.

According to the algorithm, the program first will have the user enter the five input items. It then will convert the two annual rates to monthly rates, and the term, which is stated in years, to months. The program then will use the periodic payment formula to calculate the two monthly car payments, and it will display the result of both calculations on the screen.

Notice that the periodic payment formula appears in Steps 5 and 6 in the algorithm. Rather than having to enter the code for such a complex formula two times in the program, it would be more efficient to enter the code once, in a program-defined value-returning function, which you will name `calcPayment`. You then can have the program's `main` function call the `calcPayment` function twice: first to calculate and return the monthly payment if David finances the car through the credit union, and again to calculate and return the monthly payment if he finances through the car dealer. Each time the `main` function calls the `calcPayment` function, the `main` function will need to pass the `calcPayment` function the appropriate information. Figure 6-17 shows the revised IPO chart for the program's `main` function, and Figure 6-18 shows the IPO chart for the `calcPayment` function. (Changes made to the original IPO chart are shaded in Figure 6-17.)

Input	Processing	Output

car price
rebate
credit union rate (annual)
dealer rate (annual)
term (years)
	Processing items:
	    monthly credit union rate
	    monthly dealer rate
	    number of months
	
	Algorithm:
	1. enter the car price, rebate, credit union rate, dealer rate, and term
	2. calculate the monthly credit union rate by dividing the credit union rate by 12
	3. calculate the monthly dealer rate by dividing the dealer rate by 12
	4. calculate the number of months by multiplying the term by 12
	5. calculate the credit union payment = calcPayment(car price - rebate, monthly credit union rate, number of months)
	6. calculate the dealer payment = calcPayment(car price, monthly dealer rate, number of months)
	7. display the credit union payment and the dealer payment
		credit union payment
		dealer payment

the values of the items in parentheses will be passed to the `calcPayment` function

Figure 6-17: Revised IPO chart for the program's `main` function

Input	Processing	Output
principal monthly rate number of months	Processing items: none Algorithm: 1. calculate the monthly payment = principal * monthly rate / (1 - (monthly rate + 1)$^{-\text{number of months}}$) 2. return the monthly payment	monthly payment

Figure 6-18: IPO chart for the `calcPayment` function

Notice that the **calcPayment** function's output is the monthly payment. Also notice that the function needs to know three items of information to calculate the monthly payment: the principal, monthly rate, and number of months. The values of these items will be passed to the **calcPayment** function by the **main** function, as indicated in the shaded steps shown in Figure 6-17. For example, when calling the **calcPayment** function to calculate the credit union payment, the **main** function will pass the difference between the car price and the rebate as the principal; it also will pass the monthly credit union rate and the number of months. Likewise, when calling the `calcPayment` function to calculate the dealer payment, the `main` function will pass the car price as the principal, and also the monthly dealer rate and the number of months.

Recall that you should desk-check an algorithm several times before you begin coding it. In this case, you will use the following two sets of data to desk-check the algorithms shown in Figures 6-17 and 6-18:

Data for first desk-check		Data for second desk-check	
Principal:	16000	Principal:	18000
Rebate:	3000	Rebate:	2000
Credit union rate:	.08	Credit union rate:	.09
Dealer rate:	.03	Dealer rate:	.02
Term (years):	4	Term (years):	5

Figure 6-19 shows the completed desk-check table, with the payment amounts rounded to two decimal places.

`main` function

rounded up from .00666

rounded up from .001666

car price	rebate	credit union rate	dealer rate	term	monthly credit union rate	monthly dealer rate	number of months	credit union payment	dealer payment
~~16000~~	~~3000~~	~~.08~~	~~.03~~	~~4~~	~~.007~~	~~.0025~~	~~48~~	~~317.37~~	~~354.15~~
18000	2000	.09	.02	5	.0075	.002	60	332.13	315.50

`calcPayment` function

principal	monthly rate	number of months	monthly payment
~~16000~~	~~.007~~	~~48~~	~~317.37~~
~~16000~~	~~.0025~~	~~48~~	~~354.15~~
~~18000~~	~~.0075~~	~~60~~	~~332.13~~
18000	.002	60	315.50

Figure 6-19: Completed desk-check table for the algorithms shown in Figures 6-17 and 6-18

After desk-checking the algorithm to verify its accuracy, you are ready to translate it into a language the computer can understand. Begin by coding the program's `main` function.

Coding the `main` Function

First determine how many memory locations the `main` function will need to reserve. In this case, the `main` function will require 10 memory locations to store the values of its input, processing, and output items. You will store the values in variables, because the values will be different each time the program is executed. You will use the `int` data type for the variables that store the car price, rebate, term, and number of months, which are whole numbers. You will use the `float` data type for the variables that store the interest rates and monthly payments, which will contain a decimal place. Figure 6-20 shows the C++ statements that you will use to reserve the 10 variables in the `main` function.

IPO chart information	C++ instructions
Input	
car price	`int carPrice = 0;`
rebate	`int rebate = 0;`
credit union rate (annual)	`float creditRate = 0.0;`
dealer rate (annual)	`float dealerRate = 0.0;`
term (years)	`int term = 0;`
Processing	
monthly credit union rate	`float mthCreditRate = 0.0;`
monthly dealer rate	`float mthDealerRate = 0.0;`
number of months	`int numMonths = 0;`
Output	
credit union payment	`float creditPay = 0.0;`
dealer payment	`float dealerPay = 0.0;`

Figure 6-20: C++ statements to reserve variables in the `main` function

The variables shown in Figure 6-20 are local to the `main` function and will remain in memory until the `main` function's `return` statement is processed.

Now you can begin translating the `main` function's algorithm into C++ statements. Figure 6-21 shows the C++ statements corresponding to the first four steps in the algorithm.

IPO chart information	C++ instructions
Input	
car price	`int carPrice = 0;`
rebate	`int rebate = 0;`
credit union rate (annual)	`float creditRate = 0.0;`
dealer rate (annual)	`float dealerRate = 0.0;`
term (term)	`int term = 0;`
Processing	
monthly credit union rate	`float mthCreditRate = 0.0;`
monthly dealer rate	`float mthDealerRate = 0.0;`
number of months	`int numMonths = 0;`
Output	
credit union payment	`float creditPay = 0.0;`
dealer payment	`float dealerPay = 0.0;`
Algorithm	
1. enter the car price, rebate, credit union rate, dealer rate, and term	`cout << "Enter the car price: ";`
	`cin >> carPrice;`
	`cout << "Enter the rebate: ";`
	`cin >> rebate;`
	`cout << "Enter the credit union rate: ";`
	`cin >> creditRate;`
	`cout << "Enter the dealer rate: ";`
	`cin >> dealerRate;`
	`cout << "Enter the term (years): ";`
	`cin >> term;`

Figure 6-21: C++ statements corresponding to the first four steps in the `main` function's algorithm

IPO chart information	C++ instructions
2. calculate the monthly credit union rate by dividing the credit union rate by 12	`mthCreditRate = creditRate / 12;`
3. calculate the monthly dealer rate by dividing the dealer rate by 12	`mthDealerRate = dealerRate / 12;`
4. calculate the number of months by multiplying the term by 12	`numMonths = term * 12;`

Figure 6-21: C++ statements corresponding to the first four steps in the `main` function's algorithm (continued)

The appropriate statement to use for the fifth step in the algorithm is `creditPay = calcPayment(carPrice - rebate, mthCreditRate, numMonths);`. The statement calls the `calcPayment` function, passing it the information necessary to calculate the credit union payment. It assigns the value returned by the `calcPayment` function to the `main` function's `creditPay` variable.

The sixth step in the algorithm is to call the `calcPayment` function again—this time passing it the information necessary to calculate the dealer payment. The statement should assign the value returned by the function to the `main` function's `dealerPay` variable. The appropriate statement to use in this case is `dealerPay = calcPayment(carPrice, mthDealerRate, numMonths);`.

The last step in the `main` function's algorithm is to display the monthly payments, which are stored in the `creditPay` and `dealerPay` variables, on the screen; you can use the `cout` stream and the `<<` operator to do so. Figure 6-22 shows the C++ code corresponding to the `main` function's algorithm.

tip

Recall that the items of information within parentheses in a function call are called actual arguments.

IPO chart information	C++ instructions
Input	
car price	`int carPrice = 0;`
rebate	`int rebate = 0;`
credit union rate (annual)	`float creditRate = 0.0;`
dealer rate (annual)	`float dealerRate = 0.0;`
term (years)	`int term = 0;`
Processing	
monthly credit union rate	`float mthCreditRate = 0.0;`
monthly dealer rate	`float mthDealerRate = 0.0;`
number of months	`int numMonths = 0;`
Output	
credit union payment	`float creditPay = 0.0;`
dealer payment	`float dealerPay = 0.0;`

Figure 6-22: C++ instructions for the `main` function

IPO chart information	C++ instructions
Algorithm	

1. enter the car price, rebate, credit union rate, dealer rate, and term	`cout << "Enter the car price: ";`
	`cin >> carPrice;`
	`cout << "Enter the rebate: ";`
	`cin >> rebate;`
	`cout << "Enter the credit union rate: ";`
	`cin >> creditRate;`
	`cout << "Enter the dealer rate: ";`
	`cin >> dealerRate;`
	`cout << "Enter the term (years): ";`
	`cin >> term;`

2. calculate the monthly credit union rate by dividing the credit union rate by 12	`mthCreditRate = creditRate / 12;`
3. calculate the monthly dealer rate by dividing the dealer rate by 12	`mthDealerRate = dealerRate / 12;`
4. calculate the number of months by multiplying the term by 12	`numMonths = term * 12;`
5. calculate the credit union payment = calcPayment(car price - rebate, monthly credit union rate, number of months)	`creditPay = calcPayment(carPrice -` `rebate, mthCreditRate, numMonths);`
6. calculate the dealer payment = calcPayment(car price, monthly dealer rate, number of months)	`dealerPay = calcPayment(carPrice,` `mthDealerRate, numMonths);`

7. display the credit union payment and the dealer payment	`cout << "Credit union payment: " <<`
	`creditPay << endl;`
	`cout << "Dealer payment: " << dealerPay`
	`<< endl;`

Figure 6-22: C++ instructions for the `main` function (continued)

Next, you will code the `calcPayment` function.

Coding the `calcPayment` Function

Recall that the data type and sequence of the formal parameters in a function's *parameterList* must match the data type and sequence of the actual arguments passed to the function and listed in the *argumentList*.

As the IPO chart shown earlier in Figure 6-18 indicates, the `calcPayment` function requires four memory locations: three for the input items and one for the output item. The values of the input items—principal, monthly rate, and number of months—will be passed to the `calcPayment` function when the function is called by the `main` function. Recall that when you pass variables to a function *by value*, which is the default way variables are passed in C++, the function stores the value of each item it receives in a separate memory location. The name and data type of the memory locations a function uses to store the information it receives are listed in the function's *parameterList*, which appears in the function header. In this case, you will need to list three variables in the `calcPayment` function's *parameterList*: an `int` variable to store the principal, a `float` variable to store the monthly rate, and an `int` variable to store the number of months.

Unlike the `calcPayment` function's input items, the value of its output item (monthly payment) is not passed by the `main` function. Rather, the value is calculated in the `calcPayment` function itself, and then returned to the `main` function. You will store the calculated value in a `float` variable, because the value might contain a decimal place and will change each time the function is called.

Figure 6-23 shows the function header and the C++ statement that you will use to reserve the four variables required by the `calcPayment` function. Notice that the IPO chart's input items, which are passed to the `calcPayment` function, appear in the function header. Also notice that the function's data type is the same as the data type of the value returned by the function: `float`.

The variables shown in Figure 6-23 are local to the `calcPayment` function and will remain in memory until the function's `return` statement is processed.

returnDataType agrees with data type of variable whose value is returned

variables in the *parameterList*

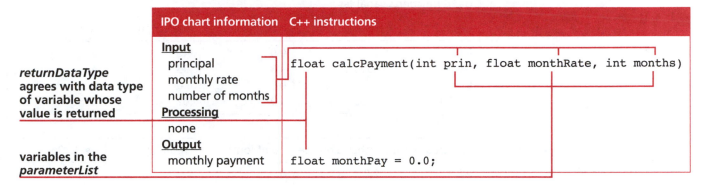

IPO chart information	C++ instructions
Input	
principal	`float calcPayment(int prin, float monthRate, int months)`
monthly rate	
number of months	
Processing	
none	
Output	
monthly payment	`float monthPay = 0.0;`

Figure 6-23: Function header and C++ statement to reserve variables in the `calcPayment` function

According to the `calcPayment` function's algorithm, the function should calculate the monthly payment, and then return the monthly payment to the `main` function. The appropriate C++ statements to use for this are shown in Figure 6-24.

IPO chart information	C++ instructions
Input	
principal	`float calcPayment(int prin, float monthRate, int months)`
monthly rate	
number of months	
Processing	
none	
Output	
monthly payment	`float monthPay = 0.0;`
Algorithm	
1. calculate the monthly payment = principal * monthly rate / (1 - (monthly rate + 1)$^{-months}$)	`monthPay =` `    prin * monthRate / (1 - pow(monthRate + 1, -months));`
2. return the monthly payment	`return monthPay;`

Figure 6-24: C++ instructions for the `calcPayment` function

After coding the algorithm, you then need to desk-check the program, using the same data you used to desk-check the algorithm. Figure 6-25 shows the data and the completed desk-check table for the program. The payment amounts are rounded to two decimal places.

Data for first desk-check		Data for second desk-check	
Principal:	16000	Principal:	18000
Rebate:	3000	Rebate:	2000
Credit union rate:	.08	Credit union rate:	.09
Dealer rate:	.03	Dealer rate:	.02
Term (years):	4	Term (years):	5

Desk-check table

`main` function's variables

carPrice	rebate	creditRate	dealerRate	term
~~0~~	~~0~~	~~0.0~~	~~0.0~~	~~0~~
~~16000~~	~~3000~~	~~.08~~	~~.03~~	4
~~0~~	~~0~~	~~0.0~~	~~0.0~~	~~0~~
18000	2000	.09	.02	5

mthCreditRate	mthDealerRate	numMonths	creditPay	dealerPay
~~0.0~~	~~0.0~~	~~0~~	~~0.0~~	~~0.0~~
~~.007~~	~~.0025~~	48	~~317.37~~	~~354.15~~
~~0.0~~	~~0.0~~	~~0~~	~~0.0~~	~~0.0~~
.0075	.002	60	332.13	315.50

`calcPayment` function's variables

prin	monthRate	months	monthPay
~~16000~~	~~.007~~	~~48~~	~~0.0~~
~~16000~~	~~.0025~~	48	~~317.37~~
~~18000~~	~~.0075~~	~~60~~	~~0.0~~
18000	.002	60	~~354.15~~
			~~0.0~~
			~~332.13~~
			~~0.0~~
			315.50

Figure 6-25: Data and completed desk-check table for the program

The results obtained when desk-checking the program agree with the results obtained when desk-checking the algorithm. You now are ready to enter the C++ instructions into the computer.

Completing the David Liu Program

Your computer's hard disk contains a partially completed C++ program that includes most of the instructions shown in Figure 6-22. Open that program now.

To open the partially completed C++ program:

1 Start Visual C++. Open the **T6App.cpp** file contained in the Cpp\Tut06\T6App folder on your computer's hard disk.

2 If necessary, maximize the T6App.cpp window. Figure 6-26 shows the instructions contained in the partially completed T6App.cpp program.

```cpp
//T6App.cpp - displays monthly payments

#include <iostream>
#include <cmath>
using namespace std;

int main()
{
    int carPrice        = 0;
    int rebate          = 0;
    float creditRate    = 0.0;
    float dealerRate    = 0.0;
    int term            = 0;
    float mthCreditRate = 0.0;
    float mthDealerRate = 0.0;
    int numMonths       = 0;
    float creditPay     = 0.0;
    float dealerPay     = 0.0;

    //enter input items
    cout << "Enter the car price: ";
    cin >> carPrice;
    cout << "Enter the rebate: ";
    cin >> rebate;
    cout << "Enter the credit union rate: ";
    cin >> creditRate;
    cout << "Enter the dealer rate: ";
    cin >> dealerRate;
    cout << "Enter the term (years): ";
    cin >> term;

    //convert annual rates and term to monthly
    mthCreditRate = creditRate /12;
    mthDealerRate = dealerRate /12;
    numMonths = term * 12;
```

Figure 6-26: Instructions contained in the partially completed T6App.cpp program

function calls are missing

```
        //calculate monthly payments

        //display monthly payments
        cout << "Credit union payment: " << creditPay << endl;
        cout << "Dealer payment: " << dealerPay << endl;

        return 0;
}       //end of main function

//*****program-defined functions*****
```

function definition
is missing

Figure 6-26: Instructions contained in the partially completed T6App.cpp program (continued)

Missing from the program are the statements that call the `calcPayment` function, as well as the `calcPayment` function definition. You will enter the missing instructions in the next set of steps, and then you will test the program to verify that it is working correctly.

To enter the missing instructions, then test the program:

1 Position the insertion point in the blank line below the `//calculate monthly payments` comment.

First enter the two function calls.

2 Press the **Tab** key, if necessary, to indent the insertion point, then type **creditPay = calcPayment(carPrice - rebate, mthCreditRate, numMonths);** and press the **Enter** key.

3 Type **dealerPay = calcPayment(carPrice, mthDealerRate, numMonths);** and press the **Enter** key.

Next, enter the `calcPayment` function definition. Most C++ programmers enter the definitions of program-defined functions below the `main` function in the program.

4 Position the insertion point in the blank line below the `//*****program-defined functions*****` comment.

First enter the function header.

5 Type **float calcPayment(int prin, float monthRate, int months)** and press the **Enter** key.

Next, enter the function body.

6 Type the additional lines of code shaded in Figure 6-27, which shows the completed function definition for the `calcPayment` function.

```
//*****program-defined functions*****
float calcPayment(int prin, float monthRate, int months)
{
        //calculates and returns a monthly payment
        float monthPay = 0.0;
        monthPay = prin * monthRate / (1 - pow(monthRate + 1, -months));
        return monthPay;
}       //end of calcPayment function
```

enter these 6 lines of code

Figure 6-27: Function definition for the `calcPayment` function

7 Save and then build the program. The compiler indicates that it found two errors in the program.

8 Scroll up the Output window as shown in Figure 6-28, and then double-click the first error message.

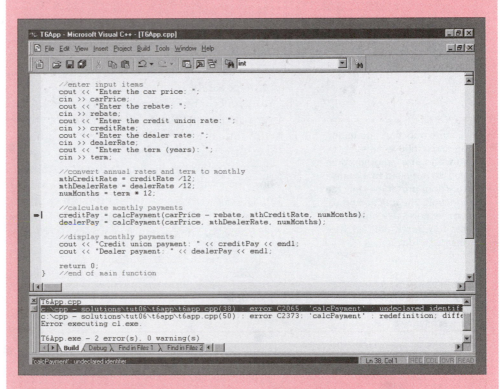

Figure 6-28: Screen showing that the compiler found two errors in the program

When you double-click an error message in the Output window, the Visual C++ editor displays a pointer at the location where the error was encountered in the program. In this case, the pointer is pointing to the statement that calculates the credit union payment. The Output window indicates that `calcPayment`, which is used in that statement, is an undeclared identifier (name). This simply means that the compiler does not recognize the function name. Hide the Output window before learning about this error.

9 Hide the Output window, and then scroll up the T6App.cpp window to view the beginning of the program.

tip

▶ The number that appears in parentheses after the file-name in the Output window refers to the line number in the program.

Before you can call a function in C++, you first must either define it or declare it. You define a function with a function definition, and you declare it with a function prototype, which you will learn about in the next section. One way to fix the undeclared identifier problem in the current program is to move the `calcPayment` function definition to a location above the `main` function, so that it appears before the function call in the `creditPay = calcPayment(carPrice - rebate, mthCreditRate, numMonths);` statement. When you enter a function definition above the `main` function, the computer does not process the statements within the function until the function is called. Rather, the computer merely remembers the function's name and the data type of its formal parameters so that calling the function later in the program will not produce the undeclared identifier error.

Another way to fix the undeclared identifier problem in the current program is to leave the function definition in its current location below the `main` function, and then declare the function by entering a function prototype above the `main` function.

Using a Function Prototype

You declare a program-defined function by using a **function prototype**, which is simply a statement that specifies the function's name, the data type of its return value (if any), and the data type of each of its formal parameters. A program will have one function prototype for each function defined below the `main` function. You usually place the function prototypes at the beginning of the program, after the `#include` and `using` directives.

A function prototype alerts the compiler that the function will be defined later in the program. It may help to think of the function prototypes in a program as being similar to the table of contents in a book. Each prototype, like each entry in a table of contents, is simply a preview of what will be expanded on later in the program (or in the book). In the programs you will create in the tutorials in this book, you will place the function definitions after the `main` function, and then use function prototypes to declare the functions above the `main` function.

Figure 6-29 shows the syntax of a function prototype, as well as the function prototype for the current program's `calcPayment` function.

If the function definition appears above the `main` function in a program, then you do not need to include a function prototype for the function. The function prototype is necessary only when the function is defined after the `main` function.

only the data types of the formal parameters are necessary

Syntax:	*returnDataType functionName([parameterList])*;
Example:	`float calcPayment(int, float, int);`

Figure 6-29: Syntax and an example of a function prototype

If you compare the function prototype shown in Figure 6-29 with the function header shown in Figure 6-27, you will notice two differences: First, the function prototype ends in a semicolon, whereas the function header does not. Second, the function header contains both the data type and name of each formal parameter, but the function prototype contains only the data type.

Now enter the function prototype for the `calcPayment` function, and then test the program using the same data you used to desk-check the algorithm and program.

Some programmers also include the name of each formal parameter in the function prototype, but this is optional.

To enter the function prototype, then test the program:

1 In the blank line below the `using namespace std;` directive, press the **Enter** key, then type **//function prototype** and press the **Enter** key.

2 Type **float calcPayment(int, float, int);** and press the **Enter** key. Figure 6-30 shows the completed T6App.cpp program.

```cpp
//T6App.cpp - displays monthly payments

#include <iostream>
#include <cmath>
using namespace std;

//function prototype
float calcPayment(int, float, int);

int main()
{
    int carPrice        = 0;
    int rebate          = 0;
    float creditRate    = 0.0;
    float dealerRate    = 0.0;
    int term            = 0;
    float mthCreditRate = 0.0;
    float mthDealerRate = 0.0;
    int numMonths       = 0;
    float creditPay     = 0.0;
    float dealerPay     = 0.0;

    //enter input items
    cout << "Enter the car price: ";
    cin >> carPrice;
    cout << "Enter the rebate: ";
    cin >> rebate;
    cout << "Enter the credit union rate: ";
    cin >> creditRate;
    cout << "Enter the dealer rate: ";
    cin >> dealerRate;
    cout << "Enter the term (years): ";
    cin >> term;

    //convert annual rates and term to monthly
    mthCreditRate = creditRate /12;
    mthDealerRate = dealerRate /12;
    numMonths = term * 12;

    //calculate monthly payments
    creditPay = calcPayment(carPrice - rebate, mthCreditRate, numMonths);
dealerPay = calcPayment(carPrice, mthDealerRate, numMonths);

//display monthly payments
cout << "Credit union payment: " << creditPay << endl;
cout << "Dealer payment: " << dealerPay << endl;

return 0;
}       //end of main function
```

function prototype

Figure 6-30: Completed T6App.cpp program

```
//*****program-defined functions*****
float calcPayment(int prin, float monthRate, int months)
{
        //calculates and returns a monthly payment
        float monthPay = 0.0;
        monthPay = prin * monthRate / (1 - pow(monthRate + 1, -months));
        return monthPay;
}       //end of calcPayment function
```

Figure 6-30: Completed T6App.cpp program (continued)

3 Save and then build the program. This time the undeclared identifier error does not occur, because the function prototype declares the `calcPayment` function before the function is called in the program.

4 Hide the Output window, then execute the program. When prompted for the car price, type **16000** and press the **Enter** key. When prompted for the rebate, type **3000** and press the **Enter** key.

5 When prompted for the credit union rate, type **.08** and press the **Enter** key. When prompted for the dealer rate, type **.03** and press the **Enter** key.

6 When prompted for the term, type **4** and press the **Enter** key. The program calculates and displays the two monthly payments, as shown in Figure 6-31.

tip

Be sure that you don't use a comma when entering large numbers into your C++ programs. For example, typing 16,000 instead of 16000 will result in incorrect output when you execute the program.

Figure 6-31: DOS window showing results of first test

The DOS window shows that the monthly payments are 317.368 and 354.149, which agree with the results shown earlier in the desk-check tables. (You will add the code to round the monthly payments to two decimal places in this lesson's Exercise 1.) In this case, it would be better for David to take the dealer's rebate and finance the car through the credit union.

7 Press the **Enter** key to close the DOS window.

8 Execute the program again. Enter **18000** as the car price, **2000** as the rebate, **.09** as the credit union rate, **.02** as the dealer rate, and **5** as the term. The DOS window shows that the monthly payments are 332.134 and 315.5, which agree with the results shown earlier in the desk-check tables. In this case, it would be better for David to finance the car through the dealer.

9 Press the **Enter** key to close the DOS window. Use the File menu to close the workspace. When prompted to close all document windows, click the **Yes** button.

10 Exit Visual C++.

You now have completed Tutorial 6's Application lesson. You can either take a break or complete the end-of-lesson exercises.

E X E R C I S E S

1. In this exercise, you will modify the program you created in this lesson so that it displays the monthly payments in fixed-point notation with two decimal places.
   a. Open the T6AppE01.cpp file contained in the Cpp\Tut06\T6AppE01 folder on your computer's hard disk.
   b. Modify the program so that it displays the monthly payments in fixed-point notation with two decimal places.
   c. Save, build, and execute the program. Enter 15000 as the car price, 1000 as the rebate, .09 as the credit union rate, .025 as the dealer rate, and 3 as the term. Is it better to finance the car through the credit union or through the car dealer?
   d. When the program is working correctly, hide the Output window, then use the File menu to close the workspace.

2. In this exercise, you will modify the program you created in this lesson. You will do so by removing the processing items from the `main` function. This will show you another way to solve the monthly payment problem.
   a. Open the T6AppE02.cpp file contained in the Cpp\Tut06\T6AppE02 folder on your computer's hard disk.
   b. Delete the lines of code declaring the `mthCreditRate`, `mthDealerRate`, and `numMonths` variables in the `main` function.
   c. Modify the `main` function according to the revised IPO chart shown in Figure 6-32. The revisions are shaded in the figure. (*Hint*: Rather than using processing items for the monthly rates and term, you simply can perform the appropriate calculation and then assign the result to the `creditRate`, `dealerRate`, and `term` variables.)

Input	Processing	Output
car price rebate credit union rate (annual) dealer rate (annual) term (years)	Processing items: none Algorithm: 1. enter the car price, rebate, credit union rate, dealer rate, and term 2. convert the credit union rate to monthly by dividing the rate by 12 3. convert the dealer rate to monthly by dividing the rate by 12 4. convert the term to months by multiplying the term by 12 5. calculate the credit union payment = calcPayment(car price - rebate, credit union rate, term) 6. calculate the dealer payment = calcPayment(car price, dealer rate, term) 7. display the credit union payment and the dealer payment	credit union payment dealer payment

Figure 6-32

d. Save, build, and execute the program. Enter 20000 as the car price, 2500 as the rebate, .07 as the credit union rate, .025 as the dealer rate, and 4 as the term. Is is better to finance the car through the credit union or through the car dealer?

e. When the program is working correctly, hide the Output window, then use the File menu to close the workspace.

3. In this exercise, you will create a program that converts a Fahrenheit temperature to a Celsius temperature.

a. Open the T6AppE03.cpp file contained in the Cpp\Tut06\T6AppE03 folder on your computer's hard disk.

b. Use the IPO charts shown in Figure 6-33 to complete the program. Display the Celsius temperature as an integer. (Notice that the program contains three functions: `main`, `getFahrenheit`, and `calcCelsius`. Be sure to enter the formula using 5.0 and 9.0, rather than 5 and 9.)

`main` function

Input	Processing	Output
Fahrenheit temperature	Processing items: none Algorithm: 1. Fahrenheit temperature = getFahrenheit() 2. Celsius temperature = calcCelsius(Fahrenheit temperature) 3. display the Celsius temperature	Celsius temperature

`getFahrenheit` function

Input	Processing	Output
	Processing items: Fahrenheit temperature Algorithm: 1. enter the Fahrenheit temperature 2. return the Fahrenheit temperature	Fahrenheit temperature

`calcCelsius` function

Input	Processing	Output
Fahrenheit temperature	Processing items: none Algorithm: 1. Celsius temperature = 5.0 / 9.0 * (Fahrenheit temperature - 32) 2. return the Celsius temperature	Celsius temperature

Figure 6-33

c. Complete a desk-check table for the program, using the following Fahrenheit temperatures: 32 F and 212 F.

d. Save, build, and execute the program. Use the data from Step c to test the program.

e. When the program is working correctly, hide the Output window, then use the File menu to close the workspace.

4. In this exercise, you will create a program that displays a bonus.

a. Open the T6AppE04.cpp file contained in the Cpp\Tut06\T6AppE04 folder on your computer's hard disk.

b. Use the IPO charts shown in Figure 6-34 to complete the program. Display the bonus amount in fixed-point notation with two decimal places. (Notice that the program contains three functions: `main`, `getSales`, and `calcBonus`.)

`main` function

Input	Processing	Output
sales	Processing items: none Algorithm: 1. sales = getSales() 2. bonus = calcBonus(sales) 3. display the bonus	bonus

`getsales` function

Input	Processing	Output
	Processing items: sales Algorithm: 1. enter the sales 2. return the sales	sales

`calcBonus` function

Input	Processing	Output
sales	Processing items: none Algorithm: 1. bonus = sales * .1 2. return the bonus	bonus

Figure 6-34

c. Complete a desk-check table for the program, using the following sales amounts: 24500 and 134780.

d. Save, build, and execute the program. Use the data from Step c to test the program.

e. When the program is working correctly, hide the Output window, then use the File menu to close the workspace.

5. In this exercise, you will modify the program you created in Tutorial 5's Application lesson by adding two additional program-defined value-returning functions to the program.

    a. Open the T6AppE05.cpp file contained in the Cpp\Tut06\T6AppE05 folder on your computer's hard disk.

    b. Modify the program so that it uses a program-defined function to get and return the interest rate, and a program-defined function to calculate and return the principal.

    c. Save, build, and execute the program. Enter .07 as the interest rate.

    d. When the program is working correctly, hide the Output window, then use the File menu to close the workspace.

6. In this exercise, you will create a program that calculates the average of three test scores.

    a. Write the IPO charts for a program that contains three program-defined value-returning functions: `main`, `getTestScore`, and `calcAverage`. The `main` function should call the `getTestScore` function to get and return each of three test scores. The test scores may contain a decimal place. (*Hint*: The `main` function will need to call the `getTestScore` function three times.) It then should call the `calcAverage` function to calculate the average of the three test scores. When the `calcAverage` function has completed its task, the `main` function should display the average on the screen.

    b. Create a console application. Name the project workspace T6AppE06, and save it in the Cpp\Tut06 folder on your computer's hard disk. Add a new C++ source file to the project. Name the source file T6AppE06.

    c. Use the IPO charts you created in Step a to code the program. Display the average in fixed-point notation with one decimal place.

    d. Complete a desk-check table for the program, using the following two groups of test scores: 95, 83, 76 and 54, 89, 77.

    e. Save, build, and execute the program. Use the data from Step d to test the program.

    f. When the program is working correctly, hide the Output window, then use the File menu to close the workspace.

7. In this exercise, you will create a program that displays an employee's name and gross pay.

    a. Write the IPO charts for a program that contains five program-defined value-returning functions: `main`, `getName`, `getHoursWorked`, `getPayRate`, and `calcGross`. The `main` function's responsibility is to call each function, and then display the employee's name and gross pay on the screen. When coding the `calcGross` function, you do not have to worry about overtime pay; you can assume everyone works 40 or fewer hours per week. The hours worked and rate of pay may contain a decimal place.

    b. Create a console application. Name the project workspace T6AppE07, and save it in the Cpp\Tut06 folder on your computer's hard disk. Add a new C++ source file to the project. Name the source file T6AppE07.

    c. Use the IPO charts you created in Step a to code the program. Display the gross pay in fixed-point notation with two decimal places.

    d. Complete a desk-check table for the program, using the following two sets of data: Mary Smith, 25.5 hours, $12 per hour, and Jack Vitor, 40 hours, $11.55 per hour.

    e. Save, build, and execute the program. Use the data from Step d to test the program.

    f. When the program is working correctly, hide the Output window, then use the File menu to close the workspace.

Exercise 8 is a Discovery Exercise. Discovery Exercises, which may include topics that are not covered in this lesson, allow you to "discover" the solutions to problems on your own.

8. In this exercise, you will modify the program you created in this lesson so that it uses a function that does not return a value.

    a. Open the T6AppE08.cpp file contained in the Cpp\Tut06\T6AppE08 folder on your computer's hard disk.

    b. Create a program-defined function named `displayPayment`. The function should accept a monthly payment, and then display the monthly payment on the screen. After displaying the monthly payment, the function should advance the cursor to the next line on the screen. (*Hint*: Unlike the functions you learned about in this tutorial, the `displayPayment` function will not return a value. Functions that do not return a value have a *returnDataType* of `void`.)

    c. Enter the appropriate function prototype for the `displayPayment` function.

    d. Change the `cout << "Credit union payment: " << creditPay << endl;` statement to `cout << "Credit union payment: ";`. Insert a blank line below the modified statement, then enter the statement `displayPayment(creditPay);` in the blank line.

    e. Change the `cout << "Dealer payment: " << dealerPay << endl;` statement to `cout << "Dealer payment: ".` Insert a blank line below the modified statement, then enter the statement `displayPayment(dealerPay);` in the blank line.

    f. Save, build, and execute the program. Enter 9000 as the principal, 500 as the rebate, .09 as the credit union rate, .03 as the dealer rate, and 2 as the term. Is is better to finance the car through the credit union or through the car dealer?

    g. When the program is working correctly, hide the Output window, then use the File menu to close the workspace.

A computer program is good only if it works. Errors in either an algorithm or programming code can cause the program to run incorrectly. Therefore, a programmer needs to know how to locate and fix these errors. Exercises 9 through 11 are Debugging Exercises. Debugging Exercises allow you to practice recognizing and solving errors in a program.

debugging

9. In this exercise, you will debug an existing C++ program.

    a. Open the T6AppE09.cpp file contained in the Cpp\Tut06\T6AppE09 folder on your computer's hard disk. The program should calculate and display the miles per gallon, but it is not working correctly. Study the program's code, then build the program.

    b. Correct any errors in the program, then save, build, and execute the program again. When the program is working correctly, hide the Output window, then use the File menu to close the workspace.

10. In this exercise, you will debug an existing C++ program.

    a. Open the T6AppE10.cpp file contained in the Cpp\Tut06\T6AppE10 folder on your computer's hard disk. This program should calculate and display the product of two numbers, but it is not working correctly. Study the program's code, then build and execute the program. Test the program by entering the numbers 4 and 5.

    b. Correct any errors in the program, then save, build, and execute the program. When the program is working correctly, hide the Output window, then use the File menu to close the workspace.

debugging

11. In this exercise, you will debug an existing C++ program.

    a. Open the T6AppE11.cpp file contained in the Cpp\Tut06\T6AppE11 folder on your computer's hard disk. This program should calculate and display the product of two numbers, but it is not working correctly. Study the program's code, then build the program. (Do not be overwhelmed by the number of errors shown in the Output window. Begin by correcting the first error, then save and build the program again. Usually you will find that correcting one error corrects many of the errors that follow it.)

    b. Correct any errors in the program, then save, build, and execute the program. Test the program by entering the numbers 6 and 3. When the program is working correctly, hide the Output window, then use the File menu to close the workspace.

Program-Defined Void Functions

After completing this tutorial, you will be able to:

- Create and invoke a function that does not return a value
- Pass information, by reference, to a function

Concept Lesson

More About Program-Defined Functions

As you learned in Tutorial 6, programmers use program-defined functions for two reasons. First, program-defined functions allow the programmer to avoid duplicating code in different parts of a program. If a program needs to perform the same task several times, it is more efficient to enter the appropriate code once, in a program-defined function, and then simply call the function to perform its task when needed. Second, program-defined functions allow large and complex programs, which typically are written by a team of programmers, to be broken into small and manageable tasks; each member of the team is assigned one of the tasks to code as a function. When writing a payroll program, for example, one team member might code the function that calculates the federal withholding tax, while another might code the function that calculates the state income tax. When each programmer has completed his or her function, all of the functions then are gathered together into one program. The `main` function in the program typically is responsible for calling each of the other functions when needed.

Recall that all functions fall into one of two categories: value-returning or void. Value-returning functions return precisely one value to the statement that called the function. You learned how to create and invoke value-returning functions in Tutorial 6. Figure 7-1 shows the syntax and an example of creating a value-returning function in a C++ program.

As indicated in Figure 7-1, the function header for a value-returning function specifies the data type of the return value, as well as the function's name and any formal parameters. The function body contains the instructions necessary for the function to perform its assigned task. Recall that the last instruction in the function body of a value-returning function in C++ typically is **return** *expression*;, where *expression* represents the value the function returns to the statement that called it. In Figure 7-1's example, for instance, the cube of the number entered by the user is returned to the `cout << calcCube(number);` statement in the `main` function.

tip

▶ Any program-defined function, not just `main`, can call another program-defined function.

function header

function body

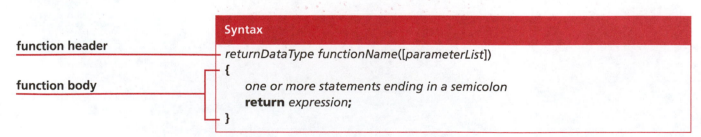

Syntax
returnDataType functionName([parameterList])
{
one or more statements ending in a semicolon
return *expression*;
}

Figure 7-1: Syntax and an example of creating and invoking a value-returning function in C++

Example

```
int main()
{
   int number = 0;
   cout << "Enter an integer: ";
   cin >> number;
   cout << calcCube(number);
   return 0;
}  //end of main function


//*****program-defined functions*****
int calcCube(int num)
{
      return num * num * num;
}  //end of calcCube function
```

function call

function definition

Figure 7-1: Syntax and an example of creating and invoking a value-returning function in C++
(continued)

Unlike value-returning functions, void functions do not return a value. You will learn how to create and invoke void functions in this tutorial.

Creating and Invoking Void Functions

A **void function** is a function that does not return a value after completing its assigned task. You might want to use a void function in a program simply to display information, such as a title and column headings, at the top of each page in a report. Rather than repeat the necessary code several times in the program, you can enter the code once, in a program-defined void function, and then call the function whenever the program needs to display the information. A void function is appropriate in this situation because the function does not need to return a value after completing its task.

Figure 7-2 (on the next page) shows the syntax used to create (or define) a void function in a C++ program. It also shows an example of a program-defined void function whose task is to display a straight line.

There are two differences between the syntax of a value-returning function (shown earlier in Figure 7-1) and the syntax of a void function. First, the function header in a void function begins with the keyword void, rather than with a data type. The keyword void indicates that the function does not return a value. Second, the function body in a void function does not contain a **return** *expression*; statement, which is required in the function body of a value-returning function. The return statement is not necessary in a void function body because a void function does not return a value.

As you do with a value-returning function, you call a void function by including its name and actual arguments (if any) in a statement. Unlike a call to a value-returning function, however, a call to a void function appears as a statement by itself, rather than as part of another statement. For example, compare the function call shown in Figure 7-1 with the two function calls shown in Figure 7-2. Notice that the call to the value-returning calcCube function in Figure 7-1 is included in the cout << calcCube(number); statement, which displays the function's return value on the screen, whereas each call to the void displayLine function in Figure 7-2 is a self-contained statement.

The close function you learned about in Tutorial 5's Application lesson is an example of a void function built into the C++ language.

In some programming languages—for example, Visual Basic—void functions are referred to as sub procedures; *sub* is short for *subroutine*.

tip

Recall that a function header in a C++ program does not end with a semicolon, because it is not considered a statement.

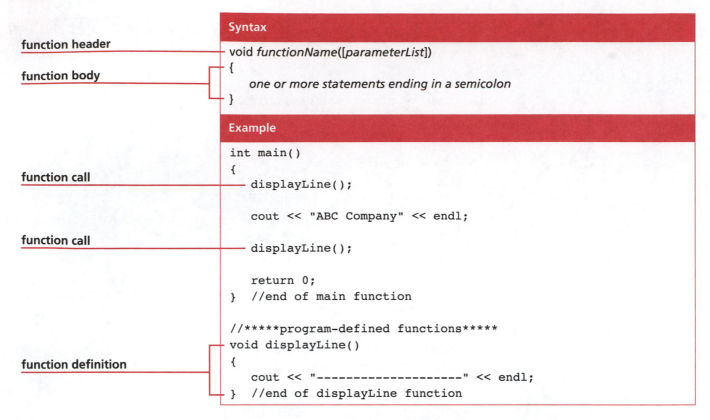

function header

function body

function call

function call

function definition

Figure 7-2: Syntax and an example of creating and invoking a void function in C++

When the computer processes a statement that calls a program-defined void function, the computer first locates the function's code in the program. If the function call contains an *argumentList*, the computer passes the values of the actual arguments (assuming variables included in the *argumentList* are passed *by value*) to the called function. Recall that the function receives these values and stores them in the formal parameters listed in its *parameterList*. After doing so, the computer processes the function's code and then it continues program execution with the statement immediately following the one that called the function. In Figure 7-2's example, for instance, the computer would continue program execution with the statement `cout << "ABC Company" << endl;` after processing the `displayLine` function's code the first time. It would continue with the statement `return 0;` after processing the function's code the second time.

In Tutorial 6, you learned that, unless specified otherwise, variables are passed to functions *by value*. In the remainder of this lesson, you will review the concept of passing *by value*, and you will learn another way of passing variables to a function—*by reference*.

Mini-Quiz 1

1. A void function header in C++ begins with the keyword _____.

2. Which of the following C++ statements can be used to call a void function named `displayTaxes`, passing it two `float` variables named `federal` and `state`?

   a. `cout << displayTaxes(federal, state);`

   b. `taxes = displayTaxes(federal, state);`

   c. `displayTaxes(federal, state);`

   d. All of the above

3. Write the function header for Question 2's `displayTaxes` function. Use the names `fedTax` and `stateTax` for the formal parameters.

4. The `return` statement is typically the last statement in a C++ void function.

   a. True

   b. False

> **tip**
>
> Recall from the Overview that the internal memory of a computer is like a large post office, where each memory cell, like each post office box, has a unique address.

Passing Variables

Each variable you reserve in a program has both a value and a unique address that represents the location of the variable in memory. Most programming languages allow you to pass either the variable's value (referred to as passing *by value*) or its address (referred to as passing *by reference*) to the receiving function. The method you choose—*by value* or *by reference*—will depend on whether you want the receiving function to have access to the variable in memory—in other words, whether you want to allow the receiving function to change the contents of the variable.

Although the idea of passing information *by value* and *by reference* may sound confusing at first, it is a concept with which you already are familiar. To illustrate, assume that you have a savings account at a local bank. During a conversation with a friend, you mention the amount of money you have in the account. Telling someone the amount of money in your account is similar to passing a variable *by value*. Knowing the balance in your account doesn't give your friend access to your bank account; it merely gives your friend some information that he or she can use—perhaps to compare to the amount of money he or she has saved.

> **tip**
>
> The default method used to pass variables is language-dependent. Some languages, such as C++ and Java, automatically pass variables *by value*. Other languages—for example, Visual Basic—automatically pass variables *by reference*. (To pass a variable *by value* in Visual Basic, you must include the keyword `ByVal` before the variable's name in the function header.) You will need to check the programming language's documentation to determine which method the language uses.

The savings account example also provides an illustration of passing information *by reference*. To deposit money to or withdraw money from your account, you must provide the bank teller with your account number. The account number represents the location of your account at the bank and allows the teller to change the account balance. Giving the teller your bank account number is similar to passing a variable *by reference*. The account number allows the teller to change the contents of your bank account; the variable's address allows the receiving function to change the contents of the variable passed to the function.

Before learning how to pass a variable *by reference*, review passing *by value*.

Passing Variables by Value

As you learned in Tutorial 6, when you pass a variable *by value*, the computer passes only the contents of the variable to the receiving function. When only the contents are passed, the receiving function is not given access to the variable in memory, so it cannot change the value stored inside the variable. You pass a variable *by value* when the receiving function needs to *know* the variable's contents, but the receiving function does not need to *change* the contents. Recall that, unless specified otherwise, variables are passed *by value* in C++. In the C++ programs you created in Tutorials 5 and 6, for example, all of the variables passed to functions were passed *by value*, because none of the programs required the receiving function to change the contents of the variables passed to it.

Figure 7-3 shows a C++ program that calculates and displays a salesperson's total sales and his or her bonus. Notice that the program's `main` function calls a void function named `calcAndDisplay`, passing it three variables *by value*.

function prototype

function call

function definition

```
//function prototype
void calcAndDisplay(float, float, float);

int main()
{
    float sale1    = 0.0;
    float sale2    = 0.0;
    float bonusRate = 0.0;
    //enter input items
    cout << "Enter first sale: ";
    cin >> sale1;
    cout << "Enter second sale: ";
    cin >> sale2;
    cout << "Enter bonus rate: ";
    cin >> bonusRate;
    //calculate and display total sales and bonus
    calcAndDisplay(sale1, sale2, bonusRate);
    return 0;
}   //end of main function

//*****program-defined functions*****
void calcAndDisplay(float s1, float s2, float rate)
{
    float total = 0.0;
    float bonus = 0.0;
    total = s1 + s2;
    bonus = total * rate;
    cout << "Total: " << total << endl;
    cout << "Bonus: " << bonus << endl;
}   //end of calcAndDisplay function
```

Figure 7-3: Example of passing variables *by value*

Because the `calcAndDisplay` function shown in Figure 7-3 is a void function, its function call, which is shaded in the figure, appears as a statement by itself. Notice that the number, data type, and sequence of the actual arguments in the function call match the number, data type, and sequence of the corresponding formal parameters in both the function header and function prototype. Also notice that the names of the formal parameters do not need to be identical to the names of the actual arguments to which they correspond. In fact, for clarity, it usually is better to use different names for the actual arguments and formal parameters. To review the concept of passing *by value*, you will desk-check the program shown in Figure 7-3.

Desk-Checking Figure 7-3's Program

The first three statements in the `main` function shown in Figure 7-3 reserve and initialize three `float` variables named `sale1`, `sale2`, and `bonusRate`. These variables are local to the `main` function, and they remain in memory until the `main` function's `return 0;` statement is processed.

The next six statements prompt the user to enter two sale amounts and the bonus rate, and then store the user's responses in the three `float` variables. Assume that the user enters the numbers 2350.25, 3000.75, and .1. Figure 7-4 shows the contents of memory after the first nine statements are processed.

`main` **function's variables**

sale1	sale2	bonusRate
~~0.0~~ 2350.25	~~0.0~~ 3000.75	~~0.0~~ .1

Figure 7-4: Contents of memory after the first nine statements in the `main` function are processed

The tenth statement, `calcAndDisplay(sale1, sale2, bonusRate);`, calls the `calcAndDisplay` function, passing it three variables *by value*, which means that only the contents of the variables are passed to the function. In this case, the computer passes the numbers 2350.25, 3000.75, and .1 to the `calcAndDisplay` function.

At this point, the computer leaves the `main` function, temporarily, to process the code contained in the `calcAndDisplay` function. The `calcAndDisplay` function header indicates that the computer should reserve three local `float` variables named `s1`, `s2`, and `rate`. The computer stores the values passed to the function in these local variables, as shown in Figure 7-5.

tip

▶ Recall that variables in a C++ program are passed, automatically, *by value*.

`calcAndDisplay` **function's variables**

`main` **function's variables**

sale1	sale2	bonusRate		s1	s2	rate
~~0.0~~ 2350.25	~~0.0~~ 3000.75	~~0.0~~ .1		2350.25	3000.75	.1

Figure 7-5: Contents of memory after the `calcAndDisplay` function header is processed

tip

▶ Recall that the variables listed in a function header are local to the function, which means they can be used only by the function.

Next, the computer processes the statements contained in the `calcAndDisplay` function body. The first two statements create and initialize two local `float` variables named `total` and `bonus`. The third statement adds together the contents of the `s1` and `s2` variables, and then assigns the sum (5351.00) to the `total` variable. The fourth statement multiplies the contents of the `total` variable by the contents of the `rate` variable, and then assigns the product (535.10) to the `bonus` variable, as shown in Figure 7-6.

`calcAndDisplay`
function's variables

`main` **function's variables**

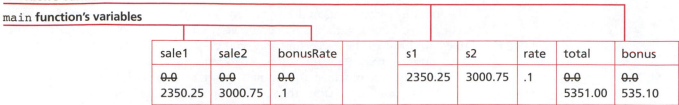

sale1	sale2	bonusRate		s1	s2	rate	total	bonus
~~0.0~~	~~0.0~~	~~0.0~~		2350.25	3000.75	.1	~~0.0~~	~~0.0~~
2350.25	3000.75	.1					5351.00	535.10

Figure 7-6: Contents of memory after the first four statements in the `calcAndDisplay` function are processed

The last two statements in the `calcAndDisplay` function display the contents of the `total` and `bonus` variables on the screen. When the computer encounters the `calcAndDisplay` function's closing brace (}), which marks the end of the function, it removes the function's local variables (`s1`, `s2`, `rate`, `total`, and `bonus`) from memory. It then continues program execution with the statement immediately following the one that called the function. In this case, program execution continues with the `return 0;` statement in the `main` function. Figure 7-7 shows the contents of memory after the `calcAndDisplay` function has completed its task. Notice that only the `main` function's local variables (`sale1`, `sale2`, and `bonusRate`) remain in the computer's memory.

`main` **function's variables**

sale1	sale2	bonusRate
~~0.0~~	~~0.0~~	~~0.0~~
2350.25	3000.75	.1

Figure 7-7: Contents of memory after the `calcAndDisplay` function ends

The `return 0;` statement in the `main` function, which is the next statement processed, returns the number 0 to the operating system to indicate that the program ended normally. The computer then removes the `main` function's local variables (`sale1`, `sale2`, and `bonusRate`) from memory before ending the program.

Next, learn how to pass variables *by reference*.

Passing Variables by Reference

In addition to passing a variable's value to a function, most languages also allow you to pass a variable's address—in other words, its location in the computer's memory. Passing a variable's address is referred to as passing *by reference*, and it gives the receiving function access to the variable being passed. You pass a variable *by reference* when you want the receiving function to change the contents of the variable.

To pass a variable *by reference* to a C++ function, you simply include an ampersand (&), called the **address-of operator**, before the name of the corresponding formal parameter in the function header. If the function definition appears below the `main` function in the program, you also must include the address-of operator in the function prototype, after the formal parameter's data type and a space. The address-of operator tells the computer to pass the variable's address rather than its contents.

tip

The statement that calls a function does not indicate if an item is passed *by value* or *by reference*. To determine how an item is passed, you need to examine the *parameterList* in either the function header or function prototype.

Figure 7-8 shows a C++ program that calculates and displays the average of two test scores. Notice that the program's `main` function calls a void function named `getScores`, passing it two variables *by reference*, as indicated by the address-of operators (`&`) in both the function prototype and function header.

Because the `getScores` function is a void function, its function call, which is shaded in the figure, appears as a statement by itself. Notice that the number, data type, and sequence of the actual arguments in the function call match the number, data type, and sequence of the corresponding formal parameters in both the function header and function prototype. Also notice that the names of the formal parameters do not need to be identical to the names of the actual arguments to which they correspond. Additionally, notice that the address-of operator appears before the name of the formal parameter in the function header; it appears after the data type and a space in the function prototype. Desk-checking the program shown in Figure 7-8 will help you understand the concept of passing *by reference*.

address-of operator

function call

address-of operator

```cpp
//function prototype
void getScores(float &, float &);

int main()
{
    float test1 = 0.0;
    float test2 = 0.0;
    float avg   = 0.0;
    //enter input items
    getScores(test1, test2);
    //calculate and display average
    avg = (test1 + test2) / 2;
    cout << "Average: " << avg << endl;
    return 0;
}   //end of main function

//*****program-defined functions*****
void getScores(float &score1, float &score2)
{
    cout << "Enter first test score: ";
    cin >> score1;
    cout << "Enter second test score: ";
    cin >> score2;
}   //end of getScores function
```

Figure 7-8: Example of passing variables *by reference*

Desk-Checking Figure 7-8's Program

The first three statements in the `main` function shown in Figure 7-8 reserve and initialize three `float` variables named `test1`, `test2`, and `avg`. Figure 7-9 shows the contents of memory after these statements are processed.

main function's variables

test1	test2	avg
0.0	0.0	0.0

Figure 7-9: Contents of memory after the first three statements in the main function are processed

The fourth statement, getScores(test1, test2);, calls the getScores function, passing it two variables. Both variables will be passed *by reference*, which means that each variable's address in memory, rather than its contents, will be passed. At this point, the computer temporarily leaves the main function to process the code contained in the getScores function.

The getScores function header indicates that the function will be receiving the addresses of two **float** variables. When you pass a variable's address to a function, the computer uses the address to locate the variable in memory; it then assigns the name appearing in the function header to the memory location. In this case, for example, the computer first locates the test1 and test2 variables in memory. After doing so, it assigns the names score1 and score2, respectively, to these locations. At this point, each of the two memory locations has two names: one assigned by the main function, and the other assigned by the getScores function, as shown in Figure 7-10.

variable belonging only to main

variables belonging to both main and getScores

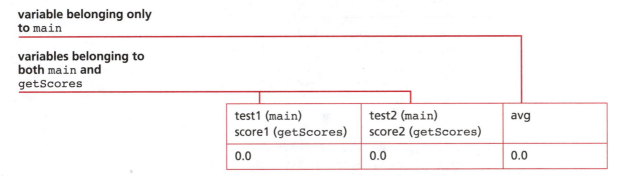

test1 (main) score1 (getScores)	test2 (main) score2 (getScores)	avg
0.0	0.0	0.0

Figure 7-10: Contents of memory after the getScores function header is processed

As Figure 7-10 indicates, only one of the memory locations shown in the figure—the one named **avg**—belongs strictly to the **main** function. The other two memory locations shown in the figure belong to both the **main** and **getScores** functions. Although both functions can access these memory locations, each function uses a different name to do so. The **main** function, for example, uses the names test1 and test2 to refer to these memory locations. The **getScores** function, on the other hand, uses the names score1 and score2.

After processing the **getScores** function header, the computer processes the statements contained in the function body. Those statements prompt the user to enter two test scores, and then store the user's responses in the **score1** and **score2** variables. Assume the user enters the numbers 93 and 84. Figure 7-11 shows the contents of memory after the four statements in the **getScores** function are processed.

**variable belonging only
to** main

**variables belonging to
both** main **and**
getScores

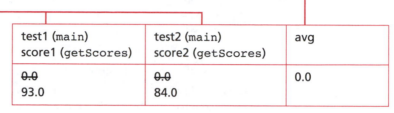

test1 (main) score1 (getScores)	test2 (main) score2 (getScores)	avg
~~0.0~~ 93.0	~~0.0~~ 84.0	0.0

Figure 7-11: Contents of memory after the four statements in the getScores function are processed

tip

· · · · · · · · · · · · · · · · · ·

► A value-returning function uses its return value to send information back to the function that called it. A void function, on the other hand, uses variables that are passed *by reference*.

Changing the contents of the score1 and score2 variables also changes the contents of the test1 and test2 variables, respectively. This is because the names refer to the same locations in memory.

When the computer encounters the getScores function's closing brace (}), it removes the score1 and score2 names assigned to the main function's test1 and test2 variables. Program execution then continues with the statement immediately following the one that called the function. In this case, program execution continues with the avg = (test1 + test2) / 2; statement in the main function. Figure 7-12 shows the contents of memory after the getScores function ends. Notice that only the main function's local variables (test1, test2, and avg) remain in the computer's memory.

main **function's variables**

test1	test2	avg
~~0.0~~ 93.0	~~0.0~~ 84.0	0.0

Figure 7-12: Contents of memory after the getScores function ends

The avg = (test1 + test2) / 2; statement in the main function adds the contents of the test1 variable to the contents of the test2 variable. It then divides the sum (177) by two and assigns the result (88.5) to the avg variable, as shown in Figure 7-13.

main **function's variables**

test1	test2	avg
~~0.0~~ 93.0	~~0.0~~ 84.0	~~0.0~~ 88.5

Figure 7-13: Contents of memory after the average is calculated

The next statement processed, cout << "Average: " << avg << endl;, displays the average test score on the screen. When the computer encounters the return 0; statement, it removes the main function's local variables (test1, test2, and avg) from memory before ending the program.

Mini-Quiz 2

1. Write the function header for a C++ void function named `calcTaxes`. The function will be passed the value of the `main` function's `gross` variable, and the addresses of the `main` function's `federal` and `state` variables. The three variables have a data type of `float`. Use the names `pay`, `fedTax`, and `stateTax` for the formal parameters.

2. Write the statement to call Question 1's `calcTaxes` function.

3. Write the function prototype for Question 1's `calcTaxes` function.

4. A void function's local variables are removed from memory when the computer encounters the function's _____.

Before ending this lesson, you will view one more program that passes variables to a function.

Passing Variables by Value and by Reference

In the program shown earlier in Figure 7-3, the variables passed to the `calcAndDisplay` function were passed *by value*. In Figure 7-8's program, on the other hand, the variables were passed to the `getScores` function *by reference*. You also can mix the way variables are passed when a function is called, passing some *by reference* and others *by value*, as shown in Figure 7-14's program.

```
//function prototype
void calc(float, float, float &, float &);

int main()
{
    float salary    = 0.0;
    float raiseRate = 0.0;
    float raise     = 0.0;
    float newSalary = 0.0;
    //enter input items
    cout << "Enter current salary: ";
    cin >> salary;
    cout << "Enter raise rate: ";
    cin >> raiseRate;
    //calculate raise and new salary
    calc(salary, raiseRate, raise, newSalary);
    //display raise and new salary
    cout << "Raise: " << raise << endl;
    cout << "New salary: " << newSalary << endl;
    return 0;
}  //end of main function

//*****program-defined functions*****
void calc(float current, float rate, float &increase, float &pay)
{
    increase = current * rate;
    pay = current + increase;
}  //end of calc function
```

passed by value

passed by reference

function call

Figure 7-14: Example of passing variables *by value* and *by reference*

The program shown in Figure 7-14 calculates and displays an employee's raise and new salary, given the employee's current salary and the raise rate. The first four statements in the `main` function reserve and initialize four `float` variables named `salary`, `raiseRate`, `raise`, and `newSalary`. The next four statements prompt the user to enter the current salary and the raise rate, and then store the user's responses in the `salary` and `raiseRate` variables. Assume that the user enters the numbers 34500 and .06 for the salary and rate, respectively. Figure 7-15 shows the contents of memory after the first eight statements are processed.

`main` function's variables

salary	raiseRate	raise	newSalary
~~0.0~~	~~0.0~~	0.0	0.0
34500.0	.06		

Figure 7-15: Contents of memory after the first eight statements in the `main` function are processed

> Recall that when you pass a variable *by value*, only the variable's contents are passed. When you pass a variable *by reference*, only the variable's address in memory is passed.

The next statement to be processed, `calc(salary, raiseRate, raise, newSalary);`, calls the `calc` function, passing it four variables. Two of the variables, `salary` and `raiseRate`, are passed *by value*, because the receiving function needs to know only the values stored in these variables. The other two variables, `raise` and `newSalary`, are passed *by reference*, because it is the receiving function's responsibility to calculate the raise and new salary amounts and then store the results in these memory locations.

At this point, the computer temporarily leaves the `main` function to process the code contained in the `calc` function. The `float current, float rate` portion of the `calc` function header indicates that the computer will need to reserve two `float` memory locations named `current` and `rate`. These memory locations will store the values of the `salary` and `raiseRate` variables passed to the function. The `float &increase, float &pay` portion of the `calc` function header tells the computer to assign the name `increase` to the `main` function's `raise` variable, and assign the name `pay` to the `main` function's `newSalary` variable. Figure 7-16 shows the contents of memory after the `calc` function header is processed.

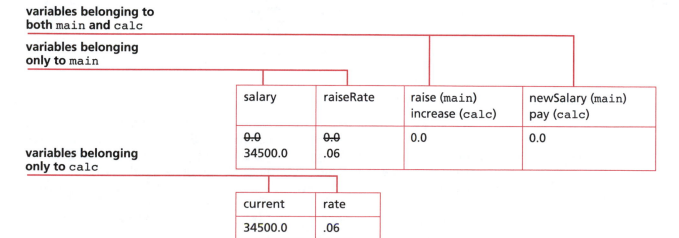

Figure 7-16: Contents of memory after the `calc` function header is processed

The statements contained in the `calc` function body are processed next. The first statement multiplies the contents of the `current` variable by the contents of the `rate` variable, and then assigns the result (2070) to the `increase` variable. The second statement adds together the contents of the `current` and `increase` variables, and then assigns the sum (36570) to the `pay` variable, as shown in Figure 7-17.

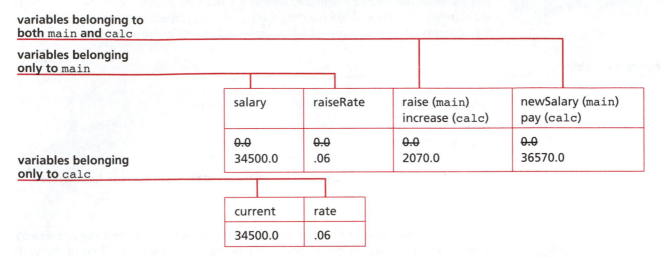

variables belonging to both main **and** calc

variables belonging only to main

variables belonging only to calc

salary	raiseRate	raise (main) increase (calc)	newSalary (main) pay (calc)
0.0 34500.0	0.0 .06	0.0 2070.0	0.0 36570.0

current	rate
34500.0	.06

Figure 7-17: Contents of memory after the two statements in the `calc` function are processed

When the computer encounters the `calc` function's closing brace, it removes the `increase` and `pay` names assigned to the `main` function's `raise` and `newSalary` variables. It also removes the `calc` function's `current` and `rate` variables from memory. Program execution then continues with the statement immediately following the one that called the function. In this case, program execution continues with the `cout << "Raise: " << raise << endl;` statement in the `main` function. Figure 7-18 shows the contents of memory after the `calc` function ends. Notice that only the main function's local variables (`salary`, `raiseRate`, `raise`, and `newSalary`) remain in the computer's memory.

main **function's variables**

salary	raiseRate	raise	newSalary
0.0 34500.0	0.0 .06	0.0 2070.0	0.0 36570.0

Figure 7-18: Contents of memory after the `calc` function ends

The `cout << "Raise: " << raise << endl;` statement in the `main` function is the next statement processed and displays the raise amount on the screen. The `cout << "New salary: " << newSalary << endl;` statement then displays the new salary amount. When the computer processes the last statement in the `main` function—`return 0;`—it returns the number 0 to the operating system to indicate that the program ended normally. The computer then removes the `main` function's local variables (`salary`, `raiseRate`, `raise`, and `newSalary`) from memory before ending the program.

You now have completed Tutorial 7's Concept lesson. You can either take a break or complete the end-of-lesson questions and exercises before moving on to the Application lesson.

SUMMARY

All functions fall into one of two categories: value-returning or void. A value-returning function returns precisely one value to the statement that called the function. A void function, on the other hand, does not return a value after completing its assigned task.

Like a value-returning function, a void function is composed of a function header and a function body. However, unlike a value-returning function, the function header for a void function begins with the keyword `void`. Also unlike a value-returning function, the function body for a void function does not contain a `return` statement.

As you do with a value-returning function, you call a void function by including its name and actual arguments (if any) in a statement. Unlike a call to a value-returning function, however, a call to a void function appears as a statement by itself, rather than as part of another statement. When the computer finishes processing a void function's code, it continues program execution with the statement immediately following the one that called the function.

Variables can be passed to functions either *by value* or *by reference*. When you pass a variable *by value*, only the value stored inside the variable is passed to the receiving function. The receiving function is not given access to a variable passed *by value*, so it cannot change the variable's contents. When you pass a variable *by reference*, on the other hand, its address in memory is passed to the receiving function, allowing the receiving function to change the variable's contents. Unless specified otherwise, variables in C++ are passed automatically *by value*. To pass a variable *by reference* in a C++ program, you include the address-of operator (&) before the corresponding formal parameter's name in the function header. If the function definition appears below the `main` function in the program, you also must include the address-of operator in the function prototype. The address-of operator tells the computer to pass the variable's address rather than its contents.

ANSWERS TO MINI-QUIZZES

Mini-Quiz 1

1. `void`
2. c. `displayTaxes(federal, state);`
3. `void displayTaxes(float fedTax, float stateTax)`
4. b. False

Mini-Quiz 2

1. `void calcTaxes(float pay, float &fedTax, float &stateTax)`
2. `calcTaxes(gross, federal, state);`
3. `void calcTaxes(float, float &, float &);`
4. closing brace (})

QUESTIONS

1. Which of the following is false?
   a. A void function does not return a value after completing its assigned task.
   b. A void function call typically appears as its own statement in a C++ program.
   c. A void function cannot receive any items of information when it is called.
   d. A void Von header begins with the keyword `void`.

2. Which of the following C++ statements can be used to call a void function named `displayHeading`, passing it one `string` variable named `companyName`?
   a. `cout << displayHeading(string companyName);`
   b. `cout << displayHeading(companyName);`
   c. `displayHeading(string companyName);`
   d. `displayHeading(companyName);`

3. Which of the following function prototypes can be used for a void function named `calcEndingBalance`? The function will be passed the value of two `int` variables.
   a. `void calcEndingBalance(int, int);`
   b. `void calcEndingBalance(int, int)`
   c. `void calcEndingBalance(int &, int &);`
   d. `int calcEndingBalance(void);`

4. Assume that a void function named `calcEndingInventory` receives four `int` variables from the `main` function: `beginInventory`, `sales`, `purchases`, and `endingInventory`. The function's task is to calculate the ending inventory, based on the beginning inventory, sales, and purchase amounts passed to the function. The function should store the result in the `endingInventory` memory location. Which of the following function headers is correct?
   a. `void calcEndingInventory(&int b, &int s, &int p, &int e)`
   b. `void calcEndingInventory(int b, int s, int p, int e)`
   c. `void calcEndingInventory(int &b, int &s, int &p, int e)`
   d. `void calcEndingInventory(int b, int s, int p, int &e)`

5. Which of the following statements should you use to call the `calcEndingInventory` function described in Question 4?
   a. `calcEndingInventory(int, int, int, int);`
   b. `calcEndingInventory(beginInventory, sales, purchases, &endingInventory);`
   c. `calcEndingInventory(beginInventory, sales, purchases, endingInventory);`
   d. `calcEndingInventory(int beginInventory, int sales, int purchases, int &endingInventory);`

6. In C++, variables are passed automatically _____.
   a. by address
   b. by number
   c. by reference
   d. by value

7. If you want the receiving function to change the contents of a variable, you will need to pass the variable _____.
   a. by address
   b. by number
   c. by reference
   d. by value

8. To determine whether an item is being passed *by value* or *by reference*, you will need to examine either the _____ or the _____.
   a. function call, function header
   b. function call, function prototype
   c. function header, function prototype
   d. function header, function body

9. Which of the following is false?
   a. You enclose a function's statements in a set of braces.
   b. The function header is considered a C++ statement, so it must end with a semicolon.
   c. The keyword `void` tells the C++ compiler that the function does not return a value.
   d. An empty set of parentheses after the function's name in the function header tells you that the function does not receive any information.

10. Which of the following calls a function named `displayName`, passing it no actual arguments?
    a. `call displayName();`
    b. `displayName;`
    c. `displayName()`
    d. `displayName();`

11. Assume a program contains a void function named `displayName`. Which of the following is a correct function prototype for this function, assuming that the function requires no formal parameters?
    a. `displayName();`
    b. `void displayName;`
    c. `void displayName();`
    d. `void displayName(none);`

12. When the computer encounters a void function's closing brace (}), it continues program execution with the statement _____.
    a. immediately preceding the statement that called the function
    b. that called the function
    c. immediately following the statement that called the function

13. A program will have one function prototype for each function defined in the program-defined section of the program. (Assume that the program-defined section is located below the `main` function.)
    a. True
    b. False

14. Variables that can be used only by the function in which they are declared are called _____ variables.
    a. global
    b. local
    c. separate
    d. void

15. Which of the following is false?
    a. When you pass a variable *by reference*, the receiving function can change its contents.
    b. When you pass a variable *by value*, the receiving function creates a local variable that it uses to store the passed value.
    c. Unless specified otherwise, all variables in C++ are passed *by value*.
    d. To pass a variable *by reference* in C++, you place an ampersand (&) before the variable's name in the statement that calls the function.

16. Assume a program contains a void function named `calcNewPrice` that receives two `float` variables: `oldPrice` and `newPrice`. The function multiplies the contents of the `oldPrice` variable by 1.1, and then stores the result in the `newPrice` variable. Which of the following is the best function prototype for this function?
    a. `void calcNewPrice(float, float);`
    b. `void calcNewPrice(float &, float);`
    c. `void calcNewPrice(float, float &);`
    d. `void calcNewPrice(float &, float &);`

17. Which of the following can be used to call Question 16's `calcNewPrice` function?
    a. `calcNewPrice(float oldPrice, float newPrice);`
    b. `calcNewPrice(&oldPrice, newPrice);`
    c. `calcNewPrice(oldPrice, &newPrice);`
    d. `calcNewPrice(oldPrice, newPrice);`

18. Which of the following is false?
    a. The names of the formal parameters in the function header must be identical to the names of the actual arguments in the function call.
    b. When listing the formal parameters in a function header, you must include each parameter's data type and name.
    c. The formal parameters should be the same data type as the actual arguments.
    d. If a function call passes an `int` variable first and a `char` variable second, the receiving function must receive an `int` variable first and a `char` variable second.

EXERCISES

1. Write the C++ code for a void function that receives an integer passed to it. The function, named `halveNumber`, should divide the integer by 2, and then display the result.

2. Write the C++ code for a void function that prompts the user to enter a character, and then stores the user's response in the `char` variable whose address is passed to the function. Name the function `getChar`.

3. Write the C++ code for a void function that receives four `int` variables: the first two *by value* and the last two *by reference*. The function should calculate the sum and the difference of the two variables passed *by value*, and then store the results in the variables passed *by reference*. (When calculating the difference, subtract the contents of the second variable from the contents of the first variable.) Name the function `calcSumAndDiff`.

4. Write the C++ code for a void function that receives three `float` variables: the first two *by value* and the last one *by reference*. The function should divide the first variable by the second variable, and then store the result in the third variable. Name the function `quotient`.

5. Write the C++ code for a void function that prompts the user to enter a name, and then stores the user's response in the `string` variable whose address is passed to the function. Name the function `getName`.

6. Write the C++ code for a void function that generates a random integer within the range *lowerbound* to *upperbound*. As you learned in Tutorial 5, you can use the formula *lowerbound* + **rand**() **%** (*upperbound* - *lowerbound* **+ 1**) to specify the range of integers you want to generate. The function will receive three variables: the first two *by value* and the last one *by reference*. The first variable represents the *lowerbound*, and the second variable represents the *upperbound*. The function should store the random number in the third variable.

7. Desk-check the program shown in Figure 7-19. Show the desk-check table after the first four instructions in the `main` function are processed, after the `calcEnd` function's `ending = beg + pur − sale;` statement is processed, and after the `calcEnd` function ends.

```
//function prototype
void calcEnd(int, int, int, int &);

int main()
{
    int begVal   = 1000;
    int purchase = 500;
    int sale     = 200;
    int endVal   = 0;

    calcEnd(begVal, purchase, sale, endVal);
```

Figure 7-19

```
      cout << endVal << endl;
      return 0;
}   //end of main function


//*****program-defined functions*****
void calcEnd(int beg, int pur, int sale, int &ending)
{
      ending = beg + pur - sale;
}   //end of calcEnd function
```

Figure 7-19 (continued)

Exercise 8 is a Discovery Exercise. Discovery Exercises, which may include topics that are not covered in this lesson, allow you to "discover" the solutions to problems on your own.

8. In this exercise, you will experiment with passing *by value* and *by reference*.
   a. Open the T7ConE08.cpp file contained in the Cpp\Tut07\T7ConE08 folder on your computer's hard disk. Notice that the **main** function passes the **name** variable *by value* to the **getName** function.
   b. Build and execute the program. When prompted to enter a name, type your name and press the Enter key. Because the **name** variable was passed *by value*, the program does not display your name.
   c. Modify the program so that it passes the **name** variable *by reference* to the **getName** function.
   d. Save, build, and execute the program. When prompted to enter a name, type your name and press the Enter key. Because the **name** variable was passed *by reference*, the program displays your name.
   e. Hide the Output window, then use the File menu to close the workspace.

A computer program is good only if it works. Errors in either an algorithm or programming code can cause the program to run incorrectly. Therefore, a programmer needs to know how to locate and fix these errors. Exercises 9 and 10 are Debugging Exercises. Debugging Exercises allow you to practice recognizing and solving errors in a program.

debugging

9. In this exercise, you will debug an existing C++ program.
   a. Open the T7ConE09.cpp file contained in the Cpp\Tut07\T7ConE09 folder on your computer's hard disk. The program should display a name entered by a user, but it is not working correctly. Study the program's code, then build and execute the program. Enter Harry Thomas as the name.
   b. Correct any errors in the program, then save, build, and execute the program. When the program is working correctly, hide the Output window, then use the File menu to close the workspace.

debugging

10. In this exercise, you will debug an existing C++ program.
   a. Open the T7ConE10.cpp file contained in the Cpp\Tut07\T7ConE10 folder on your computer's hard disk. The program should calculate and display the sum of two numbers, but it is not working correctly. Study the program's code, then build and execute the program.
   b. Correct any errors in the program, then save, build, and execute the program. When the program is working correctly, hide the Output window, then use the File menu to close the workspace.

Application Lesson

Using Void Functions in a C++ Program

case ▶ Jane Hernandez is employed by the public works office in Allenton, a small rural town with a population of 500. Each month, Jane manually calculates each customer's water bill—a time-consuming task and one that is prone to errors. She has asked you to create a program that will make the appropriate calculations, and then display the customer's name, gallons of water used, and water charge. Currently, the charge for water is $1.75 per 1000 gallons, or .00175 per gallon.

Analyzing, Planning, and Desk-Checking the Water Bill Algorithm

Figure 7-20 shows the IPO chart for the water bill problem outlined in this lesson's Case.

Input	Processing	Output
customer name current reading (gallons) previous reading (gallons) rate per gallon (.00175)	Processing items: none Algorithm: 1. enter the customer name, current reading, and previous reading 2. calculate the gallons used by subtracting the previous reading from the current reading 3. calculate the water charge by multiplying the gallons used by the rate per gallon 4. display the customer name, gallons used, and water charge	customer name gallons used water charge

Figure 7-20: IPO chart for the water bill problem

According to the IPO chart, the program's output is the customer name, gallons used, and water charge. To display the output, the program needs to know the customer name, the current and previous water meter readings (in gallons), and the rate per gallon. According to the algorithm, the program first will have the user enter the customer name and the current and previous readings. It then will calculate both the gallons used and the water charge, and it will display the result of both calculations, along with the customer name, on the screen.

As you learned in Tutorial 2, most algorithms follow a format similar to the one shown in Figure 7-20. That is, they first get the input data, then they process that data (typically by performing calculations on it), and then they display the output data. For simple algorithms (such as the water bill algorithm), the input, processing, and output tasks can be performed quite easily by the `main` function itself. As programs become larger and more complex, however, it is helpful to assign these tasks to program-defined functions, and then have the `main` function call each program-defined function when needed. Doing this allows the programmer to code and test one small portion of the program at a time. It also allows a team of programmers to work on a program, with each member of the team responsible for coding one or more of the functions.

Although the water bill algorithm is small and very simple, it can be used to demonstrate the concept of assigning major tasks to multiple program-defined functions, and then using the `main` function to call each program-defined function at the appropriate time. Toward that end, you will assign the water bill algorithm's four tasks to three program-defined void functions named `getInput`, `calculate`, and `displayBill`. The `getInput` function will be assigned the task of getting the user input (customer name, current reading, and previous reading). A void function is appropriate in this case, because the `getInput` function needs to get three values for the `main` function (recall that a value-returning function can return only one value). The `calculate` function will be responsible for calculating both the gallons used and the water charge. Here again, a void function is appropriate because the `calculate` function needs to calculate more than one value for the `main` function. The `displayBill` function will be responsible for displaying the output (customer name, gallons used, and water charge) on the screen. The `displayBill` function also should be a void function, because it will not need to return a value to the `main` function after completing its task. Figure 7-21 shows the IPO charts for the water bill problem using program-defined functions.

tip

The processing task for large and complex programs typically is assigned to more than one program-defined function. For example, a payroll program's processing task might be assigned to four functions that calculate the gross pay, calculate the tax deductions, calculate the insurance deductions, and calculate the net pay.

tip

Rather than using one void function to get the three input items in the water bill problem, you could use three value-returning functions, one to get each input item. You also could use two value-returning functions, rather than one void function, to calculate and return the gallons used and the water charge.

main function

Input	Processing	Output
customer name current reading (gallons) previous reading (gallons) rate per gallon (.00175)	Processing items: none Algorithm: 1. getInput(customer name, current reading, previous reading) 2. calculate(current reading, previous reading, rate per gallon, gallons used, water charge) 3. displayBill(customer name, gallons used, water charge)	customer name gallons used water charge

Figure 7-21: Revised IPO charts for the water bill problem

`getInput` **function**

Input	Processing	Output
address of customer name address of current reading address of previous reading	Processing items: none Algorithm: 1. enter the customer name, current reading, and previous reading	customer name current reading previous reading

`calculate` **function**

Input	Processing	Output
current reading previous reading rate per gallon address of gallons used address of water charge	Processing items: none Algorithm: 1. calculate the gallons used by subtracting the previous reading from the current reading 2. calculate the water charge by multiplying the gallons used by the rate per gallon	gallons used water charge

`displayBill` **function**

Input	Processing	Output
customer name gallons used water charge	Processing items: none Algorithm: 1. display the customer name, gallons used, and water charge	customer name gallons used water charge

Figure 7-21: Revised IPO charts for the water bill problem (continued)

First compare the `main` function's IPO chart shown in Figure 7-21 with the IPO chart shown in Figure 7-20. Notice that the `main` function's input and output items are the same in both charts; the algorithms, however, are different. Figure 7-20's algorithm indicates that the `main` function will perform the required input, processing, and output tasks, while Figure 7-21's algorithm indicates that the `main` function will call three program-defined functions to perform those tasks.

According to the IPO charts shown in Figure 7-21, the `main` function first will call the `getInput` function, whose task is to get the required information from the user. Notice that the `getInput` function's output is the customer name, current reading, and previous reading. For the function to perform its task, the `main` function will need to pass to the `getInput` function the addresses of the variables where the customer name, current reading, and previous reading should be stored.

After the `getInput` function performs its task, the `main` function will call the `calculate` function to make the appropriate calculations. Notice that the `calculate` function's output is the gallons used and the water charge. For the function to perform the necessary calculations, the `main` function will need to pass it the current reading, the previous reading, the rate per gallon, and the memory addresses of the variables where the gallons used and water charge should be stored.

Finally, the `main` function will call the `displayBill` function, whose task is to display the appropriate information on the screen. Notice that the `displayBill` function's output is the customer name, gallons used, and water charge. For the function to perform its task, it will need to receive the name, usage, and charge information from the `main` function.

Recall that you should desk-check an algorithm several times before you begin coding it. In this case, you will use the following two sets of data to desk-check the algorithms shown in Figure 7-21:

Data for first desk-check		Data for second desk-check	
Customer name:	Joe Smith	Customer name:	Suman Patel
Current reading (gallons):	9000	Current reading (gallons):	14000
Previous reading (gallons):	8000	Previous reading (gallons):	7500
Rate per gallon:	.00175	Rate per gallon:	.00175

Figure 7-22 shows the completed desk-check tables, with the water charge amounts rounded to two decimal places.

main function

customer name	current reading	previous reading	rate per gallon	gallons used	water charge
~~Joe Smith~~ Suman Patel	~~9000~~ 14000	~~8000~~ 7500	~~.00175~~ .00175	~~1000~~ 6500	~~1.75~~ 11.38

calculate function

current reading	previous reading	rate per gallon
~~9000~~ 14000	~~8000~~ 7500	~~.00175~~ .00175

displayBill function

customer name	gallons used	water charge
~~Joe Smith~~ Suman Patel	~~1000~~ 6500	~~1.75~~ 11.38

Figure 7-22: Completed desk-check tables for the algorithms shown in Figure 7-21

> **tip**
>
> The `getInput` function does not need a separate desk-check table, because it receives the addresses of items appearing in the `main` function's desk-check table. For the same reason, the `calculate` function's desk-check table does not include the gallons used and water charge items.

After desk-checking an algorithm to verify its accuracy, you are ready to translate it into a language the computer can understand. Begin by coding the current program's `main` function.

Coding the `main` Function

According to its IPO chart, the `main` function will require six memory locations: five variables and one named constant. After reserving the memory locations, the `main` function will call each of the three program-defined functions. Figure 7-23 shows the C++ statements corresponding to the `main` function.

IPO chart information	C++ instructions
Input	
customer name	`string name = "";`
current reading (gallons)	`int current = 0;`
previous reading (gallons)	`int previous = 0;`
rate per gallon (.00175)	`const float RATE = float(.00175);`
Processing	
none	
Output	
customer name	
gallons used	`int gallons = 0;`
water charge	`float charge = 0.0;`
Algorithm	
1. getInput(customer name, current reading, previous reading)	`getInput(name, current, previous);`
2. calculate(current reading, previous reading, rate per gallon, gallons used, water charge)	`calculate(current, previous, RATE, gallons, charge);`
3. displayBill(customer name, gallons used, water charge)	`displayBill(name, gallons, charge);`

Figure 7-23: C++ statements corresponding to the main function

Next, you will code the `getInput` function.

Coding the `getInput` Function

tip

Recall that the number, data type, and sequence of the formal parameters in a function header should match the number, data type, and sequence of the corresponding actual arguments passed to the function.

Recall that the `main` function will pass the memory addresses of three of its variables—`name`, `current`, and `previous`—to the `getInput` function. The `getInput` function will use the formal parameters `&cust`, `&cur`, and `&prev` to receive the information. Recall that the address-of operator (`&`) alerts the computer that what is being passed to the function is a variable's address rather than its value. Figure 7-24 shows the C++ code for the `getInput` function.

IPO chart information	C++ instructions

Input
  address of customer name
  address of current reading
  address of previous reading
Processing
  none
Output
  customer name
  current reading
  previous reading
	`void getInput(string &cust, int &cur, int &prev)`

Algorithm
1. enter the customer name,
   current reading, and
   previous reading
	`cout << "Customer name: ";`
	`getline(cin, cust);`
	`cout << "Current reading: ";`
	`cin >> cur;`
	`cout << "Previous reading: ";`
	`cin >> prev;`

Figure 7-24: C++ code for the `getInput` function

Next, you will code the `calculate` function.

Coding the `calculate` Function

The IPO charts shown in Figure 7-21 indicate that the `main` function will pass the values of three memory locations (`current`, `previous`, and `RATE`), along with the addresses of two memory locations (`gallons` and `charge`), to the `calculate` function. The `calculate` function will use the formal parameters `c`, `p`, `r`, `&gal`, and `&due` to receive the information. Figure 7-25 shows the C++ code for the `calculate` function.

tip

The variable names `cust`, `cur`, and `prev` are local to the `getInput` function and will be removed from memory when the computer encounters the function's closing brace.

tip

The variable names `c`, `p`, `r`, `gal`, and `due` are local to the `calculate` function and will be removed from memory when the computer encounters the function's closing brace.

IPO chart information	C++ instructions

Input
　current reading
　previous reading
　rate per gallon
　address of gallons used
　address of water charge
Processing
　none
Output
　gallons used
　water charge
 	
Algorithm
1. calculate gallons used by subtracting previous reading from current reading
 	
2. calculate water charge by multiplying gallons used by rate per gallon
	`void calculate(int c, int p, float r, int &gal, float &due)`
	
	`gal = c - p;`
	
	`due = gal * r;`

Figure 7-25: C++ code for the `calculate` function

Finally, code the `displayBill` function.

Coding the `displayBill` Function

tip

The variable names `cust`, `used`, and `amtDue` are local to the `displayBill` function and will be removed from memory when the computer encounters the function's closing brace.

Recall that the `main` function will pass the values of its `name`, `gallons`, and `charge`) variables to the `displayBill` function. The `displayBill` function will use the formal parameters `cust`, `used`, and `amtDue` to receive the information. Figure 7-26 shows the C++ code for the `displayBill` function.

IPO chart information	C++ instructions

Input
　customer name
　gallons used
　water charge
Processing
　none
Output
　customer name
　gallons used
　water charge
 	
Algorithm
1. display the customer name, gallons used, and water charge
	`void displayBill(string cust, int used, float amtDue)`
	
	`cout << "Customer name: " << cust << endl;`
	`cout << "Gallons used: " << used << endl;`
	`cout << "Water charge: " << amtDue << endl;`

Figure 7-26: C++ code for the `displayBill` function

Now that you have finished coding the algorithms, you need to desk-check the program, using the same data you used to desk-check the algorithms. Figure 7-27 shows the data and the completed desk-check tables for the program, with the payment amounts rounded to two decimal places.

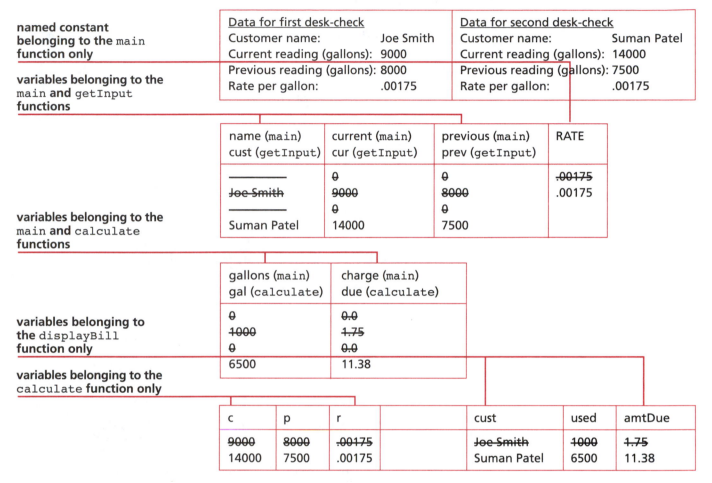

named constant belonging to the main **function only**

variables belonging to the main **and** getInput **functions**

variables belonging to the main **and** calculate **functions**

variables belonging to the displayBill **function only**

variables belonging to the calculate **function only**

Data for first desk-check		Data for second desk-check	
Customer name: Joe Smith		Customer name: Suman Patel	
Current reading (gallons): 9000		Current reading (gallons): 14000	
Previous reading (gallons): 8000		Previous reading (gallons): 7500	
Rate per gallon: .00175		Rate per gallon: .00175	

name (main) cust (getInput)	current (main) cur (getInput)	previous (main) prev (getInput)	RATE
—————	~~0~~	~~0~~	~~.00175~~
~~Joe Smith~~	~~9000~~	~~8000~~	.00175
—————	~~0~~	~~0~~	
Suman Patel	14000	7500	

gallons (main) gal (calculate)	charge (main) due (calculate)
~~0~~	~~0.0~~
~~1000~~	~~1.75~~
~~0~~	~~0.0~~
6500	11.38

c	p	r		cust	used	amtDue
~~9000~~	~~8000~~	~~.00175~~		~~Joe Smith~~	~~1000~~	~~1.75~~
14000	7500	.00175		Suman Patel	6500	11.38

Figure 7-27: Data and completed desk-check tables for the program

The results obtained when desk-checking the program agree with the results obtained when desk-checking the algorithm. You now are ready to enter the C++ instructions into the computer.

Completing the Water Bill Program

Your computer's hard disk contains a partially completed C++ program containing many of the instructions for the water bill program. Open that program now.

To open the partially completed C++ program:

1 Start Visual C++. Open the **T7App.cpp** file contained in the Cpp\Tut07\T7App folder on your computer's hard disk. Figure 7-28 shows the instructions contained in the partially completed T7App.cpp program.

```
//T7App.cpp - displays a water bill

#include <iostream>
#include <string>
using namespace std;

//function prototypes

int main()
{
    const float RATE = float(.00175);

    string name  = "";
    int current  = 0;
    int previous = 0;
    int gallons  = 0;
    float charge = 0.0;

    //enter input items

    //calculate gallons used and water charge

    //display water bill


    return 0;
}     //end of main function

//*****program-defined functions*****
```

Figure 7-28: Instructions contained in the partially completed T7App.cpp program

Missing from the program are the statements that call the three program-defined functions, as well as the prototypes and definitions of those functions.

To enter the missing instructions:

1 Position the insertion point in the blank line below the `//function prototypes` comment.

First enter the `getInput` function prototype. Recall that the function prototype is simply the function header (shown earlier in Figure 7-24) without the names of the formal parameters, but with a semicolon at the end.

2 Type **void getInput(string &, int &, int &);** and press the **Enter** key.

Now, enter the `getInput` function call shown earlier in Figure 7-23.

3 Position the insertion point in the blank line below the `//enter input items` comment in the `main` function. Press the **Tab** key, if necessary, then type **getInput(name, current, previous);**.

Next, enter the `getInput` function definition, which was shown earlier in Figure 7-24.

4   Position the insertion point in the blank line below the `//*****program-defined functions*****` comment, then type the `getInput` function definition, which is shaded in Figure 7-29.

```cpp
//T7App.cpp - displays a water bill

#include <iostream>
#include <string>
using namespace std;

//function prototypes
void getInput(string&, int&, int&);

int main()
{
    const float RATE = float(.00175);

    string name  = "";
    int current  = 0;
    int previous = 0;
    int gallons  = 0;
    float charge = 0.0;

    //enter input items
    getInput(name, current, previous);
    //calculate gallons used and water charge

    //display water bill


    return 0;
}    //end of main function

//*****program-defined functions*****
void getInput(string &cust, int &cur, int &prev)
{
    cout << "Customer name: ";
    getline(cin, cust);
    cout << "Current reading: ";
    cin >> cur;
    cout << "Previous reading: ";
    cin >>prev;
}    //end of getInput function
```

function prototype → `void getInput(string&, int&, int&);`

function call → `getInput(name, current, previous);`

enter this function definition → (shaded `getInput` function definition)

Figure 7-29: T7App.cpp program showing `getInput` function definition

Next, enter the instructions pertaining to the **calculate** and **displayBill** functions.

5   Enter the two function prototyes, two function calls, and two function definitions shaded in Figure 7-30, which shows the completed T7App.cpp program.

enter these function
prototypes

enter these function calls

```cpp
//T7App.cpp - displays a water bill

#include <iostream>
#include <string>
using namespace std;

//function prototypes
void getInput(string &, int &, int &);
void calculate(int, int, float, int &, float &);
void displayBill(string, int, float);

int main()
{
    const float RATE = float(.00175);

    string name  = "";
    int current  = 0;
    int previous = 0;
    int gallons  = 0;
    float charge = 0.0;

    //enter input items
    getInput(name, current, previous);
    //calculate gallons used and water charge
    calculate(current, previous, RATE, gallons, charge);
    //display water bill
    displayBill(name, gallons, charge);

    return 0;
}     //end of main function
//*****program-defined functions*****
void getInput(string &cust, int &cur, int &prev)
{
    cout << "Customer name: ";
    getline(cin, cust);
    cout << "Current reading: ";
    cin >> cur;
    cout << "Previous reading: ";
    cin >>prev;
}    //end of getInput function
```

Figure 7-30: Completed T7App.cpp program

```
void calculate(int c, int p, float r, int &gal, float &due)
{
      gal = c - p;      //calculate gallons used
      due = gal * r;   //calculate water charge
}     //end of calculate function

void displayBill(string cust, int used, float amtDue)
{
      cout << fixed;
      cout.precision(2);
      cout << "Customer name: " << cust << endl;
      cout << "Gallons used: " << used << endl;
      cout << "Water charge: " << amtDue << endl;
}     //end of displayBill function
```

enter these function definitions

Figure 7-30: Completed T7App.cpp program (continued)

6   Verify the accuracy of your code by comparing the code on your screen with the code shown in Figure 7-30.

Now test the program to verify that it works correctly.

To test the program:

1   Save, build, and execute the program. When prompted for the customer's name, type **Joe Brown** and press the **Enter** key.

2   When prompted for the current reading, type **9000** and press the **Enter** key. When prompted for the previous reading, type **8000** and press the **Enter** key. The program calculates and displays the water bill, as shown in Figure 7-31.

HELP? If you needed to press the **Enter** key twice after typing the customer's name, refer to the Read This Before You Begin section found at the beginning of this book.

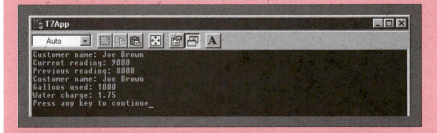

Figure 7-31: DOS window showing results of first test

The DOS window shows that the gallons used and water charge are 1000 and 1.75, respectively, which agree with the results shown earlier in the desk-check tables.

3   Press the **Enter** key to close the DOS window, then hide the Output window.

4 Execute the program again. Enter **Suman Patel** as the customer name, **14000** as the current reading, and **7500** as the previous reading. The DOS window shows that the gallons used and the water charge are 6500 and 11.38, respectively, which agree with the results shown earlier in the desk-check tables.

5 Press the **Enter** key to close the DOS window, then use the File menu to close the workspace. When prompted to close all document windows, click the **Yes** button.

6 Exit Visual C++.

You now have completed Tutorial 7's Application lesson. You can either take a break or complete the end-of-lesson exercises.

EXERCISES

1. In this exercise, you will modify the program you created in this lesson so that it uses two void functions, rather than one, to calculate the gallons used and the water charge.
   a. Open the T7AppE01.cpp file contained in the Cpp\Tut07\T7AppE01 folder on your computer's hard disk.
   b. Complete the program by entering the function prototypes, function calls, and function definitions for two void functions named calcGallons and calcCharge. The calcGallons function should calculate the number of gallons used, and the calcCharge function should calculate the water charge.
   c. Save, build, and execute the program. Enter Sue Jones as the name, 6000 as the current reading, and 3000 as the previous reading.
   d. When the program is working correctly, hide the Output window, then use the File menu to close the workspace.

2. In this exercise, you will create a simple payroll program using a main function and four void functions.
   a. Figure 7-32 shows the partially completed IPO charts for the payroll program. Complete the Input and Output columns of the IPO charts for the four void functions named getInput, calcFedTaxes, calcNetPay, and displayInfo. The FWT (Federal Withholding Tax) rate is 20% of the weekly salary, and the FICA (Federal Insurance Contribution Act) rate is 8% of the weekly salary.

main function

Input	Processing	Output
name weekly salary FWT rate (.2) FICA rate (.08)	Processing items: none Algorithm: 1. getInput(name, weekly salary) 2. calcFedTaxes(weekly salary, FWT rate, FICA rate, FWT, FICA) 3. calcNetPay(weekly salary, FWT, FICA, weekly net pay) 4. displayInfo(name, FWT, FICA, weekly net pay)	name FWT FICA weekly net pay

Figure 7-32

getInput function

Input	Processing	Output
	Processing items: none Algorithm: 1. enter the name and weekly salary	

calcFedTaxes function

Input	Processing	Output
	Processing items: none Algorithm: 1. calculate the FWT by multiplying the weekly salary by the FWT rate 2. calculate the FICA by multiplying the weekly salary by the FICA rate	

calcNetPay function

Input	Processing	Output
	Processing items: none Algorithm: 1. calculate the weekly net pay by subtracting the FWT and FICA from the weekly salary	

displayInfo function

Input	Processing	Output
	Processing items: none Algorithm: 1. display the name, FWT, FICA, and weekly net pay	

Figure 7-32 (continued)

    b. Open the T7AppE02.cpp file contained in the Cpp\Tut07\T7AppE02 folder on your computer's hard disk. Use the IPO charts you completed in Step a to complete the program.

    c. Complete a desk-check table for the program, using Samuel Montez as the employee's name and 500 as the weekly salary, and then using Barbara Jacks as the employee's name and 650 as the weekly salary.

    d. Save, build, and execute the program. Use the data from Step c to test the program.

    e. When the program is working correctly, hide the Output window, then use the File menu to close the workspace.

3.   In this exercise, you will create a program that converts a Fahrenheit temperature to a Celsius temperature. The program will use a main function and three void functions.

    a. Figure 7-33 shows the partially completed IPO charts for the temperature program. Complete the IPO charts for the main function and the three void functions named getFahrenheit, calcCelsius, and displayCelsius.

main function

Input	Processing	Output
Fahrenheit temperature	Processing items: none Algorithm: 1. getFahrenheit( ) 2. calcCelsius( ) 3. displayCelsius( )	Celsius temperature

getFahrenheit function

Input	Processing	Output
	Processing items: none Algorithm: 1. enter the Fahrenheit temperature	

calcCelsius function

Input	Processing	Output
	Processing items: none Algorithm: 1. calculate the Celsius temperature as follows: 5.0/9.0 * (Fahrenheit temperature – 32)	

displayCelsius function

Input	Processing	Output
	Processing items: none Algorithm: 1. display the Celsius temperature	

Figure 7-33

    b. Open the T7AppE03.cpp file contained in the Cpp\Tut07\T7AppE03 folder on your computer's hard disk. Use the IPO charts you completed in Step a to complete the program. (Be sure to use 5.0 and 9.0 in the equation that calculates the Celsius temperature.) Display the Celsius temperature as an integer.

    c. Complete a desk-check table for the program, using the following Fahrenheit temperatures: 32 F and 212 F.

    d. Save, build, and execute the program. Use the data from Step c to test the program.

    e. When the program is working correctly, hide the Output window, then use the File menu to close the workspace.

4. In this exercise, you will create a program that displays a 10% bonus. The program will use a main function and three void functions.

    a. Figure 7-34 shows the partially completed IPO charts for the bonus program. Complete the IPO charts for the main function and the three void functions named getSales, calcBonus, and displayBonus.

main function

Input	Processing	Output
sales bonus rate (.1)	Processing items: none Algorithm: 1. getSales( ) 2. calcBonus( ) 3. displayBonus( )	bonus

getSales function

Input	Processing	Output
	Processing items: Algorithm:	

calcBonus function

Input	Processing	Output
	Processing items: Algorithm:	

displayBonus function

Input	Processing	Output
	Processing items: Algorithm:	

Figure 7-34

b. Open the T7AppE04.cpp file contained in the Cpp\Tut07\T7AppE04 folder on your computer's hard disk. Use the IPO charts you completed in Step a to complete the program. Display the bonus amount in fixed-point notation with two decimal places.

c. Complete a desk-check table for the program, using the following sale amounts: 24500 and 134780.

d. Save, build, and execute the program. Use the data from Step c to test the program.

e. When the program is working correctly, hide the Output window, then use the File menu to close the workspace.

5. In this exercise, you will modify the program you created in Tutorial 5's Application lesson. The modified program will use a **main** function and two void functions.

a. Open the T7AppE05.cpp file contained in the Cpp\Tut07\T7AppE05 folder on your computer's hard disk.

b. Modify the program so that it uses a program-defined void function to get the interest rate, and a program-defined void function to calculate the principal.

c. Save, build, and execute the program. Enter .07 as the interest rate.

d. Use the C++ editor to open the T7AppE05.dat file and verify the file's contents. (The file is contained in the Cpp\Tut07\T7AppE05 folder on your computer's hard disk.)

e. When the program is working correctly, hide the Output window, then use the File menu to close the workspace.

6. In this exercise, you will create a program that calculates the average of three test scores. The program will use two value-returning functions and two void functions.

    a. Write the IPO charts for a program that contains four program-defined functions: `main`, `getTestScores`, `calcAverage`, and `displayAverage`. The `main` function should call the void `getTestScores` function, whose task is to get three test scores. (The test scores might contain a decimal place.) The `main` function then should call the value-returning `calcAverage` function to calculate and return the average of the three test scores. When the `calcAverage` function has completed its task, the `main` function should call the void `displayAverage` function to display the average of the three scores on the screen.

    b. Create a console application. Name the project workspace T7AppE06, and save it in the Cpp\Tut07 folder on your computer's hard disk. Add a new C++ source file to the project. Name the source file T7AppE06.

    c. Use the IPO charts you created in Step a to code the program. Display the average in fixed-point notation with one decimal place.

    d. Complete a desk-check table for the program, using the following two groups of test scores: 95.5, 83, 76 and 54, 89, 77.

    e. Save, build, and execute the program. Use the data from Step d to test the program.

    f. When the program is working correctly, hide the Output window, then use the File menu to close the workspace.

7. In this exercise, you will modify the program you created in this lesson so that it uses two value-returning functions, rather than one void function, to calculate the gallons used and the water charge.

    a. Open the T7AppE07.cpp file contained in the Cpp\Tut07\T7AppE07 folder on your computer's hard disk.

    b. Complete the program by entering the function prototypes, function calls, and function definitions for two value-returning functions named `calcGallons` and `calcCharge`. The `calcGallons` function should calculate and return the number of gallons used, and the `calcCharge` function should calculate and return the water charge.

    c. Save, build, and execute the program. Enter Sue Jones as the name, 6000 as the current reading, and 3000 as the previous reading.

    d. When the program is working correctly, hide the Output window, then use the File menu to close the workspace.

8. In this exercise, you will create a simple payroll program. The program will use four value-returning functions (`main`, `calcFwt`, `calcFica`, and `calcNetPay`), and two void functions (`getInput` and `displayInfo`).

    a. Figure 7-35 shows the partially completed IPO charts for the payroll program. Complete the IPO charts appropriately. The FWT (Federal Withholding Tax) rate is 20% of the weekly salary, and the FICA (Federal Insurance Contribution Act) rate is 8% of the weekly salary. (Remember that only the `getInput` and `displayInfo` functions are void functions.)

main function

Input	Processing	Output
name weekly salary FWT rate (.2) FICA rate (.08)	Processing items: none Algorithm: 1. getInput( ) 2. FWT = calcTax( ) 3. FICA = calcTax( ) 4. weekly net pay = calcNetPay( ) 5. displayInfo( )	name FWT FICA weekly net pay

Figure 7-35

getInput function

Input	Processing	Output
	Processing items: none Algorithm:	

calcFwt function

Input	Processing	Output
	Processing items: none Algorithm:	

calcFica function

Input	Processing	Output
	Processing items: none Algorithm:	

calcNetPay function

Input	Processing	Output
	Processing items: none Algorithm:	

displayInfo function

Input	Processing	Output
	Processing items: none Algorithm:	

Figure 7-35 (continued)

b. Open the T7AppE08.cpp file contained in the Cpp\Tut07\T7AppE08 folder on your computer's hard disk. Use the IPO charts you completed in Step a to complete the program.

c. Complete a desk-check table for the program, using Bonnie James as the employee's name and 350 as the weekly salary, and then using Drew Carlisle as the employee's name and 700 as the weekly salary.

d. Save, build, and execute the program. Use the data from Step c to test the program.

e. When the program is working correctly, hide the Output window, then use the File menu to close the workspace.

Exercises 9 and 10 are Discovery Exercises. Discovery Exercises, which may include topics that are not covered in this lesson, allow you to "discover" the solutions to problems on your own.

discovery

9. In this exercise, you will learn about including type casts in an arithmetic expression.

a. Open the T7AppE09.cpp file contained in the Cpp\Tut07\T7AppE09 folder on your computer's hard disk.

b. Initialize the RATE named constant to 1.75, rather than to .00175.

c. Change the due = gal * r; statement in the calculate function to due = gal * r / 1000;. Save, build, and execute the program. Enter Carol Price as the name, 8000 as the current reading, and 6500 as the previous reading. The gallons used and the water charge should be 1500 and 2.63, respectively.

d. Change the due = gal * r / 1000; statement to due = gal / 1000 * r;. Save, build, and execute the program. Enter Carol Price as the name, 8000 as the current reading, and 6500 as the previous reading. The gallons used is correctly displayed as 1500. The water charge, however, is incorrectly displayed as 1.75.

In C++, dividing an integer by an integer results in an integer. In this case, dividing the gal variable (which is an int variable) by the integer 1000 results in the integer 1. Multiplying the integer 1 by 1.75 results in the incorrect water charge: 1.75. One way to fix this problem is to type cast the gal variable to float.

e. Change the due = gal / 1000 * r; statement to due = float(gal) / 1000 * r;.

f. Save, build, and execute the program. Enter Carol Price as the name, 8000 as the current reading, and 6500 as the previous reading. The gallons used and the water charge should be 1500 and 2.63, respectively.

g. Another way to fix the integer division problem is to change the 1000 in the statement that calculates the water charge to 1000.0. Change the due = float(gal) / 1000 * r; statement to due = gal / 1000.0 * r;.

h. Save, build, and execute the program. Enter Carol Price as the name, 8000 as the current reading, and 6500 as the previous reading. The gallons used and the water charge should be 1500 and 2.63, respectively.

i. Hide the Output window, then use the File menu to close the workspace.

discovery

10. In this exercise, you will learn how to pass a named constant so that the receiving function cannot change the value passed to it.

a. Open the T7AppE10.cpp file contained in the Cpp\Tut07\T7AppE10 folder on your computer's hard disk. The water bill program that you created in this lesson passed the value of the RATE named constant to the calculate function. The calculate function stored the value it received (.00175) in the r variable. Because the passed value was stored in a variable, the value could be changed by the calculate function.

b. First verify that the calculate function can change the value stored in the r variable. In the blank line above the gal = c - p; statement in the calculate function, type r = float(1.5). Save, build, and execute the program. Enter your name as the customer name, 3000 as the current reading, and 2000 as the previous reading. Rather than displaying 1.75 as the water charge, the program shows 1500.00 as the water charge, which is incorrect.

c. To prevent the function from changing the water rate passed to it, change the float r in the calculate function header to const float r. Also change the first float in the calculate function prototype to const float.

d. Save and build the program. The compiler displays an error message indicating that the r variable in the statement r = float(1.5); is a constant.

e. Delete the r = float(1.5); statement from the calculate function.

f. Save, build, and execute the program. Enter your name as the customer name, 3000 as the current reading, and 2000 as the previous reading. The program correctly displays 1000 and 1.75 as the gallons used and water charge, respectively.

g. Hide the Output window, then use the File menu to close the workspace.

A computer program is good only if it works. Errors in either an algorithm or programming code can cause the program to run incorrectly. Therefore, a programmer needs to know how to locate and fix these errors. Exercises 11 and 12 are Debugging Exercises. Debugging Exercises allow you to practice recognizing and solving errors in a program.

debugging

11. In this exercise, you will debug an existing C++ program.

   a. Open the T7AppE11.cpp file contained in the Cpp\Tut07\T7AppE11 folder on your computer's hard disk. The program should display an employee's gross pay, but it is not working correctly. Study the program's code, then build and execute the program.

   b. Correct any errors in the program, then save, build, and execute the program again. Test the program by entering 35 as the hours worked, and 10 as the pay rate.

   c. When the program is working correctly, hide the Output window, then use the File menu to close the workspace.

debugging

12. In this exercise, you will debug an existing C++ program.

   a. Open the T7AppE12.cpp file contained in the Cpp\Tut07\T7AppE12 folder on your computer's hard disk. The program should display a bonus amount, but it is not working correctly. Study the program's code, then build and execute the program.

   b. Correct any errors in the program, then save, build, and execute the program again. Test the program by entering 10500 as the sales, and .05 as the bonus rate.

   c. When the program is working correctly, hide the Output window, then use the File

The Selection Structure

objectives

After completing this tutorial, you will be able to:

■ Use the selection structure in a program

■ Write pseudocode for the selection structure

■ Create a flowchart for the selection structure

■ Code the `if` and `if/else` forms of the selection structure

■ Write code that uses comparison operators and logical operators

■ Return a floating-point number when dividing two integers

Concept Lesson

Using the Selection Structure

The programs you created in Tutorials 2 through 7 used the sequence programming structure only, where the program instructions were processed, one after another, in the order in which each appeared in the program. In many programs, however, the next instruction to be processed will depend on the result of a decision or comparison that the program must make. For example, a payroll program typically will need to compare the number of hours the employee worked with the number 40 to determine whether the employee should receive overtime pay in addition to regular pay. Based on the result of that comparison the program then will select either an instruction that computes regular pay only, or an instruction that computes regular pay plus overtime pay.

You use the **selection structure**, also called the **decision structure**, when you want a program to make a decision or comparison and then, based on the result of that decision or comparison, select one of two paths. Although the idea of using the selection structure in a program is new, the concept of the selection structure is one with which you already are familiar, because you use it each day to make hundreds of decisions. For example, every morning you have to decide if you are hungry and, if you are, what you are going to eat. Figure 8-1 shows other examples of selection structures you might use today.

	Example 1	Example 2
condition	if (it is raining)	if (you have a test tomorrow)
	wear a rain coat	study tonight
condition	bring an umbrella	else
		watch a movie

Figure 8-1: Selection structures you might use today

tip

As you may remember from Tutorial 1, the selection structure is one of the three programming structures. The other two programming structures are sequence, which was covered in the previous seven tutorials, and repetition, which is covered in Tutorial 10.

In the examples shown in Figure 8-1, the portion in parentheses, called the **condition**, specifies the decision you are making and is phrased so that it results in either a true or false answer only. For example, either it's raining (true) or it's not raining (false); either you have a test tomorrow (true) or you don't have a test tomorrow (false).

If the condition is true, you will perform a specific set of tasks. If the condition is false, on the other hand, you might or might not need to perform a different set of tasks. For instance, look at the first example shown in Figure 8-1. If it is raining (a true condition), then you will wear a raincoat and bring an umbrella. Notice that you do not have anything in particular to do if it is not raining (a false condition). Compare this with the second example shown in Figure 8-1. If you have a test tomorrow (a true condition), then you will study tonight. If you do not have a test tomorrow (a false condition), however, then you will watch a movie.

Like you, the computer also can evaluate a condition and then select the appropriate tasks to perform based on that evaluation. When using the selection structure in a program, the programmer must be sure to phrase the condition so that it results in either a true or a false answer only. The programmer also must specify the tasks to be performed when the condition is true and, if necessary, the tasks to be performed when the condition is false.

Most programming languages offer three forms of the selection structure: `if`, `if/else`, and `switch` (also called `case`). You will learn about the `if` and `if/else` forms of the selection structure in this tutorial. You will learn about the `switch` form in Tutorial 9. Begin by learning how to show the `if` and `if/else` selection structures in pseudocode.

Including the Selection Structure in Pseudocode

Figure 8-2 shows examples of both the `if` and the `if/else` selection structures written in pseudocode.

if selection structure

1. enter the part number and price

condition

2. if (the part number is "AB203")

true path
 calculate price by multiplying price by 1.1
 display "Price increase" message
end if
3. display the part number and price

if/else selection structure

1. enter the sales amount

condition

2. if (the sales amount is greater than 1500)

true path
 calculate the commission by multiplying the sales amount by .02
else
false path
 calculate the commission by multiplying the sales amount by .01
end if
3. display the commission

Figure 8-2: Examples of the `if` and `if/else` selection structures written in pseudocode

Although pseudocode is not standardized—every programmer has his or her own version—you will find some similarities among the various versions. For example, many programmers begin the selection structure with the word `if` and end the structure with the two words `end if`; they also use the word `else` to designate the instructions to be performed when the condition is false.

In the examples shown in Figure 8-2, the portion within parentheses indicates the condition to be evaluated. Notice that each condition results in either a true or a false answer only. In Example 1, either the part number is "AB203" or it isn't. In Example 2, either the sales amount is greater than the number 1500 or it isn't.

When the condition is true, the set of instructions following the condition is selected for processing. The instructions following the condition are referred to as the **true path**—the path you follow when the condition is true. The true path ends when you come to the `else` or, if there is no `else`, when you come to the end of the selection structure (the `end if`). After the true path instructions are processed, the instruction following the `end if` is processed. In the examples shown in Figure 8-2, the display instructions are processed after the instructions in the true path.

The instructions processed when the `if` structure's condition is false depend on whether the selection structure contains an `else`. When there is no `else`, as in the first example shown in Figure 8-2, the `if` structure ends when its condition is false, and processing continues with the instruction following the `end if`. In the first example, for instance, the "display the part number and price" instruction is processed when the part number is not "AB203." In cases where the selection structure contains an `else`, as in the second example shown in Figure 8-2, the instructions between the `else` and the `end if`—referred to as the **false path**—are processed before the instruction after the `end if` is processed. In the second example, the "calculate the commission by multiplying the sales amount by .01" instruction is processed first, followed by the "display the commission" instruction.

In addition to using pseudocode to plan algorithms, recall from Tutorial 2 that programmers also use flowcharts. In the next section, you will learn how to show the selection structure in a flowchart.

Drawing a Flowchart of a Selection Structure

Unlike pseudocode, which consists of short English statements, a flowchart uses standardized symbols to show the steps the computer needs to take to accomplish the program's goal. Figure 8-3 shows Figure 8-2's examples in flowchart form.

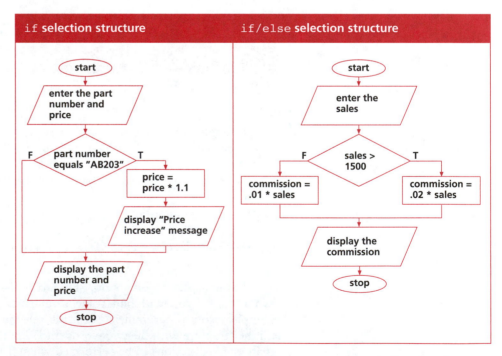

Figure 8-3: Examples of the `if` and `if/else` selection structures drawn in flowchart form

You also can mark the flowlines leading out of the diamond with a "Y" and an "N" (for yes and no).

Recall that flowlines are the lines that connect the flowchart symbols.

As you learned in Tutorial 2, the oval in the figure is the start/stop symbol, the rectangle is the process symbol, and the parallelogram is the input/output symbol. The new symbol in the flowchart, the diamond, is called the **selection/repetition symbol**, because it is used to represent both selection and repetition. In Figure 8-3's flowcharts, the diamonds represent the selection structure. (You will learn how to use the diamond to represent repetition in Tutorial 10.) Notice that inside each diamond is a comparison that evaluates to either true or false only. Each diamond also has one flowline entering the symbol and two flowlines leaving the symbol. The two flowlines leading out of the diamond should be marked so that anyone reading the flowchart can distinguish the true path from the false path. You mark the flowline leading to the true path with a "T" (for true), and you mark the flowline leading to the false path with an "F" (for false).

Next, learn how to code the `if` and `if/else` forms of the selection structure.

Coding the Selection Structure

Figure 8-4 shows the syntax of the statement you use to code the `if` and `if/else` forms of the selection structure in C++, Java, and Visual Basic. In C++ and Java, this statement is referred to as the `if` statement; in Visual Basic, it is referred to as the `If...Then...Else` statement.

<u>C++ and Java</u>

if (*condition***)**
    one statement, or a block of statements enclosed in braces, to be processed
    when the condition is true
[**else**
    one statement, or a block of statements enclosed in braces, to be processed
    when the condition is false]
//end if

<u>Visual Basic</u>

If *condition* **Then**
    one or more statements to be processed when the condition is true
[**Else**
    one or more statements to be processed when the condition is false]
End If

Important note: In the syntax, items in **bold** are required. Items in square brackets ([]), on the other hand, are optional. Items in *italics* indicate places where the programmer must supply information pertaining to the current program.

Figure 8-4: Syntax of the statement used to code the `if` and `if/else` forms of the selection structure

The items in square brackets ([ ]) in each syntax are optional. For example, you do not always need to include the `else` portion of the syntax, referred to as the `else` clause, in an `if` statement in C++ and Java. You also do not always need to include the `Else` clause in the `If...Then...Else` statement in Visual Basic.

Items in **bold** in each syntax are essential components of the statement. For example, the keyword `if` and the parentheses that surround the *condition* are required in the `if` statement in C++ and Java. The keyword `else` must be included only if the statement uses that clause. In Visual Basic, on the other hand, the keywords `If`, `Then`, and `End If` are essential components of the `If...Then...Else` statement. Similar to C++ and Java, the Visual Basic keyword `Else` is necessary only if the statement uses that clause. Notice that Visual Basic does not require you to enclose the `If...Then...Else` statement's *condition* in parentheses.

Items in italics in each syntax indicate where the programmer must supply information pertaining to the current program. For instance, the programmer must supply the *condition* to be evaluated. The *condition* must be a Boolean expression, which is an expression that results in a Boolean value (true or false).

In addition to supplying the *condition*, the programmer also must supply the statements to be processed when the *condition* evaluates to true and, optionally, when the *condition* evaluates to false. If more than one statement needs to be processed in C++ and Java, the statements must be entered as a statement block. You create a **statement block** by enclosing the statements in a set of braces ({}). Unlike in C++ and Java, braces are not used in Visual Basic.

Although it is not required to do so, it is a good programming practice to use a comment, such as `//end if`, to mark the end of the `if` statement in C++ and Java. The comment will make your program easier to read and understand. It also will help you to keep track of the required `if` and `else` clauses when you nest `if` statements—in other words, when you include one `if` statement inside another `if` statement. You will learn how to nest `if` statements in Tutorial 9. You do not need to use a comment to mark the end of the `If...Then...Else` statement in Visual Basic, as this is the purpose of the `End If` clause.

Figure 8-5 shows the different ways of using the C++ `if` statement to code the `if` and `if/else` forms of the selection structure. Notice that, whenever multiple statements are included in a path, the statements are entered as a statement block by enclosing them in braces.

tip

Some C++ programmers include the braces even when only one statement needs to be processed, but this is optional.

`if` form with one statement	`if` form with multiple statements

if (*condition*)
  one statement
//end if
	if (*condition*)
	{
	   multiple statements
	   require braces
	} //end if

`if/else` form with one statement in each path	`if/else` form with multiple statements in true path and one statement in false path	`if/else` form with multiple statements in false path and one statement in true path	`if/else` form with multiple statements in true and false paths

if (*condition*)
  one statement
else
  one statement
//end if
	if (*condition*)
	{
	   multiple statements
	   require braces
	}
	else
	  one statement
	//end if
		if (*condition*)
		  one statement
		else
		{
		   multiple statements
		   require braces
		} //end if
			if (*condition*)
			{
			   multiple statements
			   require braces
			}
			else
			{
			   multiple statements
			   require braces
			} //end if

Figure 8-5: Different ways of coding the `if` and `if/else` selection structures in C++

As mentioned earlier, the *condition* specified in the `if` and `If…Then…Else` statements must be a Boolean expression, which is an expression that evaluates to either true or false. The expression can contain variables, constants, functions, arithmetic operators, comparison operators, and logical operators. You already know about variables, constants, functions, and arithmetic operators. You will learn about comparison operators and logical operators in the following sections.

Comparison Operators

Figure 8-6 lists the **comparison operators**, also referred to as **relational operators**, that you can use to make comparisons in a C++ program. The figure also shows the order of precedence for these operators. The precedence numbers indicate the order in which C++ performs the comparisons in an expression. Comparisons with a precedence number of 1 are performed before comparisons with a precedence number of 2. However, you can use parentheses to override the order of precedence.

Operator	Operation	Precedence number
<	less than	1
<=	less than or equal to	1
>	greater than	1
>=	greater than or equal to	1
==	equal to	2
!=	not equal to	2

Important note: Notice that four of the operators contain two symbols. When using these operators, do not include any spaces between the symbols. Also be sure you do not reverse the symbols—in other words, use >=, but don't use =>.

Figure 8-6: Comparison operators in C++

Notice that you use two equal signs (==) to test for equality in C++ . You test for inequality by using an exclamation point, which stands for *not*, followed by an equal sign (!=).

It is easy to confuse the equality operator (==), which is used to compare two values, with the assignment operator (=), which is used to assign a value to a memory location. Keep in mind that you use the C++ statement `num = 1;` to assign the number 1 to the `num` variable. However, you use the C++ *condition* `num == 1` to compare the contents of the `num` variable to the number 1.

Figure 8-7 shows some examples of using comparison operators in the `if` statement's *condition* in C++.

if **statement's** *condition*	**Meaning**
`if (quantity < 50)`	Compares the contents of the `quantity` variable to the number 50. The *condition* will evaluate to true if the `quantity` variable contains a number that is less than 50; otherwise, it will evaluate to false.
`if (age >= 25)`	Compares the contents of the `age` variable to the number 25. The *condition* will evaluate to true if the `age` variable contains a number that is greater than or equal to 25; otherwise, it will evaluate to false.
`if (onhand == target)`	Compares the contents of the `onhand` variable to the contents of the `target` variable. The *condition* will evaluate to true if the `onhand` variable contains a number that is equal to the number in the `target` variable; otherwise, it will evaluate to false. (Both variables are `int` variables.)
`if (quantity != 7500)`	Compares the contents of the `quantity` variable to the number 7500. The *condition* will evaluate to true if the `quantity` variable contains a number that is not equal to 7500; otherwise, it will evaluate to false. (The `quantity` variable is an `int` variable.)

Figure 8-7: Examples of comparison operators in an `if` statement's *condition* in C++

Notice that the expression contained in each *condition* evaluates to either true or false. All expressions containing a comparison operator will result in an answer of either true or false only.

As with arithmetic operators, if an expression contains more than one comparison operator with the same precedence number, the computer evaluates the operators from left to right in the expression. Keep in mind, however, that comparison operators are evaluated after any arithmetic operators in the expression. In other words, in the expression 5 − 2 > 1 + 2, the two arithmetic operators (− and +) will be evaluated before the comparison operator (>). The result of the expression is false, as shown in Figure 8-8.

Evaluation steps	**Result**
Original expression	5 − 2 > 1 + 2
5 − 2 is evaluated first	3 > 1 + 2
1 + 2 is evaluated second	3 > 3
3 > 3 is evaluated last	false

Figure 8-8: Evaluation steps for an expression containing arithmetic and comparison operators

In the next section, you will view the pseudocode, flowchart, and C++ code for two programs that contain comparison operators in an `if` statement.

Using Comparison Operators in a Program

Assume you want to swap the values in two variables, but only if the first value is greater than the second value. Figure 8-9 shows the pseudocode, flowchart, and C++ code for a program that will accomplish this task.

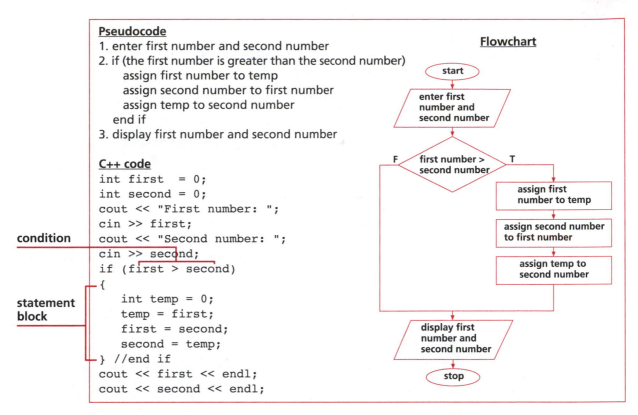

Figure 8-9: Pseudocode, flowchart, and C++ code showing the `if` form of the selection structure

The (`first > second`) *condition* in the C++ code shown in Figure 8-9 tells the computer to compare the contents of the `first` variable to the contents of the `second` variable. If the *condition* is true, which means that the value in the `first` variable is greater than the value in the `second` variable, then the four instructions in the `if` statement's true path swap the values contained in those variables. Notice that the four instructions are enclosed in braces, forming a statement block. As you learned earlier, when more than one instruction needs to be processed when the `if` statement's *condition* is true (or false), the C++ syntax requires those instructions to be entered as a statement block.

Study closely the four instructions used to swap the two values. The first instruction, `int temp = 0;`, creates and initializes a local variable named `temp`. The `temp` variable is local only to the statement block in which it is declared; in this case, it is local only to the `if` statement's true path. The second instruction, `temp = first;`, assigns the value in the `first` variable to the `temp` variable. In other words, it stores a copy of the `first` variable's contents in the `temp` variable. Next, the `first = second;` instruction assigns the value in the `second` variable to the `first` variable. Finally, the `second = temp;` instruction assigns the value in the `temp` variable to the `second` variable. The `temp` variable is necessary to store the contents of the `first` variable temporarily so that the swap can be made. If you did not store the `first` variable's value in the `temp` variable, the `second` variable's value would write over the value in the `first` variable, and the value in the `first` variable would be lost. Figure 8-10 illustrates the concept of swapping.

	temp	first	second
Values stored in the variables after the `cin` statements are processed	0	8	4
Result of the `temp = first;` statement	8	8	4
Result of the `first = second;` statement	8	4	4
Result of the `second = temp;` statement (completes the swapping process)	8	4	8

values were swapped

Figure 8-10: Illustration of the swapping concept

In the next program, assume you want to give the user the option of displaying either the sum of two numbers he or she enters, or the difference between the two numbers. Figure 8-11 shows the pseudocode, flowchart, and C++ code for a program that will accomplish this task.

Pseudocode

1. enter operation, first number, and second number
2. if (the operation is equal to 1)
   calculate the sum by adding together
   the first number and the second number
   display the sum
   else
   calculate the difference by subtracting
   the second number from the first number
   display the difference
   end if

Flowchart

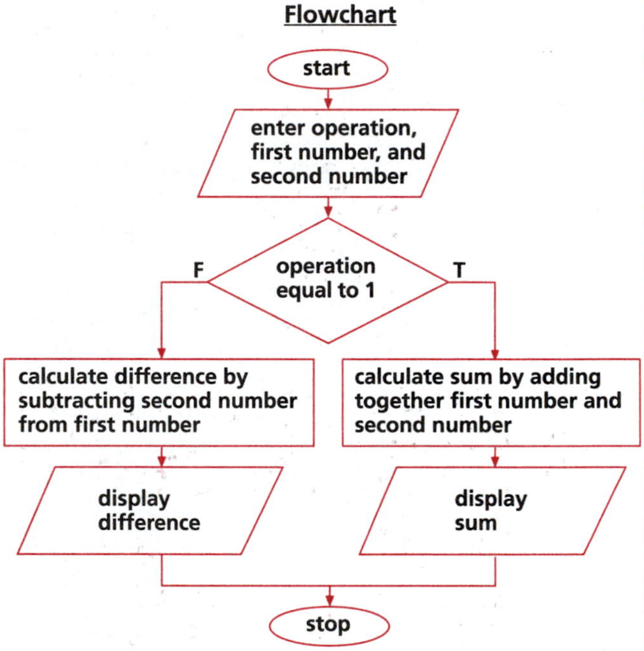

start

enter operation,
first number, and
second number

operation
equal to 1

F — calculate difference by subtracting second number from first number → display difference

T — calculate sum by adding together first number and second number → display sum

stop

C++ code
```cpp
int operation = 0;
int num1     = 0;
int num2     = 0;
int answer   = 0;
cout << "Enter 1 (add) or 2 (subtract): ";
cin >> operation;
cout << "Enter first number: ";
cin >> num1;
cout << "Enter second number: ";
cin >> num2;
if (operation == 1)
{
    answer = num1 + num2;
    cout << "Sum: " << answer << endl;
}
else
{
    answer = num1 - num2;
    cout << "Difference: " << answer << endl;
}  //end if
```

Figure 8-11: Pseudocode, flowchart, and C++ code showing the `if/else` form of the selection structure

The (`operation == 1`) *condition* in the C++ code shown in Figure 8-11 tells the computer to compare the contents of the `operation` variable to the number 1. If the *condition* is true, then the selection structure calculates and displays the sum of the two numbers entered by the user. If the *condition* is false, however, the selection structure calculates and displays the difference between the two numbers. Here again, because more than one instruction appears in both the true and false paths of the `if` statement, the instructions in each path are entered as a statement block.

Mini-Quiz 1

1. Assume that a program needs to determine if a student's score is less than 70. If it is, display the "Fail" message; otherwise, display the "Pass" message. Write the pseudocode for this selection structure.

2. Write a C++ `if` statement that corresponds to the pseudocode you wrote in Question 1. The student's score is stored in an `int` variable named `score`.

3. Which of the following C++ `if` clauses determines whether the `quantity` variable, which is of data type `int`, contains the number 100?

   a. `if (quantity = 100)`

   b. `if (quantity = 100);`

   c. `if (quantity == 100)`

   d. `if (quantity == 100);`

4. Which of the following C++ statements assigns the number 5 to a variable named `area`?

   a. `area = 5`

   b. `area = 5;`

   c. `area == 5`

   d. `area == 5;`

5. Write an `if` clause that determines whether an `int` variable named `area` has the value 5 stored in it.

Recall that you also can use logical operators to form the `if` statement's *condition*. You will learn about logical operators next.

Java uses the same symbols as C++ does to represent the And and Or logical operators. Visual Basic, however, uses the keywords `And` and `Or`.

Logical Operators

The most commonly used logical operators, sometimes referred to as Boolean operators, are And and Or. Both of these operators allow you to combine two or more *conditions* into one compound *condition*. When the And logical operator is used to create a compound condition, all of the conditions must be true for the compound condition to be true. However, when the Or logical operator is used, only one of the conditions needs to be true for the compound condition to be true.

C++ uses special symbols to represent the And and Or logical operators in a program. The And operator in C++ is two ampersands (&&), and the Or operator is two pipe symbols (||). The pipe symbol (|) usually is located on the same key as the backslash (\) on the computer's keyboard.

You will learn about another logical operator, Not (!), in a later tutorial.

Truth table for the && (And) operator		
Value of *condition1*	Value of *condition2*	Value of *condition1 && condition2*
true	true	true
true	false	false
false	true	false
false	false	false
Truth table for the || (Or) operator		
Value of *condition1*	Value of *condition2*	Value of *condition1 || condition2*
true	true	true
true	false	true
false	true	true
false	false	false

Figure 8-12: Truth tables for the And and Or logical operators

tip

If you use the && (And) operator to combine two conditions, C++ does not evaluate the second condition if the first condition is false. Because both conditions combined with the && operator need to be true for the compound condition to be true, there is no need to evaluate the second condition if the first condition is false. If, on the other hand, you use the \|\| (Or) operator to combine two conditions, C++ does not evaluate the second condition if the first condition is true. Because only one of the conditions combined with the \|\| operator needs to be true for the compound condition to be true, there is no need to evaluate the second condition if the first condition is true.

The tables shown in Figure 8-12, called **truth tables**, summarize how programming languages evaluate the logical operators in an expression.

As Figure 8-12 indicates, when you use the And (&&) operator to combine two conditions (*condition1* && *condition2*), the resulting compound condition is true only when both conditions are true. If either condition is false, or if both conditions are false, then the compound condition is false. Compare the And operator with the Or operator. When you combine conditions using the Or (\|\|) operator, as in *condition1* \|\| *condition2*, notice that the compound condition is false only when both conditions are false. If either condition is true, or if both conditions are true, then the compound condition is true. In the next section, you will use the truth tables to determine which logical operator is appropriate for the if statement's *condition*.

Using the Truth Tables

Assume that you want to pay a bonus to your A-rated salespeople—those whose monthly sales total more than $10,000. To receive a bonus, the salesperson must be rated A and he or she must sell more than $10,000 in product. Assuming the program uses the two variables rate and sales, you can phrase *condition1* as rate == 'A' and *condition2* as sales > 10000. Now the question is, should you use the And operator or the Or operator to combine both conditions into one compound condition? You will use the truth tables shown in Figure 8-12 to answer this question.

For a salesperson to receive a bonus, remember that both *condition1* (rate == 'A') and *condition2* (sales > 10000) must be true at the same time. If either condition is false, or if both conditions are false, then the compound condition should be false, and the salesperson should not receive a bonus. According to the truth tables, both the And and the Or operators will evaluate the compound condition as true when both conditions are true. Only the And operator, however, will evaluate the compound condition as false when either one or both of the conditions are false. The Or operator, you will notice, evaluates the compound condition as false only when *both* conditions are false. Therefore, the correct compound condition to use here is (rate == 'A' && sales > 10000).

Now assume that you want to send a letter to all A-rated salespeople and all B-rated salespeople. Assuming the program uses the variable rate, you can phrase *condition1* as rate == 'A' and *condition2* as rate == 'B'. Now which operator do you use—And or Or?

At first it might appear that the And operator is the correct one to use, because the example says to send the letter to "all A-rated salespeople and all B-rated salespeople." In everyday conversations, you will find that people sometimes use the word *and* when what they really mean is *or*. Although both words do not mean the same thing, using *and* instead of *or* generally does not cause a problem because we are able to infer what another person means. Computers, however, cannot infer anything; they simply process the directions you give them, word for word. In this case, you actually want to send a letter to all salespeople with either an A or a B rating, so you will need to use the Or operator. As the truth tables indicate, the Or operator is the only operator that will evaluate the compound condition as true if at least one of the conditions is true. The correct compound condition to use here is (rate == 'A' || rate == 'B').

Like expressions containing comparison operators, expressions containing logical operators always result in an answer of either true or false. If an expression contains both an And and an Or logical operator, the And operator is evaluated first, and then the Or operator is evaluated. Figure 8-13 shows the order of precedence for the arithmetic, comparison, and logical operators you have learned so far.

Operator	Operation	Precedence number
()	Overrides all other normal precedence rules	1
−	Performs negation	2
*, /, %	Performs multiplication, division, and modulus arithmetic	3
+, −	Performs addition and subtraction	4
<, <=, >, >=	Less than, less than or equal to, greater than, greater than or equal to	5
==, !=	Equal to, not equal to	6
&& (And)	All conditions connected by the And operator must be true for the compound condition to be true	7
|| (Or)	Only one of the conditions connected by the Or operator needs to be true for the compound condition to be true	8

Figure 8-13: Order of precedence for arithmetic, comparison, and logical operators

Notice that both the And and the Or logical operators are evaluated after any arithmetic operators or comparison operators in the expression. In other words, in the expression 12 > 0 && 12 < 10 * 2, the arithmetic operator (*) is evaluated first, followed by the two comparison operators (> and <), followed by the And logical operator (&&). The expression evaluates to true, as shown in Figure 8-14.

Evaluation steps	Result
Original expression	12 > 0 && 12 < 10 * 2
10 * 2 is evaluated first	12 > 0 && 12 < 20
12 > 0 is evaluated second	true && 12 < 20
12 < 20 is evaluated third	true && true
true && true is evaluated last	true

Figure 8-14: Evaluation steps for an expression containing arithmetic, comparison, and logical operators

tip

When included in a C++ program, the expression shown in Figure 8-14 results in the number 1. In C++, the number 1, as well as any nonzero number, represents the Boolean value True. You also can use the C++ keyword `true`, whose value is 1, to represent the Boolean value True.

In the next section, you will view the C++ code for three programs that contain a logical operator in an `if` statement.

Using Logical Operators in a Program

Assume you want to create a program that calculates and displays an employee's gross pay. To keep this example simple, assume that no one at the company works more than 40 hours per week, and everyone earns the same hourly rate, $10.65. Before making the gross pay calculation, the program should verify that the number of hours entered by the user is greater than or equal to zero, but less than or equal to 40. Programmers refer to the process of verifying that the input data is within the expected range as **data validation**. In this case, if the number is valid, the program should calculate and display the gross pay; otherwise, it should display an error message alerting the user that the input data is incorrect. Figure 8-15 shows two ways of writing the C++ code for this program. Notice that the `if` statement in the first example uses the And (&&) logical operator, whereas the `if` statement in the second example uses the Or (||) logical operator.

Example 1: using the && (And) operator	Example 2: using the || (Or) operator
```float hours = 0.0;```	```float hours = 0.0;```

```
Example 1: using the && (And) operator        Example 2: using the || (Or) operator

float hours = 0.0;                            float hours = 0.0;
float gross = 0.0;                            float gross = 0.0;
cout << "Enter hours worked: ";               cout << "Enter hours worked: ";
cin >> hours;                                 cin >> hours;
if (hours >= 0 && hours <= 40)                if (hours < 0 || hours > 40)
{                                                 cout << "Input error" << endl;
   gross = hours * 10.65;                     else
   cout << gross << endl;
}                                             {
else                                              gross = hours * 10.65;
   cout << "Input error" << endl;                cout << gross << endl;
//end if                                      }  //end if
```

Figure 8-15: C++ code showing the And and Or logical operators in the `if` statement's *condition*

The `(hours >= 0 && hours <= 40)` *condition* in the first example shown in Figure 8-15 tells the computer to determine whether the value stored in the `hours` variable is greater than or equal to the number 0 and, at the same time, less than or equal to the number 40. If the *condition* is true, then the selection structure calculates and displays the gross pay; otherwise, it displays an error message.

The (`hours < 0 || hours > 40`) *condition* in the second example shown in Figure 8-15 tells the computer to determine whether the value stored in the `hours` variable is less than the number 0 or greater than the number 40. If the *condition* is true, then the selection structure displays an error message; otherwise, it calculates and displays the gross pay. Both `if` statements shown in Figure 8-15 produce the same results, and simply represent two different ways of performing the same task.

In this next program, assume you want to display the word "Pass" if the user enters the letter P, and the word "Fail" if the user enters anything else. Figure 8-16 shows three ways of writing the C++ code for this program.

Example 1: using the || (Or) operator	Example 2: using the && (And) operator

```char letter = ' ';```
 ```cout << "Enter a letter: ";```
 ```cin >> letter;```
 ```if (letter == 'P' || letter == 'p')```
 ```   cout << "Pass" << endl;```
 ```else```
 ```   cout << "Fail" << endl;```
 ```//end if```
	```char letter = ' ';```
	 ```cout << "Enter a letter: ";```
	 ```cin >> letter;```
	 ```if (letter != 'P' && letter != 'p')```
	 ``` cout << "Fail" << endl;```
	 ```else```
	 ``` cout << "Pass" << endl;```
	 ```//end if```

Example 3: correct, but less efficient, solution

```
char letter = ' ';
cout << "Enter a letter: ";
cin >> letter;
if (letter == 'P' || letter == 'p')
   cout << "Pass" << endl;
//end if
if (letter != 'P' && letter != 'p')
   cout << "Fail" << endl;
//end if
```

Figure 8-16: C++ code showing the Or and And logical operators used to compare characters in the `if` statement's *condition*

> **tip**
>
> ▶ As you learned in Tutorial 4, character literal constants (for example, the letter 'P') are enclosed in single quotation marks, and string literal constants (for example, the word "Pass") are enclosed in double quotation marks.

> **tip**
>
> ▶ You learned about the ASCII codes, which are listed in Appendix A, in Tutorial 4's Concept lesson.

The (`letter == 'P' || letter == 'p'`) *condition* in Example 1 shown in Figure 8-16 tells the computer to determine whether the value stored in the `letter` variable is either the uppercase letter P or the lowercase letter p. If the *condition* is true, which means that the variable contains one of those two letters, then the selection structure displays the word "Pass" on the screen; otherwise, it displays the word "Fail". You may be wondering why you needed to tell the computer to compare the contents of the `letter` variable to both the uppercase and lowercase version of the letter P. As is true in many programming languages, character comparisons in C++ are case sensitive. That means that the uppercase version of a letter is not the same as its lowercase counterpart. So, although a human recognizes P and p as being the same letter, a computer does not; to a computer, a P is different from a p. The reason for this differentiation is that each character on the computer's keyboard is stored differently in the computer's internal memory. The uppercase letter P, for example, is stored using the eight bits 01010000 (ASCII code 80), whereas the lowercase letter p is stored using the eight bits 01110000 (ASCII code 112).

Many programming languages provide a function that you can use, instead of the Or operator, to perform a case-insensitive comparison of two characters. C++, for example, provides the `toupper` function for this purpose. You can learn about this function in Discovery Exercise 11 at the end of this lesson. The function also is covered in Tutorial 11.

The (`letter != 'P' && letter != 'p'`) *condition* in Example 2 shown in Figure 8-16 tells the computer to determine whether the value stored in the `letter` variable is not equal to either the uppercase letter P or the lowercase letter p. If the *condition* is true, which means that the variable does not contain either of those two letters, then the selection structure displays the word "Fail" on the screen; otherwise, it displays the word "Pass".

Rather than using one `if` statement with an `else` clause, as in Examples 1 and 2, Example 3 in Figure 8-16 uses two `if` statements with no `else` clause in either one. Although the `if` statement in Example 3 produces the same results as the `if` statements in Examples 1 and 2, it does so less efficiently. For example, assume that the user enters the letter P in response to the "Enter a letter: " prompt. The *condition* in the first `if` statement shown in Example 3 determines whether the value stored in the `letter` variable is equal to either P or p; in this case, the *condition* evaluates to true, because the `letter` variable contains the letter P. The first `if` statement's true path displays the word "Pass" on the screen, and then the first `if` statement ends. Although the appropriate word ("Pass") already appears on the screen, the program instructs the computer to evaluate the second `if` statement's *condition* to determine whether to display the "Fail" message. The second evaluation is unnecessary and makes Example 3's code less efficient than the code shown in Examples 1 and 2.

In addition to performing numeric and character comparisons in an `if` statement's *condition*, you also can perform string comparisons. For example, assume you want to display the message "We have a store in this state." if the user enters any of the following three state IDs: Il, In, Ky. If the user enters an ID other than these, you want to display the message "We don't have a store in this state." Figure 8-17 shows two ways of writing the C++ code for this program. Notice that the `if` statement in the first example uses the Or (||) logical operator, whereas the `if` statement in the second example uses the And (&&) logical operator.

Example 1: using the || (Or) operator

```
string state = "";
cout << "Enter a state ID: ";
getline(cin, state);
if (state == "Il" || state == "In" || state == "Ky")
    cout << "We have a store in this state." << endl;
else
    cout << "We don't have a store in this state." << endl;
//end if
```

Example 2: using the && (And) operator

```
string state = "";
cout << "Enter a state ID: ";
getline(cin, state);
if (state != "Il" && state != "In" && state != "Ky")
    cout << "We don't have a store in this state." << endl;
else
    cout << "We have a store in this state." << endl;
//end if
```

Figure 8-17: C++ code showing the Or and And logical operators used to compare strings in the `if` statement's *condition*

The (state == "Il" || state == "In" || state == "Ky") *condition* in Example 1 shown in Figure 8-17 tells the computer to compare the contents of the state variable to each of the three state IDs. If one of the three IDs is stored in the state variable, the *condition* will evaluate to true, and the selection structure will display the message "We have a store in this state." If, on the other hand, neither of the three IDs is stored in the state variable, the *condition* will evaluate to false, and the selection structure will display the message "We don't have a store in this state."

Similar to the *condition* in the first example, the *condition* in Example 2 (state != "Il" && state != "In" && state != "Ky") also compares the contents of the state variable to each of the three state IDs; however, the second example's *condition* compares for inequality, rather than equality. In this case, if neither of the three IDs is stored in the state variable, the *condition* will evaluate to true, and the selection structure will display the message "We don't have a store in this state." If, however, one of the three IDs is stored in the state variable, the *condition* will evaluate to false, and the selection structure will display the message "We have a store in this state." Here again, both if statements shown in Figure 8-17 produce the same results and simply represent two different ways of performing the same task.

As is true of char data, string data also is case sensitive. This means that the two letters "Ky" are not equivalent to "KY", "ky", or "kY". You will learn how to perform case-insensitive string comparisons in Tutorial 11. For now, when you are entering a string from the keyboard, always be sure to enter it using the exact case shown in the if statement's *condition*.

mini-quiz

Mini-Quiz 2

1. Evaluate the following compound condition: (true || false) using the truth tables shown in Figure 8-12.

2. Evaluate the following compound condition: (7 > 3 && 5 < 2) using the truth tables shown in Figure 8-12.

3. Evaluate the following compound condition: (5 * 4 < 20 || false) using the truth tables shown in Figure 8-12.

4. Write a compound condition for a C++ if statement that determines whether the value in the age variable is between 30 and 40, including 30 and 40.

5. Write a compound condition for a C++ if statement that determines whether the age variable contains a value that is either less than 30 or greater than 50.

6. Write a condition for a C++ if statement that determines whether the char variable named key contains the letter R (in any case).

7. Write a condition for a C++ if statement that determines whether the string variable named department contains the word "Accounting".

You now have completed Tutorial 8's Concept lesson. You can either take a break or complete the end-of-lesson questions and exercises before moving on to the Application lesson.

SUMMARY

The selection structure, also called the decision structure, is one of the three programming structures; the other two programming structures are sequence and repetition. You use the selection structure when you want a program to make a decision or comparison and then, based on the result of that decision or comparison, to select one of two paths: either the true path or the false path. Most programming languages offer three forms of the selection structure: `if`, `if/else`, and `switch` (also referred to as `case`).

A diamond, called the selection/repetition symbol, is used in a flowchart to represent the selection structure. The diamond contains a question that has a true or false answer only. Each selection diamond has one flowline entering the symbol and two flowlines leaving the symbol. The two flowlines leading out of the diamond should be marked so it is clear to the reader which path is the true path and which is the false path.

You can use the C++ `if` statement to code both the `if` and `if/else` forms of the selection structure. If either the `if` statement's true path or false path contains more than one statement, you must enclose the statements in a set of braces ({}). Statements enclosed in braces are referred to as a statement block. It is a good programming practice to include an `//end if` comment to identify the end of the `if` statement in a program.

The *condition* in an `if` statement can contain variables, constants, functions, arithmetic operators, comparison operators, and logical operators. The comparison operators in C++ are <, <=, >, >=, ==, and !=. The logical operators—And and Or—are represented in C++ by the symbols && and ||, respectively. If more than one operator with the same precedence number appears in an expression, C++ evaluates those operators from left to right in the expression. All expressions containing either a comparison or logical operator will result in an answer of either true or false only.

As is true in many programming languages, character and string comparisons in C++ are case sensitive.

ANSWERS TO MINI-QUIZZES

Mini-Quiz 1

1. if (score < 70)
     display "Fail"
   else
     display "Pass"
   end if

2. ```
   if (score < 70)
        cout << "Fail" << endl;
   else
        cout << "Pass" << endl;
   //end if
   ```

3. c. if (quantity == 100)

4. b. area = 5;

5. if (area == 5)
   ```

Mini-Quiz 2

1. true

2. false

3. false

4. `(age >= 30 && age <= 40)`

5. `(age < 30 || age > 50)`

6. `(key == 'R' || key == 'r')`

7. `(department == "Accounting")`

QUESTIONS

1. Which of the following symbols is used in a flowchart to represent the selection structure?
   a. diamond
   b. oval
   c. parallelogram
   d. rectangle

2. Which of the following is the equality operator in C++?
   a. !=
   b. =
   c. ==
   d. ->

3. Which of the following is the inequality operator in C++?
   a. !=
   b. ==
   c. ->
   d. <>

4. Assume you want to determine if the `item` variable contains either the word Chair or the word Desk. Which of the following *conditions* should you use in the `if` statement?
   a. `(item = "Chair" || item = "Desk")`
   b. `(item == 'Chair' || item == 'Desk')`
   c. `(item == "Chair" || item == "Desk")`
   d. `(item == "Chair" || "Desk")`

5. Assume you want to compare the character stored in the `initial` variable to the letter a. Which of the following *conditions* should you use in the `if` statement? (Be sure the *condition* will handle the letter a entered in any case.)
   a. `(initial = 'a' or 'A')`
   b. `(initial == 'a' or 'A')`
   c. `(initial == 'A' && initial == 'a')`
   d. `(initial == 'A' || initial == 'a')`

6. The expression 3 > 6 && 7 > 4 evaluates to _____.
   a. true   b. false

7. The expression 4 > 6 || 10 < 2 * 6 evaluates to _____.
   a. true   b. false

8. The expression 7 >= 3 + 4 || 6 < 4 && 2 < 5 evaluates to _____.
   a. true   b. false

9. The expression 4 * 3 < (6 + 7) && 7 < 6 + 9 evaluates to _____.
   a. true   b. false

10. Assuming the expression does not contain parentheses, which of the following operators will be performed first in the expression?
   a. arithmetic
   b. comparison
   c. logical

EXERCISES

1. Write the C++ `if` statement that compares the contents of the `quantity` variable to the number 10. If the `quantity` variable contains a number that is greater than 10, display the string "Over 10"; otherwise, display the string "Not over 10".

2. Write the C++ statements that correspond to the flowchart shown in Figure 8-18.

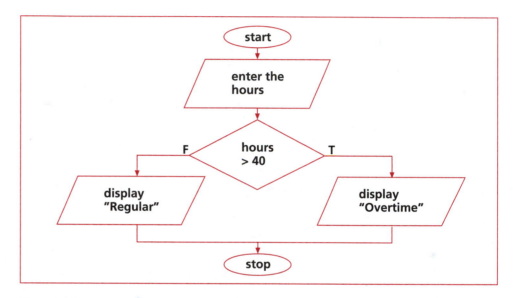

Figure 8-18

3. Open the T8ConE03.cpp file contained in the Cpp\Tut08\T8ConE03 folder on your computer's hard disk. Complete the program by writing an `if` statement that displays the string "Firebird" if the user enters the letter F (in any case). Save, build, and execute the program. Test the program three times, using the following letters: F, f, and x. When the program is working correctly, hide the Output window, then use the File menu to close the workspace.

4. Open the T8ConE04.cpp file contained in the Cpp\Tut08\T8ConE04 folder on your computer's hard disk. Complete the program by writing an `if` statement that displays the string "Entry error" if the user enters a number that is less than 0; otherwise, display the string "Valid number". Save, build, and execute the program. Test the program three times, using the following numbers: 5, 0, -3. When the program is working correctly, hide the Output window, then use the File menu to close the workspace.

5. Open the T8ConE05.cpp file contained in the Cpp\Tut08\T8ConE05 folder on your computer's hard disk. Complete the program by writing an `if` statement that displays the string "Reorder" if the user enters a number that is less than 10; otherwise, display the string "OK". Save, build, and execute the progrm. Test the program three times, using the following numbers: 5, 10, 19. When the program is working correctly, hide the Output window, then use the File menu to close the workspace.

6. Open the T8ConE06.cpp file contained in the Cpp\Tut08\T8ConE06 folder on your computer's hard disk. Complete the program by writing an `if` statement that assigns the number 10 to the `bonus` variable if the user enters a sales amount that is less than or equal to $250. If the user enters a sales amount that is greater than $250, prompt the user to enter the bonus rate, and then multiply the user's response by the sales amount and assign the result to the `bonus` variable. After assigning the appropriate bonus amount, display the bonus amount on the screen. Save, build, and execute the program. Test the program three times. For the first test, use 240 as the sales amount. For the second test, use 250 as the sales amount. For the third test, use 251 as the sales amount, and .05 as the bonus rate. When the program is working correctly, hide the Output window, then use the File menu to close the workspace.

7. Open the T8ConE07.cpp file contained in the Cpp\Tut08\T8ConE07 folder on your computer's hard disk. Assume that employees working more than 40 hours receive overtime pay (time and one-half) for the hours over 40. Complete the program by entering an `if` statement that calculates the overtime pay (if any) and the gross pay. Display the overtime pay (if any) and the gross pay. Save, build, and execute the program. Test the program using 40 as the hours and 7 as the rate. The program should display 0 as the overtime pay and 280 as the gross pay. Test the program again, using 42 as the hours and 10 as the rate. The program should display 30 as the overtime pay and 430 as the gross pay. When the program is working correctly, hide the Output window, then use the File menu to close the workspace.

8. Open the T8ConE08.cpp file contained in the Cpp\Tut08\T8ConE08 folder on your computer's hard disk. The program should prompt the user to enter an animal ID, and then store the user's response in a `char` variable named `animal`. The program should display the string "Dog" if the `animal` variable contains the letter D (in any case); otherwise, it should display the string "Cat". Complete the program appropriately, then save, build, and execute the program. Test the program three times, using the letters D, d, and h. When the program is working correctly, hide the Output window, then use the File menu to close the workspace.

9. Open the T8ConE09.cpp file contained in the Cpp\Tut08\T8ConE09 folder on your computer's hard disk. Complete the program by writing an `if` statement that displays the string "Valid entry" when the user enters either the integer 1, the integer 2, or the integer 3; otherwise, display the string "Entry error". Save, build, and execute the program. Test the program four times, using the integers 1, 2, 3, and 4. When the program is working correctly, hide the Output window, then use the File menu to close the workspace.

Exercises 10 and 11 are Discovery Exercises. Discovery Exercises, which may include topics that are not covered in this lesson, allow you to "discover" the solutions to problems on your own.

10. Recall that you must be careful when comparing two `float` values for either equality or inequality, because some `float` values cannot be stored, precisely, in memory. To determine if two `float` values are either equal or unequal, test that the difference between the values you are comparing is less than some acceptable small value, such as .00001.

   a. Open the T8ConE10.cpp file contained in the Cpp\Tut08\T8ConE10 folder on your computer's hard disk. Study the program's code. Notice that the code divides the contents of the `num1` variable (10.0) by the contents of the `num2` variable (3.0), and then stores the result (approximately 3.33333) in the `quotient` variable. An `if` statement is used to compare the contents of the `quotient` variable to the number 3.33333. The `if` statement then displays an appropriate message, indicating whether the numbers are equal.

   b. Build and execute the program. Although the DOS window shows that the quotient is 3.33333, the `if` statement displays the message "No, the quotient 3.33333 is not equal to 3.33333". Press the Enter key to close the DOS window.

   The proper procedure for comparing two `float` values is first to find the difference between the values, and then compare the absolute value of that difference to a small number, such as .00001. You can use the C++ `fabs` function, which is defined in the cmath header file, to find the absolute value of a `float` number. (`fabs` stands for *float absolute value*.) The absolute value of a number is a positive number that represents how far the number is from 0 on the number line. The absolute value of 5 is 5; the absolute value of -5 also is 5.

c. Enter the `#include <cmath>` directive below the `#include <iostream>` directive in the program.

d. Change the `if` clause to `if (fabs(quotient - 3.33333) < .00001)`.

e. Save, build, and execute the program. The DOS window displays the message "Yes, the quotient 3.33333 is equal to 3.33333". Press the Enter key to close the DOS window.

f. Hide the Output window, then use the File menu to close the workspace.

discovery

11. In this exercise, you will learn about the C++ `toupper` function.

a. Open the T8ConE11.cpp file contained in the Cpp\Tut08\T8ConE11 folder on your computer's hard disk.

b. Study the code, then build and execute the program. Enter the letter P. The DOS window displays "Pass". Press the Enter key to close the DOS window.

c. Execute the program again. This time, enter the letter p. The DOS window displays "Fail" because, to a computer, the letter P is not equivalent to the letter p. Press the Enter key to close the DOS window.

Rather than using the Or (`||`) operator to fix the problem encountered in Step c, you can use the C++ `toupper` (which stands for *to uppercase*) function. The syntax of the `toupper` function, which is defined in the cctype library file, is **toupper**(*charVariable*), where *charVariable* is the name of a `character` variable. The `toupper` function returns the uppercase equivalent of the character stored in the *charVariable*, but does not actually change the character in the variable to an uppercase letter.

d. Enter the `#include <cctype>` directive below the `directive`, then change the `if` statement's condition to `(toupper(letter) == 'P')`. The revised condition tells the computer to compare the uppercase version of the letter stored in the `letter` variable with the uppercase letter P.

e. Save, build, and execute the program. Enter the letter p. The DOS window displays "Pass". Press the Enter key to close the DOS window.

f. Hide the Output window, then use the File menu to close the workspace.

A computer program is good only if it works. Errors in either an algorithm or programming code can cause the program to run incorrectly. Therefore, a programmer needs to know how to locate and fix these errors. Exercises 12 and 13 are Debugging Exercises. Debugging Exercises allow you to practice recognizing and solving errors in a program.

debugging

12. In this exercise, you will debug an existing C++ program.

a. Open the T8ConE12.cpp file contained in the Cpp\Tut08\T8ConE12 folder on your computer's hard disk. The program should display a message based on the age entered by the user, but it is not working correctly.

b. Study the program's code, then build the program. Correct any errors in the program, then save, build, and execute the program. Test the program twice. For the first test, use John as the name and 32 as the age. For the second test, use Mary as the name and 16 as the age.

c. When the program is working correctly, hide the Output window, then use the File menu to close the workspace.

debugging

13. In this exercise, you will debug an existing C++ program.

a. Open the T8ConE13.cpp file contained in the Cpp\Tut08\T8ConE13 folder on your computer's hard disk. The program should display a message based on the sales amount entered by the user, but it is not working correctly.

b. Study the program's code, then build the program. Correct any errors in the program, then save, build, and execute the program. Test the program twice. For the first test, use 5000 as the sales amount. For the second test, use 20000 as the sales amount.

c. When the program is working correctly, hide the Output window, then use the File menu to close the workspace.

Application Lesson

Using the Selection Structure in a C++ Program

case ▶ Marshall Cabello is the manager of Willow Springs Health Club. Every other month, Marshall teaches a three-hour seminar titled "Healthy Living." The seminar stresses the importance of daily exercise (at least 20 minutes per day) and eating a low-fat diet (no more than 30% of the calories consumed should come from fat). Each time Marshall teaches the seminar, many of the participants ask him how to determine if a specific food item is considered low-fat. For demonstration at the seminar, Marshall has asked you to create a program that will allow him to enter the number of calories and grams of fat contained in a specific food. The program then should calculate and display two values: the food's fat calories (the number of calories attributed to fat) and its fat percentage (the ratio of the food's fat calories to its total calories).

Analyzing, Planning, and Desk-Checking the Health Club Program

You can calculate the number of fat calories in a food by multiplying the number of fat grams contained in the food by the number nine, because each gram of fat contains nine calories. To calculate the fat percentage, which is the percentage of a food's total calories derived from fat, you divide the food's fat calories by its total calories, and then multiply the result by 100. You will use both of these calculations in the health club's algorithm.

Recall that most algorithms follow a similar format: first they get the input data, then they process that data (typically by performing calculations on it), and then they display the output data. For simple algorithms (such as the health club algorithm), the input, processing, and output tasks can be performed by the `main` function itself. However, to help reinforce the concept of functions, which are important for most real-world programs, you will use one additional function in the health club algorithm. The additional function's task will be to calculate the fat calories and fat percentage. Figure 8-19 shows the IPO charts for one possible solution to the health club problem.

`main` **function**

Input	Processing	Output

total calories grams of fat	Processing items: none
	
	Algorithm:
	1. enter the total calories and grams of fat
	2. if (the total calories are greater than or equal to zero and the grams of fat are greater than or equal to zero)
	    calcFatInfo(total calories, grams of fat, fat calories, fat percentage)
	    display fat calories and fat percentage
	else
	    display error message
	end if
		fat calories fat percentage

`calcFatInfo` **function**

Input	Processing	Output
total calories grams of fat address of fat calories address of fat percentage	Processing items: none Algorithm: 1. calculate fat calories by multiplying grams of fat by 9 2. calculate fat percentage by dividing fat calories by total calories, then multiplying the result by 100	fat calories fat percentage

Figure 8-19: IPO charts for the health club problem

As Figure 8-19 indicates, the `main` function's output is the fat calories and fat percentage, and its input is the total calories and grams of fat. According to its algorithm, the `main` function first has the user enter the two input values; it then validates both values. If both values are greater than or equal to zero, the `main` function calls the `calcFatInfo` function to calculate the fat calories and fat percentage. For the `calcFatInfo` function to perform its task, the `main` function needs to pass it the values of the total calories and grams of fat, as well as the addresses of the variables in which to store the fat calories and fat percentage. After the `calcFatInfo` function completes its task, the `main` function displays the fat calories and fat percentage on the screen.

Notice, however, that if both input values are not greater than or equal to zero—which means that at least one of the values is less than zero—the `main` function should not call the `calcFatInfo` function, nor should it display the fat calories and fat percentage on the screen. Rather, it simply should display an error message to alert the user that one of the values he or she entered is incorrect.

Recall that you should desk-check an algorithm several times before you begin coding it, using both valid and invalid data. As you learned in Tutorial 2, **valid data** is data that the programmer is expecting the user to enter. In the health club algorithm, for example, the programmer expects the user to provide positive numbers for the input items (total calories and grams of fat). **Invalid data** is data that the programmer is not expecting the user to enter. In this case, the programmer is not expecting the user to enter negative values for the input items. A negative value entered as either the number of calories or grams of fat is obviously an input error. In this case, you will use the following three sets of data to desk-check the algorithms shown in Figure 8-19:

Data for first desk-check	Data for second desk-check	Data for third desk-check
Total calories: 150	Total calories: 105	Total calories: 100
Grams of fat: 6	Grams of fat: 2	Grams of fat: -3

Figure 8-20 shows the completed desk-check tables, with the fat percentage amounts rounded to two decimal places.

`main` function

total calories	grams of fat	fat calories	fat percentage
~~150~~	~~6~~	~~54~~	~~36.00~~
~~105~~	~~2~~	18	17.14
100	-3		

`calcFatInfo` function

total calories	grams of fat
~~150~~	~~6~~
~~105~~	~~2~~
100	-3

Figure 8-20: Completed desk-check tables for the algorithms shown in Figure 8-19

tip

You will notice that the `calcFatInfo` desk-check table does not include the fat calories and fat percentage items, which are passed to the function *by reference*. As you learned in Tutorial 7, when a function receives the address of an item from the `main` function, any changes it makes to the item are recorded in the `main` function's desk-check table.

After desk-checking an algorithm to verify its accuracy, you are ready to translate it into a language the computer can understand. Begin by coding the program's `main` function.

Coding the `main` Function

According to its IPO chart, the `main` function requires four memory locations to store the values of its input and output items. You will store the values in variables, because the values will be different each time the program is executed. You will use the `int` data type for the variables that store the total calories, grams of fat, and fat calories, since the variables will need to store whole numbers only. You will use the `float` data type for the variable that stores the fat percentage, which will contain a decimal place.

After reserving the memory locations, the `main` function will use the `cout` stream and the `<<` operator to prompt the user to enter the total calories and grams of fat. It then will use the `cin` stream and the `>>` operator to allow the user to enter the requested information.

The next step in the algorithm is to use the `if/else` form of the selection structure to determine if the user's input is valid, and then take the appropriate action based on the result. As you learned in the Concept lesson, you use the C++ `if` statement to code the `if/else` form of the selection structure. Figure 8-21 shows the C++ code corresponding to the `main` function.

IPO chart information	C++ instructions

Input
 total calories
 grams of fat
Processing
 none
 	
Output
 fat calories
 fat percentage
	`int totalCal = 0;`
	`int fatGrams = 0;`
	
	`int fatCal = 0;`
	`float fatPercent = 0.0;`

Algorithm
1. enter the total calories and
   grams of fat
 	
2. if (the total calories are greater than or
   equal to zero and the grams of fat are
   greater than or equal to zero)
     calcFatInfo(total calories, grams of fat,
     fat calories, fat percentage)
     display fat calories and fat percentage
   else
     display error message
   end if
	`cout << "Total calories: ";`
	`cin >> totalCal;`
	`cout << "Grams of fat: ";`
	`cin >> fatGrams;`
	
	`if (totalCal >= 0 && fatGrams >= 0)`
	`{`
	`    calcFatInfo(totalCal, fatGrams,`
	`        fatCal, fatPercent);`
	`    cout << "Fat calories: " <<`
	`        fatCal << endl;`
	`    cout << "Fat percentage: " <<`
	`        fatPercent << endl;`
	`}`
	`else`
	`    cout << "Input error" << endl;`
	`//end if`

Figure 8-21: C++ statements corresponding to the `main` function

tip

The four variables declared in the code shown in Figure 8-21 are local to the `main` function and will remain in memory until the function's `return 0;` statement is processed.

Next, you will code the `calcFatInfo` function.

Coding the `calcFatInfo` Function

Recall that the `main` function will pass the values of two of its variables (`totalCal` and `fatGrams`), along with the addresses of two of its variables (`fatCal` and `fatPercent`), to the `calcFatInfo` function. You will use the formal parameters `tCal`, `grams`, `&fCal`, and `&fPer` to receive the information. Figure 8-22 shows the C++ code for the `calcFatInfo` function.

IPO chart information	C++ instructions

Input
  total calories
  grams of fat
  address of fat calories
  address of fat percentage
Processing
  none
Output
  fat calories
  fat percentage
	`void calcFatInfo(int tCal, int grams, int &fCal, float &fPer)`

Algorithm
1. calculate fat calories
    by multiplying grams
    of fat by 9
2. calculate fat
    percentage by
    dividing fat calories
    by total calories, then
    multiplying the result
    by 100
	`fCal = grams * 9;`
	
	`fPer = fCal / tCal * 100;`

Figure 8-22: C++ code for the `calcFatInfo` function

Now that you have finished coding the algorithms, you need to desk-check the program, using the same data you used to desk-check the algorithms. Figure 8-23 shows the data and the completed desk-check table for the program, with the fat percentage amounts rounded to two decimal places.

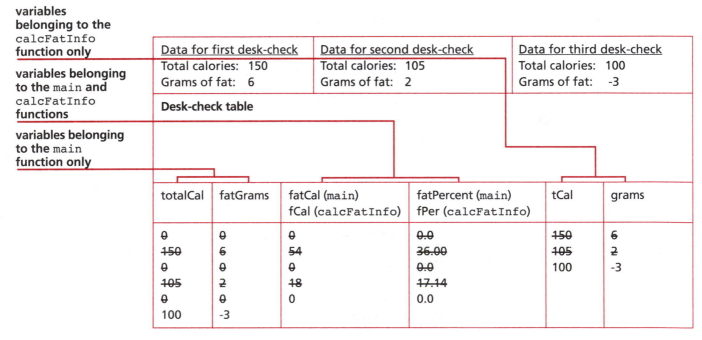

variables belonging to the `calcFatInfo` function only

variables belonging to the `main` and `calcFatInfo` functions

variables belonging to the `main` function only

Data for first desk-check		Data for second desk-check		Data for third desk-check	
Total calories: 150		Total calories: 105		Total calories: 100	
Grams of fat: 6		Grams of fat: 2		Grams of fat: -3	

Desk-check table

totalCal	fatGrams	fatCal (main) fCal (calcFatInfo)	fatPercent (main) fPer (calcFatInfo)	tCal	grams
~~0~~	~~0~~	~~0~~	~~0.0~~	~~150~~	~~6~~
~~150~~	6	54	36.00	~~105~~	~~2~~
~~0~~	~~0~~	~~0~~	~~0.0~~	100	-3
~~105~~	2	~~18~~	~~17.14~~		
~~0~~	~~0~~	0	0.0		
100	-3				

Figure 8-23: Data and completed desk-check table for the program

▶ Recall that the address-of operator (&) alerts the computer that what is being passed to the function is a variable's address rather than its value.

▶ The four variables appearing in the `calcFatInfo` function header are local to the `calcFatInfo` function. When the function's closing brace is encountered, the `tCal` and `grams` variables and the `fCal` and `fPer` variable names will be removed from memory.

The results obtained when desk-checking the program agree with the results obtained when desk-checking the algorithm. You now are ready to enter the C++ instructions into the computer.

Completing the Health Club Program

Your computer's hard disk contains a partially completed C++ program containing most of the instructions for the health club program. Open that program now.

To open the partially completed C++ program:

1 Start Visual C++.

2 Open the **T8App.cpp** file contained in the Cpp\Tut08\T8App folder on your computer's hard disk. Figure 8-24 shows the instructions contained in the partially completed T8App.cpp program.

```cpp
//T8App.cpp - displays fat calories and fat percentage

#include <iostream>
using namespace std;

//function prototype
void calcFatInfo(int, int, int &, float &);

int main()
{
    int totalCal      = 0;
    int fatGrams      = 0;
    int fatCal        = 0;
    float fatPercent = 0.0;

    //enter input data
    cout << "Total calories: ";
    cin >> totalCal;
    cout << "Grams of fat: ";
    cin >> fatGrams;
    //validate input data

    return 0;
}   //end of main function

//*****program-defined functions*****
void calcFatInfo(int tCal, int grams, int &fCal, float &fPer)
{
    //calculate fat calories and fat percentage
    fCal = grams * 9;
    fPer = fCal / tCal * 100;
}   //end of calcFatInfo function
```

Figure 8-24: Instructions contained in the partially completed T8App.cpp program

Missing from the program is the `if` statement in the `main` function.

To enter the `if` statement, then test the program:

1   Position the insertion point in the blank line below the `//validate input data` comment. Press the **Tab** key, if necessary, then enter the additional instructions shaded in Figure 8-25.

```cpp
//T8App.cpp - displays fat calories and fat percentage

#include <iostream>
using namespace std;

//function prototype
void calcFatInfo(int, int, int &, float &);

int main()
{
    int totalCal    = 0;
    int fatGrams    = 0;
    int fatCal      = 0;
    float fatPercent = 0.0;

    //enter input data
    cout << "Total calories: ";
    cin >> totalCal;
    cout << "Grams of fat: ";
    cin >> fatGrams;
    //validate input data
    if (totalCal >= 0 && fatGrams >= 0)
    {
        //valid data
        calcFatInfo(totalCal, fatGrams, fatCal, fatPercent);
        cout << fixed;
        cout.precision(0);
        cout << "Fat calories: " << fatCal << endl;
        cout << "Fat percentage: " << fatPercent << "%" << endl;
    }
    else //invalid data
        cout << "Input error" << endl;
    //end if

    return 0;
}   //end of main function

//*****program-defined functions*****
void calcFatInfo(int tCal, int grams, int &fCal, float &fPer)
{
    //calculate fat calories and fat percentage
    fCal = grams * 9;
    fPer = fCal / tCal * 100;
}   //end of calcFatInfo function
```

enter these 12 lines of code

Figure 8-25: Program showing `if` statement entered in the `main` function

2 Save, build, and execute the program.

3 When prompted for the total calories, type **150** and press the **Enter** key. When prompted for the grams of fat, type **6** and press the **Enter** key. The program calculates and displays the fat calories and fat percentage, as shown in Figure 8-26.

Figure 8-26: DOS window showing results of first test

The DOS window shows that the fat calories are 54, which agrees with the desk-check tables. However, it shows that the fat percentage is 0%, which is incorrect.

4 Press the **Enter** key to close the DOS window, then hide the Output window.

According to the desk-check tables, the fat percentage for a food with 150 total calories and 6 grams of fat should be 36% (54 fat calories / 150 total calories * 100). Why doesn't the program produce the correct result? The reason for the discrepancy is the manner in which C++ performs division between two integers. When C++ divides an integer by another integer, it returns only the integer portion of the quotient. In other words, if the quotient contains a decimal portion, the decimal portion is truncated (dropped from the number). In this case, when C++ divides the fat calories (the integer 54) by the total calories (the integer 150), it returns 0, which is the integer portion of the quotient 0.36. You can fix this problem by type casting the variables involved in the division operation to the `float` data type. When C++ divides two `float` numbers, the result is always a `float` number that contains the entire quotient—both the integer and decimal portions. Recall that you type cast an item of data by enclosing the data in parentheses, and then preceding it with the C++ keyword that represents the desired data type.

To type cast the statement that calculates the fat percentage, then save and build the program:

1 Change the **fPer = fCal / tCal * 100;** statement in the **calcFatInfo** function to **fPer = float(fCal) / float(tCal) * 100;**.

2 Save, build, and execute the program. When prompted for the total calories, type **150** and press the **Enter** key. When prompted for the grams of fat, type **6** and press the **Enter** key. The program correctly calculates and displays the fat calories and fat percentage as 54 and 36%, respectively.

3 Press the **Enter** key to close the DOS window.

4 Execute the program again. When prompted for the total calories, type **105** and press the **Enter** key. When prompted for the grams of fat, type **2** and press the **Enter** key. The program correctly calculates and displays the fat calories and fat percentage as 18 and 17%, respectively.

5 Press the **Enter** key to close the DOS window, then execute the program again. When prompted for the total calories, type **100** and press the **Enter** key. When prompted for the grams of fat, type **-3** and press the **Enter** key. The program displays the "Input error" message.

6 Press the **Enter** key to close the DOS window. Hide the Output window, then use the File menu to close the workspace. When prompted to close all document windows, click the **Yes** button.

7 Exit Visual C++.

You now have completed Tutorial 8's Application lesson. You can either take a break or complete the end-of-lesson exercises.

EXERCISES

1. In this exercise, you will create a program that displays an employee's gross pay.
    a. Figure 8-27 shows the partially completed IPO chart for the payroll program. Employees working over 40 hours should be paid time and one-half for the hours worked over 40. Complete the IPO chart.

Input	Processing	Output
name hours worked pay rate	Processing items: none Algorithm:	name gross pay

Figure 8-27

    b. Open the T8AppE01.cpp file contained in the Cpp\Tut08\T8AppE01 folder on your computer's hard disk. Use the IPO chart you completed in Step a to complete the program. Display the gross pay amount in fixed-point notation with two decimal places.
    c. Complete a desk-check table for the program. First, use Jack Henderson as the name, 35 as the hours worked, and 10 as the hourly pay rate. Then, use Mary Matiez as the name, 45 as the hours worked, and 7.50 as the hourly pay rate.
    d. Save, build, and execute the program. Use the data from Step c to test the program.
    e. When the program is working correctly, hide the Output window, then use the File menu to close the workspace.

2. In this exercise, you will create a program that displays a bonus amount.
    a. Figure 8-28 shows the partially completed IPO charts for the bonus program. Complete the IPO charts. The `calcBonus` function should be a value-returning function that calculates and returns the appropriate bonus amount. The bonus rate is 10% on the first $12,000 of sales, and 15% on sales over $12,000. (For example, a salesperson selling $15,000 in product should receive a bonus of $1650.)

`main` **function**

Input	Processing	Output
sales	Processing items: none Algorithm:	bonus

`calcBonus` **function**

Input	Processing	Output
	Processing items: Algorithm:	

Figure 8-28

 b. Open the T8AppE02.cpp file contained in the Cpp\Tut08\T8AppE02 folder on your computer's hard disk. Use the IPO charts you completed in Step a to complete the program. Display the bonus amount in fixed-point notation with zero decimal places.

 c. Complete a desk-check table for the program, using the following sale amounts: 5000 and 96000.

 d. Save, build, and execute the program. Use the data from Step c to test the program.

 e. When the program is working correctly, hide the Output window, then use the File menu to close the workspace.

3. In this exercise, you will modify the present value program you created in Tutorial 5's Application lesson. The modified program will validate the interest rate entered by the user.

 a. Open the T8AppE03.cpp file contained in the Cpp\Tut08\T8AppE03 folder on your computer's hard disk.

 b. Modify the program so that it allows the user to enter the interest rate as either an integer or a decimal number. (*Hint*: If the user enters the rate as a decimal number, the program will need to divide the rate by 100.)

 c. Save, build, and execute the program. Enter .06 as the interest rate. The amount that can be borrowed should be $15329. Execute the program again. This time, enter the number 6 as the interest rate. The amount that can be borrowed should be $15329.

 d. When the program is working correctly, hide the Output window, then use the File menu to close the workspace.

4. In this exercise, you will create a program that displays the average of three test scores entered by the user. The program will use a `main` function and one void function named `calcAverage`.

 a. Write the IPO charts for the average program, which should contain two program-defined functions: `main` and `calcAverage`. Before calling the `calcAverage` function to calculate the average, have the `main` function validate the input data. To be valid, each test score must be greater than or equal to zero. If one or more test scores is not valid, the program should display an appropriate error message.

 b. Create a console application. Name the project workspace T8AppE04, and save it in the Cpp\Tut08 folder on your computer's hard disk. Add a new C++ source file to the project. Name the source file T8AppE04.

 c. Use the IPO charts you created in Step a to code the program. Display the average in fixed-point notation with one decimal place.

 d. Complete a desk-check table for the program, using the following two groups of test scores: 95.5, 76, 59 as the first group and 45, -78, 30 (notice the minus sign before the number 78) as the second group.

e. Save, build, and execute the program. Use the data from Step d to test the program.

f. When the program is working correctly, hide the Output window, then use the File menu to close the workspace.

5. In this exercise, you will modify the water bill program you created in Tutorial 7's Application lesson.

a. Open the T8AppE05.cpp file contained in the Cpp\Tut08\T8AppE05 folder on your computer's hard disk.

b. Modify the program so that the `main` function calls the `calculate` and `displayBill` functions only if the input data (the two meter readings) is valid. To be valid, both meter readings must be greater than zero, and the current meter reading must be greater than the previous meter reading. If the data is not valid, display an appropriate error message.

c. Save, build, and execute the program. Enter Eunice Smith as the name, 25000 as the current reading, and 33000 as the previous reading. An error message should appear on the screen.

d. Execute the program again. Enter Henry Ivalli as the name, 3000 as the current reading, and -1 as the previous reading. An error message should appear on the screen.

e. Execute the program again. Enter Mary Johnson as the name, -5000 as the current reading, and 3000 as the previous reading. An error message should appear on the screen.

f. Execute the program again. Enter your name, 4000 as the current reading, and 2000 as the previous reading. The water bill should appear on the screen.

g. When the program is working correctly, hide the Output window, then use the File menu to close the workspace.

6. In this exercise, you will create a program that displays the total amount a company owes for a seminar. The seminar charge is $80 per person.

a. Write an IPO chart for the seminar program. The input will be the number of seminar registrants. The number of registrants should be greater than 0, but less than 50. Display an appropriate error message if the number of registrants is invalid.

b. Open the T8AppE06.cpp file contained in the Cpp\Tut08\T8AppE06 folder on your computer's hard disk. Use the IPO chart you completed in Step a to complete the program.

c. Complete a desk-check table for the program, using the following data: 5 and -20.

d. Save, build, and execute the program. Use the data from Step c to test the program.

e. When the program is working correctly, hide the Output window, then use the File menu to close the workspace.

7. In this exercise, you will create a program that displays a shipping charge.

a. Write an IPO chart for the shipping charge program. The shipping charge is based on the state entered by the user, as shown in the following table:

State	Shipping charge ($)
Hawaii	30
Oregon	30

If the user enters any other state, the result should be an "Incorrect state" message.

b. Open the T8AppE07.cpp file contained in the Cpp\Tut08\T8AppE07 folder on your computer's hard disk. Use the IPO chart you completed in Step a to complete the program.

c. Complete a desk-check table for the program, using the following data: Oregon and Kentucky.

d. Save, build, and execute the program. Use the data from Step c to test the program.

e. When the program is working correctly, hide the Output window, then use the File menu to close the workspace.

Exercise 8 is a Discovery Exercise. Discovery Exercises, which may include topics that are not covered in this lesson, allow you to "discover" the solutions to problems on your own.

discovery

8. In this exercise, you will create a program that displays a shipping charge.
   a. Write an IPO chart for the shipping charge program. The shipping charge is based on the state entered by the user, as shown in the following table:

State	Shipping charge ($)
Alabama	25
Alaska	50

   If the user enters any other state, the shipping charge should be 0.
   (*Hint*: You can nest an if statement, which means you can place one if statement inside another if statement.)
   b. Open the T8AppE08.cpp file contained in the Cpp\Tut08\T8AppE08 folder on your computer's hard disk. Use the IPO chart you completed in Step a to complete the program.
   c. Complete a desk-check table for the program, using the following data: Alabama, Alaska, and Illinois.
   d. Save, build, and execute the program. Use the data from Step c to test the program.
   e. When the program is working correctly, hide the Output window, then use the File menu to close the workspace.

A computer program is good only if it works. Errors in either an algorithm or programming code can cause the program to run incorrectly. Therefore, a programmer needs to know how to locate and fix these errors. Exercise 9 is a Debugging Exercise. Debugging Exercises allow you to practice recognizing and solving errors in a program.

debugging

9. In this exercise, you will debug an existing C++ program.
   a. Open the T8AppE10.cpp file contained in the Cpp\Tut08\T8AppE10 folder on your computer's hard disk. The program should display a message based on the sales amount entered by the user, but it is not working correctly. Study the program's code, then build and execute the program.
   b. Correct any errors in the program, then save, build, and execute the program again. When the program is working correctly, hide the Output window, then use the File menu to close the workspace.

More on the Selection Structure

Concept Lesson

Nested Selection Structures

As you learned in Tutorial 8, you use the selection structure when you want a program to make a decision and then select one of two paths—either the true path or the false path—based on the result of that decision. Both paths in a selection structure can include instructions that declare and initialize variables, perform calculations, and so on; both also can include other selection structures. When either a selection structure's true path or its false path contains another selection structure, the inner selection structure is referred to as a **nested selection structure**, because it is contained (nested) within the outer selection structure.

You use a nested selection structure if more than one decision needs to be made before the appropriate action can be taken. For example, assume you want to create a voter eligibility program that displays one of three messages. The messages, along with the criteria for displaying each message, are shown here:

Message	Criteria
"You are too young to vote."	person is younger than 18 years old
"You can vote."	person is at least 18 years old and is registered to vote
"You need to register before you can vote."	person is at least 18 years old but is not registered to vote

As the chart indicates, the person's age and voter registration status determine which of the three messages is the appropriate one to display. If the person is younger than 18 years old, the program should display the message "You are too young to vote." However, if the person is at least 18 years old, the program should display one of two different messages. The correct message to display is determined by the person's voter registration status. If the person is registered, then the appropriate message is "You can vote."; otherwise, it is "You need to register before you can vote." Notice that determining the person's voter registration status is important only *after* his or her age is determined. You can think of the decision regarding the age as being the **primary decision**, and the decision regarding the registration status as being the **secondary decision**, because whether the registration decision needs to be made depends on the result of the age decision. The primary decision is always made by the outer selection structure, while the secondary decision is always made by the inner (nested) selection structure.

Figure 9-1 shows the pseudocode and C++ code for the voter eligbility program, and Figure 9-2 shows the corresponding flowchart. In both figures, the outer selection structure determines the age (the primary decision), and the nested selection structure determines the voter registration status (the secondary decision). Notice that the nested selection structure appears in the outer selection structure's true path in both figures.

Pseudocode

1. enter the age
2. if (the age is greater than or equal to 18)
        enter the registration status
        if (the registration status is Y)
                display "You can vote."
        else
                display "You need to register before you can vote."
        end if
    else
        display "You are too young to vote."
    end if

tip

The lines connecting the `if`, `else`, **and** `end if` **in the** pseudocode and code shown in Figure 9-1 are included in the figure to help you see which clauses are related to each other.

C++ code

```cpp
cout << "Enter your age: ";
cin >> age;
if (age >= 18)
{
    cout << "Are you registered to vote? If yes, enter Y or y: ";
    cin >> status;
    if (status == 'Y' || status == 'y')
        cout << "You can vote." << endl;
    else
        cout << "You need to register before you can vote." << endl;
    //end if
}
else
    cout << "You are too young to vote." << endl;
//end if
```

Figure 9-1: Pseudocode and C++ code showing the nested selection structure in the true path

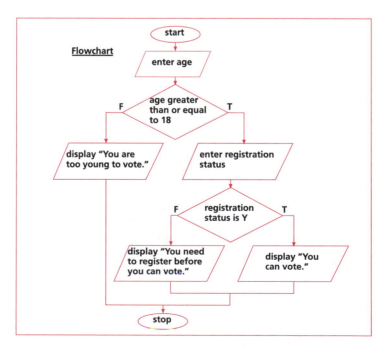

Figure 9-2: Flowchart showing the nested selection structure in the true path

As both figures indicate, the program first gets the age from the user. The condition in the outer selection structure then checks to determine if the age is greater than or equal to 18. If the condition is false, it means that the person is not old enough to vote. In that case, only one message—the "You are too young to vote." message—is appropriate. After the message is displayed, both the outer selection structure and the program end.

If the outer selection structure's condition is true, on the other hand, it means that the person *is* old enough to vote. Before displaying the appropriate message, the instructions in the outer selection structure's true path first get the registration status from the user. A nested selection structure then is used to determine if the person is registered. If he or she is registered, the instruction in the nested selection structure's true path displays the message "You can vote."; otherwise, the instruction in the nested selection structure's false path displays the message "You need to register before you can vote." After the appropriate message is displayed, both selection structures, as well as the program, end. Notice that the nested selection structure in this program is processed only when the outer selection structure's condition is true.

Figures 9-3 and 9-4 show the pseudocode, C++ code, and flowchart for a different version of the voter eligibility program. As in the previous version, the outer selection structure in this version determines the age (the primary decision), and the nested selection structure determines the voter registration status (the secondary decision). In this version of the program, however, the nested selection structure appears in the false path of the outer selection structure.

Pseudocode

```
1. enter the age
2. if (the age is less than 18)
        display "You are too young to vote."
   else
        enter the registration status
        if (the registration status is Y)
            display "You can vote."
        else
            display "You need to register before you can vote."
        end if
   end if
```

C++ code

```
cout << "Enter your age: ";
cin >> age;
if (age < 18)
    cout << "You are too young to vote." << endl;
else
{
    cout << "Are you registered to vote? If yes, enter Y or y: ";
    cin >> status;
    if (status == 'Y' || status == 'y')
        cout << "You can vote." << endl;
    else
        cout << "You need to register before you can vote." << endl;
    //end if
}   //end if
```

Figure 9-3: Pseudocode and C++ code showing the nested selection structure in the false path

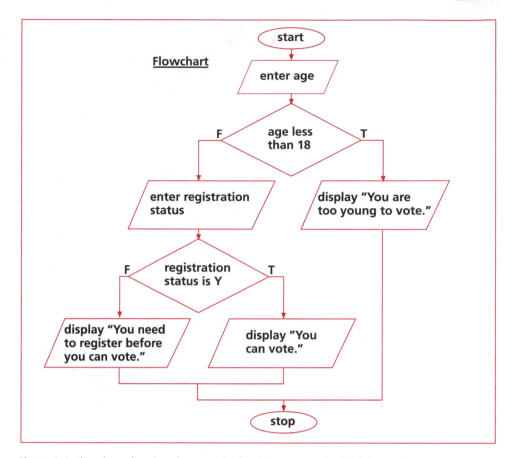

Figure 9-4: Flowchart showing the nested selection structure in the false path

Like the version shown earlier, this version of the voter eligibility program first gets the age from the user. However, rather than checking to determine if the age is greater than or equal to 18, the outer selection structure in this version checks to determine whether the age is less than 18. If the condition is true, the instruction in the outer selection structure's true path displays the message "You are too young to vote." If the condition is false, the instructions in the outer selection structure's false path first get the registration status from the user, and then use a nested selection structure to determine if the person is registered. If the person is registered, the instruction in the nested selection structure's true path displays the message "You can vote."; otherwise, the instructions in the nested selection structure's false path displays the message "You need to register before you can vote." Unlike in the previous version, the nested selection structure in this version of the program is processed only when the outer selection structure's condition is false.

Notice that both versions of the voter eligibility program produce the same results. Neither version is better than the other; each simply represents a different way of solving the same problem.

Next, view another example of a nested selection structure.

Another Example of a Nested Selection Structure

In Tutorial 8's Application lesson, you created a program for Marshall Cabello, the manager of Willow Springs Health Club. As you may remember, the program allows Marshall to enter the number of calories and grams of fat contained in a specific food. The program then calculates and displays two values: the food's fat calories (the number of calories attributed to fat) and its fat percentage (the ratio of the food's fat calories to its total calories). Now suppose that Marshall wants you to modify the program so that it displays the message "This food is high in fat." if a food's fat percentage is greater than 30%; otherwise, the program should display the message "This food is not high in fat." The modified health club program, which uses a nested selection structure, is shown in Figure 9-5.

In this case, the outer selection structure's condition, which represents the primary decision, determines if the user's input (total calories and grams of fat) is valid. If the condition is false, the instruction in the outer selection structure's false path displays an error message on the screen. However, if the condition is true, the instructions in the outer selection structure's true path both calculate and display the fat calories and fat percentage, and then use a nested selection structure to determine if the secondary decision—whether the fat percentage is greater than 30—is true or false. If the fat percentage is greater than 30, the nested selection structure's true path displays the message "This food is high in fat."; otherwise, the nested selection structure's false path displays the message "This food is not high in fat." As in the voter eligibility program, the result of the primary decision determines whether it is necessary to make the secondary decision in the health club program.

```cpp
//Modified T8App.cpp program
//displays fat calories, fat percentage, and message

#include <iostream>
using namespace std;

//function prototype
void calcFatInfo(int, int, int &, float &);

int main()
{
        int totalCal     = 0;
        int fatGrams     = 0;
        int fatCal       = 0;
        float fatPercent = 0.0;

        //enter input data
        cout << "Total calories: ";
        cin >> totalCal;
        cout << "Grams of fat: ";
        cin >> fatGrams;
        //validate input data
```

Figure 9-5: Health club program containing a nested selection structure

```
        if (totalCal >= 0 && fatGrams >= 0)
        {
            //valid data
            calcFatInfo(totalCal, fatGrams, fatCal, fatPercent);
            cout << fixed;
            cout.precision(0);
            cout << "Fat calories: " << fatCal << endl;
            cout << "Fat percentage: " << fatPercent << "%" << endl;
            if (fatPercent > 30)
                cout << "This food is high in fat." << endl;
            else
                cout << "This food is not high in fat." << endl;
            //end if
        }
        else  //invalid data
            cout << "Input error" << endl;
        //end if

        return 0;
}   //end of main function

//*****program-defined functions*****
void calcFatInfo(int tCal, int grams, int &fCal, float &fPer)
{
    //calculate fat calories and fat percentage
    fCal = grams * 9;
    fPer = float(fCal) / float(tCal) * 100;
}   //end of calcFatInfo function
```

outer selection structure

nested selection structure

Figure 9-5: Health club program containing a nested selection structure (continued)

mini-quiz

Mini-Quiz 1

1. Assume you want to create a program that displays the message "Highest honors" if a student's test score is 90 or above. If the test score is 70 through 89, the program should display the message "Good job". For all other test scores, the program should display the message "Retake the test". Write the pseudocode for this program's selection structure.

2. Write the C++ code that corresponds to the pseudocode you wrote in Question 1. The student's score is stored in an **int** variable named **score**.

3. Assume that the manager of a golf course has asked you to create a program that displays the appropriate fee to charge a golfer. The golf course uses the following fee schedule:

Fee	Criteria
0	Members
15	Non-members golfing on Monday through Thursday
25	Non-members golfing on Friday through Sunday

In this program, which is the primary decision and which is the secondary decision? Why?

In the next section, you will learn some of the common logic errors made when writing selection structures. Being aware of these errors will help to prevent you from making them.

Logic Errors in Selection Structures

Typically, logic errors commonly made when writing selection structures are a result of one of the following mistakes:

1. Using a logical operator when a nested selection structure is needed
2. Reversing the primary and secondary decisions
3. Using an unnecessary nested selection structure

The XYZ Company's vacation program can be used to demonstrate each of these logic errors. Assume that the company employs both full-time and part-time employees. Only full-time employees receive a paid vacation, as shown here:

Vacation weeks	Criteria
0	Part-time employees
2	Full-time employees working at the company for 5 years or fewer
3	Full-time employees working at the company for over 5 years

The company has asked you to create a program that allows the user to enter the employee's status—either F for full-time or P for part-time—and the number of years the employee has worked for the company. If the employee is full-time, the program should display the number of vacation weeks to which the employee is entitled, and then the program should end. If the employee is not full-time, the program should simply end without displaying anything.

As the vacation chart indicates, the employee's status—either full-time or part-time—is a factor in determining whether the employee receives any paid vacation. If the employee is entitled to a paid vacation, then the number of years he or she has worked for the company determines the appropriate number of vacation weeks. In this case, the decision regarding the employee's status is the primary decision, and the decision regarding the years employed is the secondary decision, because whether the years employed decision needs to be made depends on the result of the status decision.

Figure 9-6 shows a correct algorithm for the vacation program.

tip
....

You also could have written the nested selection structure's condition as follows: *if (the years are less than or equal to 5)*. The nested structure's true path then would contain the instruction *display "2-week vacation"*; its false path would contain the instruction *display "3-week vacation"*.

Correct algorithm for the vacation program

1. enter the status and years
2. if (the status is F)
      if (the years are greater than 5)
            display "3-week vacation"
      else
            display "2-week vacation"
      end if
  end if

Figure 9-6: A correct algorithm for the vacation program

To observe why the algorithm shown in Figure 9-6 is correct, you will desk-check it using the following test data:

Data for first desk-check	Data for second desk-check	Data for third desk-check
Status: F	Status: F	Status: P
Years: 4	Years: 15	Years: 11

The algorithm should display "2-week vacation" for the first set of test data, "3-week vacation" for the second set, and nothing for the third set.

Using the first set of test data, the user enters F as the status and 4 as the years employed. The outer selection structure's condition determines if the status is F; it is, so the nested selection structure's condition checks if the years are greater than 5. The years are not greater than 5, so the nested selection structure's false path displays the message "2-week vacation," which is correct. After doing so, both selection structures and the program end.

Using the second set of data, the user enters F as the status and 15 as the years. The outer selection structure's condition determines if the status is F; it is, so the nested selection structure's condition checks if the years are greater than 5. The years are greater than 5, so the nested selection structure's true path displays the message "3-week vacation," which is correct. After doing so, both selection structures and the program end.

Using the third set of data, the user enters P as the status and 11 as the years. The outer selection structure's condition determines if the status is F. The status is not F, so the outer selection structure and the program end. Notice that the nested selection structure is not processed when the outer selection structure's condition is false. Figure 9-7 shows the results of desk-checking the correct algorithm shown in Figure 9-6.

Desk-check	Result
First: using F as the status and 4 as the years	"2-week vacation" displayed
Second: using F as the status and 15 as the years	"3-week vacation" displayed
Third: using P as the status and 11 as the years	Nothing is displayed

Figure 9-7: Results of desk-checking the correct algorithm shown in Figure 9-6

In the next section, you will view and desk-check another algorithm for the vacation program. You will find that the algorithm does not produce the desired results because it contains a logical operator instead of a nested selection structure.

Using a Logical Operator Rather Than a Nested Selection Structure

One common error made when writing selection structures is to use a logical operator in the outer selection structure's condition when a nested selection structure is needed. Figure 9-8 shows an example of this error in the vacation algorithm. The correct algorithm is included in the figure for comparison.

logical operator used rather than a nested selection structure

Correct algorithm	Incorrect algorithm

1. enter the status and years
2. if (the status is F)
    if (the years are greater than 5)
        display "3-week vacation"
    else
        display "2-week vacation"
    end if
end if
	1. enter the status and years
	2. if (the status is F and the years are greater than 5)
	    display "3-week vacation"
	else
	    display "2-week vacation"
	end if

Figure 9-8: Correct algorithm and an incorrect algorithm containing the first logic error

Notice that the incorrect algorithm uses one selection structure, rather than two selection structures, and the selection structure's condition contains the logical operator *and*. Consider why the selection structure in the incorrect agorithm cannot be used in place of the selection structures in the correct algorithm. In the correct algorithm, the outer and nested selection structures indicate that a hierarchy exists between the status and years employed decisions: the status decision is always made first, followed by the years employed decision (if necessary). In the incorrect algorithm, on the other hand, the logical operator in the selection structure's condition indicates that no hierarchy exists between the status and years employed decisions; each has equal weight and neither is dependent on the other, which is incorrect. To better understand why this algorithm is incorrect, you will desk-check it using the same test data used to desk-check the correct algorithm.

After the user enters the first set of test data—F as the status and 4 as the years—the selection structure's condition in the incorrect algorithm determines if the status is F and, at the same time, the years are greater than 5. Only one of these conditions is true, so the compound condition evaluates to false and the selection structure's false path displays the message "2-week vacation" before both the selection structure and the program end. Even though the algorithm's selection structure is phrased incorrectly, notice that the incorrect algorithm produces the same result as the correct algorithm using the first set of data.

After the user enters the second set of test data—F as the status and 15 as the years—the selection structure's condition in the incorrect algorithm determines if the status is F and, at the same time, the years are greater than 5. Both conditions are true, so the compound condition is true and the selection structure's true path displays the message "3-week vacation" before both the selection structure and the program end. Here again, using the second set of test data, the incorrect algorithm produces the same result as the correct algorithm.

After the user enters the third set of test data—P as the status and 11 as the years—the selection structure's condition in the incorrect algorithm determines if the status is F and, at the same time, the years are greater than 5. Only one of these conditions is true, so the compound condition is false and the selection structure's false path displays the message "2-week vacation" before both the selection structure and the program end. Notice that the incorrect algorithm produces erroneous results for the third set of test data; according to Figure 9-7, the algorithm should not have displayed anything using this data. As you learned in Tutorial 2, it is important to desk-check an algorithm several times, using different test data. In this case, if you had used only the first two sets of data to desk-check the incorrect algorithm, you would not have discovered the error.

tip

As you learned in Tutorial 8, when you use the logical operator *and* to combine two conditions in a selection structure, both conditions must be true for the compound condition to be true. If at least one of the conditions is false, then the compound condition is false and the instructions in the selection structure's false path (assuming there is a false path) are processed.

Figure 9-9 shows the results of desk-checking the incorrect algorithm shown in Figure 9-8. As indicated in the figure, the results of the first and second desk-checks are correct, but the result of the third desk-check is not correct.

Desk-check	Result
First: using F as the status and 4 as the years	"2-week vacation" displayed
Second: using F as the status and 15 as the years	"3-week vacation" displayed
Third: using P as the status and 11 as the years	"2-week vacation" displayed

correct results

incorrect result

Figure 9-9: Results of desk-checking the incorrect algorithm shown in Figure 9-8

Next, you will view and desk-check another algorithm for the vacation program. You will find that this algorithm also does not produce the desired results, because the primary and secondary decisions are reversed in the selection structures.

Reversing the Primary and Secondary Decisions

Another common error made when writing a selection structure that contains a nested selection structure is to reverse the primary and secondary decisions—in other words, put the secondary decision in the outer selection structure, and put the primary decision in the nested selection structure. Figure 9-10 shows an example of this error in the vacation algorithm. The correct algorithm is included in the figure for comparison.

Correct algorithm	Incorrect algorithm

1. enter the status and years
2. if (the status is F)
    if (the years are greater than 5)
      display "3-week vacation"
    else
      display "2-week vacation"
    end if
end if
	1. enter the status and years
	2. if (the years are greater than 5)
	    if (the status is F)
	      display "3-week vacation"
	    else
	      display "2-week vacation"
	    end if
	end if

primary and secondary decisions reversed

Figure 9-10: Correct algorithm and an incorrect algorithm containing the second logic error

Unlike the selection structures in the correct algorithm, which determine the employment status before determining the number of years employed, the selection structures in the incorrect algorithm determine the number of years employed before determining the employment status. Consider how this difference changes the algorithm. In the correct algorithm, the selection structures indicate that only employees whose status is full-time receive a paid vacation, which is correct. The selection structures in the incorrect algorithm, on the other hand, indicate that all employees who have been with the company for more than 5 years receive a paid vacation, which is not correct. Desk-check the incorrect algorithm to see the results.

After the user enters the first set of test data—F as the status and 4 as the years—the condition in the outer selection structure determines if the years are greater than 5. The years are not greater than 5, so both the outer selection structure and the program end. Notice that the incorrect algorithm does not display the expected message, "2-week vacation."

After the user enters the second set of test data—F as the status and 15 as the years—the condition in the outer selection structure determines if the years are greater than 5; they are, so the condition in the nested selection structure checks to determine if the status is F. The status is F, so the nested selection structure's true path displays the message "3-week vacation," which is correct.

After the user enters the third set of test data—P as the status and 11 as the years—the condition in the outer selection structure determines if the years are greater than 5; they are, so the condition in the nested selection structure checks to determine if the status is F. The status is not F, so the nested selection structure's false path displays the message "2-week vacation," which is not correct.

Figure 9-11 shows the results of desk-checking the incorrect algorithm shown in Figure 9-10. As indicated in the figure, only the results of the second desk-check are correct.

Desk-check	Result
First: using F as the status and 4 as the years	Nothing is displayed
Second: using F as the status and 15 as the years	"3-week vacation" displayed
Third: using P as the status and 11 as the years	"2-week vacation" displayed

only this result is correct

Figure 9-11: Results of desk-checking the incorrect algorithm shown in Figure 9-10

Next, you will view and desk-check another algorithm for the vacation program. This one contains the third logic error—using an unnecessary nested selection structure. Like the correct algorithm, this algorithm will produce the desired results; however, it will do so in a less efficient manner than the correct algorithm.

Using an Unnecessary Nested Selection Structure

Another common error made when writing selection structures is to include an unnecessary nested selection structure. In most cases, a selection structure containing this error still will produce the correct results; the only problem is that it does so less efficiently than selection structures that are properly structured. Figure 9-12 shows an example of this error in the vacation algorithm. The correct algorithm is included in the figure for comparison.

Correct algorithm	Inefficient algorithm

1. enter the status and years
2. if (the status is F)
    if (the years are greater than 5)
      display "3-week vacation"
    else
      display "2-week vacation"
    end if
  end if
	1. enter the status and years
	2. if (the status is F)
	    if (the years are greater than 5)
	      display "3-week vacation"
	    else
	      if (the years are less than or equal to 5)
	        display "2-week vacation"
	      end if
	    end if
	  end if

unnecessary nested selection structure

Figure 9-12: Correct algorithm and an inefficient algorithm containing the third logic error

Unlike the correct algorithm, which contains two selection structures, the inefficient algorithm contains three selection structures. Notice that the condition in the third selection structure checks to determine if the years are less than or equal to 5, and is processed only when the condition in the second selection structure is false; in other words, it is processed only when the years are not greater than 5. However, if the years are not greater than 5, then they would have to be either less than or equal to 5, so the third selection structure is unnecessary. To better understand the error in the inefficient algorithm, you will desk-check it.

After the user enters the first set of data—F as the status and 4 as the years—the first selection structure's condition determines if the status is F; it is, so the second selection structure's condition checks if the years are greater than 5. The years are not greater than 5, so the third selection structure's condition checks if the years are less than or equal to 5—an unnecessary decision. In this case, the years (4) are less than or equal to 5, so the third selection structure's true path displays the message "2-week vacation," which is correct. After doing so, the three selection structures and the program end.

After the user enters the second set of data—F as the status and 15 as the years—the first selection structure's condition determines if the status is F; it is, so the second selection structure's condition checks to determine if the years are greater than 5. The years are greater than 5, so the second selection structure's true path displays the message "3-week vacation," which is correct. After doing so, the first and second selection structures and the program end.

After the user enters the third set of data—P as the status and 11 as the years—the condition in the first selection structure determines if the status is F; it isn't, so the first selection structure and the program end.

Figure 9-13 shows the results of desk-checking the inefficient algorithm shown in Figure 9-12. As indicated in the figure, although the results of the three desk-checks are correct, the result of the first desk-check is obtained in a less efficient manner.

correct result is obtained in a less efficient manner

Desk-check	Result
First: using F as the status and 4 as the years	"2-week vacation" displayed
Second: using F as the status and 15 as the years	"3-week vacation" displayed
Third: using P as the status and 11 as the years	Nothing is displayed

Figure 9-13: Results of desk-checking the inefficient algorithm shown in Figure 9-12

Mini-Quiz 2

1. List the three errors commonly made when writing selection structures.

2. Which error makes the selection structure inefficient, but still produces the correct results?

Some algorithms require selection structures that are capable of choosing from several alternatives. You can create such selection structures, commonly referred to as multiple-path or extended selection structures, using either the `if/else` or `switch` form of the selection structure. First learn how to use the `if/else` form.

Using the `if/else` Form to Create Multiple-Path Selection Structures

At times, you may need to create a selection structure that can choose from several alternatives. For example, assume you are asked to create a program that displays a message based on a letter grade that the user enters. Figure 9-14 shows the valid letter grades and their corresponding messages.

Letter grade	Message
A	Excellent
B	Above Average
C	Average
D	Below Average
F	Below Average

Figure 9-14: Letter grades and messages

As Figure 9-14 indicates, if the letter grade is an A, then the program should display the message "Excellent." If the letter grade is a B, then the program should display the message "Above Average," and so on. Figure 9-15 shows two versions of the C++ code for the grade problem. Both versions use the `if/else` form of the selection structure to display the appropriate message.

you can include another statement on the same line as the `else`

Version 1	Version 2

```
cout << "Grade: ";
cin  >> grade;

if (grade == 'A' || grade == 'a')
  cout << "Excellent" << endl;
else
  if (grade == 'B' || grade == 'b')
    cout << "Above Average" << endl;
  else
    if (grade == 'C' || grade == 'c')
      cout << "Average" << endl;
    else
      if (grade == 'D' || grade == 'd'
        || grade == 'F' || grade == 'f')
        cout << "Below Average" << endl;
      else
        cout << "Error" << endl;
      //end if
    //end if
  //end if
//end if
```

```
cout << "Grade: ";
cin  >> grade;

if (grade == 'A' || grade == 'a')
    cout << "Excellent" << endl;
else if (grade == 'B' || grade == 'b')
    cout << "Above Average" << endl;
else if (grade == 'C' || grade == 'c')
    cout << "Average" << endl;
else if (grade == 'D' || grade == 'd'
    || grade == 'F' || grade == 'f')
    cout << "Below Average" << endl;
else cout << "Error" << endl;
//end ifs
```

you can use one comment to mark the end of the entire structure

Figure 9-15: Two versions of the C++ code for the grade problem

Although you can write the `if/else` selection structure using either of the two methods shown in Figure 9-15, the second version of the code provides a much more convenient way of writing this logic.

In addition to using the `if/else` form to create multiple-path selection structures, you also can use the `switch` form.

tip

In some languages—for example, Visual Basic, the `switch` form of the selection structure is called the `case` form.

Using the `switch` Form to Create Multiple-Path Selection Structures

It is often simpler and clearer to use the `switch` form, rather than the `if/else` form, in situations where the selection structure has many paths from which to choose. Figure 9-16 shows the flowchart and pseudocode for the grade problem, using the `switch` form of the selection structure.

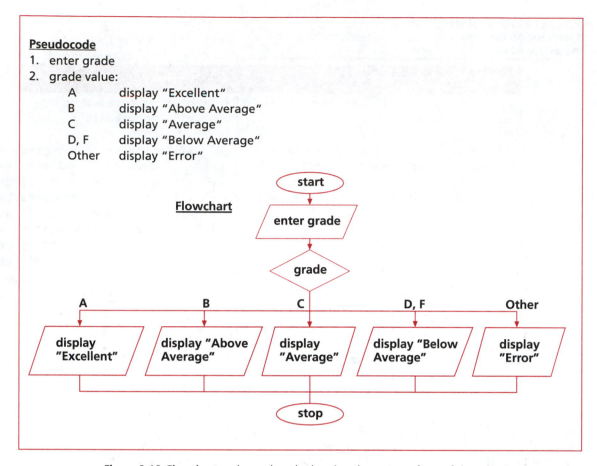

Pseudocode
1. enter grade
2. grade value:
   A   display "Excellent"
   B   display "Above Average"
   C   display "Average"
   D, F   display "Below Average"
   Other   display "Error"

Figure 9-16: Flowchart and pseudocode showing the `switch` form of the selection structure

Notice that the flowchart symbol for the `switch` form of the selection structure is the same as the flowchart symbol for the `if` and `if/else` forms—a diamond. Unlike the `if` and `if/else` diamond, however, the `switch` diamond does not contain a condition requiring a true or false answer. Instead, the `switch` diamond contains an expression—in this case, `grade`—whose value determines which path is chosen.

Like the `if` and `if/else` diamond, the `switch` diamond has one flowline leading into the symbol. Unlike the `if` and `if/else` diamond, however, the `switch` diamond has many flowlines leading out of the symbol. Each flowline represents a possible path for the selection structure. The flowlines must be marked appropriately, indicating which value(s) are necessary for each path to be chosen.

Figure 9-17 shows the syntax of the statement used to code the `switch` form of the selection structure in C++, Java, and Visual Basic. In C++ and Java, the statement is the `switch` statement, while in Visual Basic, it is the `Select Case` statement.

C++ and Java	Visual Basic

switch (*selectorExpression*)
{
case *value1*:   *one or more statements*
[case *value2*:   *one or more statements*]
[case *valueN*:   *one or more statements*]
[default: *one or more statements*
              processed when the
              selectorExpression does
              not match any of the
              values]
} //end switch
	Select Case *selectorExpression*
	    Case *expressionList1*
	        [*instructions for the first Case*]
	    [**Case** *expressionList2*
	        [*instructions for the second Case*]]
	    [**Case** *expressionListn*
	        [*instructions for the nth case*]]
	    [**Case Else**
	        [*instructions for when the*
	        selectorExpression does not match any of
	        the expressionLists]]
	End Select

Figure 9-17: Syntax of the statements used to code the switch form of the selection structure in C++, Java, and Visual Basic

Figure 9-18 shows how to use the C++ switch statement to code the grade problem.

break **statements tell the computer to exit the** switch **statement**

selectorExpression

case **clause**

switch **statement**

default **clause**

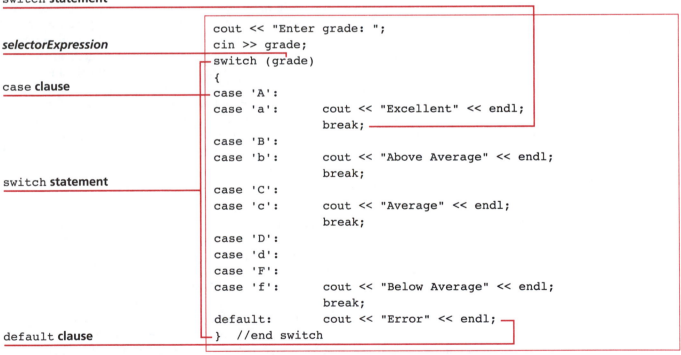

```
cout << "Enter grade: ";
cin >> grade;
switch (grade)
{
case 'A':
case 'a':        cout << "Excellent" << endl;
                 break;
case 'B':
case 'b':        cout << "Above Average" << endl;
                 break;
case 'C':
case 'c':        cout << "Average" << endl;
                 break;
case 'D':
case 'd':
case 'F':
case 'f':        cout << "Below Average" << endl;
                 break;
default:         cout << "Error" << endl;
}   //end switch
```

Figure 9-18: Grade problem coded using the C++ switch statement

Compare the switch statement shown in Figure 9-18 with the syntax shown in Figure 9-17. The switch statement begins with the switch clause, followed by an opening brace; the statement ends with a closing brace. It is a good programming practice to document the end of the switch statement with the //end switch comment, as shown in both figures.

You learned about the C++ data types in Tutorial 4.

The `default` clause can appear anywhere within the `switch` statement. However, for clarity, it is recommended that you place it at the end of the `switch` statement.

Recall from Tutorial 4 that character literal constants are enclosed in single quotation marks in C++ code.

Complete Exercises 10 and 11 at the end of this lesson to learn what happens when you do not use the `break` statement to break out of the `switch` statement.

The `switch` clause is composed of the keyword `switch` followed by a *selectorExpression* enclosed in parentheses. The *selectorExpression* can contain any combination of variables, constants, functions, and operators, as long as the combination results in a value whose data type is either `bool`, `char`, `short`, `int`, or `long`. In the `switch` statement shown in Figure 9-18, the *selectorExpression* contains a `char` variable named `grade`.

Between the `switch` statement's opening and closing braces are the individual `case` clauses, each representing a different path that the selection structure can follow. You can have as many `case` clauses as necessary in a `switch` statement. If the `switch` statement includes a `default` clause, it usually is the last clause in the statement.

Each of the individual clauses within the `switch` statement (except for the `default` clause) contains a *value*, followed by a colon. The data type of the *value* should be compatible with the data type of the *selectorExpression*. In other words, if the *selectorExpression* is a numeric variable, the *values* in the `case` clauses should be numeric. Likewise, if the *selectorExpression* is a `char` variable, the *values* should be characters. The *values* in the `case` clauses can be literal constants, named constants, or expressions composed of literal and named constants. In the `switch` statement shown in Figure 9-18, the data types of the *values* in the `case` clauses ('A', 'a', 'B', 'b', 'C', 'c', 'D', 'd', 'F', 'f') are `char` to match the data type of the *selectorExpression* (`grade`).

Following the colon in each `case` clause are one or more statements that will be processed when the *selectorExpression* matches that case's *value*. Notice that the statements within a `case` clause are not entered as a statement block—in other words, the statements are not enclosed in braces.

After the computer processes the instructions in the `case` clause whose *value* matches the *selectorExpression*, you typically will want the computer to leave the `switch` statement without processing the remaining instructions in the statement. You do so by including the `break` statement as the last statement in the `case` clause. The `break` statement tells the computer to leave ("break out of") the `switch` statement at that point. If you do not use the `break` statement to leave the `switch` statement, the computer will continue processing the remaining instructions in the statement, which may or may not be what you want to happen. After processing the `break` statement, the computer then processes the instruction that follows the `switch` statement's closing brace. To better understand the `switch` statement, you will desk-check the code shown in Figure 9-18 using the grades *a*, *B*, *D*, and *X*.

Desk-Checking the Grade Program

Assume the user enters the letter *a* in response to the "Enter grade:" prompt shown in Figure 9-18. The code stores the user's input in the `grade` variable, which then is used as the *selectorExpression* in the program's `switch` statement. When processing the `switch` statement, the computer compares the value of the *selectorExpression* with the *value* listed in each of the `case` clauses, one `case` clause at a time beginning with the first. If a match is found, the computer processes the instructions contained in that `case` clause until it encounters either a `break` statement or the `switch` statement's closing brace (which marks the end of the selection structure). The computer then skips to the instruction following the `switch` statement's closing brace. In this case, the value of the *selectorExpression*—the letter *a*—does not match the letter contained in the first `case` clause (which is 'A'); however, it does match the letter contained in the second `case` clause. The first statement in the second `case` clause is `cout << "Excellent" << endl;`, which displays the message "Excellent" on the screen. The next statement in the second `case` clause is `break;`, which tells the computer to skip the remaining instructions in the `switch` statement, and continue processing with the instruction that follows the `switch` statement's closing brace.

Now, assume the user enters the letter *B* in response to the "Enter grade:" prompt shown in Figure 9-18. As before, the code stores the user's input in the `grade` variable, which then is used as the *selectorExpression* in the program's `switch` statement. The computer compares the value of the *selectorExpression*—in this case, the letter *B*—with the *value* listed in each of the `case` clauses, one `case` clause at a time beginning with the first. In this case, the letter *B* matches the letter listed in the third case clause. However, notice that there is no statement immediately following the `case 'B':` clause—what follows `case 'B'` is the next `case` clause (`case 'b'`). So, what, if anything, will appear when the grade is *B*?

Recall that, when the *value* of the *selectorExpression* matches the *value* in a `case` clause, the computer processes the instructions contained in that clause until it encounters either a `break` statement or the `switch` statement's closing brace. In this case, not finding any instructions in the `case 'B':` clause, the computer continues processing with the instructions in the next clause—the `case 'b':` clause. The first instruction in the `case 'b':` clause displays the message "Above Average," which is the correct message to display, and the second instruction tells the computer to break out of the `switch` statement. In other words, the `cout << "Above Average" << endl;` and `break;` statements are processed when the grade is either the letter *B* or the letter *b*. As this example shows, you can process the same instructions for more than one *value* by listing each *value* in a separate `case` clause, as long as the clauses appear together in the `switch` statement. The last clause in the group of related clauses should contain the instructions you want the computer to process when one of the *values* in the group matches the *selectorExpression*. Only the last `case` clause in the group of related clauses should contain the `break` statement.

Next, assume the user enters the letter *D* as the grade. The letter *D* matches the letter listed in the `case 'D':` clause. Not finding any statements in that clause, the computer processes the next statement it encounters—in this case, it processes the `cout << "Below Average" << endl;` statement contained in the `case 'f':` clause, followed by that clause's `break;` statement. The computer then skips to the instruction following the `switch` statement's closing brace.

Finally, assume that the user enters the letter *X* as the grade. Notice that the letter *X* does not appear as a *value* in any of the `case` clauses. If the *selectorExpression* does not match any of the *values* listed in the `case` clauses, the computer processes the instructions contained in the `default` clause (if there is one). The instruction in the `default` clause shown in Figure 9-18 displays the message "Error" on the screen. If the `default` clause is the last clause in the `switch` statement, as it is in Figure 9-18, the computer then skips to the instruction following the `switch` statement's closing brace. Figure 9-19 shows the results of desk-checking the code shown in Figure 9-18.

tip

If the `default` clause is not the last clause in the `switch` statement, you will need to include a `break` statement at the end of the default clause.

Desk-check	Result
First: using a	"Excellent" displayed
Second: using B	"Above Average" displayed
Third: using D	"Below Average" displayed
Fourth: using X	"Error" displayed

Figure 9-19: Results of desk-checking the grade program shown in Figure 9-18

mini-quiz

Mini-Quiz 3

1. Assume you want to create a program that displays the message "Highest honors" if a student's test score is 90 or above. If the test score is 70 through 89, the program should display the message "Good job". For all other test scores, the program should display the message "Retake the test". Write the appropriate C++ code, using the shorter version of the if/else form of the selection structure.

2. If the *selectorExpression* used in the switch statement is a numeric variable, then the values listed in each case clause should be _____ .

3. The _____ statement tells the computer to leave the switch statement at that point.

4. If the *selectorExpression* used in the switch statement is the int variable code, which of the following case clauses is valid?

   a. `case "2":`

   b. `case 2:`

   c. `case 2;`

   d. `case == 2`

You now have completed Tutorial 9's Concept lesson. You can either take a break or complete the end-of-lesson questions and exercises before moving on to the Application lesson.

SUMMARY

You can nest a selection structure within either the true path or false path of another selection structure. You would use a nested selection structure if more than one decision needs to be made before the appropriate action can be taken. The outer selection structure always represents the primary decision, while the nested (or inner) selection structure always represents the secondary decision.

Logic errors commonly made when writing selection structures typically are a result of either using a logical operator when a nested selection structure is needed, or reversing the primary and secondary decisions, or using an unnecessary nested selection structure.

Some algorithms require selection structures that are capable of choosing from several alternatives. You can code such selection structures using either the if/else or switch form of the selection structure.

The flowchart symbol for the switch form of the selection structure is a diamond. The diamond should contain an expression; the expression's value controls which alternative is chosen. The switch diamond has one flowline leading into the symbol, and many flowlines leading out of the symbol. Each flowline represents a possible path for the selection structure, and should be marked to indicate which value(s) are necessary for each path to be chosen. In C++, you use the switch statement, along with the break statement, to code the switch form of the selection structure.

ANSWERS TO MINI·QUIZZES

Mini-Quiz 1

1.
```
if (score >= 90)
    display "Highest honors"
else
    if (score >= 70)
        display "Good job"
    else
        display "Retake the test"
    end if
end if
```

2.
```
if (score >= 90)
    cout << "Highest honors" << endl;
else
    if (score >= 70)
        cout << "Good job" << endl;
    else
        cout << "Retake the test" << endl;
    //end if
//end if
```

3. The decision regarding the member status is the primary decision. The decision regarding the day of the week is the secondary decision, because whether it needs to be made depends on the result of the member status decision.

Mini-Quiz 2

1. Using a logical operator when a nested selection structure is needed

   Reversing the primary and secondary decisions

   Using an unnecessary nested selection structure

2. Using an unnecessary nested selection structure

Mini-Quiz 3

1.
```
if (score >= 90)
        cout << "Highest honors" << endl;
else if (score >= 70)
        cout << "Good job" << endl;
else cout << "Retake the test" << endl;
//end ifs
```

2. numeric

3. break

4. b. case 2:

QUESTIONS

Use the following code to answer Questions 1 through 3. You can assume that the `number` variable was declared as an `int` variable and was initialized to 0.

```
if (number <= 100)
        number = number * 2;
else
        if (number > 500)
                number = number * 3;
        //end if
//end if
```

1. Assume the `number` variable contains the number 90. What value will be in the `number` variable after the preceding code is processed?
   a. 0
   b. 90
   c. 180
   d. 270

2. Assume the `number` variable contains the number 1000. What value will be in the `number` variable after the preceding code is processed?
   a. 0
   b. 1000
   c. 2000
   d. 3000

3. Assume the `number` variable contains the number 200. What value will be in the `number` variable after the preceding code is processed?
   a. 0
   b. 200
   c. 400
   d. 600

Use the following code to answer Questions 4 through 7.

```
if (id == 1)
   cout << "Janet" << endl;
else if (id == 2 || id == 3)
   cout << "Paul" << endl;
else if (id == 4)
   cout << "Jerry" << endl;
else cout << "Sue" << endl;
//end ifs
```

4. What, if anything, will the preceding code display if the `id` variable contains the number 2?
   a. Jerry
   b. Paul
   c. Sue
   d. nothing

5. What, if anything, will the preceding code display if the `id` variable contains the number 4?
   a. Jerry
   b. Paul
   c. Sue
   d. nothing

6. What, if anything, will the preceding code display if the id variable contains the number 3?
   a. Jerry
   b. Paul
   c. Sue
   d. nothing

7. What, if anything, will the preceding code display if the id variable contains the number 8?
   a. Jerry
   b. Paul
   c. Sue
   d. nothing

8. You can use the C++ _____ statement to code the switch form of the selection structure.
   a. case
   b. case of
   c. struc
   d. switch

9. Which of the following flowchart symbols represents the switch form of the selection structure?
   a. diamond
   b. hexagon
   c. parallelogram
   d. rectangle

10. If the *selectorExpression* used in the switch statement is the char variable code, which of the following case clauses is valid?
    a. case "3":
    b. case '3':
    c. case 3;
    d. case = 3

Use the following switch statement to answer Questions 11 through 13.

```
switch (id)
{
case 1:     cout << "Janet" << endl;
            break;
case 2:     cout << "Paul" << endl;
            break;
case 3:
case 5:     cout << "Jerry" << endl;
            break;
default:    cout << "Sue" << endl;
} //end switch
```

11. What will the preceding switch statement display if the id variable contains the number 2?
    a. Jerry
    b. Paul
    c. Sue
    d. nothing

12. What will the preceding switch statement display if the id variable contains the number 4?
    a. Jerry
    b. Paul
    c. Sue
    d. nothing

13. What will the preceding `switch` statement display if the `id` variable contains the number 3?
a. Jerry
b. Paul
c. Sue
d. nothing

EXERCISES

1. Write the C++ `if` statement that compares the contents of the `quantity` variable to the number 10. If the `quantity` variable contains a number that is equal to 10, display the string "Equal". If the `quantity` variable contains a number that is greater than 10, display the string "Over 10". If the `quantity` variable contains a number that is less than 10, display the string "Not over 10".

2. Write the C++ code that corresponds to the flowchart shown in Figure 9-20.

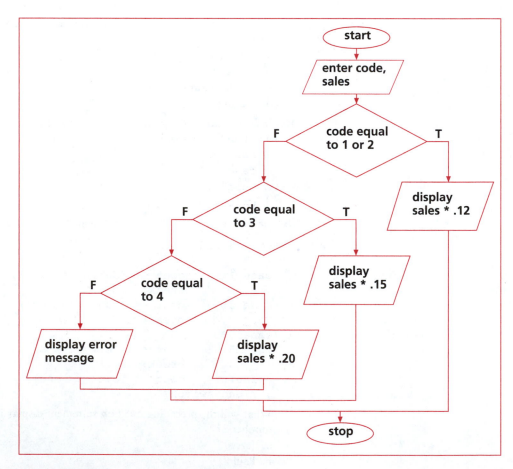

Figure 9-20

3. Write the C++ code that corresponds to the flowchart shown in Figure 9-21.

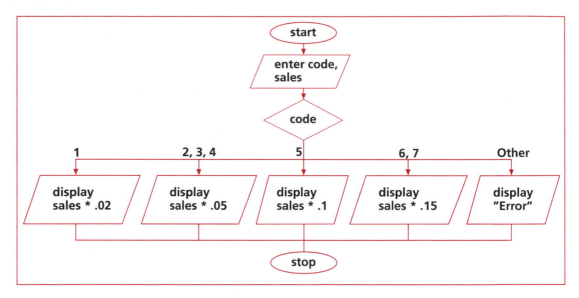

Figure 9-21

4. Open the T9ConE04.cpp file contained in the Cpp\Tut09\T9ConE04 folder on your computer's hard disk. Complete the program by writing an `if` statement that displays the string "Dog" if the `animal` variable contains the number 1. Display the string "Cat" if the `animal` variable contains the number 2. Display the string "Bird" if the `animal` variable contains anything other than the number 1 or the number 2. Save, build, and execute the program. Test the program three times, using the numbers 1, 2, and 5. When the program is working correctly, hide the Output window, then use the File menu to close the workspace.

5. Open the T9ConE05.cpp file contained in the Cpp\Tut09\T9ConE05 folder on your computer's hard disk. Complete the program by writing a `switch` statement that displays the month corresponding to the number entered by the user. For example, if the user enters the number 1, the program should display the string "January". If the user enters an invalid number (one that is not in the range 1 through 12), display an appropriate error message. Save, build, and execute the program. Test the program three times, using the numbers 3, 7, and 20. When the program is working correctly, hide the Output window, then use the File menu to close the workspace.

6. Open the T9ConE06.cpp file contained in the Cpp\Tut09\T9ConE06 folder on your computer's hard disk. Complete the program by writing an `if` statement that assigns the number 25 to the `bonus` variable if the user enters a sales amount that is greater than or equal to 100, but less than or equal to $250. If the user enters a sales amount that is greater than $250, assign the number 50 to the `bonus` variable. If the user enters a sales amount that is less than $100, assign the number 0 as the `bonus`. Save, build, and execute the program. Test the program three times, using sales amounts of 100, 300, and 40. When the program is working correctly, hide the Output window, then use the File menu to close the workspace.

7. Open the T9ConE07.cpp file contained in the Cpp\Tut09\T9ConE07 folder on your computer's hard disk. The program should display the appropriate seminar fee, which is based on the membership status and age entered by the user. Use the following information to complete the program:

Seminar fee	Criteria
10	Club member less than 65 years old
5	Club member at least 65 years old
20	Non-member

Save, build, and execute the program. Test the program three times. For the first test, use M as the status and 65 as the age. For the second test, use m as the status and 40 as the age. For the third test, use N as the status. When the program is working correctly, hide the Output window, then use the File menu to close the workspace.

8. Open the T9ConE08.cpp file contained in the Cpp\Tut09\T9ConE08 folder on your computer's hard disk. The program should display the appropriate grade based on the average of three test scores entered by the user. (Each test is worth 100 points.) Use the following information to complete the program:

Test average	Grade
90%-100%	A
80%-89%	B
70%-79%	C
60%-69%	D
below 60%	F

Save, build, and execute the program. Test the program three times. For the first test, use scores of 90, 95, and 100. For the second test, use scores of 83, 72, and 65. For the third test, use scores of 40, 30, and 20. When the program is working correctly, hide the Output window, then use the File menu to close the workspace.

9. Open the T9ConE09.cpp file contained in the Cpp\Tut09\T9ConE09 folder on your computer's hard disk. The program should display the class rank, which is based on the code entered by the user. Use the information below to complete the program. Be sure to use the `switch` statement.

Code	Rank
1	Freshman
2	Sophomore
3	Junior
4	Senior
other	Error

Save, build, and execute the program. Test the program three times, using codes of 1, 3, and 5. When the program is working correctly, hide the Output window, then use the File menu to close the workspace.

10. In this exercise, you will practice using the `switch` statement.
   a. Open the T9ConE10.cpp file contained in the Cpp\Tut09\T9ConE10 folder on your computer's hard disk.
   b. Build and execute the program. When prompted to enter a grade, type d and press the Enter key. What, if anything, did the `switch` statement display on the screen? Press the Enter key to close the DOS window.
   c. Enter a `break;` statement in the `case 'd':` clause. Save, build, and execute the program. When prompted to enter a grade, type d and press the Enter key. What, if anything, did the `switch` statement display on the screen? Press the Enter key to close the DOS window.
   d. Remove the `break;` statement from the `case 'd':` clause. Also remove the `break;` statement from the `case 'f':` clause. Save, build, and execute the program. When prompted to enter a grade, type d and press the Enter key. What, if anything, did the `switch` statement display on the screen? Press the Enter key to close the DOS window.
   e. Put the `break;` statement back in the `case 'f':` clause. Save the program.
   f. Hide the Output window, then use the File menu to close the workspace.

11. In this exercise, you will practice using the `switch` statement.

    a. Open the T9ConE11.cpp file contained in the Cpp\Tut09\T9ConE11 folder on your computer's hard disk. The program uses the `switch` statement to display the names of the gifts mentioned in the song "The Twelve Days of Christmas."

    b. Build and then execute the program. When prompted to enter the day, type the number 1 and press the Enter key. You will notice that the names of the gifts for the first through the twelfth day appear in the DOS window. Press the Enter key to close the DOS window.

    c. Execute the program again. When prompted to enter the day, type the number 9 and press the Enter key. The names of the gifts for the ninth through twelfth days appear in the DOS window. Press the Enter key to close the DOS window.

    d. Modify the program so that it displays only the name of the gift corresponding to the day entered by the user. For example, if the user enters the number 4, the program should display "4 calling birds" only.

    e. Save, build, and execute the program. When prompted to enter the day, type the number 4 and press the Enter key. The "4 calling birds" message should appear. Press the Enter key to close the DOS window.

    f. Hide the Output window, then use the File menu to close the workspace.

Exercise 12 is a Discovery Exercise. Discovery Exercises, which may include topics that are not covered in this lesson, allow you to "discover" the solutions to problems on your own.

12. In this exercise, you will use the `if` and `switch` statements.

    a. Open the T9ConE12.cpp file contained in the Cpp\Tut09\T9ConE12 folder on your computer's hard disk. The program should calculate and display the price of an order, based on the number of units ordered and the customer's status (either 1 for wholesaler or 2 for retailer). The price per unit is as follows:

Wholesaler		Retailer	
Number of units	Price per unit ($)	Number of units	Price per unit ($)
1 – 4	10	1 – 3	15
5 and over	9	4 – 8	14
		9 and over	12

    b. Complete the program appropriately. Use a `switch` statement to determine the customer's status. If the user enters a status other than 1 or 2, display an appropriate error message. Use an `if` statement to determine the price per unit. If the user enters an invalid number of units (in other words, a negative number or zero), display an appropriate error message.

    c. Save, build, and execute the program. Test the program using the number 1 as the status and 5 as the number of units ordered. The DOS window should show that the price of the order is $45. Press the Enter key to close the DOS window.

    d. Execute the program again. Test the program using 2 as the status and 2 as the number of units ordered. The DOS window should show that the price of the order is $30. Press the Enter key to close the DOS window.

    e. Execute the program again. Test the program using 4 as the status and 3 as the number of units ordered. An appropriate error message should appear in the DOS window.

    f. Execute the program again. Test the program using 2 as the status and -5 as the number of units ordered. An appropriate error message should appear in the DOS window.

    g. When the program is working correctly, hide the Output window, then use the File menu to close the workspace.

A computer program is good only if it works. Errors in either an algorithm or programming code can cause the program to run incorrectly. Therefore, a programmer needs to know how to locate and fix these errors. Exercise 13 is a Debugging Exercise. Debugging Exercises allow you to practice recognizing and solving errors in a program.

debugging

13. In this exercise, you will debug an existing C++ program.
   a. Open the T9ConE13.cpp file contained in the Cpp\Tut09\T9ConE13 folder on your computer's hard disk. Study the program's code. A state code of 1 should display "Illinois", 2 should display "Kentucky", 3 should display "New Hampshire", 4 should display "Vermont", and 5 should display "Massachusetts".
   b. Study the program's code, then build the program. Correct any errors in the program, then save, build, and execute the program. Test the program six times, using state codes of 1, 2, 3, 4, 5, and 6.
   c. When the program is working correctly, hide the Output window, then use the File menu to close the workspace.

Application Lesson

Using the Selection Structure in a C++ Program

case ▶ Jennifer Yardley is the owner of Golf Pro, a U.S. company that sells golf equipment both domestically and abroad. Each of Golf Pro's salepeople receives a commission based on the total of his or her domestic and foreign sales. Jennifer has asked you to create a program that she can use to calculate and display the commission.

Analyzing, Planning, and Desk-Checking the Golf Pro Commission Problem

Many companies pay their sales force a commission rather than, or in addition to, a salary or hourly wage. A commission is simply a percentage of the sales made by the salesperson. Some companies use a fixed rate to calculate the commission, while others—like Golf Pro—use a rate that varies with the amount of sales. Figure 9-22 shows Golf Pro's commission schedule, along with examples of using the schedule to calculate the commission on three different sales amounts.

Sales	Commission
1 – 100,000	2% * sales
100,001 – 400,000	2,000 + 5% * sales over 100,000
400,001 and over	17,000 + 10% * sales over 400,000
Example 1: Sales: 15,000 Commission: 2% * 15,000 = $300	
Example 2: Sales: 250,000 Commission: 2000 + 5% * (250,000 – 100,000) = $9500	
Example 3: Sales 500,000 Commission: 17,000 + 10% * (500,000 – 400,000) = $27,000	

Figure 9-22: Commission schedule and examples

Notice that the commission for each range in the schedule is calculated differently. For instance, the commission for sales in the first range—1 through 100,000—is calculated by multiplying the sales amount by 2%. As Example 1 shows, sales of $15,000 would earn a $300 commission. The commission for sales in the second range—100,001 through 400,000—is calculated by multiplying the amount of sales over 100,000 by 5%, and then adding $2000 to the result. As Example 2 shows, sales of $250,000 would earn a $9500 commission. The commission for sales starting at 400,001 is calculated by multiplying the amount of sales over 400,000 by 10%, and then adding $17,000 to the result. Example 3 indicates that sales of $500,000 would earn a $27,000 commission.

In addition to the `main` function, you will use a program-defined value-returning function named `calcCommission` to solve the commission problem. The `calcCommission` function's task is to calculate and return the commission amount. Figure 9-23 shows the IPO charts for the commission problem.

`main` **function**

Input	Processing	Output

sales	Processing items: none
	
	Algorithm:
	1. enter the sales
	2. if (the sales are greater than 0)
	    calculate the commission = calcCommission(sales)
	    display the commission
	  else
	    display "No commission calculated" message
	  end if
		commission

`calcCommission` **function**

Input	Processing	Output
sales	Processing items: none Algorithm: 1. if (the sales are less than or equal to 100,000) calculate the commission by multiplying the sales by .02 else if (the sales are less than or equal to 400,000) calculate the commission using the following expression: 2000 + .05 * (sales − 100,000) else calculate the commission using the following expression: 17,000 + .1 * (sales − 400,000) end ifs 2. return the commission	commission

Figure 9-23: IPO charts for the commission problem

As Figure 9-23 indicates, the `main` function's output is the commission and its input is the sales. According to its algorithm, the `main` function first gets the sales amount from the user. It then validates the user's input; in this case, only numbers that are greater than zero are valid. If the sales amount is greater than zero, the `main` function calls the `calcCommission` function to calculate the commission.

For the `calcCommission` function to perform its task, the `main` function must pass it the value of the sales amount entered by the user. After the `calcCommission` function completes its task, it returns the commission amount to the `main` function. The `main` function then displays the commission amount on the screen.

If, on the other hand, the sales amount is invalid—which means that it is less than or equal to zero—the `main` function displays a message alerting the user that no commission calculation was made.

Recall that you should desk-check an algorithm several times before you begin coding it. In this case, you will use the following four sales amounts to desk-check the algorithms shown in Figure 9-23: 15000, 250000, 500000, -1. Figure 9-24 shows the completed desk-check tables.

`main` function

sales	commission
~~15000~~	~~300~~
~~250000~~	~~9500~~
~~500000~~	27000
-1	

`calcCommission` function

sales	commission
~~15000~~	~~300~~
~~250000~~	~~9500~~
500000	27000

Figure 9-24: Completed desk-check tables for the algorithms shown in Figure 9-23

After desk-checking an algorithm to verify its accuracy, you are ready to translate it into a language the computer can understand. Begin by coding the program's `main` function.

Coding the `main` Function

According to its IPO chart, the `main` function requires two memory locations to store the values of its input and output items. You will store the values in variables, because the values will be different each time the program is executed. You will use the `int` data type for the variable that stores the sales amount, and the `float` data type for the variable that stores the commission amount.

After reserving the memory locations, the `main` function will use the `cout` stream and the insertion operator (`<<`) to prompt the user to enter the sales amount, and the `cin` stream and the extraction operator (`>>`) to allow the user to enter that information.

The next step in the algorithm is to use the `if/else` form of the selection structure to determine if the user's input is valid, and then take the appropriate action based on the result. As you learned in Tutorial 8, you use the C++ `if` statement to code the `if/else` form of the selection structure. Figure 9-25 shows the C++ code corresponding to the `main` function.

IPO chart information	C++ instructions

<u>Input</u>
sales
<u>Processing</u>
none
<u>Output</u>
commission
	`int sales = 0;`
	
	`float commission = 0.0;`

<u>Algorithm</u>
1. enter the sales
 	
2. if (the sales are greater than 0)
 	
    calculate the commission =
       calcCommission(sales)
    display the commission
 	
  else
    display "No commission calculated"
    message
  end if
	`cout << "Enter sales: ";`
	`cin >> sales;`
	`if (sales > 0)`
	`{`
	`   commission = calcCommission(sales);`
	
	`   cout << "Commission: " <<`
	`           commission << endl;`
	`}`
	`else`
	`   cout << "No commission calculated"`
	`           << endl;`
	`//end if`

Figure 9-25: C++ statements for the `main` function

tip

The two variables declared in the code shown in Figure 9-25 are local to the `main` function and will remain in memory until the `main` function's return statement is processed.

Next, you will code the `calcCommission` function.

Coding the `calcCommission` Function

As its IPO chart indicates, the `calcCommission` function requires two memory locations: one for the input item and one for the output item. The value of the input item—sales—will be passed to the `calcCommission` function when the function is called; you will use the formal parameter `amountSold` to receive this information. Within the `calcCommission` function, you will declare and initialize a variable to store the output item—commission. You will name the variable `commDollars` and declare it as a `float` variable.

According to its algorithm, the `calcCommission` function needs to use two selection structures to calculate the commission. The outer selection structure's condition will determine if the sales fall in the 1 through 100,000 range. If they do, the outer selection structure's true path will calculate the commission by multiplying the sales by .02. If the sales do not fall in the 1 through 100,000 range, the outer selection structure's false path will use a nested selection structure to determine if the sales fall in the 100,001 through 400,000 range. If they do, the nested selection structure's true path will calculate the commission using the following expression: 2000 + .05 * (sales – 100,000). Otherwise—which means that the sales are over 400,000—the nested selection structure's false path will use the following expression to calculate the commission: 17,000 + .1 * (sales – 400,000). Figure 9-26 shows the C++ code for the `calcCommission` function.

IPO chart information	C++ instructions

Input
 sales
Processing
 none
Output
 commission
	`float calcCommission(int amountSold)`
	
	`float commDollars = 0.0;`

Algorithm
1. if (the sales are less than or equal to 100,000)
  calculate the commission by multiplying the
  sales by .02
  else if (the sales are less than or equal to 400,000)
  calculate the commission using the following
  expression: 2000 + .05 * (sales – 100,000)
  else calculate the commission using the following
  expression: 17,000 + .1 * (sales – 400,000)
  end ifs
2. return the commission
	`if (amountSold <= 100000)`
	`   commDollars = amountSold * .02;`
	`else if (amountSold <= 400000)`
	`   commDollars = 2000 + .05 *`
	`   (amountSold – 100000);`
	`else commDollars = 17000 + .1 *`
	`   (amountSold - 400000);`
	`//end ifs`
	
	`return commDollars;`

Figure 9-26: C++ statements for the `calcCommission` function

> The `calcCommission` function does not need to verify that the sales amount is valid (in other words, greater than zero), as this task is handled by the `main` function.

variables belonging to the `calcCommission` function

variables belonging to the `main` function

Now that the coding for the algorithms is complete, you need to desk-check the program, using the same data you used to desk-check the algorithms. Figure 9-27 shows the data and the completed desk-check table for the commission program.

Data for first desk-check Sales: 15000	Data for second desk-check Sales: 250000	Data for third desk-check Sales: 500000	Data for fourth desk-check Sales: -1

Desk-check tables

sales	commission	amountSold	commDollars
~~0~~	~~0.0~~	~~15000~~	~~0.0~~
~~15000~~	~~300.0~~	~~250000~~	~~300.0~~
~~0~~	~~0.0~~	500000	~~0.0~~
~~250000~~	~~9500.0~~		~~9500~~
~~0~~	~~0.0~~		~~0.0~~
~~500000~~	~~27000.0~~		27000.0
~~0~~	0.0		
-1			

Figure 9-27: Data and completed desk-check table for the commission program

> The `amountSold` and `commDollars` variables are local to the `calcCommission` function and will remain in memory until the `calcCommission` function's `return` statement is processed.

The results obtained when desk-checking the program agree with the results obtained when desk-checking the algorithm. You now are ready to enter the C++ instructions into the computer.

Completing the Commission Program

Your computer's hard disk contains a partially completed C++ program containing most of the instructions for the commission program. Open that program now.

To open the partially completed C++ program, then complete the program and test it:

1 Start Visual C++.

2 Open the **T9App.cpp** file contained in the Cpp\Tut09\T9App folder on your computer's hard disk.

Missing from the program is the code for the `calcCommission` function.

3 Position the insertion point in the blank line below the `//*****program-defined functions*****` comment, then enter the additional instructions shaded in Figure 9-28.

```cpp
//T9App.cpp - displays the commission

#include <iostream>
using namespace std;

//function prototype
float calcCommission(int);

int main()
{
    int sales        = 0;
    float commission = 0.0;

    //enter input data
    cout << "Enter sales: ";
    cin >> sales;
    if (sales > 0)
    {
        //calculate and display commission
        commission = calcCommission(sales);
        cout << "Commission: " << commission << endl;
    }
    else
        cout << "No commission calculated" << endl;
    //end if

    return 0;
}   //end of main function
```

Figure 9-28: Program showing code entered in the `calcCommission` function

```
//*****program-defined functions*****
float calcCommission(int amountSold)
{
    //calculates and returns the commission
    float commDollars = 0.0;

    if (amountSold <= 100000)
        commDollars = amountSold * .02;
    else if (amountSold <= 400000)
        commDollars = 2000 + .05 * (amountSold - 100000);
    else commDollars = 17000 + .1 * (amountSold - 400000);
    //end ifs
    return commDollars;
}    //end of calcCommission function
```

enter this code

Figure 9-28: Program showing code entered in the `calcCommission` function (continued)

4 Save, build, and execute the program.

5 When prompted for the sales, type **15000** and press the **Enter** key. The program calculates and displays the commission, as shown in Figure 9-29.

Figure 9-29: DOS window showing result of first test

The DOS window shows that the commission is 300, which agrees with the desk-check tables.

6 Press the **Enter** key to close the DOS window, then execute the program again. Type **250000** as the sales, then press the **Enter** key. The program correctly calculates and displays the commission as 9500.

7 Press the **Enter** key to close the DOS window, then execute the program again. Type **500000** as the sales, then press the **Enter** key. The program correctly calculates and displays the commission as 27000.

8 Press the **Enter** key to close the DOS window. Hide the Output window, then execute the program again. Type **-1** as the sales, then press the **Enter** key. The program displays the message "No commission calculated."

9 Press the **Enter** key to close the DOS window. Hide the Output window, then use the File menu to close the workspace. When prompted to close all document windows, click the **Yes** button, then exit Visual C++.

You now have completed Tutorial 9's Application lesson. You can either take a break or complete the end-of-lesson exercises.

EXERCISES

1. In this exercise, you will modify the program that you created in this lesson so that it calculates the commission for five, rather than three, sales ranges.
    a. Open the T9AppE01.cpp file contained in the Cpp\Tut09\T9AppE01 folder on your computer's hard disk. Figure 9-30 shows Golf Pro's new commission rate schedule.

Sales	Commission
1 – 100,000	2% * sales
100,001 – 200,000	4% * sales
200,001 – 300,000	6% * sales
300,001 – 400,000	8% * sales
400,001 and over	10% * sales

Figure 9-30

    b. Modify the `calcCommission` function to accommodate the new commission rate schedule. Use the shorter version of the `if/else` form of the selection structure.
    c. Save, build, and execute the program. Use the following sales amounts to test the program: 15,000, 250,000, 500,000, -1. (The DOS window should display the following commissions: 300, 15000, 50000, "No commission calculated", respectively.)
    d. When the program is working correctly, hide the Output window, then use the File menu to close the workspace.

2. In this exercise, you will create a program that displays the total amount of money a company owes for a seminar.
    a. Write one or more IPO charts for the problem. The seminar fee per person is based on the number of people the company registers, as shown in the following table. (For example, if the company registers seven people, then the total amount owed by the company is $560.)

Number of registrants	Fee per person
1 – 4	$100
5 – 10	$ 80
11 or more	$ 60

    If the user enters the number 0 or a negative number, the program should display an appropriate error message.
    b. Create a console application. Name the project workspace T9AppE02, and save it in the Cpp\Tut09 folder on your computer's hard disk. Add a new C++ source file to the project. Name the source file T9AppE02.
    c. Use the IPO chart(s) you completed in Step a to code the program.
    d. Complete a desk-check table for the program, using the following data: 4, 8, 12, 0, -2.
    e. Save, build, and execute the program. Use the data from Step d to test the program.
    f. When the program is working correctly, hide the Output window, then use the File menu to close the workspace.

3. In this exercise, you will create a program that displays a shipping charge.
   a. Write one or more IPO charts for the problem. The shipping charge is based on the state code, as shown in the following table. Use the `switch` form of the selection structure to display the appropriate shipping charge.

State code	Shipping charge ($)
1	25
2	30
3	40
4	40
5	30
6	30

   If the user enters any other state code, the program should display an "Incorrect state code" message.
   b. Create a console application. Name the project workspace T9AppE03, and save it in the Cpp\Tut09 folder on your computer's hard disk. Add a new C++ source file to the project. Name the source file T9AppE03.
   c. Use the IPO chart(s) you completed in Step a to code the program.
   d. Complete a desk-check table for the program, using the following data: 1, 2, 3, 4, 5, 6, 7, -2.
   e. Save, build, and execute the program. Use the data from Step d to test the program.
   f. When the program is working correctly, hide the Output window, then use the File menu to close the workspace.

4. In this exercise, you will create a program that displays the price of a concert ticket.
   a. Write one or more IPO charts for the problem. The concert ticket's price is based on the seat location, as shown in the following table. (The user should be able to enter the seat location using either an uppercase or lowercase letter.)

Seat location	Concert ticket price ($)
B (box)	75
P (Pavilion)	30
L (Lawn)	21

   If the user enter any other seat location, the program should display an "Invalid location" message.
   b. Create a console application. Name the project workspace T9AppE04, and save it in the Cpp\Tut09 folder on your computer's hard disk. Add a new C++ source file to the project. Name the source file T9AppE04.
   c. Use the IPO chart(s) you completed in Step a to code the program.
   d. Complete a desk-check table for the program, using the following data: B, p, L, g.
   e. Save, build, and execute the program. Use the data from Step d to test the program.
   f. When the program is working correctly, hide the Output window, then use the File menu to close the workspace.

5. In this exercise, you will create a program that displays the number of vacation weeks due an employee.
   a. Write one or more IPO charts for the problem. The number of vacation weeks is based on the number of years the employee has been with the company, as shown in the following table.

Years with the company	Weeks of vacation
0	0
1 – 5	1
6 – 10	2
11 and over	3

   If the user enters a negative number of years, the program should display an "Invalid years" message.

b. Create a console application. Name the project workspace T9AppE05, and save it in the Cpp\Tut09 folder on your computer's hard disk. Add a new C++ source file to the project. Name the source file T9AppE05.

c. Use the IPO chart(s) you completed in Step a to code the program.

d. Complete a desk-check table for the program, using the following data: 0, 2, 10, 11, -2.

e. Save, build, and execute the program. Use the data from Step d to test the program.

f. When the program is working correctly, hide the Output window, then use the File menu to close the workspace.

6. In this exercise, you will modify the program that you created in Tutorial 8's Application lesson so that it displays a message that informs the user whether a food is high or low in fat.

a. Open the T9AppE06.cpp file contained in the Cpp\Tut09\T9AppE06 folder on your computer's hard disk.

b. Modify the program so that it displays the message "Low-fat food" if the fat percentage is less than or equal to 30%; otherwise, display the message "High-fat food".

c. Save, build, and execute the program. Test the program two times. For the first test, use 150 as the total calories and 6 as the grams of fat. For the second test, use 105 as the total calories and 2 as the grams of fat.

d. When the program is working correctly, hide the Output window, then use the File menu to close the workspace.

7. In this exercise, you will create a program that displays the number of daily calories needed to maintain your current weight.

a. Write one or more IPO charts for the problem, using the information shown in Figure 9-31.

Female:

*To maintain your current weight:
Moderately active: total calories per day = weight multiplied by 12 calories per pound
Relatively inactive: total calories per day = weight multiplied by 10 calories per pound

Male:

*To maintain your current weight:
Moderately active: total calories per day = weight multiplied by 15 calories per pound
Relatively inactive: total calories per day = weight multiplied by 13 calories per pound

*Formulas from ViaHealth

Figure 9-31

b. Create a console application. Name the project workspace T9AppE07, and save it in the Cpp\Tut09 folder on your computer's hard disk. Add a new C++ source file to the project. Name the source file T9AppE07.

c. Use the IPO chart(s) you completed in Step a to code the program.

d. Complete a desk-check table for the program, using the following data: (F stands for female, M for male, A for active, and I for inactive.)

- F, I, 150
- F, A, 120
- M, I, 180
- M, A, 200

Also desk-check the program two additional times: first, using an invalid gender status of G, and then using a valid gender status of F, but an invalid activity status of B.

e. Save, build, and execute the program. Use the data from Step d to test the program.

f. When the program is working correctly, hide the Output window, then use the File menu to close the workspace.

8. In this exercise, you will create a program that displays a message indicating whether a student passed or failed a course.

a. Write one or more IPO charts for the problem. The program will need to get two test scores from the user; both scores should be positive numbers and can include 0. Both numbers also can contain a decimal place. If the first number is negative, don't ask the user to enter the second number; rather, display an appropriate error message and end the program. However, if both numbers are positive, the program should calculate the average. If the average is at least 70, the program should display "Pass"; otherwise, it should display "Fail".

b. Create a console application. Name the project workspace T9AppE08, and save it in the Cpp\Tut09 folder on your computer's hard disk. Add a new C++ source file to the project. Name the source file T9AppE08.

c. Use the IPO chart(s) you completed in Step a to code the program.

d. Complete a desk-check table for the program, using the following data: 95 and 73, 65 and 50, 0 and 100, 80 and -3, -1.

e. Save, build, and execute the program. Use the data from Step d to test the program.

f. When the program is working correctly, hide the Output window, then use the File menu to close the workspace.

9. In this exercise, you will create a program that displays either the sum of or the difference between two integers entered by the user.

a. Write one or more IPO charts for the problem. The program will need to get a letter (either A for addition or S for subtraction) and two integers from the user. However, if the user enters a letter that is not A, a, S, or s, do not ask the user for the two integers; rather, display an appropriate error message and end the program. If the letter is A (or a), the program should calculate and display the sum of both numbers entered by the user. If the letter is S (or s), the program should calculate and display the difference between both numbers (subtracting the second number from the first number), but only if the first number is larger than, or equal to, the second number. If the first number is smaller than the second number, the program should swap both numbers before calculating and displaying the difference.

b. Create a console application. Name the project workspace T9AppE09, and save it in the Cpp\Tut09 folder on your computer's hard disk. Add a new C++ source file to the project. Name the source file T9AppE09.

c. Use the IPO chart(s) you completed in Step a to code the program.

d. Complete a desk-check table for the program, using the following five sets of data:
   - A, 10, 20
   - a, 45, 15
   - S, 65, 50
   - s, 7, 13
   - G

e. Save, build, and execute the program. Use the data from Step d to test the program.

f. When the program is working correctly, hide the Output window, then use the File menu to close the workspace.

Exercise 10 is a Discovery Exercise. Discovery Exercises, which may include topics that are not covered in this lesson, allow you to "discover" the solutions to problems on your own.

10. In this exercise, you will modify the program that you created in this lesson so that it uses a value-returning function to get and validate the sales amount entered by the user. The function will return a value that indicates if the sales amount is valid.

   a. Open the T9AppE10.cpp file contained in the Cpp\Tut09\T9AppE10 folder on your computer's hard disk.

   b. Modify the program so that it uses a value-returning function named getAndValidateSales to get and validate the sales amount. (*Hint*: Pass the address of the sales variable to the getAndValidateSales function. Have the getAndValidateSales function return a value—for example, Y or N—that indicates whether the sales are valid. This value is commonly referred to as a *flag*, because its purpose is to indicate (or flag) when a specific condition exists. In this case, the flag value should indicate if the data entered by the user is valid (Y) or invalid (N). Use the return value to determine whether to calculate and display the commission.)

   c. Save, build, and execute the program. Use the following sales amounts to test the program: 15000, -10.

   d. When the program is working correctly, hide the Output window, then use the File menu to close the workspace.

A computer program is good only if it works. Errors in either an algorithm or programming code can cause the program to run incorrectly. Therefore, a programmer needs to know how to locate and fix these errors. Exercise 11 is a Debugging Exercise. Debugging Exercises allow you to practice recognizing and solving errors in a program.

debugging

11. In this exercise, you will debug an existing C++ program.

   a. Open the T9AppE11.cpp file contained in the Cpp\Tut09\T9AppE11 folder on your computer's hard disk. The program should display the salary amount corresponding to the code entered by the user. (A code of 1 corresponds to a salary amount of $45000. Codes of 2 and 5 correspond to a salary amount of $33000. Codes of 3 and 4 correspond to a salary amount of $25000.)

   b. Study the program's code, then build the program. Correct any errors in the program, then save, build, and execute the program. Test the program using a code of 2. The salary amount of $33000 should appear in the DOS window.

   c. When the program is working correctly, hide the Output window, then use the File menu to close the workspace.

The Repetition Structure

o b j e c t i v e s

After completing this tutorial, you will be able to:

- Write pseudocode for the repetition structure
- Create a flowchart for the repetition structure
- Code the repetition structure
- Initialize and update counters and accumulators
- Nest repetition structures

Concept Lesson

Using the Repetition Structure

As you learned in Tutorial 1, the three control structures used in programs are sequence, selection, and repetition. Every program contains the sequence structure, where the program instructions are processed, one after another, in the order in which each appears in the program. Most programs also contain the selection structure; you learned about the selection structure in Tutorials 8 and 9. Recall that programmers use the selection structure when they need the computer to make a decision and then take the appropriate action based on the result of that decision.

In addition to including the sequence and selection structures, most programs also include the repetition structure. Programmers use the repetition structure, referred to more simply as a loop, when they need the computer to repeatedly process one or more program instructions until some condition is met, at which time the repetition structure ends.

A repetition structure can be either a pretest loop or a posttest loop. In both types of loops, the condition is evaluated with each repetition, or iteration, of the loop. In a pretest loop, the evaluation occurs before the instructions within the loop are processed, while in a posttest loop, the evaluation occurs after the instructions within the loop are processed. Of the two types of loops, the pretest loop is the most commonly used. You will learn about the pretest loop in this tutorial; the posttest loop is covered in Appendix C.

As with the sequence and selection structures, you already are familiar with the repetition structure. For example, shampoo bottles typically include a direction that tells you to repeat the "apply shampoo to hair," "lather," and "rinse" steps until your hair is clean.

Pretest and posttest loops also are called top-driven and bottom-driven loops, respectively.

Pretest Loops

As you already know, not all problems require a loop in their solutions. Consider, for example, Acme Hardware's problem description and IPO chart shown in Figure 10-1.

Problem description		
At the beginning of each year, the president of Acme Hardware is paid a 10% bonus. The bonus is based on the amount of sales made by the company during the previous year. The payroll clerk wants a program that he or she can use to calculate and display the amount of the president's bonus.		

Input	Processing	Output
bonus rate (10%) sales	Processing items: none Algorithm: 1. enter the sales 2. calculate the bonus by multiplying the sales by the bonus rate 3. display the bonus	bonus

Figure 10-1: Problem description and IPO chart for Acme Hardware

The problem description for Acme Hardware indicates that the bonus for only one employee needs to be displayed. Therefore, the enter, calculate, and display steps contained in the algorithm need to be processed only once. Because no steps in the algorithm need to be repeated, the algorithm does not require a loop.

Now, however, consider O'Donnell Incorporated's problem description and IPO chart shown in Figure 10-2.

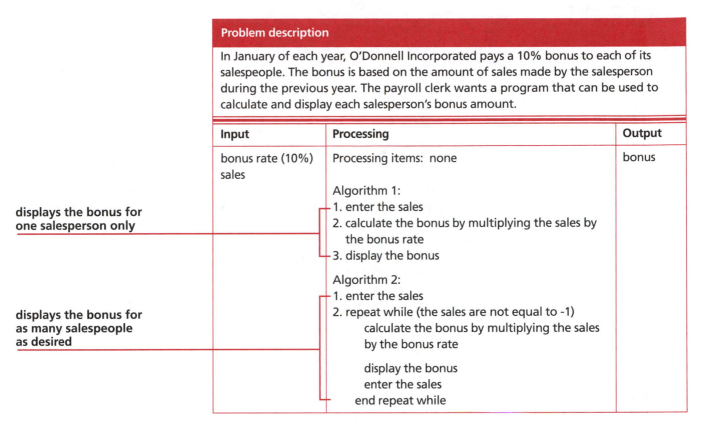

Figure 10-2: Problem description and IPO chart for O'Donnell Incorporated

The problem description for O'Donnell Incorporated is similar to the problem description for Acme Hardware, except it indicates that the bonus for more than one employee needs to be calculated and displayed. You could use either of the algorithms shown in Figure 10-2's IPO chart to solve O'Donnell Incorporated's problem; however, as you will learn shortly, the second algorithm is a much better choice.

The first algorithm shown in Figure 10-2 is identical to the Acme Hardware algorithm shown in Figure 10-1; neither algorithm contains a loop. Although the first algorithm shown in Figure 10-2 can be used to solve O'Donnell Incorporated's problem, the algorithm is inefficient for that purpose, because it displays only one bonus amount. A program based on this algorithm will need to be executed once for each salesperson receiving a bonus. In other words, if O'Donnell Incorporated has 100 salespeople, the payroll clerk will need to execute the program 100 times to calculate and display each salesperson's bonus amount.

The second algorithm shown in Figure 10-2 contains a loop and represents a more efficient solution to the O'Donnell Incorporated problem. After executing a program based on the second algorithm, the payroll clerk can calculate and display the bonus amount for as many salepeople as desired, one after another. The payroll clerk indicates when he or she is finished calculating and displaying bonus amounts by entering -1 (a negative number one) as the sales amount. Figure 10-3 identifies the important components of the loop shown in the second algorithm.

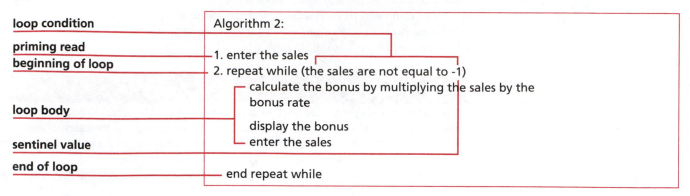

Figure 10-3: Components of a loop

With very rare exceptions, every loop has a loop condition and a loop body. The **loop condition**, which appears at the beginning of a pretest loop, determines the number of times the instructions within the loop, referred to as the **loop body**, are processed. Similar to a selection structure condition, a loop condition must result in either a true or false answer only. In the loop condition shown in Figure 10-3, for example, if the sales amount entered by the user is not equal to -1, then the loop condition evaluates to true; otherwise, in which case the user entered -1 as the sales amount, the loop condition evaluates to false.

Some loops, such as the one shown in Figure 10-3, require the user to enter a special value to end the loop. Values that are used to end loops are referred to as **sentinel values**. In the loop shown in Figure 10-3, the sentinel value is -1. The sentinel value should be one that is easily distinguishable from the valid data recognized by the program. The number 1000, for example, would not be a good sentinel value for the loop in Figure 10-3's algorithm, because it is possible that a salesperson could have made that amount of sales. The number -1, on the other hand, is a good sentinel value for the loop, because a sales amount cannot be negative.

When the loop condition evaluates to true, the one or more instructions listed in the loop body are processed; otherwise, these instructions are skipped. Because the loop condition in a pretest loop is evaluated before any of the instructions within the loop body are processed, it is possible that the loop body instructions may not be processed at all; this would occur when the loop condition initially evaluates to false. For example, if the payroll clerk at O'Donnell Incorporated enters the number -1 as the first sales amount, the loop condition shown in Figure 10-3 will evaluate to false, and the instructions in the loop body will be skipped over.

After each processing of the loop body instructions, the loop condition is reevaluated to determine if the instructions should be processed again. The loop's instructions will be processed and its condition evaluated until the condition evaluates to false, at which time the loop ends and processing continues with the instruction immediately following the end of the loop.

tip

Values used to end loops also are called trip values or trailer values.

The flowchart shown in Figure 10-4 illustrates why the loop is referred to as a pretest loop. Notice that the repetition diamond, which contains the loop condition, appears *before* the symbols in both the true and false paths.

Notice that the pseudocode shown in Figure 10-3 contains two "enter the sales" instructions: one of the instructions appears in Step 1, which is above the loop, and the other appears as the last instruction in the loop body. The "enter the sales" instruction that appears above the loop is referred to as the **priming read**, because it is used to prime (prepare or set up) the loop. In this case, the priming read will get only the first salesperson's sales from the user. This first value, when compared to the sentinel value (-1), will determine whether the loop body instructions are processed at all. If the loop body instructions are processed, the "enter the sales" instruction that appears within the loop body will get the sales amounts for the remaining salespeople (if any) from the user.

It may be easier to visualize a loop by viewing it in a flowchart.

Flowcharting a Loop

Figure 10-4 shows the O'Donnell Incorporated algorithm in flowchart form.

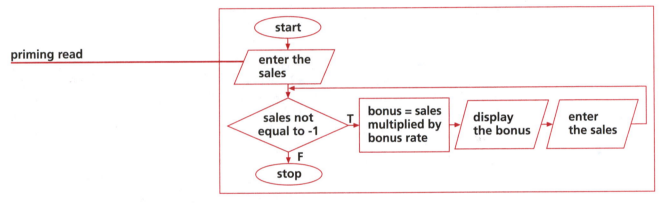

Figure 10-4: O'Donnell Incorporated algorithm shown in flowchart form

The symbol located immediately above the repetition diamond represents the instruction that will be processed immediately before the loop condition is evaluated the first time.

Recall that the oval in a flowchart is the start/stop symbol, the rectangle is the process symbol, the parallelogram is the input/output symbol, and the diamond is the selection/repetition symbol. In Figure 10-4's flowchart, the diamond indicates the beginning of a repetition structure (loop). As with the selection structure diamond, which you learned about in Tutorial 8, the repetition structure diamond contains a comparison that has a true or false answer only. The comparison represents the loop condition, which determines whether the instructions within the loop body are processed.

Like the selection diamond, the repetition diamond has two flowlines leaving the symbol. The flowline marked with a "T" (for true) leads to the loop body—the instructions to process when the loop condition evaluates to true. The flowline marked with an "F" (for false) leads to the instructions that will be processed once the loop condition evaluates to false.

The input parallelogram located within the loop in Figure 10-4's flowchart will get any additional sales amounts from the user.

Unlike the selection diamond, the repetition diamond has two flowlines leading into the diamond, rather than one. One of the flowlines comes from the symbol located immediately above the diamond. In the flowchart shown in Figure 10-4, this symbol is the parallelogram that represents the priming read, which gets only the first salesperson's sales from the user. Notice that the parallelogram has a flowline that flows into the repetition diamond.

The second flowline leading into the repetition diamond flows from the repetition structure's true path, which contains the loop body instructions. In the flowchart shown in Figure 10-4, the flowline leading out of the "enter the sales" parallelogram in the true path flows back up to the repetition diamond. Notice that the two flowlines leading into the repetition diamond, as well as the symbols and flowlines within the true path, form a circle or loop. It is this loop that distinguishes the repetition structure from the selection structure in a flowchart.

To help you understand how a loop operates in a program, you will desk-check the algorithm shown in Figure 10-4 using the following sales data: 10000, 25000, and -1. The first input parallelogram shown in Figure 10-4's flowchart gets the amount of the first salesperson's sales from the user. Figure 10-5 shows the first salesperson's sales amount—10000—recorded in the desk-check table.

bonus rate	sales	bonus
.10	10000	

Figure 10-5: First salesperson's sales amount recorded in the desk-check table

The next symbol in the flowchart is the repetition diamond. This diamond represents the beginning of a pretest loop that will repeat its instructions as long as (or while) the user enters something other than the number -1 as the sales amount. Before processing the loop instructions, the loop condition, which compares the sales amount entered by the user to -1, is evaluated. In this case, the loop condition evaluates to true, because 10000 is not equal to -1. Recall that when the loop condition evaluates to true, the instructions in the loop body are processed. The first two instructions in the loop body shown in Figure 10-4 calculate and then display the bonus amount. Figure 10-6 shows the first salesperson's information recorded in the desk-check table.

bonus rate	sales	bonus
.10	10000	1000

Figure 10-6: First salesperson's bonus information recorded in the desk-check table

The last instruction in the loop body shown in Figure 10-4 is contained in an input parallelogram, and it gets the next salesperson's sales—in this case, 25000—from the user. After getting the sales, the loop condition, which appears in the repetition diamond located at the top of the loop, is reevaluated to determine whether the loop should be processed again (a true condition) or end (a false condition). In this case, the condition evalutes to true, because 25000 is not equal to -1. Because of this, the bonus amount is calculated and then displayed on the screen. Figure 10-7 shows the second salesperson's information recorded in the desk-check table.

bonus rate	sales	bonus
.10	~~10000~~	~~1000~~
	25000	2500

Figure 10-7: Second salesperson's information recorded in the desk-check table

The input parallelogram that appears as the last flowchart symbol in the loop body then gets the next salesperson's sales from the user. In this case, the user enters the sentinel value (-1) as the sales, as shown in Figure 10-8.

bonus rate	sales	bonus
.10	~~10000~~	~~1000~~
	~~25000~~	2500
	-1	

sentinel value

Figure 10-8: Sentinel value recorded in the desk-check table

Next, the loop condition is reevaluated to determine whether the loop should be processed again (a true condition) or end (a false condition). In this case, the loop condition evaluates to false, because the sales amount entered by the user is equal to -1. Recall that when the loop condition evaluates to false, the loop instructions are skipped over and processing continues with the instruction immediately following the end of the loop. In Figure 10-4's flowchart, the stop oval, which marks the end of the algorithm, follows the loop.

Next, learn how to code the pretest loop.

Coding the Pretest Loop

You can code a pretest loop using the `while` statement in both C++ and Java, and the `Do While` statement in Visual Basic. Figure 10-9 shows the syntax of these statements.

C++ and Java

while (*loop condition***)**
    one statement, or a block of statements enclosed in braces, to be processed
    as long as the loop condition is true
 //end while

Visual Basic
Do While *loop condition*   *one or more statements to be processed as long as the loop condition is true*   **Loop**
Note: In the syntax, items in **bold** are required. Items in *italics* indicate places where the programmer must supply information pertaining to the current program.

Figure 10-9: Syntax of the `while` and `Do While` statements in C++, Java, and Visual Basic

tip

You also can use the `for` statement in C++ and Java, and the `For Next` statement in Visual Basic, to code a pretest loop. You will learn about the C++ `for` statement in Appendix D.

Items in bold in each syntax are essential components of the statement. For example, the keyword `while` and the parentheses that surround the loop condition are required in the `while` statement in C++ and Java. In Visual Basic, the keywords `Do While` and `Loop` are essential components of the `Do While` statement. Unlike C++ and Java, Visual Basic does not require you to enclose the `Do While` statement's loop condition in parentheses.

tip

Some C++ programmers enclose the loop body in braces even when it contains only one statement, but this is not required by the C++ syntax. However, including the braces in a loop that contains only one statement is convenient, because you will not need to remember to enter the braces if additional statements are added to the loop in the future. Forgetting to enter the braces around a statement block is a common error made by programmers.

Items in italics in each syntax indicate where the programmer must supply information pertaining to the current program. For instance, the programmer must supply the loop condition to be evaluated. The loop condition must be a Boolean expression, which is an expression that evaluates to either true or false. The loop condition can contain variables, constants, functions, arithmetic operators, comparison operators, and logical operators.

In addition to supplying the loop condition, the programmer also must supply the statements to be processed when the loop condition evaluates to true. If more than one statement needs to be processed in C++ and Java, the statements must be entered as a statement block. Recall that you create a statement block by enclosing the statements in a set of braces ({}). Unlike in C++ and Java, braces are not used in Visual Basic.

Although it is not required to do so, it is a good programming practice to use a comment, such as `//end while`, to mark the end of the `while` statement in C++ and Java. The comment will make your program easier to read and understand. You do not need to use a comment to mark the end of the `Do While` statement in Visual Basic, as this is the purpose of the `Loop` clause.

Figure 10-10 shows the C++ code for the O'Donnell Incorporated algorithm, which contains a pretest loop.

IPO chart information	C++ instructions

Input
  bonus rate (10%)
  sales
Processing
  none
Output
  bonus
	`const float RATE = float(.1);`
	`float sales = 0.0;`
	
	`float bonus = 0.0;`

Algorithm 1. enter the sales	`cout << "Enter the first sales amount: ";` `cin >> sales;`
2. repeat while (the sales are not equal to -1)	`while (sales != -1)`

calculate the bonus by multiplying the sales by the bonus rate	`{`
	
	`    bonus = sales * RATE;`

display the bonus	`    cout << "Bonus: " << bonus << endl;`
enter the sales	`    cout << "Enter the next sales amount: ";` `    cin >> sales;`
end repeat while	`}   //end while`

Figure 10-10: C++ statements for the O'Donnell Incorporated algorithm

Take a closer look at the statements shown in Figure 10-10. The first three statements declare and initialize the `RATE` named constant and the `sales` and `bonus` variables. The `cout << "Enter the first sales amount: ";` statement prompts the user to enter the first sales amount, and the `cin >> sales;` statement stores the user's response in the `sales` variable. The `while (sales != -1)` clause then compares the value stored in the `sales` variable to the sentinel value (-1). If the `sales` variable does not contain the sentinel value, the instructions within the loop body are processed. Those instructions calculate the bonus, display the bonus, then prompt the user to enter the next sales amount, and finally allow the user to enter the sales amount. Each time the user enters a sales amount, the `while` clause compares the sales amount to the sentinel value (-1). When the user enters the sentinel value—in this case, -1—as the sales amount, the loop instructions are skipped over, and processing continues with the line immediately below the end of the loop.

Important note: If you forget to enter the cin >> sales; statement within the program's loop, the loop will process its instructions indefinitely. A loop that processes its instructions indefinitely is referred to as either an **endless loop** or an **infinite loop**. Usually, you can stop a program that contains an endless loop by pressing Ctrl+c (press and hold down the Ctrl key as you press the letter c); you also can use the DOS window's Close button.

tip

You can practice stopping a program that contains an endless loop by completing this lesson's Discovery Exercise 17.

mini-quiz

Mini-Quiz 1

1. Write a C++ `while` clause that processes the loop instructions as long as the value in the `quantity` variable is greater than the number 0.

2. Write a C++ `while` clause that stops the loop when the value in the `quantity` variable is less than the number 0.

3. Write a C++ `while` clause that processes the loop instructions as long as the value in the `inStock` variable is greater than the value in the `reorder` variable.

4. Write a C++ `while` clause that processes the loop instructions as long as the value in the `letter` variable is either Y or y. (The `letter` variable is a `char` variable.)

5. Which of the following is a good sentinel value for a program that inputs the number of hours each employee worked this week?

   a. -9   c. 45.5

   b. 32   d. 7

6. The input instruction that appears above a pretest loop is called the

   _____ .

Many times a program will need to display a subtotal, a total, or an average. To do so, you will need to use a repetition structure that includes a counter, an accumulator, or both.

Using Counters and Accumulators

Counters and accumulators are used within a repetition structure to calculate subtotals, totals, and averages. A counter is a numeric variable used for counting something—such as the number of employees paid in a week. An accumulator is a numeric variable used for accumulating (adding together) something—such as the total dollar amount of a week's payroll.

Two tasks are associated with counters and accumulators: initializing and updating. Initializing means to assign a beginning value to the counter or accumulator. Although the beginning value usually is zero, counters and accumulators can be initialized to any number; the initial value you use will depend on the algorithm. The initialization task typically is done outside the loop body in a program, because it needs to be done only once.

tip

Counters are used to answer the question, "How many?"—for example, "How many salespeople live in Virginia?" Accumulators are used to answer the question, "How much?"—for example, "How much did the salespeople sell this quarter?"

Updating, also called incrementing, means adding a number to the value stored in the counter or the accumulator; the number can be either positive or negative. A counter is always incremented by a constant value—typically the number 1—whereas an accumulator is incremented by a value that varies. The assignment statement that updates a counter or an accumulator is placed within the loop body in a program, because the update task must be performed each time the loop body instructions are processed. You will use both a counter and an accumulator in the Sales Express program, which you will view next.

The Sales Express Program

Assume that Sales Express wants a program that the sales manager can use to display the average amount the company sold during the prior year. The sales manager will enter the amount of each salesperson's sales. The program will use both a counter and an accumulator to calculate the average sales amount, which then will be displayed on the screen. Figure 10-11 shows the IPO chart information and C++ code for the Sales Express program.

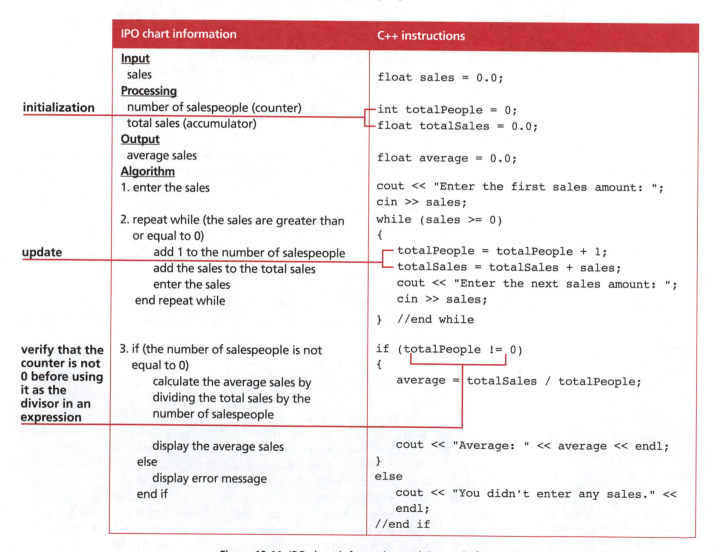

Figure 10-11: IPO chart information and C++ code for Sales Express

The "enter the sales" step located above the loop in the algorithm shown in Figure 10-11 is the priming read.

As Figure 10-11 indicates, the input for the Sales Express problem is each salesperson's sales amount, and the output is the average sales amount. The algorithm will use two processing items: a counter that keeps track of the number of salespeople, and an accumulator that keeps track of the total sales. Notice in the C++ code that the counter and accumulator are initialized to 0.

To better understand counters and accumulators, you will desk-check the Sales Express code using the following sales data: 30000, 40000, -3. After declaring and initializing the appropriate variables, the program prompts the user to enter the first sales amount, and then stores the user's response in the `sales` variable, as shown in Figure 10-12.

sales	totalPeople	totalSales	average
~~0.0~~ 30000.0	0	0.0	0.0

Figure 10-12: First sales amount recorded in the desk-check table

The `while (sales >= 0)` clause begins a pretest loop that will repeat the loop body instructions as long as (or while) the user enters a sales amount that is greater than or equal to zero. The loop will stop when the user enters the sentinel value, which, in this program, is any sales amount that is less than zero. Notice that, unlike the loop in the O'Donnell Incorporated algorithm, the loop in the Sales Express algorithm has more than one sentinel value. In the Sales Express algorithm, any number that is less than zero can be used to stop the loop.

If the sales amount entered by the user is greater than or equal to 0, as it is in this case, the instructions in the loop body are processed. The first two instructions update the `totalPeople` counter variable by adding 1 to it, and update the `totalSales` accumulator variable by adding the sales amount to it. The updates are shown in Figure 10-13's desk-check table.

sales	totalPeople	totalSales	average
~~0.0~~ 30000.0	~~0~~ 1	~~0.0~~ 30000.0	0.0

Figure 10-13: Desk-check table showing the first update to the counter and accumulator

The last two instructions in the loop body prompt the user to enter the next sales amount, and then store the user's response—in this case, 40000—in the `sales` variable. The loop condition `while (sales >= 0)` then is reevaluated to determine whether the loop should be processed again (a true condition) or simply end (a false condition). Here again, the loop condition will evaluate to true, because 40000 is greater than or equal to zero. Because of this, the loop instructions will increment the `totalPeople` variable by 1, and increment the `totalSales` variable by the sales amount, as shown in Figure 10-14.

sales	totalPeople	totalSales	average
~~0.0~~	~~0~~	~~0.0~~	0.0
~~30000.0~~	~~1~~	~~30000.0~~	
40000.0	2	70000.0	

Figure 10-14: Desk-check table showing the second update to the counter and accumulator

The last two instructions in the loop body prompt the user to enter the next sales amount, and then store the user's response—in this case, -3, which is a sentinel value—in the `sales` variable. The loop condition `while (sales >= 0)` then is reevaluated to determine whether the loop should be processed again or simply end. In this case, the loop condition will evaluate to false, because -3 is not greater than or equal to zero. When the loop condition evaluates to false, the loop ends, and processing continues with the statement immediately following the loop.

In the Sales Express program, the statement following the loop is an `if` statement, whose condition verifies that the `totalPeople` variable does not contain the number zero. This verification is necessary because the first instruction in the `if` statement's true path uses the `totalPeople` variable as the divisor when calculating the average, and the computer cannot divide by zero. If the `totalPeople` variable contains the number zero, the `if` statement's false path displays an appropriate message. However, if the `totalPeople` variable contains a value other than zero, as it does in this case, the `if` statement's true path calculates and displays the average sales amount (35000) on the screen before the program ends. Figure 10-15 shows the completed desk-check table for the Sales Express program.

	sales	totalPeople	totalSales	average
	~~0.0~~	~~0~~	~~0.0~~	~~0.0~~
	~~30000.0~~	~~1~~	~~30000.0~~	35000.0
	~~40000.0~~	2	70000.0	
sentinel value	-3			

Figure 10-15: Completed desk-check table for the Sales Express program

Mini-Quiz 2

1. A(n) _____ is updated by an amount that varies.

2. Write a C++ assignment statement that updates the `quantity` counter variable by 2.

3. Write a C++ assignment statement that updates the `total` counter variable by -3.

4. Write a C++ assignment statement that updates the `totalPurchases` accumulator variable by the value stored in the `purchases` variable.

5. Write a C++ assignment statement that updates the `sales` accumulator variable by -100.

In both the O'Donnell Incorporated and Sales Express programs, the termination of the loop is controlled by the user entering a sentinel value. The termination of a loop also can be controlled by the program itself. Typically, this is done using a counter.

Counter-Controlled Pretest Loops

Assume you want to create a program that displays the squares of the numbers from one through three on the screen. Figure 10-16 shows the IPO chart information and C++ code for the squaring problem.

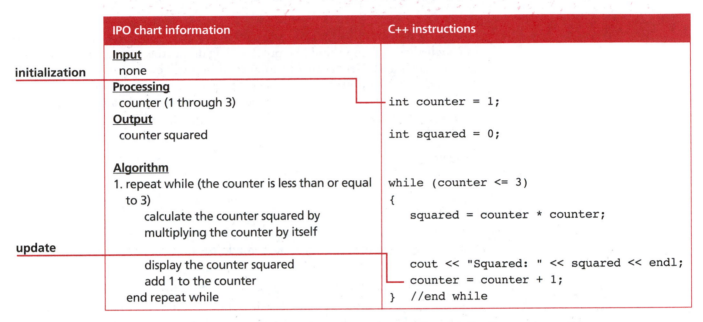

Figure 10-16: IPO chart information and C++ code for the squaring problem

As Figure 10-16 indicates, the solution to the squaring problem requires one processing item and one output item. The processing item is a counter that the program will use to keep track of the values to be squared—in this case, the numbers 1, 2, and 3. Notice in the C++ code that the counter variable, named `counter`, is initialized to the first value you want the program to square—the number 1. The output item is the square of each counter value, and its corresponding variable is named `squared` and initialized to 0, as shown in Figure 10-17.

counter	squared
1	0

Figure 10-17: Desk-check table showing initialization of variables

The `while (counter <= 3)` clause in the code begins a pretest loop that will repeat its instructions as long as (or while) the value in the `counter` variable is less than or equal to three. The loop will stop when the value in the `counter` variable is greater than three. At this point in the program, the value stored in the `counter` variable is less than three, so the loop condition evaluates to true and the loop instructions are processed. The first instruction in the loop body squares the `counter` variable's value, and stores the result in the `squared` variable. The second instruction in the loop body increments the `counter` variable by 1, as shown in Figure 10-18.

counter	squared
~~1~~	~~0~~
2	1

Figure 10-18: Results of processing the loop instructions the first time

The loop condition while (counter <= 3) then is reevaluated to determine whether the loop should be processed again (a true condition) or simply end (a false condition). Here again, the loop condition will evaluate to true, because the value stored in the counter variable (2) is less than or equal to three. Because of this, the loop instructions will square the counter variable's value, and then increment the counter variable by 1, as shown in Figure 10-19.

counter	squared
~~1~~	~~0~~
~~2~~	~~1~~
3	4

Figure 10-19: Results of processing the loop instructions the second time

The loop condition while (counter <= 3) then is reevaluated to determine whether the loop should be processed again or simply end. Here again, the loop condition will evaluate to true, because the value stored in the counter variable (3) is less than or equal to three. Because of this, the loop instructions will square the counter variable's value, and then increment the counter variable by 1, as shown in Figure 10-20.

counter	squared
~~1~~	~~0~~
~~2~~	~~1~~
~~3~~	~~4~~
4	9

Figure 10-20: Results of processing the loop instructions the third time

The loop condition while (counter <= 3) then is reevaluated to determine whether the loop should be processed again or simply end. At this point, the loop condition will evaluate to false, because the value stored in the counter variable (4) is not less than or equal to three. Because of this, the loop ends and processing continues with the instruction located immediately below the loop. Notice that the counter variable, rather than the user, controlled the termination of the loop.

In Tutorial 9, you learned how to nest selection structures. You also can nest repetition structures, which means you can place one repetition structure inside another repetition structure.

Nested Repetition Structures

In a nested repetition structure, one loop, referred to as the inner loop, is placed entirely within another loop, called the outer loop. Although the idea of nested loops may sound confusing, you already are familiar with the concept. A clock, for instance, uses nested loops to keep track of the time. For simplicity, consider a clock's second and minute hands only. You can think of the second hand as being the inner loop and the minute hand as being the outer loop. As you know, the second hand on a clock moves one position, clockwise, for every second that has elapsed. Only after the second hand completes its processing—in this case, only after it moves 60 positions—does the minute hand move one position, clockwise; the second hand then begins its journey around the clock again. Figure 10-21 illustrates the logic used by a clock's second and minute hands.

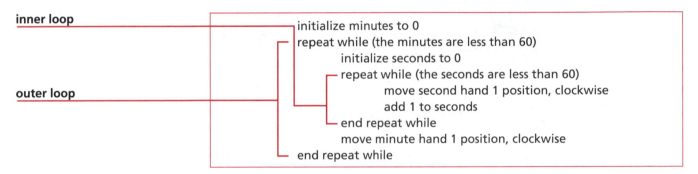

```
inner loop
                     initialize minutes to 0
                     repeat while (the minutes are less than 60)
                         initialize seconds to 0
outer loop              repeat while (the seconds are less than 60)
                             move second hand 1 position, clockwise
                             add 1 to seconds
                         end repeat while
                         move minute hand 1 position, clockwise
                     end repeat while
```

Figure 10-21: Nested loops used by a clock

As indicated in Figure 10-21, the outer loop corresponds to a clock's minute hand, and the inner loop corresponds to a clock's second hand. Notice that the entire inner loop is contained within the outer loop, which must be true for the loops to be nested and to work correctly.

You will use both an outer and inner loop in the Max Beauty Supply program, which you will view next.

The Max Beauty Supply Program

Assume that Max Beauty Supply divides its sales territory into two regions: region 1 and region 2. The company's sales manager wants a program in which he can enter each region's sales amounts. The program should use this information to calculate and display the total amount sold in each region. Figure 10-22 shows the IPO chart information and C++ code for the Max Beauty Supply program. Notice that the program contains an outer loop and an inner loop, and that the entire inner loop is contained within the outer loop.

IPO chart information	C++ instructions

Input
  sales
Processing
  region counter (1 and 2)
	`float sales = 0.0;`
	
	`int region = 1;`

Output
  total region sales (accumulator)
Algorithm
1. repeat while (the region counter is less than 3)
    enter the sales
    repeat while (the sales are greater than 0)
        add the sales to the total region sales
        enter the sales
    end repeat while
 	
    display the total region sales
    add 1 to the region counter
    assign 0 to the total region sales
end repeat while
	`float totRegSales = 0.0;`
	
	`while (region < 3)`
	`{`
	  `cout << "Enter the first sales amount: ";`
	  `cin >> sales;`
	  `while (sales > 0)`
	  `{`
	    `totRegSales = totRegSales + sales;`
	    `cout << "Enter the next sales amount: ";`
	    `cin >> sales;`
	  `} //end while`
	
	  `cout << "Total: " << totRegSales << endl;`
	  `region = region + 1;`
	  `totRegSales = 0.0;`
	`} //end while`

outer loop — inner loop

Figure 10-22: IPO chart information and C++ code for Max Beauty Supply

As Figure 10-22 indicates, the input for the Max Beauty Supply problem is the sales amounts made in each region, and the output is each region's total sales amount. The problem will require the use of an accumulator to total the sales amounts made in each region. The problem also requires one processing item: a counter that will keep track of the region numbers (1 and 2). Notice in the C++ code that the `region` counter variable is initialized to the first region number, 1.

After declaring and intializing the appropriate variables, the outer loop's `while (region < 3)` clause begins a pretest loop that will repeat its instructions while the value in the `region` variable is less than three. At this point in the program, the value stored in the `region` variable (1) is less than three, so the outer loop condition evaluates to true and the outer loop instructions are processed.

The first two instructions in the outer loop prompt the user to enter the first sales amount, and then store the user's response in the `sales` variable. The third instruction in the outer loop is the inner loop's `while (sales > 0)` clause, which begins a pretest loop that will repeat its instructions while the sales amount entered by the user is greater than zero.

The first instruction in the inner loop increments the accumulator variable, `totRegSales`, by the sales amount stored in the `sales` variable. The last two instructions in the inner loop prompt the user to enter the next sales amount, and then store the user's response in the `sales` variable. The inner loop condition then is reevaluated to determine whether the inner loop instructions should be processed again. The inner loop will continue to process its instructions until the user enters either the number zero or a negative number, at which time the inner loop will end. Figure 10-23 shows the status of the desk-check table, assuming the user enters the following sales amounts for region 1: 25000, 30000, 10000, -1.

sales	region	totRegSales
0.0	1	0.0
25000.0		25000.0
30000.0		55000.0
10000.0		65000.0
-1.0		

Figure 10-23: Desk-check table after processing region 1's data

tip

When loops are nested, the outer loop typically will need to reinitialize the counters and accumulators updated within the inner loop. In the Max Beauty Supply program, only the `totRegSales` accumulator is updated within the inner loop, so that is the only variable reinitialized by the outer loop.

The next statement processed is the `cout << "Total: " << totRegSales << endl;` statement, which appears immediately below the inner loop in the program. This statement displays the total sales made in region 1 (65000). The `region = region + 1;` statement then increments the counter variable by 1, and the `totRegSales = 0.0;` statement reinitializes the accumulator variable to zero, as shown in Figure 10-24.

sales	region	totRegSales
0.0	1	0.0
25000.0	2	25000.0
30000.0		55000.0
10000.0		65000.0
-1.0		0.0

Figure 10-24: Desk-check table after updating counter and reinitializing accumulator

The outer loop condition `while (region < 3)` then is reevaluated to determine whether the outer loop should be processed again. Here again, the outer loop condition will evaluate to true, because the value stored in the `region` variable (2) is less than three. Because of this, the outer loop instructions will be processed again.

The first two instructions in the outer loop prompt the user to enter the first sales amount, and then store the user's response in the `sales` variable. The third instruction in the outer loop is the inner loop's `while (sales > 0)` clause, which begins a pretest loop that will repeat its instructions while the sales amount entered by the user is greater than zero.

The first instruction in the inner loop increments the accumulator variable, `totRegSales`, by the sales amount stored in the `sales` variable. The last two instructions in the inner loop prompt the user to enter the next sales amount, and then store the user's response in the `sales` variable. The inner loop condition then is reevaluated to determine whether the inner loop instructions should be processed again. The inner loop will continue to process its instructions until the user enters either the number zero or a negative number, at which time the inner loop will end. Figure 10-25 shows the status of the desk-check table, assuming the user enters the following sales amounts for region 2: 13000, 10000, -1.

sales	region	totRegSales
~~0.0~~	~~1~~	~~0.0~~
~~25000.0~~	2	~~25000.0~~
~~30000.0~~		~~55000.0~~
~~10000.0~~		~~65000.0~~
~~-1.0~~		~~0.0~~
~~13000.0~~		~~13000.0~~
~~10000.0~~		23000.0
-1.0		

Figure 10-25: Desk-check table after processing region 2's data

The next statement processed is the `cout << "Total: " << totRegSales << endl;` statement, which appears immediately below the inner loop and displays the total sales made in region 2 (23000). The `region = region + 1;` statement then increments the counter variable by 1, and the `totRegSales = 0.0;` statement reinitializes the accumulator variable to zero, as shown in Figure 10-26.

sales	region	totRegSales
~~0.0~~	~~1~~	~~0.0~~
~~25000.0~~	~~2~~	~~25000.0~~
~~30000.0~~	3	~~55000.0~~
~~10000.0~~		~~65000.0~~
~~-1.0~~		~~0.0~~
~~13000.0~~		~~13000.0~~
~~10000.0~~		~~23000.0~~
-1.0		0.0

Figure 10-26: Desk-check table after updating counter and reinitializing accumulator

The outer loop condition `while (region < 3)` then is reevaluated to determine whether the outer loop should be processed again. At this point, the outer loop condition will evaluate to false, because the value stored in the `region` variable (3) is not less than three. Because of this, the outer loop ends and processing continues with the instruction located immediately below the loop.

mini-quiz

Mini-Quiz 3

1. Assume that a program declares an `int` variable named `evenNum` and initializes it to 2. Write a C++ `while` loop that uses the `evenNum` variable to display the even integers between 1 and 9.

2. For nested loops to work correctly, the entire _____ loop must be contained within the _____ loop.

   a. inner, outer
   b. outer, inner

3. Assume that a program has declared and initialized two `int` variables named `firstLoop` and `secondLoop`. Both variables are initialized to the number 1. Write the C++ code that uses these variables to display the numbers 1 through 3 on four lines, as follows.

   ```
   1   2   3
   1   2   3
   1   2   3
   1   2   3
   ```

You now have completed Tutorial 10's Concept lesson. You can either take a break or complete the end-of-lesson questions and exercises before moving on to the Application lesson.

SUMMARY

Programmers use the repetition structure, also called a loop, when they need the computer to repeatedly process one or more program instructions until some condition is met, at which time the repetition structure ends. A repetition structure can be either a pretest loop or a posttest loop. In a pretest loop, the loop condition is evaluated before the instructions within the loop are processed, while in a posttest loop, the evaluation occurs after the instructions within the loop are processed. Of the two types of loops, the pretest loop is the most commonly used.

Almost every loop has a loop condition and a loop body. The loop condition appears at the beginning of a pretest loop and determines the number of times the instructions within the loop, referred to as the loop body, are processed. The loop condition must result in either a true or false answer only. When the loop condition evaluates to true, the one or more instructions listed in the loop body are processed; otherwise, these instructions are skipped over.

Some loops require the user to enter a special value, called a sentinel value, to end the loop. You should use a sentinel value that is easily distinguishable from the valid data recognized by the program. Other loops are terminated by the program itself, through the use of a counter.

The input instruction that appears above the pretest loop is referred to as the priming read, because it is used to prime (prepare or set up) the loop. The priming read gets only the first value from the user. The input instruction that appears within the loop gets the remaining values.

The flowchart symbol for the repetition structure (loop) is the repetition/selection diamond. You can use the `while` statement to code a pretest loop in C++.

Counters and accumulators are used within a repetition structure to calculate subtotals, totals, and averages. All counters and accumulators must be initialized and updated. Counters are updated by a constant value, whereas accumulators are updated by an amount that varies.

You can nest repetition structures, similar to the way you can nest selection structures. For repetition structures to be nested and work correctly, the entire inner loop must be contained within the outer loop.

ANSWERS TO MINI-QUIZZES

Mini-Quiz 1

1. `while (quantity > 0)`
2. `while (quantity >= 0)`
3. `while (inStock > reorder)`
4. `while (letter == 'Y' || letter == 'y')`
5. a. -9
6. priming read

Mini-Quiz 2

1. accumulator
2. `quantity = quantity + 2;`
3. `total = total + -3;` (or `total = total - 3;`)
4. `totalPurchases = totalPurchases + purchases;`
5. `sales = sales + -100;` (or `sales = sales - 100;`)

Mini-Quiz 3

1. ```
   while (evenNum < 9) (or while (evenNum <= 8))
   {
        cout << evenNum << endl;
        evenNum = evenNum + 2;
   }   //end while
   ```
2. a. inner, outer
3. ```
   while (firstLoop <= 4)
   {
        while (secondLoop <= 3)
        {

             cout << secondLoop << " ";
             secondLoop = secondLoop + 1;
        }   //end while
        cout << endl;
        firstLoop = firstLoop + 1;
        secondLoop = 1;
   }  //end while
   ```

Q U E S T I O N S

1. The while loop is referred to as _____ loop, because the loop condition is tested at the beginning of the loop.
    a. a beginning
    b. an initial
    c. a pretest
    d. a priming

2. The loop condition in a flowchart is represented by _____.
    a. a diamond
    b. an oval
    c. a parallelogram
    d. a rectangle

3. A numeric variable used for counting something is called _____.
    a. an accumulator
    b. an adder
    c. a constant
    d. a counter

4. Counters and accumulators must be initialized and _____.
    a. added
    b. displayed
    c. updated
    d. none of the above

5. _____ are always incremented by a constant amount, whereas _____ are incremented by an amount that varies.
    a. Accumulators, counters
    b. Counters, accumulators

6. Which of the following will correctly update the counter variable named `numEmployees`?
    a. `numEmployees = 0;`
    b. `numEmployees = numEmployees + numEmployees;`
    c. `numEmployees = numEmployees + sumSalary;`
    d. `numEmployees = numEmployees + 1;`

7. Which of the following will correctly update the accumulator variable named `total`?
    a. `total = 0;`
    b. `total = total + total;`
    c. `total = total + sales;`
    d. `total = total + 1;`

8. Which of the following would be a good sentinel value for a program that allows the user to enter a person's age?
    a. -4
    b. 350
    c. 999
    d. all of the above

9. Which of the following `while` clauses will stop the loop when the value in the `age` variable is less than the number 0?
    a. `while (age < 0)`
    b. `while age >= 0;`
    c. `while (age >= 0);`
    d. `while (age >= 0)`

Refer to Figure 10-27 to answer Questions 10 through 13.

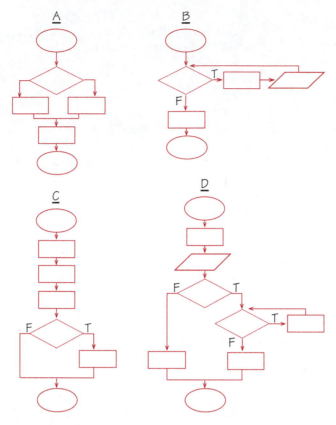

Figure 10-27

10. Which of the following control structures are used in Figure 10-27's flowchart A? (Select all that apply.)
    a. sequence
    b. selection
    c. repetition

11. Which of the following control structures are used in Figure 10-27's flowchart B? (Select all that apply.)
    a. sequence
    b. selection
    c. repetition

12. Which of the following control structures are used in Figure 10-27's flowchart C? (Select all that apply.)
    a. sequence
    b. selection
    c. repetition

13. Which of the following control structures are used in Figure 10-27's flowchart D? (Select all that apply.)
    a. sequence
    b. selection
    c. repetition

14. Values that are used to end loops are referred to as _____ values.
    a. end
    b. finish
    c. sentinel
    d. stop

15. Assume that a program allows the user to enter one or more numbers. The first input instruction will get the first number only and is referred to as the _____ read.

a. entering
b. initializer
c. priming
d. starter

E X E R C I S E S

1. Open the T10ConE01.cpp file contained in the Cpp\Tut10\T10ConE01 folder on your computer's hard disk. Complete the program by entering a `while` clause that stops the loop when the user enters a number that is less than 0. Save, build, and execute the program. Test the program by entering the following numbers: 4, 10, 0, and -3. When the program is working correctly, hide the Output window, then use the File menu to close the workspace.

2. Open the T10ConE02.cpp file contained in the Cpp\Tut10\T10ConE02 folder on your computer's hard disk. Complete the program by entering a `while` clause that stops the loop when the user enters either the letter N or the letter n. Save, build, and execute the program. Test the program by entering the following characters: a, 4, $, n. When the program is working correctly, hide the Output window, then use the File menu to close the workspace.

3. Open the T10ConE03.cpp file contained in the Cpp\Tut10\T10ConE03 folder on your computer's hard disk. Complete the program by entering a `while` clause that processes the loop as long as the user enters a number that is greater than 0. Save, build, and execute the program. Test the program by entering the following numbers: 8, 100, 0. When the program is working correctly, hide the Output window, then use the File menu to close the workspace.

4. Open the T10ConE04.cpp file contained in the Cpp\Tut10\T10ConE04 folder on your computer's hard disk. Complete the program by entering a `while` clause that processes the loop as long as the user enters either the letter Y or the letter y. Save, build, and execute the program. Test the program by entering the following three sets of data: y and 100, y and 200, n. (The total sales should be 300.) Execute the program again. When you are asked if you want to enter a sales amount, type N and press the Enter key. Notice that you were not asked to enter the sales amount. Why? When the program is working correctly, hide the Output window, then use the File menu to close the workspace.

5. In this exercise, you will create a program that displays the word "Hello" on the screen 10 times.
a. Create a console application. Name the project workspace T10ConE05, and save it in the Cpp\Tut10 folder on your computer's hard disk. Add a new C++ source file to the project. Name the source file T10ConE05.
b. Enter the appropriate C++ instructions into the source file.
c. Save, build, and execute the program. The word "Hello" (without the quotation marks) should appear on the screen 10 times.
d. When the program is working correctly, hide the Output window, then use the File menu to close the workspace.

6. In this exercise, you will create a program that uses a loop to display the numbers 20, 40, 60, 80, 100, 120, 140, 160, and 180 on the screen.
a. Create a console application. Name the project workspace T10ConE06, and save it in the Cpp\Tut10 folder on your computer's hard disk. Add a new C++ source file to the project. Name the source file T10ConE06.
b. Use the flowchart shown in Figure 10-28 to enter the appropriate C++ instructions into the source file.

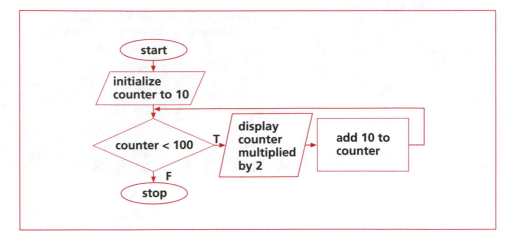

Figure 10-28

   c. Save, build, and execute the program. The numbers 20, 40, 60, 80, 100, 120, 140, 160, and 180 should appear on the screen.

   d. When the program is working correctly, hide the Output window, then use the File menu to close the workspace.

7. What will appear on the screen when the following code is processed, assuming the code is included in a valid C++ program? What is the value in the `temp` variable when the loop stops? Complete a desk-check table for this code.

```
int temp = 0;
while (temp < 5)
{
        cout << temp << endl;
        temp = temp + 1;
} //end while
```

8. What will appear on the screen when the following code is processed, assuming the code is included in a valid C++ program? What is the value in the `totEmp` variable when the loop stops? Complete a desk-check table for this code.

```
int totEmp = 0;
while (totEmp <= 5)
{
        cout << totEmp << endl;
        totEmp = totEmp + 2;
}//end while
```

9. Write an assignment statement that updates a counter variable named `numStudents` by 1.

10. Write an assignment statement that updates a counter variable named `quantity` by -5.

11. Write an assignment statement that updates an accumulator variable named `total` by the value in the `sales` variable.

12. Write an assignment statement that updates an accumulator variable named `total` by the value in the `gross` variable.

13. In this exercise, you will use a nested loop to display a pattern of asterisks.

   a. Create a console application. Name the project workspace T10ConE13, and save it in the Cpp\Tut10 folder on your computer's hard disk. Add a new C++ source file to the project. Name the source file T10ConE13.

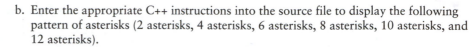

b. Enter the appropriate C++ instructions into the source file to display the following pattern of asterisks (2 asterisks, 4 asterisks, 6 asterisks, 8 asterisks, 10 asterisks, and 12 asterisks).

```
* *
* * * *
* * * * * *
* * * * * * * *
* * * * * * * * * *
* * * * * * * * * * * *
```

c. Save, build, and execute the program. When the program is working correctly, hide the Output window, then use the File menu to close the workspace.

14. In this exercise, you will use a nested loop to display a pattern of asterisks.

a. Create a console application. Name the project workspace T10ConE14, and save it in the Cpp\Tut10 folder on your computer's hard disk. Add a new C++ source file to the project. Name the source file T10ConE14.

b. Enter the appropriate C++ instructions into the source file to display the following pattern of asterisks (9 asterisks, 8 asterisks, 7 asterisks, 6 asterisks, 5 asterisks, 4 asterisks, 3 asterisks, 2 asterisks, and 1 asterisk).

```
* * * * * * * * *
* * * * * * * *
* * * * * * *
* * * * * *
* * * * *
* * * *
* * *
* *
*
```

c. Save, build, and execute the program. When the program is working correctly, hide the Output window, then use the File menu to close the workspace.

15. In this exercise, you will modify the program that you created in Exercise 13 so that it allows the user to specify the outer loop's ending value (which determines the largest number of asterisks to display) and its increment value (the number of asterisks to repeat).

a. Create a console application. Name the project workspace T10ConE15, and save it in the Cpp\Tut10 folder on your computer's hard disk. Add a new C++ source file to the project. Name the source file T10ConE15.

b. Use the File menu to open the T10ConE13.cpp file contained in the Cpp\Tut10\T10ConE13 folder on your computer's hard disk. Select all of the program's code, then copy the code to the clipboard. Close the T10ConE13.cpp window, then paste the code in the T10ConE15.cpp window.

c. Change the **T10ConE13.cpp** in the first comment to **T10ConE15.cpp**. Modify the T10ConE15.cpp program so that it allows the user to specify the outer loop's ending and increment values.

d. Save, build, and execute the program. Test the program by entering the number 4 as the maximum number of asterisks, and the number 1 as the increment value. The program should display the following pattern of asterisks (4 asterisks, 3 asterisks, 2 asterisks, and 1 asterisk).

```
* * * *
* * *
* *
*
```

e. Execute the program again. This time, enter the number 9 as the maximum number of asterisks, and the number 3 as the increment value. The program should display the following pattern of asterisks (3 asterisks, 6 asterisks, and 9 asterisks).

```
* * *
* * * * * *
* * * * * * * * *
```

f. When the program is working correctly, hide the Output window, then use the File menu to close the workspace.

16. In this exercise, you will modify the program that you created in Exercise 14 so that it allows the user to display the asterisks using either of the following two patterns:

Pattern 1 (9 asterisks, 8 asterisks, 7 asterisks, 6 asterisks, 5 asterisks, 4 asterisks, 3 asterisks, 2 asterisks, and 1 asterisk):

```
* * * * * * * * *
* * * * * * * *
* * * * * * *
* * * * * *
* * * * *
* * * *
* * *
* *
*
```

Pattern 2 (1 asterisk, 2 asterisks, 3 asterisks, 4 asterisks, 5 asterisks, 6 asterisks, 7 asterisks, 8 asterisks, and 9 asterisks).

```
*
* *
* * *
* * * *
* * * * *
* * * * * *
* * * * * * *
* * * * * * * *
* * * * * * * * *
```

a. Create a console application. Name the project workspace T10ConE16, and save it in the Cpp\Tut10 folder on your computer's hard disk. Add a new C++ source file to the project. Name the source file T10ConE16.

b. Use the File menu to open the T10ConE14.cpp file contained in the Cpp\Tut10\T10ConE14 folder on your computer's hard disk. Select all of the program's code, then copy the code to the clipboard. Close the T10ConE14.cpp window, then paste the code in the T10ConE16.cpp window.

c. Change the `T10ConE14.cpp` in the first comment to `T10ConE16.cpp`. Modify the T10ConE16.cpp program appropriately.

d. Save, build, and execute the program. Display the asterisks using pattern 1. Execute the program again. This time, display the asterisks using pattern 2.

e. When the program is working correctly, hide the Output window, then use the File menu to close the workspace.

Exercises 17 and 18 are Discovery Exercises. Discovery Exercises, which may include topics that are not covered in this lesson, allow you to "discover" the solutions to problems on your own.

17. In this exercise, you will learn two ways to stop a program that is in an endless (infinite) loop.

   a. Open the T10ConE17.cpp file contained in the Cpp\Tut10\T10ConE17 folder on your computer's hard disk.

   b. Build and execute the program. Notice that the program results in an endless (infinite) loop. (You can tell that the program is in an endless loop because it displays the number 0 over and over again in the DOS window.)

   c. On most systems, you can stop a program that is in an endless loop by pressing Ctrl + c (press and hold down the Ctrl key as you press the letter c). Use the Ctrl + c key combination to stop the program. The DOS window closes.

   d. Execute the program again. You also can use the DOS window's Close button to stop a program that is in an endless loop. Click the DOS window's Close button. A dialog box containing the message "Do you wish to terminate this program now and lose any unsaved information in the program?" appears on the screen. Click the Yes button in the dialog box. The DOS window closes.

   e. Hide the Output window, then use the File menu to close the workspace.

18. In this exercise, you will modify the program that you created in Exercise 13 so that it allows the user to process the program's code as many times as desired.

   a. Create a console application. Name the project workspace T10ConE18, and save it in the Cpp\Tut10 folder on your computer's hard disk. Add a new C++ source file to the project. Name the source file T10ConE18.

   b. Use the File menu to open the T10ConE13.cpp file contained in the Cpp\Tut10\T10ConE13 folder on your computer's hard disk. Select all of the program's code, then copy the code to the clipboard. Close the T10ConE13.cpp window, then paste the code in the T10ConE18.cpp window.

   c. Change the `T10ConE13.cpp` in the first comment to `T10ConE18.cpp`. Modify the T10ConE18.cpp program so that it allows the user to process the program's code as many times as desired.

   d. Save, build, and execute the program. Test the program appropriately.

   e. When the program is working correctly, hide the Output window, then use the File menu to close the workspace.

A computer program is good only if it works. Errors in either an algorithm or programming code can cause the program to run incorrectly. Therefore, a programmer needs to know how to locate and fix these errors. Exercises 19 and 20 are Debugging Exercises. Debugging Exercises allow you to practice recognizing and solving errors in a program.

debugging

19. When included in a valid C++ program, the following code should display the numbers 1, 2, 3, and 4. However, the code is not working properly. Correct the code.

```cpp
int num = 1;
while (num < 5)
{
        cout << num << endl;
} //end while
```

debugging

20. When included in a valid C++ program, the following code should print the commission (sales * .1) for each sales amount that is entered. However, the code is not working properly. Correct the code.

```cpp
float sales = 0.0;
cout << "Enter a sales amount: ";
cin >> sales;
while (sales > 0)
{
        cout << "Commission: " << sales * .1 << endl;
}//end while
```

Application Lesson

Using the Repetition Structure in a C++ Program

case ▶ Next Monday is career day at your alma mater. Professor Krelina, one of your computer programming instructors, has asked you to be a guest speaker in her Introduction to Programming class. You gladly accept this speaking engagement and begin planning your presentation. You decide to show the students how to create a program that will calculate their grade in Professor Krelina's class.

Analyzing, Planning, and Desk-Checking the Grade Problem

Professor Krelina assigns four projects and two tests to the students in her Introduction to Programming class. Each project is worth 50 points, and each test is worth 100 points. Figure 10-29 shows the grading scale that Professor Krelina uses to assign a grade to each student in her class.

Total points earned	Grade
360 – 400	A
320 – 359	B
280 – 319	C
240 – 279	D
below 240	F

Figure 10-29: Professor Krelina's grading scale

In addition to the `main` function, you will use two program-defined value-returning functions named `getPointsEarned` and `assignGrade` in the grade problem's solution. The `getPointsEarned` function's task will be to both get and accumulate the student's project and test scores, and then return the accumulated total to the `main` function. The `assignGrade` function's task will be to assign the appropriate grade based on the total points earned, and then return the grade to the `main` function. Figure 10-30 shows the IPO charts for one possible solution to the grade problem.

main function

Input	Processing	Output
total points earned grade	Processing items: none Algorithm: 1. total points earned = getPointsEarned() 2. grade = assignGrade(total points earned) 3. display the grade	grade

getPointsEarned function

Input	Processing	Output

project or test score	Processing items: none
	
	Algorithm:
	1. enter the first project or test score
	2. repeat while (the project or test score
	    is greater than or equal to 0)
	        add the project or test score to the total
	        points earned
	
	        enter the next project or test score
	    end repeat while
	3. return the total points earned
		total points earned

assignGrade function

Input	Processing	Output

total points earned	Processing items: none
	
	Algorithm:
	1. if (the total points earned >= 360)
	    assign A to grade
	  else if (the total points earned >= 320)
	    assign B to grade
	  else if (the total points earned >= 280)
	    assign C to grade
	  else if (the total points earned >= 240)
	    assign D to grade
	  else assign F to grade
	2. return grade
		grade

Figure 10-30: IPO charts for one possible solution to the grade problem

Notice that the main function's output is the student's grade. To display the grade, the main function will need to know the total number of points the student earned and his or her grade. As the main function's algorithm indicates, the main function will get the total number of points earned by calling the getPointsEarned function, and then assigning the function's return value to a memory location. The main function will get the grade by calling the assignGrade function, passing it the total number of points the student earned. The main function will store the grade returned by the assignGrade function in a memory location. After getting the grade, the main function then will display the grade on the screen.

Next, study the getPointsEarned function's IPO chart. The function's output is the total number of points earned by the student, and its input is the student's score on each project or test. Step 1 in the algorithm is to get the first project or test score from the user. Step 2 is a pretest loop that repeats its instructions as long as (or while) the user enters a score that is greater than or equal to zero. Notice that the instructions within the loop add the score entered by the user to the total points earned (an accumulator) and then get another score from the user. The loop will stop when the user enters the sentinel value. In this case, the sentinel value is any number that is less than zero.

Finally, study the assignGrade function's IPO chart. The function's output is the grade and its input, which it receives from the main function, is the total number of points earned by the student. As its algorithm indicates, the assignGrade function uses a selection structure to assign the appropriate grade, which is based on the total number of points earned.

Recall that you should desk-check an algorithm several times before you begin coding it. In this case, you will use the following scores to desk-check the algorithms shown in Figure 10-30:

Data for first desk-check		Data for second desk-check	
Project 1:	45	Project 1:	35
Project 2:	40	Project 2:	35
Project 3:	45	Project 3:	40
Project 4:	41	Project 4:	43
Test 1:	96	Test 1:	75
Test 2:	89	Test 2:	69
Sentinel:	-1	Sentinel:	-3

Figure 10-31 shows the completed desk-check tables.

main function

total points earned	grade
~~356~~	~~B~~
297	C

getPointsEarned function

project or test score	total points earned
~~45~~	~~45~~
~~40~~	~~85~~
~~45~~	~~130~~
~~41~~	~~171~~
~~96~~	~~267~~
~~89~~	~~356~~
~~-1~~	~~35~~
~~35~~	~~70~~
~~35~~	~~110~~
~~40~~	~~153~~
~~43~~	~~228~~
~~75~~	297
~~69~~	
-3	

Figure 10-31: Completed desk-check tables for the grade problem algorithms shown in Figure 10-30

assignGrade function

total points earned	grade
~~356~~	~~B~~
297	C

Figure 10-31: Completed desk-check tables for the grade problem algorithms shown in Figure 10-30 (continued)

After desk-checking an algorithm to verify its accuracy, you are ready to translate it into a language the computer can understand. Begin by coding the program's main function.

Coding the `main` Function

According to its IPO chart, the main function will require two memory locations to store the values of its input and output items. You will store the values in variables, because the values probably will be different each time the program is executed. You will use the int data type for the variable that stores the total points earned, and the char data type for the variable that stores the grade. Figure 10-32 shows the C++ code corresponding to the main function.

IPO chart information	C++ instructions
Input total points earned grade **Processing** none **Output** grade	`int totalEarned = 0;` `char grade = ' ';`

Algorithm
 1. total points earned = getPointsEarned()
 2. grade = assignGrade(total points earned)
 3. display the grade
	`totalEarned = getPointsEarned();`
	 `grade = assignGrade(totalEarned);`
	 `cout << "Grade: " << grade << endl;`

Figure 10-32: C++ statements for the main function

Next, you will code the getPointsEarned function.

Coding the `getPointsEarned` Function

As its IPO chart indicates, the getPointsEarned function requires two memory locations to store the values of its input and output items. You will use int variables for both items, because the values of both items will be integers and will vary as the program is running. The total points earned variable will be an accumulator, because it will need to accumulate, or add together, the project and test scores entered by the user.

The first step in the getPointsEarned function's algorithm is the priming read, which gets either a project or test score from the user. You can use the cout stream and the `<<` operator to prompt the user to enter the score, and then use the `cin` stream and `>>` operator to allow the user to enter the score, as shown in Figure 10-33.

IPO chart information	C++ instructions
Input project or test score	`int score = 0;`
Processing none	
Output total points earned	`int total = 0;`
Algorithm 1. enter the first project or test score	`cout << "Enter the first score: ";` `cin >> score;`
2. repeat while (the project or test score is greater than or equal to 0) add the project or test score to the total points earned	
priming read enter the next project or test score end repeat while 3. return the total points earned	

Figure 10-33: C++ instructions showing the priming read in the `getPointsEarned` function

Step 2 in the `getPointsEarned` function's algorithm is a pretest loop that processes its instructions each time the user enters a score that is greater than or equal to zero, and ends when the user enters the sentinel value, which is any score that is less than 0. The appropriate clause to begin the loop is `while (score >= 0)`.

The first instruction inside the loop updates the total points earned accumulator by adding to the accumulator the score entered by the user. You can use the C++ statement `total = total + score;` to perform this task.

The second instruction in the loop gets the next score from the user. You can use the `cout` stream and the `<<` operator to prompt the user to enter the score, and then use the `cin` stream and `>>` operator to allow the user to enter the score.

Step 3 in the `getPointsEarned` function's algorithm is to return the total number of points earned to the `main` function. Figure 10-34 shows the C++ instructions for the `getPointsEarned` function.

IPO chart information	C++ instructions
Input project or test score	`int score = 0;`
Processing none	
Output total points earned	`int total = 0;`
Algorithm 1. enter the first project or test score	`cout << "Enter the first score: ";` `cin >> score;`

Figure 10-34: C++ instructions for the `getPointsEarned` function

IPO chart information	C++ instructions

2. repeat while (the project or test score is greater than or equal to 0)
    add the project or test score to the total points earned
 	
    enter the next project or test score
end repeat while
3. return the total points earned
	```while (score >= 0)```
	```{```
	``` total = total + score;```
	
	``` cout << "Enter the next score: ";```
	``` cin >> score;```
	```} //end while```
	```return total;```

Figure 10-34: C++ instructions for the `getPointsEarned` function (continued)

Next, you will code the `assignGrade` function.

Coding the `assignGrade` Function

As its IPO chart indicates, the `assignGrade` function requires two memory locations to store the values of its input and output items. The value of the input item—total points earned—will be passed to the `assignGrade` function when the function is called; you will use the formal parameter `points` to receive this information. Within the `assignGrade` function, you will declare and initialize a variable to store the output item—grade. You will name the variable `letterGrade` and declare it as a `char` variable.

According to its algorithm, the `assignGrade` function will use a selection structure to assign the appropriate grade, based on the total number of points earned by the student. The function then will return the grade to the `main` function. Figure 10-35 shows the C++ instructions for the `assignGrade` function.

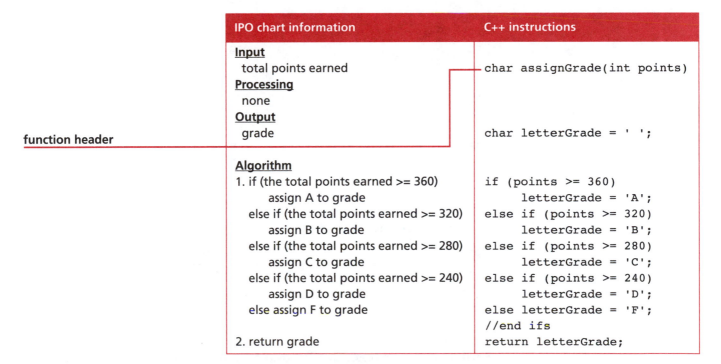

IPO chart information	C++ instructions

Input
  total points earned
Processing
  none
Output
  grade
	```char assignGrade(int points)```
	
	```char letterGrade = ' ';```

Algorithm
1. if (the total points earned >= 360)
    assign A to grade
  else if (the total points earned >= 320)
    assign B to grade
  else if (the total points earned >= 280)
    assign C to grade
  else if (the total points earned >= 240)
    assign D to grade
  else assign F to grade
 	
2. return grade
	```if (points >= 360)```
	``` letterGrade = 'A';```
	```else if (points >= 320)```
	``` letterGrade = 'B';```
	```else if (points >= 280)```
	``` letterGrade = 'C';```
	```else if (points >= 240)```
	``` letterGrade = 'D';```
	```else letterGrade = 'F';```
	```//end ifs```
	```return letterGrade;```

function header

Figure 10-35: C++ instructions for the `assignGrade` function

Now that you have finished coding the algorithms, you need to desk-check the program, using the same data you used to desk-check the algorithms. Figure 10-36 shows the data and the completed desk-check table for the program.

Data for first desk-check	Data for second desk-check
Project 1: 45	Project 1: 35
Project 2: 40	Project 2: 35
Project 3: 45	Project 3: 40
Project 4: 41	Project 4: 43
Test 1: 96	Test 1: 75
Test 2: 89	Test 2: 69
Sentinel: -1	Sentinel: -3

Desk-check tables

`main` function's variables

totalEarned	grade
~~0~~	~~–~~
~~356~~	~~B~~
~~0~~	~~–~~
297	C

`getPointsEarned` function's variables

score	total
~~0~~	~~0~~
~~45~~	~~45~~
~~40~~	~~85~~
~~45~~	~~130~~
~~41~~	~~171~~
~~96~~	~~267~~
~~89~~	~~356~~
~~-1~~	~~0~~
~~0~~	~~35~~
~~35~~	~~70~~
~~35~~	~~110~~
~~40~~	~~153~~
~~43~~	~~228~~
~~75~~	297
~~69~~	
-3	

`assignGrade` function's variables

points	letterGrade
~~356~~	~~–~~
297	~~B~~
	~~–~~
	C

Figure 10-36: Data and completed desk-check table for the program

The results obtained when desk-checking the program agree with the results obtained when desk-checking the algorithm. You now are ready to enter the C++ instructions into the computer.

Completing the Grade Program

Your computer's hard disk contains a partially completed C++ program containing most of the instructions for the grade program. Open that program now.

To open the partially completed C++ program, then complete the program and test it:

1 Start Visual C++. Open the T10App.cpp file contained in the Cpp\Tut10\ T10App folder on your computer's hard disk.

   Missing from the program is the code for the `getPointsEarned` function.

2 Position the insertion point in the blank line below the `//*****program-defined functions*****` comment, then enter the instructions shaded in Figure 10-37.

```cpp
//T10App.cpp - displays a student's grade

#include <iostream>
using namespace std;

//function prototypes
int getPointsEarned();
char assignGrade(int);

int main()
{
    //declare variables
    int totalEarned = 0;
    char grade = ' ';

    //get total points earned
    totalEarned = getPointsEarned();
    //assign grade
    grade = assignGrade(totalEarned);
    //display grade
    cout << "Grade: " << grade << endl;

    return 0;
}    //end of main function
```

Figure 10-37: Program showing the code for the `getPointsEarned` function

enter the function's code

```
//*****program-defined functions*****
int getPointsEarned()
{
     //gets and accumulates the scores, then returns the total
     int score = 0;
     int total = 0;

     cout << "Enter the first score: ";
     cin >> score;
     while (score >= 0)
     {
          total = total + score;
          cout << "Enter the next score: ";
          cin >> score;
     }//end while
     return total;
}    //end of getPointsEarned function

char assignGrade(int points)
{
     //assigns the letter grade
     char letterGrade = ' ';

     if (points >= 360)
          letterGrade = 'A';
     else if (points >= 320)
          letterGrade = 'B';
     else if (points >= 280)
          letterGrade = 'C';
     else if (points >= 240)
          letterGrade = 'D';
     else letterGrade = 'F';
     //end ifs
     return letterGrade;
}    //end of assignGrade function
```

Figure 10-37: Program showing the code for the `getPointsEarned` function (continued)

3 Save, build, and execute the program.

4 When prompted for the first score, type **45** and press the **Enter** key. Then enter the following scores, one at a time: **40, 45, 41, 96, 89, -1**. The program displays a grade of B, as shown in Figure 10-38.

Figure 10-38: DOS window showing results of first test

The B grade displayed by the program agrees with the desk-check tables.

5 Press the **Enter** key to close the DOS window, then execute the program again. When prompted for the first score, type **35** and press the **Enter** key. Then enter the following scores, one at a time: **35, 40, 43, 75, 69, -3.** The program displays a grade of C, which agrees with the desk-check tables.

6 Press the **Enter** key to close the DOS window. Hide the Output window, then use the File menu to close the workspace. When prompted to close all document windows, click the **Yes** button, then exit Visual C++.

You now have completed Tutorial 10's Application lesson. You can either take a break or complete the end-of-lesson exercises.

EXERCISES

1. In this exercise, you will modify the program that you created in this lesson so that it allows the user to display the grade for any number of students.
   a. Open the T10AppE01.cpp file contained in the Cpp\Tut10\T10AppE01 folder on your computer's hard disk.
   b. Modify the program appropriately. (*Hint*: You will need to add another loop to the program. Be sure to use an appropriate sentinel value.)
   c. Save, build, and execute the program. Use the test data from the lesson to test the program.
   d. When the program is working correctly, hide the Output window, then use the File menu to close the workspace.

2. In this exercise, you will create a program that displays the sum of the monthly sales amounts made in four regions: North, South, East, and West.
   a. Write one or more IPO charts for the problem. Use a `while` loop to allow the user to enter each of the four sales amounts, one at a time.
   b. Create a console application. Name the project workspace T10AppE02, and save it in the Cpp\Tut10 folder on your computer's hard disk. Add a new C++ source file to the project. Name the source file T10AppE02.
   c. Use the IPO chart(s) you completed in Step a to code the program.
   d. Complete a desk-check table for the program, using 2000, 3000, 2500, and 1500 as the first set of data, and 39000, 45000, 25000, and 56000 as the second set of data.
   e. Save, build, and execute the program. Use the first set of data from Step d to test the program. Execute the program again. Use the second set of data from Step d to test the program.
   f. When the program is working correctly, hide the Output window, then use the File menu to close the workspace.

3. In this exercise, you will modify the program you created in Exercise 2 so that it allows the user to enter the sales made in each of three months. In addition to displaying the total sales made during each month, the program also should display the total sales made during the three months.

   a. Create a console application. Name the project workspace T10AppE03, and save it in the Cpp\Tut10 folder on your computer's hard disk. Add a new C++ source file to the project. Name the source file T10AppE03.

   b. Use the File menu to open the T10AppE02.cpp file contained in the Cpp\Tut10\T10AppE02 folder on your computer's hard disk. Select all of the program's code, then copy the code to the clipboard. Close the T10AppE02.cpp window, then paste the code in the T10AppE03.cpp window.

   c. Change the `T10AppE02.cpp` in the first comment to `T10AppE03.cpp`. Modify the T10AppE03.cpp program so that it allows the user to enter three sets of sales amounts, then calculates and displays the total sales made during the three months.

   d. Save, build, and execute the program. Use the following three sets of data to test the program:
   2000, 2000, 3000, 4000
   4000, 5000, 2000, 1000
   3000, 5000, 1000, 6000

   e. When the program is working correctly, hide the Output window, then use the File menu to close the workspace.

4. In this exercise, you will create a program that displays an employee's name when the employee's ID is entered at the keyboard. The IDs and their corresponding names are as follows:

ID	Name
1234	Sue Nguyen
1345	Janice Blackfeather
3456	Allen Kraus
4567	Margie O'Donnell

   If the user enters an ID other than the ones listed above, the program should display the message "Incorrect ID – Please try again".

   a. Write one or more IPO charts for the problem. Use a `while` loop to allow the user to enter each ID, one at a time. (Be sure to use an appropriate sentinel value.)

   b. Create a console application. Name the project workspace T10AppE04, and save it in the Cpp\Tut10 folder on your computer's hard disk. Add a new C++ source file to the project. Name the source file T10AppE04.

   c. Use the IPO chart(s) you completed in Step a to code the program.

   d. Complete a desk-check table for the program, using 1345 as the first ID, 4567 as the second ID, and your sentinel value as the third ID.

   e. Save, build, and execute the program. Use the data from Step d to test the program.

   f. When the program is working correctly, hide the Output window, then use the File menu to close the workspace.

5. In this exercise, you will create a program that Software Workshop can use to both display and print registration information. Software Workshop offers programming seminars to companies. The price per person depends on the number of people a company registers. (For example, if a company registers four people, then the amount owed by that company is $400.) The following table shows the charges per registrant.

Number of registrants	Charge per person ($)
1–3	150
4–9	100
10 or more	90

   a. Write one or more IPO charts for the problem. Use a `while` loop to allow the user to enter the number of people registered for as many companies as desired. (Be sure to use an appropriate sentinel value.) The program should display the total number of people registered, the total charge, and the average charge per registrant. (For example, if one company registers four people and a second company registers two people, then the total number of people registered is six, the total charge is $700, and the average charge per registrant is $116.67.)

b. Create a console application. Name the project workspace T10AppE05, and save it in the Cpp\Tut10 folder on your computer's hard disk. Add a new C++ source file to the project. Name the source file T10AppE05.

c. Use the IPO chart(s) you completed in Step a to code the program. Display the average charge in fixed-point notation with two decimal places.

d. Complete a desk-check table for the program, using 3 as the number of people registered by the first company, 12 as the number of people registered by the second company, 9 as the number of people registered by the third company, and your sentinel value as the number of people registered by the fourth company.

e. Save, build, and execute the program. Use the data from Step d to test the program.

f. When the program is working correctly, hide the Output window, then use the File menu to close the workspace.

6. In this exercise, you will add a loop to an existing program. The program displays a ticket price based on a seat location entered by the user.

a. Open the T10AppE06.cpp file contained in the Cpp\Tut10\T10AppE06 folder on your computer's hard disk. The program prompts the user to enter a seat location, then displays the ticket price.

b. Modify the program so that it allows the user to enter as many seat locations as desired.

c. Save, build, and execute the program. Test the program using the following seat locations: L, b, p, a, and your sentinel value.

d. When the program is working correctly, hide the Output window, then use the File menu to close the workspace.

7. In this exercise, you will add a loop and counter to an existing program. The program displays the number of vacation weeks based on the number of years an employee has been with the company.

a. Open the T10AppE07.cpp file contained in the Cpp\Tut10\T10AppE07 folder on your computer's hard disk. The program prompts the user to enter the number of years an employee has been with the company, then displays the appropriate number of vacation weeks.

b. Modify the program so that it allows the user to enter the number of years for as many employees as desired. Also add the appropriate code to calculate and display the total number of employees entered.

c. Save, build, and execute the program. Test the program using the following years: 0, 4, 7, 20, and your sentinel value.

d. When the program is working correctly, hide the Output window, then use the File menu to close the workspace.

8. In this exercise, you will modify the program that you created in this lesson so that it uses two void functions.

a. Open the T10AppE08.cpp file contained in the Cpp\Tut10\T10AppE08 folder on your computer's hard disk.

b. Modify the program so that the `getPointsEarned` and `assignGrade` functions are void functions rather than value-returning functions.

c. Save, build, and execute the program. Use the test data from the lesson to test the program.

d. When the program is working correctly, hide the Output window, then use the File menu to close the workspace.

Exercise 9 is a Discovery Exercise. Discovery Exercises, which may include topics that are not covered in this lesson, allow you to "discover" the solutions to problems on your own.

9. In this exercise, you will learn about the C++ increment and decrement operators.

a. Open the T10AppE09.cpp file contained in the Cpp\Tut10\T10AppE09 folder on your computer's hard disk. The program gets the test scores for one or more students from the user. A student must earn at least 70 points to pass the test. If the test score is greater than or equal to 70, a counter variable named `totalPass` is incremented by 1. The program then displays the total number of students passing the test.

C++ provides a more convenient way of writing an assignment statement that increments and decrements a variable by a value of 1. Rather than using the `totalPass = totalPass + 1;` statement to update the `totalPass` variable by 1, you can use the `totalPass++;` statement. The ++ (two plus signs with no spaces between) after the variable name is called the increment operator. In this case, the increment operator tells C++ to add 1 to the `totalPass` variable and then store the result in the `totalPass` variable.

b. Change the `totalPass = totalPass + 1;` statement to `totalPass++;`.

c. Save, build, and execute the program. Test the program by entering the following scores: 78, 65, 43, 89, 100, and -1. The DOS window shows that three students passed the test. Press the Enter key to close the DOS window.

C++ also has a decrement operator, which is two minus signs (or hyphens) with no space between, like this: `--`. The decrement operator tells C++ to subtract 1 from a variable, and then store the result in the variable. The `totalPass--` statement, for example, tells C++ to subtract 1 from the `totalPass` variable, and then store the result in the `totalPass` variable.

d. Modify the code as follows:

- assign the number 5 (rather than the number 1) to the `counter` variable
- stop the `while` loop when the `counter` variable reaches 0
- use the decrement operator to subtract 1 from the `counter` variable—in other words, to update the variable by –1

e. Save, build, and execute the program. Enter the following five scores: 88, 85, 73, 89, and 54. The DOS window shows that four students passed the test. Press the Enter key to close the DOS window.

f. Hide the Output window, then use the File menu to close the workspace.

A computer program is good only if it works. Errors in either an algorithm or programming code can cause the program to run incorrectly. Therefore, a programmer needs to know how to locate and fix these errors. Exercises 10 and 11 are Debugging Exercises. Debugging Exercises allow you to practice recognizing and solving errors in a program.

debugging

10. In this exercise, you will debug a C++ program.

a. Open the T10AppE10.cpp file contained in the Cpp\Tut10\T10AppE10 folder on your computer's hard disk. This program should display the squares of the numbers from 1 through 5—in other words, it should display the numbers 1, 4, 9, 16, and 25.

b. Build and execute the program. Notice that the program results in an endless loop. Stop the program either by pressing Ctrl+c or by clicking the DOS window's Close button.

c. Correct the program's code. Save, build, and execute the program. When the program is working correctly, hide the Output window, then use the File menu to close the workspace.

debugging

11. In this exercise, you will debug a C++ program.

a. Open the T10AppE11.cpp file contained in the Cpp\Tut10\T10AppE11 folder on your computer's hard disk.

b. Build and execute the program. The program should display the number of positive integers entered by the user, and the number of negative integers entered by the user. The program should stop when the user enters the number 0. Test the program by entering the following integers: 4, 6, -4, 23, -9, and 0. Notice that the program is not working correctly.

c. Correct the program's code. Save, build, and execute the program. Use the data from Step b to test the program. When the program is working correctly, hide the Output window, then use the File menu to close the workspace.

Manipulating Characters and Strings

After completing this tutorial, you will be able to:

- Control the case of characters and strings
- Determine the number of characters contained in a string
- Compare a portion of a `string` variable's contents to another string
- Determine whether a string is contained within a `string` variable
- Replace a portion of a `string` variable's contents with another string
- Assign a portion of a `string` variable's contents to another `string` variable
- Duplicate a character within a `string` variable
- Concatenate strings
- Clear the contents of the DOS window

Concept Lesson

Character and String Manipulation

Many times, a program will need to manipulate (process) character or string data. For example, a program may need to verify that an inventory part number begins with a specific letter; or it may need to determine if the last three characters in a part number are valid. Most programming languages provide built-in functions that make character and string manipulation an easy task. In this tutorial, you will learn how to use many of these functions. Begin by learning how to use the functions that allow you to control the case of a character.

> **Important note:** Most of the functions discussed in this lesson have more than one syntax. However, because the purpose of this tutorial is simply to introduce you to character and string manipulation, you typically will be shown only one syntax for each function. If a function has more than one syntax, a Tip stating that fact will be shown in the margin next to the explanation of the function. For a more thorough discussion of each function, you should consult a C++ book.

Controlling the Case of a Character

As you learned in Tutorial 8, character comparisons involving letters of the alphabet are case-sensitive. In other words, the character 'K' is not the same as the character 'k' when both characters are processed by a computer, because both characters are stored in the computer's internal memory using different ASCII values. A problem occurs when you need to include a letter, entered by the user, in a comparison. The problem occurs because you cannot control the case in which the user enters the letter.

In Tutorial 8, you learned how to use logical operators—And (&&) and Or (||)—to solve the character comparison problem. For example, to determine if the `code` variable contains the character 'K' in either uppercase or lowercase, recall that you can use either the condition (`code == 'K' || code == 'k'`) or the condition (`code != 'K' && code != 'k'`) in an `if` or `while` statement.

Rather than using a logical operator when comparing characters that represent letters of the alphabet, you also can use a function that temporarily converts one or both of the letters to either uppercase or lowercase before the comparison is made. Figure 11-1 shows the built-in functions that allow you to control the case of a character in C++, Java, and Visual Basic.

Purpose	C++	Java	Visual Basic
Convert a letter to uppercase	`toupper`	`toUpperCase`	`UCase`
Convert a letter to lowercase	`tolower`	`toLowerCase`	`LCase`

Figure 11-1: Functions you can use to control the case of a character in C++, Java, and Visual Basic

Figure 11-2 shows the syntax of the C++ `toupper` and `tolower` functions, which are defined in the cctype library file. The figure also shows several examples of using the functions in a C++ statement.

Syntax
To convert a character to uppercase: **toupper(***charVariable***)**
To convert a character to lowercase: **tolower(***charVariable***)**

Examples	Results

Example 1
```char repeat = ' ';```
```cout << "Continue? (Y or N) ";```
```cin >> repeat;```
```while (toupper(repeat) == 'Y')```
```{```
    instructions to process when the loop condition is true
    ```cout << "Continue? (Y or N) ";```
    ```cin >> repeat;```
```}   //end while```
	gets a letter from the user, and then repeats the loop body instructions while the uppercase version of the letter is equal to the uppercase letter Y

Example 2
```char code1 = ' ';```
```char code2 = ' ';```
```cout << "Enter letter code 1: ";```
```cin >> code1;```
```cout << "Enter letter code 2: ";```
```cin >> code2;```
```if (tolower(code1) == tolower(code2))```
```{```
    instructions to process when the condition is true
```}   //end if```
	gets two letters from the user, and then determines if the lowercase version of both letters is equal

Example 3
```char letter = ' ';```
```cout << "Enter a letter: ";```
```cin >> letter;```
```letter = toupper(letter);```
```switch (letter)```
```{```
```case 'A':``` *one or more instructions*
      ```break;```
```case 'B':``` *one or more instructions*
      ```break;```
```default:``` *one or more instructions*
```} //end switch```
	gets a letter from the user, and then assigns the uppercase version of the letter to the `letter` variable before using the variable in a switch statement

Example 4
```char letter = ' ';```
```char lowerLetter = ' ';```
```cout << "Enter a letter: ";```
```cin >> letter;```
```lowerLetter = tolower(letter);```
```cout << lowerLetter << endl;```
	gets a letter from the user, and then assigns the lowercase version of the letter to the `lowerLetter` variable before displaying the contents of the variable on the screen

Figure 11-2: Syntax and examples of the C++ `toupper` and `tolower` functions

As Figure 11-2 shows, the `toupper` and `tolower` functions have one actual argument, *charVariable*. The *charVariable* argument is the name of a `char` variable, and is passed *by value* to both functions. The `toupper` function converts the value it receives to uppercase, and then returns the result. The `tolower` function, on the other hand, returns the result of converting the value it receives to lowercase. Neither function changes the value stored in the *charVariable* argument.

Study the examples shown in Figure 11-2. The code shown in Example 1 prompts the user to enter either Y or N, and then stores the user's response in a `char` variable named `repeat`. Although the user is prompted to enter his or her response using an uppercase letter, it is possible that the user will instead enter a lowercase letter. To solve this problem, the loop condition in the `while (toupper(repeat) == 'Y')` clause first uses the `toupper` function to convert the user's response to uppercase; it then compares the result of the conversion to the uppercase character 'Y'. The loop condition will evaluate to true if the user enters either the letter Y or the letter y, because the character 'Y' is the uppercase equivalent of both letters.

Notice that the condition in the `while` clause in Example 1 compares the uppercase equivalent of one character to the uppercase equivalent of another character. For the `toupper` function to work correctly when comparing characters, both characters included in the comparison must be uppercase. In other words, the clause `while (toupper(repeat) == 'y')` will not work correctly; the loop condition always will evaluate to false, because the uppercase version of a letter will never be equal to its lowercase counterpart.

The code shown in Example 2 in Figure 11-2 prompts the user to enter two letter codes, and it stores the user's responses in two `char` variables named `code1` and `code2`. The condition in the `if (tolower(code1) == tolower(code2))` clause uses the `tolower` function to convert both of the user's responses to lowercase; it then compares both results for equality. In other words, the condition checks to determine if the lowercase versions of the codes entered by the user are the same. The condition will evaluate to true if the user enters the same letter, in any case, for both codes. For example, the condition will evaluate to true if the user enters the letters A and a as code 1 and code 2, respectively; it also will evaluate to true if the user enters the letters C and C. The condition will evaluate to false, however, if the user enters the letters A and C.

Notice that the condition in the `if` clause in Example 2 compares the lowercase equivalent of one character to the lowercase equivalent of another character. For the `tolower` function to work correctly, both characters included in the comparison must be lowercase. In other words, the clause `if (tolower(code1) == toupper(code2))` will not work correctly; the condition always will evaluate to false, because the lowercase version of a letter will never be equal to its uppercase counterpart.

You also can use the `toupper` and `tolower` functions to assign the uppercase and lowercase versions of a character to a variable, as shown in Examples 3 and 4 in Figure 11-2. Example 3's code, for instance, converts the letter entered by the user to uppercase, and then assigns the result to the `letter` variable, which then is used as the *selectorExpression* in the `switch` statement. Notice that the *values* in the first two `case` clauses ('A' and 'B') are uppercase to match the case of the *selectorExpression*.

Example 4's code converts the letter entered by the user to lowercase, and then assigns the result to the `lowerLetter` variable before displaying the contents of the `lowerLetter` variable on the screen.

Next, you will learn how to control the case of a string.

Controlling the Case of a String

Like character comparisons, string comparisons are case-sensitive, which means that the string "Yes" is not the same as the string "YES" or the string "yes". Before using a string in a comparison, you can convert it to either uppercase or lowercase, and then use the converted string in the comparison. Figure 11-3 shows the built-in functions that allow you to control the case of a string in C++, Java, and Visual Basic.

Purpose	C++	Java	Visual Basic
Convert a string to uppercase	`transform`	`toUpperCase`	`UCase`
Convert a string to lowercase	`transform`	`toLowerCase`	`LCase`

Figure 11-3: Functions you can use to control the case of a string in C++, Java, and Visual Basic

Figure 11-4 shows the syntax of the C++ `transform` function and two examples of using the function in a C++ statement. The `transform` function is defined in the algorithm library file, so you will need to include the `#include algorithm` directive in any program that uses the `transform` function.

Syntax
To transform the entire contents of a `string` variable: **transform(**_string_.**begin()**, _string_.**end()**, _string_.**begin()**, _function_**)**
Examples and results

Example 1
```
string name = "";
cout << "Name (enter Done to end the program): ";
getline(cin, name);
transform(name.begin(), name.end(), name.begin(), tolower);
while (name != "done")
{
    instructions to process when the loop condition is true
    cout << "Name (enter Done to end the program): ";
    getline(cin, name);
}   //end while
```

Result
gets a string from the user, then converts the contents of the `name` variable to lowercase, and then repeats the loop body instructions while the `name` variable does not contain "done"

Figure 11-4: Syntax and examples of the C++ `transform` function

The `transform` function has more than one syntax.

Examples and results

Example 2
```
string item1 = "";
string item2 = "";
cout << "Enter item 1: ";
getline(cin, item1);
cout << "Enter item 2: ";
getline(cin, item2);
transform(item1.begin(), item1.end(), item1.begin(), toupper);
transform(item2.begin(), item2.end(), item2.begin(), toupper);
if (item1 == item2)
{
        instructions to process when the condition is true
}    //end if
```

Result
gets two strings from the user, then converts the contents of the item1 and
item2 variables to uppercase, and then determines if the contents of both
variables are equal

Figure 11-4: Syntax and examples of the C++ `transform` function (continued)

> The `transform` function
> also can be used to trans-
> form numeric data, but this
> topic is beyond the scope of
> this book.

string in the syntax of the C++ `transform` function is the name of a `string` variable that contains the string you want converted, or transformed, to either uppercase or lowercase. The first two arguments in the `transform` function specify the range of characters that are to be transformed in the *string*. To transform the entire contents of a `string` variable, you use *string*.**begin**() as the first argument, and you use *string*.**end**() as the second argument. *string*.**begin**() refers to the first character in the *string*, and *string*.**end**() refers to the location that is just past the end of the string in the computer's memory. For example, if a `string` variable named `state` contains the string "Iowa", then `state.begin()` refers to the letter I, and `state.end` refers to the memory location following the letter a, as illustrated in Figure 11-5.

Memory locations

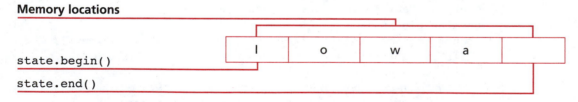

Figure 11-5: Illustration of `state.begin()` and `state.end()`

> Learn how to use the
> `transform` function to
> convert only a portion of
> a string to uppercase or
> lowercase by completing
> Discovery Exercise 9 at the
> end of this lesson.

The `transform` function converts (transforms) each of the characters contained in the range specified in the function's first two arguments—beginning with the character whose location is specified in the first argument [in this case, *string*.**begin**()] and continuing up to, but not including, the character whose location is specified in the second argument [in this case, *string*.**end**()]. The function stores the results of the conversion beginning in the location specified in the function's third argument,

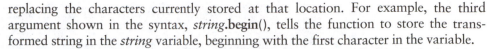

replacing the characters currently stored at that location. For example, the third argument shown in the syntax, *string*.**begin**(), tells the function to store the transformed string in the *string* variable, beginning with the first character in the variable.

The last argument in the **transform** function's syntax is the name of a function, and it indicates the task to be performed on the string contained in the *string* variable. To transform the string to uppercase, you use **toupper** as the *function* argument. To transform the string to lowercase, you use **tolower** as the *function* argument.

Study the examples shown in Figure 11-4. The code shown in Example 1 prompts the user to enter a name, indicating that the user should enter the string "Done" to end the program. The code stores the user's response in the **name** variable. As with **char** data, there is no way to control the case in which the user enters **string** data. In this case, for example, the user might enter "Done", "done", "DONE", or even "doNE". To solve this problem, the statement `transform(name.begin(), name.end(), name.begin(), tolower);` converts the contents of the **name** variable to lowercase. It makes this conversion by changing each character in the **name** variable to lowercase—beginning with `name.begin()` (the first character) and continuing up to, but not including, `name.end()`—and then storing the lowercase characters in the **name** variable, beginning with the first character [`name.begin()`] in the variable. Notice that the loop condition in Example 1 compares the lowercase string contained in the **name** variable to the lowercase string "done". The loop will end when the user enters the string "done", in any case, in response to the name prompt.

Example 2's code prompts the user to enter two items, storing the user's responses in the **item1** and **item2** variables. The code then uses the **transform** function to convert the contents of both variables to uppercase before using the variables in the **if** statement's condition. Notice that the condition compares the **item1** variable, whose contents are uppercase, to the **item2** variable, whose contents also are uppercase.

tip

▶ You do not need to enter any information between the parentheses at the end of the *string*.**begin**() and *string*.**end**() arguments.

tip

▶ Do not include a set of parentheses after the function name in the **transform** function's *function* argument. Doing so—for example, entering a *function* argument of **toupper()** rather than **toupper**—will produce a syntax error when the program is compiled.

mini-quiz

Mini-Quiz 1

1. Which of the following C++ **while** clauses processes the loop instructions as long as the value in a **char** variable named **letter** is either A or a?

   a. `while (upper(letter) = 'A')`

   b. `while (toupper(letter) = 'A')`

   c. `while (toupper(letter) == 'A')`

   d. `while (toupper(letter = 'A'))`

2. Write a C++ **if** clause that determines if the **code** variable contains either X or x. (The **code** variable is a **char** variable.) Use the **tolower** function in the **if** clause.

3. Write a C++ statement that converts the contents of a **char** variable named **answer** to uppercase.

4. Which of the following C++ statements converts the contents of a **string** variable named **emp** to uppercase?

   a. `transform(emp.begin(), emp.end(), emp.begin(), toupper);`

   b. `transform(emp.begin, emp.end, emp.end, toupper);`

   c. `transform(emp.begin, emp.end, emp.begin, upper);`

   d. `transform(emp.begin(), emp.end(), emp.begin(), toupper());`

Next, learn how to determine the number of characters contained in a string.

Determining the Number of Characters Contained in a String

In many programs, it is necessary to determine the number of characters contained in a string. For example, a program that prompts the user to enter a 10-digit phone number needs to verify that the user entered the required number of characters. In some programming languages, the number of characters contained in a string is referred to as the *size* of the string, while in others it is referred to as the *length* of the string. Figure 11-6 shows the built-in functions you use to determine the size (length) of a string in C++, Java, and Visual Basic.

Purpose	C++	Java	Visual Basic
Determine the size (length) of a string	size	length	Len

Figure 11-6: Functions used to determine the size (length) of a string in C++, Java, and Visual Basic

Figure 11-7 shows the syntax of the C++ `size` function, which is defined in the string library file, and two examples of using the function in a C++ statement.

Syntax
To determine the size of a string: *string*.**size( )**

Examples	Results

Example 1
`string name = "Paul Blackfeather";`
`cout << name.size() << endl;`
	displays the number 17 on the screen

Example 2
`string phone = "";`
`cout << "10-digit phone number: ";`
`getline(cin, phone);`
`while (phone.size() == 10)`
`{`
　　instructions to process when the loop condition is true
　　`cout << "10-digit phone number: ";`
　　`getline(cin, phone);`
`}   //end while`
	gets a string from the user, and then repeats the loop body instructions while the number of characters contained in the phone variable is equal to the number 10

Example 3
`string partNumber = "";`
`cout << "Part Number: ";`
`getline(cin, partNumber);`
`if (partNumber.size() >= 4)`
`{`
　　instructions to process when the condition is true
`}   //end if`
	gets a string from the user, and then determines if the partNumber variable contains at least four characters

Figure 11-7: Syntax and examples of the C++ `size` function

In the `size` function's syntax, *string* is the name of a `string` variable whose size, or length, you want to determine. The `size` function returns the number of characters contained in the `string` variable.

The code shown in Example 1 in Figure 11-7 assigns the string "Paul Blackfeather" to a `string` variable named `name`. It then uses the `size` function to display the number of characters contained in the `name` variable; the number 17 will appear on the screen.

The code shown in Example 2 prompts the user to enter a 10-digit phone number, and stores the user's response in a `string` variable named `phone`. The `while (phone.size() == 10)` clause uses the `size` function to return the number of characters contained in the `phone` variable, comparing the function's return value to the number 10.

Example 3's code prompts the user to enter a part number, and stores the user's response in a `string` variable named `partNumber`. The `if (partNumber.size() >= 4)` clause then determines if the `partNumber` variable contains at least four characters.

Next, you will learn how to compare a portion of a `string` variable's contents to another string.

Comparing a Portion of a `string` Variable's Contents to Another String

As you already know, you can use the comparison operators (>, >=, <, <=, ==, and !=) to compare two strings. For example, the condition in the `while (name != "done")` clause uses the inequality comparison operator (!=) to compare the contents of the `name` variable to the string "done". In some programs, rather than comparing two entire strings, you may need to compare a portion of one string to another string. For example, you may need to compare the last two characters in the `employNum` variable to the string "12" to determine if the employee works in the Accounting department, which has a department code of 12. Figure 11-8 shows the built-in functions you can use to compare a portion of a `string` variable's contents to another string in C++, Java, and Visual Basic.

Purpose	C++	Java	Visual Basic
Compare a portion of a `string` variable's contents to another string	compare	regionMatches	Mid (in combination with a comparison operator)

Figure 11-8: Functions used to compare a portion of a `string` variable's contents to another string in C++, Java, and Visual Basic

Figure 11-9 shows the syntax of the C++ `compare` function, which is defined in the string library file, and five examples of using the function in a C++ statement.

Syntax
To compare a portion of a `string` variable's contents to another string: *string1*.**compare**(*startCompare, numberOfCharsToCompare, string2*)

Examples	Results

Example 1
 `int x = 0;`
 `string employNum = "24012";`
 `x = employNum.compare(0, 2, "24");`
	`compare` function assigns 0 to `x`, because the first two characters in the `employNum` variable are equal to the string "24"

Example 2
 `int x = 0;`
 `string empNum = "24012";`
 `x = employNum.compare(3, 2, "12");`
	`compare` function assigns 0 to `x`, because the two characters in the `employNum` variable, beginning with the character in position 3 (the number 1), are equal to the string "12"

Example 3
 `int x = 0;`
 `string name = "Smith, Janet";`
 `x = name.compare(0, 5, "Jones");`
	`compare` function assigns 1 to `x`, because the first character in the `name` variable (S) comes after the first character in the string "Jones" (J) in the ASCII coding scheme

Example 4
 `int x = 0;`
 `string name = "Smith, Janet";`
 `x = name.compare(0, 5, "Smyth");`
	`compare` function assigns -1 to `x`, because the character in position 2 in the `name` variable (i) comes before the character in position 2 in the string "Smyth" (y) in the ASCII coding scheme

Example 5
 `int x = 0;`
 `string item1 = "33442AB";`
 `string item2 = "2AB";`
 `x = item1.compare(4, 3, item2);`
	`compare` function assigns 0 to `x`, because the three characters in the `item1` variable, beginning with the character in position 4 (the number 2), are equal to the string stored in the `item2` variable

Figure 11-9: Syntax and examples of the C++ `compare` function

The C++ `compare` function is case-sensitive.

The `compare` function has more than one syntax.

In the `compare` function's syntax, *string1* and *string2* are the two strings you want to compare. *string1* is the name of a `string` variable, and *string2* can be a string literal constant or the name of a `string` variable.

The `compare` function's *startCompare* and *numberOfCharsToCompare* arguments can be numeric literal constants or the names of numeric variables. *startCompare* specifies where in *string1*—in other words, with which character in *string1*—the comparison should begin. The first character in a string is in position 0, the second character is in position 1, and so on. The *numberOfCharsToCompare* argument indicates the number of characters in *string1* to compare to the characters in *string2*.

The `compare` function compares *string2* to the *numberOfCharsToCompare* in *string1*, starting in position *startCompare* in *string1*. The function returns the number 0 if *string2*'s characters are equal to the specified characters in *string1*. If *string2*'s characters are not equal to the specified characters in *string1*, the function returns either the number -1 or the number 1, depending on the ASCII values of the first characters that are different in each string. For example, assume *string1* is "bill" and *string2* is "belt". The first characters in both strings are the same—*b*.

The ASCII codes are shown in Appendix A.

The second characters, however, are different: *string1*'s second character is the letter *i* (which has an ASCII value of 105) and *string2*'s second character is the letter *e* (which has an ASCII value of 101). Because *string1*'s character comes after (is greater than) *string2*'s character in the ASCII coding scheme, the `compare` function returns the number 1. However, if the situation is reversed—in other words, if *string1* is "belt" and *string2* is "bill"—the `compare` function returns -1 to indicate that *string1*'s character (*e*) comes before (is less than) *string2*'s character (*i*).

Study each of the examples shown in Figure 11-9. The `compare` function shown in Example 1 compares the string "24" (*string2*) to two characters in the `employNum` variable (*string1*), beginning with the first character in the `employNum` variable. The function returns the number 0, because the first two characters contained in the `employNum` variable (24) are equal to the string "24". The code assigns the function's return value to an `int` variable named `x`.

The `compare` function shown in Example 2 compares the string "12" (*string2*) to two characters in the `employNum` variable (*string1*), beginning with the character located in position 3 in the `employNum` variable. The character located in position 3 in the `employNum` variable is the number 1, which is actually the fourth character in the variable. (Recall that the first character in a string is in position 0.) Therefore, the two characters that will be compared in the `employNum` are the characters 1 and 2. The function returns the number 0, because the two characters contained in the `employNum` variable, beginning with the character in position 3, are equal to the two characters in the string "12". The code assigns the function's return value to an `int` variable named `x`.

The `compare` function shown in Example 3 compares the string "Jones" (*string2*) to the first five characters in the `name` variable (*string1*). Notice that the first character in each string is different: it is S in *string1* and J in *string2*. In this case, the function returns the number 1, because the first character in *string1* (S) comes after the first character in *string2* (J) in the ASCII coding scheme. The code assigns the function's return value to an `int` variable named `x`.

The `compare` function shown in Example 4 compares the string "Smyth" (*string2*) to the first five characters in the `name` variable (*string1*). Notice that both strings are equal up to the third character: the third character in *string1* is i, and the third character in *string2* is y. In this case, the function returns the number -1, because the third character in *string1* (i) comes before the third character in *string2* (y) in the ASCII coding scheme. The code assigns the function's return value to an `int` variable named `x`.

The `compare` function shown in Example 5 in Figure 11-9 compares the contents of the `item2` variable (*string2*) to three characters in the `item1` variable (*string1*), beginning with the character in position 4 in the `item1` variable. The three characters that will be compared in the `item1` variable are 2AB. In this example, the function returns the number 0, because the three characters contained in the `item1` variable, beginning with the character in position 4, are equal to the contents of the `item2` variable (2AB). The code assigns the function's return value to an `int` variable named x.

Next, you will learn how to determine whether a string is contained within a `string` variable.

Determining Whether a String is Contained Within a `string` Variable

In some programs, you may need to determine whether a specific string is contained within a `string` variable. For example, you may need to determine if the name of a certain street appears within a string variable containing a street address. Figure 11-10 shows the built-in functions you can use to determine whether a string is contained within a string variable in C++, Java, and Visual Basic.

Purpose	C++	Java	Visual Basic
Determine whether a string is contained within a string variable	find	indexOf	Instr

Figure 11-10: Functions used to determine whether a string is contained within a string variable in C++, Java, and Visual Basic

Figure 11-11 shows the syntax of the C++ **find** function, which is defined in the string library file, and two examples of using the function in a C++ statement.

Syntax
To determine whether a string is contained within a string variable: *string*.**find**(*subString*, *startFind*)

Examples and results

Example 1
```
string zip = "60611";
cout << zip.find("61", 0) << endl;
```

Result
searches the zip variable, beginning with the first character (which is in position 0), to determine if the variable contains the string "61", then displays the result (2) on the screen

Example 2
```
string address = "";
int location = 0;
cout << "Enter the address: ";
getline(cin, address);
transform(address.begin(), address.end(), address.begin(), toupper);
location = address.find("MAIN", 0);
if (location >= 0)
      instructions to process when the condition is true
//end if
```

Result
gets a string from the user, then converts the string to uppercase, then searches the address variable, beginning with the first character (which is in position 0), to determine if the variable contains the string "MAIN", then assigns the result to the location variable, and then determines if the location variable contains a value that is greater than or equal to 0

Figure 11-11: Syntax and examples of the C++ find function

Examples and results

Example 3

```
string part = "";
int location = 0;
cout << "Part Number: ";
getline(cin, part);
transform(part.begin(), part.end(), part.begin(), tolower);
location = part.find("x", 3);
if (location >= 0)
      instructions to process when the condition is true
//end if
```

Result

gets a string from the user, then converts the string to lowercase, then searches the `part` variable, beginning with the fourth character (which is in position 3), to determine if the variable contains the string "x", then assigns the result to the `location` variable, and then determines if the `location` variable contains a value that is greater than or equal to 0

Figure 11-11: Syntax and examples of the C++ `find` function (continued)

▶ The `find` **function is case-sensitive.**

▶ The `find` **function has more than one syntax.**

In the `find` function's syntax, *string* is the name of a `string` variable whose contents you want to search, and *subString* is the string for which you are searching. *subString* can be a string literal constant or it can be the name of a `string` variable that contains the string you want to find. *startFind*, which can be either a numeric literal constant or the name of a numeric variable, specifies the starting position for the search—in other words, the character at which the search should begin. As you learned earlier, the first character in a string is in position 0, the second character is in position 1, and so on.

The `find` function searches for the *subString* in the *string*, starting with the character in position *startFind* in the *string*. If the *subString* is contained within the *string*, then the `find` function returns a number that indicates the beginning position of the *subString* within the *string*. The function returns the number -1 if the *subString* is not contained within the *string*.

Study the examples shown in Figure 11-11. The `cout << zip.find("61", 0) << endl;` statement shown in Example 1 searches for the *subString* "61" in the `zip` variable, beginning with the first character (which is in position 0) in the variable. It then displays the result—in this case, the number 2—on the screen. The number 2 is displayed because the *subString* "61" begins in character position 2 in the `zip` variable.

The code shown in Example 2 prompts the user to enter an address, and stores the user's response in a `string` variable named `address`. The `transform` function converts the contents of the `address` variable to uppercase. The statement `location = address.find("MAIN", 0);` searches for the *subString* "MAIN" in the `address` variable, beginning with the first character in the `address` variable. The statement assigns the number returned by the `find` function to an `int` variable named `location`. For example, if the `address` variable contains the address "123 MAIN STREET", the `find` function stores the number 4 in the `location` variable, because the *subString* "MAIN" begins in character position 4 in the `address` variable. However, if the `address` variable contains the address "12 HAMPTON AVENUE", the `find` function stores the number -1 in the `location` variable, because the *subString* "MAIN" is not contained within the `address` variable.

The if (location >= 0) clause uses the value stored in the location variable to determine whether the *subString* was located within the *string*. If the *subString* was found, the location variable's value will be greater than or equal to 0; otherwise, the value will be -1.

The code shown in Example 3 in Figure 11-11 prompts the user to enter a part number, storing the user's response in a string variable named part. The transform function converts the contents of the part variable to lowercase. The statement location = part.find("x", 3); searches for the *subString* "x" in the part variable, beginning with the character in position 3 (the fourth character) in the variable. The statement assigns the number returned by the find function to an int variable named location. For example, if the part variable contains the part number "678x34", the find function stores the number 3 in the location variable, because the *subString* "x" begins in character position 3 in the part variable. Similarly, if the part variable contains the part number "34561x", the find function stores the number 5 in the location variable, because the *subString* "x" begins in character position 5 in the part variable. However, if the part variable contains the part number "12x533", the find function stores the number −1 in the location variable, because the *subString* "x" does not appear in character positions 3 through 5 in the part variable. The if (location >= 0) clause uses the number stored in the location variable to determine whether the *subString* is contained within the *string*.

mini-quiz

Mini-Quiz 2

1. Which of the following C++ while clauses processes the loop instructions as long as the number of characters contained in a string variable named employee is greater than 20?

    a. while (employee.size > 20)

    b. while (employee.size() > 20)

    c. while (size(employee) > 20)

    d. while (size.employee > 20)

2. Write a C++ if clause that determines if a string variable named code contains five characters.

3. Assume a string variable named state contains two uppercase letters. Which of the following C++ statements compares the first character stored in the state variable to the string "I", and assigns the return value to an int variable named returnValue?

    a. returnValue = compare(state, 0, 1, "I");

    b. returnValue = compare(state, 1, 0, "I");

    c. returnValue = state.compare("I", 0, 1);

    d. returnValue = state.compare(0, 1, "I");

4. Assume a string variable named name contains a string in uppercase letters. Write a C++ statement that compares the first two characters in the name variable to the string "SM", and assigns the return value to an int variable named returnValue.

Mini-Quiz 2 (continued)

5. Which of the following C++ statements searches for the name "SMITH" in a `string` variable named `name`, and then assigns the beginning location of the name to an `int` variable named `startLocation`? (The search should begin with the first character in the `name` variable. You can assume that the `name` variable's contents are uppercase.)

    a. `startLocation = find(name, "SMITH", 0);`

    b. `startLocation = find.name("SMITH", 0);`

    c. `startLocation = name.find("SMITH", 0);`

    d. `startLocation = name.find("SMITH", 1);`

6. Write a C++ statement that searches for the percent sign (%) in a `string` variable named `rate`, and then assigns the location of the percent sign to an `int` variable named `location`. (Begin the search with the second character in the variable.)

In the next section, you will learn how to replace a portion of a `string` variable's contents with another string.

Replacing a Portion of a `string` Variable's Contents

As you observed in previous tutorials, when you use the assignment operator (=) to assign a string to a `string` variable, the string replaces all of the characters previously stored in the variable. For example, if the `name` variable contains "Bill", the assignment statement `name = "John";` replaces the entire contents of the `name` variable ("Bill") with the name "John". But what if you wanted to replace only a portion of the `name` variable's contents? For example, what if you just wanted to change the first character in the `name` variable from *B* to *J*? In situations where you need to replace only a portion of a `string` variable's contents, rather than the entire contents, you need to use a function. Figure 11-12 shows the built-in functions that you can use in C++ and Java, and the statement you can use in Visual Basic, to replace one or more characters in a string.

Purpose	C++	Java	Visual Basic
Replace a portion of a `string` variable's contents with another string	`replace`	`replace`	`Mid`

Figure 11-12: Functions and statement used to replace a portion of a `string` variable's contents with another string in C++, Java, and Visual Basic

Figure 11-13 shows the syntax of the C++ `replace` function, which is defined in the string library file, and two examples of using the function in a C++ statement.

Syntax	
To replace a portion of a `string` variable's contents with another string: `string`.**replace(***startReplace, numberOfCharsToReplace, replacementString***)**	
Examples	**Results**

Example 1
 `string item = "ABX34";`
 `item.replace(2, 1, "C");`
	replaces the letter X (which is located in position 2 in the `item` variable) with the letter C, changing the value stored in the `item` variable to "ABC34"

Example 2
 `string name = "Jamie Leonard";`
 `name.replace(6, 7, "Kent");`
	replaces the name Leonard (the seven characters beginning in position 6) in the `name` variable, with the name "Kent", changing the value stored in the `name` variable to "Jamie Kent"

Figure 11-13: Syntax and examples of the C++ `replace` function

The C++ language also provides a function named `insert` that you can use to insert one string within another string. You can learn about the `insert` function by completing Discovery Exercise 8 at the end of this tutorial's Application lesson.

The `replace` function has more than one syntax.

In the `replace` function's syntax, *string* is the name of a `string` variable that contains the one or more characters you want to replace. The first argument in the `replace` function, *startReplace*, specifies where—in other words, in what character position—to begin replacing characters in the *string*. The second argument, *numberOfCharsToReplace*, indicates the number of characters to replace. The *startReplace* and *numberOfCharsToReplace* arguments can be numeric literal constants or the names of numeric variables. The last argument in the `replace` function, *replacementString*, contains the string that will replace the characters in the *string*. The *replacementString* argument can be a string literal constant or the name of a `string` variable.

In Example 1 in Figure 11-13, the statement `item.replace(2, 1, "C");` replaces the letter X, which is located in position 2 in the `item` variable, with the letter C. In other words, the statement changes the value stored in the `item` variable from "ABX34" to "ABC34".

In Example 2 in Figure 11-13, the statement `name.replace(6, 7, "Kent");` replaces the string "Leonard"—which is the seven characters, beginning in position six, in the `name` variable—with the string "Kent". The statement changes the value stored in the `name` variable from "Jamie Leonard" to "Jamie Kent".

In the next section, you will learn how to assign a portion of one `string` variable to another `string` variable.

Assigning a Portion of One string Variable to Another string Variable

As you already know, you can use the assignment operator (=) to assign the entire contents of one `string` variable to another `string` variable. For example, the assignment statement `employee = fullName;` assigns the entire contents of the `fullName` variable to the `employee` variable. If the `fullName` variable contains the name "Jose Martinez", the `employee` variable will contain "Jose Martinez" after the statement is processed. But what if you wanted to assign only a portion of the string stored in the `fullName` variable to the `employee` variable? For example, what if you wanted to store only the employee's first name (Jose) in the `employee` variable? Most programming languages provide a built-in function that you can use to assign a portion of one `string` variable's contents to another `string` variable. Figure 11-14 shows the built-in functions that you can use for this purpose in C++, Java, and Visual Basic.

Purpose	C++	Java	Visual Basic
Assign a portion of one string variable's contents to another string variable	assign	subString (in combination with the assignment operator)	Mid (in combination with the assignment operator)

Figure 11-14 Functions used to assign a portion of one `string` variable's contents to another `string` variable in C++, Java, and Visual Basic

Figure 11-15 shows the syntax of the C++ `assign` function, which is defined in the string library file, and two examples of using the function in a C++ statement.

Syntax
To assign a portion of one `string` variable's contents to another `string` variable: *destinationString*.**assign**(*sourceString*, *startAssign*, *numberOfCharsToAssign*)

Examples	Results

Example 1
`string employNum = "234512";`
`string depart = "";`
`depart.assign(employNum, 4, 2);`
	assigns the string "12" (the two characters in the `employNum` variable beginning with the character in position 4) to the `depart` variable

Example 2
`string fullName = "Bess O'Brien";`
`string first = "";`
`string last = "";`
`first.assign(fullName, 0, 4);`
`last.assign(fullName, 5, 7);`
	assigns the string "Bess" (the first four characters in the `fullName` variable) to the `first` variable, and assigns the string "O'Brien" (the seven characters in the `fullName` variable beginning with the character in position 5) to the `last` variable

Figure 11-15: Syntax and examples of the C++ `assign` function

▶ The `assign` function has more than one syntax. Figure 11-16 shows another version of the `assign` function's syntax.

In the `assign` function's syntax, *destinationString* and *sourceString* are the names of `string` variables, and *startAssign* and *numberOfCharsToAssign* are either numeric literal constants or the names of numeric variables. *startAssign* indicates the location of the first character in the *sourceString* to assign to the *destinationString*, and *numberOfCharsToAssign* indicates the number of characters to assign from the *sourceString*. The `assign` function will assign *numberOfCharsToAssign* from the *sourceString* to the *destinationString*, beginning with the character in position *startAssign* in the *sourceString*.

The `assign` function changes only the contents of the *destinationString*; it does not change the contents of the *sourceString*.

In Example 1 in Figure 11-15, the statement `depart.assign(employNum, 4, 2);` assigns the two characters in the `employNum` variable, beginning with the character in position 4, to the `depart` variable. After this statement is processed, the `depart` variable contains the string "12".

In Example 2 in Figure 11-15, the statement `first.assign(fullName, 0, 4);` assigns the first four characters in the `fullName` variable to the `first` variable. After this statement is processed, the `first` variable contains the string "Bess". The last statement in Example 2, `last.assign(fullName, 5, 7);`, assigns the seven characters in the `fullName` variable, beginning with the character in position 5, to the `last` variable. After this statement is processed, the `last` variable contains the string "O'Brien".

The C++ `assign` function also has a syntax that can be used to duplicate one character a specified number of times, and then assign the resulting string to a `string` variable. Figure 11-16 shows this version of the `assign` function's syntax and two examples of using the syntax in a C++ statement.

Syntax
To duplicate a character, and then assign the result to a `string` variable: *string*.**assign**(*number, character*)

Examples	Results

Example 1
`string hyphens = "";`
`hyphens.assign(10, '-');`
	assigns 10 hyphens to the `hyphens` variable

Example 2
`char letter = ' ';`
`string letters = "";`
`cout << "Enter a letter: ";`
`cin >> letter;`
`letters.assign(4, letter);`
	prompts the user to enter a letter, then duplicates the letter four times and assigns the result to the `letters` variable

Figure 11-16: Another version of the `assign` function's syntax, and examples of using the function to duplicate a character

string in the syntax is the name of a `string` variable that will store the duplicated characters. The *number* argument is either a numeric literal constant or the name of a numeric variable, and it indicates the number of times you want the character specified in the function's *character* argument to be duplicated. The *character* argument can be either a character literal constant or the name of a `char` variable.

In Example 1 in Figure 11-16, the statement `hyphens.assign(10, '-');` duplicates the hyphen character 10 times, and then stores the resulting string in the `hyphens` variable. In Example 2, the statement `letters.assign(4, letter);` duplicates the contents of the `letter` variable four times, and then assigns the resulting string to the `letters` variable. If the `letter` variable contains the asterisk (*), the statement assigns four asterisks(****) to the `letters` variable.

Finally, learn how to concatenate strings (link them together).

If the *character* argument is a character literal constant, it must be enclosed in single quotation marks.

Concatenating Strings

Connecting (or linking) strings together is called **concatenating**. Most programming languages provide a special operator, called the **concatenation operator**, that you use to concatenate strings. Figure 11-17 shows the string concatenation operator in C++, Java, and Visual Basic.

Purpose	C++	Java	Visual Basic
Concatenate strings	+	+	you can use either + or &

Figure 11-17: String concatenation operator in C++, Java, and Visual Basic

Figure 11-18 shows examples of using the C++ concatenation operator in a C++ statement.

Examples	Results

Example 1
`string first = "Jerome";`
`string last = "Jacobs";`
`string full = "";`
`full = first + " " + last;`
	concatenates the contents of the `first` variable, a space, and the contents of the `last` variable, and then assigns the result (Jerome Jacobs) to the `full` variable

Example 2
`string sentence = "How are you";`
`sentence = sentence + "?";`
`cout << sentence << endl;`
	concatenates the contents of the `sentence` variable and a question mark, and then assigns the result (How are you?) to the `sentence` variable, and then displays the contents of the variable on the screen

Example 3
`string hyphens = "";`
`int count = 1;`
`while (count <= 5)`
`{`
`    hyphens = hyphens + "-";`
`    count = count + 1;`
`}   //end while`
`cout << hyphens << endl;`
	concatenates five hyphens within the `hyphens` variable, and then displays the contents of the `hyphens` variable (-----) on the screen

Figure 11-18: Examples of using the C++ concatenation operator

In Example 1 in Figure 11-18, the statement `full = first + " " + last;` concatenates the contents of the `first` variable (Jerome), a space, and the contents of the `last` variable (Jacobs). It assigns the concatenated string (Jerome Jacobs) to the `full` variable.

In Example 2 in Figure 11-18, the statement `sentence = sentence + "?";` concatenates the contents of the `sentence` variable (How are you) and a question mark (?). It assigns the concatenated string (How are you?) to the `sentence` variable before the contents of the variable are displayed on the screen.

In Example 3 in Figure 11-18, the statement `hyphens = hyphens + "-";` concatenates a hyphen (-) to the current contents of the `hyphens` variable. Because the instruction appears within a loop whose instructions will be processed five times, five hyphens will be assigned to the `hyphens` variable. After the loop completes its processing, the contents of the `hyphens` variable (-----) are displayed on the screen. Although you could use the code shown in Example 3 to assign five hyphens to the `hyphens` variable, it is much easier to use the statement `hyphens.assign(5, '-');`.

mini-quiz

Mini-Quiz 3

1. Write a C++ statement that replaces the first character in a `string` variable named `code` with the letter B.

2. Write a C++ statement that assigns the first four characters in a `string` variable named `street` to a `string` variable named `number`.

3. Which of the following C++ statements assigns four exclamation points to a `string` variable named `temp`, and then concatenates the contents of the `temp` variable to a `string` variable named `sentence`?

    a. `sentence = sentence & temp.assign(4, '!');`

    b. `sentence = temp + temp.assign('!', 4);`

    c. `sentence = sentence.assign(temp, 4, '!');`

    d. `sentence = sentence + temp.assign(4, '!');`

4. Which of the following C++ statements concatenates the opening parenthesis, the contents of the `areaCode` variable, and the closing parenthesis, and then assigns the result to the `displayAreaCode` variable?

    a. `displayAreaCode = "(" + areaCode + ")";`

    b. `displayAreaCode = "(" & areaCode & ")";`

    c. `displayAreaCode = "(" + "areaCode" + ")";`

    d. `displayAreaCode = "( & areaCode & )";`

You now have completed Tutorial 11's Concept lesson. You can either take a break or complete the end-of-lesson questions and exercises before moving on to the Application lesson.

SUMMARY

Most programming languages provide built-in functions for processing character and string data—a common task performed by many programs. The C++ language, for example, provides the `toupper` and `tolower` functions for converting characters to uppercase and lowercase, respectively. To convert a string to uppercase or lowercase, the C++ language provides the `transform` function.

You can use the C++ `size` function to determine the number of characters contained in a string, and the C++ `compare` function to compare a portion of a `string` variable's contents to another string. The C++ language also provides a function, named `find`, that you can use to determine if a string is contained within a `string` variable.

You can use the C++ `replace` function to replace a portion of a `string` variable's contents with another string. You can use the C++ `assign` function to assign a portion of one `string` variable's contents to another `string` variable. You also can use the C++ `assign` function to duplicate one character a specified number of times, and then assign the resulting string to a `string` variable.

Connecting (or linking) strings together is called concatenating. The concatenation operator in C++ is the plus sign (+).

ANSWERS TO MINI-QUIZZES

Mini-Quiz 1

1. c. `while (toupper(letter) == 'A')`
2. `if (tolower(code) == 'x')`
3. `answer = toupper(answer);`
4. a. `transform(emp.begin(), emp.end(), emp.begin(), toupper);`

Mini-Quiz 2

1. b. `while (employee.size() > 20)`
2. `if (code.size() == 5)`
3. d. `returnValue = state.compare(0, 1, "I");`
4. `returnValue = name.compare(0, 2, "SM");`
5. c. `startLocation = name.find("SMITH", 0);`
6. `location = rate.find("%", 1);`

Mini-Quiz 3

1. `code.replace(0, 1, "B");`
2. `number.assign(street, 0, 4);`
3. d. `sentence = sentence + temp.assign(4, '!');`
4. a. `displayAreaCode = "(" + areaCode + ")";`

QUESTIONS

1. Which of the following functions temporarily converts the contents of a C++ `char` variable named `insured` to uppercase?
   a. `toupper(insured)`
   b. `ucase(insured)`
   c. `upper(insured)`
   d. `upperCase(insured)`

2. Which of the following C++ statements converts the contents of a `string` variable named `state` to uppercase?
   a. `toupper(state);`
   b. `upper(insured);`
   c. `transform(state.begin(), state.end(), state.begin(), toupper);`
   d. `transform(state.begin(), state.end(), state.begin(), upper);`

3. Which of the following C++ statements displays the number of characters contained in a `string` variable named `address`?
   a. `cout << address.size();`
   b. `cout << numChars(address);`
   c. `cout << size(address);`
   d. `cout << size.address;`

4. Which of the following C++ statements compares the first four characters in a `string` variable named `address` to the string "1123", and then assigns the result to an `int` variable named `result`?
   a. `result = address.compare(0, 4, "1123");`
   b. `result = address.compare(1, 4, "1123");`
   c. `result = address.compare(4, 0, "1123");`
   d. `result = compare(address, 0, 4, "1123");`

5. If the `address` variable contains the string "1125", what will the correct statement in Question 4 assign to the `result` variable?
   a. -1
   b. 0
   c. 1
   d. 4

6. Which of the following C++ statements searches for the string "CA" in a `string` variable named `state`, and then assigns the result to an `int` variable named `result`? The search should begin with the character located in position 5 in the `state` variable. (You can assume that the `state` variable's contents are uppercase.)
   a. `result = find(state, 5, "CA");`
   b. `result = state.find(5, "CA");`
   c. `result = state.find("CA", 5);`
   d. `result = state.find('CA', 5, 2);`

7. If the `state` variable contains the string "San Francisco, CA", what will the correct statement in Question 6 assign to the `result` variable?
   a. -1
   b. 0
   c. 11
   d. 15

8. Which of the following C++ statements replaces the two characters located in positions 4 and 5 in a `string` variable named `code` with the string "AB"?
   a. `code.replace(2, 4, "AB");`
   b. `code.replace(4, 2, "AB");`
   c. `code.replace(4, 5, "AB");`
   d. `replace(code, 4, "AB");`

9. Which of the following C++ statements assigns the first two characters in a `string` variable named `code` to a `string` variable named `partNum`?
   a. `code.assign(0, 2, partNum);`
   b. `code.assign(partNum, 0, 2);`
   c. `partNum.assign(0, 2, code);`
   d. `partNum.assign(code, 0, 2);`

10. Which of the following C++ statements assigns 5 asterisks (*) to a `string` variable named `divider`?
    a. `divider.assign(5, '*');`
    b. `divider.assign(5, "*");`
    c. `divider.assign('*', 5);`
    d. `assign(divider, '*', 5);`

11. Which of the following C++ statements concatenates the contents of a `string` variable named `city`, a comma, a space, and the contents of a `string` variable named `state`, and then assigns the result to a `string` variable named `cityState`?

    a. `cityState = "city" + ", "  + "state";`

    b. `cityState = city + ", " + state;`

    c. `cityState = city & ", " & state;`

    d. `cityState = "city,  + state";`

E X E R C I S E S

1. Open the T11ConE01.cpp file contained in the Cpp\Tut11\T11ConE01 folder on your computer's hard disk. Complete the program by entering a `while` clause that processes the loop when the user enters the letter Y (in either uppercase or lowercase) when asked if he or she wants to repeat the loop. (Use the appropriate function rather than a logical operator). Save, build, and execute the program. Use the program to display the square root of the numbers 4, 100, and 25. Be sure to verify that the `while` clause works correctly when the user enters either the letter Y or the letter y. When the program is working correctly, hide the Output window, then use the File menu to close the workspace.

2. Open the T11ConE02.cpp file contained in the Cpp\Tut11\T11ConE02 folder on your computer's hard disk. Complete the program by entering a `while` clause that stops the loop when the user enters the letter X (in either uppercase or lowercase) as the city. Also enter the instructions that convert the contents of the `city` and `state` variables to uppercase. Save, build, and execute the program. Use the program to display the following cities and states:

   bowling green, ky
   San Francisco, ca

   Be sure to verify that the `while` clause works correctly when the user enters either the letter X or the letter x. When the program is working correctly, hide the Output window, then use the File menu to close the workspace.

3. Open the T11ConE03.cpp file contained in the Cpp\Tut11\T11ConE03 folder on your computer's hard disk. The program prompts the user to enter one or more words. Complete the program by entering a statement that uses the C++ `size` and `assign` functions to display a row of hyphens below the word(s) on the screen. Display the same number of hyphens as there are characters in the word(s). (*Hint*: You can use the `size` function within the `assign` function.) Save, build, and execute the program. Test the program two times, using the words "Las Vegas" and "computer". When the program is working correctly, hide the Output window, then use the File menu to close the workspace.

4. Open the T11ConE04.cpp file contained in the Cpp\Tut11\T11ConE04 folder on your computer's hard disk. The program prompts the user to enter two one-character strings. Complete the program by entering a statement that uses the `compare` function to compare the two strings, and then assigns the function's return value to the `compareValue` variable. (Do not change the case of either string.) Also enter an `if` statement that displays the message "Equal" if the two strings are equal. However, if the two strings are not equal, the `if` statement should display the string that comes first in the ASCII coding scheme, followed by a space and the remaining string. (Display the information on the same line.) Save, build, and execute the program. Test the program by entering the following three sets of data: a and a, b and d, f and C. (*Hint*: Uppercase letters come before lowercase letters in the ASCII coding scheme, which is shown in Appendix A.) When the program is working correctly, hide the Output window, then use the File menu to close the workspace.

5. Open the T11ConE05.cpp file contained in the Cpp\Tut11\T11ConE05 folder on your computer's hard disk. The program prompts the user to enter one or more letters. Complete the program by entering a statement that converts the user's response to lowercase. Also enter a statement that assigns to the `location` variable the beginning location of the letters in the `alphabet` variable. Save, build, and execute the program. Test the program four times, using the following strings: A, z, mnop, and $. When the program is working correctly, hide the Output window, then use the File menu to close the workspace.

6. Open the T11ConE06.cpp file contained in the Cpp\Tut11\T11ConE06 folder on your computer's hard disk. The program prompts the user to enter a phone number that includes a hyphen. Complete the program by entering a statement that replaces the hyphen with the empty string. Save, build, and execute the program. Test the program two times, using the following phone numbers: *555-5555* and *999-9999*. When the program is working correctly, hide the Output window, then use the File menu to close the workspace.

7. Open the T11ConE07.cpp file contained in the Cpp\Tut11\T11ConE07 folder on your computer's hard disk. The program prompts the user to enter a five-character part number. Complete the program by entering an `if` statement that verifies that the user entered exactly five characters. If the user did not enter exactly five characters, display an appropriate error message. However, if the user entered five characters, assign the first three characters to the `item` variable, and assign the last two characters to the `color` variable. After making the appropriate assignments, display the contents of the `item` and `color` variables. Save, build, and execute the program. Test the program two times, using the following part numbers: 123ab and 456. When the program is working correctly, hide the Output window, then use the File menu to close the workspace.

8. Open the T11ConE08.cpp file contained in the Cpp\Tut11\T11ConE08 folder on your computer's hard disk. The program prompts the user to enter a city name, state name, and ZIP code. Complete the program by entering a statement that concatenates the city name, a comma, a space, the state name, two spaces, and the ZIP code. Assign the concatenated string to the `cityStateZip` variable. Save, build, and execute the program. Test the program by entering your city, state, and ZIP code. When the program is working correctly, hide the Output window, then use the File menu to close the workspace.

Exercise 9 is a Discovery Exercise. Discovery Exercises, which may include topics that are not covered in this lesson, allow you to "discover" the solutions to problems on your own.

9. In this exercise, you will learn how to specify various ranges for the `transform` function.
   a. Open the T11ConE09.cpp file contained in the Cpp\Tut11\T11ConE09 folder on your computer's hard disk. The program prompts the user to enter the name of a state.
   b. Complete the program by entering a statement that transforms the first letter in the `state` variable to uppercase. Also enter a statement that transforms the remaining letters in the `state` variable to lowercase. (*Hint*: You can use `state.begin() + 1` to refer to the second character in the `state` variable. Recall that the `transform` function performs the *function* argument's task on the range of characters specified in the `transform` function's first and second arguments. Recall that the range includes the character specified in the first argument, but it does not include the character specified in the second argument.)
   c. Save, build, and execute the program. Test the program twice, using the following state names: kentucky and iOWA.
   d. When the program is working correctly, hide the Output window, then use the File menu to close the workspace.

A computer program is good only if it works. Errors in either an algorithm or programming code can cause the program to run incorrectly. Therefore, a programmer needs to know how to locate and fix these errors. Exercise 10 is a Debugging Exercise. Debugging Exercises allow you to practice recognizing and solving errors in a program.

debugging **10.** In this exercise, you will debug a C++ program.

a. Open the T11ConE10.cpp file contained in the Cpp\Tut11\T11ConE10 folder on your computer's hard disk. Study the program's code. The program should display the price based on the last character in the customer number.

b. Build the program. Correct any syntax errors, then save, build, and execute the program. Test the program four times, using the following customer numbers: 12x, 34W, 56a, and 23. If necessary, correct any logic errors in the program.

c. When the program is working correctly, hide the Output window, then use the File menu to close the workspace.

Application Lesson

Manipulating Characters and Strings in a C++ Program

case ▶ On days when the weather is bad and the students cannot go outside to play, Mr. Mitchell, who teaches second grade at Hinsbrook School, spends recess time playing a simplified version of the Hangman game with his class. Mr. Mitchell feels that the game is both fun (the students love playing the game) and educational (the game allows the students to observe how letters are used to form words). Mr. Mitchell has asked you to write a program that the students can use to play the game on the computer.

Analyzing, Planning, and Desk-Checking the Hangman Algorithm

Mr. Mitchell's simplified version of the Hangman game requires two people to play. Currently, Mr. Mitchell thinks of a word that has five letters. He then draws five dashes on the chalkboard—one for each letter in the word. One student then is chosen to guess the word, letter by letter. If the student guesses a correct letter, Mr. Mitchell replaces the appropriate dash or dashes with the letter. For example, if the original word is *moose* and the student guesses the letter *o*, Mr. Mitchell changes the five dashes on the chalkboard to -*oo*--. The student is allowed to guess letters until he or she has guessed all of the letters in the word.

Figure 11-19 shows the IPO chart for one possible solution to the Hangman game problem.

Input	Processing	Output

original word (from player 1)
 	
letter (one or more from player 2)
	Processing items:
	    position
	    number of dashes replaced
	
	Algorithm:
	1. get the original word (from player 1)
	2. if (the original word does not contain exactly five characters)
	    display an error message
	else
	    convert the original word to uppercase
	    clear the contents of the DOS window
	    display the five dashes in the guessed word
	    repeat while (the number of dashes replaced is less than five)
	        get a letter (from player 2)
	        convert the letter to uppercase
	        use the find function to determine the position of the letter in the original word, beginning with the first character in the original word
	        repeat while (the position is greater than or equal to zero)
	            use the replace function to replace the appropriate dash (in the guessed word) with the letter
	            add 1 to the number of dashes replaced
	            use the find function to determine the position of the letter in the remaining characters in the original word, beginning with the character located in position + 1
	        end repeat while
	        display the contents of the guessed word
	    end repeat while
	    display "Great Job!" message
	end if
		guessed word (five dashes when program begins)

outer loop — **nested loop**

Figure 11-19: IPO chart for one possible solution to the Hangman game problem

The IPO chart shows that the output is the guessed word, and the input is the original word (provided by player 1) and one or more letters (provided by player 2). The Output column indicates that the guessed word will contain five dashes when the program begins; each dash represents a letter in the original word. Each time player 2 enters a letter that is contained in the original word, the program will replace one or more of the dashes in the guessed word with the letter.

The IPO chart shows that the program will use two processing items: position and number of dashes replaced. The position item will be used to store the character position of player 2's letter within the original word. For example, if the letter is the first character in the original word, the program will store the number 0 in the position item. The program will need to know the position of the letter in the original word, because it will need to replace the dash located in the same position in the guessed word.

The second processing item—number of dashes replaced—will be used as a counter to keep track of the number of dashes replaced in the guessed word. When a total of five dashes are replaced, it indicates that player 2 has guessed all of the letters in the original word.

The first step in the algorithm shown in Figure 11-19 is to get the original word from player 1. If the original word does not contain exactly five characters, the program will display an error message, and then the program will end. However, if the original word contains exactly five characters, the program will convert the word to uppercase. It then will clear the contents of the DOS window (which will remove the original word from view) before displaying the five dashes contained in the guessed word. (You will learn how to clear the contents of the DOS window later in this lesson.)

Next, the program will use an outer loop that repeats its instructions while the number of dashes replaced (in the guessed word) is less than five. If fewer than five dashes are replaced, it means that player 2 has not guessed all of the letters in the original word. Notice that the outer loop instructions first get a letter from player 2, and then convert the letter to uppercase. The next instruction in the outer loop is to use the `find` function to determine the position of the letter within the original word. The `find` function should begin its search with the first character in the word. As you learned in the Concept lesson, if the letter is located in the word, the `find` function will return a number that is greater than or equal to zero; otherwise, it will return the number -1. The number returned by the `find` function will be stored in the position item.

The next instruction in the outer loop is the beginning of a nested loop that repeats its instructions while the value in the position item is greater than or equal to zero. Recall that a position value greater than or equal to zero indicates that the letter entered by player 2 is located in the original word. The first instruction in the nested loop is to use the `replace` function to replace the appropriate dash with the letter. The appropriate dash is located in the guessed word, in the character position whose value is stored in the position item. The second instruction in the nested loop adds the number 1 to the counter that is counting the number of dashes replaced. The last instruction in the nested loop indicates that the `find` function will be used again—this time to determine whether the letter appears in the remaining characters in the original word. The remaining characters begin with the character in position + 1 in the original word, and this is where the `find` function should begin searching for the letter. The nested loop will end when the position item contains a value that is less than zero, which indicates that the `find` function did not find the letter.

The last instruction in the outer loop displays the contents of the guessed word. When the outer loop has completed its processing, which is when player 2 has guessed all of the letters in the original word, the program will display the message "Great Job!".

Recall that you should desk-check an algorithm several times before you begin coding it. In this case, you will use the following words and letters to desk-check the algorithm shown in Figure 11-19:

Data for first desk-check	Data for second desk-check
Original word: apple	Original word: orange
Letters: e, a, w, p, k, l	

Figure 11-20 shows the completed desk-check table.

original word	letter	position	number of dashes replaced	guessed word
~~apple~~	~~e~~	4	~~1~~	~~-----~~
~~APPLE~~	~~E~~	~~-1~~	~~2~~	~~----E~~
orange	~~a~~	~~0~~	~~3~~	~~A---E~~
	~~A~~	~~-1~~	4	~~AP--E~~
	~~w~~	~~-1~~	5	~~APP-E~~
	~~W~~	~~1~~		~~APPLE~~
	~~p~~	~~2~~		-----
	~~P~~	~~-1~~		
	~~l~~	~~3~~		
	L	-1		

Figure 11-20: Completed desk-check table for the algorithm shown in Figure 11-19

After desk-checking an algorithm to verify its accuracy, you are ready to translate it into a language the computer can understand.

Coding the Hangman Game Algorithm

The program will require five variables to store the values of its input, processing, and output items. You will use the `string` data type for the three variables that store the input and output items; you will name the variables `origWord`, `letter`, and `guessWord`. The `guessWord` variable will be initialized to five dashes ("-----"). You will use the `int` data type for the two variables that store the processing items. The names of the variables will be `position` and `dashesReplaced`.

The first step in the algorithm shown in Figure 11-19 is to get the original word from player 1, and the second step is to verify that the word contains exactly five characters. You can use the C++ `size` function to determine the number of characters contained in the `origWord` variable, where the original word is stored. If the `origWord` variable does not contain exactly five characters, the program should display an appropriate error message; otherwise, it should convert the contents of the variable to uppercase. You can use the C++ `transform` function to convert the contents of the `origWord` variable to uppercase. Figure 11-21 shows the current status of the code.

IPO chart information	C++ instructions

Input
  original word (from player 1)
  letter (from player 2)
Processing
  position
  number of dashes replaced
Output
  guessed word (five dashes when
  program begins)
 	
Algorithm
1. get the original word (from
   player 1)
2. if (the original word does not
   contain exactly five characters)
      display an error message
   else
      convert the original word to
      uppercase
	`string origWord = "";`
	`string letter = "";`
	
	`int position = 0;`
	`int dashesReplaced = 0;`
	
	`string guessWord = "-----";`
	
	`cout << "Enter the original word: ";`
	`getline(cin, origWord);`
	
	`if (origWord.size() != 5)`
	  `cout << "Enter a five-letter word" << endl;`
	`else`
	`{`
	    `transform(origWord.begin(), origWord.end(),`
	    `origWord.begin(), toupper);`

Figure 11-21: Current status of the program's code

The next step in the algorithm is to clear the contents of the DOS window; this will prevent player 2 from viewing the original word.

Clearing the Contents of the DOS Window

You can use the C++ `system` function to clear the contents of the DOS window. The syntax of the `system` function is **system**(*command*), where *command* is an operating system instruction enclosed in quotation marks. For example, you can clear the contents of the DOS window by using the operating system instruction "cls" (which stands for "clear screen") as the *command* argument. You can display the names, sizes, dates, and times pertaining to files located on your computer's hard disk by using the operating system instruction "dir" (which stands for "directory") as the *command* argument. In the current program, you will use the statement `system("cls");` to clear the contents of the DOS window.

After clearing the contents of the DOS window, the program should display the five dashes contained in the guessed word. You can use the statement `cout << "Guess this word: " << guessWord << endl;` for this purpose.

The next step in the algorithm is the beginning of the outer loop, which repeats its instructions while the number of dashes replaced in the guessed word in less than five. The appropriate `while` clause to use is `while (dashesReplaced < 5)`.

The instructions in the outer loop first get a letter from player 2, then convert the letter to uppercase, and then use the `find` function to return the location of the letter within the original word. The value returned by the `find` function should be assigned to the `position` variable. Figure 11-22 shows the current status of the code.

IPO chart information	C++ instructions

Input
  original word (from player 1)
  letter (from player 2)
	```string origWord = "";```
	```string letter = "";```

Processing
  position
  number of dashes replaced
	```int position = 0;```
	```int dashesReplaced = 0;```

Output
  guessed word (five dashes when
  program begins)
	```string guessWord = "-----";```

Algorithm
1. get the original word (from
  player 1)
2. if (the original word does not
  contain exactly five characters)
    display an error message
  else
 	
    convert the original word to
    uppercase
 	
    clear the contents of the DOS
    window
 	
    display the five dashes in the
    guessed word
 	
    repeat while (the number of
    dashes replaced is less than
    five)
      get a letter (from player 2)
 	
      convert the letter to
      uppercase
 	
      use the find function to
      determine the position of
      the letter in the original
      word, beginning with the
      first character in the
      original word
	```cout << "Enter the original word: ";```
	```getline(cin, origWord);```
	
	```if (origWord.size() != 5)```
	``` cout << "Enter a five-letter word" << endl;```
	```else```
	```{```
	``` transform(origWord.begin(), origWord.end(),```
	``` origWord.begin(), toupper);```
	``` system("cls");```
	
	``` cout << "Guess this word: " << guessWord <<```
	``` endl;```
	
	``` while (dashesReplaced < 5)```
	``` {```
	
	``` cout << "Enter a letter: ";```
	``` cin >> letter;```
	
	``` transform(letter.begin(), letter.end(),```
	``` letter.begin(), toupper);```
	
	``` position = origWord.find(letter, 0);```

Figure 11-22: Current status of the program's code

The next step in the algorithm is the beginning of the nested loop, which repeats its instructions while the value in the `position` variable is greater than or equal to zero. The appropriate `while` clause to use is `while (position >= 0)`.

The first instruction in the nested loop is to use the `replace` function to replace the appropriate dash (in the guessed word) with the letter entered by player 2. The appropriate statement to use is `guessWord.replace(position, 1, letter);`. The next instruction is to add the number 1 to the counter; you can do so using the statement `dashesReplaced = dashesReplaced + 1;`. The last instruction in the nested loop is to use the `find` function to search for the letter in the remaining characters in the original word. The statement `position = origWord.find(letter, position + 1);` will accomplish the task.

When the inner loop ends, you will use the statement `cout << "Your guess: " << guessWord << endl;` to display the contents of the `guessWord` variable. Finally, when the outer loop ends, you will use the statement `cout << "Great Job!" << endl;` to display the "Great Job!" message. Figure 11-23 shows the completed code for the Hangman game program.

IPO chart information	C++ instructions
Input original word (from player 1) letter (from player 2)	`string origWord = "";` `string letter = "";`
Processing position number of dashes replaced	`int position = 0;` `int dashesReplaced = 0;`
Output guessed word (five dashes when program begins)	`string guessWord = "-----";`

Algorithm
1. get the original word (from player 1)
2. if (the original word does not contain exactly five characters)
   display an error message
else
	`cout << "Enter the original word: ";`
	`getline(cin, origWord);`
	
	`if (origWord.size() != 5)`
	`  cout << "Enter a five-letter word" << endl;`
	`else`
	`{`

convert the original word to uppercase	`  transform(origWord.begin(), origWord.end(), origWord.begin(), toupper);`
clear the contents of the DOS window	`  system("cls");`
display the five dashes in the guessed word	`  cout << "Guess this word: " << guessWord << endl;`
repeat while (the number of dashes replaced is less than five)	`  while (dashesReplaced < 5)` `  {`
get a letter (from player 2)	`    cout << "Enter a letter: ";` `    cin >> letter;`
convert the letter to uppercase	`    transform(letter.begin(), letter.end(), letter.begin(), toupper);`
use the find function to determine the position of the letter in the original word, beginning with the first character in the original word	`    position = origWord.find(letter, 0);`

Figure 11-23: Completed code for the Hangman game program

IPO chart information	C++ instructions
repeat while (the position is greater than or equal to zero)	```while (position >= 0)
{```
use the replace function to replace the appropriate dash (in the guessed word) with the letter	```guessWord.replace(position, 1,
letter);```
add 1 to the number of dashes replaced	```dashesReplaced = dashesReplaced + 1;```
use the find function to determine the position of the letter in the remaining characters in the original word, beginning with the character located in position + 1	```position = origWord.find(letter,
position + 1);```
end repeat while	```} //end while```
display the contents of the guessed word	```cout << "Your guess: " << guessWord <<
endl;```
end repeat while	```} //end while```
display "Great Job!" message	```cout << "Great Job!" << endl;```
end if	```} //end if```

Figure 11-23: Completed code for the Hangman game program (continued)

Now that you have finished coding the algorithm, you need to desk-check the program, using the same data you used to desk-check the algorithm. Figure 11-24 shows the data and the completed desk-check table for the program.

Data for first desk-check	Data for second desk-check
Original word: apple	Original word: orange
Letters: e, a, w, p, k, l	

Desk-check table

origWord	letter	position	dashesReplaced	guessWord
~~————~~	~~—~~	~~0~~	~~0~~	~~————~~
~~apple~~	~~e~~	~~4~~	~~1~~	~~———E~~
~~APPLE~~	~~E~~	~~-1~~	~~2~~	~~A——E~~
~~————~~	~~a~~	~~0~~	~~3~~	~~AP—E~~
orange	~~A~~	~~-1~~	4	~~APP—E~~
	~~w~~	~~-1~~	~~5~~	~~APPLE~~
	~~W~~	~~-1~~	0	-----
	~~p~~	2		
	~~P~~	~~-1~~		
	~~l~~	3		
	~~L~~	~~-1~~		
		0		

Figure 11-24: Data and completed desk-check table for the program

The results obtained when desk-checking the program agree with the results obtained when desk-checking the algorithm. You now are ready to enter the C++ instructions into the computer.

Completing the Hangman Program

Your computer's hard disk contains a partially completed C++ program containing most of the instructions for the Hangman program. Open that program now.

To open the partially completed C++ program, then complete the program and test it:

1 Start Visual C++. Open the **T11App.cpp** file contained in the Cpp\Tut11\ T11App folder on your computer's hard disk.

Seven statements are missing from the program.

2 Enter the seven statements that are shaded in Figure 11-25, which shows the completed Hangman program.

```
//T11App - simplified version of the Hangman game

#include <iostream>
#include <string>
#include <algorithm>
using namespace std;int main()
```

Figure 11-25: Completed Hangman game program

```
{
    //declare variables
    string origWord     = "";
    string letter       = "";
    int position        = 0;
    int dashesReplaced = 0;
    string guessWord    = "-----";

    //get the original word from player 1
    cout << "Enter the original word: ";
    getline(cin, origWord);

    //verify that the original word contains exactly 5 characters
    if (origWord.size() != 5)
        cout << "Enter a five-letter word" << endl;
    else
    {
        //convert the original word to uppercase
        transform(origWord.begin(), origWord.end(), origWord.begin(), toupper);
        //clear the contents of the DOS window
        system("cls");
        //display the five dashes in the guessed word
        cout << "Guess this word: " << guessWord << endl;
        //repeat loop instructions while all dashes have not been replaced
        while (dashesReplaced < 5)
        {
            //get a letter from player 2
            cout << "Enter a letter: ";
            cin >> letter;
            //convert the letter to uppercase
            transform(letter.begin(), letter.end(), letter.begin(), toupper);
            //search for the letter in the original word
            position = origWord.find(letter, 0);
            //repeat while the letter is found in the original word
            while (position >= 0)
            {
                //replace the appropriate dash with the letter
                guessWord.replace(position, 1, letter);
                //add 1 to the counter
                dashesReplaced = dashesReplaced + 1;
                //search for the letter in the remaining characters
                position = origWord.find(letter, position + 1);
            } //end while
            //display the contents of the guessed word
            cout << "Your guess: " << guessWord << endl;
        } //end while
        //display message indicating that the word has been guessed
        cout << "Great job!" << endl;
    }  //end if
    return 0;
}   //end of main function
```

Figure 11-25: Completed Hangman game program (continued)

3   Save, build, and execute the program.

4   When you are prompted to enter the original word, type **apple** and press the **Enter** key. The program clears the contents of the DOS window, then displays the message "Guess this word: -----" and the prompt "Enter a letter: ", as shown in Figure 11-26.

Figure 11-26: DOS window showing message and prompt

HELP? If you needed to press the Enter key twice after typing the original word, refer to the Read This Before You Begin section found at the beginning of this book.

5   Type **e** and press the **Enter** key. The program displays the message "Your guess: -----E", followed by the prompt "Enter a letter: ", as shown in Figure 11-27.

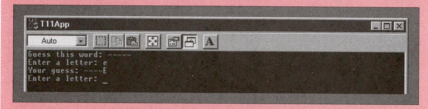

Figure 11-27: Contents of the DOS window after the letter e is entered

6   Type the following letters, one at a time, pressing the Enter key after typing each letter: **a, w, p, k, l**. When you are finished, the program correctly displays the "Great Job!" message, as shown in Figure 11-28.

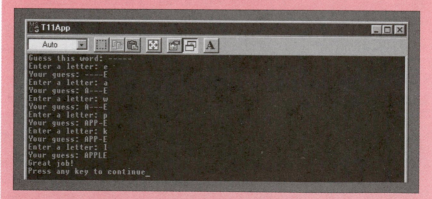

Figure 11-28: DOS window showing result of first test

Important Note: The hangman program will not work as intended if the user inadvertently enters the same letter again. You will fix this problem in Exercise 7 at the end of this lesson.

7 Press the **Enter** key to close the DOS window, then execute the program again. When you are prompted to enter the original word, type **orange** and press the **Enter** key. The program displays the message "Enter a five-letter word", which is correct.

8 Press the **Enter** key to close the DOS window. Hide the Output window, then use the File menu to close the workspace. When prompted to close all document windows, click the **Yes** button, then exit Visual C++.

You now have completed Tutorial 11's Application lesson. You can either take a break or complete the end-of-lesson exercises.

E X E R C I S E S

1. In this exercise, you will modify the program that you created in this lesson so that it allows player 1 to enter a word that contains any number of characters.
   a. Open the T11AppE01.cpp file contained in the Cpp\Tut11\T11AppE01 folder on your computer's hard disk.
   b. Modify the program appropriately. (*Hint*: Remove the selection structure that determines whether the user entered five characters.)
   c. Save, build, and execute the program. Test the program using the word "encyclopedia".
   d. When the program is working correctly, hide the Output window, then use the File menu to close the workspace.

2. In this exercise, you will complete a program that displays the color of an item.
   a. Open the T11AppE02.cpp file contained in the Cpp\Tut11\T11AppE02 folder on your computer's hard disk. The program should display the color of the item whose item number is entered by the user. All item numbers contain exactly five characters. All items are available in four colors: blue, green, red, and white. The third character in the item number indicates the item's color, as follows:

Character	Color
B or b	Blue
G or g	Green
R or r	Red
W or w	White

   If the third character is not one of these characters, the program should display an error message.
   b. Study the existing code. Complete the program appropriately. Be sure to include a loop that allows the user to enter as many item numbers as desired. Also be sure to verify that the user entered exactly five characters for the item number. If the user entered five characters, then display the item's color; otherwise, display an error message. (*Hint*: Assign the letter that indicates the item's color to a `string` variable, and then use the `string` variable in the selection structure that displays the appropriate color.)
   c. Save, build, and execute the program. Use the following item numbers to test the program: 12x, 12b45, 99G44, abr55, 78w99, 23abc. Enter your sentinel value to stop the program.
   d. When the program is working correctly, hide the Output window, then use the File menu to close the workspace.

3. In this exercise, you will complete a program that allows the user to enter a name (the first name followed by a space and the last name). The program then displays the name (the last name followed by a comma, a space, and the first name) on the screen.

    a. Open the T11AppE03.cpp file contained in the Cpp\Tut11\T11AppE03 folder on your computer's hard disk. The program prompts the user to enter the first name, a space, and the last name. The prompt indicates that the user should enter the number 9 to end the program.

    b. Complete the program appropriately.

    c. Save, build, and execute the program. Use the following names to test the program: Carol Smith, Jose Martinez, and Sven Miller. Enter 9 to stop the program.

    d. When the program is working correctly, hide the Output window, then use the File menu to close the workspace.

4. In this exercise, you will create a program that allows the user to enter a phone number. The program then removes any hyphens from the phone number before displaying the phone number on the screen.

    a. Open the T11AppE04.cpp file contained in the Cpp\Tut11\T11AppE04 folder on your computer's hard disk. The program prompts the user to enter a phone number. The prompt indicates that the user should enter the number 9 to end the program.

    b. Complete the program appropriately.

    c. Save, build, and execute the program. Use the following following phone numbers to test the program: 555-111-1111, 555-5555, and 1234567. Enter 9 to stop the program.

    d. When the program is working correctly, hide the Output window, then use the File menu to close the workspace.

5. In this exercise, you will complete a program that displays a message indicating if a portion of a string begins with another string.

    a. Open the T11AppE05.cpp file contained in the Cpp\Tut11\T11AppE05 folder on your computer's hard disk. The program prompts the user to enter a name (first name followed by a space and the last name) and the search text. The prompt indicates that the user can end the program by entering the number 9 as the search text. The program should determine if the last name portion of the name begins with the search text. (Keep in mind that the name and search text might be entered in uppercase letters, lowercase letters, or a combination of uppercase and lowercase letters.) If the last name begins with the search text, display the message "The last name begins with" followed by a space and the search text. If the characters in the last name come before the search text in the ASCII coding scheme, display the message "The last name comes before" followed by a space and the search text. If the characters in the last name come after the search text in the ASCII coding scheme, display the message "The last name comes after" followed by a space and the search text.

    b. Complete the program appropriately.

    c. Save, build, and execute the program. To test the program, enter Helga Swanson as the name, then use the following strings for the search text: g, ab, he, s, SY, sw, swan, and TW.

    d. When the program is working correctly, hide the Output window, then use the File menu to close the workspace.

6. In this exercise, you will complete a program that allows the user to guess a letter chosen randomly by the computer.

    a. Open the T11AppE06.cpp file contained in the Cpp\Tut11\T11AppE06 folder on your computer's hard disk. The program assigns the letters of the alphabet to a `string` variable named `letters`. It also prompts the user to enter a letter. Complete the program by entering instructions to do the following:

       ■ generate a random number that can be used to select one of the letters from the `letters` variable, and assign the selected letter to the `randomLetter` variable

       ■ verify that the user entered exactly one letter

       ■ if the user did not enter exactly one letter, display an appropriate error message

- if the user entered exactly one letter, compare the lowercase version of the letter to the random letter
- allow the user to enter a letter until he or she guesses the random letter
- if the letter entered by the user is the same as the random letter, display the message "You guessed the correct letter.", then end the program
- if the random letter appears after the user's letter in the alphabet, display the message "The correct letter comes after the letter", followed by a space, the user's letter, and a period
- if the random letter appears before the user's letter in the alphabet, display the message "The correct letter comes before the letter", followed by a space, the user's letter, and a period

b. Save, build, and execute the program. Test the program by entering one or more letters. The program should stop when you have guessed the correct letter.

c. When the program is working correctly, hide the Output window, then use the File menu to close the workspace.

7. In this exercise, you will modify the program that you created in this lesson so that it allows the user to enter the same letter more than once.

a. Open the T11AppE07.cpp file contained in the Cpp\Tut11\T11AppE07 folder on your computer's hard disk.

b. Build and execute the program. When you are prompted to enter the original word, type apple and press the Enter key. When you are prompted to enter a letter, type a and press the Enter key. A---- appears on the screen. When you are prompted to enter another letter, type p and press the Enter key. APP-- appears on the screen.

c. Although unlikely, it is possible that the user might inadvertently enter the same letter again. Observe what happens when you enter the letter p again. Type p and press the Enter key. Notice that the program displays the "Great Job!" message, even though each letter in the word has not been guessed. Press the Enter key to close the DOS window.

d. Modify the program so that it works correctly when the user enters the same letter more than once.

e. Save, build, and execute the program. When you are prompted to enter the original word, type apple and press the Enter key. Then enter the following letters, one at a time: a, p, p, l, a, e. After entering the letter e, the program should display the "Great Job!" message.

f. When the program is working correctly, hide the Output window, then use the File menu to close the workspace.

Exercise 8 is a Discovery Exercise. Discovery Exercises, which may include topics that are not covered in this lesson, allow you to "discover" the solutions to problems on your own.

8. In this exercise, you will learn about the C++ **insert** function.

a. Open the T11AppE08.cpp file contained in the Cpp\Tut11\T11AppE08 folder on your computer's hard disk. The program prompts the user to enter a phone number (without any hyphens). If the phone number contains exactly seven characters, the program uses the C++ **insert** function to insert a hyphen before the character currently in position 3 in the **phone** variable. The syntax of the **insert** function is *string*.**insert**(*position*, *insertString*), where *string* is the name of a **string** variable in which the *insertString* will be inserted. *insertString* can be a string literal constant or the name of a **string** variable. *position* is a number (either a numeric literal constant or a numeric variable) that indicates where to insert the *insertString*.

b. Build and execute the program. When you are prompted to enter the phone number, type 2224444 and press the Enter key. The program inserts a hyphen before the character in position 3 in the **phone** variable, and displays 222-4444 as the phone number. Press the Enter key to close the DOS window.

c. Modify the program so that it also allows the user to enter a phone number containing 10 characters. In addition to displaying the hyphen in the phone number, as the program does now, also display parentheses around the area code and a space after the closing parenthesis. For example, if the user enters the 10 characters 1112223333 as the phone number, display the phone number as (111) 222-3333.

d. Save, build, and execute the program. Test the program twice, using the following phone numbers: 333-5555 and 1112223333.

e. When the program is working correctly, hide the Output window, then use the File menu to close the workspace.

A computer program is good only if it works. Errors in either an algorithm or programming code can cause the program to run incorrectly. Therefore, a programmer needs to know how to locate and fix these errors. Exercise 9 is a Debugging Exercise. Debugging Exercises allow you to practice recognizing and solving errors in a program.

debugging

9. In this exercise, you will debug a C++ program.

a. Open the T11AppE09.cpp file contained in the Cpp\Tut11\T11AppE09 folder on your computer's hard disk. This program should display the city portion of the string entered by the user.

b. Build and execute the program. When prompted for the city and state, enter Tampa, Florida. The program displays the letter T in the DOS window, which is incorrect; it should display the word Tampa. Press the Enter key to close the DOS window.

c. Correct the program's code, then save, build, and execute the program. Test the program again, using Tampa, Florida as the city and state.

d. When the program is working correctly, hide the Output window, then use the File menu to close the workspace.

Classes and Objects

Concept Lesson

Programming Methods

Currently, the two most popular methods used to create computer programs are the procedure-oriented method and the object-oriented method. When using the procedure-oriented method to create a program, the programmer concentrates on the major tasks that the program needs to perform. A payroll program, for example, will perform several major tasks, such as calculating the gross pay, calculating the taxes, and calculating the net pay. A programmer using the procedure-oriented method typically assigns each major task to a function, which is the primary component in a procedure-oriented program. You used the procedure-oriented method to develop the programs that you created in the previous 11 tutorials.

Different from the procedure-oriented method, which focuses on the individual tasks the program must perform, the object-oriented method requires the programmer to focus on the objects that a program can use to accomplish its goal. A payroll program, for example, might utilize a time card object, an employee object, and a pay check object. The primary component in an object-oriented program is an object. In this tutorial, you will learn more about object-oriented programming. You also will learn how to create simple object-oriented programs.

Object-Oriented Programming

Unlike the procedure-oriented method of programming, the object-oriented method allows the programmer to use familiar objects to solve problems. The ability to use objects that model things found in the real world makes problem solving much easier. For example, assume that the manager of a flower shop asks you to create a program that keeps track of the shop's daily sales revenue. Thinking in terms of the objects used to represent revenue—cash, checks, credit card receipts, and so on—will make the sales revenue problem easier to solve. Additionally, because each object is viewed as an independent unit, an object can be used in more than one program, usually with little or no modification. A check object used in the sales revenue program, for example, also can be used in a payroll program (which issues checks to employees) and an accounts payable program (which issues checks to creditors). The ability to use an object for more than one purpose saves programming time and money—an advantage that contributes to the popularity of object-oriented programming.

You may be surprised to learn that you have been using objects in programs ever since you created your first C++ program in Tutorial 3. The keywords `cin` and `cout`, for example, are actually the names of objects created for you by C++. The `cin` object represents the keyboard, and the `cout` object represents the monitor. Each of these objects contains the code that allows it to communicate with the peripheral device it represents. C++ provides these objects to save you (the programmer) the time and effort it would take to write the code yourself. As you know, you can use (or reuse) the `cin` and `cout` objects in any program that contains the `#include <iostream>` directive.

A program does not have to be based on the object-oriented method to use objects.

C++ creates the `cin` and `cout` objects in the iostream file.

Although you may have either heard or read that object-oriented programming is difficult to learn, do not be intimidated. Admittedly, creating object-oriented programs does take some practice. However, you already are familiar with many of the concepts upon which object-oriented programming is based. Much of the anxiety of object-oriented programming stems from the terminology used when discussing it. Many of the terms are unfamiliar, because they typically are not used in everyday conversations. The next section will help to familiarize you with the terms used in discussions about object-oriented programming.

Object-Oriented Programming Terminology

When discussing object-oriented programs, you will hear programmers use the term "OOP" (pronounced like *loop*). **OOP** is an acronym for object-oriented programming, which, as you know, is a programming methodology based on objects. An **object** is anything that can be seen, touched, or used; in other words, an object is nearly any *thing*. The objects used in an object-oriented program can take on many different forms. The menus, option buttons, and command buttons included in most Windows programs are objects. An object also can represent something encountered in real life—such as a wristwatch, a car, a credit card receipt, and an employee.

Every object has attributes and behaviors. The **attributes** are the characteristics that describe the object. When you tell someone that your wristwatch is a Farentino Model 35A, you are describing the watch (an object) in terms of some of its attributes—in this case, its maker and model number. A watch also has many other attributes, such as a crown, dial, hour hand, minute hand, movement, and so on.

An object's **behaviors**, on the other hand, are the operations (actions) that the object is capable of performing. A watch, for example, can keep track of the time. Some watches also can keep track of the date. Still others can illuminate their dials when a button on the watch is pushed.

In OOP, behaviors are also referred to as methods.

You also will hear the term "class" in OOP discussions. A **class** is a pattern or blueprint used to create an object. Every object used in an object-oriented program comes from a class. A class contains—or, in OOP terms, it **encapsulates**—all of the attributes and behaviors that describe the object the class creates. The blueprint for the Farentino Model 35A watch, for example, encapsulates all of the watch's attributes and behaviors. Objects created from a class are referred to as **instances** of the class, and are said to be "instantiated" from the class. All Farentino Model 35A watches are instances of the Farentino Model 35A class.

The class itself is not an object; only an instance of the class is an object.

"Abstraction" is another term used in OOP discussions. **Abstraction** refers to the hiding of the internal details of an object from the user; hiding the internal details helps prevent the user from making inadvertent changes to the object. The internal mechanism of a watch, for example, is enclosed (hidden) in a case to protect the mechanism from damage. Attributes and behaviors that are not **hidden** are said to be **exposed** to the user. Exposed on a Farentino Model 35A watch are the crown used to set the hour and minute hands, and the button used to illuminate the dial. The idea behind abstraction is to expose to the user only those attributes and behaviors that are necessary to use the object, and to hide everything else.

The term "encapsulate" means "to enclose in a capsule." In the context of OOP, the "capsule" is a class.

Another OOP term, **inheritance**, refers to the fact that you can create one class from another class. The new class, called the **derived class**, inherits the attributes and behaviors of the original class, called the **base class**. For example, the Farentino company might create a blueprint of the Model 35B watch from the blueprint of the Model 35A watch. The Model 35B blueprint (the derived class) will inherit all of the attributes and behaviors of the Model 35A blueprint (the base class), but it then can be modified to include an additional feature, such as an alarm.

Keep the OOP terms and definitions in mind as you proceed through the remaining sections in this lesson.

Mini-Quiz 1

1. OOP is an acronym for _____ .
2. A class is an object.
    a. True
    b. False
3. An object created from a class is called _____ .
    a. an attribute
    b. an instance of the class
    c. the base class
    d. the derived class
4. The operations (actions) that an object can perform are called its
    _____ .

> **tip**
>
> Although you can define and code a C++ class in just a matter of minutes, the objects produced by such a class probably will not be of much use. The creation of a good class—one whose objects can be used in a variety of ways by many different programs—requires a lot of time, patience, and planning.

> **tip**
>
> *istream* stands for *input stream*, and *ostream* stands for *output stream*.

> **tip**
>
> Recall that you use the `#include` directive to include a header file in a program.

Now that you are familiar with OOP terminology, you will learn how to define a class in C++.

Defining a Class in C++

Every object used in a program is created from a class. The `cin` and `cout` objects, for example, are created from the C++ `istream` and `ostream` classes, respectively. Each of these classes defines the attributes and behaviors of the object it creates.

In addition to using objects provided by C++, you also can create your own objects. Before you can do so, however, you first must create the object's class. Like the C++ classes, your classes also must specify the attributes and behaviors of the objects they create.

In C++, you create a class using a **class definition**. You typically enter the code for the class definition in a header file. You then can use the class to create objects in any program that contains the appropriate `#include` directive.

In C++, a class definition contains two sections: a declaration section and an implementation section. You'll learn first about the declaration section.

The Declaration Section of the Class Definition

The **declaration section** of the class definition contains the C++ `class` statement, which specifies the name of the class, as well as the attributes and behaviors included in the class. Figure 12-1 shows the syntax of the `class` statement and an example of using the statement to describe a simple `Date` class. You can use the `Date` class to create a Date object in any program that requires a date—such as a payroll program, a personnel program, or an airline reservation program.

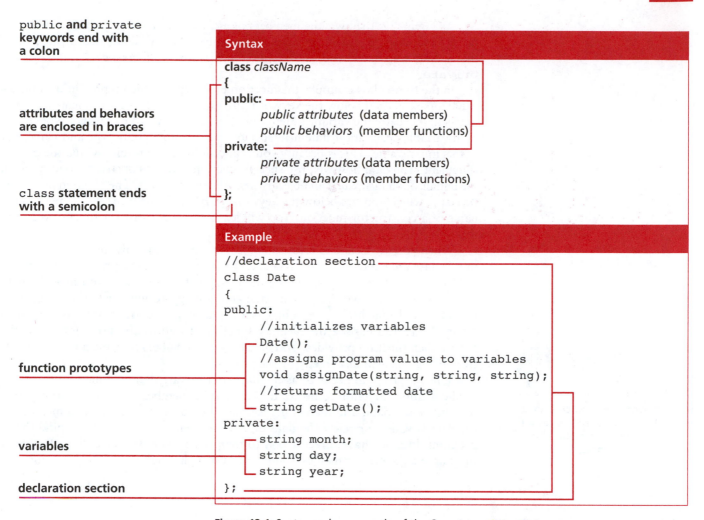

public **and** private
**keywords end with
a colon**

**attributes and behaviors
are enclosed in braces**

class **statement ends
with a semicolon**

function prototypes

variables

declaration section

Syntax

```
class className
{
public: ────────
        public attributes  (data members)
        public behaviors  (member functions)
private: ────────
        private attributes (data members)
        private behaviors (member functions)
};
```

Example

```
//declaration section
class Date
{
public:
        //initializes variables
        Date();
        //assigns program values to variables
        void assignDate(string, string, string);
        //returns formatted date
        string getDate();
private:
        string month;
        string day;
        string year;
};
```

Figure 12-1: Syntax and an example of the C++ class statement

The C++ class statement begins with the keyword class, followed by the name of the class. The name of the class shown in Figure 12-1 is Date. Although it is not required by the C++ syntax, many C++ programmers capitalize the first letter in a class name to distinguish it from the name of a variable or function, which typically begins with a lowercase letter. You will use this naming convention for the classes you create in this book.

As Figure 12-1 indicates, you enclose the attributes and behaviors that describe the class in braces ({}), and you end the class statement with a semicolon. The attributes, called **data members**, are represented by variables within the class statement, and the behaviors, called **member functions**, are represented by function prototypes. The Date class shown in Figure 12-1, for example, contains three variables: month, day, and year. Each variable is associated with an attribute of a Date object. The Date class also contains three function prototypes: Date, assignDate, and getDate. Each function prototype represents a task that a Date object can perform.

tip

· · · · · · · · · · · · · · · ·

▶ When determining an object's attributes, it is helpful to consider how you would describe the object. A date, for example, typically is described in terms of a month, day, and year. The month, day, and year items, therefore, are the attributes of a Date object, and will need to be included in the Date **class.**

As Figure 12-1 shows, the members of a class can be either public members or private members. You record the public members below the keyword `public` in the `class` statement, and you record the private members below the keyword `private`.

In the `Date` class example, the function prototypes, which represent the object's behaviors, are listed below the keyword `public` in the `class` statement; the statements that declare the variables are listed below the keyword `private`. Notice that each variable declaration statement specifies the variable's data type and name, but not its initial value. This is because you cannot initialize variables within the `class` statement. You can, however, use special functions, called constructors, to perform the initialization task when an object is created from the class. The function prototype `Date()`, which appears below the keyword `public` in the `class` statement, is the name of a constructor function. You will learn about constructor functions later in this lesson.

When you use a class to create an object in a program, only the public members of the class are exposed (made available) to the program; the private members are hidden. In most classes, you expose the member functions and you hide the data members. In other words, you list the function prototypes below the keyword `public`, and you list the variables below the keyword `private`, as shown in Figure 12-1. You expose the member functions to allow the program to use the service each function provides. You hide the data members to protect their contents from being changed incorrectly by the program.

When a program needs to assign data to a private data member, it must use a public member function to do so. It is the public member function's responsibility to validate the data, and then either assign the data to the private data member (if the data is valid), or reject the data (if the data is not valid). Keep in mind that a program does not have direct access to the private members of a class. Rather, it must access the private members indirectly, through a public member function.

tip

The private members in a class can be directly accessed only by the member functions in the class.

mini-quiz

Mini-Quiz 2

1. A program cannot access a public member function directly.
   a. True
   b. False

2. In C++, you use the `class` statement in the _____ section of a class definition.

3. The data members (attributes) are represented by _____ in a class definition.
   a. constants
   b. member functions
   c. public data members
   d. variables

4. A private data member can be accessed directly by a public member function.
   a. True
   b. False

Next, you'll learn about the implementation section of the class definition.

The Implementation Section of the Class Definition

Each function listed in the declaration section must be defined in the **implementation section** of the class definition. The implementation section of the Date class definition is shown in Figure 12-2.

declaration section

Example

```
//declaration section
class Date
{
public:
      //initializes variables
      Date();
      //assigns program values to variables
      void assignDate(string, string, string);
      //returns formatted date
      string getDate();
private:
      string month;
      string day;
      string year;
};
```

function prototypes

variables

class name

scope resolution operator

```
//implementation section
Date::Date()
{
      //constructor
      month = "";
      day   = "";
      year  = "";
} //end of default constructor
```

default constructor function

```
void Date::assignDate(string m, string d, string y)
{
      month = m;
      day   = d;
      year  = y;
} //end of assignDate function

string Date::getDate()
{
      return month + "/" + day + "/" + year;
} //end of getDate function
```

implementation section

Figure 12-2: Implementation section shown in the Date class definition

The implementation section shown in Figure 12-2 contains three function definitions; each definition corresponds to a function prototype listed in the declaration section. The first definition recorded in the implementation section, as well as the first prototype listed in the declaration section, pertains to the default constructor function.

You will learn about the default constructor in this tutorial. Constructors having formal parameters are covered in Tutorial 14.

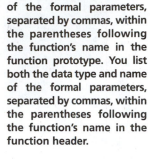

As you do with other functions, you list the data type of the formal parameters, separated by commas, within the parentheses following the function's name in the function prototype. You list both the data type and name of the formal parameters, separated by commas, within the parentheses following the function's name in the function header.

Recall that the + sign in the getDate function's return statement is the string concatenation operator.

The Default Constructor Function

A **constructor function**, often simply called a **constructor**, is a member function that C++ automatically calls when you use the class to create—or in OOP terms, **instantiate**—an object. The sole purpose of a constructor is to initialize the class's variables. Every class should have at least one constructor. Each constructor included in a class must have the same name as the class, but its formal parameters (if any) must be different from any other constructor in the class. A constructor that has no formal parameters is called the **default constructor**.

You list each constructor's function prototype below the keyword `public` in the declaration section of the class definition, and you list its function definition in the implementation section. Unlike other function prototypes and function definitions, a constructor's prototype and definition do not begin with a data type. Because the sole purpose of a constructor is to initialize the class's variables, a constructor will never return a value, so no data type—not even `void`—is included in the prototype or definition.

The `Date` class shown in Figure 12-2 has one constructor, `Date()`. Because the constructor has no formal parameters, it is the default constructor for the `Date` class. Notice that the default constructor's function header contains the name of the class— `Date`—and the name of the constructor— `Date()`. The two colons (::) that separate the class name from the constructor name are called the **scope resolution operator**, and they indicate that the `Date()` constructor belongs to the `Date` class.

Recall that a program does not have direct access to the private members of a class. Rather, it must access the private members through a public member function.

Public Member Functions

The public member functions in a class define the tasks that an object can perform. You already have learned about one public member function: a constructor. Recall that a constructor automatically initializes an object's private data members when the object is created in a program.

In addition to one or more constructors, most classes also contain public member functions that programs can use to assign new values to an object's private data members and also view the contents of the private data members. For example, a program can use the `Date` class's `assignDate` function to assign new values to a `Date` object's `month`, `day`, and `year` variables. A program can use the `Date` class's `getDate` function, on the other hand, to view the contents of a `Date` object's variables.

As Figure 12-2 indicates, the `assignDate` function is a void function, and the `getDate` function is a value-returning function. Notice that the `assignDate` function receives three `string` values from the program. The first value represents the month, the second value the day, and the third value the year. The `assignDate` function assigns these values to the three variables listed in the private area of the class. Unlike the `assignDate` function, the `getDate` function does not receive any information from the program that calls it. The function simply returns the contents of the `month`, `day`, and `year` variables, separated by a slash (/).

Next, learn how to use a class to create an object in a program.

Using the Class in a Program

Once a class is defined, you can then create an instance of it—in other words, an object—in a program. The hire date program shown in Figure 12-3, for example, uses the `Date` class to create a Date object.

```
//displays a formatted hire date

#include <iostream>
using namespace std;
#include "c:\cpp\myclasses\date"

int main()
{
    //create object
    Date dateObj;

    //declare variables
    string hireMonth = "";
    string hireDay   = "";
    string hireYear  = "";

    //get month, day, and year
    cout << "Enter the month: ";
    getline(cin, hireMonth);
    cout << "Enter the day: ";
    getline(cin, hireDay);
    cout << "Enter the year: ";
    getline(cin, hireYear);

    //set the date
    dateObj.assignDate(hireMonth, hireDay, hireYear);

    //display the date
    cout << "Employee hire date " << dateObj.getDate() << endl;

    return 0;
} //end of main function
```

creates a Date object

calls the assignDate member function

calls the getDate member function

Figure 12-3: Hire date program

As mentioned earlier, you typically enter the code for a class definition in a header file. In this case, the class definition for the **Date** class is in a header file named Date. To use the **Date** class to create a Date object, you will need to include the Date header file in the program. When including a C++ standard header file in a program, you enclose the header file's name in angle brackets, like this: `#include <iostream>`. As you learned in Tutorial 2, the angle brackets indicate that the file is located in the C++ include folder, which comes with the C++ system. However, if the header file is not located in the include folder, you enclose the header file's name along with the full path to the file in a set of double quotation marks (""). For example, you will enter the `#include "c:\cpp\myclasses\date"` directive in the current program.

After the user enters the month, day, and year that the employee was hired, the program calls the class's public **assignDate** function, passing it the hire date information. The **assignDate** function assigns the hire date information to the private data members of the class—the **month**, **day**, and **year** variables. The program then calls the public **getDate** function to return the contents of the **month**, **day**, and **year** variables, separated by a slash (/); the program displays the returned information on the screen.

Notice that you call a public member function by preceding its name with the object's name and a period. The period that separates the object name from the function name is called the **dot member selection operator**, and it indicates that the function is a member of the class used to create the object. In this case, for example, the dot member selection operator indicates that the `assignDate` and `getDate` functions are members of the class used to create the `dateObj` object.

Mini-Quiz 3

1. The scope resolution operator is _____ .

2. Write the default constructor function prototype for a class named `Item`.

3. Assume the `Item` class in Question 2 contains two private data members: a `char` variable named `code` and an `int` variable named `price`. Write the function definition for the default constructor.

You now have completed Tutorial 12's Concept lesson. You can either take a break or complete the end-of-lesson questions and exercises before moving on to the Application lesson.

SUMMARY

A class is a pattern for creating one or more instances of the class—in other words, one or more objects. A class encapsulates all of an object's attributes and behaviors. An object's attributes are the characteristics that describe the object, and its behaviors are the operations (actions) that the object can perform.

The OOP term "abstraction" refers to the hiding of an object's internal details from the user; this is done to prevent the user from making inadvertent changes to the object. The idea behind abstraction is to expose to the user only the attributes and behaviors that are necessary to use the object, and to hide everything else. In most classes, you expose an object's behaviors (member functions) and you hide its attributes (data members).

If you enter a class definition in a C++ header file, you then can use the class to create an object in any program, as long as the program contains the appropriate `#include` directive.

You can use a constructor to initialize the data members in a class when an object is created. A class can have more than one constructor. Each constructor has the same name, but its formal parameters (if any) must be different from any other constructor. A constructor that has no formal parameters is called the default constructor. Unlike other functions, a constructor does not have a data type because it cannot return a value.

ANSWERS TO MINI-QUIZZES

Mini-Quiz 1

1. object-oriented programming

2. b. False

3. b. an instance of the class

4. behaviors

Mini-Quiz 2

1. b. False

2. declaration

3. d. variables

4. a. True

Mini-Quiz 3

1. :: (two colons)

2. `Item();`

3.
```
Item::Item()
{
    code = ' ';
    price = 0;
}  //end of default constructor
```

QUESTIONS

1. A blueprint for creating an object in C++ is called _____.
   a. a class
   b. an instance
   c. a map
   d. a pattern

2. Which of the following statements is false?
   a. An example of an attribute is the `minutes` variable in a `Time` class.
   b. An example of a behavior is the `setTime` function in a `Time` class.
   c. An object created from a class is referred to as an instance of the class.
   d. A class is considered an object.

3. You hide a member of a class by recording the member below the _____ keyword in the `class` statement.
   a. `confidential`
   b. `hidden`
   c. `private`
   d. `restricted`

4. You expose a member of a class by recording the member below the _____ keyword in the `class` statement
   a. `common`
   b. `exposed`
   c. `public`
   d. `unrestricted`

5. A program can access the private members of a class _____.
   a. directly
   b. only through the public members of the class
   c. only through other private members of the class
   d. none of the above—the program cannot access the private members of a class in any way

6. If you want to use a class to define objects in many different programs, you should enter the class definition in a C++ _____ file.
   a. header
   b. program
   c. source
   d. text

7. In most classes, you expose the _____ and hide the _____.
   a. attributes, data members
   b. data members, member functions
   c. member functions, data members
   d. variables, member functions

8. The function definitions for a class are entered in the _____ section in the class definition.
   a. declaration
   b. function
   c. implementation
   d. program-defined

9. Assume that the userclass file is located in the Cpp\Tut12\MyClasses folder on the computer's C drive. Which of the following instructions will include this header file in a program?
   a. `#include <c:\cpp\tut12\MyClasses\userclass>`
   b. `#include "c:\cpp\tut12\MyClasses\userclass"`
   c. `#include "<c:\cpp\tut12\MyClasses\userclass>"`
   d. `#include <"c:\cpp\tut12\MyClasses\userclass">`

10. Which of the following is the scope resolution operator?
    a. :: (two colons)
    b. * (asterisk)
    c. . (period)
    d. & (ampersand)

11. The name of the constructor function for a class named `Animal` is _____.
    a. `Animal`
    b. `AnimalConstructor`
    c. `ConstAnimal`
    d. any of the above could be used as the name of the constructor function

12. Which of the following statements is false?
    a. You typically use a public member function to change the value in a private data member.
    b. Because the constructor function does not return a value, you place the keyword `void` before the constructor's name.
    c. The public member functions in a class can be accessed by any program that uses an object created from the class.
    d. An instance of a class is considered an object.

13. Which of the following creates an Animal object named `dog`?
    a. `Animal "dog";`
    b. `Animal dog;`
    c. `dog "Animal";`
    d. `dog Animal;`

14. Which of the following indicates that the `displayBreed` function is a member of the `Animal` class?
    a. `Animal::displayBreed()`
    b. `Animal.displayBreed()`
    c. `displayBreed()::Animal`
    d. `displayBreed&Animal()`

E X E R C I S E S

1. Write the class definition for a class named `Employee`. The class should include data members for an employee object's name and salary. (The salary will be an integer.) The class should contain two member functions: the constructor and a function that allows a program to assign values to the data members.

2. Add two member functions to the `Employee` class you created in Exercise 1. One member function should allow any program using an employee object to view the contents of the salary data member. The other member function should allow the program to view the contents of the employee name data member. (*Hint*: Have the member functions simply return the contents of the appropriate data member.)

3. Add another member function to the `Employee` class you modified in Exercise 2. The member function should calculate an employee object's new salary, based on a raise percentage provided by the program using the object. Before calculating the raise, the member function should verify that the raise percentage is greater than or equal to zero. If the raise percentage is less than zero, the member function should display an error message.

4. In this exercise, you will enter the `Employee` class definition from Exercise 3 in a header file. You also will use the class in a program to create an object.
   a. Open the T12ConE04 header file contained in the Cpp\MyClasses folder on your computer's hard disk. (Note: You will need to change the Files of type list box in the Open dialog box to All Files (*.*).) Complete the header file by entering the class definition from Exercise 3. Save and then close the file.
   b. Open the T12ConE04.cpp file contained in the Cpp\Tut12\T12ConE04 folder on your computer's hard disk. If necessary, change the `#include "c:\cpp\myclasses\T12ConE04"` statement to reflect the location of the header file on your computer's hard disk.
   c. The instructions to create an employee object, assign values to the object, display the name and current salary, calculate the new salary, and then display the new salary are missing from the program. Complete the program, using the comments as a guide.
   d. Save, build, and execute the program. Test the program by entering your name, a salary amount of 54000, and a raise rate of .1. The program should display your name, the number 54000, and the number 59400.
   e. When the program is working correctly, hide the Output window, then use the File menu to close the workspace.

5. In this exercise, you will modify the `getDate` member function contained in this lesson's `Date` class. The modified function will return the formatted date separated by either slashes (/) or dashes (-).
   a. Open the T12ConE05 header file contained in the Cpp\MyClasses folder on your computer's hard disk. (Note: You will need to change the Files of type list box in the Open dialog box to All Files (*.*).) The `getDate` function will need to receive a string (passed to it by a program) that indicates whether the user wants slashes (/) or dashes (-) in the date. Modify the `getDate` function's code accordingly. Save and then close the file.
   b. Open the T12ConE05.cpp file contained in the Cpp\Tut12\T12ConE05 folder on your computer's hard disk. If necessary, change the `#include "c:\cpp\myclasses\T12ConE05"` statement to reflect the location of the header file on your computer's hard disk.
   c. Save, build, and execute the program. Test the program by entering 12 as the month, 5 as the day, 2000 as the year, and a - (dash) as the separator. The formatted date, 12-5-2000, should appear in the DOS window. Press the Enter key to close the DOS window.
   d. Execute the program again. This time, enter 9 as the month, 30 as the day, 02 as the year, and a / (slash) as the separator. The formatted date, 9/30/02, should appear in the DOS window. Press the Enter key to close the DOS window.
   e. When the program is working correctly, hide the Output window, then use the File menu to close the workspace.

6. In this exercise, you will modify the Date class created in this lesson. The modified class will allow the program to view the contents of the private data members individually.

    a. Open the T12ConE06 header file contained in the Cpp\MyClasses folder on your computer's hard disk. (Note: You will need to change the Files of type list box in the Open dialog box to All Files (*.*).) Add three member functions to the class; each function should allow a program to view the contents of one of the three private data members. Save and then close the file.

    b. Open the T12ConE06.cpp file contained in the Cpp\Tut12\T12ConE06 folder on your computer's hard disk. If necessary, change the #include "c:\cpp\myclasses\T12ConE06" statement to reflect the location of the header file on your computer's hard disk.

    c. Complete the three statements that display the month, day, and year, using the member functions you created in Step a.

    d. Save, build, and execute the program. Test the program by entering 3 as the month, 7 as the day, and 2003 as the year. The month, day, and year should appear on separate lines in the DOS window. Press the Enter key to close the DOS window.

    e. When the program is working correctly, hide the Output window, then use the File menu to close the workspace.

7. In this exercise, you will view a Date class that is different from the one you viewed in the lesson. You will modify the class so that it validates the month and day values entered by the user.

    a. Open the T12ConE07 header file contained in the Cpp\MyClasses folder on your computer's hard disk. (Note: You will need to change the Files of type list box in the Open dialog box to All Files (*.*).) Study the existing code. Modify the assignDate function so that it validates the month and day values passed by the program. For example, valid month values are the numbers 1 through 12. If the month is 1, then only the numbers 1 through 31 are valid day values. However, if the month is 6, then valid day values are the numbers 1 through 30. If the month is 2, then valid day values are the numbers 1 through 29 if the year is a leap year; otherwise, the valid values are the numbers 1 through 28. (*Hint:* If the remainder after dividing the year by 4 is 0, then the year is a leap year.) Save and then close the file.

    b. Open the T12ConE07.cpp file contained in the Cpp\Tut12\T12ConE07 folder on your computer's hard disk. If necessary, change the #include "c:\cpp\myclasses\T12ConE07" statement to reflect the location of the header file on your computer's hard disk.

    c. The instruction to assign values to the object is missing from the program. Enter the appropriate instruction.

    d. Also enter the instructions to display the date, but only if the month and day values are valid. If the month and day values are not valid, display an error message.

    e. Save, build, and execute the program. Test the program by entering 6 as the month, 4 as the day, and 2002 as the year. The date 6/4/2002 should appear in the DOS window. Press the Enter key to close the DOS window.

    f. Execute the program again. This time enter 6 as the month, 31 as the day, and 2002 as the year. An error message should appear in the DOS window. Press the Enter key to close the DOS window.

    g. Execute the program again. This time enter 2 as the month, 29 as the day, and 2000 as the year. The date 2/29/2000 should appear in the DOS window. Press the Enter key to close the DOS window.

    h. Execute the program again. This time enter 2 as the month, 29 as the day, and 2001 as the year. An error message should appear in the DOS window. Press the Enter key to close the DOS window.

    i. When the program is working correctly, hide the Output window, then use the File menu to close the workspace.

Exercise 8 is a Discovery Exercise. Discovery Exercises, which may include topics that are not covered in this lesson, allow you to "discover" the solutions to problems on your own.

8. In this exercise, you will learn how to create a header file using the Visual C++ editor.
   a. Click File on the Visual C++ menu bar, and then click New.
   b. When the New dialog box appears, click the Files tab, then click C/C++ Header File in the list of file types.
   c. Click the ellipsis button (...) that appears to the right of the Location text box in the New dialog box. When the Choose Directory dialog box appears, open the Cpp\MyClasses folder, and then click the OK button. Click the File name text box, then type T12ConE08 and click the OK button.

   As the title bar indicates, the Visual C++ editor saves the file using .h as the file extension. The .h indicates that the file is a header file. However, the new standard in C++ is to omit the .h from the names of header files. To do so, you will need to use Windows to rename the file. First, however, you will enter a comment in the header file.

   d. Type the comment //My first header file and press the Enter key, then save the file.
   e. Close the header file, then use Windows to rename the file T12ConE08.

A computer program is good only if it works. Errors in either an algorithm or programming code can cause the program to run incorrectly. Therefore, a programmer needs to know how to locate and fix these errors. Exercise 9 is a Debugging Exercise. Debugging Exercises allow you to practice recognizing and solving errors in a program.

debugging

9. Correct the errors in the `Item` class shown in Figure 12-4.

```
class Item
private:
    item();
    void assignItem(string, float);
public:
    string name;
    float price;
}

Item()
{
    name  = "";
    price = 0.0;
} //end of default constructor

void assignItem(string n, float p)
{
    name = n;
    price = p;
} //end of assignItem function
```

Figure 12-4

Application Lesson

Using Classes and Objects in a C++ Program

case ▶ The owners of two small businesses asked you to create programs for them. Sharon Terney of Terney Landscaping wants a program that the salespeople can use to estimate the cost of laying sod. Jack Sysmanski, the owner of All-Around Fence Company, wants a program that he can use to calculate the cost of installing a fence.

Analyzing the Problems

While analyzing the Terney Landscaping and All-Around Fence Company problems, you notice that each involves a rectangular shape. For example, in the Terney Landscaping program, you need to find the area of a rectangle on which the sod is to be laid. In the All-Around Fence Company program, on the other hand, you need to find the perimeter of the rectangle around which a fence is to be constructed. To save time, you decide to create a `Rectangle` class that contains the attributes and behaviors of a rectangle. You will use the `Rectangle` class to create a Rectangle object in the Terney Landscaping and All-Around Fence Company programs. (You will complete the Terney Landscaping program in this lesson. You will complete the All-Around Fence Company program in this lesson's Exercise 1.)

Creating the `Rectangle` Class

As you learned in the Concept lesson, before you can create an object in C++, you first must create a class that specifies the object's attributes and behaviors. When determining an object's attributes, it is helpful to consider how you would describe the object. Rectangles, for example, typically are described in terms of two dimensions: length and width. The length and width dimensions are the attributes of a rectangle object. You will include both attributes as private data members in the `Rectangle` class, using the `float` variables `length` and `width`.

Next, you determine the object's behaviors, which are the tasks that the object can perform. A Rectangle object will need to be capable of performing the four tasks shown in Figure 12-5.

Tasks
1. initialize private data members (default constructor)
2. assign values to the private data members
3. calculate and return the area of the object
4. calculate and return the perimeter of the object

Figure 12-5: Tasks a Rectangle object should be capable of performing

As Figure 12-5 indicates, a Rectangle object will need to initialize its private data members; you will include a default constructor function in the class for this purpose. A Rectangle object also will need to provide a means for the program to assign values to the private data members; this task will be handled by a void member function named `setDimensions`. You will use two value-returning member functions named `area` and `perimeter` to perform the third and fourth tasks listed in Figure 12-5, which are to calculate and return the area and perimeter of a Rectangle object. Figure 12-6 shows the completed declaration section for the `Rectangle` class.

store the length and width values passed by the program

```
//declaration section
class Rectangle
{
public:
    Rectangle();
    void setDimensions(float, float);
    float area();
    float perimeter();
private:
    float length;
    float width;
};
```

Figure 12-6: Declaration section of the `Rectangle` class

Now that the declaration section of the class is complete, you can move on to the implementation section, which contains the function definitions for the member functions.

Completing the Implementation Section of the `Rectangle` Class

First you will code the Rectangle object's default constructor function. As you learned in the Concept lesson, the default constructor function simply initializes the data members (variables) in the class. In this case, the data members are `float` variables, so you will initialize each to 0.0, as shown in Figure 12-7.

```
//implementation section
Rectangle::Rectangle()
{
    length = 0.0;
    width  = 0.0;
}   //end of default constructor
```

Figure 12-7: Constructor function code shown in the implementation section

Listed second in the declaration section is the function prototype for the setDimensions member function. This function will need to receive the length and width values from the program, and then assign those values to the private members of the class. However, the values should be assigned only if both values are greater than zero. Figure 12-8 shows the appropriate code.

```
//implementation section
Rectangle::Rectangle()
{
    length = 0.0;
    width  = 0.0;
} //end of default constructor

void Rectangle::setDimensions(float len, float wid)
{
    //assigns length and width
    if (len > 0 && wid > 0)
    {
        length = len;
        width = wid;
    } //end if
} //end of setDimensions function
```

assign to private data members only if both values are greater than zero

Figure 12-8: setDimensions code included in the implementation section

The last two function prototypes listed in the declaration section are for the area and perimeter member functions. The area function will calculate the area by multiplying the contents of the private length variable by the contents of the private width variable; it then will return the result. The perimeter member function will add together the contents of the length and width variables, and then multiply the sum by 2; it then will return the result. Figure 12-9 shows both functions in the completed class definition.

```
//Rectangle - defines a Rectangle class

//declaration section
class Rectangle
{
public:
    Rectangle();
    void setDimensions(float, float);
    float area();
    float perimeter();
private:
    float length;
    float width;
};
```

Figure 12-9: Completed class definition for the Rectangle class

```
//implementation section
Rectangle::Rectangle()
{
     length = 0.0;
     width  = 0.0;
}   //end of default constructor
void Rectangle::setDimensions(float len, float wid)
{
     //assigns length and width
     if (len > 0 && wid > 0)
     {
          length = len;
          width = wid;
     } //end if
}   //end of setDimensions function

float Rectangle::area()
{
     return length * width;
}   //end of area function

float Rectangle::perimeter()
{
     return (length + width) * 2;
}   //end of perimeter function
```

Figure 12-9: Completed class definition for the `Rectangle` class (continued)

On your computer's hard disk is a header file that contains some of the class definition instructions shown in Figure 12-9. You will complete the header file in the next set of steps.

To complete the header file:

1 Start Visual C++. Open the **Rectangle** file, which is located in the Cpp\MyClasses folder on your computer's hard disk. (Note: You will need to change the Files of type list box in the Open dialog box to All Files (*.*).) The partially completed class definition appears on the screen.

2 Enter the additional instructions shaded in Figure 12-10, which shows the completed header file.

enter this code

```
//Rectangle - defines a Rectangle class

//declaration section
class Rectangle
{
public:
      Rectangle();
      void setDimensions(float, float);
      float area();
      float perimeter();
private:
      float length;
      float width;
};

//implementation section
Rectangle::Rectangle()
{
      length = 0.0;
      width  = 0.0;
}  //end of default constructor

void Rectangle::setDimensions(float len, float wid)
{
      //assigns length and width
      if (len > 0 && wid > 0)
      {
           length = len;
           width = wid;
      } //end if
}  //end of setDimensions function

float Rectangle::area()
{
      return length * width;
}  //end of area function

float Rectangle::perimeter()
{
      return (length + width) * 2;
}  //end of perimeter function
```

Figure 12-10: Completed Rectangle header file

3 Save and then close the header file.

Now that you have defined the Rectangle class, you can begin creating the Terney Landscaping program.

Analyzing, Planning, and Desk-Checking the Terney Landscaping Program

Figure 12-11 shows the IPO chart for the Terney Landscaping program.

Input	Processing	Output
length in feet width in feet sod price per square yard	Processing items: Rectangle object Algorithm: 1. enter length in feet, width in feet, and sod price per square yard 2. use the Rectangle object's setDimensions function to assign the length and width to the Rectangle object 3. use the Rectangle object's area function to calculate the area in square feet, then divide the result by 9 to get the area in square yards 4. calculate the total price by multiplying the area in square yards by the sod price per square yard 5. display the area in square yards and the total price	area in square yards total price

Figure 12-11: IPO chart for the Terney Landscaping program

The IPO chart shows that the output is the area (in square yards) and the total price. The input is the length and width of the rectangle (both in feet), and the price of a square yard of sod. Notice that a Rectangle object will be used as a processing item in the program.

As the algorithm shown in Figure 12-11 indicates, the program first will get the length, width, and price information from the user. The program will pass the length and width information to the Rectangle object's setDimensions function, which will assign the values (assuming that both are greater than zero) to the Rectangle object's private data members.

Step 3 in the algorithm is to calculate the area of the Rectangle object in square yards. To do so, the program first will call the Rectangle object's area function to calculate the area in square feet. It then will convert the value returned by the area function from square feet to square yards by dividing the return value by the number 9—the number of square feet in a square yard.

Step 4 in the algorithm is to calculate the total price by multiplying the number of square yards by the price per square yard of sod. The last step in the algorithm is to display the area (in square yards) and the total price on the screen. Notice that, although the Rectangle object also is capable of calculating its perimeter, the current program does not require the object to perform that task.

Your computer's hard disk contains a partially completed program for Terney Landscaping. You will complete the program in the next set of steps.

tip

You will use the perimeter function in Exercise 1 at the end of this lesson.

To complete the Terney Landscaping program:

1 Open the **T12App.cpp** file, which is located in the Cpp\Tut12\T12App folder on your computer's hard disk. The Terney Landscaping program appears in the T12App.cpp window.

2 Enter the additional instructions shaded in Figure 12-12. (If the full path to the Rectangle header file on your system differs from the one shown in the figure, then change the #include directive to reflect the full path used on your system.)

modify this directive,
if necessary

enter these three
lines of code

```cpp
//T12App.cpp - displays the cost of laying sod

#include <iostream>
#include "c:\cpp\myclasses\rectangle"

using namespace std;

int main()
{
    //declare rectangle object
    Rectangle lawnObj;

    //declare variables
    float lawnLength = 0.0;
    float lawnWidth  = 0.0;
    float lawnArea   = 0.0;
    float priceSqYd  = 0.0;
    float totalPrice = 0.0;

    //get the length, width, and price
    cout << "Enter the length, in feet: ";
    cin >> lawnLength;
    cout << "Enter the width, in feet: ";
    cin >> lawnWidth;
    cout << "Enter the price per square yard: ";
    cin >> priceSqYd;

    //assign data
    lawnObj.setDimensions(lawnLength, lawnWidth);

    //calculate the area in square yards
    lawnArea = lawnObj.area() / 9;

    //calculate the total price
    totalPrice = lawnArea * priceSqYd;

    //display the area and the total price
    cout << fixed;
    cout.precision(2);
    cout << "Square yards: " << lawnArea << endl;
    cout << "Total price: " << totalPrice << endl;

    return 0;
} //end of main function
```

Figure 12-12: Completed Terney Landscaping program

3 Save, build, and execute the program. When you are prompted to enter the length, type **120** and press the **Enter** key. When you are prompted to enter the width, type **75** and press the **Enter** key. When you are prompted to enter the price per square yard of sod, type **1.55** and press the **Enter** key. The DOS window shows that the area in square yards is 1000.00 and the total price is $1550.00.

4 Press the **Enter** key to close the DOS window. Hide the Output window, then use the File menu to close the workspace.

5 When prompted to close all document windows, click the **Yes** button, then exit Visual C++.

You now have completed Tutorial 12's Application lesson. You can either take a break or complete the end-of-lesson exercises.

EXERCISES

1. In this exercise, you will use the `Rectangle` class that you created in this lesson to declare a `Rectangle` object in the All-Around Fence program. (Recall that the `Rectangle` class is defined in the Cpp\MyClasses\Rectangle file on your computer's hard disk.)

Jack Sysmanski, the owner of All-Around Fence Company, wants a program that he can use to calculate the cost of installing a fence.

a. Open the T12AppE01.cpp file contained in the Cpp\Tut12\T12AppE01 folder on your computer's hard disk.

b. Complete the program, using the IPO chart shown in Figure 12-13. Display the perimeter and price using fixed-point notation with two decimal places.

Input	Processing	Output
length in feet width in feet fence cost per linear foot	Processing items: Rectangle object Algorithm: 1. enter length in feet, width in feet, and fence cost per linear foot 2. use the Rectangle object's setDimensions function to assign the length and width to the Rectangle object 3. use the Rectangle object's perimeter function to calculate the perimeter 4. calculate the total price by multiplying the perimeter by the fence cost per linear foot 5. display the perimeter and total price	perimeter total price

Figure 12-13

c. Save, build, and execute the program. Test the program using 120 as the length, 75 as the width, and 10 as the price. The program should display 390.00 as the perimeter and 3900.00 as the total price.

d. When the program is working correctly, hide the Output window, then use the File menu to close the workspace.

2. In this exercise, you will modify the `Rectangle` class that you created in this lesson so that it allows a program to view the contents of the `length` and `width` data members.

a. Open the T12AppE02 header file contained in the Cpp\MyClasses folder on your computer's hard disk. (Note: You will need to change the Files of type list box in the Open dialog box to All Files (*.*).) Add two value-returning member functions to the class; each function should return the value of one of the attributes.

b. Save and then close the header file.

c. Open the T12AppE02.cpp file contained in the Cpp\Tut12\T12AppE02 folder on your computer's hard disk. If necessary, change the `#include "c:\cpp\myclasses\t12appe02"` directive to reflect the location of the header file on your computer's hard disk.

d. Modify the program so that it displays the length and width of the rectangle, in addition to the area and total price. (Use the functions you created in Step a.)

e. Save, build, and execute the program. Use 120 feet as the length, 75 feet as the width, and 1.55 as the price. The program should display 120.00 as the length, 75.00 as the width, 1000.00 as the area, and $1550.00 as the price.

f. When the program is working correctly, hide the Output window, then use the File menu to close the workspace.

3. In this exercise, you will modify the `Rectangle` class that you created in this lesson so that its `setDimensions` function returns a value. You also will modify the Terney Landscaping program.

a. Open the T12AppE03 header file contained in the Cpp\MyClasses folder on your computer's hard disk. (Note: You will need to change the Files of type list box in the Open dialog box to All Files (*.*).) Modify the `setDimensions` function so that it returns a value that indicates whether the length and width dimensions passed to the function are greater than zero.

b. Save and then close the header file.

c. Open the T12AppE03.cpp file contained in the Cpp\Tut12\T12AppE03 folder on your computer's hard disk. If necessary, change the `#include "c:\cpp\myclasses\t12appe03"` directive to reflect the location of the header file on your computer's hard disk.

d. If the `setDimensions` function indicates that the length and width dimensions are greater than zero, the program should calculate and display both the area and the total price; otherwise, it should display an error message. Modify the program appropriately.

e. Save, build, and execute the program. Enter 120 as the length, 75 as the width, and 1.55 as the price. The program should display 1000.00 as the area and $1550.00 as the total price. Press the Enter key to close the DOS window.

f. Execute the program again. Enter -5 as the length, 6 as the width, and 3 as the price. The program should display an error message, because the length dimension is less than zero. Press the Enter key to close the DOS window.

g. When the program is working correctly, hide the Output window, then use the File menu to close the workspace.

4. In this exercise, you will create a `Triangle` class. You also will complete a program that uses the `Triangle` class to declare a `Triangle` object.

a. Open the T12AppE04 header file contained in the Cpp\MyClasses folder on your computer's hard disk. (Note: You will need to change the Files of type list box in the Open dialog box to All Files (*.*).)

b. Create a `Triangle` class. The class should include a void member function that allows the program to set the triangle's dimensions. The member function should verify that all of the dimensions are greater than zero before assigning the values to the private data members. The class also should include two value-returning member functions.

One value-returning member function should calculate the area of a triangle, and the other should calculate the perimeter of a triangle. (*Hint*: The formula for calculating the area of a triangle is 1/2 * b * h, where b is the base and h is the height. The formula for calculating the perimeter of a triangle is a + b + c, where a, b, and c are the lengths of the sides.) Determine the appropriate variables to include in the class. Be sure to include a constructor function that initializes the variables.

c. Save and then close the header file.

d. Open the T12AppE04.cpp file contained in the Cpp\Tut12\T12AppE04 folder on your computer's hard disk. Declare a `Triangle` object. Prompt the user for the triangle's dimensions, then display the triangle's area and perimeter amounts. Display the amounts using fixed-point notation with two decimal places.

e. Save, build, and execute the program. Test the program by entering 10 as the base, 7 as the height, and 7, 10, and 7 as the three side lengths. The program should display 35.00 as the area and 24.00 as the perimeter.

f. When the program is working correctly, hide the Output window, then use the File menu to close the workspace.

5. In this exercise, you will modify an existing header file.

a. Open the T12AppE05 header file contained in the Cpp\MyClasses folder on your computer's hard disk. (Note: You will need to change the Files of type list box in the Open dialog box to All Files (*.*).) The header file defines a class named `Date`. Study the code. Because the header file uses the `cout` stream, it must include the `#include <iostream>` and `using namespace std;` directives.

b. Close the header file.

c. Open the T12AppE05.cpp file contained in the Cpp\Tut12\T12AppE05 folder on your computer's hard disk. If necessary, change the `#include "c:\cpp\myclasses\t12appe05"` directive to reflect the location of the header file on your computer's hard disk.

The program uses the `Date` class to create an object named `today`. Study the code. Notice that the program prompts the user to enter the month, day, and year. It then uses the `Date` class's public member functions (`setDate` and `displayDate`) both to set and display the date entered by the user. The program also uses a public member function named `updateDate` to increase the day by 1. It then displays the new date on the screen.

d. Build and execute the program. Enter 3 as the month, 15 as the day, and 2002 as the year. The DOS window shows that today is 3/15/2002 and tomorrow is 3/16/2002, which is correct. Press the Enter key to close the DOS window.

e. Execute the program again. Enter 3 as the month, 31 as the day, and 2002 as the year. The DOS window shows that today is 3/31/2002 and tomorrow is 3/32/2002, which is incorrect. Press the Enter key to close the DOS window.

f. Open the T12AppE05 header file. Modify the `updateDate` function so that it updates the date correctly. For example, if today is 3/31/2002, then tomorrow is 4/1/2002. If today is 12/31/2002, then tomorrow is 1/1/2003. You do not have to worry about leap years; treat February as though it always has 28 days.

g. Save and then close the header file.

h. Save, build, and then execute the program. Test the program four times, using the following dates: 3/15/2001, 4/30/2002, 2/28/2003, and 12/31/2002. The DOS window should show that tomorrow's dates are 3/16/2001, 5/1/2002, 3/1/2003, and 1/1/2003.

i. When the program is working correctly, hide the Output window, then use the File menu to close the workspace.

6. In this exercise, you will create a class that converts a full name to uppercase letters.

a. Open the T12AppE06 header file contained in the Cpp\MyClasses folder on your computer's hard disk. (Note: You will need to change the Files of type list box in the Open dialog box to All Files (*.*).) Notice that the file contains three directives: `#include <string>`, `#include <algorithm>`, and `using namespace std;`. These directives must be included because the header file will create a `string` variable and also use a function contained in the algorithm library.

b. Create a class named Name. Include one private data member in the class: a string variable named firstLast. Include three public member functions in the class. The first member function should be the constructor function. The second member function should be a value-returning function that allows a program to view the contents of the firstLast data member; name the function getName. The third member function, named upperCase, should be a void function that converts the name (which is passed to the function by a program) to uppercase letters, and then assigns the name to the firstLast data member.

c. Save and then close the header file.

d. Open the T12AppE06.cpp file contained in the Cpp\Tut12\T12AppE06 folder on your computer's hard disk. If necessary, change the #include "c:\cpp\myclasses\t12appe06" directive to reflect the location of the header file on your computer's hard disk.

e. Complete the program, which should allow the user to enter a full name (first name followed by a space and the last name). It then should use the upperCase function defined in the Name class to convert the full name to uppercase letters, and use the getName function to display the name on the screen.

f. Save, build, and execute the program. When prompted to enter a name, type your full name, using all lowercase letters, and press the Enter key. Your full name should be displayed in uppercase letters in the DOS window. Press the Enter key to close the DOS window.

g. When the program is working correctly, hide the Output window, then use the File menu to close the workspace.

7. In this exercise, you will modify the class that you created in Exercise 6. You will add a member function that converts a name (first and last) to the proper case.

a. Use Windows to copy the T12AppE06 header file contained in the Cpp\MyClasses folder on your computer's hard disk. Rename the copy T12AppE07.

b. Open the T12AppE07 header file contained in the Cpp\MyClasses folder on your computer's hard disk. (Note: You will need to change the Files of type list box in the Open dialog box to All Files (*.*).)

c. Add another public member function named properCase to the class. The function should be a void function that converts the name (which is passed to the function by a program) to the proper case, and then assigns the name to the firstLast data member. Proper case means that only the first letter in the first and last name should be uppercase; the remaining letters should be lowercase, like this: Donald Tailer. (Hint: Use a string function to search for the space that separates the first name from the last name.)

d. Save and then close the header file.

e. Open the T12AppE07.cpp file contained in the Cpp\Tut12\T12AppE07 folder on your computer's hard disk. If necessary, change the #include "c:\cpp\myclasses\t12appe07" directive to reflect the location of the header file on your computer's hard disk.

f. Complete the program, which should allow the user to enter a full name (first name followed by a space and the last name). It then should use the properCase function defined in the Name class to convert the full name to the proper case, and use the getName function to display the name on the screen.

g. Save, build, and execute the program. When prompted to enter a name, type GEORGE SMITH and press the Enter key. The name George Smith should appear in the DOS window. Press the Enter key to close the DOS window.

h. Execute the program again. This time, type your full name, using all lowercase letters, and press the Enter key. When your name appears in the DOS window, only the first letter in your first name and the first letter in your last name should be uppercase; the remaining letters should be lowercase. Press the Enter key to close the DOS window.

i. When the program is working correctly, hide the Output window, then use the File menu to close the workspace.

8. In this exercise, you will modify the Terney Landscaping program that you created in the lesson so that it passes an object to a function.

    a. Use Windows to create a folder named T12AppE08 in the Cpp\Tut12 folder on your computer's hard disk. Copy the T12App.cpp file from the Cpp\Tut12\T12App folder to the T12AppE08 folder. Rename the file T12AppE08.cpp.

    b. Open the T12AppE08.cpp file. Modify the program so that it uses a function named `calcAndDisplay` to calculate and display the area. Pass the `Rectangle` object and the price per square yard to the function.

    c. Save, build, and execute the program. Enter 120 as the length, 75 as the width, and 1.55 as the price per square yard of sod. The program should display 1000.00 as the area and $1550.00 as the total price. Press the Enter key to close the DOS window.

    d. When the program is working correctly, hide the Output window, then use the File menu to close the workspace.

Exercise 9 is a Discovery Exercise. Discovery Exercises, which may include topics that are not covered in this lesson, allow you to "discover" the solutions to problems on your own.

9. In this exercise, you will learn how to overload a function.

    Pool-Time, which sells in-ground pools, wants a program that its salespeople can use to determine the number of gallons of water required to fill an in-ground pool—a question commonly asked by customers. To calculate the number of gallons, you will need to find the volume of the pool. (The volume formula is length * width * depth.)

    a. Open the T12AppE09 header file contained in the Cpp\MyClasses folder on your computer's hard disk. (Note: You will need to change the Files of type list box in the Open dialog box to All Files (*.*).) Modify the `Rectangle` class appropriately. You will need to include an additional private data member for the depth attribute, and an additional public member function that calculates and returns the volume. Name the function `volume`. You also will need to modify the constructor function so that it initializes the new private data member. Additionally, the `setDimensions` function will need to receive the depth value from the program, and it should verify that the depth value is greater than zero before assigning the value to the private data member.

    b. Save and then close the header file.

    c. Open the T12AppE09.cpp file contained in the Cpp\Tut12\T12AppE09 folder on your computer's hard disk.

    d. Complete the program, using the IPO chart shown in Figure 12-14. Display the volume and number of gallons using fixed-point notation with two decimal places.

Input	Processing	Output
length in feet width in feet depth in feet	Processing items: Rectangle object Algorithm: 1. enter length in feet, width in feet, and depth in feet 2. use the Rectangle object's setDimensions function to assign the length, width, and depth to the Rectangle object 3. use the Rectangle object's volume function to calculate the volume in cubic feet 4. calculate the number of gallons of water by dividing the volume by .13368 5. display the volume and number of gallons of water	volume in cubic feet number of gallons of water

Figure 12-14

e. Save, build, and execute the program. Use 25 feet as the length, 15 feet as the width, and 6.5 feet as the depth. The program should display 2437.50 as the volume, and 18233.84 as the number of gallons.

f. When the program is working correctly, hide the Output window, then use the File menu to close the workspace.

Now observe what happens when you use the modified Rectangle class in the Terney Landscaping program that you created in the lesson.

g. Use Windows to copy the T12App.cpp file, which is contained in the Cpp\Tut12\T12App folder on your computer's hard disk, to the Cpp\Tut12\T12AppE09 folder.

h. Open the T12App.cpp file contained in the Cpp\Tut12\T12AppE09 folder. Change the #include "c:\cpp\myclasses\rectangle" directive to #include "c:\cpp\myclasses\t12appe09" (or the location of the header file on your computer's hard disk). Study the code. Notice that the program passes two actual arguments to the setDimensions function. Build the program. The C++ compiler displays an error message indicating that the setDimensions function does not take two parameters.

In C++, you can assign the same name to more than one function, as long as each function has a different set of formal parameters. To use the Rectangle class in the Terney Landscaping and Pool-Time programs, for example, you will provide two setDimensions functions in the Rectangle class: one having two formal parameters (for the Terney Landscaping program) and the other having three formal parameters (for the Pool-Time program). When two functions have the same name but different parameters, the functions are said to be *overloaded*.

i. Open the T12AppE09 header file contained in the Cpp\MyClasses folder on your computer's hard disk. Enter the prototype and definition for a setDimensions function that accepts two float values, verifies that the values are greater than zero, and then assigns the values to the private data members.

j. Save and then close the header file.

k. Build and then execute the T12App.cpp program. Enter 120 as the length, 75 as the width, and 1.55 as the price per square yard of sod. The program displays 1000.00 as the area and $1550.00 as the total price. Press the Enter key to close the DOS window.

l. When the program is working correctly, hide the Output window, then use the File menu to close the workspace.

A computer program is good only if it works. Errors in either an algorithm or programming code can cause the program to run incorrectly. Therefore, a programmer needs to know how to locate and fix these errors. Exercise 10 is a Debugging Exercise. Debugging Exercises allow you to practice recognizing and solving errors in a program.

debugging

10. In this exercise, you will debug an existing C++ program.

a. Open the T12AppE10 header file contained in the Cpp\MyClasses folder on your computer's hard disk. (Note: You will need to change the Files of type list box in the Open dialog box to All Files (*.*).)

b. Study the Inventory class code, then close the header file.

c. Open the T12AppE10.cpp program contained in the Cpp\Tut12\T12AppE10 folder on your computer's hard disk. The program prompts the user to enter an item name and the amount of the item in inventory. It then displays the name and amount on the screen.

d. Build the program. Correct any errors in the program and/or header file.

e. Save, build, and execute the program. Enter Chair as the item name and 10 as the amount. The program should display "Name: Chair" and "Amount: 10" in the DOS window.

f. When the program is working correctly, hide the Output window, then use the File menu to close the workspace.

Sequential Access Files

After completing this tutorial, you will be able to:

- Open and close a sequential access data file
- Write information to a sequential access data file
- Read information from a sequential access data file
- Test for the end of a sequential access data file
- Consume characters using the `ignore` function
- Include a delimeter character in the `getline` function

Concept Lesson

Data Files

In all of the programs you created in the previous tutorials, the data processed by the program was entered from the keyboard each time the program was executed. This approach works fine in programs that require only a small amount of data. However, most real-world programs—such as payroll and inventory programs—process large amounts of data. Consider how time-consuming it would be to have a payroll clerk enter every employee's data—Social Security number, name, rate of pay, and so on—each time he or she processed the weekly payroll!

In addition to getting data from the keyboard, a program also can get data from a file, called a data file, stored on the computer's disk. This means that, rather than having the payroll clerk enter the employee data each week, you can save the data to a data file, and then instruct the payroll program to get its input data from there as often as needed.

Typically, the information in a data file is organized into fields and records. A **field** is a single item of information about a person, place, or thing—for example, a Social Security number, a city, or a price. A **record** is one or more related fields that contain all of the necessary data about a specific person, place, or thing. The college you are attending keeps a student record on you. Your student record might contain the following fields: your Social Security number, name, address, phone number, credits earned, grades earned, grade point average, and so on. The place where you are employed also keeps a record on you. Your employee record might contain your Social Security number, name, address, phone number, starting date, salary or hourly wage, and so on. A collection of related records is called a **data file**. The collection of records for each of the students in your class forms the class data file; the collection of employee records forms the employee data file. Figure 13-1 illustrates the concept of fields and records in a data file.

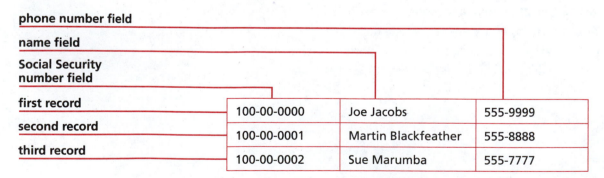

Figure 13-1: Illustration of fields and records in a data file

In most programming languages, you can create three different types of data files: sequential, random, and binary. The data file type refers to how the data is accessed. The data in a sequential access file is always accessed sequentially—in other words, in consecutive order. The data in a random access file, on the other hand, can be accessed either in consecutive order or in random order. The data in a binary access file can be accessed by its byte location in the file. You will learn about sequential access files in this tutorial. Random and binary access files are advanced programming topics that are beyond the scope of this book.

Sequential Access Data Files

Sequential access files are similar to cassette tapes in that each record in the file, like each song on a cassette tape, is both stored and retrieved in consecutive order (sequentially). Sequential access files have the advantage of being very easy to create. The drawback of this file type is the same drawback encountered with cassette tapes: the records in a sequential access file, like the songs on a cassette tape, can be processed only in the order in which they are stored. In other words, if you want to listen to the third song on a cassette tape, you must play (or fast-forward through) the first two songs. Likewise, if you want to read the third record in a sequential access file, you first must read the two records that precede it. Sequential access files work best when you want to process either a small file—one that contains fewer than 100 records—or a large file whose records are always processed in consecutive order.

Before a sequential access file can be written to or read from, it must be created and opened.

Creating and Opening a Sequential Access Data File

As you know, you use stream objects to perform standard input and output operations in C++. The standard input stream object, `cin`, refers to the keyboard, and the standard output stream object, `cout`, refers to the computer screen. For a program to use the standard input and output stream objects, recall that it must include the iostream header file. The header file contains the definitions of the `istream` and `ostream` classes, from which the `cin` and `cout` objects, respectively, are created. Recall that you do not have to create the `cin` and `cout` objects, as C++ creates these objects in the iostream header file for you.

In addition to getting information from the keyboard and sending output to the computer screen, a program also can get information from and send information to a file on a disk. Getting information from a file is referred to as "reading the file," and sending information to a file is referred to as "writing to the file." Data files to which information is written are called **output files**, because the files store the output produced by a program. Data files that are read by the computer are called **input files**, because a program uses the data in these files as input.

Just as you do to perform standard input and output operations, you use objects to perform file input and output operations. Unlike the standard `cin` and `cout` objects, which C++ creates, the programmer must create the input and output file objects used in a program. To create a file object, you must include the fstream header file in the program. The fstream header file contains the definitions of the `ifstream` (*input file stream*) and `ofstream` (*output file stream*) classes that allow you to create input and output file objects, respectively. Figure 13-2 shows examples of statements that use the `ifstream` and `ofstream` classes to create input and output file objects.

tip

As you learned in Tutorial 12, all objects are created from a class and are referred to as instances of the class. For example, an input file object is an instance of the `ifstream` class, and an output file object is an instance of the `ofstream` class.

Syntax	Examples	Result
ifstream *object*;	`ifstream inFile;`	creates an input file object named `inFile`
	`ifstream inEmploy;`	creates an input file object named `inEmploy`
ofstream *object*;	`ofstream outFile;`	creates an output file object named `outFile`
	`ofstream outSales;`	creates an output file object named `outSales`

Figure 13-2: Examples of using the `ifstream` and `ofstream` classes to create file objects

As Figure 13-2 shows, the syntax for creating an input file object is **ifstream** *object*; and the syntax for creating an output file object is **ofstream** *object*;. In each syntax, *object* is the name of the file object you want to create. Notice that the names of the input file objects (`inFile` and `inEmploy`) in the figure begin with the two letters `in`, and the names of the output file objects (`outFile` and `outSales`) begin with the three letters `out`. Although the C++ syntax does not require you to begin file object names with either `in` or `out`, using this naming convention helps to distinguish a program's input file objects from its output file objects.

You use the input and output file objects, along with the C++ **open** function, to open actual files on your computer's disk. The **open** function is a public member function defined in both the **ifstream** and **ofstream** classes. The syntax of the **open** function is *object*.**open(***filename* [, *mode*]**);**. In the syntax, *object* is the name of either an **ifstream** or an **ofstream** file object, and *filename*, which must be enclosed in quotation marks, is the name of the file you want to open on the computer's disk. If the file you want to open is not in the same location as the program file, you will need to enter the file's full path in the *filename* argument. For example, to open the scores.dat file contained in the Tut13 folder on the A drive, you would use "a:\tut13\scores.dat" as the *filename* argument in the **open** function. The **open** function associates the opened file with the file object whose name is specified in the syntax as *object*.

The *mode* argument, which is optional in the **open** function's syntax, indicates how the file is to be opened. Figure 13-3 lists the most commonly used *mode*s and describes their meaning. The `ios::in` *mode* is used when opening input files; the `ios::out` and `ios::app` *mode*s are used when opening output files.

If you do not supply the file's full path in the *filename* argument, the `open` function assumes that the file is located in the same folder as the program file.

As you learned in Tutorial 12, the functions within a class are referred to as member functions, because they are members (parts) of the class. Also recall that the period (.) between *object* and the name of the member function is called the dot member selection operator.

input file *mode*s	Description
`ios::in`	Opens the file for input, which allows the program to read the file's contents. This is the default *mode* for input files.
output file *mode*s	**Description**
`ios::app`	Opens the file for append, which allows the program to write new data to the end of the existing data in the file. If the file does not exist, the file is created before data is written to it.
`ios::out`	Opens the file for output, which creates a new, empty file to which data can be written. If the file already exists, its contents are erased before the new data is written. This is the default *mode* for output files.

Figure 13-3: Most commonly used `open` function *mode*s

As you learned in Tutorial 12, a base class is a class from which another class, referred to as the derived class, is created. In this case, the ios **class is the base class for the derived classes** ifstream **and** ofstream.

Notice that `ios::` appears in each *mode* shown in Figure 13-3. The two colons (::), called the **scope resolution operator**, indicate that the `in`, `out`, and `app` keywords, which follow the scope resolution operator in each *mode*, are defined in the `ios` class. The `ios` class is the base class that defines all input/output operations in C++.

The `ios::in` *mode* tells the computer to open the file for input, which allows the program to read the data stored in the file. You can use the `ios::in` *mode* in `open` functions that open input files only. You can use either the `ios::app` *mode* or the `ios::out` *mode*, on the other hand, in `open` functions that open output files only. Both of these *modes* allow the program to write data to the files. You use the `ios::app` (app stands for *append*) *mode* when you want to add data to the end of an existing file. If the file does not exist, the computer creates the file for you. You use the `ios::out` *mode* to open a new, empty file for output. If the file already exists, the computer erases the contents of the file before writing any data to it. Figure 13-4 shows examples of using the `open` function to open input and output files.

Examples of opening input files	Results
`inFile.open("sales.dat", ios::in);`	opens the sales.dat file for input
`inFile.open("sales.dat");`	opens the sales.dat file for input
Examples of opening output files	**Results**
`outFile.open("payroll.dat", ios::out);`	opens the payroll.dat file for output
`outFile.open("payroll.dat");`	opens the payroll.dat file for output
`outFile.open("employ.dat", ios::app);`	opens the employ.dat file for append
`outFile.open("a:\employ.dat", ios::app);`	opens the employ.dat file contained on the A drive for append

Important note: In the above examples, `inFile` is the name of an `ifstream` object and `outFile` is the name of an `ofstream` object. All but the last example assume that the file being opened is in the same location as the program file.

Figure 13-4: Examples of using the `open` function to open input and output files

You should assign meaningful names to the files you create. For example, a meaningful name for a data file that contains test scores is scores.dat. Many programmers use a .dat filename extension to indicate that a file is a data file.

As Figure 13-4 indicates, you can use either the statement `inFile.open("sales.dat", ios::in);` or the statement `inFile.open("sales.dat");` to open the sales.dat file for input. In C++, all files associated with an `ifstream` file object are opened automatically for input. Therefore, if you do not specify a *mode* when opening an input file, C++ uses the default *mode* `ios::in`.

Files associated with an `ofstream` file object, on the other hand, are opened automatically for output. In other words, `ios::out` is the default *mode* when opening output files, which explains why you can use either the statement `outFile.open("payroll.dat", ios::out);` or the statement `outFile.open("payroll.dat");` to open the payroll.dat file for output. In cases where the program needs to add data to the end of the existing data stored in an output file, you will need to specify the `ios::app` *mode* in the `open` function. The statement `outFile.open("employ.dat", ios::app);`, for example, tells the computer to open the employ.dat file, which is contained in the same location as the program file, for append. Notice, however, that you would need to use the statement `outFile.open("a:\employ.dat", ios::app);` to open the employ.dat file located on the A drive for append. For most data files, you will want to append new information to the end of the existing information, rather than erase the existing information, so in most cases you will use the `ios::app` *mode* when opening output data files.

The computer uses a record indicator to keep track of the next record either to read or write in a data file. When you open a file for input, the computer positions the record indicator at the beginning of the file, immediately before the first record. When you open a file for output, the computer also positions the record indicator at the beginning of the file, but recall that the file is empty. (As you learned earlier, opening a file for output tells the computer to create a new, empty file or erase the contents of an existing file.) However, when you use the `ios::app` *mode* to open a file for append, the computer positions the record indicator immediately after the last record in the file. Figure 13-5 illustrates the positioning of the record indicator when files are opened for input, output, and append.

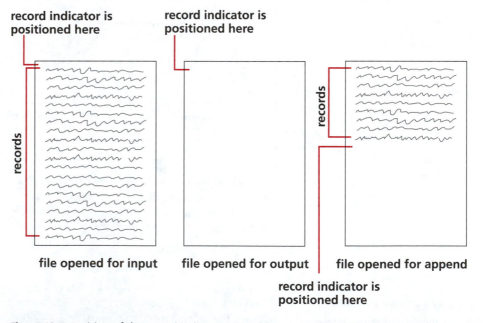

Figure 13-5: Position of the record indicator when files are opened for input, output, and append

mini-quiz

Mini-Quiz 1

1. A collection of related records is called a(n) _____ .

2. To use either an input or output file, the program must include the _____ header file.

    a. filestream

    b. fstream

    c. instream

    d. iostream

3. The _____ mode tells the computer to open a file for input.

    a. `add::ios`

    b. `in::file`

    c. `ios::app`

    d. `ios::in`

4. Write the C++ statement that creates an output file object named `outName`.

5. Which of the following statements uses the `outName` file object created in Question 4 to open an output file named items.dat? New information should be written following the current information in the file.

    a. `outName.open("items.dat", ios::in);`

    b. `outName.open("items.dat", ios::out);`

    c. `outName.open("items.dat", ios::app);`

    d. `outName.open("items.dat", ios::add);`

Before attempting either to read data from or write data to a file, you always should verify that the file was opened successfully.

Determining Whether a File Was Opened Successfully

It is possible for the `open` function to fail when attempting to open a file. For example, the `open` function will not be able to create an output file on a disk that is either full or write-protected. It also will not be able to open an input file that does not exist. Before attempting either to read from or write to a file, you should use the C++ `is_open` function to determine if the file was opened successfully. The `is_open` function is a public member function defined in both the `ifstream` and `ofstream` classes.

The syntax of the `is_open` function is *object*.**is_open**(), where *object* is the name of a file object in the program. If the file was opened successfully, the `is_open` function returns the Boolean value `true`; otherwise, the function returns the Boolean value `false`. Most times, you will use the `is_open` function in an `if` statement's *condition*, as shown in Figure 13-6.

Determining whether the open **function was successful in opening the file**

Example 1:
```
if (outFile.is_open() == true)
    instructions to process if the file was opened
else
    instructions to process if the file could not be opened
//end if
```

Example 2:
```
if (outFile.is_open())
    instructions to process if the file was opened
else
    instructions to process if the file could not be opened
//end if
```

Determining whether the open **function was unsuccessful in opening the file**

Example 3:
```
if (outFile.is_open() == false)
    instructions to process if the file could not be opened
else
    instructions to process if the file was opened
//end if
```

Example 4:
```
if (!outFile.is_open())
    instructions to process if the file could not be opened
else
    instructions to process if the file was opened
//end if
```

Not logical operator

Figure 13-6: Examples of using the is_open function in an if statement's *condition*

As Figure 13-6 shows, you can use either of the *conditions* shown in Examples 1 and 2 to determine if the open function was successful. Example 1's *condition*, outFile.is_open() == true, compares the is_open function's return value to the value true; recall that a return value of true indicates that the function was able to open the file. Notice in Example 2 that you can omit the text == true from the *condition*, and simply use outFile.is_open().

Unlike the *conditions* contained in Examples 1 and 2, the *conditions* contained in Examples 3 and 4 determine if the open function was unsuccessful rather than successful. Example 3's *condition*, outFile.is_open() == false, compares the is_open function's return value to the value false; recall that a return value of false indicates that the function was unable to open the file. Notice in Example 4 that you can omit the text == false from the *condition*, but to do so you must begin the *condition* with an exclamation point (!). The ! is the Not logical operator in C++, and its purpose is simply to reverse the truth value of the *condition*. In other words, if the value of the *condition* is true, then the value of !*condition* is false. Likewise, if the value of the *condition* is false, then the value of !*condition* is true.

Before learning how to write records to and read records from a file, you will learn how to close an open file.

Closing a File

To prevent the loss of data, you should close any files opened by a program before the program ends. You close an open file using the C++ `close` function, which is a public member function defined in both the `ifstream` and `ofstream` classes. The syntax of the `close` function is *object*.**close**(), where *object* is the name of a file object in the program. The `close` function does not require the name of the file to close, because the computer automatically closes the file whose name is associated with the file object specified as *object*. Recall that the `open` function associates the filename with the file object when the file is opened. Figure 13-7 shows two examples of using the `close` function in a statement to close files.

Examples of using the `close` function in a statement	Results
`outFile.close();`	closes the file associated with the file object named `outFile`
`inFile.close();`	closes the file associated with the file object named `inFile`

Figure 13-7: Examples of the `close` function

As Figure 13-7 indicates, you use the statement `outFile.Close();` to close the output file associated with the file object named `outFile`, and you use the statement `inFile.close();` to close the input file associated with the file object named `inFile`.

Next, you will learn how to write records to a sequential access data file.

> **tip**
>
> Because it is so easy to forget to close the files used in a program, you should enter the statement to close the file as soon as possible after entering the one that opens it. Forgetting to close an open file can result in a loss of data.

> **tip**
>
> Because the newline character is invisible, you will not see it when you open a data file.

Writing Records to a Sequential Access Data File

In C++, the syntax for writing a record to a sequential access data file is similar to the syntax for displaying information on the computer screen. Recall that the syntax for displaying information is **cout** << *data* << **endl;**, where *data* is one or more variables or constants. The statement `cout << score << endl;`, for example, displays the contents of the `score` variable and then advances the cursor to the next line on the screen.

Similarly, the syntax for writing a record to a sequential access data file is *object* << *data* << **endl;**, where *object* is the name of the program's `ofstream` object, and *data* is the one or more fields included in each record. To distinguish one record from another in the data file, programmers typically write each record on a separate line in the file. The `endl` stream manipulator included at the end of the syntax accomplishes this by writing an invisible character—referred to as the newline character—at the end of each record. The **newline character**, which is designated as '\n' (the backslash and letter n in single quotation marks) in C++, advances the cursor to the next line in the file immediately after a record is written. In other words, the newline character is equivalent to pressing the Enter key.

When writing to a file a record that contains more than one field, programmers typically separate each field with a character literal constant; '#' is most commonly used. Figure 13-8 shows examples of writing records to a sequential access data file.

Examples	Results
| ```cpp
//Example 1 — records contain one numeric field
int pay = 0;
cout << "Pay (-1 to stop): ";
cin >> pay;
while (pay > 0)
{
    //write pay to file
    outFile << pay << endl;
    cout << "Pay (-1 to stop): ";
    cin >> pay;
} //end while
``` | Assuming the user enters 450, 530, 250, 670, 800, and -1, the file would contain the following records:<br><br>450<br>530<br>250<br>670<br>800 |
| ```cpp
//Example 2 - records contain two string fields
string state   = "";
string capital = "";
cout << "State (X to stop): ";
getline(cin, state);
while (state != "X" && state != "x")
{
    cout << "Capital: ";
    getline(cin, capital);
    //write record to file
    outFile << state << '#' << capital << endl;
    cout << "State (X to stop): ";
    getline(cin, state);
} //end while
``` | Assuming the user enters Oregon, Salem, New Jersey, Trenton, Ohio, Columbus, and X, the file would contain the following records:<br><br>Oregon#Salem<br>New Jersey#Trenton<br>Ohio#Columbus |
| ```cpp
//Example 3 - records contain a string field
//and a numeric field
string name = "";
int sales   = 0;
cout << "Name (X to stop): ";
getline(cin, name);
while (name != "X" && name != "x")
{
    cout << "Sales: ";
    cin >> sales;
    cin.ignore(1);
    //write record to file
    outFile << name << '#' << sales << endl;
    cout << "Name (X to stop): ";
    getline(cin, name);
} //end while
``` | Assuming the user enters Mary Jones, 2000, Susan Carello, 1000, John Hilo, 4000, and X, the file would contain the following records:<br><br>Mary Jones#2000<br>Susan Carello#1000<br>John Hilo#4000 |

ignore **function** ← (points to `cin.ignore(1);` in Example 3)

Figure 13-8: Examples of writing records to a sequential access data file
```

In the first example shown in Figure 13-8, each record contains one numeric field: a pay amount. The statement `outFile << pay << endl;` shown in the example writes each record on a separate line in the file, as indicated in the figure.

In the second example shown in Figure 13-8, each record contains two `string` fields: the name of a state and the name of the state's capital. In this example, the statement `outFile << state << '#' << capital << endl;` writes each record on a separate line in the file, with the # character separating the data in the state field from the data in the capital field.

Each record in the third example shown in Figure 13-8 also contains two fields: a salesperson's name and a sales amount. The name field is of type `string` and the sales field is of type `int`. In this example, the statement `outFile << name << '#' << sales << endl;` writes each record on a separate line in the file, with the # character separating the salesperson's name from his or her sales amount.

Notice that the `while` loop shown in Example 3 in Figure 13-8 uses the `ignore` function. You will learn about the `ignore` function in the next section.

The `ignore` Function

In some programs, you may need the computer to disregard, or skip, characters entered at the keyboard or read in from a file. In a C++ program, you instruct the computer to disregard characters using the `ignore` function. The function actually reads and then discards the characters—a process C++ programmers refer to as **consuming** the characters.

The syntax of the `ignore` function is *object*.**ignore**(*[nCount]* [, *delimCharacter*]);, where *object* is either `cin` or the name of an input file object. The *nCount* argument, which is optional, is an integer that represents the maximum number of characters you want the `ignore` function to consume. To consume one character, you use the number 1 as *nCount*; to consume three characters, you use the number 3.

The `ignore` function's *delimCharacter* (short for *delimiter character*) argument is a character that, when consumed, stops the `ignore` function from reading and discarding any additional characters. The `ignore` function stops reading and discarding characters either when it consumes *nCount* characters or when it consumes the *delimCharacter*, whichever occurs first. For example, if the `cin` stream contains the five characters 'A', 'B', 'C', 'D', and '\n' (the newline character), the statement `cin.ignore(3, '\n');` stops reading and discarding characters after it consumes the first three characters ('A', 'B', and 'C'); the fourth and fifth characters ('D' and '\n') remain in the `cin` stream and will be read by the next statement looking for keyboard input. The statement `cin.ignore(5, 'B');`, on the other hand, reads and discards only the first two characters ('A' and 'B'), leaving the remaining characters ('C', 'D', and '\n') in the `cin` stream. Figure 13-9 shows examples of using the `ignore` function to consume characters entered at the keyboard and read from a file.

tip

If you omit the *nCount* argument from the `ignore` function, the default value for the argument is 1. In other words, the statement `cin.ignore();` is equivalent to the statement `cin.ignore(1);`. Both statements consume one character entered at the keyboard.

tip

The `ignore` function is a public member function defined in the `istream` class.

Example	Result
`cin.ignore(100, '\n');`	Stops reading and discarding characters from the keyboard either after consuming the next 100 characters or after consuming the newline character, whichever occurs first.
`cin.ignore(25, '#');`	Stops reading and discarding characters from the keyboard either after consuming the next 25 characters or after consuming the # character, whichever occurs first.
`inFile.ignore(10, '#')`	Stops reading and discarding characters from an input file either after consuming the next 10 characters or after consuming the # character, whichever occurs first.
`inPay.ignore(1)`	Stops reading and discarding characters from an input file either after consuming the next character or after encountering the end of the file, whichever occurs first.

Figure 13-9: Examples of the `ignore` function

The first two examples shown in Figure 13-9 read and discard characters contained in the `cin` stream. The first example, `cin.ignore(100, '\n');`, reads and discards either 100 characters from the `cin` stream or all of the characters in the `cin` stream through the newline character. The second example, `cin.ignore(25, '#');`, consumes either 25 characters from the `cin` stream or all of the characters in the `cin` stream through the # delimiter character.

The third and fourth examples shown in Figure 13-9 read and discard characters contained in an input file. The third example, `inFile.ignore(10,'#');`, reads and discards either 10 characters from the input file or all of the characters in the input file through the # delimiter character. Notice that the fourth example, `inPay.ignore(1);`, does not specify a delimiter character. When using the `ignore` function to consume characters from an input file, the default delimiter character is `EOF`, a keyword that stands for "end of file." The statement `inPay.ignore(1);`, therefore, stops reading and discarding characters after it consumes one character or after it encounters the end of the input file, whichever occurs first.

To understand why the `ignore` function is necessary in Example 3 shown earlier in Figure 13-8, you will desk-check the example's program using "Sue" as the name and 250 as the sales amount. The program begins by declaring and initializing a `string` variable named `name` and an `int` variable named `sales`. The program then prompts the user to enter the name. Before allowing the user to enter the name, the `getline` function in the next statement, `getline(cin, name);`, looks in the `cin` stream to determine whether the stream contains any characters. Not finding any characters in the `cin` stream at this point, the `getline` function waits for the user to make an entry from the keyboard. In this case, the user types the letters S, u, and e, and then presses the Enter key to indicate that he or she is finished entering the name. The computer stores the characters entered by the user—'S', 'u', 'e', and '\n'— in the `cin` stream, and alerts the `getline` function that the `cin` stream now contains data. The `getline` function, which stops reading characters from the `cin` stream when it encounters the newline character, reads and then removes the letters S, u, and e from the `cin` stream; it stores the letters in the `name` variable. The `getline` function also removes the newline character ('\n') from the `cin` stream, but it discards this character.

The next line of code in Example 3's program is the beginning of a `while` loop that repeats its instructions as long as the `name` variable does not contain either the letter X or the letter x. The first instruction in the `while` loop prompts the user to enter a sales amount. Before allowing the user to enter the sales amount, the second instruction in the loop, `cin >> sales;`, looks in the `cin` stream to determine whether the stream contains any characters. Because the `cin` stream is empty at this point, the `>>` (extraction) operator waits for the user to enter a sales amount. In this case, the user enters the numbers 2, 5, and 0, and then presses the Enter key to indicate that he or she is finished entering the sales amount. The computer stores the numbers 2, 5, and 0, along with the newline character ('\n'), and in the `cin` stream, and alerts the `>>` operator that the `cin` stream now contains data. The `>>` operator removes the numbers 2, 5, and 0 from the `cin` stream and stores them (in binary format) in the `sales` variable, but leaves the newline character in the `cin` stream.

The next statement in the loop, `cin.ignore(1);`, tells the computer to read and discard the character currently in the `cin` stream. In this case, the `ignore` function will consume the newline character that was left in the stream after the sales amount was entered. If you do not use the `ignore` function at this point, the next `getline` function, which appears in the last statement in the loop, will find the newline character in the `cin` stream, and will interpret the newline character as the end of the name entry. As a result, rather than allowing the user to enter the salesperson's name, the `getline` function will assign the empty string to the `name` variable before reading and discarding the newline character from the `cin` stream. The user then will be prompted to enter a sales amount.

In the next section, you will view a program that demonstrates what you have learned so far about sequential access files.

tip

> You can learn more about the problem that occurs when using the `getline` function and the `>>` operator by completing Exercise 13 at the end of this lesson.

The Sales Program

Assume that a company wants to record each salesperson's quarterly sales in a sequential access file. You can use the sales program shown in Figure 13-10 to perform this task. (The lines of code pertaining to the sequential access file are shaded in the figure.)

```
//writes records to a sequential access file
#include <iostream>
#include <string>
#include <fstream>
using namespace std;

int main()
{
    //create file object and open file
    ofstream outFile;
    outFile.open("sales.dat", ios::app);
    //determine if the file was opened successfully
    if (outFile.is_open())
    {
        //declare variables
        string name = "";
        int sales    = 0;
        //get sales information
        cout << "Name (X to stop): ";
        getline(cin, name);
        while (name != "X" && name != "x")
        {
            cout << "Sales: ";
            cin >> sales;
            cin.ignore(1);
            //write record to file
            outFile << name << '#' << sales << endl;
            cout << "Name (X to stop): ";
            getline(cin, name);
        } //end while
        //close file
        outFile.close();
    }
    else
        cout << "File could not be opened." << endl;
    //end if
    return 0;
} //end of main function
```

Figure 13-10: The sales program that writes records

Notice that the #include <fstream> directive appears in the sales program shown in Figure 13-10; recall that the fstream header file is necessary to create file objects. In this case, the program creates an output file object named outFile using the statement ofstream outFile;.

After creating the output file object, the program uses the statement `outFile.open("sales.dat", ios::app);` to open the sales.dat file for append. If the file does not exist, the statement creates it and positions the record indicator at the beginning of the file; otherwise, it opens the existing file and positions the record indicator after the last record in the file. Recall that the `open` function also associates the file object (`outFile`) with the data file (sales.dat).

The `if  (outFile.is_open())` clause in the sales program uses the `is_open` function to determine whether the sales.dat file was opened successfully. If the `is_open` function returns the value false, the program displays an appropriate error message. If the `is_open` function returns the value true, the program gets the salesperson's name and his or her sales amount from the user, and then writes the information as a record to the file. Notice that the program uses the statement `outFile << name << '#' << sales << endl;` to write the record, which contains two fields, on a separate line in the file. In this case, the '#' character separates the data in the name field from the data in the sales field in the file.

As mentioned earlier, any files opened by a program should be closed before the program ends. The sales program opens one file only—sales.dat; the file will be closed by the statement `outFile.close();`, which appears after the `while` loop in the program. (Recall that the sales.dat file is associated with the `outFile` object.)

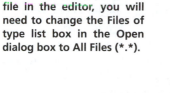

tip

> You can verify that the records were written correctly to a data file by opening the file in the Visual C++ editor. When opening the file in the editor, you will need to change the Files of type list box in the Open dialog box to All Files (*.*).

mini-quiz

Mini-Quiz 2

1. The `is_open` function returns _____ if the `open` function could not open the file.

2. Which of the following statements will write the contents of the `quantity` variable to the inventory.dat file, which is associated with a file object named `outInv`?

   a. `inventory.dat << quantity << endl;`

   b. `ofstream << quantity << endl;`

   c. `outInv << quantity << endl;`

   d. `outInv >> quantity << endl;`

3. Which of the following statements will write the contents of the `score1` and `score2` variables to the test.dat file, which is associated with a file object named `outFile`?

   a. `test.dat << score1 << score2 << endl;`

   b. `ofstream << score1 << score2 << endl;`

   c. `outFile << score1 << '#' << score2 << endl;`

   d. `outFile >> score1 << '#' << score2 << endl;`

4. Write the statement that will close the inventory.dat file, which is associated with a file object named `outInv`.

Next, learn how to read the data contained in a sequential access file.

Reading Records from a Sequential Access File

In C++, the syntax for reading information from a file is similar to the syntax for getting information from the keyboard. Recall that the syntax for getting numeric and **char** information from the keyboard is **cin >>** *variable*;. The statement **cin >> score;**, for example, gets a test score from the user at the keyboard and then stores the user's response in the **score** variable. Similarly, the syntax for reading numeric and **char** information from a file is *object >> variable*, where *object* is the name of an **ifstream** object in the program, and *variable* is the name of either a numeric or **char** variable. The statement **inFile >> score;**, for example, gets a test score from an input file and stores the score in the **score** variable.

The syntax used to read string information from a file is similar to the syntax used to get string information from the keyboard. To get string information from the keyboard, you use the syntax **getline(cin,** *variable*);. The statement **getline(cin, state);**, for example, gets a state name from the user at the keyboard and then stores the user's response in the **state** variable. To read string information from an input file, you use the syntax **getline(***object, variable*[, *delimCharacter*]);, where *object* is the name of an **ifstream** object in the program. The *delimCharacter* (short for *delimiter character*) argument, which is optional, indicates where the string ends by specifying the character that follows the last character in the string. For example, the statement **getline(inFile, state, '#');** indicates that the state field ends with the character immediately preceding the # character. After storing the string in the *variable* argument, the **getline** function consumes the *delimCharacter*. If you omit the *delimCharacter* argument from the **getline** function, the default *delimCharacter* is the newline character ('\n'). Figure 13-11 shows examples of reading records from a sequential access data file. (The records in each example were written to the file using the code shown earlier in Figure 13-8.)

Examples	Results
```//Example 1 — records contain one numeric field` `int pay = 0;` `inFile >> pay;` `while (!inFile.eof())` `{` ` //display record` ` cout << pay << endl;` ` inFile >> pay;` `} //end while```	Assuming the file contains the following records: 450 530 250 670 800 The following will be displayed: 450 530 250 670 800

Figure 13-11: Examples of reading records from a sequential access data file

```
//Example 2 - records contain two string fields      Assuming the file
string state   = "";                                 contains the
string capital = "";                                 following records:
getline(inFile, state, '#');                         Oregon#Salem
while (!inFile.eof())                                 New Jersey#Trenton
{                                                     Ohio#Columbus
    getline(inFile, capital, '\n');
    //display record                                 The following will
    cout << capital << ", " << state << endl;        be displayed:
    getline(inFile, state, '#');                     Salem, Oregon
} //end while                                        Trenton, New Jersey
                                                     Columbus, Ohio
```

```
//Example 3 - records contain a string field         Assuming the file
//and a numeric field                                contains the
string name = "";                                    following records:
int sales   = 0;                                     Mary Jones#2000
getline(inFile, name, '#');                          Susan Carello#1000
while (!inFile.eof())                                John Hilo#4000
{
    inFile >> sales;
    inFile.ignore(1);                                The following will
    //display record                                 be displayed:
    cout << name << " " << sales << endl;            Mary Jones 2000
    getline(inFile, name, '#');                      Susan Carello 1000
} //end while                                        John Hilo 4000
```

Figure 13-11: Examples of reading records from a sequential access data file (continued)

As Figure 13-11 indicates, each record in Example 1 appears on a separate line in the file and contains one numeric field: a pay amount. The code shown in the example uses the statement `inFile >> pay;` to read each record from the file.

The records in Example 2 in Figure 13-11 contain two `string` fields: the name of a state and the name of the state's capital. Notice that each record appears on a separate line in the file, and the # character separates the state field from the capital field. The code shown in this example uses the statement `getline(inFile, state, '#');` to read the state field in each record, and uses the statement `getline(inFile, capital, '\n');` to read the capital field.

The records in the third example shown in Figure 13-8 also contain two fields: a `string` field for the salesperson's name and an `int` field for the sales amount. Notice that each record appears on a separate line in the file, and the # character separates the name field from the sales field. In this example, the statement `getline(inFile, name, '#');` reads the name field in each record, and the statement `inFile >> sales;` reads the sales amount field. The statement `inFile.ignore(1);`, which appears below the statement `inFile >> sales;`, instructs the computer to consume (discard) the newline character that is at the end of each record in the file.

Each of the examples shown in Figure 13-11 includes a function named `eof`. You will learn about the `eof` function in the next section.

tip

As you may remember from Figure 11-8, the records in Example 1 were written to the file using the statement `outFile << pay << endl;`. The records in Examples 2 and 3 were written using the statements `outFile << state << '#' << capital << endl;`, and `outFile << name << '#' << sales << endl;`, respectively.

The eof Function

Recall that the computer uses a record indicator to keep track of the current record in the file. When a program first opens a sequential access file for input, the computer positions the record indicator before the first record in the file. Each time the program reads a record, the computer moves the record indicator to the beginning of the next record in the file. The only exception to this positioning occurs when the last record is read: at that time, the computer positions the record indicator after the last record in the file.

In most programs, the records in a sequential access file are read from the first record through the last record. You can use the C++ eof (*end of file*) function to determine whether the last record has been read—in other words, to determine whether the record indicator is located after the last record in the file. The syntax of the eof function is *object*.eof(), where *object* is the name of an input file object in the program. If the record indicator is located after the last record in the input file, the eof function returns the Boolean value true when the program attempts to read the next record; otherwise, it returns the Boolean value false.

In each of the examples shown in Figure 13-11, the while(!inFile.eof()) clause uses the eof function along with the ! (Not) logical operator to control the processing of the loop instructions. If the record indicator is *not* at the end of the file, the !inFile.eof() condition evaluates to true and the loop instructions are processed. However, if the record indicator *is* at the end of the file, the !inFile.eof() condition evaluates to false and the loop stops.

Mini-Quiz 3

1. Which of the following statements reads the contents of the quantity variable from the inventory.dat file, which is associated with a file object named inInv?

    a. ifstream >> quantity;

    b. inventory.dat >> quantity;

    c. inInv << quantity;

    d. inInv >> quantity;

2. Which of the following while clauses reads each record in the inventory.dat file while the record indicator is not at the end of the file? The file object is named inInv.

    a. while (inventory.dat.end())

    b. while (inInv.end())

    c. while (!inInv.eof())

    d. while (!inventory.dat.eof())

3. If the record indicator is not at the end of the file, the eof function returns the value _____ .

Next, view a program that reads records from a sequential access file.

Reading the Sales Program Records

The sales program shown earlier in Figure 13-10 wrote the sales records—names and sales amounts—to a sequential access file named sales.dat. The sales program shown in Figure 13-12 reads each record from the file, displaying the record on the screen. (The lines of code pertaining to the sequential access file are shaded in the figure.)

```cpp
//reads records from a sequential access file
#include <iostream>
#include <string>
#include <fstream>
using namespace std;

int main()
{
    //create file object and open file
    ifstream inFile;
    inFile.open("sales.dat", ios::in);
    //determine if the file was opened successfully
    if (inFile.is_open())
    {
        //declare variables
        string name = "";
        int sales   = 0;
        //read and display records
        getline(inFile, name, '#');
        while (!inFile.eof())
        {
            inFile >> sales;
            inFile.ignore(1);
            //display record
            cout << name << "   " << sales << endl;
            getline(inFile, name, '#');
        } //end while
        //close file
        inFile.close();
    }
    else
        cout << "File could not be opened." << endl;
    //end if
    return 0;
} //end of main function
```

Figure 13-12: The sales program that reads records

Notice that the `#include <fstream>` directive, which is necessary to create file objects, appears in the sales program shown in Figure 13-12. In this case, the program creates an input file object named `inFile` using the statement `ifstream inFile;`. After creating the input file object, the program uses the statement `inFile.open("sales.dat", ios::in);` to open the sales.dat file for input.

If the file cannot be opened, the program displays an appropriate error message; otherwise, it opens the file and positions the record indicator before the first record in the file.

The statement `getline(inFile, name, '#');` reads all of the characters in the first record, up to and including the # character. The statement stores the characters to the left of the # character in the `name` variable, and it consumes the # character. Next, the `while (!inFile.eof())` clause determines if the record indicator is at the end of the file. If it is, the file is closed and the program ends; otherwise, the statement `inFile >> sales;` reads the remaining characters in the first record, up to but not including the newline character located at the end of the record. The statement `inFile.ignore(1);` instructs the computer to ignore (consume) the newline character at the end of the record before the statement `getline(inFile, name, '#');`, which appears within the `while` loop, reads the name from the next record.

You now have completed Tutorial 13's Concept lesson. You can either take a break or complete the end-of-lesson questions and exercises before moving on to the Application lesson.

SUMMARY

In addition to saving the C++ program instructions in a file, called a program file, you also can save input data in a file, called a data file. The information in a data file typically is organized into fields and records. A field is a single item of information about a person, place, or thing. A record is a group of related fields that contains all of the necessary data about a specific person, place, or thing. A data file is a collection of related records.

In most programming languages, you can create three different types of data files: sequential, random, and binary. The data file type refers to how the data is accessed. The data in a sequential access file is always accessed sequentially—in other words, in consecutive order. The data in a random access file, on the other hand, can be accessed either in consecutive order or in random order. The data in a binary access file can be accessed by its byte location in the file. This book covers sequential access data files only.

Sequential access data files can be either input data files or output data files. Input data files are those whose contents are read by a program, and output data files are those to which a program writes data.

For a program to use a sequential access file, it must include the fstream header file. You use the `ifstream` and `ofstream` classes, which are defined in the fstream header file, to create input or output file objects, respectively; these file objects are used to represent the actual files stored on your computer's disk. After creating the file object, you then use the C++ `open` function to open the file for either input, output, or append.

Before attempting either to read data from or write data to a file, you always should verify that the data file was opened successfully. You can use the C++ `is_open` function, which is defined in both the `ifstream` and `ofstream` classes, to test if the file was opened successfully. The `is_open` function returns the value `true` if the `open` function was able to open the file; it returns the value `false` if the `open` function could not open the file. You typically test the file immediately after opening it.

When a program is finished with a data file, you should use the C++ `close` function, which is defined in both the `ifstream` and `ofstream` classes, to close it. Failing to close an open data file can result in the loss of data.

To distinguish one record from another in a file, programmers usually write each record on a separate line in the file. You do in C++ so by including the `endl` stream manipulator at the end of the statement that writes the record to the file. If the record contains more than one field, C++ programmers use a character to separate the data in one field from the data in another field; the '#' character is most commonly used.

When reading records from a data file, you use the C++ eof function to determine if the record indicator is at the end of the file. If a program attempts to read past the end of the file, the eof function returns true; otherwise, it returns false.

ANSWERS TO MINI-QUIZZES

Mini-Quiz 1
1. data file
2. b. fstream
3. d. `ios::in`
4. `ofstream outName;`
5. c. `outName.open("items.dat", ios::app);`

Mini-Quiz 2
1. false
2. c. `outInv << quantity << endl;`
3. c. `outFile << score1 << '#' << score2 << endl;`
4. `outInv.close();`

Mini-Quiz 3
1. d. `inInv >> quantity;`
2. c. `while (!inInv.eof())`
3. false

QUESTIONS

1. A _____ is a single item of information about a person, place, or thing.
   a. data file
   b. field
   c. program file
   d. record

2. A group of related fields that contains all of the data about a specific person, place, or thing is called a _____.
   a. data file
   b. field file
   c. program file
   d. record

3. For a program to create a file object, it must include the _____ file.
   a. file
   b. fstream
   c. outFile
   d. sequential

4. You use the _____ class to instantiate an output file object.
   a. cout
   b. fstream
   c. ofstream
   d. outstream

5. Which of the following statements will create an object named `outPayroll` that represents an output file in the program?
   a. `fstream outPayroll;`
   b. `ofstream outPayroll;`
   c. `outPayroll as ofstream;`
   d. `outPayroll as outstream;`

6. Which of following statements will open the payroll.dat file for output?
   a. `outPayroll.open("payroll.dat");`
   b. `outPayroll.open("payroll.dat", ios::out);`
   c. `outPayroll.open("payroll.dat", ios::output);`
   d. both a and b

7. To add records to the end of an existing output file, you use the _____ *mode* in the `open` function.
   a. add
   b. ios::add
   c. ios::app
   d. ios::out

8. You use the _____ function to close a data file.
   a. close
   b. end
   c. exit
   d. finish

9. To determine if the `open` function was successful, you use the _____ function.
   a. is_open
   b. isopen
   c. isFileOpen
   d. is_FileOpen

10. Which of the following will write the `city` variable to an output file named address.dat?
    a. `address.dat << city << endl;`
    b. `ofstream << city << endl;`
    c. `outFile << city << endl;`
    d. `outFile >> city >> endl;`

11. Which of the following will read the `salary` variable from an input file named managers.dat?
    a. `managers.dat >> salary;`
    b. `ifstream >> salary;`
    c. `inFile >> salary;`
    d. `inFile << salary;`

12. Which of the following will write the `city` and `state` variables to an output file named address.dat?
    a. `address.dat << city << state << endl;`
    b. `ofstream << city << state << endl;`
    c. `outFile >> city >> '#' >> state >> endl;`
    d. `outFile << city << '#' << state << endl;`

13. Which of the following `while` clauses will repeat the loop instructions until the end of the file associated with the `inFile` object is reached?
    a. `while(inFile.eof())`
    b. `while(!ifstream.eof())`
    c. `while(!inFile.eof())`
    d. `while(!ifstream.fail())`

14. Which of the following statements will create an object, named inPayroll, that represents an input file in the program?
    a. `instream inPayroll;`
    b. `ifstream inPayroll;`
    c. `inPayroll as ifstream;`
    d. `inPayroll as ifstream;`

15. Which of the following statements will open the payroll.dat file for input?
    a. `inFile.open("payroll.dat", ios::app);`
    b. `inFile.open("payroll.dat");`
    c. `inFile.open("payroll.dat", ios::in);`
    d. both b and c

E X E R C I S E S

1. Mary Conrad wants a program that will allow her to save each letter of the alphabet in a sequential access file. She will enter the letters from the keyboard.
   a. Create an IPO chart for the program.
   b. Open the T13ConE01.cpp file contained in the Cpp\Tut13\T13ConE01 folder on your computer's hard disk.
   c. Use the IPO chart you created in Step a to code the program. Name the sequential access data file T13ConE01.dat and open it for output.
   d. Save, build, and execute the program. Enter the 26 letters of the alphabet.
   e. Open the T13ConE01.dat file. (Note: You will need to change the Files of type list box in the Open dialog box to All Files (*.*).) The file should contain 26 letters. Each letter should appear on a separate line in the file. Close the data file.
   f. When the program is working correctly, hide the Output window, then use the File menu to close the workspace.

2. Cheryl Perry wants a program that will save the squares of the numbers from 1 through 25 in a sequential access file.
   a. Create an IPO chart for the program.
   b. Open the T13ConE02.cpp file contained in the Cpp\Tut13\T13ConE02 folder on your computer's hard disk.
   c. Use the IPO chart you created in Step a to code the program. Name the sequential access data file T13ConE02.dat and open it for output.
   d. Save, build, and execute the program.
   e. Open the T13ConE02.dat file. (Note: You will need to change the Files of type list box in the Open dialog box to All Files (*.*).) The file should contain 25 numbers that represent the squares of the numbers from 1 through 25. Each number should appear on a separate line in the file. Close the data file.
   f. When the program is working correctly, hide the Output window, then use the File menu to close the workspace.

3. The manager of Checks Inc. wants a program that she can use to save each week's total payroll amount in a sequential access file.
   a. Create an IPO chart for the program. (Use a negative number as the sentinel value.)
   b. Open the T13ConE03.cpp file contained in the Cpp\Tut13\T13ConE03 folder on your computer's hard disk.

c. Use the IPO chart you created in Step a to code the program. Name the sequential access data file T13ConE03.dat and open it for append.

d. Save, build, and execute the program. Enter the following two payroll amounts: 25000.89 and 35600.50. Stop the loop.

e. Execute the program again. Enter the following two payroll amounts: 45678.99 and 67000.56. Stop the loop.

f. Open the T13ConE03.dat file. (Note: You will need to change the Files of type list box in the Open dialog box to All Files (*.*).) The file should contain the four amounts listed in Steps d and e. Each amount should appear on a separate line in the file. Close the data file.

g. When the program is working correctly, hide the Output window, then use the File menu to close the workspace.

4. The manager of Boggs Inc. wants a program that he can use to save the price of each inventory item in a sequential access file.

a. Create an IPO chart for the program. (Use a negative number as the sentinel value.)

b. Open the T13ConE04.cpp file contained in the Cpp\Tut13\T13ConE04 folder on your computer's hard disk.

c. Use the IPO chart you created in Step a to code the program. Name the sequential access file T13ConE04.dat and open it for append.

d. Save, build, and execute the program. Enter the following two prices: 10.50 and 15.99. Stop the loop.

e. Execute the program again. Enter the following three prices: 20, 76.54, and 17.34. Stop the loop.

f. Open the T13ConE04.dat file. (Note: You will need to change the Files of type list box in the Open dialog box to All Files (*.*).) The file should contain the five amounts listed in Steps d and e. Each amount should appear on a separate line in the file. Close the data file.

g. When the program is working correctly, hide the Output window, then use the File menu to close the workspace.

5. Mary Conrad wants a program that will allow her to count the number of letters stored in the data file that you created in Exercise 1.

a. Create an IPO chart for the program.

b. Open the T13ConE05.cpp file contained in the Cpp\Tut13\T13ConE05 folder on your computer's hard disk.

c. Copy the T13ConE01.dat file, which is contained in the Cpp\Tut13\T13ConE01 folder on your computer's hard disk, to the T13ConE05 folder. Rename the file T13ConE05.dat.

d. Use the IPO chart you created in Step a to code the program.

e. Save, build, and execute the program. The program should display the number 26 in the DOS window.

f. When the program is working correctly, hide the Output window, then use the File menu to close the workspace.

6. Cheryl Perry wants a program that will display the sum of the numbers stored in the data file that you created in Exercise 2.

a. Create an IPO chart for the program.

b. Open the T13ConE06.cpp file contained in the Cpp\Tut13\T13ConE06 folder on your computer's hard disk.

c. Copy the T13ConE02.dat file, which is contained in the Cpp\Tut13\T13ConE02 folder on your computer's hard disk, to the T13ConE06 folder. Rename the file T13ConE06.dat.

d. Use the IPO chart you created in Step a to code the program.

e. Save, build, and execute the program. The program should display the number 5525 as the sum.

f. When the program is working correctly, hide the Output window, then use the File menu to close the workspace.

7. The manager of Checks Inc. wants a program that she can use to calculate and display the total of the weekly payroll amounts stored in the data file that you created in Exercise 3.
   a. Create an IPO chart for the program.
   b. Open the T13ConE07.cpp file contained in the Cpp\Tut13\T13ConE07 folder on your computer's hard disk.
   c. Copy the T13ConE03.dat file, which is contained in the Cpp\Tut13\T13ConE03 folder on your computer's hard disk, to the T13ConE07 folder. Rename the file T13ConE07.dat.
   d. Use the IPO chart you created in Step a to code the program. Display the payroll total in fixed-point notation with two decimal places.
   e. Save, build, and execute the program. The program should display 173280.94 as the total payroll amount.
   f. When the program is working correctly, hide the Output window, then use the File menu to close the workspace.

8. The manager of Boggs Inc. wants a program that he can use to calculate and display the average price of the company's inventory items. The price of each inventory item is stored in the data file that you created in Exercise 4.
   a. Create an IPO chart for the program.
   b. Open the T13ConE08.cpp file contained in the Cpp\Tut13\T13ConE08 folder on your computer's hard disk.
   c. Copy the T13ConE04.dat file, which is contained in the Cpp\Tut13\T13ConE04 folder on your computer's hard disk, to the T13ConE08 folder. Rename the file T13ConE08.dat.
   d. Use the IPO chart you created in Step a to code the program. Display the average price in fixed-point notation with two decimal places.
   e. Save, build, and execute the program. The program should display 28.07 as the average price.
   f. When the program is working correctly, hide the Output window, then use the File menu to close the workspace.

9. The manager of Stellar Company wants a program that will allow him to save the company's five payroll codes and corresponding salaries in a sequential access file.
   a. Create an IPO chart for the program.
   b. Open the T13ConE09.cpp file contained in the Cpp\Tut13\T13ConE09 folder on your computer's hard disk.
   c. Use the IPO chart you created in Step a to code the program. Name the sequential access data file T13ConE09.dat and open it for output. When writing the records to the file, use the '#' character to separate one field from another.
   d. Save, build, and execute the program. Enter the following codes and salaries:

Code	Salary
A	27200
B	15000
C	23000
D	12000
E	25500

   e. Open the T13ConE09.dat file. (Note: You will need to change the Files of type list box in the Open dialog box to All Files (*.*).) The file should contain five records, each having two fields separated by the '#' character. Close the data file.
   f. When the program is working correctly, hide the Output window, then use the File menu to close the workspace.

10. The manager of Boggs Inc. wants a program that he can use to record, in a sequential access file, the inventory number, quantity, and price of the items in inventory.
    a. Create an IPO chart for the program.
    b. Open the T13ConE10.cpp file contained in the Cpp\Tut13\T13ConE10 folder on your computer's hard disk.

c. Use the IPO chart you created in Step a to code the program. Name the sequential access data file T13ConE10.dat and open it for output. When writing the records to the file, use the '#' character to separate one field from another.

d. Save, build, and execute the program. Enter the following inventory numbers, quantities, and prices:

Inventory number	Quantity	Price ($)
20AB	400	5
30CD	550	9
45XX	600	20

e. Open the T13ConE10.dat file. (Note: You will need to change the Files of type list box in the Open dialog box to All Files (*.*).) The file should contain three records, each having three fields separated by the '#' character. Close the data file.

f. When the program is working correctly, hide the Output window, then use the File menu to close the workspace

11. The manager of Stellar Company wants a program that he can use to display the codes and salaries stored in the data file that you created in Exercise 9.

a. Create an IPO chart for the program.

b. Open the T13ConE11.cpp file contained in the Cpp\Tut13\T13ConE11 folder on your computer's hard disk.

c. Copy the T13ConE09.dat file, which is contained in the Cpp\Tut13\T13ConE09 folder on your computer's hard disk, to the T13ConE11 folder. Rename the file T13ConE11.dat.

d. Use the IPO chart you created in Step a to code the program.

e. Save, build, and execute the program. The program should display the five codes and salaries.

f. When the program is working correctly, hide the Output window, then use the File menu to close the workspace.

12. The manager of Boggs Inc. wants a program that he can use to calculate and display the total dollar value of the items in inventory. The inventory numbers, quantities, and prices are stored in the data file that you created in Exercise 10.

a. Create an IPO chart for this program.

b. Open the T13ConE12.cpp file contained in the Cpp\Tut13\T13ConE12 folder on your computer's hard disk.

c. Copy the T13ConE10.dat file, which is contained in the Cpp\Tut13\T13ConE10 folder on your computer's hard disk, to the T13ConE12 folder. Rename the file T13ConE12.dat.

d. Use the IPO chart you created in Step a to code the program.

e. Save, build, and then execute the program. The program should display 18950 as the total dollar value.

f. When the program is working correctly, hide the Output window, then use the File menu to close the workspace.

Exercise 13 is a Discovery Exercise. Discovery Exercises, which may include topics that are not covered in this lesson, allow you to "discover" the solutions to problems on your own.

13. In this exercise, you will learn about the problem that occurs when using `getline` along with the >> operator.

a. Open the ConE13.cpp file contained in the Cpp\Tut13\T13ConE13 folder on your computer's hard disk.

b. Build and execute the program. When prompted for the name, type Jack Rodney and press the Enter key. When prompted for the sales amount, type 2000 and press the Enter key. The text "Bonus: 300" appears in the DOS window, followed by the text "Salesperson name: Sales: ". Notice that you cannot enter the salesperson's name at this point; this is because the Enter key, which was pressed after entering the sales amount, was read by the `getline` function.

c. Press Ctrl + c (or click the DOS window's Close button, and then click the Yes button) to stop the program.

    d. Enter the statement `cin.ignore(1);` in the blank line below the `cin >>` `sales;` statement. This statement tells the computer to ignore the Enter key that is pressed after the sales amount is entered.

    e. Save, build, and execute the program. Enter your name and 3000. The text "Bonus: 450" appears in the DOS window, followed by the prompt "Salesperson name: ".

    f. Type x and press the Enter key to stop the program. Press the Enter key to close the DOS window.

    g. Hide the Output window, then use the File menu to close the workspace.

A computer program is good only if it works. Errors in either an algorithm or programming code can cause the program to run incorrectly. Therefore, a programmer needs to know how to locate and fix these errors. Exercise 14 is a Debugging Exercise. Debugging Exercises allow you to practice recognizing and solving errors in a program.

debugging 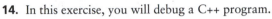   **14.** In this exercise, you will debug a C++ program.

    a. Open the T13ConE14.cpp file contained in the Cpp\Tut13\T13ConE14 folder on your computer's hard disk.

    b. Build the program. Correct any errors in the program.

    c. Save, build, and execute the program. Enter the numbers 7, 10, 6, and -1. Press the Enter key to close the DOS window.

    d. Open the T13ConE14.dat file. (Note: You will need to change the Files of type list box in the Open dialog box to All Files (*.*).) The file should contain the numbers 7, 10, and 6. Each number should appear on a separate line. Close the data file.

    e. When the program is working correctly, hide the Output window, then use the File menu to close the workspace.

Application Lesson

Using Sequential Access Data Files in a C++ Program

case ▶ Your nephew John recently completed two C++ courses at a community college, and already has accepted a programming job at a company; he starts in two weeks. Although he performed well in the C++ courses, receiving a grade of A in both, he feels he needs more practice creating classes and objects before he starts his new job. He has asked for your help. You decide to show John the class and program you created for the owner of Flowers Express, a small flower shop.

Viewing the Salesperson Class

Last month, you created a program for Bob Marquart, the owner of Flowers Express. The program allows Bob to record each salesclerk's name and monthly sales amount in a sequential access file. It also allows him to total the sales amounts contained in the file, and then display the total on the screen.

Before creating the Flowers Express program, you defined a `Salesperson` class, which you used to create a Salesperson object in the program. Figure 13-13 shows the declaration section of the `Salesperson` class.

```
//Salesperson - defines a Salesperson class

#include <fstream>
#include <string>
#include <algorithm>
using namespace std;
```

Figure 13-13: Declaration section of the `Salesperson` class

```
//declaration section
class Salesperson
{
    public:
        Salesperson();
        void writeRecordToFile(string, int, ofstream &);
        void readRecordFromFile(ifstream &);
        string getName();
        int getSales();
    private:
        string name;
        int sales;
};
```

Figure 13-13: Declaration section of the `Salesperson` class (continued)

tip

Although the Flowers Express program that you will complete in this lesson will not need to view the contents of the `name` data member included in the `Salesperson` class, other programs using the class to create Salesperson objects may need to do so. Therefore, you should include the `getName` function in the class. Recall from Tutorial 12 that a good class is one whose objects can be used in a variety of ways by many different programs.

Notice that the `Salesperson` class contains two private data members (variables) named `name` and `sales`; these data members represent the attributes of a Salesperson object. The class also contains five public member functions. Each member function corresponds to a task that a Salesperson object can perform. In this case, a Salesperson object can initialize its private data members, write a record to a file, read a record from a file, and return the values stored in its private data members.

Figure 13-14 shows the implementation section of the `Salesperson` class.

```
//implementation section
Salesperson::Salesperson()
{
    name  = "";
    sales = 0;
} //end of default constructor

void Salesperson::writeRecordToFile(string n, int s, ofstream &outF)
{
        transform(n.begin(), n.end(), n.begin(), toupper);
        name = n;
        sales = s;
        outF << name << '#' << sales << endl;
} //end of writeRecordToFile function

void Salesperson::readRecordFromFile(ifstream &inF)
{
    getline(inF, name, '#');
    inF >> sales;
    inF.ignore(1);
} //end of readRecordFromFile function

string Salesperson::getName()
{
    return name;
} //end of getName function

int Salesperson::getSales()
{
    return sales;
} //end of getSales function
```

Figure 13-14: Implementation section of the `Salesperson` class

The first member function listed in the implementation section is the default constructor. As you learned in Tutorial 12, the default constructor's task is simply to initialize the private data members of the class. In this case, the constructor does so by assigning the empty string and the number 0 to the `name` and `sales` variables, respectively.

The second member function, `writeRecordToFile`, writes a salesperson's record, which consists of a name and a sales amount, to a sequential access file. The information written to the file, as well as the address of the output file, is passed to the `writeRecordToFile` function when a program calls it; notice that the output file must be passed to the function *by reference*. Before writing a record to the file, the `writeRecordToFile` function uses the `transform` function, which you learned about in Tutorial 11, to convert the name field to uppercase letters.

The third member function, `readRecordFrom File`, reads a record from a sequential access file, and assigns the field values to the private data members of the class. Notice that the address of the input file is passed to the `readRecordFromFile` function.

The fourth and fifth member functions, `getName` and `getSales`, simply return the values stored in the private data members of the class.

Next, view the Flowers Express program.

The Flowers Express Program

The Flowers Express program contains four program-defined functions: `main`, `displayMenu`, `addRecords`, and `displayTotal`. Figure 13-15 shows the code entered in the program's `main` and `displayMenu` functions.

```
int main()
{
    //declare variable
    int menuChoice = 0;

    //display menu and get choice
    menuChoice = displayMenu();

    while (menuChoice != 3)
    {
        if (menuChoice == 1)
            addRecords();
        else if (menuChoice == 2)
            displayTotal();
        else
            cout << "Invalid menu choice";
        //end ifs
        menuChoice = displayMenu();
    } //end while


    return 0;
} //end of main function
```

Figure 13-15: Code entered in the `main` and `displayMenu` functions

```
//*****program-defined functions*****
int displayMenu()
{
      int choice = 0;
      //display options
      cout << "Options" << endl;
      cout << "1    Add Records" << endl;
      cout << "2    Display Total Sales" << endl;
      cout << "3    Exit Program" << endl;
      cout << "Enter menu option: ";
      cin >> choice;
      cin.ignore(1);   //consume Enter key
      return choice;
} //end of displayMenu function
```

Figure 13-15: Code entered in the main and displayMenu functions (continued)

The main function begins by declaring and initializing an int variable named menuChoice. It then calls the displayMenu function to display a menu that contains three options: Add Records, Display Total Sales, and Exit Program. After displaying the menu, the displayMenu function prompts the user to enter his or her menu choice: either 1 to add records, 2 to display the total sales, or 3 to exit the program. The user's response is returned to the main function, which assigns the returned value to the menuChoice variable.

The while (menuChoice != 3) clause in the main function repeats the loop body instructions as long as (or while) the menuChoice variable does not contain the number 3. (Recall that menu choice 3 indicates that the user wants to exit the program.) The first instruction in the loop body is a selection structure that compares the contents of the menuChoice variable to the number 1. If the menuChoice variable contains the number 1, the main function calls the addRecords function to add one or more records to the sequential access file. When the addRecords function completes its processing, the main function calls the displayMenu function to display the menu.

If the menuChoice variable does not contain the number 1, the nested selection structure in the loop body compares the contents of the menuChoice variable to the number 2. If the menuChoice variable contains the number 2, the main function calls the displayTotal function to total the sales amounts in the sequential access file and then display the total on the screen. When the displayTotal function completes its processing, the main function calls the displayMenu function to display the menu.

If the menuChoice variable contains a value other than 1, 2, or 3, the main function displays an appropriate error message before calling the displayMenu function to display the menu.

Next, view the Flowers Express program's addRecords function.

The addRecords Function

Figure 13-16 shows the code entered in the Flowers Express program's addRecords function. The lines of code pertaining to the Salesperson object and sequential access file are shaded in the figure.

```cpp
void addRecords()
{
     //create file object and open file
     ofstream outFile;
     outFile.open("sales.dat", ios::app);

     //determine if the file was opened successfully
     if (outFile.is_open())
     {
          //declare variables
          string name = "";
          int sales    = 0;

          //create Salesperson object
          Salesperson salesObj;

          //get name
          cout << "Enter name (X to stop adding records): ";
          getline(cin, name);
          while (name != "X" && name != "x")
          {
               //get sales
               cout << "Enter sales: ";
               cin >> sales;
               cin.ignore();   //consume Enter key

               //write record to file
               salesObj.writeRecordToFile(name, sales, outFile);

               //get name
               cout << "Enter name (X to stop adding records): ";
               getline(cin, name);
          } //end while

          //close file
          outFile.close();
     }
     else
          cout << "File could not be opened." << endl;
     //end if
} //end of addRecords function
```

Figure 13-16: Code entered in the addRecords function

The `addRecords` function begins by creating an output file object named `outFile`. It then uses the `open` function to open a file named sales.dat for append, and uses the `is_open` function to determine whether the file was opened successfully. If the `is_open` function returns the value false, the `addRecords` function displays an appropriate error message; otherwise, the instructions in the `if` statement's true path are processed.

The first two statements in the `if` statement's true path declare and initialize a `string` variable named `name` and an `int` variable named `sales`. The third statement, `Salesperson salesObj;`, creates a Salesperson object named `salesObj`. Recall that the constructor function in the `Salesperson` class initializes the `salesObj` object when the object is created.

After creating the variables and object, the true path instructions prompt the user to enter a name, and then store the user's response in the `name` variable. The next instruction is the `while` clause, which indicates that the loop should repeat its instructions as long as the `name` variable contains a value other than X or x.

The first two statements in the loop body prompt the user to enter a sales amount and store the user's response in the `sales` variable. The third statement, `cin.ignore(1);`, instructs the computer to consume the newline character that remains in the `cin` stream after the sales amount is entered. The next statement, `salesObj.writeRecordToFile(name, sales, outFile);`, calls the `writeRecordToFile` function, which is a public member function defined in the `Salesperson` class, to write the name and sales information to the sequential access file. The last two statements in the loop prompt the user to enter a name, and then store the user's response in the `name` variable. When the loop completes its processing, which occurs when the user enters either the letter X or the letter x, the `outFile.close()` instruction in the `if` statement's true path closes the output file before the `addRecords` function ends.

Next, view the Flowers Express program's `displayTotal` function.

The `displayTotal` Function

Figure 13-17 shows the code entered in the Flowers Express program's `displayTotal` function. The lines of code pertaining to the Salesperson object and sequential access file are shaded in the figure.

```
void displayTotal()
{
      //create file object and open file
      ifstream inFile;
      inFile.open("sales.dat", ios::in);

      //determine if the file was opened successfully
      if (inFile.is_open())
      {
            //declare variables
            int total = 0;

            //create Salesperson object
            Salesperson salesObj;

            //read records from file
            salesObj.readRecordFromFile(inFile);
            while (!inFile.eof())
            {
                  total = total + salesObj.getSales();
                  salesObj.readRecordFromFile(inFile);
            } //end while

            //display total
            cout << endl << "Total sales $"
                  << total << endl << endl;

            //close file
            inFile.close();
      }
      else
            cout << "File could not be opened." << endl;
      //end if
} //end of displayTotal function
```

Figure 13-17: Code entered in the displayTotal function

The displayTotal function begins by creating an input file object named inFile. It then uses the open function to open the sales.dat file for input, and uses the is_open function to determine whether the file was opened successfully. If the is_open function returns the value false, the displayTotal function displays an appropriate error message; otherwise, the instructions in the if statement's true path are processed.

The first statement in the if statement's true path declares and initializes an int variable named total, which will be used to accumulate the sales amounts stored in the sequential access file. The second statement, Salesperson salesObj;, creates a Salesperson object named salesObj. As you know, the constructor function in the Salesperson class will initialize the salesObj object when the object is created. The third statement in the true path, salesObj.readRecordFromFile(inFile);, calls the readRecordFromFile function, which is a public member function defined in the Salesperson class, to read the first record from the sequential access file and store the field values in the private data members of the class. The next instruction in the true path is a while clause that repeats the loop body instructions as long as the record indicator is not at the end of the file.

The first statement in the loop body calls the getSales function, which is a public member function defined in the Salesperson class, to return the value stored in the sales data member. The statement adds the value returned by the getSales function to the accumulator variable, total. The second statement in the loop body calls the readRecordFromFile function to read another record from the file. When the loop completes its processing, which occurs when the record indicator is at the end of the sequential access file, the last two statements in the if statement's true path display the total sales amount on the screen, then close the input file before the displayTotal function ends.

Next, you will complete the Flowers Express program by entering the missing instructions in the program.

Completing the Flowers Express Program

On your computer's hard disk is a C++ header file that contains the Salesperson class definition. Before completing the Flowers Express program, you will open the header file to view its contents.

To open the header file that contains the Salesperson class definition:

1 Start Visual C++. Open the **Salesperson** file contained in the Cpp\MyClasses folder on your computer's hard disk. Figure 13-18 shows the **Salesperson** class definition contained in the file.

```
//Salesperson - defines a Salesperson class

#include <fstream>
#include <string>
#include <algorithm>
using namespace std;
```

Figure 13-18: Header file showing the Salesperson class definition

```
//declaration section
class Salesperson
{
    public:
        Salesperson();
        void writeRecordToFile(string, int, ofstream &);
        void readRecordFromFile(ifstream &);
        string getName();
        int getSales();
    private:
        string name;
        int sales;
};


//implementation section
Salesperson::Salesperson()
{
    name  = "";
    sales = 0;
} //end of default constructor

void Salesperson::writeRecordToFile(string n, int s, ofstream&
outF)
{
        transform(n.begin(), n.end(), n.begin(), toupper);
        name = n;
        sales = s;
        outF << name << '#' << sales << endl;
} //end of writeRecordToFile function

void Salesperson::readRecordFromFile(ifstream &inF)
{
    getline(inF, name, '#');
    inF >> sales;
    inF.ignore(1);
} //end of readRecordFromFile function

string Salesperson::getName()
{
    return name;
} //end of getName function

int Salesperson::getSales()
{
    return sales;
} //end of getSales function
```

Figure 13-18: Header file showing the `Salesperson` class definition (continued)

2 Close the header file.

Your computer's hard disk also contains a partially completed program for Flowers Express. You will complete the program in the next set of steps.

To complete the Flowers Express program, then test the program:

1 Open the **T13App.cpp** file contained in the Cpp\Tut13\T13App folder on your computer's hard disk. If necessary, change the `#include "c:\cpp\myclasses\salesperson"` directive to reflect the location of the Salesperson header file on your computer's hard disk.

Eleven instructions are missing from the program.

2 Enter the 11 instructions shaded in Figure 13-19, which shows the completed Flowers Express program. (The missing instructions are in the `addRecords` and `displayTotal` functions.)

```cpp
//T13App.cpp - Flowers Express program

#include <iostream>
#include <string>
#include <fstream>
#include "c:\cpp\myclasses\salesperson"
using namespace std;

//function prototypes
int displayMenu();
void addRecords();
void displayTotal();

int main()
{
    //declare variable
    int menuChoice = 0;

    //display menu and get choice
    menuChoice = displayMenu();

    while (menuChoice != 3)
    {
        if (menuChoice == 1)
            addRecords();
        else if (menuChoice == 2)
            displayTotal();
        else
            cout << "Invalid menu choice";
        //end ifs
        menuChoice = displayMenu();
    } //end while


    return 0;
} //end of main function
```

Figure 13-19: Completed Flowers Express program

```
//*****program-defined functions*****
int displayMenu()
{
     int choice = 0;
     //display options
     cout << "Options" << endl;
     cout << "1    Add Records" << endl;
     cout << "2    Display Total Sales" << endl;
     cout << "3    Exit Program" << endl;
     cout << "Enter menu option: ";
     cin >> choice;
     cin.ignore(1);   //consume Enter key
     return choice;
} //end of displayMenu function

void addRecords()
{
     //create file object and open file
     ofstream outFile;
     outFile.open("sales.dat", ios::app);

     //determine if the file was opened successfully
     if (outFile.is_open())
     {
          //declare variables
          string name = "";
          int sales   = 0;

          //create Salesperson object
          Salesperson salesObj;

          //get name
          cout << "Enter name (X to stop adding records): ";
          getline(cin, name);
          while (name != "X" && name != "x")
          {
               //get sales
               cout << "Enter sales: ";
               cin >> sales;
               cin.ignore();   //consume Enter key

               //write record to file
               salesObj.writeRecordToFile(name, sales, outFile);

               //get name
               cout << "Enter name (X to stop adding records): ";
               getline(cin, name);
          } //end while

          //close file
          outFile.close();
     }
     else
          cout << "File could not be opened." << endl;
     //end if
} //end of addRecords function
```

enter these five
instructions

Figure 13-19: Completed Flowers Express program (continued)

```
void displayTotal()
{
    //create file object and open file
    ifstream inFile;
    inFile.open("sales.dat", ios::in);

    //determine if the file was opened successfully
    if (inFile.is_open())
    {
        //declare variables
        int total = 0;

        //create Salesperson object
        Salesperson salesObj;

        //read records from file
        salesObj.readRecordFromFile(inFile);
        while (!inFile.eof())
        {
            total = total + salesObj.getSales();
            salesObj.readRecordFromFile(inFile);
        } //end while

        //display total
        cout << endl << "Total sales $"
             << total << endl << endl;

        //close file
        inFile.close();
    }
    else
        cout << "File could not be opened." << endl;
    //end if
} //end of displayTotal function
```

enter these six
instructions

Figure 13-19: Completed Flowers Express program (continued)

3 Save, build, and execute the program. The menu appears in the DOS window, as shown in Figure 13-20.

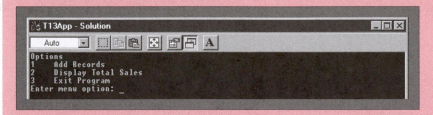

Figure 13-20: Menu shown in the DOS window

4 Type the number 1 as the menu option and press the **Enter** key to add records to the sales.dat file. When prompted to enter the name, type **John Hammil** and press the **Enter** key. When prompted to enter the sales amount, type **3000** and press the **Enter** key.

5 Use the program to enter the following names and sales amount:

Name	Sales amount
Carol Wroberg	2000
Sean Nunez	1000
Drew Merriweather	4500
Jake Treadle	4650
x	

6 When the menu appears in the DOS window, type **2** as the menu option and press the **Enter** key to display the total sales amount. The DOS window indicates that the total sales amount is $15150, as shown in Figure 13-21.

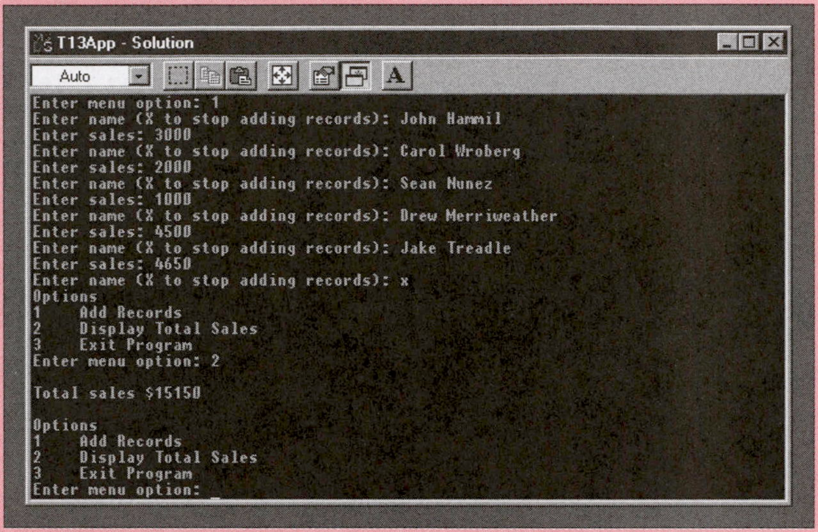

Figure 13-21: DOS window showing the total sales amount

7 Type **3** as the menu option and press the **Enter** key to exit the program.

8 Press the **Enter** key to close the DOS window. Hide the Output window, then use the File menu to close the workspace. When prompted to close all document windows, click the **Yes** button, then exit Visual C++.

You now have completed Tutorial 13's Application lesson. You can either take a break or complete the end-of-lesson exercises.

EXERCISES

1. The manager of Stellar Company wants a program that he can use to display the codes and salaries stored in a sequential access file named T13AppE01.dat.

   a. Open the T13AppE01.dat file contained in the Cpp\Tut13\T13AppE01 folder on your computer's hard disk. Notice that the file contains five records. Each record contains two fields: a code followed by a salary. Close the data file.

    b. Open the T13AppE01 header file contained in the Cpp\MyClasses folder on your computer's hard disk. Create an appropriate class for the codes and salaries. Name the class EmployCodes. Include a constructor function, a function to read a record, a function to view the code, and a function to view the salary. Save and then close the header file.

    c. Open the T13AppE01.cpp file contained in the Cpp\Tut13\T13AppE01 folder on your computer's hard disk.

    d. Complete the program, using the program comments as a guide.

    e. Save, build, and execute the program. The program should display the codes and salaries stored in the T13AppE01.dat file.

    f. When the program is working correctly, hide the Output window, then use the File menu to close the workspace.

2. In this exercise, you will modify the program that you created in Exercise 1 so that it displays the salary corresponding to the code entered by the user.

    a. Use Windows to copy the T13AppE01 header file, which is contained in the Cpp\MyClasses folder, to the Cpp\MyClasses folder. Rename the copied file to T13AppE02. Open the T13AppE02 header file. Change the T13AppE01 name in the first comment to T13AppE02. Close the header file.

    b. Use Windows to copy the T13AppE01 folder, which is contained in the Cpp\Tut13 folder on your computer's hard disk, to the Cpp\Tut13 folder. Rename the copied folder T13AppE02.

    c. Open the T13AppE02 folder. Rename the T13AppE01.cpp file T13AppE02.cpp. Also rename the T13AppE01.dat file T13AppE02.dat.

    d. Open the T13AppE02.cpp file. Change the T13AppE01.cpp name in the first comment to T13AppE02.cpp. Also change the header filename in the `#include` directive to "t13appe02", and change the data filename in the `open` function to "t13appe02.dat".

    e. Modify the program to allow the user to enter the code. Display the salary corresponding to the code entered by the user. If the code is not contained in the file, display an appropriate message.

    f. Save, build, and execute the program. Enter the letter c. The DOS window should show that the salary is 23000. Press the Enter key to close the DOS window.

    g. Execute the program again. Enter the letter k. A message indicating that the code is not valid should appear in the DOS window. Press the Enter key to close the DOS window.

    h. When the program is working correctly, hide the Output window, then use the File menu to close the workspace.

3. Consolidated Advertising wants a program that its managers can use to record various ZIP codes and their corresponding cities in a sequential access file.

    a. Open the T13AppE03 header file contained in the Cpp\MyClasses folder on your computer's hard disk. Create an appropriate class for the ZIP codes and cities. Name the class AddressInfo. Include a constructor function, a function to assign data to the private data members, and a function to write a record. The function that assigns data to the private data members should convert the city name to uppercase letters. It also should verify that the ZIP code contains five characters. If the zip code does not contain five characters, the record should not be written to the file. (*Hint*: Have the function return a value to the program indicating whether the ZIP code length is valid.) Save and then close the header file.

    b. Open the T13AppE03.cpp file contained in the Cpp\Tut13\T13AppE03 folder on your computer's hard disk.

    c. Complete the program. Save the ZIP codes and cities in a sequenial access file named T13AppE03.dat. (Open the sequential access file for append.)

d. Save, build, and execute the program. Enter the ZIP codes and cities shown here:

ZIP code	City
60561	Darien
60544	Hinsdale
60137	Glen Ellyn
6	Westmont
60135	Downers Grove
60136	Burr Ridge

e. Stop the program. Open the T13AppE03.dat file. The file should contain five records, each having two fields (a ZIP code and a city name). The city name should appear in uppercase letters. Close the data file.

f. When the program is working correctly, hide the Output window, then use the File menu to close the workspace.

4. Each salesperson at BobCat Motors is assigned a code that consists of two characters. The first character is either the letter F for full-time employee, or the letter P for part-time employee. The second character is either a 1 (indicating the salesperson sells new cars) or a 2 (indicating the salesperson sells used cars). The names of BobCat's salespeople, along with their codes, are contained in the T13AppE04.dat sequential file.

a. Open the T13AppE04.dat file contained in the Cpp\Tut13\T13AppE04 folder on your computer's hard disk. Print the contents of the file, then close the file.

b. Open the T13AppE04.cpp file contained in the Cpp\Tut13\T13AppE04 folder on your computer's hard disk. Create a program that prompts the user to enter a code—either F1, F2, P1, or P2. The program should search the T13AppE04.dat file for the code, and should display only the names of the salespeople assigned that code.

c. Save, build, and execute the program. Test the program by entering F2 as the code. The program should display three records: Mary Jones, Joel Adkari, and Janice Paulo.

d. When the program is working correctly, hide the Output window, then use the File menu to close the workspace.

5. In this exercise, you will update a sequential access file.

a. Open the T13AppE05.dat file contained in the Cpp\Tut13\T13AppE05 folder on your computer's hard disk. The sequential access file contains the numbers 10 through 15; each number appears on a separate line in the file. Close the data file.

b. Open the T13AppE05.cpp file contained in the Cpp\Tut13\T13AppE05 folder on your computer's hard disk.

c. Create a program that reads the numbers from the T13AppE05.dat file. The program should add the number 1 to each number, and then write the new value to another sequential access file. Name the updated sequential access file T13AppE05.new.

d. Save, build, and execute the program.

e. Open the T13AppE05.new file. The file should contain the numbers 11 through 16; each number should appear on a separate line in the file. Close the data file.

f. When the program is working correctly, hide the Output window, then use the File menu to close the workspace.

6. In this exercise, you will update a sequential access file.

a. Open the T13AppE06.dat file contained in the Cpp\Tut13\T13AppE06 folder on your computer's hard disk. The sequential access file contains 10 numbers; each number appears on a separate line in the file. Close the data file.

b. Open the T13AppE06.cpp file contained in the Cpp\Tut13\T13AppE06 folder on your computer's hard disk.

    c. Create a program that reads the numbers from the T13AppE06.dat file. The program should write only the even numbers to a new sequential file named T13AppE06.new.

    d. Save, build, and execute the program.

    e. Open the T13AppE06.new file. The file should contain six even numbers; each number should appear on a separate line in the file. Close the data file.

    f. When the program is working correctly, hide the Output window, then use the File menu to close the workspace.

Exercise 7 is a Discovery Exercise. Discovery Exercises, which may include topics that are not covered in this lesson, allow you to "discover" the solutions to problems on your own.

7. In this exercise, you will modify the program that you created in Exercise 2 so that it allows the user to enter more than one code.

    a. Use Windows to copy the T13AppE02 header file, which is contained in the Cpp\MyClasses folder, to the Cpp\MyClasses folder. Rename the copied file T13AppE07.

    b. Use Windows to copy the T13AppE02 folder, which is contained in the Cpp\Tut13 folder on your computer's hard disk, to the Cpp\Tut13 folder. Rename the copied folder T13AppE07.

    c. Open the T13AppE07 folder. Rename the T13AppE02.cpp file T13AppE07.cpp. Also rename the T13AppE02.dat file T13AppE07.dat.

    d. Open the T13AppE07.cpp file. Change the T13AppE02.cpp name in the first comment to T13AppE07.cpp. Also change the header filename in the `#include` directive to "t13appe07", and change the data filename in the `open` function to "t13appe07.dat".

    e. Include a loop in the program to allow the user to enter as many codes as desired.

    f. Save, build, and execute the program. Test the program by entering the following three codes, one at a time: A, c, f. Stop the program.

    g. When the program is working correctly, hide the Output window, then use the File menu to close the workspace.

A computer program is good only if it works. Errors in either an algorithm or programming code can cause the program to run incorrectly. Therefore, a programmer needs to know how to locate and fix these errors. Exercise 8 is a Debugging Exercise. Debugging Exercises allow you to practice recognizing and solving errors in a program.

debugging

8. In this exercise, you will debug a program.

    a. Open the T13AppE08 header file contained in the Cpp\MyClasses folder on your computer's hard disk. Print the contents of the header file, then close the file.

    b. Open the T13AppE08.dat file contained in the Cpp\Tut13\T13AppE08 folder on your computer's hard disk. The sequential access file contains four records; each record contains three fields (name, quantity, and price). Close the data file.

    c. Open the T13AppE08.cpp file contained in the Cpp\Tut13\T13AppE08 folder on your computer's hard disk. The program should simply read the records from the sequential access file, and then display the records on the screen.

    d. Build the program. Correct any errors in the program.

    e. Save, build, and execute the program. The five records should appear on the screen.

    f. When the program is working correctly, hide the Output window, then use the File menu to close the workspace.

Arrays

After completing this tutorial, you will be able to:

■ Declare, initialize, and store data in an array
■ Display the contents of an array
■ Access an array element
■ Search an array
■ Compute the average of an array's contents
■ Find the highest entry in an array
■ Update the contents of an array
■ Pass an array to a function
■ Manipulate parallel arrays
■ Manipulate a two-dimensional array
■ Create a one-dimensional array of objects

Concept Lesson

Arrays

All of the variables you have used so far have been simple variables. A **simple variable** is one that is unrelated to any other variable in memory. In many programs, however, you may need to reserve a block of memory locations (variables). The block is referred to as an array.

An **array** is a group of variables that have the same name and data type and are related in some way. For example, each variable in the array might contain an inventory quantity, or each might contain a state name, or each might contain an employee record (name, Social Security number, pay rate, and so on). It may be helpful to picture an array as a group of small boxes inside the computer's memory. You can write information to the boxes and you can read information from the boxes; you just cannot *see* the boxes.

The most commonly used arrays in programs are one-dimensional and two-dimensional. A **one-dimensional** array is simply a column of variables. A **two-dimensional** array, on the other hand, resembles a table in that it has rows and columns. Figure 14-1 illustrates a one-dimensional and a two-dimensional array. (Arrays having more than two dimensions, which are used in scientific and engineering programs, are beyond the scope of this book.)

The variables in an array are stored in consecutive memory locations in the computer's internal memory.

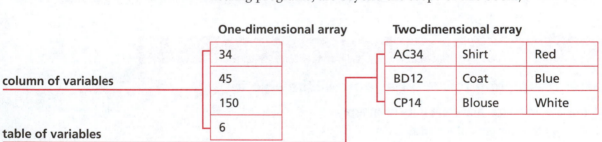

column of variables

table of variables

One-dimensional array

34
45
150
6

Two-dimensional array

AC34	Shirt	Red
BD12	Coat	Blue
CP14	Blouse	White

Figure 14-1: Illustrations of a one-dimensional and a two-dimensional array

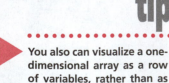

You also can visualize a one-dimensional array as a row of variables, rather than as a column of variables.

It takes longer for the computer to access the information stored in a disk file, because the computer must wait for the disk drive to locate the needed information and then read the information into internal memory.

Programmers use arrays to temporarily store related data in the internal memory of the computer. Examples of data stored in an array would be the federal withholding tax tables in a payroll program, and a price list in an order entry program. Storing data in an array increases the efficiency of a program, because data can be both written to and read from internal memory much faster than it can be written to and read from a file on a disk. Additionally, after the data is entered into an array, which typically is done at the beginning of the program, the data can be used by the program as many times as desired. A payroll program, for example, can use the federal withholding tax tables stored in an array to calculate the amount of each employee's federal withholding tax.

Now that you know what arrays are and why they are used, you will learn how to declare and initialize a one-dimensional array.

Declaring and Initializing a One-Dimensional Array

Before you can use an array, you first must declare it. It also is a good programming practice to initialize the array. Figure 14-2 shows the syntax of the statements you use to declare and initialize one-dimensional arrays in C++, Java, and Visual Basic.

statement ends with a semicolon

Language	Syntax
C++	*datatype arrayname*[*numberOfElements*] = {*initialvalues*};
Java	*datatype*[] *arrayname* = {*initialvalues*};
Visual Basic	**Dim** *arrayname(lower subscript To upper subscript)* **As** *datatype* (Visual Basic initializes arrays automatically)

Figure 14-2: Syntax of the statements used to declare and initialize one-dimensional arrays in C++, Java, and Visual Basic

The = {*initialvalues*} section of the syntax shown in Figure 14-2 is optional. Typically, optional items are enclosed in square brackets ([]) in the syntax. In this case, the square brackets were omitted so as not to confuse them with the square brackets that are required by the syntax.

As Figure 14-2 indicates, the syntax for declaring a one-dimensional array in C++ is *datatype arrayname*[*numberOfElements*] = {*initialvalues*};. The *datatype* in the syntax is the type of data the array variables, referred to as **elements**, will store. Recall that each of the elements (variables) in an array has the same data type. You can use any of the C++ data types you have learned so far to declare an array. You also can declare an array using a class that you created. You will learn how to use a class to declare an array in this tutorial's Application lesson.

In the syntax for declaring an array, *arrayname* is the name of the array. The name must follow the same rules as for variables. *numberOfElements* in the syntax is an integer that specifies the size of the array—in other words, the number of elements you want in the array. To declare an array that contains 10 elements, for example, you enter the number 10 as the *numberOfElements*. Notice that you enclose the *numberOfElements* in square brackets ([]).

As mentioned earlier, it is a good programming practice to initialize the elements (variables) in an array to ensure that they will not contain garbage. You can initialize the array elements at the same time you declare the array simply by entering one or more values, separated by commas, in the *initialvalues* section of the syntax, as shown in Figure 14-3. Notice that you enclose the *initialvalues* in braces ({}).

Examples	Results
Example 1: `char letter[3] = {'A', 'B', 'C'};`	declares and initializes a three-element `char` array

Example 2:
`string name[4] = {"Barb",`
`                  "Nancy",`
`                  "Bill",`
`                  "Samuel"};`
	declares and initializes a four-element `string` array

Example 3:
`string state[4] = {"", "", "", ""};`
    or
`string state[4] = {""};`
	declares and initializes a four-element `string` array; each element is initialized to the empty string

Example 4:
`int num[3] = {0, 0, 0};`
        or
`int num[3] = {0};`
	declares and initializes a three-element `int` array; each element is initialized to 0

Example 5: `float price[5] = {float(6.5)};`	declares and initializes a five-element `float` array; the first element is initialized to 6.5, while the others are initialized to 0.0

Figure 14-3: Examples of declaring and initializing one-dimensional arrays in C++

Carefully study the examples shown in Figure 14-3. In the first example, the statement `char letter[3] = {'A', 'B', 'C'};` declares a `char` array named `letter` that contains three elements. It initializes the first element in the array to the letter A, the second element to B, and the third element to C, as shown in Figure 14-4.

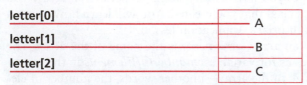

letter[0] ——————————————— A
letter[1] ——————————————— B
letter[2] ——————————————— C

Figure 14-4: Illustration of the `letter` array in memory

Similar to the way each house on a street is identified by a unique address, each element in an array is identified by a unique number, called a **subscript**. The computer assigns the subscript to each of the array elements when it creates the array in memory. The first element in a one-dimensional array is assigned a subscript of 0, the next element is assigned a subscript of 1, and so on, as indicated in Figure 14-4.

You refer to each element in the array by the array's name and the element's subscript, which is specified in square brackets ([]) immediately following the name. For example, letter[0]—read "letter sub zero"—refers to the first element in the letter array, and letter[2] refers to the third element in the array.

As Figure 14-4 indicates, a three-element array will have subscripts of 0, 1, and 2. Notice that the last subscript is one number less than the number of elements in the array; this is because the first subscript is 0 rather than 1.

The statement shown in Example 2 in Figure 14-3, string name[4] = {"Barb", "Nancy", "Bill", "Samuel"};, declares a string array that contains four elements. The elements are named name[0], name[1], name[2], and name[3]. The statement initializes the first element to the string "Barb", the second to "Nancy", and so on.

Notice that you can use either of the two statements shown in the third example in Figure 14-3 to declare and initialize a string array to the empty string. The first statement (string state[4] = {"", "", "", ""};) provides an initial value for each of the four array elements, whereas the second statement (string state[4] = {""};) provides only one value. When you do not specify an initial value for each of the elements in a string array, Microsoft Visual C++ stores the empty string in the uninitialized elements.

Example 4 in Figure 14-3 shows two statements that you can use to declare and initialize an int array to the number 0. The first statement (int num[3] = {0, 0, 0};) provides an initial value for each of the three array elements, whereas the second statement (int num[3] = {0};) provides only one value. When you do not provide an initial value for each of the elements in a numeric array, C++ stores the number 0 in the uninitialized elements. One word of caution, however: Microsoft Visual C++ initializes the uninitialized array elements only if you provide at least one value in the *initialvalues* section of the statement that declares the array. If you omit the *initialvalues* section from the declaration statement—for example, if you use the statement int num[3]; to declare an array—Microsoft Visual C++ does not automatically initialize the elements, so the array elements will contain garbage.

The last example shown in Figure 14-3, float price[5] = {float(6.5)};, declares a five-element float array named price, and it initializes the first element to the number 6.5. Because the statement does not provide an initial value for the remaining elements in the array, Microsoft Visual C++ initializes the remaining elements to 0.0.

Although Microsoft Visual C++ initializes the uninitialized elements in an array (assuming you have provided at least one initial value), not all C++ systems do.

If you inadvertently provide more values in the *initialvalues* section than the number of array elements, Microsoft Visual C++ displays a syntax error message when you compile the program. However, not all C++ systems display a message when this error occurs; some systems simply store the extra values in memory locations adjacent to, but not reserved for, the array.

Mini-Quiz 1

1. Write a C++ statement that declares and initializes a 20-element int array named number. Initialize the array elements to the number 0.
2. Write a C++ statement that declares and initializes a 10-element string array named items. Initialize the array elements to the empty string.
3. The first subscript in a 25-element array is the number _____ .
4. The last subscript in a 25-element array is the number _____ .
5. quantity[7] is read _____ .

After declaring and initializing a one-dimensional array, you can use various methods to store other data in the array.

Storing Data in a One-Dimensional Array

Typically, you declare and initialize an array at the beginning of a program. You then can use a variety of ways to enter other data into the array. The examples shown in Figure 14-5, for instance, can be used to enter data into the arrays declared and initialized in Figure 14-3.

Examples	Results

Example 1:
`letter[0] = 'X';`
`letter[1] = 'Y';`
`letter[2] = 'Z';`
	assigns the letters X, Y, and Z to the `letter` array, replacing the letters A, B, and C

Example 2: `name[1] = "Helen";`	assigns the name Helen to the second element in the `name` array, replacing the name Nancy

Example 3:
`x = 0;`
`while (x < 4 && !inFile.eof())`
`{`
`    getline(inFile, state[x]);`
`    x = x + 1;`
`} //end while`
	reads the data from a sequential access file, and stores the data in the `state` array, replacing the data stored in the array

Example 4:
`count = 1;`
`while (count <= 3)`
`{`
`    num[count - 1] = count * count;`
`    count = count + 1;`
`} //end while`
	assigns the squares of the numbers from 1 through 3 to the `num` array, replacing the data stored in the array

Example 5:
`x = 0;`
`while (x < 5)`
`{`
`    cout << "Enter price: ";`
`    cin >> price[x];`
`    x = x + 1;`
`} //end while`
	stores the values entered by the user in the `price` array, replacing the data stored in the array

Figure 14-5: Examples of entering data into a one-dimensional array

The three assignment statements shown in the first example in Figure 14-5 assign the letters X, Y, and Z to the `letter` array, replacing the array's initial values (A, B, C). In the second example, the statement `name[1] = "Helen";` assigns the name "Helen" to the second element in the `name` array, replacing the name "Nancy" that was stored in the element when the array was initialized.

The code shown in the third example in Figure 14-5 reads the data from a sequential access file and stores the data in the `state` array, replacing the empty strings stored in the array when the array was created. The code shown in the fourth example assigns the squares of the numbers from 1 through 3 to the `num` array, writing over the array's initial values. Notice that the number 1 must be subtracted from the value stored in the `count` variable when assigning the squares to the array; this is because the first array element has a subscript of 0 rather than 1. The code shown in the last example in Figure 14-5 replaces the data stored in the `price` array with the values entered by the user.

Now that you know how to declare, initialize, and enter data into a one-dimensional array, you will learn how to manipulate an array in a program.

Manipulating One-Dimensional Arrays

The variables (elements) in an array can be used just like any other variables. For example, you can assign values to them, use them in calculations, and display their contents. In the next several sections, you will view sample programs that demonstrate how one-dimensional arrays are used in a program. More specifically, the programs will show you how to perform the following tasks using a one-dimensional array:

1. Display the contents of an array
2. Access an array element using its subscript
3. Search the array
4. Calculate the average of the data stored in a numeric array
5. Find the highest value stored in an array
6. Update the array elements

Begin by viewing a program that displays the contents of a one-dimensional array.

Displaying the Contents of a One-Dimensional Array

Many times, a program will need simply to display the contents of an array used by the program. The month program shown in Figure 14-6 demonstrates how you can accomplish this task.

In most programs, the values stored in an array come from a file on the computer's disk, and are stored in the array after it is created and initialized. However, so that you can follow the code and program results more easily, most of the programs you will view in this lesson will initialize the array data to the appropriate values.

Pseudocode

1. initialize x to 0 (first subscript)
2. repeat while (x is less than array size)
      display array element located in position x
      add 1 to x
  end repeat while

Figure 14-6: Month program

Program

```
//displays the contents of a one-dimensional array
int main()
{
    //declare array
    string month[12] = {"JAN", "FEB", "MAR", "APR", "MAY",
                        "JUNE", "JULY", "AUG", "SEPT",
                        "OCT", "NOV", "DEC"};

    int x = 0;                          //first subscript
    while (x < 12)                      //repeat for each element
    {
        cout << month[x] << endl;   //display current element
        x = x + 1;                      //update subscript
    } //end while
    return 0;
} //end of main function
```

Results

```
JAN
FEB
MAR
APR
MAY
JUNE
JULY
AUG
SEPT
OCT
NOV
DEC
```

Figure 14-6: Month program (continued)

tip

Notice that the loop in the month program stops when x is 12, which is one number more than the last subscript in the array.

The month program shown in Figure 14-6 declares a 12-element **string** array named **month**, using the names of the 12 months to initialize the array. The program uses a **while** loop, along with a counter variable named **x**, to display the contents of each array element on the screen. For example, the first time the loop instructions are processed, the **x** variable contains the number 0, and the statement **cout << month[x] << endl;** displays the contents of the **month[0]** element—JAN—on the screen. The statement **x = x + 1;** then increases the value stored in **x** by 1, giving 1. When the loop instructions are processed the second time, the statement **cout << month[x] << endl;** displays the contents of the **month[1]** element—FEB—on the screen, and so on. The loop processes its instructions until the value in **x** is 12, at which time the loop stops. As Figure 14-6 indicates, the program displays the names of the 12 months on separate lines on the screen.

Next, you will view a program that uses the array subscript to access the appropriate element in an array.

Using the Subscript to Access an Element in a One-Dimensional Array

Assume that XYZ Corporation pays its managers based on six different salary codes, 1 through 6. Each code corresponds to a different salary amount. You can use the salary program shown in Figure 14-7 to display the salary amount corresponding to the code entered by the user.

Pseudocode

1. enter the code
2. if (the code is valid)
       display array element located in position (code - 1)
   else
       display an error message
   end if

Program

```
//uses the subscript to access an element in a one-dimensional
//array
int main()
{
    //declare array
    int salary[6] = {25000, 35000, 55000, 70000, 80200, 90500};
    int code = 0;
    cout << "Enter the salary code (1 through 6): ";
    cin >> code;

    //determine if the code is valid
    if (code >= 1 && code <= 6)
        cout << "Salary: " << salary[code - 1] << endl;
    else
        cout << "Invalid code" << endl;
    //end if
    return 0;
} //end of main function
```

Results

Salary: 55000   (assuming the user enters the number 3)
Invalid code   (assuming the user enters the number 8)

Figure 14-7: Salary program

Before accessing an array element, a program should always verify that the subscript is valid—in other words, that it is in range. If the program uses a subscript that is not in range, the program may write over a portion of internal memory that is not reserved for the array. This could lead to a loss of data or a system crash.

The salary program shown in Figure 14-7 declares an `int` array named `salary`, and it uses six salary amounts to initialize the array. The salary amount for code 1 is stored in `salary[0]`. Code 2's salary amount is stored in `salary[1]`, and so on. Notice that the code is one number more than the array subscript with which it is associated.

After creating and initializing the array, the program prompts the user to enter the salary code, storing the user's response in the `code` variable. The `if` statement in the program determines whether the code entered by the user is valid. In this case, valid codes are numbers that are greater than or equal to 1 and, at the same time, less than or equal to 6. If the code is not valid, the program displays an error message; otherwise, the statement `cout << "Salary: " << salary[code – 1] << endl;` displays the appropriate salary from the array. Notice that, to access the appropriate array element, the number 1 must be subtracted from the contents of the `code` variable; this is because the code entered by the user is one number more than its associated array subscript. As Figure 14-7 indicates, the program displays the number 55000 if the user enters a code of 3. If the user enters a code of 8, the program displays the message "Invalid code".

In the next section, you will learn how to search a one-dimensional array.

Searching a One-Dimensional Array

Assume that the sales manager at Jacobsen Motors wants a program that allows him to determine the number of salespeople selling above a certain amount, which he will enter when the program is executed. To accomplish this task, the program needs to search the array, looking for values that are greater than the amount entered by the sales manager. The sales program shown in Figure 14-8 shows you how to search an array.

Pseudocode
1. initialize x to 0 (first subscript)
2. initialize counter to 0
3. get the sales amount
4. repeat while (x is less than array size)
if (the value in the current array element is greater than the sales amount)
add 1 to the counter
end if
add 1 to x
end repeat while
5. display the contents of the counter

Figure 14-8: Sales program

Program

```cpp
//searches a one-dimensional array
int main()
{
    //declare array
    int sales[5] = {45000, 35000, 25000, 60000, 23000};

    //declare variables
    int x        = 0;       //keeps track of subscripts
    int count    = 0;       //counter
    int searchFor = 0;      //number to search for

    //get sales to search for
    cout << "Search for sales greater than: ";
    cin >> searchFor;

    //search array
    while (x < 5)
    {
        if (sales[x] > searchFor)   //compare values
            count = count + 1;      //add 1 to counter
        //end if
        x = x + 1;                  //update subscript
    } //end while

    //display count
    cout << "Count: " << count << endl;
    return 0;
} //end of main function
```

Results

Count: 2 (assuming the user enters the number 40000)
Count: 0 (assuming the user enters the number 60000)

Figure 14-8: Sales program (continued)

The sales program shown in Figure 14-8 declares an int array named sales, using five sales amounts to initialize the array. The program prompts the user to enter a sales amount, and it stores the user's response in the searchFor variable. The while loop in the program then repeats its instructions for each element in the array.

The first instruction in the while loop is an if statement that compares the contents of the current array element with the contents of the searchFor variable. If the array element contains a number that is greater than the number stored in the searchFor variable, the if statement's true path adds the number 1 to the value stored in the count variable. The count variable in this program is a counter that keeps track of the number of salespeople selling over the amount entered by the sales manager. The last instruction in the while loop, x = x + 1;, updates the array subscript variable by adding 1 to it.

When the `while` loop ends, which is when the `x` variable contains the number 5, the statement `cout << "Count: " << count << endl;` displays the contents of the `count` variable on the screen. As Figure 14-8 indicates, the program displays the number 2 if the sales manager enters 40000 as the sales amount, and it displays the number 0 if he enters 60000 as the sales amount.

mini-quiz

Mini-Quiz 2

1. Which of the following C++ statements assigns the string "BX45" to the third element in an array named `item`?

   a. `item[2] = "BX45";`

   b. `item[3] = "BX45";`

   c. `item[2] == "BX45";`

   d. `item[3] == "BX45";`

2. Assume that the `item` array is declared using the statement `string item[20] = {""};`. Also assume that the `x` variable, which keeps track of the array subscripts, is initialized to 0. Which of the following C++ `while` clauses will process the loop instructions for each element in the array?

   a. `while (x > 20)`

   b. `while (x < 20)`

   c. `while (x >= 20)`

   d. `while (x <= 20)`

3. Assume that the `bonus` array is declared using the statement `float bonus[10] = {0.0};`. Also assume that the `x` variable, which keeps track of the array subscripts, is initialized to 0. Write the C++ code to display the contents of the `bonus` array.

Next, you will learn how to calculate the average of the data stored in a numeric array.

Calculating the Average Amount Stored in a One-Dimensional Numeric Array

Professor Jeremiah wants a program that he can use to calculate and display the average test score earned by his students on the final exam. The test average program shown in Figure 14-9 can be used to accomplish this task.

Pseudocode
1. initialize x to 0 (first subscript)
2. initialize accumulator to 0
3. repeat while (x is less than array size)
add the contents of the current array element to the accumulator
add 1 to x
end repeat while
4. calculate the average by dividing the accumulator by the number of array elements
5. display the average

Figure 14-9: Test average program

Program

```
//calculates the average of the amounts stored in a
//one-dimensional array
int main()
{
    //declare array
    int scores[5] = {98, 100, 56, 74, 35};

    //declare variables
    int x     = 0;   //keeps track of array subscripts
    int total = 0;   //scores accumulator
    float avg = 0.0; //average of the scores

    while (x < 5)
    {
        total = total + scores[x];   //accumulate scores
        x = x + 1;                   //update subscript
    } //end while

    //calculate and display average
    avg = float(total) / 5.0;
    cout << "Average: " << avg << endl;
    return 0;
} //end of main function
```

Results

Average: 72.6

Figure 14-9: Test average program (continued)

The test average program shown in Figure 14-9 declares an `int` array named `scores`, using five test scores to initialize the array. The instructions in the `while` loop add the score contained in each array element to the `total` variable. The `total` variable in this program is an accumulator, used to add up the test scores. When the `while` loop ends, which is when the value stored in the `x` variable is 5, the program calculates and then displays the average test score. As Figure 14-9 indicates, the program displays the number 72.6.

In the next section, you will learn how to determine the highest value stored in a one-dimensional array.

Determining the Highest Value Stored in a One-Dimensional Array

Sharon Johnson keeps track of the amount of money she spends each week on groceries. She would like a program that she can use to display the highest amount spent in a week. Similar to the sales program shown earlier in Figure 14-8, this program will need to search the array. However, rather than looking in the array for values that are greater than a specific amount, the program will be looking for the highest amount in the array, as shown in Figure 14-10.

Pseudocode

1. initialize high variable to contents of first array element
2. initialize x to 1 (second subscript)
3. repeat while (x is less than array size)
   if (the value in the current array element is greater than the value in the high variable)
      assign the current array element's contents to the high variable
   end if
   add 1 to x
   end repeat while
4. display the contents of the high variable

Program

```
//searches for the highest amount stored in a one-dimensional array
int main()
{
    //declare array
    int dollars[6] = {25, 30, 50, 20, 15, 25};

    int high = dollars[0]; //assign first element value to high
    int x    = 1;          //begin search with second element
    while (x < 6)
    {
        if (dollars[x] > high)  //compare values
            high = dollars[x]; //assign element value to high
        //end if
        x = x + 1;             //update subscript
    } //end while

    //display highest value
    cout << "High: " << high << endl;
    return 0;
} //end of main function
```

Results

High: 50

Figure 14-10: Highest amount program

Recall that in most programs, the values stored in an array come from a file on the computer's disk.

The highest amount program shown in Figure 14-10 declares an int array named dollars, and it initializes the array to the amounts that Sharon spent on groceries during the last six weeks. The program also declares and initializes two int variables named high and x. The high variable is used to keep track of the highest value stored in the array, and is initialized using the value stored in the first array element. The x variable is used to keep track of the array subscripts. Notice that the program initializes the x variable to the number 1, which is the subscript corresponding to the second element in the array.

The first time the `while` loop instructions in the program are processed, the `if` statement within the loop compares the value stored in the second array element (`dollars[1]`) with the value stored in the `high` variable. (Recall that the `high` variable contains the same value as the first array element at this point.) If the value stored in the second array element is greater than the value stored in the `high` variable, then the statement `high = dollars[x];` assigns the array element value to the `high` variable. The next statement in the loop, `x = x + 1;`, adds 1 to the `x` variable, giving 2. The next time the loop instructions are processed, the `if` statement compares the value stored in the third array element (`dollars[2]`) with the value stored in the `high` variable, and so on.

When the `while` loop ends, which is when the value stored in the `x` variable is 6, the program displays the contents of the `high` variable on the screen. As Figure 14-10 indicates, the program displays the number 50.

Next, learn how to update the values stored in a one-dimensional array.

Updating the Values Stored in a One-Dimensional Array

The sales manager at Jillian Company wants a program that she can use to increase the price of each item the company sells. She also would like the program to display each item's current and new prices. The program shown in Figure 14-11 will perform these tasks.

Pseudocode

1. initialize x to 0 (first subscript)
2. enter increase amount
3. repeat while (x is less than array size)
       display contents of current array element
       add increase to current array element
       display contents of current array element
       add 1 to x
   end repeat while

Program

```
//updates the values stored in a one-dimensional array
int main()
{
    //declare array
    float prices[4] = {float(150.35), float(35.60),
                       float(75.75), float(25.30)};

    int x          = 0;      //keeps track of array subscripts
    float increase = 0.0;    //stores increase amount
    cout << "Enter the increase amount: ";
    cin >> increase;
```

Figure 14-11: Update program

Program

```
    while (x < 4)
    {
        //display current value
        cout << fixed;
        cout.precision(2);
        cout << "Current price: $" << prices[x] << endl;

        //add increase to element
        prices[x] = prices[x] + increase;

        //display new value
        cout << "New price: $" << prices[x] << endl;

        x = x + 1;        //update subscript
    } //end while
    return 0;
} //end of main function
```

Results

```
Current price: $150.35
New price: $155.35      (assuming the user enters the number 5)
Current price: $35.60
New price: $40.60
Current price: $75.75
New price: $80.75
Current price: $25.30
New price: $30.30
```

Figure 14-11: Update program (continued)

The update program shown in Figure 14-11 declares a `float` array named `prices`, using four `float` values to initialize the array. The program prompts the user to enter the amount of the increase, and stores the user's response in the `increase` variable. The `while` loop in the program then repeats its instructions for each element in the array.

The `cout << "Current price: $" << prices[x] << endl;` statement in the `while` loop displays a message and the contents of the current array element on the screen. The next statement, `prices[x] = prices[x] + increase;`, updates the contents of the array element by adding the increase to it. The next statement, `cout << "New price: $" << prices[x] << endl;`, displays the updated contents on the screen. The last statement in the loop, `x = x + 1;`, adds the number 1 to the `x` variable, which keeps track of the array subscripts. The `while` loop ends when the value stored in the `x` variable is 4. Assuming the user enters the number 5 as the increase amount, the program displays the results shown in Figure 14-11.

The program you will view next uses many of the concepts you have learned so far about arrays. It also shows you how to pass an array to a program-defined function.

The Rainfall Program

At the beginning of each year, Martha Stenwaldt records the monthly rainfall amounts for the previous year in a sequential access file named rainfall.dat. A sample file is shown in Figure 14-12. Notice that the file contains 12 amounts; each corresponds to one of the months in a year.

```
2.76
2.36
2.44
1.20
.40
.07
.04
.23
.54
.63
1.54
2.16
```

Figure 14-12: Sample rainfall.dat file

Martha would like a program that reads the data from the file, and then calculates and displays the total rainfall amount. The program shown in Figure 14-13 represents one possible solution to the rainfall problem.

Pseudocode

main function
1. initialize x to 0 (first subscript)
2. open the rainfall.dat file
3. if (the open was successful)
        repeat while (x is less than array size and it is not the end of the file)
                read record from file, storing it in the current array element
                add 1 to x
        end repeat while
        close the file
        use the calcTotal function to calculate the total rainfall amount
        display the total rainfall amount on the screen
    else
        display error message
    end if

calcTotal function
1. initialize x to 0 (first subscript)
2. initialize total to 0.0
3. repeat while (x is less than array size)
        add contents of current array element to total
        add 1 to x
    end repeat while
4. return total

Figure 14-13: Rainfall program

Program

```
//calculates and displays the total rainfall

#include <iostream>
#include <fstream>
using namespace std;

//function prototype
float calcTotal(float []);

int main()
{
        //declare variable
        int x = 0;      //keeps track of subscripts

        //declare array
        float rainFall[12] = {0.0};

        //declare file object and open file
        ifstream inFile;
        inFile.open("rainfall.dat", ios::in);

        if (inFile.is_open())
        {
            //fill array with file data
            while (x < 12 && !inFile.eof())
            {
                inFile >> rainFall[x];
                x = x + 1;
            } //end while
            inFile.close();     //close file

            //display total rainfall
            cout << "Total rainfall: "
                 << calcTotal(rainFall) << endl;
        }
        else
            cout << "File could not be opened" << endl;
        return 0;
} //end of main function

//*****program-defined functions*****
float calcTotal(float r[])
{
        int x         = 0;      //keeps track of subscripts
        float total = 0.0;   //accumulator

        while (x < 12)
        {
                total = total + r[x];
                x = x + 1;
        } //end while
        return total;
} //end of calcTotal function
```

enter the array's datatype and square brackets in the prototype → `float calcTotal(float []);`

enter the array name in the function call → `<< calcTotal(rainFall) << endl;`

enter the array's data type and name, followed by square brackets, in the function header → `float calcTotal(float r[])`

Figure 14-13: Rainfall program (continued)

tip

You also could have written the rainfall program shown in Figure 14-13 without using an array. However, in Exercise 4 at the end of the lesson, you will add other functions to the rainfall program, making the array necessary.

tip

It is a good programming practice to use a compound condition, similar to the one shown in Figure 14-13, in a `while` loop that reads records from a file into an array, even when you know that the file contains the same number of records as there are array elements. Doing so helps to ensure that the program will not end in an error if the file is somehow changed.

tip

Passing an array by reference is more efficient than passing it by value. Because many arrays are large, passing by value would consume a great deal of memory and time since the computer would need to duplicate the array in the receiving function's formal parameter.

The `main` function in the program shown in Figure 14-13 declares and initializes a 12-element `float` array named `rainFall`. It then opens the rainfall.dat file for input. If the file cannot be opened, the program displays an appropriate message. However, if the open was successful, the `while` loop reads each record from the file, storing each in the array. Notice that the `while` clause contains two conditions connected by the And (`&&`) logical operator. The `x < 12` condition ensures that the loop does not attempt to access a memory location that is not part of the array, and the `!inFile.eof()` condition ensures that the loop does not attempt to read past the end of the file.

When the `while` loop in the `main` function ends, the program closes the rainfall.dat file. It then calls the `calcTotal` function to calculate the total rainfall amount before displaying the message "Total rainfall: " and the total rainfall amount on the screen.

Study closely the `calcTotal` function prototype, function call, and function header, which are shaded in the figure. As you know, data can be passed to functions either by value or by reference. Recall that, in C++, variables are passed automatically by value. To pass a variable by reference in C++, you need to include the address-of (`&`) operator before the formal parameter's name in the receiving function's header. You also need to include the `&` operator in the receiving function's prototype.

Arrays in C++, however, are automatically passed by reference rather than by value. When you pass an array, the computer passes the address of only the first array element to the receiving function. Because array elements are stored in contiguous locations in memory, the receiving function needs to know only where the first element is located in memory. From there, the function can easily locate the other elements.

Because arrays are automatically passed by reference, you do not include the address-of (`&`) operator before the formal parameter's name in the function header, as you do when passing variables by reference. You also do not include the `&` operator in the function prototype. To pass an array to a function, you need simply to enter the data type and name of the formal parameter, followed by an empty set of brackets, in the receiving function's header. You also enter the data type and an empty set of brackets in the receiving function's prototype. As Figure 14-13 shows, you can pass the `rainFall` array to the `calcTotal` function by entering `float r[]` in the `calcTotal` function header, and entering `float []` in the `calcTotal` function prototype.

Next, learn about parallel one-dimensional arrays.

Using Parallel One-Dimensional Arrays

Takoda Tapahe owns a small gift shop named Treasures. She has asked you to create a program that she can use to display the price of the item whose product ID she enters. Figure 14-14 shows a portion of the gift shop's price list.

Product ID	Price
BX35	13
CR20	10
FE15	12
KW10	24
MM67	4

Figure 14-14: A portion of the gift shop's price list

Recall that all of the variables in an array have the same data type. So how can you store a price list, which includes a string (the product ID) and a number (the price), in an array? One way of doing so is to use two one-dimensional arrays: a `string` array to store the product IDs and an `int` array to store the prices. Both arrays are illustrated in Figure 14-15.

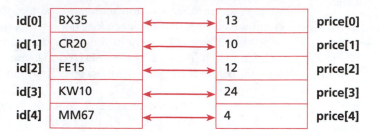

id[0]	BX35		13	price[0]
id[1]	CR20		10	price[1]
id[2]	FE15		12	price[2]
id[3]	KW10		24	price[3]
id[4]	MM67		4	price[4]

Figure 14-15: Illustration of a price list stored in two one-dimensional arrays

The arrays shown in Figure 14-15 are referred to as parallel arrays. **Parallel arrays** are simply two or more arrays whose elements are related by their position—in other words, by their subscript—in the arrays. The `id` and `price` arrays shown in Figure 14-15 are parallel because each element in the `id` array corresponds to the element located in the same position in the `price` array. For example, the first element in the `id` array corresponds to the first element in the `price` array—in other words, the item whose product ID is BX35 (`id[0]`) has a price of $13 (`price[0]`). Likewise, the second elements in both arrays—the elements with a subscript of 1—also are related; the item whose product ID is CR20 has a price of $10. The same relationship is true for the remaining elements in both arrays. If you want to know an item's price, you simply locate the item's ID in the `id` array and then view its corresponding element in the `price` array. Figure 14-16 shows a program that displays the item's price based on the ID entered by the user.

Pseudocode

1. enter product ID to search for
2. convert product ID to uppercase
3. repeat while (product ID is not X)
    initialize y to 0 (first subscript)
    repeat while (y is less than array size and product ID was not located in id array)
        add 1 to y
    end repeat while
    if (ID was found in id array)
        display appropriate price from price array
    else
        display "Product ID is not valid" message
    end if
    enter product ID to search for
    convert product ID to uppercase
end repeat while

Figure 14-16: Price list program using parallel arrays

Program

```cpp
int main()
{
    //declare arrays
    string id[5] = {"BX35", "CR20", "FE15", "KW10", "MM67"};
    int price[5]    = {13, 10, 12, 24, 4};

    string searchFor = ""; //product ID to locate

    //get product ID and convert to uppercase
    cout << "Enter product ID (X to exit program): ";
    getline(cin, searchFor);
    transform(searchFor.begin(), searchFor.end(),
        searchFor.begin(), toupper);

    while (searchFor != "X")
    {
        //locate position of product ID in the id array
        int y = 0;  //keeps track of array subscripts
        while (y < 5 && id[y] != searchFor)
            y = y + 1;
        //end while

        //if ID was found, display price from price array
        //otherwise, display error message
        if (y < 5)
        {
            cout << fixed;
            cout.precision(2);
            cout << "Price: $" << price[y] << endl;
        }
        else
            cout << "Product ID is not valid" << endl;
        //end if

        //get product ID and convert to uppercase
        cout << "Enter product ID (X to exit program): ";
        getline(cin, searchFor);
        transform(searchFor.begin(), searchFor.end(),
            searchFor.begin(), toupper);
    } //end while
    return 0;
}//end of main function
```

parallel arrays → (points to the `string id[5]` and `int price[5]` lines)

Results

Price: $12 (assuming the user enters FE15 as the product ID)
Product ID is not valid (assuming the user enters XX89 as the product ID)

Figure 14-16: Price list program using parallel arrays (continued)

The price list program shown in Figure 14-16 declares and initializes two parallel arrays: a five-element `string` array named `id` and a five-element `int` array named `price`. The program then prompts the user to enter a product ID, and it stores the user's response in the `searchFor` variable. The `transform` function is used to convert the contents of the `searchFor` variable to uppercase, to match the case of the product IDs stored in the array.

The outer `while` loop in the program repeats its loop body instructions as long as the user does not enter the letter X (in any case) as the product ID. The first instruction in the outer `while` loop declares and initializes an `int` variable named `y`. The second instruction is the beginning of a nested `while` loop.

The nested `while` loop continues to add the number 1 to the `y` variable as long as the `y` variable contains a value that is less than 5 and, at the same time, the product ID has not been located in the array. The nested `while` loop will stop when either of the following conditions is true: the `y` variable contains the number 5 (which indicates that the loop reached the end of the array without finding the product ID) or the product ID is located in the array.

After the nested `while` loop completes its processing, the `if` statement in the program compares the value in the `y` variable to the number 5. If the `y` variable's value is less than 5, it indicates that the loop stopped processing because the product ID was located in the `id` array. In that case, the statement `cout << "Price: $" << price[y] << endl;` displays the corresponding price from the `price` array. However, if the `y` variable's value is not less than 5, it indicates that the loop stopped processing because it reached the end of the array without finding the product ID; in that case, the message "Product ID is not valid" is displayed.

tip

Using parallel arrays is only one way of solving the price list problem; you also can use an array of objects. You will learn how to code the price list program using an array of objects in this tutorial's Application lesson.

mini-quiz

Mini-Quiz 3

1. Write a C++ `if` clause that determines if the value stored in the current array element is less than the value stored in the `low` variable. The name of the array is `price`. Use `x` as the name of the variable that keeps track of the subscripts.

2. Write a C++ `while` loop that subtracts the number 3 from each of the elements in an array named `numbers`. The array contains five elements. Use `x` as the name of the variable that keeps track of the subscripts. You can assume that the `x` variable was initialized to 0.

3. Assume that the `employeeNumber` and `employeeName` arrays are parallel arrays. If an employee's number is located in `employeeNumber[3]`, then his or her name is located in _____ .

Recall that, in addition to using one-dimensional arrays, many programs also utilize two-dimensional arrays.

Two-Dimensional Arrays

As you learned earlier, a two-dimensional array resembles a table in that the elements are in rows and columns. As with one-dimensional arrays, you must declare and (optionally) initialize a two-dimensional array before you can use it. Figure 14-17 compares the syntax for creating and initializing a one-dimensional array with the syntax for creating and initializing a two-dimensional array. The additional information required to create and initialize a two-dimensional array is shaded in the figure.

Syntax

One-dimensional array
datatype arrayname[*numberOfElements*] = {*initialvalues*};

Two-dimensional array
datatype arrayname[*numberOfElements*] [*numberOfElements*]
                = {{*initialvalues*}, {*initialvalues*}, ...{*initialvalues*}};

Figure 14-17: Comparison of the syntax to create and initialize one-dimensional and two-dimensional arrays in C++

Notice that the two-dimensional array syntax includes an additional *numberOfElements* enclosed in square brackets ([]) after the array's name. Recall that *numberOfElements* in the one-dimensional array syntax represents the number of elements in the array. When you create a two-dimensional array, however, the first *numberOfElements* after the array name represents the number of rows in the array, and the second *numberOfElements* represents the number of columns. To create an array that has three rows and four columns, for example, you would enter [3][4] after the array name. In other words, the number of rows is listed first in the syntax, followed by the number of columns. You can calculate the size of a two-dimensional array—or, the total number of elements in the array—by multiplying the number of rows by the number of columns. For example, a two-dimensional array created with [3][4] as the *numberOfElements* values would contain a total of 12 (3 times 4) elements.

As discussed earlier, you should always initialize the elements in an array. Recall that you can initialize the elements in a one-dimensional array at the same time you create the array simply by entering one or more values, separated by commas, in the *initialvalues* section of the syntax. You also can initialize the elements in a two-dimensional array at the same time you create the array by entering a separate *initialvalues* section, enclosed in braces, for each row in the array. If the array has two rows, for example, then the statement that declares and initializes the array can have a maximum of two *initialvalues* sections. If the array has five rows, then the declaration statement can have a maximum of five *initialvalues* sections.

Within the individual *initialvalues* sections, you enter one or more values separated by commas. The maximum number of values you enter corresponds to the maximum number of columns in the array. If the array contains 10 columns, for example, then you can include up to 10 values in each *initialvalues* section.

In addition to the set of braces that surrounds each individual *initialvalues* section, notice in the syntax that a set of braces also surrounds all of the *initialvalues* sections. Figure 14-18 shows four examples of creating and initializing two-dimensional arrays.

Examples	Results

Example 1:
`char grade[3][2]`
`    = {{'A', 'A'}, {'B', 'C'}; {'D', 'B'}};`
	declares and initializes a three-row, two-column char array

Example 2:
`string name[2][2]`
`    = {{"Bob", "Sue"}, {"Bill", "Tom"}};`
	declares and initializes a two-row, two column string array

Example 3:
`int num[2][4] = {0};`
      or
`int num[2][4] = {{0}, {0}};`
      or
`int num[2][4] = {{0,0,0,0}, {0,0,0,0}};`
	declares and initializes a two-row, four-column int array; each element is initialized to 0

Example 4: `float price[5][6] = {float(2.0)};`	declares and initializes a five-row, six-column float array; the first element is initialized to 2.0, while the others are initialized to 0.0

Figure 14-18: Examples of creating and initializing two-dimensional arrays

Carefully study the examples shown in Figure 14-18. In the first example, the statement `char grade[3][2] = {{'A', 'A'}, {'B', 'C'}, {'D', 'B'}};` declares a `char` array named `grade` that contains three rows and two columns. It initializes the first row in the array to the grades A and A, the second row to the grades B and C, and the third row to the grades D and B, as shown in Figure 14-19.

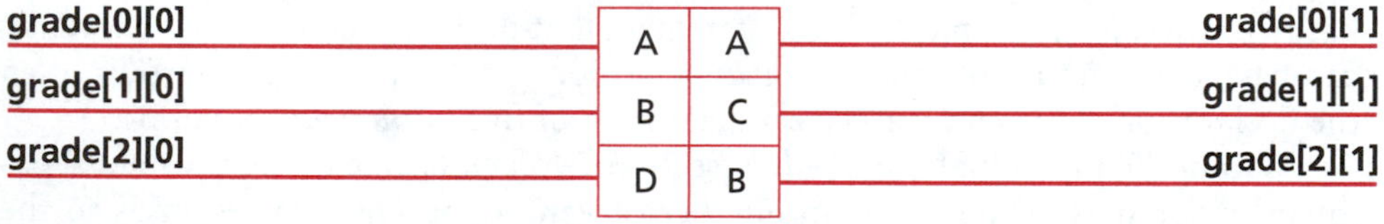

Figure 14-19: Illustration of the two-dimensional `grade` array in memory

As Figure 14-19 shows, the first row in a two-dimensional array is row 0, and the first column is column 0. You refer to each element in a two-dimensional array by the array's name followed by the row subscript (in square brackets) and the column subscript (also in square brackets). For example, `grade[0][0]`—read "grade sub zero zero"—refers to the element located in row 0, column 0 in the `grade` array, and `grade[2][1]` refers to the element located in row 2, column 1 in the array.

The second example shown in Figure 14-18, `string name[2][2] = {{"Bob", "Sue"}, {"Bill", "Tom"}};`, creates a `string` array having two rows and two columns. It uses the names "Bob" and "Sue" to initialize the first row in the array, and the names "Bill" and "Tom" to initialize the second row.

You can use either of the statements shown in Example 3 to declare and initialize a two-dimensional `int` array named `num` to 0. Recall that when you don't provide an initial value for each of the elements in a numeric array, Microsoft Visual C++ stores the number 0 in the uninitialized elements.

The last example shown in Figure 14-18 declares and initializes a two-dimensional `float` array named `price`. The element located in the first row, first column of the array will be initialized to 2.0; the remaining elements will be initialized to 0.0.

You will use a two-dimensional array in the Conway Enterprises program in the next section.

The Conway Enterprises Program

Conway Enterprises has both domestic and international sales operations. The company's sales manager wants a program that she can use to display the total sales made by the company during a six-month period. The program shown in Figure 14-20 will accomplish this task.

```
                    //calculates and displays total sales
international        int main()
                    {
domestic                //declare array
                        int sales[6][2] =  {{12000, 10000},
                                            {45000, 56000},
                                            {32000, 42000},
                                            {67000, 23000},
                                            {24000, 12000},
                                            {55000, 34000}};

                        //declare variables
                        int row     = 0;  //keeps track of row subscript
                        int col     = 0;  //keep track of column subscript
                        int company = 0;  //sales accumulator

                        while (row < 6)
                        {
                            col = 0;                //reset column subscript
                            while (col < 2)
outer loop              {
                                //accumulate sales
                                company = company + sales[row][col];
                                col = col + 1;  //update column subscript
                            } //end while
                            row = row + 1;          //update row subscript
                        } //end while
nested loop
                        //display total sales
                        cout << "Total sales: $" << company << endl;

                        return 0;
                    } //end of main function
```

Figure 14-20: Conway Enterprises program

The Conway Enterprises program declares and initializes a six-row, two-column `int` array named `sales`. The company's domestic sales amounts are stored in the first column in each row in the array, and its international sales amounts are stored in the second column in each row.

As Figure 14-20 indicates, two loops are necessary to access each element in a two-dimensional array: one loop to keep track of the row number, and another to keep track of the column number. Figure 14-21 shows the desk-check table for the Conway Enterprises program. According to the desk-check table, the total sales made during the six months is $412,000.

sales[0][0]		12000	10000		sales[0][1]
sales[1][0]		45000	56000		sales[1][1]
sales[2][0]		32000	42000		sales[2][1]
sales[3][0]		67000	23000		sales[3][1]
sales[4][0]		24000	12000		sales[4][1]
sales[5][0]		55000	34000		sales[5][1]

tip

To pass a two-dimensional array to a function, you leave the first set of brackets after the formal parameter's name empty. Recall that the first set of brackets represents the number of rows in the array. However, you must enter a number in the second set of brackets to specify the number of columns in the array. For example, to pass the `sales` array shown in Figure 14-20 to a function whose formal parameter is named `dollars`, you enter `int dollars[][2]` in the receiving function's header, and enter `int [][2]` in its prototype. You can practice passing a two-dimensional array to a function by completing Discovery Exercise 19 at the end of this lesson.

row	col	company
0	0	0
1	0	12000
2	1	22000
3	2	67000
4	0	123000
5	1	155000
6	2	197000
	0	264000
	1	287000
	2	311000
	0	323000
	1	378000
	2	412000
	0	
	1	
	2	
	0	
	1	
	2	

Figure 14-21: Desk-check table for the Conway Enterprises program

mini-quiz

Mini-Quiz 4

1. Write a C++ statement that declares a four-row, two-column `int` array named `quantity`. Initialize each element in the array to 0.

2. A five-row, four-column array has a total of _____ elements.

3. `quantity[1][7]` is read _____ .

   a. "quantity one seven"

   b. "quantity one bracket seven"

   c. "quantity sub one sub seven"

   d. "quantity sub one seven"

4. A six-row, three-column array will have row subscripts of _____ through _____ .

5. A six-row, three-column array will have column subscripts of _____ through _____ .

6. Write a C++ assignment statement that stores the number 5 in the second row, third column of a two-dimensional array named `quantity`.

You now have completed Tutorial 14's Concept lesson. You can either take a break or complete the end-of-lesson questions and exercises before moving on to the Application lesson.

SUMMARY

An array is a group of variables that have the same name and data type and are related in some way. The most commonly used arrays in programs are one-dimensional and two-dimensional. A one-dimensional array is simply a column of variables. A two-dimensional array, on the other hand, resembles a table in that it has rows and columns. Programmers use arrays to temporarily store related data in the internal memory of the computer. By doing so, a programmer can increase the efficiency of a program because data stored inside the computer can be both written and read much faster than data stored in a file on a disk. Additionally, after the data is entered into an array, which typically is done at the beginning of the program, the program can use the data as many times as desired.

You must declare an array before you can use it. You can use any C++ built-in data type, as well as a class that you create, to declare an array. It is a good programming practice to initialize the elements in an array. After declaring and initializing an array, you can use a variety of ways to enter data into the array. For example, you can enter data from the keyboard or from a file on the computer's disk.

Each of the array elements in memory is assigned a unique number, called a subscript. The first element in a one-dimensional array in C++ is assigned a subscript of 0, the next element in the array is assigned a subscript of 1, and so on. Because the first array subscript is 0, the last subscript in an array is always one less than the number of elements. You refer to each element in the array by the array's name and the element's subscript, which is specified in square brackets ([]) immediately following the name.

Unlike variables, arrays are passed automatically by reference rather than by value. When you pass an array, the address of only the first array element is passed to the receiving function. Because array elements are stored in contiguous locations in memory, the receiving function can use the address to locate the other elements.

The syntax for creating and initializing a two-dimensional array is similar to the syntax for creating and initializing a one-dimensional array. The two-dimensional array syntax, however, requires the programmer to provide two, rather than one, *numberOfElements* values after the array name. The first *numberOfElements* value represents the number of rows in the array, and the second *numberOfElements* value represents the number of columns. As with a one-dimensional array, you also can initialize a two-dimensional array at the same time you create the array.

Just as each element in a one-dimensional array is identified by a unique number, called a subscript, each element in a two-dimensional array is identified by a unique combination of two subscripts. The first subscript represents the element's row location in the array, and the second represents its column location. The computer assigns the subscripts to the elements when the array is created in memory. The first row subscript in a two-dimensional array is 0. The first column subscript also is 0.

If you want to access every element in a two-dimensional array, you will need to use two loops to do so. One of the loops keeps track of the row subscript, while the other keeps track of the column subscript.

ANSWERS TO MINI-QUIZZES

Mini-Quiz 1

1. `int number[20] = {0};`

2. `string items[10] = {""};`

3. 0

4. 24

5. "quantity sub 7"

Mini-Quiz 2

1. a. `item[2] = "BX45";`

2. b. `while (x < 20)`

3.
```
while (x < 10)
{
    cout << bonus[x] << endl;
    x = x + 1;
} //end while
```

Mini-Quiz 3

1. `if (price[x] < low)`

2.
```
while (x < 5)
{
    numbers[x] = numbers[x] − 3;
    x = x + 1;
} //end while
```

3. `employeeName[3]`

Mini-Quiz 4

1. `int quantity[4][2] = {0};`

2. 20

3. d. "quantity sub one seven"

4. 0, 5

5. 0, 2

6. `quantity[1][2] = 5;`

QUESTIONS

1. Which of the following is false?
    a. The elements in an array are related in some way.
    b. All of the elements in an array have the same data type.
    c. All of the elements in an array have the same subscript.
    d. All of the elements in an array have the same name.

2. Elements in an array are identified by a unique _____.
    a. data type
    b. order
    c. subscript
    d. symbol

Use the following array, named `sales`, to answer Questions 3 through 7. The array was declared with the following statement: `int sales[5] = {10000, 12000, 900, 500, 20000};`.

10000	12000	900	500	20000

3. The `sales[3] = sales[3] + 10;` statement will _____.
    a. replace the 500 amount with 10
    b. replace the 500 amount with 510
    c. replace the 900 amount with 910
    d. result in an error

4. The `sales[4] = sales[4 - 2];` statement will _____.
    a. replace the 20000 amount with 900
    b. replace the 20000 amount with 19998
    c. replace the 500 amount with 12000
    d. result in an error

5. The `cout << sales[0] + sales[1];` statement will _____.
    a. display 22000
    b. display 10000 + 12000
    c. display sales[0] + sales[1]
    d. result in an error

6. Which of the following `if` clauses can be used to verify that the array subscript, named `x`, is valid for the `sales` array?
    a. `if (sales[x] >= 0 && sales[x] < 4)`
    b. `if (sales[x] >= 0 && sales[x] <= 4)`
    c. `if (x >= 0 && x < 4)`
    d. `if (x >= 0 && x <= 4)`

7. Which of the following will correctly add 100 to each variable in the **sales** array?
    (You can assume that the **x** variable was initialized to 0.)
    ```
    a. while ( x <= 4)
            x = x + 100;
       //end while
    b. while (x <= 4)
       {
               sales = sales + 100;
               x = x + 1;
       } //end while
    c. while (sales < 5)
       {
               sales[x] = sales[x] + 100;
       } //end while
    d. while (x <= 4)
       {
               sales[x] = sales[x] + 100;
               x = x + 1;
       } //end while
    ```

Use the following array, named num, to answer Questions 8 through 12. The array was
declared with the following statement: `int num[4] = {10, 5, 7, 2};`. Assume that
the `total` variable is declared as an `int` and that it is initialized to 0. Assume that the `avg`
variable is declared as a `float` and is initialized to 0.0.

10	5	7	2

8. Which of the following will correctly calculate and display the average of the num
    array elements?
    ```
    a. while (x < 4)
       {
               num[x] = total + total;
               x = x + 1;
       } //end while
       avg = float(total) / float(x);
       cout << avg << endl;
    b. while (x < 4)
       {
               total = total + num[x];
               x = x + 1;
       }//end while
       avg = float(total) / float(x);
       cout << avg << endl;
    c. while (x < 4)
       {
               total = total + num[x];
               x = x + 1;
       } //end while
       avg = float(total) / float(x) - 1.0;
       cout << avg << endl;
    d. while (x < 4)
       {
               total = total + num[x];
               x = x + 1;
       } //end while
       avg = float(total) / (float(x) - 1.0);
       cout << avg << endl;
    ```

9. The code in Question 8's answer a will display _____.
   a. 0
   b. 5
   c. 6
   d. 8

10. The code in Question 8's answer b will display _____.
    a. 0
    b. 5
    c. 6
    d. 8

11. The code in Question 8's answer c will display _____.
    a. 0
    b. 5
    c. 6
    d. 8

12. The code in Question 8's answer d will display _____.
    a. 0
    b. 5
    c. 6
    d. 8

13. To pass a one-dimensional array by reference, you _____.
    a. must include the address-of (&) operator before the array's name
    b. must include the number symbol (#) before the array's name
    c. do not have to do anything because arrays are automatically passed by reference

14. Two-dimensional arrays in C++ are automatically passed by _____.
    a. reference
    b. value

15. The first element in a two-dimensional array has a row subscript of _____ and a column subscript of _____.
    a. 0, 0
    b. 0, 1
    c. 1, 0
    d. 1, 1

16. The individual elements in a two-dimensional array are identified by a unique _____.
    a. combination of two subscripts
    b. data type
    c. order
    d. subscript

17. stock[2][4] is read _____.
    a. "stock two sub four"
    b. "stock array two sub four"
    c. "stock bracket two bracket four"
    d. "stock sub two four"

Use the following array, named `sales`, to answer Questions 18 through 21. The array was declared using the statement `int sales[2][5] = {{10000, 12000, 900, 500, 20000}, {350, 600, 700, 800, 100}};`.

10000	12000	900	500	20000
350	600	700	800	100

18. The statement `sales[1][3] = sales[1][3] + 10;` will _____.

    a. replace the 900 amount with 910

    b. replace the 500 amount with 510

    c. replace the 700 amount with 710

    d. replace the 800 amount with 810

19. The statement `sales[0][4] = sales[0][4 - 2];` will _____.

    a. replace the 20000 amount with 900

    b. replace the 20000 amount with 19998

    c. replace the 20000 amount with 19100

    d. result in an error

20. The statement `cout << sales[0][3] + sales[1][3];` will _____.

    a. display 1300

    b. display 1600

    c. display sales[0][3] + sales[1][3]

    d. result in an error

21. Which of the following `if` clauses can be used to verify that the array subscripts named `row` and `column` are valid for the `sales` array?

    a. `if (sales[row][column] >= 0 && sales[row][column] < 5)`

    b. `if (sales[row][column] >= 0 && sales[row][column] <= 5)`

    c. `if (row >= 0 && row < 3 && column >= 0 && column < 6)`

    d. `if (row >= 0 && row <= 1 && column >= 0 && column <= 4)`

EXERCISES

1. Write the C++ statement to declare and initialize a 10-element, one-dimensional `int` array named `temperature`. Use the following temperatures to initialize the array: 78, 89, 65, 90, 35, 20, 88, 101, 56, 99. Then write the C++ code to display the contents of the array on the screen.

2. Write the C++ statement to declare and initialize a 50-element, one-dimensional `string` array named `state`. Initialize the array elements to the empty string. Then write a C++ function named `fillArray` that opens a sequential access file named state.dat. The function should read the state names stored in the state.dat file into the `state` array, and then close the file. The `state` array will be passed to the `fillArray` function by the `main` function.

3. In this exercise, you will create a program that displays the number of days in a month.

    a. Open the T14ConE03.cpp file contained in the Cpp\Tut14\T14ConE03 folder on your computer's hard disk.

    b. Declare a 12-element, one-dimensional array named `monthDays`. Use the number of days in each month to initialize the array. (Use 28 for February.)

    c. Enter the code that allows the user to enter the month number—1 for January, 2 for February, and so on. The program should display the number of days in the month corresponding to the number entered by the user. Include a loop that allows the user to enter as many month numbers as desired.

    d. Save, build, and execute the program. Use the program to display the number of days for month numbers 1, 6, 9, and 11.

    e. When the program is working correctly, hide the Output window, then use the File menu to close the workspace.

4. In this exercise, you will modify the rainfall program from the lesson so that it includes functions that calculate the following: the average rainfall amount, the highest rainfall amount, and the lowest rainfall amount.

    a. Open the T14ConE04.cpp file contained in the Cpp\Tut14\T14ConE04 folder on your computer's hard disk.

    b. Modify the program appropriately. In addition to displaying the total rainfall amount, the `main` function also should display the average rainfall amount, the highest rainfall amount, and the lowest rainfall amount.

    c. Save, build, and execute the program. When the program is working correctly, hide the Output window, then use the File menu to close the workspace.

5. In this exercise, you will modify an existing program so that it updates the prices stored in a one-dimensional array, and then writes the prices to a sequential access file.

    a. Open the T14ConE05.dat file contained in the Cpp\Tut14\T14ConE05 folder on your computer's hard disk. The sequential access file contains 10 prices. Print and then close the file.

    b. Open the T14ConE05.cpp file contained in the Cpp\Tut14\T14ConE05 folder on your computer's hard disk. Study the code.

    c. Add a function named `updatePrices` to the program. The function should allow the user to enter the percentage by which each element in the array should be increased. For example, if the user enters the number 15, then each element in the array should be increased by 15%. Write the code to update each element.

    d. Add a function named `writeToFile` to the program. The function should write the updated contents of the array to a file named T14ConE05.new. Write the prices using fixed-point notation with two decimal places.

    e. Modify the `main` function so that it calls the `updatePrices` function after the array is filled with data, and then calls the `writeToFile` function.

    f. Save, build, and execute the program. Increase each item's price by 20%.

    g. Open the T14ConE05.new file to verify that the prices were updated correctly, then close the file.

    h. When the program is working correctly, hide the Output window, then use the File menu to close the workspace.

6. In this exercise, you will modify the program you created in Exercise 5 so that it updates only specific elements in a one-dimensional array. The contents of the array will be written to a file after the appropriate elements are updated.

    a. Open the T14ConE06.dat file contained in the Cpp\Tut14\T14ConE06 folder on your computer's hard disk. The sequential access file contains 10 prices. Print and then close the file.

    b. Use Windows to copy the T14ConE05.cpp file, which is contained in the Cpp\Tut14\T14ConE05 folder on your computer's hard disk, to the T14ConE06 folder. Rename the copied T14ConE05.cpp file T14ConE06.cpp.

    c. Open the T14ConE06.cpp file. Change the T14ConE05.cpp in the first comment to T14ConE06.cpp. In the `open` statement in the `main` and `writeToFile` functions, change the TConE05.dat to TConE06.dat.

    d. Assume that each of the 10 prices contained in the T14ConE06.dat file is numbered 1 through 10. Modify the `updatePrices` function so that it asks the user which item number he or she wants to update before requesting the rate. For example, if the user wants to update item 1's price, which is stored in the first element of the array, the user will enter the number 1. Include a loop that will allow the user to modify as many prices as he or she desires.

    e. Save, build, and execute the program. Increase item 1's price by 20%, then increase item 3's price by 25%, and then decrease item 10's price by 15%. (*Hint:* To decrease a price, enter a negative rate.)

    f. Open the T14ConE06.new file to verify that the appropriate prices were updated, then close the file.

    g. When the program is working correctly, hide the Output window, then use the File menu to close the workspace.

7. In this exercise, you will create a program that displays the number of students earning a specific score. The scores are stored in a one-dimensional array.

    a. Open the T14ConE07.dat file contained in the Cpp\Tut14\T14ConE07 folder on your computer's hard disk. The sequential access file contains 20 test scores. Print and then close the file.

b. Open the T14ConE07.cpp file contained in the Cpp\Tut14\T14ConE07 folder on your computer's hard disk.

c. Write a program that stores the contents of the T14ConE07.dat file in an `int` array. After filling the array with data, the program should allow the user to enter a score. The program should then display the number of students who earned that score.

d. Save, build, and execute the program. Use the program to answer the following questions. (Use Step a's printout of the T14ConE07.dat file to verify your answers.)
- How many students earned 72?
- How many students earned 88?
- How many students earned 20?
- How many students earned 99?

e. When the program is working correctly, hide the Output window, then use the File menu to close the workspace.

8. In this exercise, you will create a program that displays the number of students earning a score in a specific range. The scores are stored in a one-dimensional array.

a. Open the T14ConE08.dat file contained in the Cpp\Tut14\T14ConE08 folder on your computer's hard disk. Print and then close the file.

b. Open the T14ConE08.cpp file contained in the Cpp\Tut14\T14ConE08 folder on your computer's hard disk.

c. Write a program that stores the contents of the T14ConE08.dat file in an `int` array. After filling the array with data, the program should allow the user to enter a minimum score and a maximum score. The program then should display the number of students that earned a score within that range.

d. Save, build, and execute the program. Use the program to answer the following questions. (Use Step a's printout of the T14ConE08.dat file to verify your answers.)
- How many students earned scores between 70 and 79, including 70 and 79?
- How many students earned scores between 65 and 85, including 65 and 85?
- How many students earned scores between 0 and 50, including 0 and 50?

e. When the program is working correctly, hide the Output window, then use the File menu to close the workspace.

9. Ms. Jenkins uses the grade table shown below for her Introduction to Computers course. She would like to have a program that displays the grade after she enters the total points earned. You will use two parallel arrays in this program.

Minimum points	Maximum points	Grade
0	299	F
300	349	D
350	399	C
400	449	B
450	500	A

a. Open the T14ConE09.cpp file contained in the Cpp\Tut14\T14ConE09 folder on your computer's hard disk.

b. Store the minimum points in a one-dimensional array named `minPoints`. Store the grades in a parallel, one-dimensional array named `grade`. (*Hint*: Initialize the arrays to the appropriate values when you declare the arrays.) The program should display the appropriate grade after Ms. Jenkins enters the number of points earned by a student. Include a loop that allows Ms. Jenkins to enter as many values as desired.

10. In this exercise, you will use three parallel numeric arrays. You will search one of the arrays and then display its corresponding values from the other two arrays.

    a. Open the T14ConE10.cpp file contained in the Cpp\Tut14\T14ConE10 folder on your computer's hard disk.

    b. Write a program that uses three numeric arrays. Store the even numbers from 2 through 10 in the first array. Store the square of the even numbers from 2 through 10 in the second array. Store the square root of the even numbers from 2 through 10 in the third array.

    c. After filling the arrays, the program should prompt the user to enter a number. The program should then search for the number in the first array, and then use the second and third arrays to display both the square and the square root of the number. Allow the user to display the square and square root for as many numbers as desired without having to execute the program again. Display an error message if the number is not in the first array.

    d. Save, build, and execute the program. Test the program by entering the following numbers, one at a time: 5, 10, 8, and 7.

    e. When the program is working correctly, hide the Output window, then use the File menu to close the workspace.

11. Jacques Cousard has been playing the lottery for four years and has yet to win any money. He wants a program that will select the six lottery numbers for him. Each lottery number can range from 1 through 54 only. (An example of six lottery numbers is: 4, 8, 35, 15, 20, 3.) In this exercise, you will use a two-dimensional array.

    a. Open the T14ConE11.cpp file contained in the Cpp\Tut14\T14ConE11 folder on your computer's hard disk.

    b. Write a program that generates 50 groups of six random lottery numbers—for example, the six numbers 4, 8, 35, 15, 20, and 3 would be considered one group, and the six numbers 3, 54, 78, 21, 3, and 1 would be considered another group. Store the random numbers in an int array. The program should prevent a number from appearing more than once in the same group—in other words, each number in the same group should be unique. Save the lottery numbers in a sequential access file named T14ConE11.dat. Write each group of six numbers on a separate line in the file, and separate each number in the group with a space.

    c. Save, build, and execute the program.

    d. Open the T14ConE11.dat file. Verify that each group contains six unique numbers, then close the data file.

    e. When the program is working correctly, hide the Output window, then use the File menu to close the workspace.

12. Write a `while` loop that sums the values stored in a two-dimensional `int` array named `quantity`. The array contains three rows and four columns. Use an `int` variable named `totQuantity` to accumulate the values. Use `row` and `col` as the counter variables for the loops. (You can assume that `totQuantity` has already been declared and initialized.)

13. Write a C++ statement to declare and initialize a two-dimensional `int` array named `population`. Initialize the elements to 0. The array should contain 10 rows and four columns of elements.

14. Write a C++ statement to declare and initialize a two-dimensional `int` array named `quantity`. Initialize the elements to 0. The array should have 5 rows and 4 columns. Then write the `while` loops that will store the number 5 in each element.

15. Write a C++ statement that assigns the number 10000 to the element located in the third row and fifth column in the `item` array.

16. In this exercise, you will modify the Conway Enterprises program you viewed in this lesson. The modified program will display the total domestic and total international sales, in addition to displaying the total company sales.
    a. Open the T14ConE16.cpp file contained in the Cpp\Tut14\T14ConE16 folder on your computer's hard disk.
    b. Modify the program appropriately.
    c. Save, build, and execute the program. The program should display domestic sales of $235000, international sales of $177000, and total sales of $412000. When the program is working correctly, hide the Output window, then use the File menu to close the workspace.

17. In this exercise, you will determine the number of times a value appears in an array.
    a. Open the T14ConE17.cpp file contained in the Cpp\Tut14\T14ConE17 folder on your computer's hard disk.
    b. Create a program that displays the number of times each of the numbers 1 through 9 appears in the two-dimensional numbers array. Display the nine counts. (For example, the number 1 appears 2 times, the number 2 appears 2 times, and so on. (*Hint*: Store the counts in a two-dimensional array.)
    c. Save, build, and execute the program. When the program is working correctly, hide the Output window, then use the File menu to close the workspace.

18. In this exercise, you will create a program that allows the user to display the highest score earned on the midterm and the highest score earned on the final.
    a. Open the T14ConE18.cpp file contained in the Cpp\Tut14\T14ConE18 folder on your computer's hard disk.
    b. The program uses two numbers to initialize each row in the array. The first number in each row is the midterm score; the second number is the final score.
    c. Create a program that displays the highest score earned on the midterm and the highest score earned on the final.
    d. Save, build, and execute the program. When the program is working correctly, hide the Output window, then use the File menu to close the workspace.

Exercise 19 is a Discovery Exercise. Discovery Exercises, which may include topics that are not covered in this lesson, allow you to "discover" the solutions to problems on your own.

19. In this exercise, you will learn how to pass a two-dimensional array to a function.
    a. Open the T14ConE19.cpp file contained in the Cpp\Tut14\T14ConE19 folder on your computer's hard disk.
    b. Create a value-returning function named calcTotal that calculates the total company sales. Move the appropriate code from the main function to the calcTotal function. The main function will need to call the calcTotal function, passing it the two-dimensional sales array. Add the appropriate function call to the main function.

    When passing a two-dimensional array to a function, you leave the first set of brackets after the formal parameter's name empty, but you must enter the number of array columns in the second set of brackets. You do so in both the receiving function's header and prototype.
    c. Enter the appropriate information in the calcTotal function header and function prototype.
    d. Save, build, and execute the program. The program should display total sales of $412000. When the program is working correctly, hide the Output window, then use the File menu to close the workspace.

A computer program is good only if it works. Errors in either an algorithm or programming code can cause the program to run incorrectly. Therefore, a programmer needs to know how to locate and fix these errors. Exercise 20 is a Debugging Exercise. Debugging Exercises allow you to practice recognizing and solving errors in a program.

debugging

20. In this exercise, you will debug a C++ program.

a. Open the T14ConE20.dat file contained in the Cpp\Tut14\T14ConE20 folder on your computer's hard disk. Print and then close the file.

b. Open the T14ConE20.cpp file contained in the Cpp\Tut14\T14ConE20 folder on your computer's hard disk. After filling the array with the quantities stored in the T14ConE20.dat file, the program prompts the user to enter the amount by which each quantity is to be increased or decreased. It then displays the old and new quantities.

c. Build the program. Correct any errors in the program, then save, build, and execute the program.

d. When prompted to enter a number, type 5 and press the Enter key. The DOS window should show the old and new quantities. Notice that the program is not working correctly. Press the Enter key to close the DOS window.

e. Correct any errors in the program, then save, build, and execute the program. When the program is working correctly, hide the Output window, then use the File menu to close the workspace.

Application Lesson

Using an Array in a C++ Program

case ▶ In the Concept lesson, you viewed a price list program created for Takoda Tapahe, the owner of a small gift shop named Treasures. As you may remember, the program allows Takoda to display the price of the item whose ID she enters. Recall that the program stores the gift shop's price list in two one-dimensional parallel arrays. In this lesson, you will modify the price list program so that it uses a one-dimensional array of objects, rather than two parallel arrays, to store the price list.

Creating the Product Class

Before you can store objects in an array, you need to create the class from which the objects will be made. Recall that creating a class involves determining the attributes and behaviors of the object you want to create. The attributes describe the object, while the behaviors specify the tasks the object can perform.

To keep the example simple, the Product class that you use in this lesson contains only two attributes (the item's ID and its price) and five behaviors, as indicated in the class definition shown in Figure 14-22.

```
//Product - defines the Product class
#include <string>
using namespace std;

//*****declaration section*****
class Product
{
public:
        Product();
        Product(string, int);
behaviors    void assignData(string, int);
        string getId();
        int getPrice();
private:
        string id;
attributes    int price;
};
```

Figure 14-22: Product class definition

```
//*****implementation section*****
Product::Product()
{
     id    = "";
     price = 0;
} //end of default constructor


Product::Product(string pId, int pCost)
{
     id    = pId;
     price = pCost;
} //end of constructor


void Product::assignData(string pId, int pCost)
{
     id    = pId;
     price = pCost;
} //end of assignData function


string Product::getId()
{
     return id;
} //end of getId function


int Product::getPrice()
{
     return price;
} //end of getPrice function
```

default constructor is used when no values are passed

this constructor is used when string and int values are passed

Figure 14-22: Product class definition (continued)

Notice that the attributes—ID and price—are assigned to two variables: a string variable named **id** and an int variable named **price**. As is typical in a class definition, the variables are declared as private data members in the declaration section of the class.

Also notice that the **Product** class contains five public member functions, each representing a task that objects created from the class can perform. The function prototypes are listed in the declaration section of the class, while the function definitions are entered in the implementation section.

The first member function, **Product**, is the default constructor function. Recall that the purpose of the default constructor is to initialize the private data members of an object when the object is created in a program.

The second member function, also named `Product`, is another constructor. Unlike the default constructor, this constructor allows a program to pass the initial values of the private data members when a Product object is created. (Notice that the second constructor contains two formal parameters.) You will learn more about the second constructor later in this lesson.

The third member function, `assignData`, allows a program to assign new values to a Product object's private data members. The remaining two member functions, `getId` and `getPrice`, allow a program to view the values stored in a Product object's private data members.

On your computer's hard disk is a partially completed header file named Product. To complete the file, you will need to enter the instructions shown in the implementation section of the `Product` class. You will complete the header file before modifying the gift shop program.

To complete the Product header file:

1 Start Visual C++. Open the **Product** header file contained in the Cpp\MyClasses folder on your computer's hard disk.

   HELP? You will need to change the Files of type list box in the Open dialog box to All Files (*.*).

2 Enter the additional instructions shaded in Figure 14-23.

```
//Product - defines the Product class
#include <string>
using namespace std;

//*****declaration section*****
class Product
{
public:
    Product();
    Product(string, int);
    void assignData(string, int);
    string getId();
    int getPrice();
private:
    string id;
    int price;
};
```

Figure 14-23: Completed Product header file

enter these lines of code

```
//*****implementation section*****
Product::Product()
{
    id    = "";
    price = 0;
} //end of default constructor

Product::Product(string pId, int pCost)
{
    id    = pId;
    price = pCost;
} //end of constructor

void Product::assignData(string pId, int pCost)
{
    id    = pId;
    price = pCost;
} //end of assignData function

string Product::getId()
{
    return id;
} //end of getId function

int Product::getPrice()
{
    return price;
} //end of getPrice function
```

Figure 14-23: Completed Product header file (continued)

3 Verify the accuracy of your code by comparing the code on your screen with the code shown in Figure 14-23.

4 Save and then close the header file.

Now that the class has been defined, you can use it to create Product objects in the price list program.

Completing the Price List Program

The price list program, whose instructions you viewed in Figure 14-16 in the Concept lesson, is contained on your computer's hard drive. You will open that program now.

To open the price list program:

1 Open the T14App.cpp file contained in the Cpp\Tut14\T14App folder on your computer's hard drive. Figure 14-24 shows the instructions entered in the price list program.

parallel arrays

```
//T14App.cpp - displays the price of an item
#include <iostream>
#include <string>
#include <algorithm>

using namespace std;

int main()
{
    //declare arrays
    string id[5] = {"BX35", "CR20", "FE15", "KW10", "MM67"};
    int price[5]   = {13, 10, 12, 24, 4};

    string searchFor = ""; //product ID to locate

    //get product ID and convert to uppercase
    cout << "Enter product ID (X to exit program): ";
    getline(cin, searchFor);
    transform(searchFor.begin(), searchFor.end(),
        searchFor.begin(), toupper);

    while (searchFor != "X")
    {
        //locate position of product ID
        int y = 0;  //keeps track of array subscripts
        while (y < 5 && id[y] != searchFor)
            y = y + 1;
        //end while

        //if ID was found, display price
        //otherwise, display error message
        if (y < 5)
        {
            cout << fixed;
            cout.precision(2);
            cout << "Price: $" << price[y] << endl;
        }
        else
            cout << "Product ID is not valid" << endl;
        //end if

        //get product ID and convert to uppercase
        cout << "Enter product ID (X to exit program): ";
        getline(cin, searchFor);
        transform(searchFor.begin(), searchFor.end(),
            searchFor.begin(), toupper);
    } //end while
    return 0;
} //end of main function
```

Figure 14-24: Price list program containing two parallel one-dimensional arrays

As you learned in the Concept lesson, the elements in parallel arrays are related by their position (subscript) in the arrays.

The price list program shown in Figure 14-24 declares and initializes two one-dimensional arrays: a `string` array named `id` and an `int` array named `price`. Each array has five elements, one for each item sold by the gift shop. The program stores each item's ID in the `id` array, and stores each item's price in the corresponding location in the `price` array.

After filling the arrays with data, the program prompts the user to enter a product ID, storing the user's response in the `searchFor` variable. The `transform` function then converts the contents of the `searchFor` variable to uppercase to match the case of the IDs stored in the array.

The instructions contained in the outer `while` loop use a nested `while` loop to search for the product ID in the `id` array. The nested `while` loop will repeat its one instruction, which adds the number 1 to the `y` variable, as long as the `y` variable contains a value that is less than 5 and, at the same time, the product ID has not been located in the array. (When the `y` variable's value is less than 5, it indicates that there are more array elements to search.) After the nested `while` loop completes its processing, the `if` statement in the program compares the value in the `y` variable to the number 5. If the `y` variable contains a number that is less than 5, the program displays the appropriate price from the `price` array; otherwise, it displays the message "Product ID is not valid".

You will need to make four changes to the current program to store the price list in an array of Product objects, rather than in parallel arrays. The first change will be to include the Product header file in the program.

To include the Product header file in the price list program:

1 Position the insertion point in the blank line below the `#include <algorithm>` directive.

2 Type `#include "c:\cpp\myclasses\product"`. (If necessary, change the path to reflect the location of the Product header file on your computer's hard disk.)

The next change is to replace the statements that declare and initialize the `string` and `int` arrays with a statement that declares and initializes an array of Product objects.

Declaring and Initializing a One-Dimensional Array of Objects

As you learned in the Concept lesson, the syntax used to declare and initialize a one-dimensional array is *datatype arrayname[numberOfElements] = {initialvalues};*. When declaring an array of objects, *datatype* is the name of the object's class. Figure 14-25 shows two examples of declaring and initializing a one-dimensional array of Product objects.

Recall that the *initialvalues* section of the array declaration statement is optional.

Examples	Results
`Product items[5];`	Declares a five-element one-dimensional array; each element contains a Product object. Because the declaration statement does not contain any *initialvalues*, the default constructor is used to initialize the private data members in each object stored in the array.

`Product items[5] =`
`    {Product("BX35", 13),`
`     Product("CR20", 10),`
`     Product("FE15", 12),`
`     Product("KW10", 24),`
`     Product("MM67", 4)};`
	Declares a five-element one-dimensional array; each element contains a Product object. The declaration statement calls the second constructor function to initialize the private data members in each object stored in the array.

Figure 14-25: Examples of declaring and initializing a one-dimensional array of Product objects

The first statement shown in Figure 14-25 declares a five-element one-dimensional array named `items`; each element in the `items` array contains a Product object. Because no *initialvalues* are specified in the array declaration statement, the computer uses the default constructor to initialize the objects. In this case, for example, the default constructor initializes each object's `id` and `price` data members to the empty string and the number 0, respectively.

At times, you may want to assign specific values to the objects in the array when the array is created, rather than using the values provided by the default constructor. This is the purpose of the second `Product` constructor included in the `Product` class. To use the second constructor, you need simply to call it. You call it by including its name, along with the values you want assigned to the object, in the *initialvalues* section of the array declaration statement, as shown in the second example in Figure 14-25. Notice that you enclose each object's values in parentheses, and you use a comma to separate each object's values from the next. If you refer to the function definition for the second `Product` constructor, which is shown in Figure 14-23, you will notice that the constructor assigns the values it receives to the private data members in the class. Figure 14-26 shows how the `items` array will look in memory as a result of the array declaration statements shown in Figure 14-25.

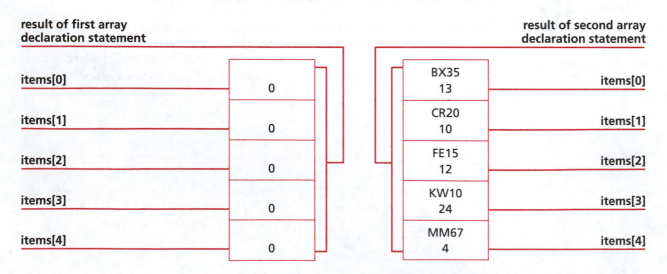

Figure 14-26: Results of the array declaration statements shown in Figure 14-25

You will use the second statement shown in Figure 14-25 to initialize the `items` array in the price list program.

To complete the modifications to the price list program, then test the program:

1 Delete the `string id[5] = {"BX35", "CR20", "FE15", "KW10", "MM67"};` and `int price[5] = {13, 10, 12, 24, 4};` statements.

2 Enter the array declaration statement shaded in Figure 14-27. Also modify the comment as shown in the figure.

```
/T14App.cpp - displays the price of an item
#include <iostream>
#include <string>
#include <algorithm>
#include "c:\cpp\myclasses\product"
using namespace std;

int main()
{
    //declare array of objects
    Product items[5] = {Product("BX35", 13),
                        Product("CR20", 10),
                        Product("FE15", 12),
                        Product("KW10", 24),
                        Product("MM67", 4)};

    string searchFor = ""; //product ID to locate

    //get product ID and convert to uppercase
    cout << "Enter product ID (X to exit program): ";
    getline(cin, searchFor);
    transform(searchFor.begin(), searchFor.end(),
        searchFor.begin(), toupper);
```

modify the comment

enter the array declaration statement

Figure 14-27: Array declaration statement entered in the price list program

You also must change the two program statements that refer to the elements in the parallel arrays. In the statement `while (y < 5 && id[y] != searchFor)`, for example, you will replace the `id[y]` with `items[y].getId()`. Recall that the `getId` function is a public member function in the `Product` class, and it allows a program to view the contents of the `id` data member. Additionally, you will replace the `price[y]` in the statement `cout << "Price: $" << price[y] << endl;` with `items[y].getPrice()`. The `getPrice` function also is a public member function in the `Product` class; it allows a program to view the contents of the `price` data member.

3 Modify the two statements shaded in Figure 14-28, which shows the completed price list program.

```cpp
//T14App.cpp - displays the price of an item
#include <iostream>
#include <string>
#include <algorithm>
#include "c:\cpp\myclasses\product"
using namespace std;

int main()
{
    //declare array of objects
    Product items[5] = {Product("BX35", 13),
                        Product("CR20", 10),
                        Product("FE15", 12),
                        Product("KW10", 24),
                        Product("MM67", 4)};

    string searchFor = ""; //product ID to locate

    //get product ID and convert to uppercase
    cout << "Enter product ID (X to exit program): ";
    getline(cin, searchFor);
    transform(searchFor.begin(), searchFor.end(),
        searchFor.begin(), toupper);
    while (searchFor != "X")
    {
        //locate position of product ID
        int y = 0;  //keeps track of array subscripts
        while (y < 5 && items[y].getId() != searchFor)
            y = y + 1;
        //end while

        //if ID was found, display price
        //otherwise, display error message
        if (y < 5)
        {
            cout << fixed;
            cout.precision(2);
            cout << "Price: $" << items[y].getPrice() << endl;
        }
        else
            cout << "Product ID is not valid" << endl;
        //end if

        //get product ID and convert to uppercase
        cout << "Enter product ID (X to exit program): ";
        getline(cin, searchFor);
        transform(searchFor.begin(), searchFor.end(),
            searchFor.begin(), toupper);
    } //end while
    return 0;
}
```

make these modifications

Figure 14-28: Completed price list program using a one-dimensional array of objects

4   Save, build, and execute the program. When you are prompted to enter a product ID, type **cr20** and press the **Enter** key. The DOS window indicates that the price of this item is $10, as shown in Figure 14-29.

Figure 14-29: DOS window showing results of first test

5   Next, type **aa22** and press the **Enter** key. The message "Product ID is not valid" appears in the DOS window.

6   Type **x** and press the **Enter** key to stop the program.

7   Press the **Enter** key to close the DOS window. Hide the Output window, then use the File menu to close the workspace. When prompted to close all document windows, click the **Yes** button.

8   Exit Visual C++.

You may have noticed that the price list program did not use the `assignData` function contained in the `Product` class. You will use the member function in Discovery Exercise 4 at the end of this lesson, where you will learn how to fill an array of objects with the data from a sequential access file.

You now have completed Tutorial 14's Application lesson. You can either take a break or complete the end-of-lesson exercises.

E X E R C I S E S

1. Ms. Jenkins uses the grade table shown below for her Introduction to Computers course. She would like to have a program that displays the grade after she enters the total points earned. You will use an array of objects in this program. (*Hint*: If you completed Exercise 9 in the Concept lesson, you can use that program as a guide when completing this program.)

Minimum points	Maximum points	Grade
0	299	F
300	349	D
350	399	C
400	449	B
450	500	A

a. Open the T14AppE01 header file contained in the Cpp\MyClasses folder on your computer's hard disk. Create a class for the grade table. Include two data members: minimum points and grade. Include a default constructor, a constructor that allows you to initialize the array at the same time the array is declared, a function that allows a program to view the contents of the minimum points data member, and a function that allows the program to view the contents of the grade data member. Save and then close the header file.

b. Open the T14AppE01.cpp file contained in the Cpp\Tut14\T14AppE01 folder on your computer's hard disk.

c. Use the class you created in Step a to declare an array of objects. The program should display the appropriate grade after Ms. Jenkins enters the number of points earned by a student. Include a loop that allows Ms. Jenkins to enter as many values as desired.

d. Save, build, and execute the program. Test the program by entering the following amounts: 455, 210, 400, and 349.

e. When the program is working correctly, hide the Output window, then use the File menu to close the workspace.

2. In this exercise, you will search an array of objects. (*Hint*: If you completed Exercise 10 in the Concept lesson, you can use that program as a guide when completing this program.)

a. Open the T14AppE02 header file contained in the Cpp\MyClasses folder on your computer's hard disk. Create a class that contains two `int` variables (named `num` and `sqNum`) and one `float` variable (named `sqRtNum`) as data members. Include a default constructor, a constructor that allows you to initialize the array at the same time the array is declared, and three functions that allow a program to view the contents of the data members. Save and then close the header file.

b. Open the T14AppE02.cpp file contained in the Cpp\Tut14\T14AppE02 folder on your computer's hard disk.

c. Use the class you created in Step a to declare an array of objects. Store the even numbers from 2 through 10, the square of the even numbers from 2 through 10, and square root of the even numbers from 2 through 10 in the array.

d. The program should prompt the user to enter a number. The program should then search for the number in the first array, and then display both the square and the square root of the number. Allow the user to display the square and square root for as many numbers as desired without having to execute the program again.

e. Save, build, and execute the program. Test the program by entering the following numbers, one at a time: 5, 10, 8, and 7.

f. When the program is working correctly, hide the Output window, then use the File menu to close the workspace.

3. In this exercise, you will modify the Conway Enterprises program you viewed in the Concept lesson. The modified program will use an array of objects to display the total domestic sales, the total international sales, and the total company sales. (*Hint*: If you completed Exercise 16 in the Concept lesson, you can use that program as a guide when completing this program.)

a. Open the T14AppE03 header file contained in the Cpp\MyClasses folder on your computer's hard disk. Create an appropriate class. Include two `int` variables as data members: one variable will represent the domestic sales, and the other will represent the international sales. Include a default constructor, a constructor that allows you to initialize the array at the same time the array is declared, and two functions that allow a program to view the contents of the data members. Save and then close the header file.

b. Open the T14AppE03.cpp file contained in the Cpp\Tut14\T14AppE03 folder on your computer's hard disk. Use the class you created in Step a to declare an array of objects. Store the sales amounts in the array. (*Hint*: Use a one-dimensional array, rather than a two-dimensional array.)

c. Modify the program so that it displays the total domestic sales, the total international sales, and the total company sales.

d. Save, build, and execute the program. The program should display domestic sales of $235000, international sales of $177000, and total sales of $412000.

e. When the program is working correctly, hide the Output window, then use the File menu to close the workspace.

Exercise 4 is a Discovery Exercise. Discovery Exercises, which may include topics that are not covered in this lesson, allow you to "discover" the solutions to problems on your own.

4. In this exercise, you will learn how to fill an array of objects with the data from a sequential access file.

a. Open the T14AppE04 header file contained in the Cpp\MyClasses folder on your computer's hard disk. Print and then close the header file.

b. Open the T14AppE04.dat file contained in the Cpp\Tut14\T14AppE04 folder on your computer's hard disk. Print and then close the file.

c. Open the T14AppE04.cpp file contained in the Cpp\Tut14\T14AppE04 folder on your computer's hard disk. If necessary, change the `#include "c:\cpp\myclasses\t14appe04"` directive to reflect the location of the header file on your computer's hard disk.

d. Remove the *initialvalues* section from the array declaration statement. Modify the code so that it reads each record from a sequential access file, and assigns each to the objects in the array. The sequential access file is named T14AppE04.dat, and is located in the Cpp\Tut14\T14AppE04 folder on your computer's hard disk. (*Hint*: Read the data into variables, and then pass the variables to the `assignData` member function.)

e. Save, build, and execute the program. The program should display five IDs and prices. When the program is working correctly, hide the Output window, then use the File menu to close the workspace.

A computer program is good only if it works. Errors in either an algorithm or programming code can cause the program to run incorrectly. Therefore, a programmer needs to know how to locate and fix these errors. Exercise 5 is a Debugging Exercise. Debugging Exercises allow you to practice recognizing and solving errors in a program.

debugging

5. In this exercise, you will debug an existing C++ program.

a. Open the T14AppE05 header file contained in the Cpp\MyClasses folder on your computer's hard disk. Study the code, then close the header file.

b. Open the T14AppE05.cpp file contained in the Cpp\Tut14\T14AppE05 folder on your computer's hard disk. The program should display the contents of the `empData` array.

c. Build the program. Correct any errors in the program, then save, build, and execute the program. The program should display five names and salary amounts.

d. When the program is working correctly, hide the Output window, then use the File menu to close the workspace.

APPENDIX A

ASCII Codes

Character	ASCII	Binary	Character	ASCII	Binary	Character	ASCII	Binary
SPACE	32	00100000	9	57	00111001	R	82	01010010
!	33	00100001	:	58	00111010	S	83	01010011
"	34	00100010	;	59	00111011	T	84	01010100
#	35	00100011	<	60	00111100	U	85	01010101
$	36	00100100	=	61	00111101	V	86	01010110
%	37	00100101	>	62	00111110	W	87	01010111
&	38	00100110	?	63	00111111	X	88	01011000
'	39	00100111	@	64	01000000	Y	89	01011001
(	40	00101000	A	65	01000001	Z	90	01011010
)	41	00101001	B	66	01000010	[	91	01011011
*	42	00101010	C	67	01000011	\	92	01011100
+	43	00101011	D	68	01000100	]	93	01011101
'	44	00101100	E	69	01000101	^	94	01011110
–	45	00101101	F	70	01000110	_	95	01011111
.	46	00101110	G	71	01000111	'	96	01100000
/	47	00101111	H	72	01001000	a	97	01100001
0	48	00110000	I	73	01001001	b	98	01100010
1	49	00110001	J	74	01001010	c	99	01100011
2	50	00110010	K	75	01001011	d	100	01100100
3	51	00110011	L	76	01001100	e	101	01100101
4	52	00110100	M	77	01001101	f	102	01100110
5	53	00110101	N	78	01001110	g	103	01100111
6	54	00110110	O	79	01001111	h	104	01101000
7	55	00110111	P	80	01010000	i	105	01101001
8	56	00111000	Q	81	01010001	j	106	01101010

Character	ASCII	Binary
k	107	01101011
l	108	01101100
m	109	01101101
n	110	01101110
o	111	01101111
p	112	01110000
q	113	01110001
r	114	01110010
s	115	01110011
t	116	01110100
u	117	01110101
v	118	01110110
w	119	01110111
x	120	01111000
y	121	01111001
z	122	01111010
{	123	01111011
|	124	01111100
}	125	01111101
~	126	01111110
DELETE	127	01111111

Mathematical Functions Included in the cmath Library File

Mathematical function	Returns
abs(x)	absolute value of x
acos(x)	arccosine of x
asin(x)	arcsine of x
atan(x)	arctangent of x
atan2(y, x)	arctangent of y/x
ceil(x)	x rounded up to an integer
cos(x)	cosine of x
cosh(x)	hyperbolic cosine of x
exp(x)	exponential value of x
fabs(x)	absolute value of the floating-point x
floor(x)	x rounded down to an integer
fmod(x, y)	floating-point remainder of x/y
hypot(x, y)	hypotenuse of a right triangle
labs(x)	absolute value of the long integer x
log(x)	natural (base e) log of x
log10(x)	common (base 10) log of x
pow(x, y)	x raised to the power of y
sin(x)	sine of x
sinh(x)	hyperbolic sine of x
sqrt(x)	square root of x
tan(x)	tangent of x
tanh(x)	hyperbolic tangent of x

The Posttest Repetition Structure

objectives

After completing this appendix, you will be able to:

■ Write pseudocode for the posttest repetition structure
■ Create a flowchart for the posttest repetition structure
■ Code the posttest repetition structure

Using a Posttest Loop

As you learned in Tutorial 10, programmers use the repetition structure, referred to more simply as a loop, when they need the computer to repeatedly process one or more program instructions until some condition is met, at which time the repetition structure ends. Recall that a repetition structure can be either a pretest loop or a posttest loop. You learned about the pretest loop in Tutorial 10; you will learn about the posttest loop in this appendix.

As is true in a pretest loop, the condition in a posttest loop is evaluated with each repetition, or iteration, of the loop. However, unlike the evaluation in a pretest loop, the evaluation in a posttest loop occurs *after* the instructions within the loop are processed, rather than *before* the instructions are processed.

Figure C-1 shows the problem description and IPO chart for O'Donnell Incorporated. The IPO chart contains two algorithms that could be used to calculate and display a bonus for each of the company's salespeople. Algorithm 1, which you viewed in Tutorial 10's Concept lesson, uses a pretest loop to repeat the appropriate instructions; Algorithm 2 uses a posttest loop to do so.

As Figure C-1 shows, the first step in Algorithm 1 is to enter a sales amount. The second step is a pretest loop whose loop condition compares the sales amount entered by the user with the sentinel value, -1. If the sales amount is not the sentinel value, the loop body instructions calculate and display the bonus amount, and then get another sales amount from the user. The loop condition then compares the sales amount with the sentinel value to determine whether the loop body instructions should be processed again. The loop will repeat the loop body instructions as long as (or while) the user does not enter the sentinel value, -1, as the sales amount.

tip

Posttest loops also are called bottom-driven loops.

	Problem description		
	In January of each year, O'Donnell Incorporated pays a 10% bonus to each of its sales-people. The bonus is based on the amount of sales made by the salesperson during the previous year. The payroll clerk wants a program that can be used to calculate and display each salesperson's bonus amount.		

	Input	Processing	Output
loop condition	bonus rate (10%) sales	Processing items: none	bonus

pretest loop		Algorithm 1:
		1. enter the sales
		2. repeat while (the sales are not equal to -1)
		     calculate the bonus by multiplying the sales by the bonus rate
		     display the bonus
		     enter the sales
		  end repeat while	

posttest loop		Algorithm 2:
		1. enter the sales
		2. do
		     calculate the bonus by multiplying the sales by the bonus rate
		     display the bonus
		     enter the sales
		  repeat while (the sales are not equal to -1)	

loop condition			

Figure C-1: Problem description and IPO chart for O'Donnell Incorporated

You often will find a posttest loop in programs that allow the user to select from a menu, such as a game program. This type of program uses the posttest loop to control the display of the menu, which must appear on the screen at least once.

Compare the steps in Algorithm 2 to the steps in Algorithm 1. Like the first step in Algorithm 1, the first step in Algorithm 2 is to enter a sales amount. The second step in Algorithm 2, however, is a posttest loop, rather than a pretest loop. You can tell that Algorithm 2's second step is a posttest loop because it begins with the keyword `do`, rather than with the keywords `repeat while` followed by the loop condition. In a posttest loop, the words `repeat while` and the loop condition appear at the *end* of the loop, which indicates that the loop condition is evaluated only *after* the instructions in the loop body are processed.

Like the loop body instructions in Algorithm 1, the loop body instructions in Algorithm 2 calculate and display the salesperson's bonus, and then get another sales amount from the user. The loop condition, which appears at the bottom of the posttest loop, then compares the sales amount with the sentinel value (-1) to determine whether the instructions in the loop body should be processed again. In a posttest loop, only the second and subsequent sales amounts are compared to the sentinel value; the first sales amount is not compared to the sentinel value, as it is in a pretest loop. While it is possible that the instructions contained in a pretest loop might never be processed, the instructions contained in a posttest loop always will be processed at least once. You should use a posttest loop only when you are sure that the loop body instructions can and should be processed at least once.

tip

• • • • • • • • • • • • •

As you learned in Tutorial 10, if the loop condition in a pretest loop initially evaluates to false, the loop body instructions will never be processed.

It may be easier to understand the difference between a pretest loop and a posttest loop by viewing both loops in flowchart form.

Flowcharting a Posttest Loop

Figure C-2 shows the O'Donnell Incorporated algorithms in flowchart form. The flowcharts illustrate why the loops are referred to as pretest and posttest loops. Notice that the repetition diamond, which contains the loop condition, appears at the top of a pretest loop, but it appears at the bottom of a posttest loop.

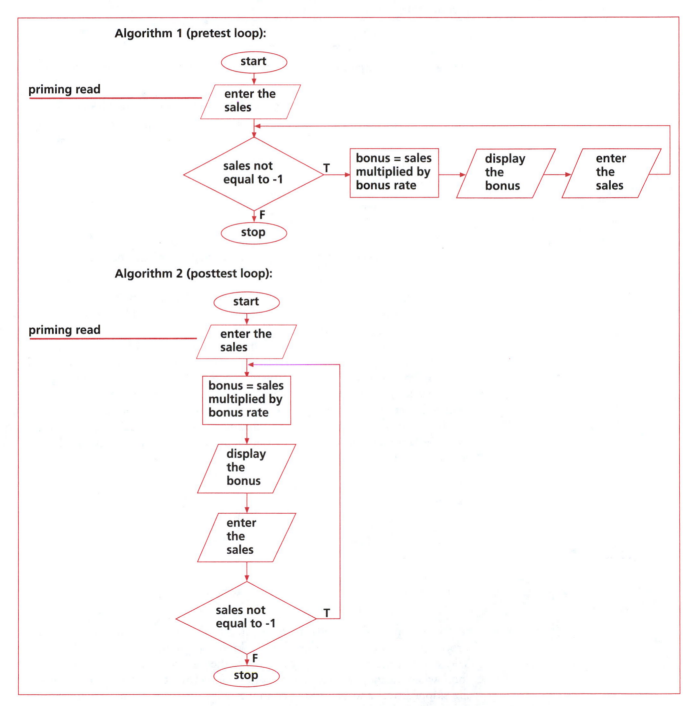

Figure C-2: O'Donnell Incorporated algorithms shown in flowchart form

To help you understand how a posttest loop operates in a program, you will desk-check Algorithm 2 shown in Figure C-2 using the following sales data: 10000, 25000, and -1. The first instruction in the flowchart gets the first sales amount (10000) from the user; recall that this instruction is referred to as the priming read. The next instruction calculates the bonus and is the first instruction in the loop body. Notice that the first sales amount is not compared to the sentinel value in a posttest loop. Figure C-3 shows the first salesperson's sales and bonus amounts recorded in the desk-check table.

bonus rate	sales	bonus
.10	10000	1000

Figure C-3: First salesperson's sales and bonus amounts recorded in the desk-check table

The second instruction in the loop body displays the bonus on the screen, and the third instruction gets the next salesperson's sales amount (25000) from the user. Figure C-4 shows the second salesperson's sales amount recorded in the desk-check table.

bonus rate	sales	bonus
.10	~~10000~~ 25000	1000

Figure C-4: Second salesperson's sales amount recorded in the desk-check table

The next symbol in the flowchart is the repetition diamond, which contains the loop condition and marks the end of the posttest loop. The loop condition compares the sales amount entered by the user with the sentinel value, -1, to determine whether the loop should be processed again (a true condition) or end (a false condition). Notice that this is the first time the loop condition is evaluated. In this case, the loop condition evaluates to true, because 25000 is not equal to -1. As is true in a pretest loop, when the loop condition in a posttest loop evaluates to true, the instructions in the loop body are processed. Those instructions calculate and display the bonus for the second salesperson, and then get another sales amount (in this case, the sentinel value) from the user. Figure C-5 shows the sentinel value recorded in the desk-check table.

bonus rate	sales	bonus
.10	~~10000~~ ~~25000~~ -1	~~1000~~ 2500

sentinel value

Figure C-5: Sentinel value recorded in the desk-check table

The loop condition then is reevaluated to determine whether the loop should be processed again or end. In this case, the loop condition evaluates to false, because the sales amount entered by the user is equal to the sentinel value, -1. As is true in a pretest loop, when the loop condition in a posttest loop evaluates to false, the loop instructions are skipped over and processing continues with the instruction immediately following the end of the loop. In Algorithm 2's flowchart, the stop oval, which marks the end of the algorithm, follows the loop.

mini-quiz

Mini-Quiz 1

1. In a _____ loop, the loop condition is evaluated *after* the loop instructions are processed, while in a _____ loop, the evaluation occurs *before* the loop instructions are processed.

   a. pretest, posttest

   b. posttest, pretest

2. The instructions in a _____ loop will always be processed at least once, while the instructions in a _____ loop might never be processed.

   a. pretest, posttest

   b. posttest, pretest

3. Assume that a program contains a posttest loop that repeats the loop body instructions until the user enters a negative number. How many times will the loop condition be evaluated if the user enters the numbers 5, 8, 9, and -1, respectively?

Next, you will learn how to code the posttest loop.

Coding the Posttest Loop

You can code a posttest loop using the `do while` statement in both C++ and Java, and the `Do Until` statement in Visual Basic. Figure C-6 shows the syntax of these statements.

notice that the `do` `while` **statement ends with a semicolon**

C++ and Java
do
one statement, or a block of statements enclosed in braces, to be processed one time, and thereafter as long as the loop condition is true
while (*loop condition***);**

Visual Basic
Do
one or more statements to be processed one time, and thereafter as long as the loop condition is true
Loop Until *loop condition*

Note: In the syntax, items in **bold** are required. Items in *italics* indicate places where the programmer must supply information pertaining to the current program.

Figure C-6: Syntax of the `do while` and `Do Until` statements in C++, Java, and Visual Basic

tip

Recall that some C++ programmers enclose the loop body in braces even when it contains only one statement, but this is not required by the C++ syntax.

Items in bold in each syntax are essential components of the statement. For example, the keywords do and while, and the parentheses that surround the loop condition, are required in the do while statement in C++ and Java. In Visual Basic, the keywords Do and Loop Until are essential components of the Do Until statement. Unlike C++ and Java, Visual Basic does not require you to enclose the Do Until statement's loop condition in parentheses.

Items in italics in each syntax indicate where the programmer must supply information pertaining to the current program. For instance, the programmer must supply the loop condition to be evaluated. As is true in the while statement in C++ and Java, and the Do While statement in Visual Basic, the loop condition in the do while and Do Until statements must be a Boolean expression, which is an expression that evaluates to either true or false. The loop condition can contain variables, constants, functions, arithmetic operators, comparison operators, and logical operators.

In addition to supplying the loop condition, the programmer also must supply the statements to be processed when the loop condition evaluates to true. If more than one statement needs to be processed in C++ and Java, the statements must be entered as a statement block. Recall that you create a statement block by enclosing the statements in a set of braces ({}). Unlike in C++ and Java, braces are not used in Visual Basic.

Figure C-7 shows how you can use the C++ do while statement to code the O'Donnell Incorporated algorithm.

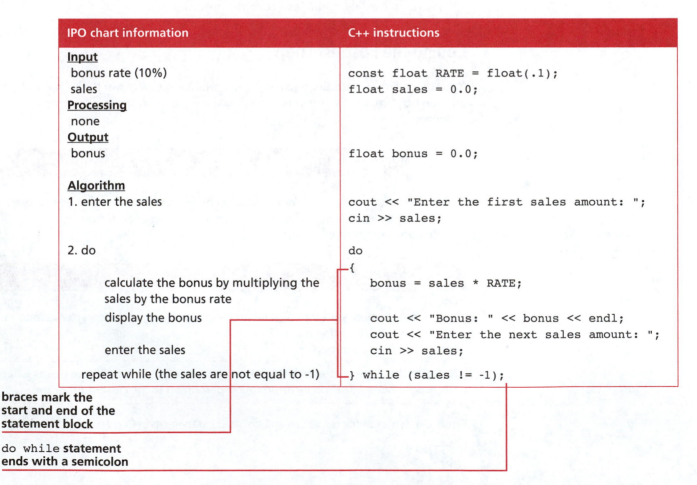

IPO chart information	C++ instructions

Input
  bonus rate (10%)
  sales
	`const float RATE = float(.1);`
	`float sales = 0.0;`

Processing none	
Output bonus	`float bonus = 0.0;`
Algorithm 1. enter the sales	`cout << "Enter the first sales amount: ";` `cin >> sales;`
2. do	`do` `{`
calculate the bonus by multiplying the sales by the bonus rate	`    bonus = sales * RATE;`
display the bonus	`    cout << "Bonus: " << bonus << endl;` `    cout << "Enter the next sales amount: ";`
enter the sales	`    cin >> sales;`
repeat while (the sales are not equal to -1)	`} while (sales != -1);`

braces mark the start and end of the statement block

do while statement ends with a semicolon

Figure C-7: C++ do while statement included in the code for the O'Donnell Incorporated algorithm

Take a closer look at the statements shown in Figure C-7. The first three statements declare and initialize the RATE named constant and the sales and bonus variables. The cout << "Enter the first sales amount: "; statement prompts the user to enter the first sales amount, and the cin >> sales; statement stores the user's response in the sales variable. The do clause, which appears next in the program, simply marks the beginning of the posttest loop.

The first instruction in the posttest loop (bonus = sales * RATE;) calculates the bonus amount, and the second instruction (cout << "Bonus: " << bonus << endl;) displays the bonus amount on the screen. The third instruction in the loop (cout << "Enter the next sales amount: ";) prompts the user to enter the next sales amount, and the fourth instruction (cin >> sales;) stores the user's response in the sales variable. The while (sales != -1) clause then compares the value stored in the sales variable to the sentinel value (-1). If the sales variable does not contain the sentinel value, the instructions within the loop body are processed again; otherwise, the instructions are skipped over, and processing continues with the code immediately following the end of the loop.

In the next section, you will learn how to use a posttest loop to display the squares of the numbers from 1 through 3.

Using a Posttest Loop to Display the Squares of Three Numbers

Assume you want to create a program that displays the squares of the numbers from 1 through 3 on the screen. Figure C-8 shows the IPO chart information and C++ code for the squaring problem.

tip

As you learned in Tutorial 10, if you forget to enter the cin >> sales; statement within the program's loop, the loop will process its instructions indefinitely and is referred to as either an endless loop or an infinite loop. Usually, you can stop a program that contains an endless loop by pressing Ctrl + c; you also can use the DOS window's Close button.

IPO chart information	C++ instructions

Input
  none
Processing
  counter (1 through 3)
Output
  counter squared
	
	`int counter = 1;`
	
	`int squared = 0;`

Algorithm
1. do
 	
    calculate the counter squared by
    multiplying the counter by itself
    display the counter squared
    add 1 to the counter
repeat while (the counter is less than or equal
to 3)
	
	`do`
	`{`
	`   squared = counter * counter;`
	
	`   cout << "Squared: " << squared << endl;`
	`   counter = counter + 1;`
	`} while (counter <= 3);`

do while **statement**
ends with a semicolon

Figure C-8: IPO chart information and C++ code for the squaring problem

You learned how to code the squaring program using a pretest loop in Tutorial 10's Concept lesson.

As Figure C-8 indicates, the solution to the squaring problem requires one processing item and one output item. The processing item is a counter that the program will use to keep track of the values to be squared—in this case, the numbers 1, 2, and 3. Notice in the C++ code that the counter variable, named `counter`, is initialized to the first value you want the program to square—the number 1. The output item is the square of each counter value, and its corresponding variable is named `squared` and is initialized to 0, as shown in Figure C-9.

counter	squared
1	0

Figure C-9: Desk-check table showing initialization of variables

The `do` clause, which appears next in the program, marks the beginning of a posttest loop. The first instruction in the loop body squares the contents of the `counter` variable, and stores the result in the `squared` variable. The second instruction displays the contents of the `squared` variable on the screen, and the third instruction increments the `counter` variable by 1, as shown in Figure C-10.

counter	squared
~~1~~	~~0~~
2	1

Figure C-10: Results of processing the loop body instructions the first time

The loop condition in the `while (counter <= 3)` clause compares the contents of the `counter` variable to the number 3 to determine whether the loop body instructions should be processed again. At this point in the program, the value stored in the `counter` variable (2) is less than or equal to three, so the loop condition evaluates to true and the loop body instructions are processed again.

The loop body instructions square the contents of the `counter` variable (2), then display the contents of the `squared` variable, and then increment the `counter` variable by 1, as shown in Figure C-11.

counter	squared
~~1~~	~~0~~
~~2~~	~~1~~
3	4

Figure C-11: Results of processing the loop body instructions the second time

The loop condition in the `while (counter <= 3)` clause then is reevaluated to determine whether the loop should be processed again or simply end. Here again, the loop condition evaluates to true, because the value stored in the `counter` variable (3) is less than or equal to three. Because of this, the loop instructions square the `counter` variable's value, then display the contents of the `squared` variable, and then increment the `counter` variable by 1, as shown in Figure C-12.

counter	squared
~~1~~	~~0~~
~~2~~	~~1~~
~~3~~	4
4	9

Figure C-12: Results of processing the loop body instructions the third time

The loop condition in the `while (counter <= 3)` clause then is reevaluated to determine whether the loop should be processed again or simply end. At this point, the loop condition evaluates to false, because the value stored in the `counter` variable (4) is not less than or equal to three. Because of this, the posttest loop ends and processing continues with the instruction located immediately following the loop.

mini-quiz

Mini-Quiz 2

1. The `do while` clause marks the beginning of the C++ `do while` statement.
   a. True
   b. False

2. The `while` clause in the C++ `do while` statement ends with a semicolon.
   a. True
   b. False

3. Write a C++ `while` clause that processes a posttest loop's instructions as long as the value in the `quantity` variable is greater than the number 0.

4. Write a C++ `while` clause that stops a posttest loop when the value in the `quantity` variable is less than the number 0.

5. Write a C++ `while` clause that processes a posttest loop's instructions as long as the value in the `inStock` variable is greater than the value in the `reorder` variable.

6. Write a C++ `while` clause that processes a posttest loop's instructions as long as the value in the `letter` variable is either Y or y. (The `letter` variable is a `char` variable.)

7. Assume that a program declares an `int` variable named `evenNum` and initializes it to 2. Write the C++ code, using the `do while` statement and the `evenNum` variable, to display the even integers between 1 and 9.

You now have completed Appendix C.

ANSWERS TO MINI-QUIZZES

Mini-Quiz 1

1. b. posttest, pretest
2. b. posttest, pretest
3. three

Mini-Quiz 2

1. b. False
2. a. True
3. `while (quantity > 0);`
4. `while (quantity >= 0);`
5. `while (inStock > reorder);`
6. `while (letter == 'Y' || letter == 'y');`
7.
```
do
{
    cout << evenNum << endl;
    evenNum = evenNum + 2;
} while (evenNum < 9); (or while (evenNum <= 8);)
```

The C++ for Statement

objectives

After completing this appendix, you will be able to:

■ Code the pretest repetition structure using the C++ `for` statement

Coding the Pretest Loop

In Tutorial 10, you learned that you can code a pretest loop using the C++ `while` statement. You also can use the C++ `for` statement to code a pretest loop. Figure D-1 shows the syntax of the `for` statement.

Syntax
for ([*initialization*]**;** *loop condition***;** [*update*]**)**
one statement, or a block of statements enclosed in braces, to be processed
as long as the loop condition is true
//end for
Note: Items in **bold** are required. Items in square brackets ([]) are optional. Items in *italics* indicate places where the programmer must supply information pertaining to the current program.

semicolon

semicolon

Figure D-1: Syntax of the C++ for statement

tip

As you can with the `while` statement, you can also use the C++ `for` statement to code any pretest loop. However, the most common use for the `for` statement is to code pretest loops whose processing is controlled by a counter. This is because the `for` statement provides a more compact way of writing that type of loop.

The `for` statement begins with the `for` clause, followed by the body of the loop, which contains the one or more statements that you want the loop to repeat. If the loop body contains more than one statement, the statements must be entered as a statement block, which means that they must be enclosed in a set of braces ({}). Although it is not required by the C++ syntax, it is helpful to use a comment, such as `//end for`, to document the end of the `for` statement.

....
▶ A common error made by C++ programmers is to separate the three items of information in the `for` clause with two commas rather than two semicolons.

As the syntax shown in Figure D-1 indicates, the `for` clause contains three arguments, separated by two semicolons. In most `for` clauses, the first argument, *initialization*, creates and initializes a counter variable, which is used by the `for` statement to keep track of the number of times the loop instructions are processed. The second argument in the `for` clause, *loop condition*, specifies the condition that must be true for the loop to continue processing the loop body instructions. The *loop condition* must be a Boolean expression, which is an expression that evaluates to either true or false. The *loop condition* can contain variables, constants, functions, arithmetic operators, comparison operators, and logical operators. The loop stops when the *loop condition* evaluates to false. The third argument in the `for` clause, *update*, usually contains an expression that updates the counter variable specified in the *initialization* argument.

In the remaining sections in this appendix, you will view three examples of the `for` statement.

Example 1 – Displaying the Numbers 1 Through 3

Figure D-2 shows a `for` statement that displays the numbers 1 through 3 on the screen.

Code
`for (int count = 1; count <= 3; count = count + 1)`
`    cout << count << endl;`
`//end for`

Results
1
2
3

initialization
loop condition

update

Figure D-2: `for` statement displays the numbers 1 through 3

Desk-checking the `for` statement shown in Figure D-2 will help you to understand how the `for` statement works. When the computer encounters a `for` statement in a program, it first processes the code shown in the `for` clause's *initialization* argument. The code shown in the *initialization* argument is processed only once, at the beginning of the loop. In the case of the `for` statement shown in Figure D-2, the computer creates an `int` variable named `count` and initializes the variable to the number 1, as shown in Figure D-3.

count
1

Figure D-3: Desk-check table showing the result of processing the *initialization* argument

Next, the computer processes the code shown in the **for** clause's *loop condition* argument to determine whether to process the loop body instructions. In the case of the *loop condition* shown in Figure D-2, the computer processes the instruction contained in the loop body only when the value stored in the **count** variable is less than or equal to the number 3. Currently, the value stored in the **count** variable is the number 1, so the loop body instruction is processed and displays the **count** variable's value (1) on the screen. Unlike the *initialization* code, which is processed only once, the *loop condition* code is processed with each repetition, or iteration, of the loop.

Next, the computer processes the code shown in the **for** clause's *update* argument. The *update* argument shown in Figure D-2 instructs the computer to add the number 1 to the value stored in the **count** variable, giving 2. Like the *loop condition* argument, the *update* argument is processed with each repetition of the loop. Figure D-4 shows the result of processing the *update* argument for the first time.

Like the **while** statement you learned about in Tutorial 10, the **for** statement evaluates the loop condition *before* the loop body instructions are processed.

count
~~1~~
2

Figure D-4: Desk-check table showing the result of processing the *update* argument for the first time

After processing the *update* code for the first time, the computer processes the *loop condition* code again to determine whether to process the loop body instructions once more. In the case of the program shown in Figure D-2, the **count** variable's value still is less than or equal to 3, so the computer displays the **count** variable's value (2) on the screen.

After processing the loop body instructions, the computer processes the *update* argument again. The *update* argument shown in Figure D-2 increments the **count** variable by 1, giving 3, as shown in Figure D-5.

count
~~1~~
~~2~~
3

Figure D-5: Desk-check table showing the result of processing the *update* argument for the second time

Next, the computer processes the *loop condition* code again to determine whether to process the loop body instructions another time. In this case, the **count** variable's value still is less than or equal to 3, so the computer displays the **count** variable's value (3) on the screen.

After processing the loop body instructions, the computer processes the *update* argument again. The *update* argument shown in Figure D-2 increments the **count** variable by 1, giving 4, as shown in Figure D-6.

count
~~1~~
~~2~~
~~3~~
4

Figure D-6: Desk-check table showing the result of processing the *update* argument for the third time

Next, the computer processes the *loop condition* code again to determine whether to process the loop body instructions another time. In this case, the `count` variable's value is not less than or equal to 3, so the computer does not process the loop body instruction. Rather, the loop ends (the *update* argument is not processed this time) and the computer processes the instruction following the end of the `for` statement. Notice that the value in the `count` variable is 4 when the loop stops.

Now view an example of a `for` statement that contains more than one instruction in the loop body.

Example 2 – Calculating and Displaying a Commission

Figure D-7 shows a `for` statement that calculates a commission using commission rates of .1, .15, .2, and .25, and then displays the commission on the screen. Notice that the loop body contains more than one instruction, and the instructions are entered as a statement block by enclosing them in a set of braces ({}).

Code

loop condition

initialization

update

```
float sales = 0.0;
float comm  = 0.0;
cout << "Enter sales: ";
cin >> sales;
for (float rate = float(.1); rate <= .25; rate = rate + float(.05)
{
    comm = sales * rate;
    cout << "Commission: $" << comm << endl;
} //end for
```

Results

Commission: $2500   (assuming the user enters 25000 as the sales amount)
Commission: $3750
Commission: $5000
Commission: $6250

Figure D-7: `for` statement calculates and displays a commission

Figure D-8 shows the steps the computer follows when processing the code shown in Figure D-7.

Processing steps

1. Computer creates and initializes the `sales` variable to 0.0.
2. Computer creates and initializes the `comm` variable to 0.0.
3. Computer prompts user for sales amount.
4. Computer stores user's response in the `sales` variable.
5. Computer creates the `rate` variable and initializes it to .1 (*initialization* code).
6. Computer determines whether value in `rate` variable is less than or equal to .25 (*loop condition* code). It is.
7. Computer calculates the commission and displays "Commission: $2500" on the screen (loop body instructions).
8. Computer adds .05 to value stored in `rate` variable, giving .15 (*update* code).
9. Computer determines whether value in `rate` variable is less than or equal to .25 (*loop condition* code). It is.
10. Computer calculates the commission and displays "Commission: $3750" on the screen (loop body instructions).
11. Computer adds .05 to value stored in `rate` variable, giving .2 (*update* code).
12. Computer determines whether value in `rate` variable is less than or equal to .25 (*loop condition* code). It is.
13. Computer calculates the commission and displays "Commission: $5000" on the screen (loop body instructions).
14. Computer adds .05 to value stored in `rate` variable, giving .25 (*update* code).
15. Computer determines whether value in `rate` variable is less than or equal to .25 (*loop condition* code). It is.
16. Computer calculates the commission and displays "Commission: $6250" on the screen (loop body instructions).
17. Computer adds .05 to value stored in `rate` variable, giving .3 (*update* code).
18. Computer determines whether value in `rate` variable is less than or equal to .25 (*loop condition* code). It is not.
19. Loop ends and the computer processes the instruction following the end of the `for` statement.

Figure D-8: Processing steps for the code shown in Figure D-7

As Figure D-8 indicates, the `for` statement stops when the value stored in the `rate` variable is .3.

Finally, view an example of a `for` statement that does not use the *initialization* and *update* arguments.

Example 3 – Calculating and Displaying a Bonus

Although the most common use for the `for` statement is to code loops whose processing is controlled by a counter, you actually can use the `for` statement to code any pretest loop. For example, the `for` statement shown in Figure D-9's code, which calculates and displays a bonus, is controlled by the user rather than by a counter.

Code

```cpp
const float RATE = float(.1);
float sales = 0.0;
float bonus = 0.0;
cout << "Enter the first sales amount: ";
cin >> sales;
for (; sales > 0;)
{
    bonus = sales * RATE;
    cout << "Bonus: $" << bonus << endl;
    cout << "Enter the next sales amount: ";
    cin >> sales;
} //end for
```

semicolon after the *initialization*

loop condition

semicolon after the *loop condition*

Results

Bonus: $400   (assuming the user enters 4000 as the sales amount)
Bonus: $300   (assuming the user enters 3000 as the sales amount)

Figure D-9: for statement calculates and displays a bonus

Notice that the for clause shown in Figure D-9 contains only the loop condition argument. Although the initialization and update arguments are omitted from the for clause, the semicolons after the initialization and loop condition arguments must be included. Figure D-10 shows the steps the computer follows when processing the code shown in Figure D-9.

You also can omit the second argument in the for clause. When doing so, however, you will need to include the break statement in the loop body to stop the loop. You learned about the break statement in Tutorial 9.

Whether you use the for statement or the while statement to code the loop shown in Figure D-9 is a matter of personal preference.

Processing steps

1. Computer creates and initializes the RATE constant to .1.
2. Computer creates and initializes the sales variable to 0.0.
3. Computer creates and initializes the bonus variable to 0.0.
4. Computer prompts user for sales amount. Assume the user enters the number 4000.
5. Computer stores the user's response (4000) in the sales variable.
6. Computer determines whether the value in the sales variable is greater than 0 (*loop condition* code). It is.
7. Computer calculates the bonus and displays "Bonus: $400" on the screen. It then prompts the user for another sales amount and stores the user's response in the sales variable (loop body instructions). Assume the user enters the number 3000.
8. Computer determines whether the value in the sales variable is greater than 0 (*loop condition* code). It is.

Figure D-10: Processing steps for the code shown in Figure D-9

Processing steps
9. Computer calculates the bonus and displays "Bonus: $300" on the screen. It then prompts the user for another sales amount and stores the user's response in the `sales` variable (loop body instructions). Assume the user enters the number -1.
10. Computer determines the whether value in the `sales` variable is greater than 0 (*loop condition* code). It is not.
11. Loop ends and the computer processes the instruction following the end of the `for` statement.

Figure D-10: Processing steps for the code shown in Figure D-9 (continued)

As Figure D-10 indicates, the `for` statement stops when the user enters either the number 0 or a negative number as the sales amount.

mini-quiz

Mini-Quiz 1

1. Which of the following `for` clauses processes the loop instructions as long as the value stored in the counter variable named **x** is less than or equal to the number 100?

   a. `for (x = 10; x <= 100; x = x + 10)`

   b. `for (x = 10, x <= 100, x = x + 10)`

   c. `for (x == 10; x <= 100; x = x + 10)`

   d. `for (x = x + 10; x <= 100; x = 10)`

2. What is the value stored in the **x** variable when the loop corresponding to the `for` clause in Question 1 ends?

   a. 100

   b. 110

   c. 101

   d. 110

3. Write a `for` clause that processes the loop instructions as long as the value stored in the counter variable named **x** is greater than 0. The **x** variable should be an `int` variable. Initialize the variable to the number 25 and increment it by -5 with each repetition of the loop.

4. What is the value stored in the **x** variable when the loop corresponding to the `for` clause in Question 3 ends?

5. Write a `for` statement that displays the even integers between 1 and 9 on the screen. Use `number` as the name of the counter variable.

6. Which of the following `for` clauses stops the loop when the user enters the letter X (in uppercase or lowercase)?

   a. `for (toupper(letter) != 'X')`

   b. `for (, toupper(letter) != 'X',)`

   c. `for (; toupper(letter) == 'X';)`

   d. `for (; toupper(letter) != 'X';)`

You now have completed Appendix D.

ANSWERS TO MINI-QUIZ

Mini-Quiz 1

1. a. for (x = 10; x <= 100; x = x + 10)

2. d. 110

3. for (int x = 25; x > 0; x = x - 5) or
for (int x = 25; x > 0; x = x + -5)

4. 0 (zero)

5. for (int number = 2; number <= 8; number = number + 2)
        cout << number << endl;

6. d. for (; toupper(letter) != 'X';)

APPENDIX E

Sorting

objectives

After completing this appendix, you will be able to:

- Sort data using the bubble sort

Sorting Data

In Tutorial 14, you learned how to store data in a one-dimensional array. One reason for storing data in an array is to **sort** the data—that is, arrange it in either alphabetical or numerical order—before displaying the data on the screen. When data is displayed in a sorted order, it allows a user to quickly find the information for which he or she is searching. For example, it is much easier to find a name in a list that is arranged alphabetically rather than randomly. Additionally, many programs require data to be in a specific sequence to work correctly. For example, programs that use the binary search algorithm, which is covered in Appendix F, require the program data to be sorted. Programs that use the control break algorithm also require the program data to be sorted.

You can sort data in either ascending (from smallest to largest) or descending (from largest to smallest) order. Over the years, many different sorting algorithms have been developed. In this appendix, you will learn how to use one of the algorithms—the bubble sort—to sort the data stored in an array.

The Bubble Sort

The bubble sort provides a quick and easy way to sort the items stored in an array, as long as the number of items is relatively small—for example, under 50. The **bubble sort** algorithm works by comparing adjacent array elements and interchanging (swapping) the ones that are out of order. The algorithm continues comparing and swapping until the data in the array is sorted. To illustrate the logic of a bubble sort, manually sort the numbers 9, 8, and 7 in ascending order. Assume that the three numbers are stored in an array named num. Figure E-1 shows the num array values before, during, and after the bubble sort.

	Comparison	Swap	Result/Comparison	Swap	Result
Pass 1:					
num [0]	9 ⌐	Yes	8		8
num [1]	8 ⌐		9 ⌐	Yes	7
num [2]	7		7 ⌐		9
Pass 2:					
num [0]	8 ⌐	Yes	7		7
num [1]	7 ⌐		8 ⌐	No	8
num [2]	9		9 ⌐		9

Figure E-1: Array values before, during, and after the bubble sort

The bubble sort algorithm begins by comparing the first value in the array to the second value. If the first value is less than or equal to the second value, then no swap is made. However, if the first value is greater than the second value, then both values are interchanged. In this case, the first value (9) is greater than the second (8), so the values are swapped as shown in Figure E-1's Result/Comparison column.

After comparing the first value in the array to the second, the algorithm then compares the second value to the third. In this case, 9 is greater than 7, so the two values are swapped as shown in Figure E-1's Result column.

At this point, the algorithm has completed its first time through the entire array—referred to as a **pass**. Notice that, at the end of the first pass, the largest value (9) is stored in the last position of the array. The bubble sort gets its name from the fact that as the larger values drop to the bottom of the array, the smaller values rise, like bubbles, to the top. Now observe what the algorithm does on its second pass through the array.

The bubble sort algorithm begins the second pass by comparing the first value in the array to the second value. In this case, 8 is greater than 7, so the two values are interchanged as shown in Figure E-1. Then the second value is compared to the third. In this case, 8 is not greater than 9, so no swap is made. Notice that at the end of the second pass, the data in the array is sorted.

Figure E-2 shows a C++ program that uses the bubble sort to sort the contents of an array. The program then displays the contents of the sorted array on the screen.

Code

```cpp
#include <iostream>
using namespace std;

int main()
{

    //declare array
    int num[4] = {3, 6, 2, 5};

    //declare variables used in bubble sort code
    int x        = 0;    //keeps track of subscripts
    int temp     = 0;    //variable used for swapping
    int maxSub   = 3;    //maximum subscript
    int lastSwap = 0;    //indicates position of last swap
    char swap    = 'Y';  //indicates whether a swap was made

    //repeat loop instructions as long as a swap was made
    while (swap == 'Y')
    {
        swap = 'N';   //assume that no swaps are necessary
        x = 0;        //begin comparing with first array
                      //element

        //compare adjacent array elements to determine
        //whether a swap is necessary
        while (x < maxSub)
        {
            if (num[x] > num[x + 1])
            {
                //a swap is necessary
                temp = num[x];
                num[x] = num[x + 1];
                num[x + 1] = temp;
                swap = 'Y';
                lastSwap = x;
            } //end if

            x = x + 1;  //increment subscript
        } //end while
        maxSub = lastSwap;  //reset maximum subscript
    } //end while

    //display sorted array
    x = 0;
    while (x < 4)
    {
        cout << num[x] << endl;
        x = x + 1;
    } //end while

    return 0;
} //end of main function
```

code for the bubble sort algorithm

Figure E-2: C++ program containing the code for the bubble sort algorithm

Results
2
3
5
6

Figure E-2: C++ program containing the code for the bubble sort algorithm (continued)

To better understand the bubble sort algorithm, desk-check the code shown in Figure E-2. Figure E-3 shows the completed desk-check tables.

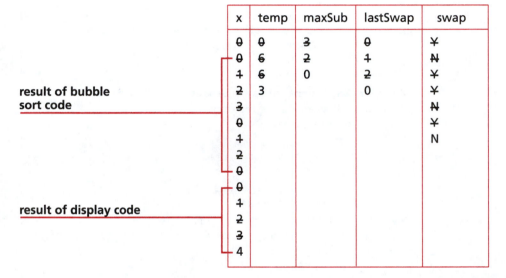

num[0]	num[1]	num[2]	num[3]
~~3~~	~~6~~	~~2~~	~~5~~
2	~~2~~	~~6~~	6
	3	5	

result of bubble sort code

result of display code

x	temp	maxSub	lastSwap	swap
~~0~~	~~0~~	~~3~~	~~0~~	~~Y~~
~~0~~	~~6~~	~~2~~	~~1~~	~~N~~
~~1~~	~~6~~	0	~~2~~	~~Y~~
~~2~~	3		0	~~Y~~
~~3~~				~~N~~
~~0~~				~~Y~~
~~1~~				N
~~2~~				
~~0~~				
~~0~~				
~~1~~				
~~2~~				
~~3~~				
4				

Figure E-3: Completed desk-check tables for the code shown in Figure E-2

Mini-Quiz 1

1. The process of arranging data in alphabetical or numerical order is called _____ .

2. The bubble sort compares the value stored in the `code[x]` element to the value stored in the _____ element.

3. To swap the values stored in two elements in the `salary` array, the bubble sort first _____ .

   a.   assigns `salary[x]` to `temp`

   b.   assigns `salary[x]` to `salary[x + 1]`

   c.   assigns `temp` to `salary[x]`

   d.   assigns `temp` to `salary[x + 1]`

You now have completed Appendix E.

ANSWERS TO MINI-QUIZ

Mini-Quiz 1

1. sorting

2. `code[x + 1]`

3. a. assigns `salary[x]` to temp

APPENDIX F

The Binary Search

objectives

After completing this appendix, you will be able to:

■ Search an array using the binary search algorithm

Performing a Binary Search

tip

Appendix E covers the bubble sort algorithm, which you can use to sort the data contained in an array.

In Tutorial 14, you learned how to use a serial search to search for a specific value contained in an array. When performing a **serial search**, the program begins the search with the first array element and then continues searching, element by element, until either a match is found or the end of the array is encountered. A serial search is useful when the amount of data that must be searched is small. However, in cases where you have a large amount of data to search, it is much more efficient to perform a binary search rather than a serial search. For a binary search to work correctly, the data in the array must be sorted; in other words, it must be arranged in either alphabetical or numerical order.

To illustrate the logic of the binary search algorithm, assume that 11 salesperson IDs are sorted in ascending numerical order and stored in an array named **num**. Also assume that you want to use the binary search to locate ID 411 in the array. Rather than beginning the search with the first array element, as a serial search does, a **binary search** begins the search in the middle of the array, as indicated in Figure F-1.

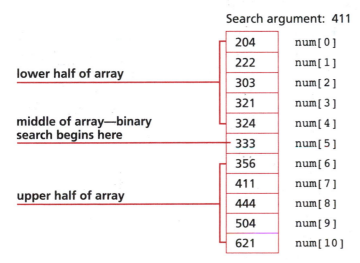

Search argument: 411

	lower half of array		204	num[0]
			222	num[1]
			303	num[2]
			321	num[3]
middle of array—binary search begins here			324	num[4]
			333	num[5]
	upper half of array		356	num[6]
			411	num[7]
			444	num[8]
			504	num[9]
			621	num[10]

Figure F-1: num array

If the value for which you are searching, called the **search argument**, is equal to the value located in the middle of the array, then the binary search ends. However, if the search argument is *greater* than the value located in the middle of the array, the binary search continues in the upper half of the array, because that is where the values greater than the search argument are located. Finally, if the search argument is *less* than the value located in the middle of the array, the binary search continues in the lower half of the array, where the values that are less than the search argument are located. In Figure F-1, the search argument (411) is greater than the value found in the middle of the array (the 333 stored in num[5]), so the binary search continues in the upper half of the array.

Before continuing the search, the upper half of the array is halved again, as shown in Figure F-2.

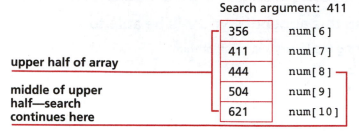

Search argument: 411

356	num[6]
411	num[7]
444	num[8]
504	num[9]
621	num[10]

upper half of array

middle of upper half—search continues here

Figure F-2: Upper half halved again

Here again, if the search argument is equal to the value in the array, then the search ends. If, on the other hand, the search argument is greater than the value in the array, the search continues in the array elements located above the current one; otherwise, it continues in the array elements located below the current one. In Figure F-2, the search argument (411) is less than the array value found in the middle of the upper half of the array (the 444 stored in num[8]). Therefore, the search continues in the elements located between the middle of the array (num[5]) and the current element (num[8]). The binary search algorithm continues to halve the remaining array elements until it either finds a match or determines that no match exists.

In the next section, you will view and desk-check a program that uses the binary search to locate a salesperson's ID in an array.

The Gifts Express Program

You learned about parallel arrays in Tutorial 14.

Figure F-3 shows the Gifts Express program. Notice that the program declares and initializes two parallel one-dimensional arrays: the num array contains salesperson IDs and the dollar array contains sales amounts. The arrays are parallel because the position of each salesperson's ID in the num array corresponds to the position of his or her sales amount in the dollar array.

```cpp
#include <iostream>
using namespace std;

int main()
{
    //declare parallel arrays
    int num[11] = {204, 222, 303, 321, 324, 333,
                   356, 411, 444, 504, 621};
    int dollar[11] = {200000, 455000, 150000, 130000, 120000, 210000,
                      150000, 310000, 180000, 213000, 141000};

    //declare variables
    int searchId = 0;    //ID to locate
    int startSub = 0;    //subscript of first element to search
    int stopSub  = 10;   //subscript of last element to search
    int middleSub = 0;   //subscript corresponding to middle element
    char found   = 'N';  //indicates whether ID was found

    //get search ID
    cout << "Enter ID: ";
    cin >> searchId;

    while(found == 'N' && startSub <= stopSub)
    {
        //use binary search to locate ID
        middleSub = (startSub + stopSub) / 2;        //halve array

        if(searchId > num[middleSub])        //search upper half
            startSub = middleSub + 1;
        else if(searchId < num[middleSub])   //search lower half
            stopSub = middleSub - 1;
        else   //ID equals array element
        {
            found = 'Y';
            cout << "Salesperson " << searchId
                 << " sales are $" << dollar[middleSub]
                 << endl << endl;
        } //end ifs
    } //end while

    if(found == 'N')
        cout << "Invalid salesperson ID" << endl;
    //end if

    return 0;
} //end of main function
```

Figure F-3: Gifts Express program

tip

In most programs, the values stored in an array come from a file on the computer's disk, and are stored in the array after it is created and initialized. However, so that you can follow the code and program results more easily, the Gifts Express program initializes the array data to the appropriate values.

The Gifts Express program prompts the user to enter an ID, then uses the binary search to locate the ID in the num array. If the ID is not contained in the num array, the program displays an appropriate message. However, if the ID is found in the num array, the program displays the sales amount contained in the corresponding position in the dollar array. To understand how the binary search algorithm works, you will desk-check the Gifts Express program twice: first using a valid ID and then using an invalid ID. A valid ID is an ID that is contained in the num array, and an invalid ID is an ID that is not contained in the num array.

Desk-Checking the Gifts Express Program Using a Valid ID

The Gifts Express program begins by declaring and initializing the num and dollar arrays. It also declares and initializes four int variables (searchId, startSub, stopSub, and middleSub) and one char variable (found). The program uses the searchId variable to store the ID number entered by the user. It uses the startSub variable to store the subscript of the first array element to search, and it uses the stopSub variable to store the subscript of the last array element to search. Notice that the startSub variable is initialized to the number 0, which is the value of the first subscript in the num array. The stopSub variable, on the other hand, is initialized to 10—the value of the last subscript in the 11-element num array.

Each time the array is halved, the program assigns the subscript of the array element located in the middle position to the middleSub variable, which has an initial value of 0. The program uses the char variable named found to keep track of whether the search ID was found in the array. When the program begins, the found variable is initialized to the literal constant 'N'.

After the arrays and variables are declared and initialized, the program prompts the user to enter an ID and stores the user's response in the searchId variable. Assume that the user enters the number 321, which corresponds to an ID contained in the num array. Figure F-4 shows the values stored in the arrays and variables before the binary search begins.

searchId	startSub	stopSub	middleSub	found
~~0~~ 321	0	10	0	N

num[0]	204	dollar[0]	200000
num[1]	222	dollar[1]	455000
num[2]	303	dollar[2]	150000
num[3]	321	dollar[3]	130000
num[4]	324	dollar[4]	120000
num[5]	333	dollar[5]	210000
num[6]	356	dollar[6]	150000
num[7]	411	dollar[7]	310000
num[8]	444	dollar[8]	180000
num[9]	504	dollar[9]	213000
num[10]	621	dollar[10]	141000

Figure F-4: Values stored in the arrays and variables before the binary search begins

The next line of code is the `while(found == 'N' && startSub <= stopSub)` clause, which determines whether the instructions in the `while` loop should be processed. In this case, the instructions will be processed, because both conditions contained in the compound condition are true: the `found` variable contains the literal constant 'N' and the `startSub` variable contains a value that is less than or equal to the value in the `stopSub` variable.

The first instruction in the loop body splits the array in half by adding the value stored in the `startSub` variable (0) to the value stored in the `stopSub` variable (10), and then dividing the sum (10) by 2. The result, 5, is assigned to the `middleSub` variable, as shown in Figure F-5.

searchId	startSub	stopSub	middleSub	found
~~0~~ 321	0	10	~~0~~ 5	N

Figure F-5: New value placed in the `middleSub` variable

After the array is halved, the first `if` statement in the `while` loop determines whether the search argument value is greater than the value stored in the middle array element (`num[middleSub]`); if it is, the search should continue in the upper half of the array only. In the Gifts Express program, the value in the `searchId` variable (321) is not greater than the value in the `num[5]` element (333), so the nested `if` statement is processed.

The nested `if` statement determines whether the search argument value is less than the value stored in the `num[middleSub]` element; if it is, the search should continue in the lower half of the array only. In the Gifts Express program, the value stored in the `searchId` variable (321) is less than the value stored in the `num[5]` element (333), so only the array elements with subscripts from 0 through 4 should be searched the next time the loop is processed. As Figure F-5 shows, the `startSub` variable, which stores the subscript of the first array element to search, already contains the correct value of 0. However, the `stopSub` variable, which stores the subscript of the last element to search, needs to be changed from its current value (10) to 4. This task is accomplished by the statement `stopSub = middleSub - 1;`, which is located in the nested `if` statement's true path. After the `stopSub` variable is assigned the correct value, both `if` statements end. At the completion of the first time through the loop, the variables have the values shown in Figure F-6.

searchId	startSub	stopSub	middleSub	found
~~0~~ 321	0	~~10~~ 4	~~0~~ 5	N

Figure F-6: Values in the variables after the `while` loop is processed the first time

The next line of code to be processed is the `while(found == 'N' && startSub <= stopSub)` clause, which determines whether the loop instructions should be processed again. In this case, the instructions will be processed again, because both conditions contained in the compound condition are true: the `found` variable contains the literal constant 'N' and the `startSub` variable contains a value that is less than or equal to the value in the `stopSub` variable.

The first instruction in the loop body halves the lower half of the array and assigns the result to the `middleSub` variable. In this case, the `middleSub` variable is assigned a value of 2, which is calculated by adding the `startSub` value of 0 to the `stopSub` value of 4 and then dividing that sum by 2. Figure F-7 shows the values in the variables after the statement `middleSub = (startSub + stopSub) / 2;` is processed.

searchId	startSub	stopSub	middleSub	found
~~0~~	0	~~10~~	~~0~~	N
321		4	~~5~~	
			2	

Figure F-7: New value placed in the `middleSub` variable

After the lower half of the array is halved, the first `if` statement in the `while` loop determines whether the search argument value is greater than the value stored in the middle array element (`num[middleSub]`); if it is, the search should continue in the upper half of the halved array. In the Gifts Express program, the value in the `searchId` variable (321) is greater than the value in the `num[2]` element (303), so only the array elements with subscripts of 3 and 4 should be searched the next time the loop is processed. As Figure F-7 shows, the `stopSub` variable, which stores the subscript of the last element to search, already contains the correct value of 4. However, the `startSub` variable, which stores the subscript of the first element to search, needs to be changed from its current value (0) to 3. This task is accomplished by the statement `startSub = middleSub + 1;`, which is located in the first `if` statement's true path. After the `startSub` variable is assigned its correct value, the `if` statement ends. At the end of the second time through the loop, the variables have the values shown in Figure F-8.

searchId	startSub	stopSub	middleSub	found
~~0~~	~~0~~	~~10~~	~~0~~	N
321	3	4	~~5~~	
			2	

Figure F-8: Values in the variables after the `while` loop is processed the second time

The next line of code to be processed is the `while(found == 'N' && startSub <= stopSub)` clause, which determines whether the loop instructions should be processed again. In this case, the instructions will be processed a third time, because both conditions contained in the compound condition are true: the `found` variable contains the literal constant 'N' and the `startSub` variable contains a value that is less than or equal to the value in the `stopSub` variable.

The first instruction in the loop body, `middleSub = (startSub + stopSub) / 2;`, adds the `startSub` value of 3 to the `stopSub` value of 4 and then divides that sum by 2, giving 3.5. The 3.5 result is truncated to 3 before being stored in the `middleSub` variable, as shown in Figure F-9.

searchId	startSub	stopSub	middleSub	found
~~0~~	~~0~~	~~10~~	~~0~~	N
321	3	4	5	
			2	
			3	

Figure F-9: New value placed in the `middleSub` variable

The first `if` statement in the `while` loop determines whether the value contained in the `searchId` variable (321) is greater than the value in `num[3]` (321); it is not. The nested `if` statement then determines whether the value in the `searchId` variable (321) is less than the value in `num[3]` (321); here again, it is not. If the `searchId` value is neither greater than nor less then the `num[3]` value, then the two values must be equal. In that case, the two statements within the nested `if` statement's false path are processed.

The first statement in the nested `if` statement's false path, `found = 'Y';`, assigns the literal constant 'Y' to the `found` variable. The 'Y' value indicates that the search argument was found in the array. The second statement, `cout << "Salesperson " << searchId << " sales are $" << dollar[middleSub] << endl << endl;`, displays a message along with the search argument and the corresponding sales amount from the `dollar` array. In this case, the program displays the text "Salesperson 321 sales are $130000." After the instructions are processed, both `if` statements end. At the end of the third time through the loop, the variables have the values shown in Figure F-10.

searchId	startSub	stopSub	middleSub	found
~~0~~	~~0~~	~~10~~	~~0~~	~~N~~
321	3	4	5	Y
			2	
			3	

Figure F-10: Values in the variables after the `while` loop is processed the third time

The next line of code to be processed is the `while(found == 'N' && startSub <= stopSub)` clause, which determines whether the loop instructions should be processed again. In this case, the loop instructions will not be processed again, because the `found` variable contains the literal constant 'Y'.

When the `while` statement has completed its processing, the `if` statement below the loop determines whether the search argument was found in the array. If the `found` variable contains the literal constant 'N', then the ID for which the user was searching was not found in the array. In that case, the program displays an appropriate message before it ends. If the `found` variable does not contain the literal constant 'N', the program simply ends. In this case, the program ends, because the `found` variable contains the literal constant 'Y'.

Next, desk-check the Gifts Express program using an ID that is not in the array.

Desk-Checking the Gifts Express Program Using an Invalid ID

The Gifts Express program begins by declaring and initializing the arrays and variables. It then prompts the user to enter an ID and stores his or her response in the searchId variable. Assume the user enters the number 322, which is not contained in the num array.

Next, the while loop determines if the loop instructions should be processed. In this case, the instructions will be processed, because the found variable contains the literal constant 'N' and the startSub variable contains a value that is less than or equal to the value in the stopSub variable. (Recall that when the program begins, the startSub variable contains the number 0 and the stopSub variable contains the number 10.)

The first instruction in the loop body splits the array in half by adding the startSub value of 0 to the stopSub value of 10, and then dividing the sum by 2. The result, 5, is assigned to the middleSub variable. The first if clause in the while loop determines whether the search argument value (322) is greater than the value stored in num[5] (333); it is not. The nested if statement then determines whether the search argument value (322) is less than the value stored in num[5] (333); it is, so only the array elements with subscripts from 0 through 4 should be searched the next time the loop is processed. At this point, the startSub variable, which stores the subscript of the first element to search, already contains the correct value of 0. However, the stopSub variable, which stores the subscript of the last element to search, needs to be changed from its current value (10) to 4. Recall that this task is accomplished by the statement stopSub = middleSub - 1;, which is located in the nested if statement's true path. After the stopSub variable is assigned its correct value, both if statements end. At the end of the first time through the loop, the variables have the values shown in F-11.

searchId	startSub	stopSub	middleSub	found
~~0~~ 322	0	~~10~~ 4	~~0~~ 5	N

Figure F-11: Values in the variables after the while loop is processed the first time

The next line of code to be processed is the while(found == 'N' && startSub <= stopSub) clause, which determines whether the loop instructions should be processed again. In this case, the instructions will be processed a second time, because both conditions contained in the compound condition are true.

The first instruction in the loop, middleSub = (startSub + stopSub) / 2;, halves the lower half of the array and assigns the result to the middleSub variable. In this case, the middleSub variable is assigned a value of 2, which is calculated by adding the startSub value of 0 to the stopSub value of 4 and then dividing the sum by 2. The first if clause in the while loop determines whether the search argument value (322) is greater than the value stored in num[2] (303); it is, so the search should continue in the upper half of the halved array, with the elements having subscripts of 3 and 4. At this point, the stopSub variable, which stores the subscript of the last element to search, already contains the correct value of 4. However, the startSub variable, which stores the subscript of the first element to search, needs to be changed from its current value (0) to 3. Recall that this task is accomplished by the statement startSub = middleSub + 1;, which is located in the first if statement's true path. After the startSub variable is assigned its correct value, the if statement ends. At the end of the second time through the loop, the variables have the values shown in Figure F-12.

searchId	startSub	stopSub	middleSub	found
~~0~~	~~0~~	~~10~~	~~0~~	N
322	3	4	5	
			2	

Figure F-12: Values in the variables after the `while` loop is processed the second time

The next line of code to be processed is the `while(found == 'N' && startSub <= stopSub)` clause, which determines whether the loop instructions should be processed again. In this case, the instructions will be processed a third time, because both conditions contained in the compound condition are true.

The first instruction in the loop, `middleSub = (startSub + stopSub) / 2;`, adds the `startSub` value of 3 to the `stopSub` value of 4, and then divides that sum by 2, giving 3.5. The 3.5 result is truncated to 3 before being stored in the `middleSub` variable. The first `if` clause in the `while` loop determines whether the search argument value (322) is greater than the value in `num[3]` (321); it is, so the search continues in the upper half of the array, with the element whose subscript is 4. At this point, the `stopSub` variable, which stores the subscript of the last element to search, already contains the correct value of 4. However, the `startSub` variable, which stores the subscript of the first element to search, needs to be changed from its current value (3) to 4. Recall that this task is accomplished by the statement `startSub = middleSub + 1;`, which is located in the first `if` statement's true path. After the `startSub` variable is assigned its correct value, the `if` statement ends. At the end of the third time through the loop, the variables have the values shown in Figure F-13.

searchId	startSub	stopSub	middleSub	found
~~0~~	~~0~~	~~10~~	~~0~~	N
322	~~3~~	4	~~5~~	
	4		~~2~~	
			3	

Figure F-13: Values in the variables after the `while` loop is processed the third time

The next line of code to be processed is the `while(found == 'N' && startSub <= stopSub)` clause, which determines whether the loop instructions should be processed again. In this case, the instructions will be processed a fourth time, because both conditions contained in the compound condition are true.

The first instruction in the loop, `middleSub = (startSub + stopSub) / 2;`, adds the `startSub` value of 4 to the `stopSub` value of 4, and then divides that sum by 2; the result (4) is assigned to the `middleSub` variable. The first `if` statement in the `while` loop determines whether the search argument value (322) is greater than the value in `num[4]` (324); it is not. The nested `if` statement then determines if the search argument value (322) is less than the value in `num[4]` (324); it is, so the statement `stopSub = middleSub - 1;`, which is located in the nested `if` statement's true path, assigns the value 3 to the `stopSub` variable. After the `stopSub` variable is assigned its value, both `if` statements end. At the end of the fourth time through the loop, the variables have the values shown in Figure F-14.

searchId	startSub	stopSub	middleSub	found
~~0~~	~~0~~	~~10~~	~~0~~	N
322	~~3~~	~~4~~	5	
	4	3	2	
			~~3~~	
			4	

Figure F-14: Values in the variables after the `while` loop is processed the fourth time

The next line of code to be processed is the `while(found == 'N' && startSub <= stopSub)` clause, which determines whether the loop instructions should be processed again. In this case, the instructions will not be processed again, because the `startSub` variable contains a value that is greater than the value in the `stopSub` variable. When the `while` statement has completed its processing, the `if` statement below the loop determines whether the search argument was found in the array. If the `found` variable contains the literal constant 'N', then the ID for which the user was searching was not found in the array. In that case, the program displays an appropriate message before it ends. If the `found` variable does not contain the literal constant 'N', the program simply ends. In this case, the program displays the message "Invalid salesperson ID" before the program ends.

mini-quiz

Mini-Quiz 1

1. A _____ search begins the search with the first array element.
   a. ascending
   b. binary
   c. descending
   d. serial

2. A _____ search begins the search with the element that is located in the middle of the array.
   a. ascending
   b. binary
   c. descending
   d. serial

3. The data for which you are searching is called the _____ .

4. Desk-check the Gifts Express program shown in Figure F-3 using a search argument of 504.

searchId	startSub	stopSub	middleSub	found

You now have completed Appendix F.

ANSWERS TO MINI-QUIZ

Mini-Quiz 1

1. d. serial
2. b. binary
3. search argument
4.

searchId	startSub	stopSub	middleSub	found
~~0~~	~~0~~	~~10~~	~~0~~	~~N~~
504	~~6~~		~~5~~	Y
	9		~~8~~	
			9	

Index